SEVEN AUTHORS
OF CRAWFORDSVILLE, INDIANA

BIBLIOGRAPHICAL STUDIES OF

Seven Authors
of Crawfordsville, Indiana

Lew and Susan Wallace,

Maurice and Will Thompson,

Mary Hannah and Caroline Virginia Krout,

and Meredith Nicholson

———————◆◆◆———————

BY DOROTHY RITTER RUSSO
AND THELMA LOIS SULLIVAN

INDIANA HISTORICAL SOCIETY

Indianapolis · 1952

THE LAKESIDE PRESS · R. R. DONNELLEY & SONS COMPANY
CHICAGO, ILLINOIS, AND CRAWFORDSVILLE, INDIANA

To

LEW WALLACE, III

Preface

THROUGH the selection of the title for this group of bibliographical studies Crawfordsville, Indiana, rather than Lew Wallace and the other authors seems to have been given first importance. This cannot be, since human beings are more important than the place where they originate or develop. To Lew Wallace and his wife, the Thompsons and the Krouts and Meredith Nicholson, we are paying full tribute. It remains an interesting fact that a town with a population of little over five thousand in 1880, when *Ben-Hur* was being published, not quite doubled by 1920, and still counted a small city, should have made this book possible. Whoever first called it "The Athens of Indiana"* ("The Athens of the West," more extravagantly), Mary Hannah Krout used the appellation for her column, "The Hoosier Athens," published in an Indianapolis newspaper, *The Saturday Herald*, from 1876–1878. All the Indiana cities, including Indianapolis with its relatively large population, must bow to the astoundingly high rate of authorship in Crawfordsville.

Maurice Thompson attempted an explanation, writing in *Literature*, June 2, 1888, "Beside Ben Hur": "In truth it is a singing city, a romancing city, a city up and down whose streets letters have been pursued with a perseverance and tact which could but end in success. There is no more chance for an original thought to slip through Crawfordsville uncaptured by some of her writers than for a crumb to escape the notice of her legion of sparrows. Here, under a spreading beech tree, Gen. Lew Wallace wrote The Fair God and Ben Hur, books whose leaves have been turned in every civilized country . . . and I, when I came to Crawfordsville a few

---

*As early as 1836 a toast was offered to "Crawfordsville—The Athens of Indiana" by William Compton at a local Fourth of July celebration, as reported in the *Crawfordsville Record* of July 9, 1836. Theodore G. Gronert commented on it in the *Crawfordsville Journal Review*, October 22, 1931.

years ago, fell into this sort of company and was soon grinding out books as recklessly as any of them." He includes other names, Henry Beebee Carrington and John Merle Coulter, who wrote books during their periods of teaching at Wabash College. This book would be indeed unwieldy if we included professors who were published authors, and numerous residents who contributed articles and poetry to periodicals.

There has been a general recognition of Indiana as a state fertile in the production of men and women who have grown to be influential in many fields of culture and activity; we have no intention of being boastful, but merely grateful; our concern is with a selected "Pleiades" of literary lights.

Meredith Nicholson, in *The Hoosiers,* attributed the "great stimulus to literary ambition in Indiana" to the success of several Indiana authors, particularly that of Maurice Thompson and James Whitcomb Riley. Nearly forty years later, in a letter addressed to J. K. Lilly, Jr., June 12, 1939, from Nicaragua, he expressed further appreciation of Thompson, of the Thompson brothers:

"I note in a recent issue of the Bulletin that you are a member of the Historical Society's committee on the bibliography of Indiana authors. Please do not take it amiss if I suggest what has long been in my mind and heart—that we Hoosiers have never done justice to the genius of Maurice and Will Thompson. I need hardly say that I yield to no one in my admiration for Riley; my tributes to him in divers ways and forms are a matter of record. Through many years I profited greatly by his friendship.

"The Thompsons were of a different intellectual species, and the differences in their make-up were not discreditable to either. You will find in my little book The Hoosiers (Macmillan, 1900; 1915) some notes on the Thompsons.

"My feeling about them is quickened by noting from time to time the lively interest in all parts of the country in archery. Our excellent magazine 'Outdoor Indiana' reports frequent archery tournaments in our state. But rarely, if ever have I seen any reference to the fact that the Thompson brothers, by their charming writings on the subject in prose and verse, started the American archery going away back in the 70's. Their book 'The Witchery of Archery' and Maurice Thompson's 'Songs of Fair Weather' have a real charm—the latter a fragrance and 'magic' rare in modern verse. I have a copy of the latter here—a beautiful little book which I prize above most other books.

"These men were contributing to the *Atlantic, Century,* and *Scribner's* among the very first Westerners to gain access to our foremost periodicals. Maurice was for years literary editor of *The Independent* (N.Y.), a weekly of distinction in its day and he printed in it many of his delightful essays and outdoor lyrics. He did his work at his home in Crawfordsville. His output was large; he was truly a scholar and a man of letters. I once had many of his books but they have got away from me. No doubt a skilled hunter in the field of bibliomania like yourself could find them. Maurice had a turn for science and was State Geologist in the natural gas days.

"I am making this too long, but I would like to infect you if possible with my warm liking for the work of these men. I am afraid our libraries may not have their books, and that lack should be remedied. Please, some day, ask the city library to copy for you from the *Century,* sometime in the 90's I think, Will Thompson's 'Together Against the Stream'—one of my favorites in all lyric poetry. His 'High Tide at Gettysburg' is in all the better anthologies."

It was at Maurice Thompson's home that William Dean Howells, "dean of American literature," chose to stay while writing the final chapters of *A Modern Instance,* and *The Literary World,* November 4, 1882, assures us that "Crawfordsville is well described in that powerful story."

A glance through the pages of this bibliography, even to those who are not book collectors and have no concern with collations, will reveal the depth and extent of our seven writers' interests, as diverse as their personalities. It is not in our scope to give details of their lives or to evaluate the literary quality of their works. All have been found worthy of some years of concentrated bibliographical study; the result is a reference tool designed for collectors, librarians, and scholars with an interest in American literature.

The general plan of the book, in its presentation of collations, follows closely that of our previous publications: *A Bibliography of James Whitcomb Riley,* by Anthony J. and Dorothy R. Russo (1944); *A Bibliography of George Ade,* by Dorothy R. Russo (1947); *A Bibliography of Booth Tarkington,* by Dorothy R. Russo and Thelma L. Sullivan (1949). It offers a guide to collectors of first editions; describes in three chronological sections books, ephemeral publications, and books by others including first edition matter by our authors. There follows a listing of periodicals which contain first newspaper and first magazine printings. Inevitably more published bits, in the way of elusive "ephemera" and obscure periodicals, will be found too late for inclusion herein.

Boundary lines between the first and second sections often are a problem. When is a "brochure" a book and when an ephemeral item? Lew Wallace's *Commodus* (1876) is slight enough in format to be the latter, and it was privately printed; because it was later republished, by Harpers, in the book, *The Wooing of Malkatoon* (1897), it has been arbitrarily placed in the first section.

Joint authorship, requiring repetition of collating, is sometimes clear, sometimes debatable. Mary H. Krout and Susan E. Wallace brought to completion Lew Wallace's *Autobiography,* but from a bibliographical standpoint it remains his book, their "contributions." Will H. Thompson probably helped Maurice in preparing *The Witchery of Archery* (1878), but no acknowledgment to him appears in it although he is the dedicatee; it is to be considered Maurice Thompson's alone. *How to Train in Archery* (1879) was their book together, collated for both authors, but Will revised it considerably after his brother's death and the third edition (1905) is herein merely mentioned in "Notes" in Maurice's bibliography, while it is separately described in Will's.

The brief introduction that precedes the study of each author is at best a poor attempt to give flesh and blood to the skeletal outline of himself, in the form of published words, that follows. The chronology of books and pamphlets may be useful for quick reference; titles not included thereon can be traced through the index. The biographical references are suggestive, but far from complete; to prepare a well-selected, balanced, and detailed list would have postponed publication of our book beyond the allotted time.

It has been a privilege and a pleasure to compile the studies, thanks to the cooperation of the many individuals who have been generous in their aid. The Lilly Endowment, Inc., made the book possible, by sponsoring it. The Eagle Crest Library and Indiana Historical Society, William Henry Smith Memorial Library provided the bulk of material from which it has been compiled. The Library of Congress and its staff, together with many collections throughout America in libraries and private homes, furthered it to completion, by giving access to items not in Indianapolis. It is hard to choose names for special mention from among the many persons who have been helpful. Librarians from New York to Honolulu have been particularly kind. Some members of our authors' families and people to whom our queries did not come in the line of duty responded graciously: Lew Wallace, III, John C. Rugenstein, William G. Sullivan, George Schumacher, Lee Burns, and F. Bates Johnson, all of Indianapolis; Wilda Thompson, Tacoma, Washington; Mrs. Eugen Eisenlohr, Terre Haute, Indiana; R. E. Banta and Roberta Krout, Crawfordsville; Maud Sansberry, Anderson, Indiana; William M. Hepburn, Lafayette, Indiana; Edwin C. Gilcher, Cherry Plains, New York; David A. Randall, Scribner Book Store, New York City; Ethel G. Martin, Hanover, New Hampshire; Clement C. Parker, Norristown, Pennsylvania; Paul E. Klopsteg, Evanston, Illinois; C. N. Hickman, Albuquerque, New Mexico; Otis Wheeler, St. Paul, Minnesota; Frank H. Ristine, Clinton, New York; Walter Buchen, Chicago; Willard E. Bishop, South Weymouth, Massachusetts; the late Dr. Robert P. Elmer, Wayne, Pennsylvania; Cecil J. Wilkinson, Washington, D. C.; H. J. Sievers, S. J., West Baden, Indiana; Mabel Major, Fort Worth, Texas; Robert Mullin, Toledo, Ohio; Maurice G. Fulton, Roswell, New Mexico; J. C. Dykes, College Park, Maryland; and other friends. To all who lent their interest and advice in large or small measure, we are indeed grateful.

Contents

		PAGE
PREFACE	. . . .	vii
CAROLINE VIRGINIA KROUT	. . . . .	[1]
FIRST EDITIONS		
BOOKS	. . . .	5
CONTRIBUTIONS	. . . .	11
PERIODICALS CONTAINING FIRST APPEARANCES	. .	12
MARY HANNAH KROUT	. . . . . .	[13]
FIRST EDITIONS		
BOOKS	. . . .	19
EPHEMERA	. . . .	35
CONTRIBUTIONS	. . . . . .	36
PERIODICALS CONTAINING FIRST APPEARANCES	. .	39
MEREDITH NICHOLSON	. . . . . .	[69]
FIRST EDITIONS		
BOOKS	. . . .	75
EPHEMERA	. . . .	134
CONTRIBUTIONS	. . . . . .	139
PERIODICALS CONTAINING FIRST APPEARANCES	. .	154
[JAMES] MAURICE THOMPSON	. . . . .	[173]
FIRST EDITIONS		
BOOKS	. . . .	179
EPHEMERA	. . . .	231
CONTRIBUTIONS	. . . . . .	238
PERIODICALS CONTAINING FIRST APPEARANCES	. .	252

CONTENTS

PAGE

WILL HENRY THOMPSON . . . . [285]

    FIRST EDITIONS

        BOOKS 289

        EPHEMERA 293

        CONTRIBUTIONS 297

    PERIODICALS CONTAINING FIRST APPEARANCES . . 300

LEW[IS] WALLACE . . . . [305]

    FIRST EDITIONS

        BOOKS 311

        EPHEMERA 351

        CONTRIBUTIONS 364

    PERIODICALS CONTAINING FIRST APPEARANCES . . 399

SUSAN ARNOLD ELSTON WALLACE . . . [417]

    FIRST EDITIONS

        BOOKS 421

        CONTRIBUTIONS 437

    PERIODICALS CONTAINING FIRST APPEARANCES . . 441

GENERAL INDEX . . . . [447]

Illustrations

FACING

Caroline Virginia Krout's four books, published as by
   Caroline Brown 10

Prospectus, Mary Hannah Krout's *Picturesque Honolulu*,
   proving her authorship of the brochure 30

The Marys, a poem by Mary Hannah Krout, issued in
   connection with a Marys' Day reunion 34

Meredith Nicholson's first book, *Short Flights*: the two
   bindings and a presentation inscription 76

The Port of Missing Men in first and second states of binding 96

[James] Maurice Thompson, *Sylvan Secrets*,
   two binding states 200

Letter from Maurice Thompson to the editor of
   The Independent, about his book reviews therein . . 266

Archery books: one by both Thompsons, the other by Maurice,
   but dedicated to his brother Will 290

Lew Wallace's *Ben-Hur* in flower-stamped cloth and in later
   undecorated bindings; all first edition copies . . . 316

Harpers' letter to Wallace, November 13, 1880, relating to
   Ben-Hur bindings 318

Susan E. Wallace's six books 424

CAROLINE VIRGINIA KROUT

BORN: *Crawfordsville, Indiana, October 13, 1852*
DIED: *Crawfordsville, Indiana, October 9, 1931*

THE NAME of Caroline Virginia Krout has almost been lost by her determination to remain a pseudonymous author. Her books were all published as "by Caroline Brown." This was her mother's maiden name, and she adopted it at the suggestion of Susan E. (Mrs. Lew) Wallace, who was a close family friend. She may have used other pseudonyms in periodical publications as yet unlocated. "Thad Winship" is signed to the manuscript of a short story, "Number '7648,'" with her own name also present (Krout Papers, Indiana State Library). What happened to the clippings that one would expect to find with the family papers is not known; their absence made it almost impossible to trace her contributions to newspapers and magazines.

Four books are the visible results of her work: three of them pieces of historical fiction; the first one printed, *Knights in Fustian* (1900) is most widely known and interesting for its Indiana background. The other is a juvenile, Robin Hood reappearing in original story form.

To find the outlines of her life is not difficult; to see her as anything but a timid, shadowy figure is not easy, so she must be viewed in the light of that forceful and vigorous woman who was her older sister: Mary Hannah Krout. It was Mary who, with Susan Wallace, urged and aided her to write during years of invalidism.

The burden that fell on her as a young girl may have made too many demands on her strength; she helped her father rear his family of nine children after her mother died. When a younger sister took over the household chores Caroline tried teaching school. After five years of it (she was still only twenty-four) her health failed and it was during the long period of convalescence that she started writing. Later she made efforts to take outside employment, court reporting in Crawfordsville and library work at Newberry, in Chicago. These were brief periods. Practically all of her long life was one of retirement with her family at home; she was born and she died in Crawfordsville.

The most dramatic incident of her life, which she frequently

3

told when asked about her work, centered around the fact that she and Maurice Thompson were both writing novels about the capture of Vincennes, at the same time, close to each other in the same town, each without the knowledge that the other was doing so; his, the famous *Alice of Old Vincennes*, hers the moderately successful *On the We-a Trail*.

CHRONOLOGY OF BOOKS

1900   *Knights in Fustian*   Houghton, Mifflin and Company
1903   *On the We-a Trail*   The Macmillan Company
1905   *Bold Robin and His Forest Rangers*   E. P. Dutton & Company
1911   *Dionis of the White Veil*   L. C. Page & Company

BIOGRAPHICAL REFERENCES

Who's Who in America, Vols. 2–14 (1901–1926); Meredith Nicholson, *The Hoosiers* (1900; 1915); Jacob P. Dunn, *Indiana and Indianans* (1919); W. J. Burke & Will D. Howe, *American Authors and Books 1640–1940* (1943); R. E. Banta, *Indiana Authors and Their Books* (1949). Letter, unpublished, February 4, 1917, to Charles T. Sansberry, Anderson, Indiana.

1900

Knights in Fustian

KNIGHTS IN FUSTIAN | A War Time Story of | Indiana | BY | CARO-LINE BROWN | [*2-line quotation*] | SHAKESPEARE | [*publishers' emblem*] | BOSTON AND NEW YORK | HOUGHTON, MIFFLIN AND COMPANY | The Riverside Press, Cambridge | 1900

COLLATION: [1]⁴, [2–18]⁸, [19]⁴. White laid paper. Leaf measures 7¹¹⁄₁₆″ x 4⅞″, all edges trimmed.

End paper; binder's leaf; title-page, p. [i]; copyright notice dated 1900, p. [ii]; dedication to the memory of Oliver Perry Morton, p. [iii]; blank, p. [iv]; *Preface*, pp. [v]–vi; table of contents, p. [vii]; blank, p. [viii]; text, pp. [1]–279; colophon, p. [280]; binder's leaf; end paper. [Note: Text, pp. (1)–279: Knights in Fustian, Chapters I–XXVIII (titled).]

BINDING: Blue, and, brown mesh cloth. Front cover gilt-stamped with ornament in each of the four corners: KNIGHTS | [*parallel rule*] IN [*parallel rule*] | FUSTIAN | [*parallel rule*] BY [*parallel rule*] | CAROLINE BROWN Spine gilt-stamped: KNIGHTS | [*parallel rule*] IN [*parallel rule*] | FUSTIAN | [*parallel rule*] | CAROLINE | [*parallel rule*] BROWN [*parallel rule*] | HOUGHTON | MIFFLIN & CO Back cover blank.

End papers same as book stock; binder's leaf front and back, conjugates pasted under lining papers.

PUBLICATION DATA: Published March 24, 1900. Deposited in the Copyright Office March 28th. Earliest review noted: *The Indianapolis Journal*, April 16, 1900.* Price, $1.50.

NOTES: No illustrations. Two states, distinguished by signature gatherings:

State 1: Sigs. [1]⁴, [2–18]⁸, [19]⁴
State 2: Sigs. [1–18]⁸.

---

*A later review in *The Independent*, June 7, 1900, p. 1389, unsigned, is believed to have been written by Maurice Thompson.

Errors that the author corrected by hand in a presentation copy,* remained unchanged in the printed book: p. 35, line 9, *whom* (should be *who*); p. 210, line 2, same correction suggested.

This was Caroline Krout's first novel, published pseudonymously, a story of the Knights of the Golden Circle and the "Copperhead" insurrection incited by Clement L. Vallandigham in Indiana in 1863; its background the "Balhinch" district of Montgomery County.†

1903

On the We-a Trail

ON THE WE-A TRAIL | A STORY OF THE GREAT | WILDERNESS | BY | CAROLINE BROWN | "'Tis Destiny, unshunnable, like death." | —SHAKESPEARE | WITH ILLUSTRATIONS | BY MAX KLEPPER | New York | THE MACMILLAN COMPANY | LONDON: MACMILLAN & CO., LTD. | 1903 | All rights reserved

COLLATION: B–I⁸, K⁸, [L]⁸, M–O⁸, [P]⁸, Q–U⁸, [V]⁸, Y–Z⁸, [*]⁸ (wherever signed, numeral appears on recto of 6th leaf). White laid paper. Leaf measures 7½" x 5⅟₁₆", top edge gilt, other edges untrimmed.

End paper; fly title, p. [i]; publishers' emblem, p. [ii]; frontispiece, inserted; title-page, p. [iii]; copyright notice with statement: *Set up, electrotyped, and published September, 1903,* and imprint of the Norwood Press, p. [iv]; dedication to the Sons and Daughters of the Revolution, the Colonial Dames, and the Daughters of the American Revolution, p. [v]; blank, p. [vi]; table of contents, pp. vii–viii; list of illustrations, p. ix; blank, p. [x]; text, pp. 1–351; blank, p. [352]; advertisements of Macmillan, New York, pp. [353–355]; blank, pp. [356–358]; end paper.

[Note: Text, pp. 1–351: On the We-a Trail, Chapters I–XL (titled).‡]

ILLUSTRATIONS: Frontispiece inserted as are illustrations facing

---

*In Indiana Historical Society, William Henry Smith Memorial Library.
†See *Indiana Authors and Their Books,* compiled by R. E. Banta (1949), p. 184.
‡Chapter XXXV, "A Game of Piquet," was reprinted in *Hoosier Caravan,* selected . . . by R. E. Banta (1951).

pp. 8, 34, 122, 194, 236, 286, and 320; all are from drawings by Max Klepper.

BINDING: Dark green mesh cloth. Front cover gilt-stamped: ON THE [*tilde-like mark under a small o*] | WE-A | TRAIL [*title bordered on each side by a brick-like design in red and white*] | [*white flower with gilt stamens, stem and leaves outlined in red, stamped on horizontal red and white brick-like panels, with 4 small designs in self-cloth and monogram in white at lower right*] | CAROLINE | BROWN [*author's name bordered the same as title*]. Spine gilt-stamped below a row of short red and white vertical rules: ON THE | WE-A | TRAIL | BROWN | [*two rows of short red and white vertical rules*] | THE MACMILLAN | COMPANY | [*row of red and white vertical rules*]. Back cover blank. Issued in a plain, transparent dust wrapper.

End papers white wove; no binder's leaf front or back.

PUBLICATION DATA: Deposited in the Copyright Office and published on October 7, 1903. Earliest review noted: *The Indianapolis News,* November 21st.* Price, $1.50.

NOTES: Published pseudonymously, under the name *Caroline Brown.* First edition has statement on copyright page: *Set up, electrotyped, and published September, 1903.*

In a letter to Charles T. Sansberry, February 4, 1917, the author wrote: "My second book, 'On the We-a Trail,' which dealt with the capture of Vincennes, had hard luck from the start; for Maurice Thompson, at the same time, the same summer, in this town, was writing his 'Alice.' Neither knew what the other was doing. His book was put on the market the day mine was ready to send to the publisher. Of course mine was overshadowed. It was rejected several times because of this, but finally after a year the American branch of the old London firm, Macmillans, accepted it. It too had very good success."†

Caroline Krout offered to withdraw her book in favor of *Alice of Old Vincennes* but Maurice Thompson encouraged her to find a publisher (see *The Indianapolis Star,* March 19, 1905); actually the two novels are quite dissimilar.

Macmillan issued the book in London the same month as in America. They reprinted it in a paper novel series, May, 1905, with *Special edition* on copyright page; this was available also in cheap cloth binding. A Grosset & Dunlap reprint was later put on the market.

---

*It was reviewed by Mrs. Lew Wallace in *The Indianapolis Journal,* December 28, 1903.
†Letter unpublished; property of Mrs. Charles T. Sansberry.

1905
Bold Robin

BOLD [*dot*] ROBIN [*initials and dot in red*] AND HIS | FOREST [*dot*]
RANGERS [*dot; initials and dots in red*] | [*colored illustration within
a parallel rule box*] | BY CAROLINE BROWN | DRAWINGS BY F. I. BEN-
NETT | [*ornament and dot*] NEW YORK [*dot and ornament*] | E P
DUTTON AND COMPANY [*in red*] | 31 WEST TWENTY THIRD ST.
    [Note: All within a single rule box.]

COLLATION: [*]⁴ (plus one unsigned sheet), [1] 2 [3]–[11] 12⁸
(Signature 6 erroneously numbered 7), 13⁴, one unsigned sheet. White
laid paper, wire marks 1³⁄₁₆″ apart; the white wove sheet inserted between 1st and 2nd leaf of the preliminary gathering is white coated
on front. Leaf measures 7⁹⁄₁₆″ x 5⅛″, top edge gilt, other edges untrimmed.

End paper; blank, pp. [i–ii]; inserted sheet: frontispiece with inserted tissue guard, its conjugate the title-page which bears on verso
the copyright notice dated 1905, with statement: *Published, September, 1905,* and imprint of the Knickerbocker Press; dedication to Robert
and Richard [Scearce], Lewis and William [Wallace],* p. [iii]; blank,
p. [iv]; table of contents, p. v; blank, p. [vi]; list of illustrations, p. vii;
blank, p. [viii]; half-title, p. 1; blank, p. [2]; text, pp. 3–200 (with divisional half-titles between stories, and statement at foot of pp. 76 and
200: [*Originally appeared in St. Nicholas*]); blank, pp. [201–204];
end paper.
    [Note: For text, pp. 3–200, see *Contents.*]

ILLUSTRATIONS: Colored frontispiece with legend quoted from
p. 181 of text, its conjugate the title-page; the sheet is folded and inserted with a tissue guard tipped in on the frontispiece. Inserted colored
illustrations face pp. 20, 50, 59, 86, 124, and 156. A colored illustration
also appears on the title-page. All are by F. I. Bennett.

BINDING: Blue mesh cloth. Front cover gilt-stamped within a deco-

---

*Robert and Richard Scearce were nephews of Miss Krout, Lewis and William
Wallace were grandsons of General and Mrs. Lew Wallace; they are introduced
on the dedication page as "Four Merry Men . . . lovers of the greenwood and
faithful henchmen of bold Robin Hood. . . ." The copy presented to the Wallace
boys, with inscription dated September 6, 1905, is in the Eagle Crest Library.

rative green-stamped design: BOLD [*dot*] ROBIN | AND [*dot*] HIS | FOREST [*dot*] RANGERS | [*the decorative green-stamped design, becoming more elaborate, encloses an inlaid colored illustration with the following gilt-stamped below the illustration:*] BY | CAROLINE BROWN | [*artist's initials,* F I B, *in green at foot; all within a green-stamped single rule box*]. Spine gilt-stamped: BOLD | ROBIN | AND | HIS | FOREST | RANGERS | [*rule*] | BROWN | [*green-stamped ornamental arrow design*] | E [*dot*] P [*dot*] DUTTON | & CO Back cover blank.

End papers white laid, wire marks $1\frac{1}{16}''$ apart (book stock, $1\frac{3}{16}''$); no binder's leaf front or back.

PUBLICATION DATA: Deposited in the Copyright Office August 12, 1905. Not listed in *The Publishers' Weekly* until September 23rd. Price, $1.25.

NOTES: First edition bears statement on copyright page: *Published, September, 1905.*

Issued in England by J. M. Dent & Co., November, 1905.

The author used her pseudonym, *Caroline Brown*, in this, her first and only "juvenile," a collection of stories told her young nephews which were original, one only (the last in the book) taken from the old ballads relating to Robin Hood.

CONTENTS: Six stories are here first collected.
Robin Hood's Pennyworth
George o' [*o* capitalized in table of contents] Green and Robin Hood *St. Nicholas,* October, 1896 (signed *Caroline Brown*)
Round Robin Hood's Barn
The Doughty Page
Jock o' [*o* capitalized in table of contents] Nimble Heels
The Feast in the Forest *St. Nicholas,* November, 1899 (signed *Caroline Brown*)

1911

Dionis of the White Veil

DIONIS OF THE | WHITE VEIL | [*parallel rule*] | BY | CAROLINE BROWN | AUTHOR OF "KNIGHTS IN FUSTIAN," "ON | THE WE-A TRAIL," ETC. | [*parallel rule*] | ILLUSTRATED BY | HENRY ROTH | [*publishers' emblem*] | [*parallel rule*] | L. C. PAGE & COMPANY | BOSTON [*two ornaments*] MDCCCCXI

[Note: All within an ornamental border which is enclosed in a double rule box.]

COLLATION: [1–20]⁸. White wove paper. Leaf measures 7$\frac{9}{16}$" (full) x 5$\frac{1}{16}$", top edge trimmed, other edges untrimmed.

End paper; fly title, p. [i]; blank, p. [ii]; frontispiece with tissue guard, inserted; title-page, p. [iii]; copyright notice with statement: *First Impression, July, 1911*, and imprint of the Colonial Press, p. [iv]; table of contents, pp. v–vi; list of illustrations, p. [vii]; blank, p. [viii]; text, pp. 1–291; blank, p. [292]; advertisements, *From L. C. Page & Company's Announcement List of New Fiction*, pp. [1]–6; *Selections from L. C. Page and Company's List of Fiction*, pp. [1]–12; blank, pp. [13–14]; end paper.

[Note: Text, pp. 1–291: Dionis of the White Veil, Chapters I–XXXII (titled).]

ILLUSTRATIONS: Frontispiece with tissue guard, inserted as are illustrations facing pp. 102, 138 (not 139 as in list of illustrations), 174, 230 (not 231), and 270 (not 271). All are by Henry Roth.

BINDING: Blue ribbed cloth. Front cover white-stamped: DIONIS OF THE | WHITE VEIL | by | CAROLINE BROWN [*all within a white-stamped decorative panel, the whole within a blind-stamped rule box*]. Spine white-stamped below blind-stamped rule: DIONIS | OF THE | WHITE | VEIL | by | CAROLINE | BROWN [*all within a white-stamped decorative panel*] | PAGE | [*rule*] | BOSTON [*publishers' imprint within a white-stamped decorative panel*] | [*blind-stamped rule*]. Back cover blank. Issued in an ivory-colored dust wrapper, with design of front cover reproduced in blue and gold.

End papers white wove; no binder's leaf front or back.

PUBLICATION DATA: Published July 17, 1911; deposited in the Copyright Office July 20th. Earliest review noted: *The Indianapolis News*, August 19, 1911. Price, $1.50.

NOTES: *First Impression, July, 1911*, so stated on copyright page.

The plot for this story of the founding of Post Vincennes was taken from *The Mission to the Ouabache*, by Jacob P. Dunn, Indiana Historical Society Publications, Vol. 3, No. 4, 1902; ". . . with the exception of the love story it follows the text faithfully."*

In this, her last book, the author maintained her pseudonym, insisting on its use by the publishers in their advertising copy.

---

*Dunn, Jacob P.: *Indiana and Indianans* (1919), Vol. V, p. 1924.

Caroline Virginia Krout's four books, published as by "Caroline Brown"

First Editions — Contributions

1901

WHO'S WHO IN AMERICA 1901–1902. [Volume 2]. Chicago, A. N. Marquis & Co. [1901]

Contains an autobiographical sketch, p. 652. This appeared, with additions, in succeeding volumes through 1926–1927, Volume 14.

1912

THE HOOSIER ALMANACK AND FAMILY MAGAZINE [for 1913]. Indiana Society of Chicago, 1912

Pictorial yellow wrappers. Souvenir of the eighth annual dinner, December 7, 1912. Contains a short story, "The Baby," signed *Caroline Brown Krout*, p. 73.

Periodicals Containing First Appearances

THE COSMOPOLITAN
    1896: August   Under the Shadow of Tyburn-Tree (*signed Caroline Brown*)*

    1898: November   The Tragedies of the Kohinoor (*signed Caroline Brown*)†

INDIANA MAGAZINE OF HISTORY
    1927: March   Dr. Ryland Thomas Brown (*signed Caroline Brown*)†

THE INDIANAPOLIS NEWS
    1898: December 9   The Story of His [Maurice Thompson's] Life and Achievements (*signed Caroline Brown*)†

MEN AND WOMEN
    1903: January   Writers of Today—II: General Lew Wallace (*signed Caroline Brown*)†

OUTING
    1903: February   Brannigan (*signed Caroline Brown*)†

ST. NICHOLAS
    1896: October   George o' Green and Robin Hood (*signed Caroline Brown*)

    1899: November   The Feast in the Forest (*signed Caroline Brown*)

SUCCESS
    1901: August   The Literary Redemption of Indiana . . . Discussed by Lewis Wallace and James Whitcomb Riley [interview, *signed Caroline Brown*]†

NOTES: Titles of three pieces written by her, but not located in print have been recorded: "Archibald Kenshaw," a story "ready for the publishers" according to an interview in *The Indianapolis Journal*, September 15, 1903; "In an Early Day," described as a typescript of a story of life in the Old Northwest Territory, with a poem, "The Pioneers"; and "The Pathfinders," typescript of a sketch of the early history of Montgomery County.

---

*Uncollected; her first story, according to a biographical sketch in *Current Literature*, August, 1900, p. 148.

†Uncollected.

MARY HANNAH KROUT

BORN: *Crawfordsville, Indiana, November 3, 1851*

DIED: *Crawfordsville, Indiana, May 31, 1927*

MARY HANNAH KROUT

Mary Hannah Krout could be done justice to only in a full-length biography. She was ahead of her times; one whose interests spread over the whole world, a writer of vigorous comments on both timely and timeless subjects. Of her eight books (and this figure includes a brochure which was anonymous and by its format might be classed as a bit of ephemera), five deal with the Hawaiian Islands, one with London, another with China, just one with generalities. The titles give only a slight clue to the wealth of writing from which they were selected.

The field of her choice was journalism, at a time when women were not common in it, especially one successful enough to secure an appointment as foreign correspondent for a leading newspaper of the nineties, *The* (Chicago) *Inter Ocean*. Her reports to the paper of the Benjamin Harrison Presidential campaign, written from Indianapolis during the summer and autumn of 1888, had given her prestige. She had already made a name for herself as a literary woman by her contributions to Indiana newspapers: poems, articles, and "gossip" columns which were far from amateurish in style and contents, not feminine, feministic; the cause of woman's rights was always a crusade for her.

Her career had started with teaching. She was employed in the local schools for about twelve years, but she had been writing since she was twelve and decided to make it a profession when she was in the early thirties. For a while she used pseudonyms: "Mynheer Heinrich Karl," "Mary Hannah Kennedy," "LeRoy Armstrong" are proven to be hers. She may have authored some "Austin Lawrence" papers on Hawaiian subjects; their presence as manuscripts among the Krout Papers in the Indiana State Library is indication (they have not been found published). A similar situation exists with a story, "An Attraction of Opposites," signed, "Jane Richardson." "Anna Dickinson" is a name she is reported to have used when she was seventeen, but neither corroboration nor publications so signed have come to light.

Before she became associate editor of *The Crawfordsville Jour-*

nal at the close of the year 1882, she is said to have served as editor of *The Terre Haute Gazette.* It has been stated, too, that she was on the staff of *The* (Peoria, Illinois) *Saturday Evening Call* in 1885 and *The* (Chicago) *Interior* in 1886. During her subsequent ten-year connection with *The* (Chicago) *Inter Ocean* she lived not only in Chicago, but also in Hawaii and London, traveled extensively on the continents of Europe and Asia, and wrote continually. She returned to Hawaii on her own responsibility after *The Inter Ocean* was sold; also took a journey to China, a country that had particular appeal to her. *The* (New York) *Sun* interviewed her; their report of "The Woman Globe Trotter" in the issue of April 7, 1901, makes interesting reading. Early in this century she spent some time in Denver, Colorado, and wrote for their *Times,* being on their staff and also contributing a column of "Odds and Ends" and signed feature stories. In 1906 she revisited Australia, in 1907, Hawaii. Herewith ended her world travels; the rest of her life was a quiet one in Crawfordsville; like her sister, Caroline, she died in this city of her birth.

Little of Mary Krout's poetry appeared in books, but much was printed in newspapers and magazines. A collection to be entitled, *Songs of the Wayside,* was projected but not published.

She tried out her talents in drama; wrote two plays and took part in their production. "A Man in the House," a comedy in two acts, was presented in Crawfordsville, December 24, 1875, and again on February 7, 1879; it was on the stage in Indianapolis at English's the week of May 25, 1885 (Susan E. Wallace reviewed the latter for *The Indianapolis Journal,* May 31st). The other, "The Widow Selby," had local production on March 31, 1876; the author played the part of the widow. It is not surprising, then, that Mary Krout was at home on the lecture platform, or that she was a speaker at Republican political rallies, or that she presided over the Chicago (Woman's) Press League.

The secret of Mary Krout's successful career probably lies in her personality, so definitely reflected in her writing, summed up in an editorial in *The Indianapolis News* the day following her death: "She was a woman of fine literary taste, great force of character, and deep religious feeling. Also she was one of the friendliest of souls, with a keen sense of humor and a zest for life."

CHRONOLOGY OF BOOKS

1898 *Hawaii and a Revolution* Dodd, Mead and Company
1899 *A Looker On in London* Dodd, Mead & Company
1900 *Alice's Visit to the Hawaiian Islands* American Book Company
1903 *Two Girls in China* American Book Company
1907 *Picturesque Honolulu* The Hawaiian Gazette Co., Ltd.
1908 *Reminiscences of Mrs. Mary S. Rice* The Hawaiian Gazette Co., Ltd. *The Memoirs of Hon. Bernice Pauahi Bishop* [Knickerbocker Press]
1910 *Platters and Pipkins* A. C. McClurg & Co.

BIOGRAPHICAL REFERENCES

Who's Who in America, Vols. 2–14 (*Who Was Who in America 1897–1942* has added information that appeared in newspaper obituaries and includes listing of a book title, *The Eleventh Hour*, of which no record has yet been found); Meredith Nicholson, *The Hoosiers* (1900; 1915); Jacob P. Dunn, *Indiana and Indianans* (1919); R. E. Banta, *Indiana Authors and Their Books* (1949). Krout Papers, from the collection of her father, Robert Kennedy Krout, a miscellany of clippings, scrapbooks, and manuscripts, in the Indiana State Library; a Mary H. Krout scrapbook in the University of Chicago Library.

1898

Hawaii and a Revolution

(American edition)

HAWAII | AND A REVOLUTION | THE PERSONAL EXPERIENCES | OF A | CORRESPONDENT IN THE SANDWICH ISLANDS | DURING THE CRISIS OF 1893 | AND SUBSEQUENTLY | BY | MARY H. KROUT | NEW YORK | DODD, MEAD AND COMPANY | 1898

COLLATION: [*]⁸, 1–20⁸, 21⁶. White laid paper. Leaf measures 7⅞″ x 5⅜″, top edge red, other edges untrimmed.

End paper; fly title, p. [i]; blank, p. [ii]; frontispiece, inserted; title-page, p. [iii]; copyright notice dated 1898, and imprint of the University Press, John Wilson and Son, Cambridge, U. S. A., p. [iv]; dedication to her father [Robert Kennedy Krout], p. [v]; blank, p. [vi]; *Preface* dated January 9th, 1898, pp. vii–x; table of contents, pp. xi–xiv; list of illustrations, p. [xv]; blank, p. [xvi]; *Introduction*, dated December, 1897, pp. [1]*–31; blank, p. [32]; text, pp. 33–321; blank, p. [322]; *Index*, pp. [323]–330; blank, pp. [331–332]; end paper.

[Note: For text, pp. 33–321, see *Contents*.]

ILLUSTRATIONS: Frontispiece inserted as are illustrations facing pp. 88 (not 89 as in list of illustrations), 94, 114, 202 (not 203), 286 (not 287), 306, and 316 (not 317). All are from photographs. A rule appears below caption on pp. vii, xi, [xv], [1], and [323], also between *Contents* and *Index*, p. xiv.

BINDING: Dark blue silk-finished mesh cloth. Front cover orange-stamped: HAWAII | AND A | REVOLUTION | [*Hawaiian scene stamped in orange, pale yellow, light blue and black; artist's initials, FB(?)S, at lower right; all within single rule black box*] | MARY [*dot*] H [*dot*] KROUT Spine orange-stamped: HAWAII | AND [*dot*] A [*dot*] | REVO- | LUTION | [*pale yellow and orange scabbard crossed with a light blue,*

---

*Numeral at foot considered a signature identification, not pagination.

orange, and black battle-ax, both outlined in black, within a black single rule box] | *[dot]* KROUT *[dot]* | DODD, MEAD & | COMPANY   Back cover blank.

End papers calendered; no binder's leaf front or back.

PUBLICATION DATA: Deposited in the Copyright Office, August 18, 1898. Earliest review noted: *The Friend,* September, 1898. Price, $2.00.

NOTES: Misprint in chapter numbering in running head, pp. 142 and 144, IX (should be X), present in all copies of the American edition.

The author's personal experiences in Hawaii during the early days of the Provisional Government, 1893–1894, were woven into this political study. Her "long-cherished hope of securing an appointment as special war correspondent from that island was finally realized when the Chicago Inter Ocean yielded its prejudices against employing a woman in that capacity and decided to avail itself of her services."* This was her first book.

Simultaneous publication took place in England (see *post* 22).

CONTENTS: Much of the text had earlier appeared as her "Special Correspondence" from Hawaii, in *The* (Chicago) *Inter Ocean,* 1893– 1895. Some of the letters from Hawaii published in the newspaper remained uncollected, others were so revised in the process of selection for the book that they have proved difficult to identify as part of it. Portions of the introduction and Chapters XXI, XXIII–XXV might have been gleaned from scattered comments in her dispatches; the first two chapters were evidently new writing for the book.

CHAPTER
    I   The First Impulse
    II   Disappointments
    III From Chicago to Hawaii   *The* (Chicago) *Inter Ocean,*
            March 13, 1893 (with caption: Hawaiians at Home)
    IV   A First Impression *The* (Chicago) *Inter Ocean,*
            March 13, 1893 (with caption: Hawaiians at Home)
    V   In Honolulu   *The* (Chicago) *Inter Ocean,* March 18,
            1893 (with caption: Hawaiian Politics); March 24,
            1893 (with caption: Life in Honolulu)

---

*The Friend, September, 1898, p. 76. The author had been reporting national as well as local events for *The* (Chicago) *Inter Ocean* since 1888. Her letters from Hawaii, and about Hawaii, began their appearance therein on March 9, 1893 (see *post* 46, 48, 50); her interest in the territory continued (for a summary of her books on Hawaii, see *post* 32).

VI The Home of Kaiulani *The* (Chicago) *Inter Ocean*, March 21, 1893 (with caption: Home of a Princess)

VII An Ostrich Farm *The* (Chicago) *Inter Ocean*, April 4, 1893

VIII A Visit to Camp Boston *The* (Chicago) *Inter Ocean*, March 27, 1893 (with caption: In Regal Quarters)

IX King Kalakaua's Palace *The* (Chicago) *Inter Ocean*, March 23, 1893 (with caption: Kalakaua's Palace); April 9, 1893 (with caption: A Hawaiian Farm)

X The President's Commissioner *The* (Chicago) *Inter Ocean*, April 6, 1893 (with caption: Support the New Government); April 16, 1893 (with caption: Royal Emissaries Return)

XI The Lowering of the American Flag *The* (Chicago) *Inter Ocean*, April 14, 1893 (with caption: Old Glory Down)

XII Violated Coronets *The* (Chicago) *Inter Ocean*, April 28, 1893 (with caption: The Crown Jewels)

XIII The Princess Kaiulani *The* (Chicago) *Inter Ocean*, March 29, 1893 (with caption: Must Annex Hawaii); November 21, 1895 (with caption: Fresh London Notes)

XIV The Chinese Population *The* (Chicago) *Inter Ocean*, May 7, 1893 (with caption: A Chinese Paradise)

XV The Queen-Dowager *The* (Chicago) *Inter Ocean*, May 13, 1893 (with caption: A Queen Dowager)

XVI The Leper Settlement *The* (Chicago) *Inter Ocean*, March 30, 1893 (with caption: Lepers and Molakai)

XVII An Audience with Queen Liliuokalani *The* (Chicago) *Inter Ocean*, May 12, 1893 (with caption: Pacific Royalty)

XVIII The Close of the Blount Administration *The* (Chicago) *Inter Ocean*, February 18, 1894 (with caption: Our Hawaii Letter)

XIX In Hilo *The* (Chicago) *Inter Ocean*, March 3, 1894 (with caption: In Halcyon Hilo); April 1, 1894 (with caption: In the Hilo Swim)

XX A Little Journey to Kileauea *The* (Chicago) *Inter Ocean*, March 31, 1894 (with caption: Visiting a Volcano)

XXI Social Life

XXII   An Interlude   *The* (Chicago) *Inter Ocean,* May 26, 1894
          (with caption: In the South Seas)
XXIII   Ancient Customs
XXIV   Products
XXV   The Passing of the Native*

1898

Hawaii and a Revolution

(English edition)

HAWAII | AND A REVOLUTION | THE PERSONAL EXPERIENCES | OF A | NEWSPAPER CORRESPONDENT IN THE SANDWICH ISLANDS | DURING THE CRISIS OF 1893 | AND SUBSEQUENTLY | BY | MARY H. KROUT | LONDON | JOHN MURRAY, ALBEMARLE STREET | 1898

COLLATION: [*]1–20⁸, 21⁴, 22². White laid paper. Leaf measures 8⁵⁄₁₆" x 5⅜", all edges untrimmed.

End paper; blank, pp. [1–2]; fly title, p. [i]; blank, p. [ii]; frontispiece with tissue guard, inserted; title-page, p. [iii]; blank, except for rule and imprint: *Printed by Hazell, Watson, & Viney, Ld., London and Aylesbury,* p. [iv]; dedication, to her father [Robert Kennedy Krout], p. [v]; blank, p. [vi]; *Preface* dated March 1898, pp. vii–x; table of contents, pp. xi–xiv (with list of illustrations also on p. xiv); *Introduction* dated December, 1897, pp. [1]†–31; blank, p. [32]; text, pp. 33–321; blank, p. [322]; *Index,* pp. 323–332 (with imprint at foot of p. 332); end paper.

[Note: Text, pp. 33–321: Hawaii and a Revolution, Introduction, and Chapters I–XXV (titled).]

ILLUSTRATIONS: Frontispiece with tissue guard, inserted as are illustrations facing pp. 84, 100, 144, 192, 256, 288, 316. A rule appears below caption on pp. [v], vii, xi, [1], 33, and 323, also between *Contents* and *List Of Illustrations,* p. xiv.

BINDING: Red silk-finished mesh cloth. Front cover gilt-stamped

---

*For this chapter she used material from a letter captioned, "Customs of Hawaii [*sic*]," written from Honolulu, March 18, year unnamed, not located in *The* (Chicago) *Inter Ocean,* 1893 or 1894; a clipping is preserved in the Krout Scrapbook in University of Chicago, Harper Library.

†Numeral at foot considered a signature identification, not pagination.

within a quadruple rule box: HAWAII | AND A REVOLUTION | [*rule*] | MARY H. KROUT Spine gilt-stamped: [*quadruple rule*] | HAWAII | [*rule*] | KROUT | [*ornament*] | LONDON | JOHN MURRAY | [*quadruple rule*]. Back cover blank except for blind-stamped quadruple rule box. Issued in a plain green dust wrapper.

End papers white laid, slightly less heavy than book stock; no binder's leaf front or back.

PUBLICATION DATA: Published 1898, apparently simultaneously with the American edition. Earliest review noted: *The Field, the Country Gentleman's Newspaper* (London), December 3rd. Price, 10s 6d.

NOTES: The book was published simultaneously in America and England according to *The Indianapolis Journal*, November 13, 1898, which quoted a review from the *London Daily News*. *The English Catalogue*, however, gives date of publication as October, 1898, while the American edition is known to have been a September publication. The preface of the New York edition is dated January 9th, 1898; the same preface in the London edition, March, 1898; this may or may not indicate earlier preparation for issuance in America; for collation see *ante* 19.

Two states of the British edition have been noted:

State 1: As collated, with final signature, 22, a single sheet (later, two sheets). Thus in a copy with contemporary inscription dated 1898

State 2: Final signature, 22, two sheets, the last leaf of which is used as back lining paper, extending pagination to p. [336] (earlier, pagination ends with p. 332, the final signature, 22, being a single sheet, followed by an end paper).

1899
A Looker On in London

A LOOKER ON | IN LONDON [*article two lines high; title in red*] | By MARY H. KROUT | Author of HAWAII IN TIME OF REVOLUTION* | [*ornament, chalice-like*] | NEW YORK: DODD, MEAD [*in red*] | & COMPANY, [*in red*] MDCCCXCIX

[Note: All within a parallel rule box.]

---

*Erroneous title; the book was published as *Hawaii and a Revolution*.

COLLATION: [1–22]⁸, [23]⁴. White wove paper. Leaf measures 7⅝″ x 5⅛″, top edge trimmed, other edges untrimmed.

End paper; title-page, p. [i]; copyright notice dated 1899, p. [ii]; dedication to Susan Elston Wallace, p. [iii]; blank, p. [iv]; table of contents, pp. v–vii; blank, p. [viii]; *Preface* dated December 1898, pp. 1–3; blank, p. [4]; text, pp. 5–352; end paper.

[Note: For text, pp. 5–352, see *Contents*.]

BINDING: Dark gray mesh cloth. Front cover has a London scene stamped in ivory and two shades of blue in a panel at left; title and author's name ivory-stamped at right: A | Looker-on | in London | Mary H Krout [*all within ivory-stamped single rule box*]. Spine ivory-stamped: [*rule*] | A Looker- | on in | London | Mary | H | Krout | DODD, MEAD | & COMPANY | [*rule*]. The font in title and author's name on front cover and spine is script-like, with some letters intertwined, some ending in a curlicue. Back cover blank.

End papers ivory calendered; no binder's leaf front or back.

PUBLICATION DATA: Deposited in the Copyright Office, September 16, 1899. Listed in *The Publishers' Weekly*, October 21, 1899; it had been advertised therein in the "Autumn Books" list of September 30th. Price, $1.50.

NOTES: First edition as collated. No illustrations. Actually contains 27 chapters although table of contents lists only I–XXVI. The table of contents does not break "The Venezuela Controversy" into two chapters, hence, beginning with Chapter XVIII, there is a discrepancy in the numbering in table of contents to the end.

A British edition is reported as published by B. F. Stevens, November, 1899; unlocated, possibly a distribution in London of the American edition.

CONTENTS: Earlier published in a series of "London letters," reports as staff correspondent for *The* (Chicago) *Inter Ocean*, 1895–1897; with selections from her column, "Woman's Kingdom."

CHAPTER

I "Going Down to London" *The* (Chicago) *Inter Ocean*, August 17, 1895 (with caption: Scottish Sketches); August 18, 1895 (with caption: England in August)

II The Opening of Parliament *The* (Chicago) *Inter Ocean*, August 25, 1895 (with caption: The House of Peers)

III Lord Leighton *The* (Chicago) *Inter Ocean*, September 10, 1895 (with caption: Prince of Painters)

IV After the Season and London Weather *The* (Chicago)

Inter Ocean, October 6, 1895 (with caption: Only a Meadow Mist); October 7, 1895 (with caption: John Bull at Home)

V Carlyle's House *The* (Chicago) *Inter Ocean,* December 27, 1895 (with caption: Late London Notes)

VI Pentonville Prison *The* (Chicago) *Inter Ocean,* February 27, 1896 (with caption: In a Great Prison)

VII In the Lower Courts *The* (Chicago) *Inter Ocean,* December 1, 1895 (with caption: Justice as Administered in Expeditious English Courts)*

VIII English Women and Their Affairs *The* (Chicago) *Inter Ocean,* December 14, 1895 (with caption: Woman's Kingdom)

IX Women's Clubs *The* (Chicago) *Inter Ocean,* January 4, 11, 1896 (with caption: Woman's Kingdom)

X Women's Schools and Colleges *The* (Chicago) *Inter Ocean,* November 30, 1895 (with caption: Woman's Kingdom)

XI The Queen's Bounty *The* (Chicago) *Inter Ocean,* April 18, 1896 (with caption: Bounty of a Queen)

XII The Annual Habitation of the Primrose League *The* (Chicago) *Inter Ocean,* May 17, 1896 (with caption: Women in Politics)

XIII In Kentish Fields *The* (Chicago) *Inter Ocean,* June 1, 1896

XIV Henley *The* (Chicago) *Inter Ocean,* July 20, 1896 (with caption: Henley's Gay Scene)

XV The Princess Maud's Wedding *The* (Chicago) *Inter Ocean,* August 10, 1896 (with caption: Hot Days in London)

XVI Death of the Prince of Battenberg *The* (Chicago) *Inter Ocean,* February 9, 1896 (with caption: London in Mourning); February 21, 1896 (with caption: Week of Funerals)

XVII The Venezuela Controversy *The* (Chicago) *Inter Ocean,* December 31, 1895 (with caption: John and Jonathan)

XVIII The Venezuela Controversy—continued† *The* (Chicago) *Inter Ocean,* December 31, 1895 (with caption:

---

*In her letters published September 28 and October 6, 1895, Mary Hannah Krout discussed women and English law, but not in the same words as in the latter portion of Chapter VII.

†See *Notes* for explanation of difference between text and table of contents in numbering Chapters XVIII–XXVII.

John and Jonathan); January 7, 1896 (with caption: She Stood Amazed); January 27, 1896 (with caption: No War with America)

XIX The Chartered Company   *The* (Chicago) *Inter Ocean,* January 27, 1896 (with caption: No War with America)

XX The Jameson Trial   *The* (Chicago) *Inter Ocean,* March 30, April 5, 1896 (with caption: Dr. Jameson's Trial) son's Trial)

XXI The Jameson Trial—continued   *The* (Chicago) *Inter Ocean,* May 10 and 12, 1896 (with caption: Dr. Jame-

XXII Cipher Messages   *The* (Chicago) *Inter Ocean,* June 27, 1896 (with caption: Dr. Jameson's Trial)

XXIII Before the Lord Chief Justice   *The* (Chicago) *Inter Ocean,* August 8, 1896 (with caption: Dr. Jameson's Trial); August 14, 1896 (with caption: Passing of "Dr. Jim")

XXIV The Diamond Jubilee   *The* (Chicago) *Inter Ocean,* July 4, 1897 (with caption: London's Big Show)

XXV The Princess of Wales' Dinner   *The* (Chicago) *Inter Ocean,* July 12, 1897 (with caption: Little Children Fed)

XXVI The Illuminations   *The* (Chicago) *Inter Ocean,* July 11, 1897 (with caption: Evening of Jubilee)

XXVII The Jubilee Commemoration at Oxford   *The* (Chicago) *Inter Ocean,* July 18, 1897 (with caption: Customs of Oxford)

1900

Alice's Visit to the Hawaiian Islands

ECLECTIC SCHOOL READINGS | [*rule*] | ALICE'S VISIT | TO | THE HA-
WAIIAN ISLANDS | BY | MARY H. KROUT | AUTHOR OF "HAWAII AND A
REVOLUTION," "A LOOKER-ON | IN LONDON," ETC. | [*ornamental
rule*] | NEW YORK [*ornament*] CINCINNATI [*ornament*] CHICAGO |
AMERICAN BOOK COMPANY

COLLATION: [1]–13^8. White calendered paper. Leaf measures 7¼" x 5", all edges trimmed.*

End paper; binder's leaf; blank, pp. [1–4]; frontispiece, inserted; title-page, p. [5]; copyright notice dated 1900, statements: *Krout's Hawaii.*, and *W. P. 1*, p. [6]; *Preface*, pp. 7–8; table of contents, pp. 9–10; text, pp. 11–206; *Pronunciation of Hawaiian Names And Terms*, pp. 207–208 (with imprint of J. S. Cushing & Co., Norwood, Mass., at foot of p. 208); binder's leaf; end paper.

[Note: Text, pp. 11–206: Alice's Visit to the Hawaiian Islands, Chapters I–XXXV (titled), followed by a key to pronunciation of names and terms.]

ILLUSTRATIONS: Frontispiece a colored map, a folded sheet on stub. Profuse text illustrations. Chapters all have tailpiece or ornament at end with the exception of II, XVIII, and XXXI.

BINDING: Light green mesh cloth. Front cover stamped in dark green: [*ornamental border*] | ECLECTIC SCHOOL READINGS | [*tree ornament*] ALICE'S VISIT [*tree ornament*] | TO THE | HAWAIIAN ISLANDS | [*vignette with tree ornaments at sides and below; all with ornamental border at each side*] | [*rule*] | [*broken rule formed of dots and dashes*] | [*rule*] | NEW YORK [*dot*] CINCINNATI [*dot*] CHICAGO | AMERICAN [*dot*] BOOK [*dot*] COMPANY | [*imprint boxed within single rules at top and bottom and side designs of single rule, wide rule, single rule*] | [*row of ornaments*] | [*parallel rule*]. Spine dark green-stamped: [*parallel rule*] | ALICE'S | VISIT | TO THE | HAWAIIAN | ISLANDS | [*rule*] | KROUT | [*ornament*] | AMERICAN | BOOK | COMPANY | [*parallel rule*]. Back cover bears dark green-stamped publisher's emblem.

End papers white wove, sewn in with a binder's sheet, half of which is pasted under the lining paper; same front and back.

PUBLICATION DATA: Deposited in the Copyright Office May 24, 1900. Listed in *The Publisher's Weekly*, June 2nd. Price, 45¢.

NOTES: First edition bears symbol on copyright page, *W. P. 1*.

D. McNetton & Company, New York, published it with statement at top of title-page: *The Youth's Library*; symbol on copyright page, *M. B. C. 1*. The book was in print as late as 1928, judging by listing in the *Cumulative Book Index*.

Material for it was gathered during her visit to the Islands 1898–1899, after the conclusion of her work as staff correspondent for *The* (Chicago) *Inter Ocean*. The background may go back to her first year there, 1893–1894.

---

*The copy in the Library of the Hawaiian Mission Children's Society, Honolulu, is reported as measuring 7½" x 5".

1903
Two Girls in China

ECLECTIC SCHOOL READINGS | [*rule*] | TWO GIRLS IN CHINA | BY | MARY H. KROUT | AUTHOR OF "HAWAII AND A REVOLUTION," "ALICE'S | VISIT TO THE HAWAIIAN ISLANDS," "A | LOOKER-ON IN LONDON," ETC. | NEW YORK [*ornament*] CINCINNATI [*ornament*] CHICAGO | AMERICAN BOOK COMPANY

COLLATION: [1]–13⁸. White calendered paper. Leaf measures 7¼″ x 4⅞″, all edges trimmed.

End paper; binder's leaf; blank, p. [1]; frontispiece, p. [2]; title-page, p. [3]; copyright notice dated 1903, statement of entry at Stationers' Hall, London, brief title, and symbol: W. P. *1*, p. [4]; *Preface*, pp. 5–6; table of contents, pp. 7–8; text, pp. 9–208; binder's leaf; end paper.

[Note: Text, pp. 9–208: Two Girls in China, I–XXI (titled).]

ILLUSTRATIONS: Frontispiece, map of China and Japan, an integral part of the book. Numerous text illustrations from photographs.

BINDING: Light green mesh cloth. Front cover stamped in dark green*: [*ornamental border*] | ECLECTIC SCHOOL READINGS | TWO GIRLS | IN | CHINA | [*vignette, wreathed and surrounded, as is the title, with Chinese ornaments and with ornamental border at each side*] | [*rule*] | [*broken rule formed of dots and dashes*] | [*rule*] | NEW YORK [*dot*] CIN-CINNATI [*dot*] CHICAGO | AMERICAN [*dot*] BOOK [*dot*] COMPANY [*imprint boxed within single rules at top and bottom and side designs of single rule, wide rule, single rule*] | [*row of ornaments*] | [*parallel rule*]. Spine dark green-stamped, reading from bottom to top: [*Chinese ornament*] TWO [*dot*] GIRLS [*dot*] IN [*dot*] CHINA [*Chinese ornament*]. Back cover bears dark green-stamped publisher's emblem.

End papers white wove, sewn in with a binder's sheet, half of which is pasted under the lining paper; same front and back.

PUBLICATION DATA: Published March 17, 1903; deposited in the Copyright Office March 18th. Price, 45¢.

NOTES: First edition bears symbol on copyright page, W. P. *1*.

---

*Possibly originally black, faded to green.

In the preface the author states that material for it was obtained during some months of travel in China in 1899–1900, preceding the Boxer rebellion. "Almost three months were spent in the capital . . . ." The book was still in print in 1928.

1907

Picturesque Honolulu

Picturesque [*green*] | Honolulu [*white, green-shadowed; title on an elaborate pictorial green panel with artist's name and date at lower right:*] E M Grosse [*white*] 1907 [*green, white-shadowed; all the foregoing hand-lettered on the above-mentioned panel within a lighter green border; price and imprint on an outer white border, at top:*] PRICE, 15 CENTS PER COPY | [*at bottom:*] PUB-LISHED BY THE HAWAIIAN GAZETTE CO., LTD., HONOLULU, T. H.

[Note: Foregoing printed on front wrapper, which serves as title page.]

COLLATION: Wire side-stitched. White calendered paper. Leaf measures 15½" x 11¼", all edges trimmed.

Illustrations, p. i; advertisements, pp. ii–iii; *The Promotion Committee*, p. iv; text, pp. [1]–72 (with title, date, publisher and place at top of p. [1]); advertisements, pp. 73–80.
[Note: For text, pp. (1)–72, see *Contents*.]

ILLUSTRATIONS: Profuse textual illustrations from photographs.

BINDING: Pictorial, green tinted on white wrappers, front serving as title-page. Spine reads, from top to bottom: PICTURESQUE HONOLULU 1907 HAWAIIAN GAZETTE CO.* Pictorial back wrapper. Inside front and back wrappers bear advertisements.

PUBLICATION DATA: Published February, 1907. An advertisement has been noted in *The Pacific Commercial Advertiser*, February 23, 1907; earlier, a prospectus in same, January 15, 1907, similarly worded, included a statement: "To be ready in February or March, 1907"; omis-

---

*Thus on rebound copies, presumably text of original spine. Thus far no copy has been found as issued. Mrs. Violet A. Silverman, of the Library of Hawaii, reports evidence of original wire stapling. The Hawaiian Historical Society's copy is also rebound, but contains both front and back wrappers.

sion of this statement in the advertisement of February 23rd indicates that the book was then available. Price, 15 cents. Number of copies: *ca.* 15,000; estimate based on the announcement in *The Pacific Advertiser,* January 15, 1907: "There will be an edition of not less than 15,000."

NOTES: Published anonymously. An advertisement in an unidentified newspaper, establishing Mary Hannah Krout as author of all the articles except those signed by others (advertisement reproduced facing here), found in her father's scrapbook, has a parenthetical three written in her hand to indicate the number of the articles not hers, but actually there were four (see *Contents*). The advertisement was evidently from an early prospectus (not the one in *The Pacific Commercial Advertiser*) since it lists "Honolulu in 1893"; the article as it appears in the book is entitled, "Honolulu in 1903," most of it pertaining to her arrival in Hawaii in 1893, but the final paragraph referring to later events, which made the earlier date inappropriate.

CONTENTS: All the articles herein are Mary Hannah Krout's with exception of four: "When I Came to Honolulu," by A. S. Cleghorn; "The Bernice Pauahi Bishop Museum," by L. G. Blackman; "Honolulu the Home of Out-Door Sports," by R. O. Matheson; "Honolulu's Mardi Gras," by Mrs. W. M. Graham. Only the poem, "Tantalus," and the article, "Honolulu in 1903," bear a Krout signature; that the other articles are hers is borne out by the prospectus mentioned in foregoing *Notes,* which stated: "The articles, with the exception of those signed, were written by Miss Mary Hannah Krout, who also carefully arranged and edited the account of historical incidents, the data for which was furnished by old residents . . . ." Her brief account of historical incidents, without titles, fill in space at end of articles. Her titled contributions are as follows:

Native Chiefs of Honolulu
Tantalus
Honolulu Literature and Authors
Founders of Honolulu
Honolulu Society
Kapiolani Park
Honolulu in 1903
The Clubs of Honolulu
The Oriental Quarter
Hawaiian Court Ladies
Honolulu's Royal Residences
What Honolulu Has
The Aquarium

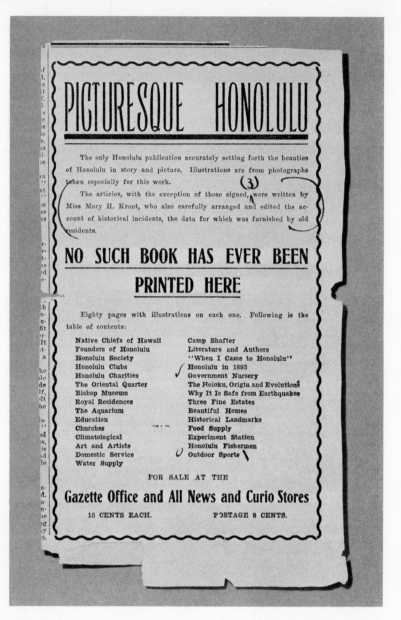

PICTURESQUE HONOLULU

The only Honolulu publication accurately setting forth the beauties of Honolulu in story and picture. Illustrations are from photographs taken especially for this work.

The articles, with the exception of those signed, were written by Miss Mary H. Krout, who also carefully arranged and edited the account of historical incidents, the data for which was furnished by old residents.

NO SUCH BOOK HAS EVER BEEN

PRINTED HERE

Eighty pages with illustrations on each one. Following is the table of contents:

Native Chiefs of Hawaii	Camp Shafter
Founders of Honolulu	Literature and Authors
Honolulu Society	"When I Came to Honolulu"
Honolulu Clubs	Honolulu in 1893
Honolulu Charities	Government Nursery
The Oriental Quarter	The Holoku, Origin and Evolution
Bishop Museum	Why It Is Safe from Earthquakes
Royal Residences	Three Fine Estates
The Aquarium	Beautiful Homes
Education	Historical Landmarks
Churches	Food Supply
Climatological	Experiment Station
Art and Artists	Honolulu Fishermen
Domestic Service	Outdoor Sports
Water Supply	

FOR SALE AT THE

Gazette Office and All News and Curio Stores

15 CENTS EACH.   POSTAGE 8 CENTS.

Prospectus, Mary Hannah Krout's PICTURESQUE HONOLULU,
proving her authorship of the brochure

Education in Honolulu
Honolulu Churches
Climate of Honolulu; Its Value as a Health Resort
Water Supply of Honolulu
Art and Artists in Honolulu
An Impression of the Government Nursery
Honolulu Charities
The Holoku—Its Origin and Evolutions
Why Honolulu Is Safe from Earthquakes
Three Fine Estates
Fine Residences
On Tantalus Heights
Historical Landmarks of Honolulu
The Food Supply of Honolulu
The Hawaii Experiment Station
Among Honolulu's Fishermen
Domestic Service in Honolulu
Camp Shafter

1908

Reminiscences of
Mrs. Mary S. Rice

REMINISCENCES | OF | MRS. MARY S. RICE | BY | MARY H. KROUT |
[*ornament, lighted candle in holder*] | HONOLULU, T. H. | THE HA-
WAIIAN GAZETTE CO., LTD. | 1908

COLLATION: [1–9]⁸. White wove paper, watermarked: EXETER [*ornament*] *1886* [*ornament*] & CO. [*ornament*]. Leaf measures 9⅛″ x
5⅞″, all edges trimmed.

End paper; blank, pp. [i–ii]; title-page, p. [iii]; blank, p. [iv]; table
of contents, p. [1]; blank, p. [2]; *Preface*, July 24, 1908, p. [3]; blank,
p. [4]; text, pp. [5]–143; blank, p. [144]; end paper.

[Note: Text, pp. (5)–143: Reminiscences of Mrs. Mary S. Rice,
Chapters I–XIX (titled).]

ILLUSTRATIONS: Reproductions from photographs, facing pp. [5],
[96], 130, and [138].

BINDING: Brown coarse mesh cloth. Parallel rule box blind-stamped on front cover which is otherwise blank. Spine gilt-stamped: [*parallel rule*] | REMINIS- | CENCES | OF | MRS. MARY | S. RICE | [*rule*] | KROUT | [*parallel rule*]. Back cover same as front.

End papers same as book stock; no binder's leaf in front; binder's leaf in back has conjugate excised or pasted under the lining paper.

PUBLICATION DATA: Privately printed, 1908, ". . . not intended for general circulation but for the family and the more intimate friends of Mrs. Rice."* Not sold.

NOTES: Written during a visit to Hawaii in 1907.

The author's historical studies of Hawaii include another biography, *The Memoirs of Hon. Bernice Pauahi Bishop* (1908); also, *Hawaii and a Revolution* (1898); also a little book for school children, *Alice's Visit to the Hawaiian Islands* (1900); and *Picturesque Honolulu* (1907).

1908

The Memoirs of
Hon. Bernice Pauahi Bishop

The Memoirs | of | Hon. Bernice Pauahi Bishop | by | Mary H. Krout

COLLATION: [*]² (plus one inserted sheet), [1]–16⁸. White laid paper, 1¾₁₆" between wire marks. Leaf measures 8¹¹⁄₁₆" x 5¾", top edge gilt, other edges untrimmed.

End paper; binder's leaf; title-page, p. [i]; copyright notice, in name of Charles R. Bishop, dated 1908, and imprint of the Knickerbocker Press, New York, p. [ii]; *Preface*, dated January 7, 1908, pp. iii–iv; table of contents, pp. v–vi; list of illustrations, p. vii; blank, p. [viii]; text, pp. 1–249; blank, p. [250]; *Index*, pp. 251–255; blank, p. [256]; binder's leaf; end paper.

[Note: Text, pp. 1–249: The Memoirs of Hon. Bernice Pauahi Bishop, Chapters I–XXVII (titled)].

ILLUSTRATIONS: Frontispiece with tissue guard, inserted as are illustrations facing pp. 6, 10 (not 11 as in list of illustrations), 28, 64

*So stated in the preface, with further explanation that therefore ". . . letters and incidents have been used which might not have been included were it designed for the public."

(not 65), 100 (not 101), 104, 110 (not 111), 116, 166, 196 (not 197), 204, 214 (not 215), 218, 222, 228, 232 (not 233), 242, and 244.

BINDING: Dark blue linen. Front cover blank. Spine gilt-stamped: The | Memoirs | of | Hon. | Bernice | Pauahi | Bishop | [*rule*] | Krout Back cover blank.

End papers white laid, $1\frac{3}{16}''$ between wire marks; binder's leaf in front has $1\frac{5}{16}''$ between wire marks, and bears an unidentified water mark; the binder's leaf in back is same as end papers.

PUBLICATION DATA: Deposited in the Copyright Office, September 23, 1908. Not sold.

NOTES: In all copies located except one (the copyright deposit copy) the legend accompanying the illustration facing p. 166 has *Nenua*, blocked out and *Vienna*, red-stamped below it. Bernice Pauahi (1831–1884) was heir to the Hawaiian throne, the last of the ancient ruling race, the Kamehamehas; she married Charles R. Bishop, Collector of Customs in Honolulu. This book was in preparation as early as August, 1907, according to *The Indianapolis Star*, August 5, 1907. *The Pacific Commercial Advertiser*, January 8, 1908, carried a story that the book, written by Miss Krout at the request of Charles R. Bishop, was then being made ready for the press. "The edition to be published will be a small one and is intended only for private distribution." Later *The Indianapolis Star*, July 11, 1915, quoted the author as saying that the manuscript, proofs, revised proofs, and printed book traveled seven times across the Pacific.

1910

Platters and Pipkins

Platters and Pipkins | By | MARY H. KROUT | "There's pippins and cheese to come" | —Merry Wives of Windsor | [*publishers' emblem*] | CHICAGO | A. C. MCCLURG & CO. | 1910
[Note: All printed in blue.]

COLLATION: [1]⁸ (plus one unsigned sheet), [2–13]⁸. Printed in blue on white wove paper. Leaf measures $6\frac{13}{16}'' \times 5''$, all edges trimmed.

End paper; blank, pp. [i–ii]; fly title, p. [1]; blank, p. [2]; title-page, p. [3]; copyright notice with statement: *Published October 15, 1910,* and imprint of the Publishers' Press, Chicago, p. [4]; dedication to all housekeepers, p. [5]; blank, p. [6]; table of contents, p. [7]; blank, p. [8]; text, pp. [9]–209; blank, p. [210]; end paper.

[Note: Text, pp. (9)–209: Platters and Pipkins: Chapters I–XXII (titled).]

ILLUSTRATIONS: Blue-gray headpiece and illuminated blue-gray initial at beginning of each chapter.

BINDING: Light blue boards. Front cover printed in white: PLATTERS | AND [*illustration of a Willow Ware platter and an orange* and white pipkin*] | PIPKINS | MARY H. KROUT   Spine and back cover blank. Issued boxed, with cover design repeated on box lid.

End papers light blue wove; no binder's leaf front or back.

PUBLICATION DATA: Published October 15, 1910; deposited in the Copyright Office October 18th. Earliest review noted: *The Indianapolis Star*, November 13, 1910. Price, 75¢.

NOTES: *Published October 15, 1910*, so stated on copyright page.

The book was in manuscript as early as October 24, 1905, according to an article in *The Indianapolis Star*, that date.

---

*Whether orange or yellow depends on light conditions to which the book has been exposed.

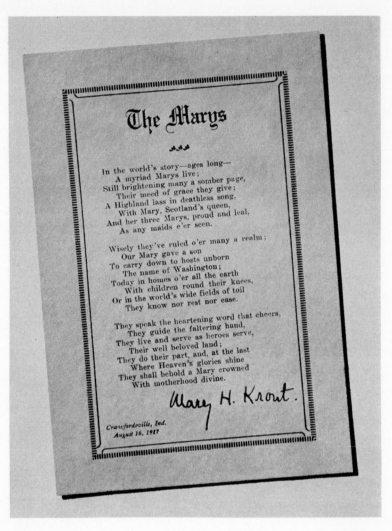

THE MARYS, *a poem by Mary Hannah Krout, issued in connection with a Marys' Day reunion*

1917

The Marys

The Marys | [3 *ornaments*] | [*text of poem*] | [*signature in facsimile:*] Mary H. Krout. | Crawfordsville, Ind. | August 16, 1917
[Note: All enclosed by an ornamental border.]

Single sheet of light brown mottle paper, 7½" x 5⅛", printed in brown on one side only.

The poem was recited by the author at a Marys' Day reunion, Noblesville, and published in *The Crawfordsville Journal*, August 17, 1917, under the title, "To the Marys."

1872

CHILD LIFE: A COLLECTION OF POEMS. Edited by John Greenleaf Whittier. Boston, James R. Osgood & Co., 1872

Contains "Little Brown Hands," p. 251. The poem was first printed in *Our Young Folks*, September, 1868, signed *M. H. K.* In *The Terre Haute Saturday Evening Mail*, June 12, 1875, it reappeared over the signature, *Mary H. Crout*, with an erroneous history of the poem; the author wrote on a clipping,* at the foot of its reprinting in *The Crawfordsville Journal*, June 19th: "The above is a fabrication." It describes the poem as written by her at the age of thirteen (she was closer to sixteen), and published in *The Crawfordsville Journal*, as three times in the *New York Citizen*, and in *Blackwood's Magazine* (in none of which was the poem found before 1875; later it did appear frequently in *The Crawfordsville Journal*).

The poem almost became a book. An illuminated manuscript copy has present a cover design, title-page, frontispiece, and ten sheets of text; all hand-lettered, illustrated, and decorated, done on Bristol boards by M. Louise McLaughlin.†

It was included in many later school readers and anthologies, more so than any of her other writings.

1894

BEACON LIGHTS OF PATRIOTISM, OR, HISTORIC INCENTIVES TO VIRTUE AND GOOD CITIZENSHIP. By Henry B. Carrington. New York, Boston, etc., Silver Burdett & Co., 1894

Contains the poem, "Once at Battle Eve," p. 222, with a note that "the poetess described an incident which occurred on the banks of the Tennessee during the year 1863." Rewritten from a poem, "Luther's Choral," earlier in *The* (Indianapolis) *Saturday Herald*, July 1, 1882.

---

*In Indiana State Library, Krout Papers.
†In Indiana Historical Society, William Henry Smith Memorial Library.

1900

POETS AND POETRY OF INDIANA . . . 1800 TO 1900. Compiled and edited by Benjamin S. Parker and Enos B. Heiney. New York, Silver, Burdett & Co. [1900]

Earliest state measures 1¼″ across sheets (later 1⅛″). Earliest binding has two-color stamping on front cover and spine, and blind-stamped publishers' emblem on back cover; a later binding state has the two-color stamping, but back cover is blank; still later, one-color (green) stamping on front cover and spine, back cover blank.

Contains "Stubble," p. 183, earlier in the (New York) Semi-Weekly Tribune, August 21, 1874, reprinted in The (Chicago) Inter Ocean, August 23, 1890, in Mary Hannah Krout's column, "Woman's Kingdom." The other poem herein, "Little Brown Hands," had earlier book appearances.

1901

WHO'S WHO IN AMERICA 1901–1902. [Volume 2]. Chicago, A. N. Marquis & Co. [1901]

Contains an autobiographical sketch of Mary H. Krout, p. 653. It appeared, with some additions, in succeeding volumes through 1926–1927, Volume 14. The account in Who Was Who in America, 1897–1942, Vol. I, is considerably enlarged, containing information that appeared in newspaper obituaries.

1903

LAUREL LEAVES FOR LITTLE FOLKS. By Mary E. Phillips. Boston, Lee & Shepard, 1903

Contains "General Lewis Wallace," p. 113, written for this book.
Mary Krout had many articles on Wallace published in newspapers and magazines: in "The Hoosier Athens," The (Indianapolis) Saturday Herald, October 12, 1878; an account in The Cincinnati Commercial Gazette, February 12, 1887; in Literature, June 2, 1888; The Indi-

anapolis News, August 25, 1888 (repeated in *The* [Chicago] *Inter Ocean,* August 26th, and in the St. Joseph, Missouri, *Herald,* September 16th); *The* (Chicago) *Inter Ocean,* November 22 & 30, 1888; "Personal Reminiscences of Lew Wallace," in *Harper's Weekly,* March 18, 1905.

1906

LEW WALLACE: AN AUTOBIOGRAPHY. 2 volumes. New York & London, Harper & Bros., MCMVI

Completed by his wife after the death of Lew Wallace, the second part of Vol. II, pp. 799–[1003], was edited by Mary H. Krout, according to the statement of Susan E. Wallace, p. 796: "And here the Autobiography ends. What follows must be a plain record of facts without attempt at polish or effect.

"Whatever merit it may have belongs to my friend, Mary H. Krout, whose careful work has made this continuation possible."

1912

THE HOOSIER ALMANACK AND FAMILY MAGAZINE [for 1913]. Indiana Society of Chicago, 1912

Pictorial yellow wrappers. Souvenir of the eighth annual dinner, December 7, 1912. Contains poem, "Fair Indiana," p. 54.

1924

EARLY DAYS IN A COLLEGE TOWN AND WABASH COLLEGE IN EARLY DAYS AND NOW. By Frank Moody Mills. Sioux Falls, S.D., Sessions Printing Co., 1924

Contains two poems: "From the Campus," p. [186], and "In Crawford's Woods," p. 207. The latter had an early newspaper appearance.*

---

*Clipping only located; lacks source and date of publication.

Periodicals Containing First Appearances

AMERICA
1888: May   5   Long Live the King [poem]*
                  26   Dead in May [poem]*
       August   25   Outward Bound [poem]*

BOSTON EVENING TRANSCRIPT
1876: April   3   The Course of True Love: The Modern Version [poem]*
                  19   An Evening Promise [poem]*
       May   25   Ferns [poem]*

THE CHAUTAUQUAN
1898: May –
       June   The United States and Hawaii*
       October   New Zealand and Its Resources*
1899: January   English Journalism*
       June   The English at Home*
       August   New Zealand Cities and Government*
1900: August   By Rail to Peking*
       September   An American Consulate in China†

1901: September   Mission Schools in China*
1902: November   American Education of Chinese Girls*
1904: July   The Women of Hawaii*

(Chicago) CURRENT (see CURRENT)

THE (Chicago) INTER OCEAN (daily)
1888: June   27   A Woman's View [report of the convention which nominated Benjamin Harrison for President of the United States]*

       July   11–12, 16–18, 20–21, 25‡–28, 30,
       August   1–2, 4, 6–8, 10–11, 13–17, 20, 22–24, 27§–30,

---

*Uncollected.

†Uncollected. Among the Mary Hannah Krout Papers is a manuscript entitled, "American Consulates and Embassies," text not same as *The Chautauquan* article. It bears a statement in her hand, "By Austin Lawrence." Other "Austin Lawrence" manuscripts are in the Krout Papers: "Hawaiian Gardens" and "The Washington Effigies," bearing her name and address.

‡Uncollected; on negro suffrage and conditions of negroes in Indiana.

§Uncollected; the dispatch of August 26th concerns Lew Wallace and his friendship for General Harrison; same as in *The Indianapolis News* a day earlier.

THE (Chicago) INTER OCEAN—*continued*

1888: September   1, 3, 5–6, 12–15, 20–28,
        October   10, 13, 16–18, 22–23, 25, 27, 30,
        November   1, 4–5, 11–12, 15–16, 19, 21–22,* 26–27 [Harrison campaign sidelights, special telegrams, series begun July 11th]†
                    30   [Lew Wallace; comments on, under caption:] Gen. Wallace Wants No Appointment [from President Harrison], but Only Time for Writing†
1889: January   1   New Years at Indianapolis†
                     7   Notes from Indianapolis [about Maurice Thompson]†
                 10, 15, 18, 19, 21, 25   Indianapolis Gossip†
                  30   Cabinet Talk;† Indianapolis Gossip†
                  31,
       February   2   Indianapolis Gossip†
                     4   Indianapolis Sensations†
                     7   Indiana Democracy†
                     9   Indianapolis Gossip†
                  16   Trials of the President Elect†
                  20   Indianapolis Gossip†
                  25   Will Not Go [many prominent Indianans will not attend the inauguration]†
       March   1   Notes from Indianapolis†
                  12   They Breathe Easier [about Indiana Legislature]†
                  14   The Indiana Legislature†
                  17   "The Romance of Dollard" [review of book by Mary Hartwell Catherwood]†
       April   7   In April [poem]†
       August   10   Woman's Kingdom‡
                  13   (weekly issue§)   The Home†
                  17   Woman's Kingdom†

---

   *Uncollected; the dispatch on November 22nd concerns Lew Wallace's efforts in Harrison's behalf.

   †Uncollected.

   ‡Uncollected; her first contibution to "The Woman's Kingdom," a column later hers frequently in whole or in part; if part only, and that part consisting of a poem reprinted from some earlier periodical, entries are here omitted.

   §Both a daily and weekly *Inter Ocean* were published on Tuesdays at this time, the latter sometimes containing original matter (noted), sometimes reprinted features from the daily issues (omitted).

THE (Chicago) INTER OCEAN—*continued*

1889: August   20   (weekly issue) The Home*
                 24   Woman's Kingdom*
                 27   (weekly issue) The Home*
                 31   Woman's Kingdom*
    September   3   (weekly issue) The Home*
                 7   Woman's Kingdom*
                 10   (weekly issue) The Home*
                 14   Woman's Kingdom*
                 17   (weekly issue) The Home*
                 21   Woman's Kingdom*
                 24   (weekly issue) The Home*
                 28   Woman's Kingdom*
    October   1   (weekly issue) The Home*
                 5   Woman's Kingdom*
                 8   (weekly issue) The Home*
                 12   Woman's Kingdom*
                 15   (weekly issue) The Home*
                 19   Woman's Kingdom*
                 22   (weekly issue) The Home*
                 26   Woman's Kingdom*
                 29   (weekly issue) The Home*
    November   2   Woman's Kingdom*
                 5   (weekly issue) The Home*
                 9   Woman's Kingdom*
                 12   (weekly issue) The Home*
                 16, 23   Woman's Kingdom*
                 30   The Home*; Woman's Kingdom*
    December   3   (weekly issue) The Home*
                 7   Woman's Kingdom*
                 10   (weekly issue) The Home*
                 14   Woman's Kingdom*
                 17   (weekly issue) The Home*
                 25   Christmas Bells [poem]*
                 28   Woman's Kingdom*; The Poem on Spring [poem; read at meeting of editors of religious publications of Chicago]*
                 31   (weekly issue) The Home*
1890: January   4, 11   Woman's Kingdom*
                 25   The Home†
    February   1   The Home*; Woman's Kingdom*

---

*Uncollected.

†Uncollected; a column irregular in appearance and not always wholly, or even in part, Mary H. Krout's; when the column has been found unsigned or bearing initials of other writers, the issues have been disregarded. Her signature is occasionally misprinted, but her writing is easy to distinguish by its style; wherever there is any doubt about authorship, omission has been made.

THE (Chicago) INTER OCEAN—*continued*

1890: February   8, 15, 22   Woman's Kingdom*
      March   8, 15, 29   The Home*; Woman's Kingdom*
      April   5   The Easter Miracle [poem]†; The Home*
                  12, 19, 26   Woman's Kingdom*; The Home*
      May   3, 10   The Home*; Woman's Kingdom*
                  17, 24   Woman's Kingdom*
                  31   The Home*; Woman's Kingdom*
      June   7, 14, 21, 28,
      July   5, 12, 19   Woman's Kingdom*; The Home*
                  26   The Home*
      August   2, 9   Woman's Kingdom*; The Home*
                  13   Indiana's Future Poet [Meredith Nicholson]*
                  16, 30,
      September   6, 13, 20, 27   The Home*; Woman's Kingdom*
      October   4   The Farm and Home‡; Woman's Kingdom*
                  11, 18, 25   The Home*; Woman's Kingdom*
      November   1   Woman's Kingdom [about Emily Meigs Rip-
                       ley, under caption:] A Woman of Genius,
                       Her Character and Her Unfinished Work*
                   8   The Home*
                  15   The Home*; Woman's Kingdom*
                  22   Woman's   Kingdom   [including   poem:]
                       Thanksgiving*; The Home*
                  29   The Home*; Woman's Kingdom*
      December   6, 13, 20   Woman's Kingdom*; The Home*
                  27   The Home*
1891: January   3   Woman's Kingdom*; The Home*
                   9   The Outsider [poem; read to Illinois Wom-
                       en's Press Association, Chicago, January
                       8th]*
                  10, 17   Woman's Kingdom*; The Home*
                  24   The Home*
                  31,
      February   7, 14, 21, 28,
      March   7, 14, 21, 28,
      April   4, 11, 18   The Home*; Woman's Kingdom*
      May   2   Woman's Kingdom*
                   6   The Home*
                   9   Woman's Kingdom*

---

*Uncollected.

†Uncollected; heads column, "Woman's Kingdom," as do her other poems of this period. Evidently there was an earlier publication, since a clipping in a Krout scrapbook has dateline, *Easter 1887*, its source unknown.

‡Uncollected; "The Home" column under different title.

The (Chicago) Inter Ocean—*continued*

1891: May	13	The Home*
	16	Woman's Kingdom*
	20	The Home*
	23	Woman's Kingdom*
	27	The Home*
	30	Woman's Kingdom*
June	4, 10	The Home*
	13, 20	Woman's Kingdom*
	24	The Home*
	27	Woman's Kingdom*
July	1	The Home*
	4	Woman's Kingdom*
	8	The Home*
	9	Indiana Politics . . . President Harrison's Strength in His Own State*
	11	Woman's Kingdom*
	13	A War-Time Horror: The Story of the Explosion of the Eclipse*
	15	The Home*
	18	Woman's Kingdom*
	22	The Home*
	25	Woman's Kingdom*
	29	The Home*
August	1	Woman's Kingdom*
	5	The Home*
	8	Woman's Kingdom*
	12	The Home*
	15	Woman's Kingdom*
	19	The Home*
	22	Woman's Kingdom*
	26	Around the Home†
	29	Woman's Kingdom*
	31	Wisconsin Wilds*
September	5	Woman's Kingdom*; Wilds of Wisconsin*
	9	Home Department†
	12	Woman's Kingdom*
	16	Home Circle†
	19	Lovely Island Lake [in Wisconsin]*; Woman's Kingdom*
	22	The Home*
	26	Woman's Kingdom*
	30	The Home*
October	3	Woman's Kingdom*

*Uncollected.
†Uncollected; "The Home" column under different title.

THE (Chicago) INTER OCEAN—*continued*

1891: October   7   The Home*
                   10   Woman's Kingdom*
                   14   The Home Circle†; [Speech before Woman's Press League, in Chicago, October 13th, captioned:] Women in Council*
                   17   Woman's Kingdom*
                   21   The Home Circle*
                   24   Woman's Kingdom*
                   28   The Home Circle*
                   31   Woman's Kingdom*
       November 7   Woman's Kingdom‡
                   24   The Home Circle*
                   28   Woman's Kingdom*
       December 1   The Home Circle*
                   5   Woman's Kingdom*
                   9   The Home Circle*
                   12, 19   Woman's Kingdom*
                   26   The Home Circle*; Woman's Kingdom*
1892: January   2   Woman's Kingdom*
                   6   The Home Circle*
                   9, 16, 23   Woman's Kingdom*
                   26   The Home Circle*
                   30   Woman's Kingdom*
       February 3   The Home Circle*
                   6, 13   Woman's Kingdom*
                   15   The Home Circle*
                   20   Woman's Kingdom*
                   24   The Home Circle*
                   27   Woman's Kingdom*
                   29   The Home Circle*
       March   5, 12 Woman's Kingdom*
                   14   Gen. Lew Wallace: His Opinion of Harrison's Administration§
                   15   The Home Circle*
                   19, 26,
       April   2, 9, 16, 23, 30,
       May   7, 14   Woman's Kingdom*
                   21   Discipline [poem]*
                   28,

---

*Uncollected.

†Uncollected; here "The Home" column's title is changed to "The Home Circle."

‡Uncollected; for two weeks following the column was evidently not hers; but her signature reappeared on the 24th and 28th.

§Uncollected; reprinted on the following day.

THE (Chicago) INTER OCEAN—*continued*

1892: June   4, 11, 18 Woman's Kingdom*
                20 The Home Circle*
                22 Hoosier Delegates: Gen. Lew Wallace Talks about the Minneapolis Convention†
                25 Woman's Kingdom*
     July   9, 16, 23, 30 Woman's Kingdom*
     August   6 The Home Circle*; Woman's Kingdom*
                8 The Home Circle‡
              13, 20 Woman's Kingdom*; The Home Circle*
              27 Woman's Kingdom*
              29 The Home Circle*
     September 3, 10, 17 Woman's Kingdom*
              27 The Home Circle*
     October   1, 8, 15, 22 Woman's Kingdom*
              29,
     November 1, 3 [Reports of the W.C.T.U. Convention, Denver, Colorado; unsigned]§
              5 Woman's Kingdom*
              10 The Home Circle*
              12 Woman's Kingdom*
              18 The Home Circle*
              19 Woman's Kingdom*
              21 Miss [Ada C.] Sweet's Paper*
              26 Woman's Kingdom*
     December 2 The Home Circle*
              3 Woman's Kingdom*
              7 The Home Circle*
              10, 17, 24 Woman's Kingdom*
              31 The Home Circle*; Woman's Kingdom*
1893: January   7 Woman's Kingdom*
              13 The Home Circle*
              14 Woman's Kingdom*
              20 The Home Circle*
              21,
     February 4, 11, 15 Woman's Kingdom*
              18 The Home Circle*; Woman's Kingdom*

---

*Uncollected.

†Uncollected; reprinted on the following day.

‡Uncollected; on August 11th the newspaper contained a reprint of "The Home Circle" of August 8th.

§Uncollected. Mary H. Krout represented the Chicago *Inter Ocean* at this convention, held October 28–November 2nd, according to a notice in *The Crawfordsville Journal*, November 5, 1892, so these "special telegrams" are undoubtedly hers! One from Denver captioned, "Women in Pulpits," published October 31st, may also be hers.

THE (Chicago) INTER OCEAN—*continued*

1893: March	4*	Woman's Kingdom†	
	9	[Hawaii: letter from]†	
	11	Woman's Kingdom†	
	13	Hawaiians at Home	
	18	Woman's Kingdom†; Hawaiian Politics	
	21	Home of a Princess	
	23	Kalakaua's Palace	
	24	Life in Honolulu	
	25	The Home Circle†; Woman's Kingdom†	
	26	[Hawaii: letter from]†	
	27	In Regal Quarters	
	29	Must Annex Hawaii	
	30	Lepers and Molakai	
April	1	Woman's Kingdom†	
	2	The Home Circle†	
	4	An Ostrich Farm	
	6	[Hawaii: letter from]†; Support the New Government	
	8	Woman's Kingdom†	
	9	A Hawaiian Farm	
	10	[Hawaii: letter from]	
	14	Old Glory Down	
	15	Woman's Kingdom†; [Hawaii: letter from]†	
	16	[Hawaii: letter from]†; Royal Emissaries Return	
	18	The Home Circle†	
	22, 24	[Hawaii: letters from]†	
	28	The Home Circle†; The Crown Jewels	
May	2, 4	[Hawaii: letters from]†	
	7	A Chinese Paradise	
	12	Pacific Royalty	
	13	A Queen Dowager	
	20	Woman's Kingdom†	
	23	The Home Circle†	
June	3, 17	Woman's Kingdom†	
	19	The Home Circle†	
	21	[World's Fair feature story]†	
	25	The Home Circle†; Woman's Kingdom†	
July	2	The Home Circle†; Woman's Kingdom†	
	5	[World's Fair feature stories (2)]†	
	8	Woman's Kingdom†	

---

*The issue of February 25th, unlocated, may have contained contributions also.

†Uncollected.

THE (Chicago) INTER OCEAN—*continued*

1893: July	9	The Home Circle*
	12	[World's Fair feature story]*
	15	Woman's Kingdom*
	19	[World's Fair feature story]*
	22	The Home Circle*
	26	[World's Fair feature stories (3)]*
	29	The Home Circle*
August	2	[World's Fair feature story]*
	5	Woman's Kingdom*
	9	[World's Fair feature stories (2)]*
	12	Woman's Kingdom*
	16	[World's Fair feature story]*
	19	Woman's Kingdom*; The Home Circle*
	23	[World's Fair feature story]*
	25	The Home Circle*
	26, 29	Woman's Kingdom*
	30	[World's Fair feature stories (2)]*
September	2	The Home Circle*; Woman's Kingdom*
	6	[World's Fair feature stories (2)]*
	9	The Home Circle*; Woman's Kingdom*
	13	The Home Circle*; [World's Fair feature stories (2)]*
	16	Woman's Kingdom*
	19	The Home Circle*
	20	[World's Fair feature stories (3)]*
	26	The Home Circle*
	27	[World's Fair feature stories (2)]*
	30	Woman's Kingdom*
October	4	[World's Fair feature story]*
	7	Woman's Kingdom*
	10	The Home Circle*
	11	[World's Fair feature stories (2)]*
	14	Woman's Kingdom*
	15	The Home Circle*
	18	[World's Fair feature stories (2)]*
	21	Woman's Kingdom*
	25	[World's Fair feature stories (2)]†
	28	Woman's Kingdom*
November	1	Woman's Work and the Fair*

---

*Uncollected.

†Uncollected; the World's Fair closed at the end of October; one wonders if Mary Hannah Krout's path had crossed that of another Hoosier, George Ade, who had been writing daily stories of the same scenes for another Chicago newspaper.

THE (Chicago) INTER OCEAN—*continued*

1893: November	4	Woman's Kingdom*
	5	The Home Circle*
	11	Woman's Kingdom*; The Home Circle*
	12	Woman's New Field: The Illinois Woman's Exposition Board*
	15	[Hawaii: story of, written in Chicago]*
	18	Woman's Kingdom*; [Hawaii: story of, written in Chicago]*
	20	Harriet Hosmer: The Distinguished Sculptress Chats*
	25	Woman's Kingdom*
	26	The Home Circle*
	30	The Season Suggestive of Thanksgiving*
December	2	Woman's Kingdom*; The Home Circle*
	8	[Hawaii: story of, written in Chicago]*
	9	Woman's Kingdom*
	15	The Home Circle*; [Hawaii: story of, written in Chicago]*
	16, 23	Woman's Kingdom*
	24	The Shepherds [poem]*
	30	The Home Circle*; Woman's Kingdom*
1894: January	13	Woman's Kingdom*
	26	The Home Circle*
	27	Woman's Kingdom*
February	10	Supplication [poem]*
	13	The Home Circle*
	17	Woman's Kingdom*
	18	Our Hawaii Letter
	19, 20	[Hawaii: letters from]*
	24	Woman's Kingdom*
	28	[Hawaii: letter from]*
March	3	In Halcyon Hilo
	16, 17, 18	[Hawaii: letters from]*
	31	Visiting a Volcano
April	1	In the Hilo Swim
May	20	[Hawaii: letter from]*
	26	In the South Seas
	27,	
June	3, 10, 17, 18	[South Pacific and New Zealand: letters from]*
	23	Woman's Kingdom*
	24	[South Pacific and New Zealand: 2 letters from]*
	30	Woman's Kingdom*

*Uncollected.

THE (Chicago) INTER OCEAN—*continued*

1894: July	1, 8	[Australia: letters about Melbourne and Sydney]*
	14, 21	Woman's Kingdom†
	22	Pullman Laid Bare†
	28	The Home Circle†; Woman's Kingdom†
	30	The Home Circle†
August	4	Woman's Kingdom†
	11	The Home Circle†; Woman's Kingdom†
	13	Work of Ida B. Wells [unsigned]†
	18	The Home Circle†; Woman's Kingdom†
	25,	
September	1, 15‡, 22	Woman's Kingdom†
	30	Jottings†; Woman's Kingdom†
October	2, 6	Woman's Kingdom†
	7	Jottings†
	12	[Speech before Republican Women's rally in Chicago, October 11th, at Central Music Hall]§
	13	Woman's Kingdom†
	14	Jottings†
	20	Woman's Kingdom†
	21	Jottings†
	27	Woman's Kingdom†
	28	Jottings†
November	3	Woman's Kingdom†
	4	Jottings†
	10	Woman's Kingdom†

---

*An article clipped from the *Hawaiian Star,* July 5, 1894, is present in the Krout Papers in the University of Chicago Harper Library: "God Save the Republic." It is unsigned; may, or may not be hers, following her series of Hawaiian articles.

†Uncollected.

‡Uncollected, the issue of the 8th, unlocated, may have contained the column also.

§Uncollected. Her scrapbook, in the University of Chicago, Harper Library, includes many clippings, probably from *The* (Chicago) *Inter Ocean,* October–November, 1894, which report political meetings and campaign speeches. Two of them quote her own speeches: one at a banquet given by the Illinois Woman's Republican Committee in honor of Mrs. Lucy L. Flower, first woman elected to a state office in Illinois (November, 1894); the other at a banquet for all the candidates for Trustees of the State University (date, "Nov. 30," written in by her, but piece not found in *Inter Ocean* this day or the next). Her "Woman's Kingdom" column was full of the campaign in which she enthusiastically took part. A letter, processed on Illinois Woman's Republican Committee stationery, October 12, 1894, bears her signature as Chairman of the Press Committee.

THE (Chicago) INTER OCEAN—*continued*

1894: November	11	Jottings*
	17, 24	Woman's Kingdom*
	25	Jottings*
1895: January	5	Woman's Kingdom*
	6	Jottings*
	12	Woman's Kingdom*
	13	Jottings*
	19	Woman's Kingdom*
	20	A Policy of Infamy [about Hawaii]*
	26	Woman's Kingdom*
	27	Jottings*; Two Famous Roads [about Hawaii]*
February	2	Woman's Kingdom*
	3	Jottings*
	9	Woman's Kingdom*
	10	Jottings*; A Matter of History [about Hawaii]*
	16	Woman's Kingdom*
	17	Jottings*
	23	Woman's Kingdom*
	24	Jottings*
March	2	Woman's Kingdom*
	3	Jottings*
	9	Woman's Kingdom*
	10	Jottings*
	16	Woman's Kingdom*
	17	Jottings*
	23	Woman's Kingdom* [includes poem:] At Last*
	24	Jottings*
	30	Woman's Kingdom*
	31	Jottings*
April	6	Woman's Kingdom*
	7	Jottings*
	13	Woman's Kingdom*
	14	Jottings*
	20	Woman's Kingdom*
	21	Jottings*
	27	Woman's Kingdom*
	28	Jottings*
May	4	Woman's Kingdom*
	5	Jottings*
	11	Woman's Kingdom*
	12	Jottings*

*Uncollected.

THE (Chicago) INTER OCEAN—*continued*

1895:	May	18	Woman's Kingdom*
		19	Jottings*
		25	Woman's Kingdom*
		26	Jottings*
	June	1	Woman's Kingdom*
		2	Jottings*
		8	Woman's Kingdom*
		9	Jottings*
		15	Woman's Kingdom*
		16	Jottings*
		22	Woman's Kingdom*
		23	Jottings*
		29	Woman's Kingdom*
		30	Jottings*
	July	6	Woman's Kingdom*
		7	Jottings*; George Meredith*
	August	17	Scottish Sketches [leading to series of London letters]
		18	[London letter, captioned:] England in August
		19	[London letter]*
		25	[London letter, captioned:] The House of Peers
		27,	
	September	8	[London letters]*
		10	[London letter concerning Sir Frederick (later, Lord) Leighton, captioned:] Prince of Painters
		21, 22, 26, 28	[London letters]*
	October	6	[London letter, captioned:] Only a Meadow Mist
		7	[London letter, captioned:] John Bull at Home
		13, 20, 26, 27, 28,	
	November	4, 24, 27	[London letters]*
		30	Woman's Kingdom
	December	1	[London letter, captioned:] Justice as Administered in Expeditious English Courts
		7	Woman's Kingdom*
		9	[London letter]*
		14	Woman's Kingdom
		16	[London letter]*
		27	[London letter, captioned:] Late London Notes

*Uncollected.

THE (Chicago) INTER OCEAN—*continued*

1895: December 28   Woman's Kingdom*
              29, 30   [London letters]*
              31   [London letter, captioned:] John and Jona-
                        than
1896: January   4   Woman's Kingdom
              7   [London letter, captioned:] She Stood Amazed
              11   Woman's Kingdom
              18   Woman's Kingdom*
              19, 23   [London letters]*
              25   Woman's Kingdom*; [London letter]*
              27   [London letter, captioned:] No War with
                        America
              30   [London letter]*
        February   1   Woman's Kingdom*
              5   [London letter]*
              8   Woman's Kingdom*
              9   [London letter, captioned:] London in Mourn-
                        ing
              15   Woman's Kingdom*; [London letter]*
              19   [London letter]*
              21   [London letter, captioned:] Week of Funerals
              22   Woman's Kingdom*
              27   [London letter, captioned:] In a Great Prison
              29   Woman's Kingdom*
        March   4, 6   [London letters]*
              7, 14   Woman's Kingdom*
              16, 20   [London letters]*
              21, 28   Woman's Kingdom*
              30   [London letter, captioned:] Dr. Jameson's
                        Trial
        April   4   Woman's Kingdom*
              5   [London letter, captioned:] Dr. Jameson's
                        Trial
              11   Woman's Kingdom*
              13   [London letter, concerning Dr. Jameson's
                        trial]*
              18   Woman's Kingdom*; [London letter, cap-
                        tioned:] Bounty of a Queen
              19, 20   [London letters]*
              25   Woman's Kingdom*
              27, 29   [London letters]*
        May   2   Woman's Kingdom*
              3, 4   [London letters, the first concerning Dr.
                        Jameson's trial]*

*Uncollected.

THE (Chicago) INTER OCEAN—*continued*

1896: May	9	Woman's Kingdom*
	10	[London letter captioned:] Dr. Jameson's Trial
	12	[London letter captioned:] Dr. Jameson's Trial; The Woman's Kingdom*
	16	Woman's Kingdom*
	17	[London letter, captioned:] Women in Politics
	23	Woman's Kingdom*
	24, 25	[London letters]*
	30	Woman's Kingdom*
June	1	[London letter, captioned:] In Kentish Fields
	6	Woman's Kingdom*
	7	[London letter]*
	13	Woman's Kingdom*
	15	[London letter]*
	20	Woman's Kingdom*
	21	[London letter]*
	27	[London letter, captioned:] Dr. Jameson's Trial; Woman's Kingdom*
July	4	Woman's Kingdom*
	6, 12	[London letters]*
	13	Woman's Kingdom*
	20	[London letter, captioned:] Henley's Gay Scene
	25	Woman's Kingdom*
	27	[London letter]*
August	1	Woman's Kingdom*
	3	[London letter]*; Woman's Kingdom*
	8	[London letter, captioned:] Dr. Jameson's Trial; Woman's Kingdom*
	10	[London letter, captioned:] Hot Days in London
	14	[London letter, captioned:] Passing of "Dr. Jim"
	15	Woman's Kingdom*
September	5	[Switzerland letter]*
	12	Woman's Kingdom*
	14	[Switzerland letter]*
	19	Woman's Kingdom*
	21	[Switzerland letter]*
	26	Woman's Kingdom*
October	3	[Paris letter]*; Woman's Kingdom*
	5	[Paris letter]*

---

*Uncollected.

THE (Chicago) INTER OCEAN—*continued*

1896:	October	11	[London letter, about Paris]*
		17	Woman's Kingdom*
		18	[London letter]*
		24, 31	Woman's Kingdom*
	November	2	[London letter]*
		7	Woman's Kingdom*
		14	[London letter]*; Woman's Kingdom*
		16	[London letter]*
		21	Woman's Kingdom*
		23	[London letter]*
		28,	
	December	5	Woman's Kingdom*
		6	[London letter]*
		12,	
1897:	January	23,	
	February	1	Woman's Kingdom*
		7	A Pioneer Englishwoman [Mrs. E. L. Mass- ingberd]†
		8	Woman's Kingdom†
		10	One Day in Society†
		15, 22	The Home Circle†; Woman's Kingdom†
		28	London Charity†
	March	1	The Home Circle†; Woman's Kingdom†
		7	[London Charity, under caption:] London's Charities†
		8	The Home Circle†; Woman's Kingdom†
		14	[London charity, captioned:] Of London Charities†
		15	The Home Circle†; Woman's Kingdom†
		21	London Restaurants†
		22	The Home Circle†; Woman's Kingdom†
		28	London Landmarks†
		29	Woman's Kingdom†; The Home Circle†
	April	5	The Home Circle*
	May	1	[London letter, about Ireland]*
		2	[London letter]*
		3	Woman's Kingdom*
		9	[London letter, about John Hay]*
		10	Woman's Kingdom*
		16	[London letter]*
		17	Woman's Kingdom*
		23	[London letter]*
		24	Woman's Kingdom*

*Uncollected.
†Uncollected. Written in Chicago during a visit before return to London.

THE (Chicago) INTER OCEAN—*continued*

1897: May	30	[London letter]*
	31	Woman's Kingdom*
June	6	[London letter]*
	7	Woman's Kingdom*
	13	[London letter]*
	14	Woman's Kingdom*
	20	[London letter]*
	21	Woman's Kingdom*
	27	[London letter]*
	28	Woman's Kingdom*
July	4	[London letter, captioned:] London's Big Show
	5	Woman's Kingdom*
	11	[London letter, captioned:] Evening of Jubilee; Woman's Kingdom*
	12	[London letter, captioned:] Little Children Fed
	18	[London letter, captioned:] Customs of Oxford
	19	Woman's Kingdom*
	26	[London letter]*; Woman's Kingdom*
August	1	[London letter]*
	2	Woman's Kingdom*
	8	[London letter]*
	9	Woman's Kingdom*
	15	[London letter]*
	16	Woman's Kingdom*
	22	[London letter]*
	23	Woman's Kingdom*
	29	[London letter]*
	30	Woman's Kingdom*
September	5	[London letter]*
	6	Woman's Kingdom*
	13	[London letter]*; Woman's Kingdom*
	26	[London letter, about Mrs. Maybrick]†
	27	Woman's Kingdom*
October	3	[London letter]*
	11	Woman's Kingdom*
	17	[London letter, about Stockholm's Fair]*

---

*Uncollected.

†Uncollected; Florence Holbrook Maybrick had been imprisoned on a charge of murdering her husband. Mary H. Krout interviewed her. Besides the story above-mentioned she wrote a later feature article published in *The New York Journal & Advertiser, American Magazine Supplement,* May 21, 1899.

THE (Chicago) INTER OCEAN—*continued*

1897: October	24	[London letter]
	25	Woman's Kingdom*
November	1	[London letter]*; Woman's Kingdom*
	7	[London letter, about Lily Langtry]*
	8	Woman's Kingdom*
	15	[London letter]*; Woman's Kingdom*
	27,	
December	4	Woman's Kingdom*
	5	[London letter]*
	11	Woman's Kingdom*
	12	[London letter]*
	14	Women Abroad*
	18	Woman's Kingdom*
	19	[London letter]*
	22	Women Abroad*
	25	Woman's Kingdom*
	26	[London letter]*
	28	Women Abroad*
1898: January	1	Woman's Kingdom*
	2, 16	[London letters]*
	17	Woman's Kingdom*
	23	[London letters (2)]*
	30	Career of the Doles: President of the Hawaiian Republic and His Helpful Wife [Mr. and Mrs. Sanford Ballard Dole]*
	31	Woman's Kingdom [unsigned]†
February	20	Roars of John Bull [about Hawaii and British attitude toward American annexation]*

THE (Chicago) INTERIOR‡

1886: April	22	Easter Praise [poem]*
May	13	Jack's Half-Holiday*

THE (Chicago) TIMES-HERALD (Sunday)

1899: May	14, 21, 28,	
June	4, 11, 18	Gold Hunters of Indiana [signed, *Le Roy Armstrong*§]

---

*Uncollected.

†Uncollected; reads like a Krout article, although unsigned.

‡Mary Hannah Krout transferred from the editorial department of the *Peoria* (Illinois) *Call* to the *Interior*, a weekly Chicago newspaper, on March 30, 1886, according to an announcement in *The Crawfordsville Journal*, March 27, 1886.

§Uncollected. Apparently hers since the issue of May 14, 1899, preserved in one of the family scrapbooks, now in Indiana State Library, bears name of Mary Hannah Krout penciled below that of Le Roy Armstrong.

THE CINCINNATI COMMERCIAL-GAZETTE
    1887: February   12   Gen. Lew Wallace: Facts concerning the Author of the "Fair God" and "Ben Hur"*

CINCINNATI GAZETTE
    1882: April   22   The Dead Painter [Wilbur W. Woodward, died March —, 1882, at Lawrenceburg, Ind.; poem]*

THE CRAWFORDSVILLE JOURNAL
1864:	March	17	My Castle in the Air [poem]†
1866:	October	4	October [poem]‡
1867:	December	19	There Is a God [poem]*
1868:	February	13	My Ship [poem]*
	May	21	World Praise [poem]*
	July	2	Beyond [poem]*
	October	8	The Rights of Women*
	November	5	A November Day [poem]*
1869:	January	28	Beautiful Songs Unsung [poem]*
	February	11	The Great [poem]*
	May	6	About Work*
	June	10	Woman's Rights This*
	July	8	"Sphere"*
	September	2	Sunbeams [poem]*
		9	The Promised Land [poem]*
	November	4	"Tell Us a Story" [poem]*
	December	30	Out in the Street [poem]*
1870:	January	13	The Little, Old Cradle [poem]*
		27	Mud Pies [poem]*
	February	17	What the Crickets Say [poem]*
	April	7	Childhood Land [poem]*
1873:	September	18	The 86th Indiana Battle Flag [poem; unsigned]*
1875:	February	13	Little Ruth [poem]*
	April	10	From My Windows [poem]§
	November	13–	

---

*Uncollected.

†Uncollected. This, her first poem, was printed with a notice predicting high rank for the young poetess, then only twelve years old. Another poem, which did bring fame to her, "Little Brown Hands," included in many later anthologies, is said to have first appeared in *The Crawfordsville Journal* when she was thirteen, *i.e.*, after November 3, 1864; file of November and December unlocated.

‡Uncollected; "For the *Crawfordsville Journal*"; accompanied by prediction of future fame for the author. The same poem, with statement, "Written for the *North Western Farmer*," was previously published therein, October 1, 1866.

§Uncollected; acknowledgment made to the *New York Tribune* but not found in the 1875 issues of that daily, before April 10th.

THE CRAWFORDSVILLE JOURNAL—*continued*

1876: March	4	Topics of the Town: Observations and Comments by Mynheer Heinrich Karl*
March	11	A Glimpse of Spring [poem]†; [Letter to Ladies and Gentlemen of Crawfordsville, *ca.* March 8th, about production of her play, "The Widow Selby"]†; Topics of the Town . . .†
	18	The Singer [poem]†; Topics of the Town . . .†
	25	"Home Talent" [synopsis, from manuscript, of "The Widow Selby"]‡; Topics of the Town . . .†
April	1–	
July	1	Topics of the Town . . .†
1880: February	14	Dodie Blair [poem]†
June	5	[Memorial Day poem]§
1881: October	22	[Civil War poem, written for 7th annual reunion of Eleventh Indiana Regiment at Crawfordsville on October 19th]‖
1883: January	27¶	The Plaint of the Country Editor [poem]†; Ben D. House†
February	3	Crawfordsville Girls [unsigned]†
	10	To Mrs. Maurice Thompson [poem]†
March	24	To St. Louis and Back†
	31	St. Louis Notes†
April	14	The Princess Perizade [poem; read at a breakfast honoring Gertrude Garrison]†
May	26	The Nation's Dead [poem]£
July	7	The Monon Route†
August	18	The Associate on Her Travels†

---

*Uncollected; a weekly "gossip column," to which her name was not attached.

†Uncollected.

‡Uncollected; the only form in which published except that the programme of the play gives a briefer synopsis. It was produced in Crawfordsville, March 31, 1876. For account of an earlier play by her, in which she took part, see Susan E. Wallace's review in *The Indianapolis Journal*, May 31, 1885, of "A Man in the House."

§Uncollected; later in *The* (Chicago) *Interior*, May 27, 1886, with title, "For Memorial Day," and in *The Denver Times*, May 30, 1903, as "Memorial Day."

‖Uncollected; part was reprinted in editorial columns of *The* (Indianapolis) *Saturday Review*, October 29, 1881, and compared with another poem on a similar subject, not hers.

¶On January 6, 1883, *The Crawfordsville Journal* announced that Mary Hannah Krout had been made associate editor.

£Uncollected; a Memorial Day poem; for a different one, earlier, see *The Crawfordsville Journal*, June 5, 1880.

The Crawfordsville Journal—*continued*

1883: August   25   M. H. K.'s St. Paul Letter*
      September 22   Taylor-Blair [report of wedding of Harold
                           Taylor and Anna Elston Blair; unsigned]*
      November 10   The Louisville Exposition*
      December 29   Some Reminiscences of George C. Harding*;
                           Doubt†
1884: January   5   A Year in Journalism*
      May   17   Dust to Dust; Death of W. F. Elston [obitu-
                           ary; unsigned]*
                   24   [Wabash schools]‡
      June   7   The Prairie City [Terre Haute, Ind.]*
                   14, 21   [Wabash schools]*
      September 6, 13   Washington Letter[s]*
                   20, 27,
      October   4, 11   Boston Letter[s]*
                   18   New England*
      November 1   Sights in New York*
      December 20   The Ghost at Christmas [poem]*
1885: February   21   "The Poets of Indiana" [speech at Woman's
                           Reading Club of Terre Haute, Febru-
                           ary 20th]*
      July   25   Chicago Letter*
1886: January   9   Beethoven [poem]*; Chicago Working
                           Women, How They Live . . .*
1891: July   11   Wabash and Co-education [plea for admis-
                           sion of women to Wabash College]*
1899: July   28   Anna E. Hall [obituary; includes a poem be-
                           ginning, "Somewhere thou livest and hast
                           need of Him"]§
1900: October   19   Manila [speech, before D. A. R., Indianapo-
                           lis]*
1918: August   23   In Lincoln Street [poem]‖

---

*Uncollected.

†Uncollected; not same as the poem with same title in *Terre Haute Daily News*, February 19, 1880; begins: "A veiled shape passed . . ."

‡Uncollected and unsigned; this May 24th article, discussing removal of six teachers from the Wabash schools, was attributed to her by the *Wabash Plain Dealer*; her replies to the latter followed in *The Crawfordsville Journal*, June 14 and 21, unsigned still.

§Uncollected. In an unidentified newspaper there appeared an obituary of Annie Rachel Hall, a Chicago schoolteacher, unsigned, but clipping present in the Krout Scrapbook in Chicago University Library; annotated in her hand: "Sat. May 21 '92."

‖Uncollected; the poem had appeared in an unidentified newspaper on August 19, 1918 (excerpt in Krout Papers).

THE CURRENT (Chicago)
    1884: October   18 Professor Emeritus [poem]*
           December 6 The Lark [poem]*
    1885: May   9 When Spring Comes [poem]*
    1886: January   2 Beethoven [poem]*

THE DAILY NEBRASKAN (University of Nebraska, Lincoln)
    1918: December 11 Letter about the *Mid-West Quarterly*, December 1st, addressed to J. E. Le Rossignol]*

THE DENVER (Colorado) TIMES
    1902:† October   2–4 Odds and Ends*
                   6 Two Poet Brothers [Maurice and Will H. Thompson]*; Odds and Ends*
                  7–
         December 27 Odds and Ends‡
                  29 Mary Hartwell Catherwood§; Odds and Ends*
                  30–
    1903: February   5 Odds and Ends*
                   6 Mrs. [James H.] Peabody*; Odds and Ends*
                   7 Miss [Zona] Vallance*; Odds and Ends*
                  9–
         April   24–25, 27–
         May   5 Odds and Ends*
                   6 Odds and Ends [about Meredith Nicholson]*
                  7–
         June   27 Odds and Ends*

GOOD COMPANY
    1881: August   Lydia Darrah: An Episode of the Revolutionary War [poem, unsigned]*

HARPER'S WEEKLY
    1905: March   18 Personal Reminiscences of Lew Wallace*

THE HOME-MAKER
    1892: June   Yesterday [poem]*

THE INDEPENDENT
    1876: March   9 The Singer [poem]*
    1901: February 21 Maurice Thompson at Home‖

---

*Uncollected.

†The contributions that Mary H. Krout made in 1900–1901 when she was on the staff of this newspaper were evidently unsigned.

‡Uncollected; this column frequently included her poems earlier published, therefore not listed here.

§Uncollected. She had earlier paid brief tribute to Mrs. Catherwood in an article, "Some Indianapolis Women" (*post* 63).

‖Uncollected; reprinted in *Phi Gamma Delta*, Vol. 23, February, 1901.

THE INDEPENDENT—*continued*
    1912: July   11   Thomas Ryan Marshall*

THE INDIANA SCHOOL JOURNAL
    1864: December   The Old Homestead [poem]*

THE INDIANAPOLIS JOURNAL
    1881: October   20   For the Veterans [poem]†
    1882: October   21   The Last Prayer [poem]‡
    1884: August   9   My Friend [poem]*
          December 7   The Lark [poem]*
    1885: March   15   When Spring Comes [poem]*
          July   5   [Untitled poem under caption:] The Fourth in Indiana§
    1888: May   13   Long Live the King [poem]*
                  30   Dead in May (In Memory of Luella G. Kunse) [poem]*
          December 23   Christmas Bells [poem]*
    1889: January 27   Professor Emeritus*
    1892: June   19   Yesterday [poem]*
    1899: January   1   English Housekeeping*
          February 19   Fair Samoa Recalled*
          April   3   At the Mansion House*

THE INDIANAPOLIS NEWS
    1888: August   25   Gen. Lew Wallace*
    1901: July   27   Noted Women of Hawaii*
    1920: March   8   Spring Ledge, a Bird Paradise near Crawfordsville*

THE INDIANAPOLIS PRESS
    1900: June   23   An American Woman at a Chinese Feast*

THE (Indianapolis) SATURDAY HERALD
    1876: August   19   The Indiana Athens [signed *Ben Offield*]‖
                  26   Crawfordsville Letter, August 24 [signed *Ben Offield*]*
          September 9   Premonition [poem]*

---

*Uncollected.

†Uncollected; part was reprinted in the editorial columns of *The* (Indianapolis) *Saturday Review*, October 29, 1881.

‡Uncollected; dated October 16, 1882; earlier, bearing date July 25, 1882, published in an unidentified newspaper under title, "Out of the Depths."

§Uncollected; read by Mrs. N. S. Joslin, July 4th, at Crawfordsville.

‖Uncollected; the pseudonym, *Ben Offield*, was used for her sporadic column of Crawfordsville correspondence until January 3, 1880, when she signed her own name. People named Offield were the first white settlers in Montgomery County, hence, probably, her choice of this pen name.

THE (Indianapolis) SATURDAY HERALD—*continued*

1876: September 23   The Story of the Bloody Shirt [poem]'
              30   Crawfordsville [signed *Ben Offield*]*
     October   14, 28,
     November 18   The Hoosier Athens [signed *Ben Offield*]*
              25   The Land of the Swallow [poem]*
     December 2, 16   The Hoosier Athens [signed *Ben Of-field*]*
              23   After Work [poem]*
1877: January   13, 20   The Hoosier Athens [signed *Ben Offield*]*
     February 10   A Sorrow [poem]*
              17,
     March   3,†
     April   7, 14   The Hoosier Athens [signed *Ben Offield*]*
              21   Apart [poem]*
     September 8   Mr. Jiggers' Toothpick [signed *Mrs. J.*]‡
              15   Faith [poem]*
     December 8, 22   The Hoosier Athens [signed *Ben Offield*]§
1878: June   22   Our Alley—A Rural Sketch‖
              29   In the East and West [poem]*
     September 7   From Chicago (Special Correspondence)*
     October   12,
     November 9,
     December   7   The Hoosier Athens [signed *Ben Offield*]*
              21   Jessies [*sic*] Guest: A Christmas Story for Children*
1879: March   22   Cornelia Chisholm [poem]*
     December 20   A Balhinch Christmas*
1880: January   3   The Hoosier Athens¶

---

*Uncollected.

†The intervening issue, February 24th, may have contained the column, but is unlocated.

‡Uncollected; established as her writing by an "M. H. K." written below the printed "Mrs. J." on the clipping in her father's scrapbook, now in the Indiana State Library.

§Uncollected. During 1877 and 1878 the column occasionally bore signatures of *Emily Hawthorne, Phoenix,* or *P,* omitted here as not hers.

‖Uncollected; reprinted twice in *The Crawfordsville Journal* (July 6, 1878, and April 12, 1879) under the title, "A Crawfordsville Alley."

¶Signed Mary H. Krout for first time; her contributions to the column, "The Hoosier Athens," were earlier signed, *Ben Offield.* The fact that this pseudonym was hers is made clear by a note in the same newspaper, September 7, 1878, that "Miss Mary H. Krout, of Crawfordsville, a valued contributor to *The Herald,* has returned from her lakeside vacation . . .," and, on October 12, 1878, the column, "The Hoosier Athens," signed *Ben Offield,* begins: "It requires a good deal of resignation to leave pleasure haunts in forest and by lakeshore . . . and turn willingly and cheerfully to work . . . especially if that work be . . . teaching

THE (Indianapolis) SATURDAY HERALD—*continued*
    1882: July   1   Luther's Choral [poem]*
    1887: February 19   Equal Suffrage Societies*

THE (Indianapolis) SATURDAY REVIEW
    1881: October 29   [Civil War poem]*
    December 31   Lydia Darrah [poem]*

THE INDIANAPOLIS STAR
    1914: March   1   Indiana Woman Recalls Incidents of Stevenson's Life in Samoa Islands*
    July   12   (Hoosier Section) Neighbors, Old and New*

THE INTERIOR (see THE [Chicago] INTERIOR)

THE INTER OCEAN (see THE [Chicago] INTER OCEAN)

KOKOMO (Indiana) SATURDAY TRIBUNE
    1879: March   8   Country Homes*
    April   5   Moral Qualifications*
    May   3   Boys and Girls*
                31   "The Silent Majority"*
    June   28   Concerning Rest*
    July   26   Professional Women*
    August   9   In a Day [poem]*
                30   Minor Trials*
    September 20   American Heathen*
    November 1   A Prologue [poem]*
                29   Dress and Its Associations*
    December 27   The Four Knights [poem]*
    1880: January 31   Two Country Towns*
    February 28   A Chapter on Shirks*
    March   27   The Wages of Sin*
    April   24   Sham*
    May   15   The Word of the King [poem]*
                29   My Thought [poem]*
    June   26   Some Old Fashions and Their Decay*
    July   31   Some Indianapolis Women*
    August   14   Aunt Polly*
    September 25   A Common Grievance*
    October 23   Children*
    November 20   Uncle Riley's Funeral*
    December 18   Popular Taste*

---

school." The scrapbooks preserved in her family also contain many of the *Ben Offield* clippings.
    *Uncollected.

THE LADIES REPOSITORY
    1869: December   Out in the Street [poem]*

LIPPINCOTT'S MAGAZINE OF POPULAR LITERATURE AND SCIENCE
    1870: December   To-Day [poem]*
    1871: January   Life [poem]*

LITERATURE: AN ILLUSTRATED WEEKLY
    1888: June   2   General Lew Wallace*

THE LITTLE CORPORAL
    1869: June   Mud Pies [poem]*
        September   Lullaby [poem]*
        November   "Tell Us a Story" [poem]*
    1870: January   The Little, Old Cradle [poem]*
        February   What the Crickets Say [poem]*
        April   Childhood Land [poem]*
        July   The Clod [poem]*
        August   Biddy*
        October   Bess [poem]*
        December   Little Purple Heartsease [poem]*
    1871: March   The Little Acorn [poem]*
        August   What the Birds Told [poem]*
        October   What Will the Baby Be? [poem]*
    1872: October   The Wood Violet [poem]*
        November   The Lost Lamb [poem]*
    1873: February   The Wind and the Rain [poem]*
    1874: April   Winter Is Over [poem]*; An Idler [poem]*
        July   A Little Dinner [poem]*
    1875: April   The Elves' Work [poem]*; Mother Earth's
                           House-cleaning [poem]*

MUNSEY'S MAGAZINE
    1901: October   The Sower [poem]*

THE NEBRASKAN (see THE DAILY NEBRASKAN)

THE NEW YORK JOURNAL & ADVERTISER, AMERICAN MAGAZINE SUPPLE-
MENT
    1899: May   21   Mrs. [Florence Holbrook] Maybrick to Be
                          Free†

NEW YORK TRIBUNE
    1874: August   21 (semi-weekly issue) Stubble [poem]*
    1900: January   7   (daily issue) Missions in China‡

---

*Uncollected.

†Uncollected; see *The* (Chicago) *Inter Ocean*, September 26, 1897, for an earlier article about Mrs. Maybrick.

‡Unsigned; uncollected. Of her "special letters" from China, sent to the *New York Tribune* between September, 1899, and June, 1900, this is the only one

THE NORTH WESTERN FARMER
    1866: October   1   October [poem]*
    1867: February   1   To the Wild Goose [poem; signed M.H.K.]†

OUR YOUNG FOLKS
    1868: September   Little Brown Hands†

THE OVERLAND MONTHLY
    1871: March   The Consummation [poem]†

THE (Peoria, Illinois) SATURDAY EVENING CALL
    1879: October   4   Elizabeth Boynton Harbert [under caption:
                               Women Who Write, Number III]‡
          December 20   Spirits Four [poem]§; The Home-Coming
                               [poem]†
    1880: April   10   An Educational Fallacy†
          October   16   From Chicago to Mackinaw‖

READER MAGAZINE
    1904: July   A Song of Birds [poem]†
          August   Opportunity [poem]†
          December   The Doves of Honolulu [poem]†
    1905: September   Tusitala: Teller of Tales [poem]†
    1906: May   The King's Road [poem]†

SYDNEY (Australia) MAIL
    1906: August   15   Brandon's Beat¶

---

that, by its style, is identifiable as from her pen; an article published April 15, 1900, "To Benefit Other Lands," may or may not be hers. Manuscripts of several articles on China, not found published, are among the Krout Papers in the Indiana State Library. The Boxer Rebellion was the subject of a lecture she gave later in Australia (mentioned but not quoted in the *Sydney Mail,* June 20, 1906).

*Uncollected; another poem written for this periodical, "The Departure of Summer," has been found in excerpt form, signed *Mary Hannah Kennedy* (Kennedy was a family name; Mary H. Krout signed the clipping with her same initials, so she evidently wrote it).

†Uncollected.

‡Uncollected. Elizabeth Boynton Harbert later wrote about Mary Krout in "Indiana Authors," *Kokomo Saturday Tribune,* January 31, 1880.

§Uncollected; reprinted without title in her column, "After Breakfast Chat," November 14, 1886 (see *post* 66); begins: "Spirits four my door have passed . . . ."

‖Uncollected. Her later contributions to the same newspaper have not yet been located; according to *The Crawfordsville Journal,* March 27, 1886, she was on the editorial staff of the *Call* from October, 1885, through March, 1886. She is thought to have had material published in this newspaper as early as 1878, but the issues are not available.

¶Uncollected; a short story written for this paper. Her talk on American journalism before the Woman's Branch of the British Empire League was mentioned but not quoted in the *Sydney Mail* on May 16, 1906. The *Sydney Morning Herald,* August 4, 1906, reported but did not quote her talk on "yellow" journalism before the Y. W. C. A. on August 2nd.

SYDNEY (Australia) MORNING HERALD
   1906: August   8   American Women Millionaires*

THE TERRE HAUTE EXPRESS
   1886: September 5, 12, 19   After Breakfast Chat*
                    26   Woman and Home*; After Breakfast Chat*
         October   3   After Breakfast Chat*
                    10, 17, 24, 31,
         November 7, 14   Woman and Home*; After Breakfast
                        Chat*
                    21   After Breakfast Chat*
                    28,
         December   5   Woman and Home*; After Breakfast Chat*
                    12, 19, 26,
   1887: January   2, 9, 16, 23, 30   After Breakfast Chat*
         February   6   Swallows at Sunset [poem]†; After Breakfast
                        Chat*
                    [13]‡ 20, 27,
         March   6, 13, 20, 27,
         April   3   After Breakfast Chat*
                    10   After Breakfast Chat* [includes poem:
                        (April)]§
                    17, 24,
         May   1, 8, 15   After Breakfast Chat*
                    22   After Breakfast Chat* [includes poem: At
                        Parting]*
                    29,
         June   5, 12, 19, 26,
         July   17, 24, 31,
         August   7, 14, 21, 28,
         September 4, 11, 18, 25,
         October   2, 9, [16]‖, 23, 30,
         November 6, 13   After Breakfast Chat*

THE TERRE HAUTE SATURDAY EVENING MAIL
   1875: June   12   Little Brown Hands [poem]¶
         October   30   Grown Old [poem]*

---

*Uncollected.
†Uncollected. Published later under the title, "The Higher Light."
‡This date's issue missing from file in Emeline Fairbanks Memorial Library,
Terre Haute. Since the column was a regular weekly feature at this time, it was
probably present.
§Uncollected; poem without title here, but called "April" in a later printing in
The Denver Times, April 25, 1903.
‖This date's issue missing from file in Emeline Fairbanks Memorial Library,
Terre Haute. Since the column was a regular weekly feature at this time, it prob-
ably was present therein.
¶Uncollected; author's name spelled *Crout*.

TERRE HAUTE DAILY NEWS
    1880: February 19 Doubt [poem]*
UNITED STATES NAVAL INSTITUTE PROCEEDINGS
    1921: February   Perry's Expedition to Japan†
    1924: March   Rear Admiral Charles Wilkes and His Ex-
                               ploits†
THE WABASH MAGAZINE
    1867: June   Twilight [poem]‡
    1869: June   Dead [poem]§
    1870: June   The Perfect [poem]‖

NOTES: The list that follows is a record of titles known to have been published in periodicals which are unidentified; all are uncollected:

Already [poem] (For the Indiana State Council of Defense). Probably published in an Indianapolis newspaper in 1917

The Answer [poem]

The Children's Wishes [poem]

A Colonial Staple [article about wool and its tariff]. Probably in *The* (Chicago) *Inter Ocean*. She wrote at the side of the clipping: "A campaign document used in Illinois in 1894." Undoubtedly by her, though unsigned. She had written much this year about the wool industry in New Zealand and Hawaii, in her signed columns

The Cow [poem]. From *The Terre Haute Express*, so stated, but not found therein

The Crocus [poem], with date line: March 31, 1868

Died [obituary poem for Walter Nicholson, "aged 19 months 17 days," who died on Sunday, July 17, year unnamed]

Down in New Zealand [poem]

The Dying Year (For the *Journal*). Poem dated Dec. 19, 1864, and probably published in *The Crawfordsville Journal* December 24 or 31, 1864, but these issues unlocated

The Empty Nest [poem]

Evelyn Claire [poem] (For the *Journal*)

Helpless Girls

In Convalescence [poem], dated March 2, 1878

In Crawford's Woods [poem]

---

*Uncollected; not same as poem with same title in *The Crawfordsville Journal*, December 29, 1883; begins: "No warmth was in the wintry sky . . . ."

†Uncollected.

‡Uncollected, signed M.H.K. According to a story in *The Northwestern Farmer*, October 1, 1866, she had a contribution earlier in *The Wabash Magazine*; not located therein, unless the poem to Beach, untitled and author unnamed, included in the class history by R.B.F. Peirce, June, 1866, was hers.

§Uncollected, signed M.H.K.; not same as "Dead in May."

‖Uncollected. On May 8, 1875, *The Crawfordsville Journal* listed this poem as one of the items deposited in the copper box sunk into the cornerstone of the Crawfordsville Court House, May 6, 1875.

Into Mischief [poem] (For the *Crawfordsville Journal*)

[Kennedy; poem, untitled, written for the birthday of "Madam" Kennedy; begins: "Bright shines the light on the hearthstone"]

[Letter to editor of *The Evening Post*, written from Chicago, Sept. 27, year unnamed; a protest against "Cecil's" comments on women who work outside the home]

My Valentine [poem]

The Old Stone House, Built in the City of Covington, Kentucky, in the Year 1791 [poem] (For the *Review*)

Patient Workers [poem]

[Poem, untitled, beginning: "O Soul, be strong! What bitter griefs are thine"]

Pointers for Women. Article undated and unsigned, but undoubtedly hers. Probably in *The* (Chicago) *Inter Ocean;* on work open to women

The Sick Boy [poem]

Some Hints to Young, Middle-aged, and Elderly Gentlemen. (In the *Inter-Ocean*)

The Soul [poem]

To Olga Nethersole [poem; date line: Chicago, Feb. 3, year unnamed.] The author dined with Olga Nethersole in Picadilly in 1895, and described the occasion in her London letter published August 19th of that year. The poem and letter have no apparent connection, but in both she expressed admiration for the actress.

[Note: Four, at least, of her poems appeared in an unlocated periodical called the *Home Journal;* two of these (clippings in her scrapbook) are stated to be written "for the *Home Journal*": "The Way of the World" and "Departed Days." *The Crawfordsville Journal*, September 9, 1869, published "The Promised Land" as "from the *Home Journal*" and, on February 24, 1870, "Through the Windows," with the same note.

Another unlocated publication, the *Sorosis*, is given credit for "The Face in the Fire," a poem reprinted therefrom in *The Crawfordsville Journal*, January 14, 1869. The Crawfordsville *Weekly Review* on the 23rd printed it also, with acknowledgment: "Copied from a recent number of *Sorosis*"; possibly a publication of the first woman's professional club in America, "Sorosis," founded in New York City in 1868.

The poem, " 'Woman's Sphere,' " which appeared on August 12, 1869, in *The Crawfordsville Journal*, made acknowledgment to *The Covington Journal*, and "The Grasshopper's Song," preserved in the form of an undated clipping, was written "For the Covington Journal." The Covington, Kentucky, newspaper of this name was searched from April to August 12, 1869, without success; the Covington, Indiana, paper was not available for checking.

Two titles listed as hers in a newspaper obituary (*The Indianapolis Star*, June 1, 1927) and carried over into *Who Was Who in America: 1897–1942*, have not been found: "The Eleventh Hour" (1921) and "The Coign of Vantage"; latter supposed to have been a serial in *Advance*, 1909–1910.]

MEREDITH NICHOLSON

BORN: *Crawfordsville, Indiana, December 9, 1866*

DIED: *Indianapolis, Indiana, December 21, 1947*

MEREDITH NICHOLSON loved Indiana! He expressed in words and actions a life-time devotion to his state. Born in Crawfordsville, he was brought by his family to Indianapolis when he was six and spent most of his eighty-one years in the capital city. He wove both cities into his stories and essays, which he saturated with his predominate theme: the wholesome culture of the people of Indiana; notably the books he considered his best, *The Hoosiers* (1900; 1915) and *A Hoosier Chronicle* (1912), the one a collection of essays, the other a novel. His works fall largely within these two classifications; he had published twenty-one novels and five volumes of essays.

When his publishers (Scribners) asked him for help in preparing a bibliography for the brochure, *Meredith Nicholson: American Man of Letters,* he suggested (June, 1923; letter unpublished, in Scribners' files) that they print the list in the latest *Who's Who in America:* "A complete bibliography would be difficult to compile as I have scattered a lot of stuff over the world. My patriotic howling during the war [World War I] distributed, and addresses and lectures through many years would make a large, fat volume. And I have written introductions for a few books—difficult to recall them now."

The contributions to books, magazines, and newspapers are indeed voluminous. Remembering that his first book was a collection of poems, *Short Flights,* published 1890, post-dated 1891, it is interesting to note the preponderance of poetry among his early accepted writings. On August 13, 1890, Mary H. Krout was predicting in *The* (Chicago) *Inter Ocean* great heights for him, "Indiana's Future Poet." In 1906 he had another volume, called, *Poems,* His fame is due to neither, although they were favorably noticed. It is as essayist and novelist that he is known. The world has agreed with his own opinion that *The Hoosiers* and *A Hoosier Chronicle* are his best, also showing appreciation of *The House of a Thousand Candles,* which is still in print. The latter is a story that the

71

author claimed "wrote itself"; usually he applied considerable time and effort to his work.

Like Mary Krout he did more in the field of journalism than appears as signed poems and articles. He served in an editorial capacity on *The Indianapolis Sentinel* in 1884 and *The Indianapolis News*, 1884–1897. After his brief sojourn in the West (he and his wife lived in Denver for about three years) he returned to Indianapolis and his writing career became really launched with the publication of *The Hoosiers*.

His signature to poems in *The Crawfordsville Journal*, 1885–1886, was *Will Meredith Nicholson*; he dropped the *Will* early and it has not been found in other publications. He apparently never used a pseudonym.

A Crawfordsville friend, Kenyon Nicholson, collaborated with him to make a play out of one of his short stories, "Honor Bright," but this was evidently not his medium.

Lacking a high school education, he was yet granted honorary degrees by colleges. Phi Gamma Delta made him an honorary member, and so did Phi Beta Kappa. He was elected to the American Academy of Arts and Letters.

His interest in politics and faith in the Democratic Party, for which he worked and wrote for years, bore fruit: he was appointed Minister to Portugal in 1913. This he refused, but later service he accepted, to Paraguay (1933–1934), Venezuela (1935–1938), and Nicaragua (1938–1941).

The ambition to be an author probably came from his high admiration for James Whitcomb Riley and other successful writers, and his own quality of determination carried him to a place with them; loyalty, integrity, and the ability to express himself in written words kept him there. It is hard to think of him apart from the little group whose association he enjoyed so much: Riley, Ade, Tarkington, Nicholson; each recalls the other. The sparks they provided built a good literary fire.

CHRONOLOGY OF BOOKS AND PAMPHLETS

1891   *Short Flights*   The Bowen-Merrill Co
1900   *The Hoosiers*   The Macmillan Company

1903 *The Main Chance* The Bobbs-Merrill Company
1904 *Zelda Dameron* The Bobbs-Merrill Company
1905 *The House of a Thousand Candles* The Bobbs-Merrill Company
1906 *Poems* The Bobbs-Merrill Company
1907 *The Port of Missing Men* The Bobbs-Merrill Company
Rosalind at Red Gate The Bobbs-Merrill Company
1908 *The Little Brown Jug at Kildare* The Bobbs-Merrill Company
1909 *The Lords of High Decision* Doubleday, Page & Company
1910 *The Siege of the Seven Suitors* Houghton Mifflin Company
1911 *Address by Meredith Nicholson at Manual Training High School . . . October 6, 1911* (Ephemera)
Style and the Man The Bobbs-Merrill Co. (Ephemera)
1912 *A Hoosier Chronicle* Houghton Mifflin Company
The Provincial American and Other Papers Houghton Mifflin Company
1913 *Otherwise Phyllis* Houghton Mifflin Company
1914 *The Poet* Houghton Mifflin Company
A Hoosier Classic (Ephemera)
1916 *The Proof of the Pudding* Houghton Mifflin Company
1917 *The Madness of May* Charles Scribner's Sons
A Reversible Santa Claus Houghton Mifflin Company
1918 *The Valley of Democracy* Charles Scribner's Sons
1919 *Lady Larkspur* Charles Scribner's Sons
1920 *Blacksheep! Blacksheep!* Charles Scribner's Sons
1921 *The Man in the Street* Charles Scribner's Sons
1922 *Best Laid Schemes* Charles Scribner's Sons
Broken Barriers Charles Scribner's Sons
1923 *Honor Bright: A Comedy in Three Acts* (with Kenyon Nicholson) Samuel French
The Hope of Happiness Charles Scribner's Sons
1924 *On the Antietam Battlefield* (Ephemera)
1925 *And They Lived Happily Ever After!* Charles Scribner's Sons
1926 *The Governor's Day Off* (Ephemera)
1928 *The Cavalier of Tennessee* The Bobbs-Merrill Company
1929 *Old Familiar Faces* The Bobbs-Merrill Company

BIOGRAPHICAL REFERENCES

Who's Who in America, Vols. 5–24; *International Who's Who*; standard encyclopedias and biographical reference works on American authors (he is named in practically all published in the twentieth century); Jacob P. Dunn, *Indiana and Indianans* (1919); *Meredith Nicholson: American Man of Letters* (Scribners, 1923); R. E. Banta,

Indiana Authors and Their Books (1949), *Hoosier Caravan* (1951); Mrs. Jean Sanders, *Meredith Nicholson: Hoosier Cavalier* (thesis for Master's degree, in preparation under Raymond Pence, DePauw University; copy to be deposited in Indiana State Library); "Without Benefit of College," (autobiographical) in Meredith Nicholson, *Old Familiar Faces* (1929).

1891

(Published 1890)

Short Flights

SHORT FLIGHTS | BY | MEREDITH NICHOLSON | [*rule*] | With a weak, uncertain wing | And a short flight, faltering | Like a heart afraid to sing. | [*rule*] | INDIANAPOLIS | THE BOWEN-MERRILL CO | 1891

COLLATION: [1–14]⁴. White laid paper. Leaf measures $5\,{}^{13}\!/_{16}''$ x $4\,{}^{1}\!/_{4}''$, all edges trimmed (edges red in parti-colored cloth-bound copies).

End paper; binder's leaf; title-page, p. [i]; copyright notice dated 1890, p. [ii]; dedication to his uncle, William Morton Meredith, p. [iii]; blank, p. [iv]; table of contents, pp. v–vii; blank, p. [viii]; half-title, p. [ix]; blank, p. [x]; *Invocation*, p. xi; blank, p. [xii;] text, pp. [1]–86; divisional half-title, p. [87]; blank, p. [88]; text, pp. 89–100; binder's leaf; end paper.

[Note: For text, pp. (1)–100, see *Contents*.]

ILLUSTRATIONS: None. A rule appears below running title on pp. vi–vii, xi, 2–86, and 89–100.

BINDING: Solid colored: green, maroon, and, light purple silk-finished mesh cloth; also, parti-colored blue, and, green: upper portion dark and lower light. Front cover gilt-stamped: SHORT FLIGHTS | [*floral decoration at left of author's name:*] MEREDITH | NICHOLSON Spine gilt-stamped: SHORT | FLIGHTS | [*rule*] | NICHOLSON Back cover blank.

End papers same as book stock; binder's leaf front and back.

[Note: For other bindings see *Notes*.]

PUBLICATION DATA: Copyrighted January 8, 1891. Earliest review noted: *The Indianapolis News*, December 24, 1890. Price, cloth, 75¢; half-calf, $1.50 (full calf-binding not mentioned in early advertisements, but available December 24th).

NOTES: This collection of poetry was Nicholson's first book. It appeared in two cloth bindings: parti-colored, and, solid colored, without priority; also, in half-calf, and, full calf. A copy with inscription dated December 24, 1890, given to O. R. Johnson, business manager of *The Indianapolis News,* is in flexible calf binding; one inscribed January, 1891, is in solid color; another, presented to Gen. Lew Wallace, also inscribed January, 1891, is in the parti-colored cloth,* as is the copyright deposit copy.

In all copies examined, the title-page, next to the last line, has final letter broken; in last line of the quotation above it, *afraid,* the first letter is separated slightly from the rest of the word; *M* in author's name defective.

James Whitcomb Riley evidently had a copy in his hands on December 23, 1890, since he wrote on that date to Charles Warren Stoddard, prophecying "a very desirable altitude for the young man later on"—*The Letters of James Whitcomb Riley,* edited by William Lyon Phelps (1930), p. 112.

"The verses in this little book were written between my seventeenth and twenty-second year," the author wrote later in a copy of his book.†

CONTENTS:

Invocation—To the Seasons
Sat Est Vixisse *The Catholic World,* October, 1889; *The Indianapolis News,* October 15, 1889
Song [beginning, "Glad and sad make rhyme, my dear"]
'Tis Never Night in Love's Domain *The Indianapolis Journal,* September 5, 1886
Estranged
When Friends Are Parted
Whereaway *The Boston Evening Transcript,* November 10, 1890 (with title: Where Away)
A Secret *The Indianapolis Journal,* January 13, 1889
Disappointment *The Indianapolis Journal,* January 17, 1886 (signed *Will Meredith Nicholson*)
Striving
An Idolater *The Indianapolis News,* September 2, 1886
Love's Midas Touch
In Ether Spaces‡ *The Catholic World,* June, 1887; *The Indianapolis Journal,* November 10, 1889
My Paddle Gleamed

---

*The first-named is John C. Rugenstein's; the second Lee Burns' copy; the latter is in Eagle Crest Library.
†Owned by the Indianapolis Public Library.
‡Reprinted in *Indiana Poetry,* by Aletha Mae Taylor (1925).

Meredith Nicholson's first book, SHORT FLIGHTS: *the two bindings and a presentation inscription*

Faithless *The Current*, October 17, 1885 (signed *Will Meredith Nicholson*)

Grape Bloom *The Indianapolis News*, May 28, 1886* (signed *Will Meredith Nicholson*)

Ill-starred *The Indianapolis News*, July 25, 1886 (without hyphen in title; signed *Will Meredith Nicholson*)

The Soldier Heart *The Indianapolis News*, May 30, 1890

An Unwritten Letter

My Lady of the Golden Heart

Dreams *The Indianapolis Journal*, July 12, 1885 (signed *Will Meredith Nicholson*); *The Catholic World*, July, 1889†

Cardinal Newman *The Catholic World*, September, 1890

On the Mediterranean: The Greek Girl's Song; The Shepherd's Song [subtitles not in table of contents] *The Indianapolis Journal*, December 22, 1889 (under caption: Greek Love Songs)

Watching the World Go By *The Indianapolis News*, March 29, 1890

Righteous Wrath *The Boston Evening Transcript*, December 26, 1889

Sunset

Rondeau of Eventide *The Catholic World*, November, 1889

A Prince's Treasure (To His Royal Highness, Russell Fortune) [subtitle not in table of contents] *The Indianapolis Journal*, April 14, 1889

Dieu Vous Garde *The Indianapolis Journal*, January 20, 1889‡

Sweetheart Time

The Road to Happiness

Guarding Shadows

Art's Lesson *The Indianapolis News*, April 5, 1890

In the Shadow *The Indianapolis Journal*, July 6, 1890

"Lead, Kindly Light" *The Indianapolis Journal*, July 13, 1890

Songs and Words

For a New Year's Morn

Three Friends (Paul Hamilton Hayne, Sidney Lanier and Robert Burns Wilson) [subtitle not in table of contents] *The Indianapolis Journal*, June 8, 1890

---

*"*For the Indianapolis News*, May, 1886," so stated in the newspaper printing. Nicholson tells in *Old Familiar Faces* (1929), p. 107, of his selling this poem to a New York weekly paper (unnamed), but he never saw it printed therein.

†The newspaper printing is from an early draft of the poem; between the versions in the periodicals and book there is evidence of rewriting.

‡Reprinted in *The Dial*, February, 1891, in a review of the book by William Morton Payne.

A Rhyme of Little Girls   *The Indianapolis Journal,* January 6,
1889

The Battles Grandsire Missed   *The Indianapolis News,* May 30,
1889

Barred   *The Current,* December 26, 1885 (signed *Will Meredith
Nicholson*)

A Slumber Son   *The Indianapolis Journal,* July 7, 1889

Before the Fire

October   *The Indianapolis Journal,* October 26, 1890

"In Winter I Was Born" [quotation marks not in table of contents]

Good Night and Pleasant Dreams   *The Indianapolis News,* February 15, 1890

Where Love Was Not   *The Indianapolis Journal,* September 12,
1886

Down the Aisles

Ruin

Half Flights   *The Indianapolis Journal,* May 1, 1887

A Kind of Man   *The Indianapolis Journal,* September 19, 1886

Transfigured   *The Indianapolis Journal,* January 2, 1887

Love's Power   *The Indianapolis Journal,* January 2, 1887

Fire-hunting   *The Current,* September 5, 1885 (signed *Will
Meredith Nicholson*)

"Heartache" (Lines naming a landscape painted by Mr. Theodore C. Steele, owned by Mr. Louis C. Gibson) [quotation
marks and subtitle not in table of contents]

Friendship's Sacrament   *The Indianapolis News,* November 8,
1890

Omar Khayyam   *Poems* (Indianapolis Flower Mission, 1890)

A Discovery (According to a Child) [subtitle not in table of con-
tents]   *The Indianapolis Journal,* January 24, 1886 (signed
Will Meredith Nicholson)

A Modern Puritan*   *The Indianapolis Journal,* July 13, 1890

The Law of Life (To Mr. Charles H. Ham, author of "Manual
Training") [subtitle not in table of contents]

To Eugene Field in England   *The Indianapolis News,* April 26,
1890 (with title: To Eugene Field in London)

Dependence

By Sheridan's Grave

Viking (Written in Du Chaillu's *Viking Age*) [subtitle not in table

---

*This poem, and those following are sonnets, introduced by a divisional half-
title.

of contents] *The Indianapolis News,* December 16, 1889 (with title: Our Debt to the Norsemen)

Violin *The Crawfordsville Journal,* November 20, 1886 (signed *Will Meredith Nicholson*)

What the Babies Say

Secrets *The Indianapolis News,* November 19, 1885 (signed *Will Meredith Nicholson*)

Blind *The Indianapolis News,* February 8, 1890

A Fancy

Thoreau *The Current,* July 10, 1886 (signed *Will Meredith Nicholson*)

1900
The Hoosiers

THE HOOSIERS | BY | MEREDITH NICHOLSON | New York | THE MAC-MILLAN COMPANY | LONDON: MACMILLAN AND CO., LTD. | 1900 | All rights reserved

COLLATION: B–I⁸, K–T⁸ (all signed on recto of 7th leaf), [U]². White laid paper. Leaf measures $7\frac{1}{8}''$ x $5''$, top edge gilt, other edges untrimmed.

End paper; fly title, p. [i]; list of books in the series of *National Studies in American Letters* edited by George Edward Woodberry, p. [ii]; title-page, p. [iii]; copyright notice dated 1900, and imprint of the Norwood Press, p. [iv]; dedication to the memory of Caleb Mills, p. [v]; blank, p. [vi]; preface dated July, 1900, pp. vii–viii; table of contents, pp. ix–x; half-title, p. [xi]; blank, p. [xii]; text, pp. 1–271; blank, p. [272]; *Index,* pp. 273–277; blank, p. [278]; publisher's advertisements, pp. [279–280]; end paper.

[Note: For text, pp. 1–271, see *Contents.*]

BINDING: Maroon mesh cloth. Front cover gilt-stamped: THE HOOSIERS | [*rule*] | NICHOLSON | NATIONAL STUDIES IN AMERICAN LET-TERS Spine gilt-stamped: [*triple rule*] | THE | HOOSIERS | NICHOLSON | THE MACMILLAN | COMPANY | [*triple rule*]. Back cover blank.

End papers white laid, heavier than book stock; no binder's leaf front or back.

PUBLICATION DATA: Deposited in the Copyright Office and published November 17, 1900. Earliest review noted: *The Indianapolis News,* November 24th. Price, $1.25.

NOTES: First edition as collated. No illustrations. Issued in the series of *National Studies in American Letters*, done at the request of George E. Woodberry.

A later binding state of the book shows all edges trimmed, top edge gilt, leaf measuring $6\frac{7}{8}$" x $4\frac{11}{16}$" (earlier, $7\frac{1}{8}$ " x 5"), bound in red ribbed cloth, of poorer quality than the original mesh.

A new impression from plates of the first edition appeared with all edges trimmed, top edge ungilded, leaf measuring only $6\frac{3}{4}$" x $4\frac{1}{2}$", bound in bright red coarse mesh cloth stamped in black.

The *Centennial Edition*, dated 1915, identified on front cover, was also printed from the original plates, but with revisions and an added chapter, IX, "A Centennial Postscript." The revisions consisted of footnotes, pp. 9, 198, 199, 211, 223, and 226; the account of George Ade reworded and added to, p. 242; a one-sentence note of Edward Eggleston's death added p. 155. It was published August, 1915 (copyrighted August 26th), reprinted twice in September, 1915, also reprinted January, February twice, March, September, and December, 1916.

In an inscription, July 5, 1919,* the author said: "This book, written in Denver, during a three year's residence there, expresses my *homesickness*. I spent much time and care in the writing . . . ." In an interview published in *The Indianapolis News*, December 5, 1900, he is quoted as declaring it written at the invitation of Prof. Woodberry, of Columbia University, editor of the series. He remarked frequently that this was his personal favorite of all his writings, the one by which he expected to be longest remembered.† In telling an interviewer in 1946 that he considered it his best book, he described it as "a long essay on Indiana culture."‡

CONTENTS:

CHAPTER

    I   Indiana and Her People§

   II The Rural Type and the Dialect [subdivisions in table of contents: The Word "Hoosier" | Pioneer Difficulties | The Dialect]

 III Bringers of the Light [subdivisions in table of contents: Religious Influences | Early Illiteracy | Caleb Mills | Julia L. Dumont and Catharine Merrill]

---

*Inscription for Charles Romm; copy in the Indiana State Library.

†*Indiana Authors and Their Books, 1816–1916*, compiled by R. E. Banta (1949), p. 238. For Riley's appreciation of the book see *Letters of James Whitcomb Riley* edited by William Lyon Phelps (1930), p. 248.

‡*The Indianapolis Times*, February 20, 1946, p. 7; interview by Henry Butler.

§Reprinted, with comment, in *Hoosier Caravan*, selected by R. E. Banta (1951).

IV   An Experiment in Socialism [subdivisions in table of contents: New Harmony | Robert Dale Owen and William Maclure | Thomas Say and the Scientists]

V   The Hoosier Interpreted
Edward Eggleston*
James Whitcomb Riley†

VI   Crawfordsville [first subdivision in table of contents: "The Hoosier Athens"]
General Lew Wallace [in table of contents: Lew Wallace]
Maurice Thompson
Mary H. Krout—Caroline V. Krout [in table of contents: *and* in place of em dash]

VII   "Of Making Many Books There Is No End" [first subdivision in table of contents: Indiana a Point of Departure]
Fiction
History and Politics
Miscellaneous

VIII   An Indiana Choir
Early Writers
Forceythe Willson [table of contents adds: and Elizabeth Conwell Willson]
Later Poets [table of contents adds a final subdivision: The Hoosier Landscape]

1903

The Main Chance

THE MAIN | CHANCE [*title in red*] | BY | MEREDITH NICHOLSON | ILLUSTRATED BY | HARRISON FISHER | INDIANAPOLIS | THE BOBBS-MERRILL COMPANY | PUBLISHERS

[Note: All within a wide rule box which is within a parallel rule box, the inner parallel rule being red.]

---

*Not same as "Edward Eggleston," a later article in *The Atlantic Monthly*, December, 1902.

†Not same as "James Whitcomb Riley," later in *The Atlantic Monthly*, October, 1916.

COLLATION: [1–28]⁸ (plus one unsigned leaf in first signature). White wove paper. Leaf measures 7⅜″ (full) x 5¹⁄₁₆″, all edges trimmed.

End paper; fly title, p. [i]; blank, p. [ii]; frontispiece with tissue guard, inserted; title-page, inserted, verso bearing copyright notice dated 1903, statement: *May,* and imprint in red of Braunworth & Co., Brooklyn, N. Y.; dedication to E. K. N. [Eugenie Kountze Nicholson], p. [iii]; blank, p. [iv]; table of contents, pp. [v–vi]; half-title, p. [vii]; blank, p. [viii]; text, pp. 1–419; blank, pp. [420–422]; divisional half-title, p. [423]; publishers' advertisements, pp. [424–438]; blank, pp. [439–440]; end paper.

[Note: Text, pp. 1–419: The Main Chance, Chapters I–XLII (titled).]

ILLUSTRATIONS: Colored frontispiece with tissue guard, inserted as are colored plates facing pp. 28, 118, 286, 294, 416. All are by Harrison Fisher.

BINDING: Light green ribbed cloth. Front cover has title and author's name gilt-stamped within a white-stamped design: THE | MAIN CHANCE [*title boxed by a wide rule, the lower part of box joined to a panel composed of vertical rules crossed by horizontal rules, single, quadruple, and parallel; the quadruple rules are intercepted in center by a vignette displaying a white-stamped trolley car; at foot, gilt-stamped:*] By MEREDITH NICHOLSON [*the wide rule forming the box for the title, continues to foot of cover, boxing all the foregoing*]. Spine has lettering gilt-stamped, rules white-stamped: [*wide rule*] | THE | MAIN | CHANCE | [*wide rule joined to vertical rules which intercept one single rule and join another one*] | NICHOLSON | [*single rule joined by vertical rules which intercept one single rule and join another*] | BOBBS | MERRILL | [*wide rule*]. Back cover blank.

End papers white wove, heavier than book stock; no binder's leaf front or back.

PUBLICATION DATA: Deposited in the Copyright Office May 9, 1903; published May 10th. Earliest review noted: *The Indianapolis News,* May 14, 1903. Price, $1.50.

NOTES: First edition bears statement on copyright page: *May.* It has been noted in several states:

    State 1: Sigs. [1–28]⁸

          Title-page in red and black, inserted

          Braunworth imprint on copyright page in red (later, black)

    State 2: Signatures and title-page as in *State* 1

Braunworth imprint on copyright page in black (earlier, red)

State 3: Sigs. [1–13]¹⁶, [14]⁸ (earlier, [1–28]⁸)

Title-page in black (earlier, red and black), and an integral part of the book (earlier, inserted)

No imprint on copyright page (earlier, present, first in red, and then in black)

Copies in State 3 have no color in illustrations.

Advertisements are in various states following p. [424] which ends the book proper:

Advertisements State 1: 16-page publisher's catalogue in back, followed by a final blank leaf (later, 18 printed pages)

15th page advertises The 13th District [Note: Thus in the copyright deposit copies and the earliest inscribed copy located*]

Advertisements State 2: 18-page catalogue in back (earlier, 16 pages plus blank leaf), last leaf advertising The Redemption of David Corson and The Puppet Crown

15th page same as Advertisements State 1

Advertisements State 3: 18-page catalogue in back with 17th page advertising Tomorrow's Tangle, 18th, The Grey Cloak (earlier, a blank leaf, then, advertising The Redemption of David Corson and The Puppet Crown)

15th page advertises The Fortunes of Fifi (earlier, The 13th District).

Copies in States 1 and 2 of sheets have combinations that are at first glance puzzling with States 2 and 3 of advertisements. But, the final signature being a publisher's catalogue, it is of no great significance in determining sequence of issue. If the catalogue advertised books published after 1903, that would be a different matter. A complete lack of advertisements seems to accompany State 3 of the sheets.

This was Nicholson's first novel, recorded as a "best-seller" in the Bookman record of November, 1903. It was also Omaha's first historical

---

*Inscription dated May 29, 1903; copy in the collection of John C. Rugenstein.

novel, according to newspaper accounts, and provoked considerable discussion there.*

Grosset & Dunlap reprinted it in 1905 and kept it in print until 1912; noted in two bindings: green coarse mesh, with title gilt-stamped but other lettering and decorations green, and, light blue with title and lettering blue-stamped but decorations brown; advertisements differ also: only 2 pages of advertisements in green-bound copy with title gilt, 14 pages in other.

A British edition was published by Ward, Lock & Co., Ltd., June, 1904.

The author made the following comments in a copy inscribed in 1923:† "This is a story of Omaha. The publishers wouldn't allow me to use the name—hence 'Clarkson,' the name of a P. E. Bishop long identified with the community. The kidnapping episode was well known; the boy was a Cudahy, of a family long identified with the meat packing business in Omaha, Chicago, and elsewhere."

Nicholson, it was said,‡ had offers from New York dramatists who in 1903 wanted to put the book on the stage, but he thought it not well adapted to such presentation.

1904
Zelda Dameron

ZELDA | DAMERON | By | MEREDITH NICHOLSON | Author of The Main Chance | With Drawings by | JOHN CECIL CLAY | INDIANAPOLIS | THE BOBBS-MERRILL COMPANY | PUBLISHERS
[Note: All within a parallel rule box.]

COLLATION: [1–13]¹⁶ (plus one inserted leaf in first signature), [14]⁸. White wove paper. Leaf measures 7⅜" (scant) x 4¹³⁄₁₆", all edges trimmed.

End paper; fly title, p. [i]; blank, p. [ii]; frontispiece with tissue guard, inserted; title-page, inserted, verso bearing copyright notice dated 1904, statement: *October,* and imprint of Braunworth & Co.,

---

*Nicholson probably got inspiration for the book from visits to his wife's people in Omaha. *The Indianapolis Journal* as early as December 17, 1897, noted that the Nicholsons were to spend the holidays there.

†For the Indiana State Library.

‡*The Indianapolis Journal,* November 5, 1903, p. 3.

Brooklyn, N. Y.; dedication to the memory of the author's father [Edward Willis Nicholson], p. [iii]; blank, p. [iv]; table of contents, pp. [v–vi]; half-title, p. [vii]; blank, p. [viii]; text, pp. 1–411; blank, pp. [412–414]; divisional half-title, p. [415]; publisher's advertisements, pp. [416–424]; end paper.

[Note: Text, pp. 1–411: Zelda Dameron, Chapters I–XXXVI (titled).]

ILLUSTRATIONS: Colored frontispiece with tissue guard, inserted as are colored plates facing pp. 22, 98, 148, 222, 258, 326, and 376. All are by John Cecil Clay.

BINDING: Tan (rose beige) silk-finished mesh cloth. Front cover white-stamped: Zelda | Dameron | [*floral design in rose, yellow, and green on white oval, with monogram,* MA; *bordered by a row of dots and dashes*] | Meredith Nicholson [*all within a white parallel rule box*]. Spine white-stamped: [*parallel rule*] | ZELDA | DAMERON | [*floral design stamped in yellow and green*] | MEREDITH | NICHOLSON | BOBBS | MERRILL | [*parallel rule*]. Back cover blank.

End papers slightly calendered; no binder's leaf front or back.

PUBLICATION DATA: Deposited in the Copyright Office October 12, 1904. Earliest review noted: *The Indianapolis News,* October 15th.*
Price, $1.50.

NOTES: First edition bears statement, *October,* on copyright page. It has been noted in two states besides a "de luxe edition":

> State 1: Printed on wove paper that bulks book to 1″ across sheets (later, 1⅛″)
> Sigs. [1–13]^{16} (plus one inserted leaf in first signature), [14]^8 (later, [1–27]^8)
> Title-page inserted (later, an integral part of the book)
> Copyright page bears 4-line printers' slug (later, 3-line slug)
> Publisher's catalogue, pp. [415–424] (later, pp. [415–422]), contents same in all copies up to p. [419]: advertising *At the Big House* by Anne Virginia Culbertson, p. [419] (later omitted and this page adver-

*The review suggests that the locale is identifiable: "Mariona" is Indianapolis; "Jefferson Street," Washington; "High Street," Virginia Avenue; "Hamilton Club," Columbia Club; and "Tippecanoe," University Club. An interview reported in *The Indianapolis Sentinel,* October 23, 1904, quoted the author as saying that his characters were not drawn from local personages, but the book was an attempt to link the old Indianapolis, "the town of the period before the Civil War, with the city of today [1904]."

tising *The Yoke*); advertising *The Yoke* on p. [422];
Her Infinite Variety by Brand Whitlock, p. [423]
(later omitted); *The Reader Magazine*, p. [424]
(later on p. [422])

State 2: Printed on wove paper that bulks book to 1⅛" across
sheets (earlier, 1")

Sigs. [1–27]⁸ (earlier, [1–13]¹⁶ [plus one inserted leaf
in first signature], [14]⁸)

Title-page an integral part of the book (earlier, an insert)

Copyright page bears 3-line printer's slug, lacking
statement: *Bookbinders And Printers* (earlier the
third line in a 4-line slug)

Publisher's catalogue, pp. [415–422] (earlier, pp.
[415–424]: advertisements same as *State* 1 up to
p. [419] which advertises *The Yoke* (earlier, *At The
Big House*); pp. [420] and [421] same as *State* 1;
p. [422] advertising *The Reader Magazine* (earlier,
p. [424]).

To compensate for the title-page being made an integral part of
the book, two pages of advertisements were omitted in the later issue,
those advertising Anne Virginia Culbertson's *At the Big House,* and
Brand Whitlock's *Her Infinite Variety.*

Both states are in the tan floral binding, white-stamped. *State* 1
copies have end papers slightly calendered; in *State* 2 copies there is
less evidence of any coating.

The "de luxe edition" was available in December, 1904.* It is
printed on white laid paper, top edge gilt, other edges untrimmed; has
title-page an integral part of the book; gatherings are [1–27]⁸; lacks
printers' slug on copyright page; has no advertisements; is bound in
light blue cloth, gilt-stamped. It probably appeared before *State* 2 of
the trade edition.

Grosset & Dunlap reprinted the novel in 1906. A copy has been reported with their imprint on title-page, original publisher's on spine.

This book does not contain characterizations of Indianapolis residents, the author told a reporter for *The Indianapolis Sentinel, ca.* October 15, 1904 (clipping examined lacks full date).

---

*A copy presented by the author to General Lew Wallace at this time is now
in Eagle Crest Library.

1905

The House of
a Thousand Candles

THE HOUSE OF A | THOUSAND CANDLES | By | MEREDITH NICHOLSON | Author of THE MAIN CHANCE | ZELDA DAMERON, ETC. | WITH ILLUSTRATIONS BY | HOWARD CHANDLER CHRISTY | "So on the morn there fell new tidings and other adventures" | MALORY | INDIANAPOLIS | THE BOBBS-MERRILL COMPANY | PUBLISHERS

COLLATION: [1–25]⁸. White laid paper. Leaf measures 7⅝″ x 5⅛″ (full), all edges trimmed.

End paper; blank, pp. [i–iv]; fly title, p. [v]; blank, p. [vi]; frontispiece with tissue guard, inserted; title-page, p. [vii]; copyright notice dated 1905, statement: *November,* and imprint of Braunworth Press, Brooklyn, N. Y., p. [viii]; dedication *To Margaret My Sister,* p. [ix]; blank, p. [x]; table of contents, p. [xi]; blank, p. [xii]; half-title, p. [xiii]; blank, p. [xiv]; text, pp. 1–382; blank, pp. [383–384]; publisher's advertisements, pp. [385–386]; end paper.

[Note: For text, pp. 1–382, see *Contents.*]

ILLUSTRATIONS: Colored frontispiece with tissue guard, inserted as are plates facing pp. 30, 100, 124, 164, 230, and 312; all by Howard Chandler Christy. A headpiece appears on first page of text and tailpiece on last.

BINDING: Blue mesh cloth. Front cover red-stamped: The HOUSE | of [*dot*] a | THOUSAND | CANDLES | [*decorative design of gilt-stamped candelabrum, with candles stamped in white, flames red; within the design are ornaments in red, white, and gilt, and gilt dots, initial R at inner left, repeated at inner right; author's name red-stamped within panel-like base:*] MEREDITH [*dot*] NICHOLSON Spine red-stamped: The | HOUSE | of a | THOUSAND | CANDLES | NICHOLSON | [*decorative design of gilt-stamped candelabrum with candles stamped in white, flames red, a red and white ornament in center, graduated gilt rules at base*] | BOBBS | MERRILL | [*gilt-stamped rule*]. Back cover blank.

End papers white wove; no binder's leaf front or back.

PUBLICATION DATA: Published November 16, 1905. Two copies of proof sheets of Chapter XVI had been deposited for copyright August 21, 1905. Advertised as "The Big November Novel" in *The Publishers' Weekly*, October 28th. Earliest review noted: *The Indianapolis News*, November 16th. Price, $1.50.

NOTES: First edition as collated, with *November* on copyright page. The *Albany* (New York) *Journal*, December 6, 1905, described the book as already in its second edition. Within the numerous issues there are distinguishable two states of text and several states of binding:

> State 1: Sigs. [1–25]⁸ (later, [1–26]⁸)
> Book stock laid paper (later, wove)
> Publisher's advertisements, pp. [385–386] (later, a catalogue extending to p. [416])
>
> State 2: Sigs. [1–26]⁸ (earlier, [1–25]⁸)
> Book stock wove paper (earlier, laid)
> Publisher's advertisements introduced by a divisional half-title (p. [385], verso blank), and extended to p. [416] (earlier, only 2 pages of advertisements).

All the books advertised were published in 1905, but in *State 2* a book is listed which was of later deposit in the Copyright Office than *The House of a Thousand Candles; i.e., Hearts and Masks*, by MacGrath.

The defective last line and folio of p. 370 are found in copies with both states of text, but in no copies of *State 1* is the correction made; some copies of *State 2* bear correction.

Bindings offer many variations, and a sequence is difficult to establish. This much is apparent: gilt stamping on front cover and spine occurs only on copies with text in *State 1*. Where it is found on copies with text in *State 2* it is accompanied by a change in the font of the red Bobbs Merrill imprint on spine, the *M* in *Merrill* 3mm. high (earlier, 4) and the word 18mm. wide (earlier, 22). Gold-colored stamping (in place of gold leaf) came later, but both the gilt and its imitation were used before Christmas, 1905. The gold color varies from pale yellow to orange (deep orange found on copies with text in *State 2* and repairs to last line and folio of p. 370); herewith the red imprint on the spine shows further variations in font and spacing of the letters, the *Merrill* being spread as far as 3cm. in width.

A copy of the book with frontispiece captioned, *Olivia*, has been reported but not located.* Frontispiece in all copies examined bears the legend: *There is something jaunty . . .* , quoted from p. 79; later a reprint used as frontispiece the plate that earlier faced p. 164 (thus in

---

*Noted by Jacob Blanck.

copy with A. Wessels' imprint on title-page, Grosset & Dunlap on spine).

Grosset & Dunlap had at least three editions: one in 1912 or earlier; another, with scenes from the photoplay, 1915; and a third, in their *Novels of Distinction* series, 1936.

McClurg issued a "new edition," in 1915.

British editions began appearing with Gay & Bird's "cheaper edition (printed from American plates)," November, 1906; Nelson issued it in March, 1911; Gay & Hancock, April, 1928; A. & C. Black, "new edition," July, 1928, and "cheap edition," July, 1936.

A Budapest edition with title, (*Az*) *Ezer Gyertyak Haza*, has been located. The novel was published as a serial in a French newspaper under the title, "La Maison des Milles Flambeaux," probably in book form also, translated by Jean Rolland. Other foreign editions are yet to be found.*

In a "self-interview," written for the *New York Herald*, September 23, 1906, the author claimed that the story followed "the wind's will," that he "never assumed any responsibility for the characters or incidents." "It was all news to me," he said, "and I shall never know again the same pleasure I experienced in running upstairs every evening to my workroom to see just what was going to happen next. The very name of the book was an inadvertence. It slipped from the pen without premeditation . . . ." His inscriptions in copies of the book told a similar story.

"This novel was written at 1500 N. Delaware Street, Indianapolis, (a new home we had built), between October, 1904 and the following May.† At this time there was a deluge of tales in imitation of Anthony Hope's 'Prisoner of Zenda.' It occurred to me to show if possible that a romantic tale could be written, without an 'imaginary kingdom,' with the scene in our own Indiana. Lake Maxinkuckee suggested the scene . . . . The success of the story surprised me. It was translated into five languages, was popular in England, and was dramatized with E. M. Holland, a distinguished actor, in the role of Bates. Two motion picture versions have been made. The title is still being paraphrased by advertisers. I have had more fun out of this tale than out of any other I have written."‡

---

*A Bobbs-Merrill advertisement on September 26, 1908 (in *The Publishers' Weekly*) mentioned a Japanese translation as contemplated.

†"Unusually quick production for me," he declared in a copy inscribed April 8, 1921, for Charles Thomas Scott, now in Eagle Crest Library.

‡Written in an Indiana State Library copy, May 23, 1932. According to the Peoria, Illinois, *Star*, December 16, 1906, a railway was advertising "The Road of a Thousand Wonders," two widely separated candy manufacturers described

His "Confessions of a 'Best-Seller,'" in *The Atlantic Monthly*, November, 1909, collected in *The Provincial American* (1912), concerned this book, though unnamed therein.

The dramatization, by George Middleton, was mentioned in *The Indianapolis Star*, May 28, 1906, and again on August 16, 1906; produced in Indianapolis September 5, 1907. The Wright Huntington stock company was playing it in Minneapolis on June 5, 1913. Of the two motion pictures before 1936, one was released in 1915, by the Selig Company, Chicago (see a story in *The Indianapolis Star*, June 20, 1915, captioned, "What's a Mere Author's Pet to the Czar of Filmland?," with statement that it would be released within six weeks); it was directed by T. N. Heffron, starred Harry Mestayer and Grace Darmond. This is evidently the one from which Grosset & Dunlap made a photoplay edition (1915). The other was released February, 1920.* An adaptation by Dorothy Davenport Reid and others was released by Republic Productions, Inc., April 3, 1936, directed by Arthur Lubin, starring Phillips Holmes, Mae Clarke and Iriving Pichel.

CONTENTS: The House of a Thousand Candles, Chapters I–XXIX (titled); earlier a serial in *The Reader Magazine*, Vol. 6, June–December, 1905.†

1906

Poems

POEMS | [*vignette within single rule box*] | MEREDITH NICHOLSON | INDIANAPOLIS | THE BOBBS-MERRILL COMPANY | PUBLISHERS

COLLATION: [1–8]⁸. White laid paper. Leaf measures 8″ x 5⅜″, top edge gilt, other edges deckled.

End paper; blank, pp. [i–iv]; fly title, p. [v]; blank, p. [vi]; title-page, p. [vii]; copyright notice dated 1906, and statement: *April*, p. [viii]; proem: *To James Whitcomb Riley*, pp. [ix–xi]; acknowledg-

---

themselves as "The House of a Thousand Candies," and a summer resort hotel was called "The House of a Thousand Delights."

*According to the author's statement in a letter to M. E. Perkins of Scribners, February 4, 1920; producer unnamed, and no record obtained from Republic Productions, Inc.

†It was a newspaper serial after book publication, in *The Indianapolis News*, October 13–November 13, 1906.

ment to periodicals, p. [xii]; table of contents, pp. [xiii–xiv]; half-title, p. [xv]; blank, p. [xvi]; text, pp. 1–110; blank, pp. [111–112]; end paper.

[Note: For text, pp. 1–110, see *Contents*.]

ILLUSTRATIONS: None except vignette on title-page. Title-page made decorative with hand-lettering, O intercepting P in title, and hyphen in *Bobbs-Merrill* being two short rules.

BINDING: Green ribbed cloth. Front cover gilt-stamped: POEMS | MEREDITH | NICHOLSON | [*vignette, similar to that on title-page, at lower right; all within a single rule box*]. Spine gilt-stamped: POEMS | MEREDITH | NICHOLSON | BOBBS | MERRILL   Back cover blank.

End papers same as book stock; no binder's leaf front or back.

PUBLICATION DATA: Published May 21, 1906 (reviewed in *The Indianapolis News*, this date, with statement, "published today"); deposited in the Copyright Office May 25th. A presentation copy to Louis Howland was signed May 19th.* Price, $1.25.

NOTES: First edition bears statement on copyright page: *April* (though not available until the month following). Two states of binding have been noted:

> *Binding State* 1: Ribbed cloth (later, smooth mesh); end papers same as book stock (later, calendered). Thus in copyright deposit copies and those with earliest inscriptions
>
> *Binding State* 2: Smooth mesh cloth (earlier, ribbed); end papers calendered (earlier, same as book stock). Thus in a copy purchased new in 1911, and in one inscribed by the author, January, 1911.†

This was Nicholson's second (and last) book of poems, the earlier one being *Short Flights* (1891).

CONTENTS: The poems herein make their first appearance in a Nicholson book with exception of "'In Winter I Was Born,'" "Watching the World Go By," "To the Seasons," and "Grace Chimes," which had appeared in *Short Flights*, the last-named under the title, "'Lead, Kindly Light.'"

[Proem] To James Whitcomb Riley‡

---

*In John C. Rugenstein's private library.

†Former in Indiana State Library, latter in Eagle Crest Library.

‡The tribute evidently pleased Riley, since he bought seventy-five copies of the book and sent them far and wide, which "constituted the greater part of the

Where Four Winds Meet   *Modern Art,* Winter, 1895; *The Indianapolis Journal,* August 8, 1895

The Wind at Whitsuntide

The Valley of Vision   *Once a Year, the Flower Mission Magazine* (1899)

Charm   *Harper's New Monthly Magazine,* June, 1898; *The Indianapolis Journal,* May 29, 1898

Wide Margins   *The Atlantic Monthly,* October, 1902

Chords   *The Century Magazine,* January, 1895

The Wind Patrol   *Once a Year* (1897)

A Prayer of the Hill-Country   *The Century Magazine,* June, 1899; *Louisville* (Kentucky) *Post,* June 20, 1903

The Spirit of Mountains   *The Hesperian Tree* ... 1903, edited by John James Piatt (1903)

The Psalms in the Mountains   *Indiana Writers of Poems and Prose,* compiled by Edward Joseph Hamilton (1902)*

In the Great Pastures   *The Atlantic Monthly,* July, 1901

A Shadow of the Rockies   *The Century Magazine,* September, 1900

Simplicity   *The Reader Magazine,* August, 1904†

An April Easter   *The Ishmaelite,* April, 1899

Asphodel

To a Débutante

Love's Music   *Once a Year, The Flower Mission Magazine* (1899)

West   *Boston Evening Transcript,* May 2, 1894

Escheat   *The University Review,* October, 1893; *The Indianapolis Journal,* October 15, 1893

Shadow Lines   *Poets and Poetry of Indiana,* edited by Benj. S. Parker & Enos B. Heiney (1900)

Youth and Winter

The Winter Wind in the Rockies

God Save the State!   [dated November, 1904]   *The Century Magazine,* November, 1904; *The* (Chicago) *Inter Ocean,* November 13, 1904

---

circulation of the book."—Meredith Nicholson's comment reported in *The Indianapolis Star,* December 11, 1910. The poem has been frequently reprinted. See *The Poet* (1914), *Notes,* for further Riley-Nicholson references.

*With acknowledgment to *Century Magazine,* but the poem has not been located therein.

†Reprinted in *Indiana Poetry* by Aletha Mae Taylor (1925), and in *Troubadour,* Indiana number, October, 1930; also on back of one issue of Scribner's booklet, *Meredith Nicholson: American Man of Letters* (1923).

The Earth *The* (New York) *Sun,* April 9, 1899*

An Old Guidon *Boston Evening Transcript,* September 28, 1894 (with title: The Old Guidons); *War Papers Read before the Indiana Commandery Military Order of the United States* (1898)

The Heart of the Bugle†

Shiloh

Cuba [dated January, 1898] *The Ishmaelite,* January, 1897

"Bless Thou the Guns" [dated April, 1898] *The Indianapolis Journal,* April 18, 1898; *Spanish-American War Songs,* compiled by Sidney A. Witherbee (1898)

The Horns *The Century Magazine,* August, 1898; *The Indianapolis Journal,* October 23, 1898; *Poets and Poetry of Indiana,* edited by Benj. S. Parker & Enos B. Heiney (1900)

Bellona | (Gêrome's Statue) *The Reader Magazine,* November, 1905

A Tenant

New Year's Collect

From Bethlehem to Calvary‡

Mea Culpa *University Magazine,* December, 1892

News *The Indianapolis Journal,* June 19, 1898§

For a Pioneer's Memorial *The Century Magazine,* July, 1899 (with title: Camps)||

Orchards by the Sea *The Century Magazine,* September, 1898

Ireland

Derelict

The Wayward Muse

Memory *Harper's New Monthly Magazine,* April, 1897

Unmapped *The Critic,* June 18, 1898; *Poets and Poetry of Indiana,* edited by Benj. S. Parker & Enos B. Heiney (1900)

John Tyndall | Obiit December 4, 1893

The Dead Archer | Maurice Thompson, Obiit February 15, 1901

---

*Reprinted in *The Indianapolis Journal,* April 16, 1899, with same title; in *The Indianapolis News,* May 24, 1902, with title, "Earth's Moods of Might."

†Reprinted in *Poetry of Today,* by Rose M. R. Mikels & Grace Shoup (1927), and in *Hoof-Marks in the Sod,* compiled by June W. Snyder (1946).

‡Reprinted in *The Master of Men,* compiled by Thomas Curtis Clark (1930).

§Signed, "Meredith Nicholson in the *Chap-Book*"; notwithstanding, it did not appear in *The Chap-Book,* which ceased publication with the issue of July 1, 1898; perhaps the poem had been accepted for publication, and acknowledgment was made in anticipation.

||Published with musical setting by Corinne L. Barcus, on a single sheet of white calendered paper [n.p.], 1916, reprinted in *Some Torch Bearers in Indiana* by Charity Dye (1917).

The Indianapolis News, February 16, 1901; *The Hesperian Tree* . . . 1903, edited by John James Piatt (1903)
"She Gathers Roses" [dated January 30, 1901]*
Voices of Children
At the Monument†
Marjorie
Horatio at Elsinore   *The Ishmaelite,* December, 1896
Labor and Art   *Harper's New Monthly Magazine,* October, 1898; *The Indianapolis Journal,* October 9, 1898
The Blind Boys
In the Street
Miriam: At a Concert
Aileen   *The Reader Magazine,* May, 1906 (with typographical error in title: Aideen)

1907

The Port of Missing Men

THE PORT | OF MISSING MEN | By | MEREDITH NICHOLSON | Author of | The House of a Thousand Candles | The Main Chance | Zelda Dameron | etc. | With Illustrations by | CLARENCE F. UNDER-WOOD | [*five-line quotation, last line reading:*] adventure.—Malory. | INDIANAPOLIS | THE BOBBS-MERRILL COMPANY | PUBLISHERS

COLLATION: [1–26]⁸. White laid paper. Leaf measures 7⅝" x 5", all edges trimmed.

End paper; fly title, p. [i]; blank, p. [ii]; frontispiece with tissue guard, inserted; title-page, p. [iii]; copyright notice dated 1907, statement: *January,* and imprint of Braunworth & Co., Brooklyn, N. Y., p. [iv]; dedication to the memory of Herman Kountze, p. [v]; blank, p. [vi]; proem: *The Shining Road,* pp. [vii–viii]; table of contents, p. [ix]; blank, p. [x]; half-title, p. [xi]; blank, p. [xii]; text, pp. 1–399; blank, p. [400]; publisher's advertisements, pp. [401–404]; end paper.

[Note: For text, pp. 1–399, see *Contents.*]

ILLUSTRATIONS: Frontispiece with tissue guard, inserted as are

---

*Later in *The Arena,* August, 1906.
†Included later in *Prose and Poetry of Today; Regional America,* edited by Harriet M. Lucas (1941).

plates facing pp. 18, 68, 190, 212, 320, and 356. All are by Clarence F. Underwood. Headpiece on first page of text.

BINDING: Bright blue silk-finished mesh cloth. Front cover red-stamped: The PORT | of | MISSING | MEN | [*pictorial design stamped in white, gold color, and green**] | [*wide rule, white, with initials of the artist (Franklin Booth?) above:* F. *at left,* B. *at right*] | [*shield-like ornament stamped in gold color, white, and red*] MEREDITH [*red dot*] NICHOLSON [*shield-like ornament stamped in gold color, white, and red*]. Spine red-stamped: The | PORT | of | MISSING | MEN | NICHOLSON | [*tree, cloud, and grass design stamped in green, gold color, and white*] | BOBBS | MERRILL Back cover blank.

End papers white calendered; no binder's leaf front or back.

PUBLICATION DATA: Deposited in the Copyright Office January 28, 1907. Earliest review noted: *The Indianapolis News*, February 8, 1907. Price, $1.50.

NOTES: First edition bears statement on copyright page: *January.* Two states noted:

> State 1: With slug on copyright page: *Press Of | Braunworth & Co. | Bookbinders And Printers | Brooklyn, N. Y.* (later, no slug)
> State 2: Without printer's slug on copyright page.

Two binding states are found, the earlier established by a reproduction of the front cover in the publisher's advertisement in *The Publishers' Weekly*, February 2, 1907, and by a copy with inscription dated February 7, 1907†:

> Binding State 1: Silk-finished (later, coarse) mesh cloth
> > Front cover bears white rule, 4mm. wide, stamped above author's name (later, a gold-colored rule, 3mm. wide)
> > Spine has no rule above or below publisher's imprint (later, gold-colored rules present). Type in publisher's imprint 4mm. high (later, 3mm.)
> > Sheets loosely cased, spine flat (later, tightly cased, spine rounded)
> > End papers white calendered (later, laid)
> Binding State 2: Coarse (earlier, silk-finished) mesh cloth‡
> > Front cover bears gold-stamped rule, 3mm.

---

*Design similar to, not same as the headpiece on p. 1.
†In collection of Earle J. Bernheimer, Beverly Hills, California.
‡Possibly fine-ribbed before pressed to the boards.

wide, above author's name (earlier, a white
rule, 4mm. wide)

Spine has gold-colored rule stamped above
and below publisher's imprint (earlier, no
rules). Type in publisher's imprint 3mm.
high (earlier 4mm.)

Sheets tightly cased, spine rounded (earlier,
loosely cased, spine flat)

End papers laid (earlier, calendered).

Other differences in stamping are difficult to describe, but apparent
when the two states are side by side: the tree trunks on front cover are
stamped in *Binding State* 1 at sides below title (in *Binding State* 2 extend up almost to the second line); the tree design on spine is from two
different engravings in the two states, measuring, from top leaf to
bottom grass, in *Binding State* 1, 4½″ high (in *Binding State* 2, less
than 4″).

Advertisements are in two states, also:

Advertisements State 1: *The Main Chance*, p. [401]; *The
House of a Thousand Candles*, p.
[402]; *Poems*, p. [403]; *Zelda Dameron*, p. [404]. Thus in the copy
inscribed February 7, 1907, in *State*
1 of both sheets and binding

Advertisements State 2: Same as *Advertisements State* 1 except
that *The House of a Thousand
Candles* is advertised on p. [401],
The Main Chance, p. [402], *Zelda
Dameron*, p. [403], and *Poems*, p.
[404]. Thus in copies in *State* 2 of
both sheets and binding.

A. Wessels Company reprinted the novel in 1908, Grosset & Dun-
lap *ca.* 1909. In one issue the latter firm's imprint is on spine, and
A. Wessels Company on title-page; in another a new title-page with
Grosset & Dunlap imprint replaces the earlier.

Albert & Charles Boni, Inc., issued it in wrappers in 1931 (Boni-
books, 47).

In England two editions were published: by Gay & Bird, June,
1907, and Amalgamated Press, June, 1912.

A dramatization by Edward E. Rose was produced in Peoria, Illinois, April 24, 1910, at the Majestic, and at Indianapolis, February 12,
1911, at the Park Theater.

A motion picture, "The Port of Missing Men," produced by Fa-

THE PORT OF MISSING MEN *in first and second states of binding*

mous Players under direction of Daniel Frohman, with Arnold Daly playing "John Armitage," was released May 1, 1914.

Nicholson wrote regarding the novel:* "This story followed 'The House of a Thousand Candles' and is of the same general character. I do not like it so well. I will say, however, that I think the poetical quotations scattered through the book are good!"

The first page of his manuscript was reproduced in facsimile with legend, "Successful Fiction of 1907," in *The Bookman*, date unestablished on clipping examined.

CONTENTS: The Port of Missing Men, Chapters I–XXVIII (titled), and proem:

The Shining Road [proem] *A November Leaf* (1896; with title: Romance)†

The Port of Missing Men *The Reader Magazine*, November, 1906–April, 1907

1907

Rosalind at Red Gate

ROSALIND AT RED GATE | By | MEREDITH NICHOLSON | WITH ILLUS-TRATIONS BY | ARTHUR I. KELLER | INDIANAPOLIS | THE BOBBS-MERRILL COMPANY | PUBLISHERS

COLLATION: [1–25]⁸. White laid paper. Leaf measures $7\frac{5}{8}''$ x 5", all edges trimmed.

End paper; fly title, p. [i]; list of books by the author, p. [ii]; frontispiece with tissue guard, inserted; title-page, p. [iii]; copyright notice dated 1907, statement: *November,* and imprint of Braunworth & Co., Brooklyn, N. Y., p. [iv]; dedication: *To My Mother,* p. [v]; blank, p. [vi]; quotations from *As You Like It,* and *Morte Darthur,* p. [vii]; blank, p. [viii]; table of contents, p. [ix]; blank, p. [x]; half-title, p. [xi]; blank, p. [xii]; text, pp. 1–387; blank, p. [388]; end paper.

[Note: Text, pp. 1–387: Rosalind at Redgate, Chapters I–XXV (titled).]

---

*In a copy inscribed April 8, 1921, for Charles T. Scott, now in Eagle Crest Library.

†A printing of the poem in *The Indianapolis News,* February 8, 1907, was in connection with a review of the book; it was later printed alone in *Current Literature,* May, 1907.

ILLUSTRATIONS: Frontispiece with tissue guard, inserted as are plates facing pp. 26, 138, 318, 364, and 372; all are by Arthur I. Keller.

BINDING: Dark green ribbed, and, mesh cloth. Front cover bears inlaid colored illustration, reproduced from the frontispiece; below is gilt-stamped: ROSALIND | AT REDGATE* | MEREDITH NICHOLSON [all boxed within blind-stamped decorative borders]. Spine gilt-stamped: ROSALIND | AT | REDGATE* | NICHOLSON | [blind-stamped rule] | [blind-stamped decoration] | BOBBS | MERRILL   Back cover blank.

End papers white calendered; no binder's leaf front or back.

PUBLICATION DATA: Deposited in the Copyright Office, November 23, 1907. Earliest review noted: The Indianapolis Star, November 23rd. Price, $1.50.

NOTES: First edition bears statement on copyright page: November. Noted in several states of sheets, illustrations, and binding; sequence of sheets thus:

> State 1: Imprint on copyright page at lower right (later, at left slightly off-center; still later, omitted). Thus in copies with leaf size 7⅝" x 5", inscriptions November and December, 1907
>
> State 2: Imprint on copyright page at lower left slightly off-center (earlier, at right; later, omitted). Thus in copies with leaf trimmed to 7½" x 5" (scant)
>
> State 3: No imprint on copyright page. Thus in copies with leaf trimmed to 7½" (scant) x 4⅞". The generally poor type on p. 375 has not been found in earlier states.

Illustrations vary in number and in color. Copies of the book are in such mixed states that attempts to establish their sequence have had to be abandoned. Seldom are two copies quite the same. At least ten different conditions exist, seven in copies inscribed November and December, 1907. It is fairly certain that the earliest state consists of either three† or five illustrations (not nine) plus the frontispiece, on a plate paper that tones in with the cream-white of the book stock (not of contrasting ivory); thus in the copyright deposit copies and a presentation copy inscribed November 29, 1907. The earliest copies of the book have a conspicuous absence of illustrations among the pages in

---

*No space between Red and Gate.

†Only one copy thus far seen with only three plates within the text, loaned by John C. Rugenstein; inscription undated; the illustrations which obviously were here never included when bound occur in other copies facing pp. 364 and 372.

the two hundreds. When four plates were added, facing pp. 220, 252, 264, and 300, they were all on ivory plate paper, definitely deeper in tone than the book stock. Beyond this point there seems to have been a random mixture, the plates being from different lots of paper, shading all the way from the cream-colored tone to a darker cream, to ivory of deep tint, and to a lighter, yellowish ivory. For example, a copy* bearing Christmas greetings from author, publisher, and printer, presumably an issue of December, 1907, with sheets in *State 2*, has nine plates plus frontispiece; the latter, as well as the plates facing pp. 138, 318, 364, and 372, tone in with the book stock as in earliest copies, but the one facing p. 26 is of a cream color, neither the early light tone, nor the ivory of the added plates, and the four that we have been calling "added" are of a very deep ivory. A copy in *Binding State 4* and sheets *State 3* has the frontispiece and nine plates of an ivory paper relatively light in tone, but differing from other plate stock which we have attempted to describe.

    Bindings noted in three states:

        Binding State 1: Ribbed cloth, dark green (later, mesh)
                        Spine has capital r's in *Merrill* long-tailed (later, not extending below the line)
                        End papers calendered (later, wove)
        Binding State 2: Mesh cloth, dark green (earlier, ribbed); with, and without Christmas greetings of publisher, author, and printer white-stamped on back cover
                        Spine and end papers as in *Binding State 1*
        Binding State 3: Binding and end papers as in *Binding State 2*
                        Spine has capital r's in *Merrill* not extending below the line (earlier, long-tailed)
        Binding State 4: Mesh cloth, dark blue (earlier dark green ribbed, and dark green mesh)
                        Spine as in *Binding State 3*
                        End papers wove (earlier, calendered).

    Binding State 1 is found on copies with sheets and illustrations in earliest state, and with presentation inscriptions dated November, 1907. *Binding State 2* occurs where sheets are in States 1 and 2; thus on a copy in latter state of sheets, bearing Christmas greetings of publisher, author, and printer white-stamped on back cover. This would seem to indicate that both states of sheets appeared before December 25, 1907 (it is not likely that publisher, author, and printer would have combined

---

*In Eagle Crest Library.

to send any but a book of the year as their Christmas greeting). *Binding State* 3 has been found on a copy with sheets in *State* 2; the fourth state of binding seems to accompany *State* 3 of sheets.

Some confusion in the preparation of this book is indicated by the fact that an advertisement in *The Publishers' Weekly*, November 30, 1907, depicts the book cover design as altogether different from the actual binding.

Grosset & Dunlap reprinted the novel in 1908 with only three illustrations besides the frontispiece present (including one of those not present in the earliest copies, but facing p. 264 later); the plate paper here differs from the original edition, being a true white.

British editions include the following: Amalgamated Press, March, 1908; Everett & Co., September, 1908; Hodder & Stoughton, *Popular Edition*, June, 1913.

The Universal Film Company contracted to produce it as a motion picture, according to *The Indianapolis Star*, June 20, 1915.

1908

The Little Brown Jug at Kildare

THE LITTLE BROWN JUG | AT KILDARE | By | MEREDITH NICHOLSON | WITH ILLUSTRATIONS BY | JAMES MONTGOMERY FLAGG | [*4-line poetical quotation*] | —H. C. BUNNER | INDIANAPOLIS | THE BOBBS-MERRILL COMPANY | PUBLISHERS

COLLATION: [1–27]⁸. White laid paper. Leaf measures 7⅝″ (scant) x 5 1/16″, all edges trimmed.

End paper; fly title, p. [i]; list of books by the author, p. [ii]; frontispiece with tissue guard, inserted; title-page, p. [iii]; copyright notice dated 1908, and statement: *September*, p. [iv]; half-title, p. [v]; blank, p. [vi]; dedication: *To You At The Gate*, dated June 30, 1908, p. [vii]; blank, p. [viii]; table of contents, p. [ix]; blank, p. [x]; text, pp. 1–422; end paper.

[Note: Text, pp. 1–422: The Little Brown Jug at Kildare, Chapters I–XXI (titled).*]

ILLUSTRATIONS: Frontispiece with tissue guard, inserted as are

---

*The story later appeared as a serial in *The Indianapolis Sunday Star*, November 21, 1909–February 20, 1910.

plates facing pp. 70, 270, 328, and 418. A headpiece appears at the beginning of Chapter I and tailpiece at end of the last chapter. All are by James Montgomery Flagg.

BINDING: Blue mesh, and, ribbed cloth. Front cover red-stamped: The | LITTLE | BROWN | JUG | at | KILDARE [*part of K and I stamped over a white cloud which is part of a pictorial design stamped in white, green, and red, depicting a southern Governor's mansion, its trees extending above at each side of the title; artist's symbol, crown above C, at lower right; author's name at foot:*] MEREDITH NICHOLSON Spine red-stamped: THE | LITTLE | BROWN | JUG | at | KILDARE | [*rule*] | NICHOLSON | [*pictorial tree and cloud design stamped in green and white; imprint at foot:*] BOBBS | MERRILL Back cover blank.

End papers white calendered; no binder's leaf front or back.

PUBLICATION DATA: Deposited in the Copyright Office September 14, 1908. Earliest review noted: *The Indianapolis News*, September 19th. Price, $1.50.

NOTES: First edition bears statement, *September*, on copyright page. Three states of book stock noted, similar in kind ($1\frac{3}{16}''$ between wire marks) but of different weights; leaf size varies between copies; indication of increase in paper weight (book thickness) and reduction in leaf size is given below:

> *State* 1: Thin paper bulking book to $1\frac{1}{16}''$ across sheets, $1\frac{3}{16}''$ across covers
>> Leaf $7\frac{5}{8}''$ (scant) x $5\frac{1}{16}''$
>
> *State* 2: Thicker paper bulking book to $1\frac{3}{16}''$ across sheets, $1\frac{5}{16}''$ across covers
>> Leaf less tall, $7\frac{1}{2}''$
>
> *State* 3: Thick paper bulking book to $1\frac{1}{4}''$ across sheets, $1\frac{7}{16}''$ across covers
>> Leaf still less tall, $7\frac{7}{16}''$.

Binding occurs in two states: ribbed, and, mesh cloth; both on copies in *State* 1. The ribbed cloth occurs on a copy having a curious arrangement of the illustrations, possibly a bindery error, possibly an advance state*: the frontispiece is the plate that is last in the book (facing p. 418) in all other copies examined. The regular edition bears as frontispiece the scene of a rifled desk; in this particular copy it faces p. 152. Until more copies in ribbed cloth come to light, it is best considered a trial binding, not a true binding state.

Copies in *States* 1 and 2 were available before Christmas, 1908. One, with inscription so dated, *State* 1, has mesh cloth binding with

---

*Copy in the collection of John C. Rugenstein.

calendered end papers; another, *State 2*, has same binding, but wove end papers. The ribbed cloth copy has them calendered. Wove end papers, occurring in *States* 2 and 3, may be considered the later condition.

Burt reprinted the novel in 1910. Nelson had published it in London in August, 1909, under the title: *The War of the Carolinas;* the same firm reprinted it in a "cheap edition," June, 1923.

The author inscribed a copy for the Indiana State Library in 1932, with a statement that the story "is just foolishness, and was not intended to have a moral purpose."

A contract was signed by the author with Universal Film Company for its production as a motion picture, according to *The Indianapolis Star,* June 20, 1915.

1909

The Lords of High Decision

The | Lords of High Decision | By | MEREDITH NICHOLSON | Illustrated by | ARTHUR I. KELLER | [*publishers' emblem*] | New York | Doubleday, Page & Company | 1909

COLLATION: [1–16]¹⁶, [17]². White wove paper. Leaf measures 7½" x 5", all edges trimmed.

End paper; fly title, p. [i]; list of books by the author, p. [ii]; frontispiece with tissue guard, inserted; title-page, p. [iii]; copyright notice dated 1909 and statement: *Published, October, 1909,* p. [iv]; dedication to Bowman Elder and Edward Robinette, dated September 20, 1909, p. [v]; quotation from "The Book of Daniel," p. [vi]; table of contents, pp. vii–viii; list of illustrations, p. [ix]; blank, p. [x]; half-title, p. [1]; blank, p. [2]; text, pp. 3–503; blank, pp. [504–506]; end paper.

[Note: Text, pp. 3–503: The Lords of High Decision, Chapters I–XLI (titled).]

ILLUSTRATIONS: Colored frontispiece with tissue guard, inserted as are colored plates facing pp. 322, 422, and 442. All are by Arthur I. Keller.

BINDING: Red coarse mesh cloth. Front cover white-stamped: THE [*two ornaments*] | LORDS [*ornament*] | OF HIGH | DECISION | [*blind-stamped ornament*] | MEREDITH | NICHOLSON [*all within a single rule box which encloses ornaments in the corners, and rules knobbed at*

ends; box, ornaments, and rules blind-stamped]. Spine white-stamped:
[*blind-stamped rule*] | THE [*ornament*] | LORDS | OF [*two ornaments*]
| HIGH [*ornament*] | DECISION | [*blind-stamped rule*] | NICHOLSON |
[*blind-stamped ornament*] | DOUBLEDAY | PAGE & CO. | [*blind-stamped
rule*]. Back cover blank.

End papers white wove; no binder's leaf front or back.

PUBLICATION DATA: Published October 29, 1909; deposited in the
Copyright Office October 30th. Earliest review noted: *The Indianapolis Star*, October 23rd. Price, $1.50.

NOTES: First edition bears statement: *Published, October, 1909*. It
occurs in two binding states, the first found in the copy presented by the
author to his son, Lionel, October 26th,* and in the copyright deposit
copy:

> *Binding State* 1: The final signature is followed by a conventional end sheet (later, last leaf of final signature used as lining paper, and end sheet present, sewed in, but wholly free)
> End papers white wove
>
> *Binding State* 2: Last leaf of final signature used as lining paper (earlier, a free leaf), and end sheet present, but sewed in and wholly free (earlier, conventionally half free, half the lining paper)
> Front end sheet wove, and, laid†; back wove.

Grosset & Dunlap reprinted the novel in 1911.

Gay & Hancock published it in England, in January, 1910.

In an inscription the author commented: ". . . I spent three years
in the coal business (in Colorado) before I had written any fiction
worth mentioning and later I made some first hand studies of labor conditions in [Pittsburgh] Pennsylvania in getting material for this
novel."‡ The aims of *The Lords of High Decision* were stated by him
in more detail in an article, "What I Tried to Do in My Latest Book,"
The World's Work, January, 1910; see also *The Indianapolis Star*, December 23, 1909, for quotations from the article.

The Universal Film Company is said to have bought photoplay
rights to this title (*The Indianapolis Star*, June 20, 1915); produced?

---

*In Indiana State Library.

†A copy presented by John C. Rugenstein for examination, with front end
sheet of laid paper, back wove, bears an inscription dated December 25, 1909.

‡Inscribed for the Indiana State Library in 1932.

1910

The Siege of the Seven Suitors

The Siege of | The Seven Suitors | BY | MEREDITH NICHOLSON | AUTHOR OF "THE HOUSE OF A THOUSAND CANDLES," ETC. | ILLUS-TRATED BY C. COLES PHILLIPS | AND REGINALD BIRCH | [*publisher's emblem with motto*] | BOSTON AND NEW YORK | HOUGHTON MIF-FLIN COMPANY | The Riverside Press Cambridge | 1910

COLLATION: [1–26]^8. White wove paper. Leaf measures 7$\frac{5}{16}$" x 4$\frac{15}{16}$", all edges trimmed.

End paper; fly title, p. [i]; blank, p. [ii]; frontispiece with tissue guard, inserted; title-page, p. [iii]; copyright notice dated 1910, state-ments: *All Rights Reserved,* and *Published October* 1910, p. [iv]; dedi-cation to the Honorable [Governor] Thomas R. Marshall, with a letter to him August 10, 1910, p. [v]; blank, p. [vi]; table of contents, p. [vii]; blank, p. [viii]; text, pp. 1–[401]; imprint of the Riverside Press, p. [402]; publisher's advertisements, pp. [403–408]; end paper.

[Note: Text, pp. 1–(401): The Siege of the Seven Suitors (Chap-ters) I–XX (titled).]

ILLUSTRATIONS: Colored frontispiece by C. Coles Phillips, with tissue guard, inserted. Text illustrations by Reginald Birch at frequent intervals throughout the book. A rule appears below the running head.

BINDING: Bluish-green, and, gray mesh cloth. Front cover white-stamped: [*illustration stamped in blue, yellow-green, black, and white*] |THE |SIEGE [*dot*] OF [*dot*] THE [*dot*] SEVEN | SUITORS | By | MEREDITH NICHOLSON Spine white-stamped: THE SIEGE | OF | THE SEVEN | SUIT-ORS | By | MEREDITH | NICHOLSON | HOUGHTON | MIFFLIN CO. Back cover blank.

End papers same as book stock; no binder's leaf front or back.

PUBLICATION DATA: Published October 22, 1910; deposited in the Copyright Office November 3rd. Earliest reviews noted: *The* (New York) *Sun* and *Herald,* October 22nd. Price, $1.20.

NOTES: First edition bears statement on copyright page: *Published October 1910.*

Grosset & Dunlap published an edition in 1912. Constable's British edition of the novel was listed in the *English Catalogue* as published November, 1910.

1912

A Hoosier Chronicle

A HOOSIER | CHRONICLE | [*rule*] | MEREDITH NICHOLSON | [*rule*] | WITH ILLUSTRATIONS | BY F. C. YOHN [*rule; single vertical rule at each side of the statement about illustrations*] | [*publisher's emblem with single vertical rule at each side*] | [*rule*] | [*single vertical rules*] | [*rule*] | BOSTON AND NEW YORK | HOUGHTON MIFFLIN COMPANY | The Riverside Press Cambridge | 1912

[Note: All within a parallel rule box.]

COLLATION: [1–39]⁸. White wove paper. Leaf measures 7⁷⁄₁₆″ x 5⅛″, all edges trimmed.

End paper; blank, p. [i]; list of books by the author, p. [ii]; fly title, p. [iii]; blank, p. [iv]; frontispiece with tissue guard, inserted; title-page, p. [v]; copyright notice dated 1912, and statement: *Published March 1912*, p. [vi]; dedication to Evans Woollen, Esq., and quotation from Emerson, p. [vii]; blank, p. [viii]; table of contents, pp. vii (should be ix)–[x]; list of illustrations, p. [xi]; blank, p. [xii]; text, pp. 1–[606]; blank, p. [607]; imprint of the Riverside Press, p. [608]; publisher's advertisements, pp. [609–612]; end paper.

[Note: Text, pp. 1–(606): A Hoosier Chronicle, Chapters I–XXXIV (titled), followed by: A Postscript by the Chronicler.]

ILLUSTRATIONS: Colored frontispiece with tissue guard, inserted as are colored plates facing pp. 284, 458, and 556. All are from drawings by Frederick Coffay Yohn.

BINDING: Brown smooth-finished mesh cloth. Front cover gilt-stamped: A [*ornament*] HOOSIER | CHRONICLE | [*silhouette of the Indianapolis Soldiers' and Sailors' Monument stamped in brown within brown wide-rule box*] | MEREDITH | NICHOLSON [*an ornamental border of conventional ear of corn design is brown-stamped on each side of the box containing the monument silhouette, and the author's name*]. Spine gilt-stamped: A HOOSIER | CHRONICLE | [*conventional ear of corn design, brown-stamped**] | NICHOLSON | [*conventional ear of corn design, brown-stamped†*] | HOUGHTON | MIFFLIN CO. Back cover blank.

*Faded to green in some copies.
†Also faded sometimes to a green cast.

End papers white wove; no binder's leaf front or back.

PUBLICATION DATA: Published March 16, 1912; deposited in the Copyright Office March 19th. Earliest review noted: *The Indianapolis Star*, March 8th. Price, $1.40.

NOTES: First edition bears statement on copyright page: *Published March 1912*. It occurs in various bindings following one in brown cloth that was apparently a trial stamping, since the author's name does not appear on the front cover and the decorations are all blind-stamped.*

Binding State 1: Decorations on spine ⅞" wide. Thus on copies in brown smooth mesh cloth binding

Binding State 2: Decorations on spine 1¼" wide. Thus on copies in the brown smooth mesh cloth binding, also, brown ribbed, and, red smooth mesh.

These variations in binding occurred early, both being available the first month of publication to judge by the author's inscriptions dated March, 1912. Precedence is given the narrow decoration because it occurred only on earliest published copies; the wider decoration was used on Grosset & Dunlap's later edition (1914).

The edition issued on the occasion of the American Booksellers Convention in May, 1912, bound in full publisher's leather, gilt top, other edges untrimmed, and printed on paper bulking sheets to only 1⁵⁄₁₆" (earlier 1⁷⁄₁₆"), bears the following printed on front end paper: *To The Members And Guests | Of The | American Booksellers Association | With The Compliments | And Good Wishes | Of | Author And Publisher | May 16th 1912*.† The advertisements in back of this edition are same as in the regular issue, offering *A Safety Match* by Ian Hay, p. [609], *Queed* by Henry Sydnor Harrison, p. [610], *The Siege of the Seven Suitors* by Nicholson, p. [611], *The Long Roll* by Mary Johnston, p. [612].

Grosset & Dunlap reprinted the novel in 1914. Copies are found in two states: earlier, sheets as in the original edition, with Grosset & Dunlap imprint on spine, but not on title-page; later, sheets provided with a new title-page.

A British edition by Constable appeared May, 1912.

The author commented at length on his book in various inscriptions. "I consider this my best novel," he wrote April 8, 1921,‡ and iden-

---

*This particular copy noted by Jacob Blanck, not located.

†The author inscribed a copy in the Indiana State Library, with a poem not found in print, entitled, "To All Gentle Book Men."

‡In a copy in Eagle Crest Library.

tified the scenes of the story as mainly Crawfordsville and Indianapolis. In another copy, inscribed April, 1932,* he said: "This is one of only a few instances where I have drawn characters 'from life.' 'Aunt Sally' was a friend of my mother [Mrs. Patteson]†; the minister was Myron Reed, of the First Presbyterian Church, Indianapolis. Others are composite. The senatorial episode was built up from an actual incident [in which John E. Lamb and Nicholson had a part, during Thomas Marshall's administration as Governor]. The lake is Maxinkuckee, used also in 'The House of a Thousand Candles.' The period is 'just before the automobile.'"

1912

The Provincial American

The Provincial American | And Other Papers | By | Meredith Nicholson | [*illustration, signed:* Franklin Booth] | Boston and New York | Houghton Mifflin Company | 1912

COLLATION: [1]⁴ (plus one inserted sheet of plate paper, plus one inserted sheet of book stock), [2–15]⁸, [16]⁴. White laid paper. Leaf measures 7⅜" x 5", top edge trimmed, other edges untrimmed.

End paper; blank, p. [i]; list of books by the author, p. [ii]; fly title, p. [iii]; blank, p. [iv]; title-page, p. [v]; copyright notice dated 1912, statements: *All Rights Reserved,* and *Published October 1912,* p. [vi] (pp. [iii–vi] on inserted sheet of plate paper); dedication to George Edward Woodberry, and date line, Indianapolis, September 1912, p. [vii]; blank, p. [viii]; table of contents, p. [ix]; blank, p. [x]; half-title, p. [1]; blank, p. [2]; text, pp. 3–[237] (pp. 3–4, the conjugate of the half-title, on inserted sheet of book stock); publisher's imprint, p. [238]; end paper.

[Note: Divisional half-titles with versos blank separate the "papers." For text, pp. 3–(237), see *Contents.*]

ILLUSTRATIONS: Title-page bears a drawing by Franklin Booth, depicting a small-town scene.

---

*In the Indiana State Library.
†Identifying this friend of his mother's, Nicholson explained "Aunt Sally" as a composite of Mrs. Patteson and his grandmother Meredith in a statement written on a sheet of added information given by him to the Indiana State Library.

BINDING: Dark blue silk-finished mesh cloth. Front cover gilt-stamped: THE PROVINCIAL | AMERICAN | By Meredith Nicholson [*all on black-stamped panel within a black-stamped single rule box*]. Spine gilt-stamped: THE | PROVINCIAL | AMERICAN | Meredith | Nicholson | HOUGHTON | MIFFLIN CO. Back cover blank.

End papers white laid, not same as book stock, 1 ⅜6″ between wire marks (book stock, 1³⁄₁₆″); no binder's leaf front or back.

PUBLICATION DATA: Published October 11, 1912; deposited in the Copyright Office October 14th. Earliest review noted: *The Indianapolis News*, November 2, 1912. Price, $1.25.

NOTES: First edition bears statement on copyright page: *Published October 1912*. There were two issues, in the following states:

State 1: As collated, with the inserted sheet, glued, not sewn, of book stock bearing half-title and pp. 3–4 of text (later, bearing dedication and table of contents)

State 2: The inserted sheet of book stock bearing dedication and table of contents (earlier, half-title and pp. 3–4 of text).

There were at least two different states of binding:

Binding State 1: Black-stamped panel on front cover (later, blind-stamped)

End papers, white laid as described (later, wove). Thus in copies with sheets in State 1

Binding State 2: Blind-stamped panel on front cover (earlier, black-stamped)

End papers, white wove (earlier, laid). Thus in a copy with sheets in State 2, purchased new in 1922.*

The book was published in London by Constable, January, 1913.

In a copy inscribed July 5, 1919, the author said of the contents: "These papers tell their own story. They cover a good many years, and are supplemented by my other volume of essays called 'The Valley of Democracy.'

"The first essay is, as you will see, somewhat autobiographical."

A more extended comment by the author was written in 1932:† "Of these papers, 'Should Smith Go to Church,' first published in the *Atlantic Monthly*, attracted the most attention. Editorials were written on it, sermons were preached about it, I was deluged with letters, and the magazine had to print an announcement that no more articles in reply

---

*In Indiana State Library.

†In the copy purchased 1922 by the Indiana State Library.

would be considered.* 'Confessions of a Best Seller' was another Atlantic paper: and, I may say, wholly truthful."

For his introduction to a book of sermons inspired by the article, "Should Smith Go to Church?," see *Smith and the Church*, by Harry H. Beattys (1913), *post* 145.

CONTENTS: A statement at foot of table of contents reads: "These papers, with one exception, have appeared in the *Atlantic Monthly*. A part of 'Experience and the Calendar,' under another title, was published in the *Reader Magazine*"; actually all of this fourth paper appeared in the latter magazine.

The Provincial American   *The Atlantic Monthly*, March, 1911
Edward Eggleston†   *The Atlantic Monthly*, December, 1902
A Provincial Capital   *The Atlantic Monthly*, June, 1904 (with title: Indianapolis: A City of Homes)
Experience and the Calendar   *The Reader*, May, 1906 (with title: Why Send for the Doctor?)
Should Smith Go to Church?   *The Atlantic Monthly*, June, 1912‡
The Tired Business Man   *The Atlantic Monthly*, October, 1912
The Spirit of Mischief: A Dialogue   *The Atlantic Monthly*, May, 1908
Confessions of a "Best-Seller"   *The Atlantic Monthly*, November, 1909 (unsigned)§

1913

Otherwise Phyllis

OTHERWISE PHYLLIS | BY | MEREDITH NICHOLSON | [*publisher's emblem*] | BOSTON AND NEW YORK | HOUGHTON MIFFLIN COMPANY | The Riverside Press Cambridge | 1913

COLLATION: [1–26]⁸. White wove paper. Leaf measures $7\frac{7}{16}$″ x $5\frac{1}{16}$″, all edges trimmed.

---

*"The Last of Smith: Some Letters on the Subject," appeared in *The Atlantic Monthly*, October, 1912, Vol. 110, p. 574.
†Not same as "Edward Eggleston" in *The Hoosiers* (1900), p. 134.
‡For response to this article see *Notes*, foregoing.
§In an interview, "Meredith Nicholson Talks about Literary Hoosierdom," *The Indianapolis Star*, December 11, 1910, he is said to have "confessed" to the writing of this essay.

End paper; blank, p. [i]; list of books by the author, p. [ii]; fly title, p. [iii]; blank, p. [iv]; frontispiece with tissue guard, inserted; title-page, p. [v]; copyright notice dated 1913, statements: *All Rights Reserved*, and *Published September 1913*, p. [vi]; dedication to Albert B. Anderson, p. [vii]; blank, p. [viii]; table of contents, pp. [ix]–viii (should be x); half-title, p. [xi]; blank, p. [xii]; text, pp. [1]–397; publisher's imprint, p. [398]; advertisements, pp. [399–402]; blank, pp. [403–404]; end paper.

[Note: Text, pp. (1)–397: Otherwise Phyllis, Chapters I–XXVII (titled).]

ILLUSTRATIONS: Frontispiece on ivory-colored plate paper with tissue guard, inserted; drawn by Charles Dana Gibson.

BINDING: Brown mesh cloth. Front cover gilt-stamped: OTHERWISE | PHYLLIS [*ornament*] | MEREDITH | NICHOLSON   Spine gilt-stamped: OTHERWISE | PHYLLIS [*ornament*] | NICHOLSON | HOUGHTON | MIFFLIN CO.   Back cover blank.

End papers white wove; no binder's leaf front or back.

PUBLICATION DATA: Published September 6, 1913; deposited in the Copyright Office September 8th. Earliest review noted: *The Indianapolis News*, September 6th. Price, $1.35.

NOTES: First edition bears statement on copyright page: *Published September 1913*.

A British edition was published by Constable, September, 1913. Burt reprinted the novel in 1915.

In an inscription, September 1, 1919, the author stated:* "The scene of this story is Crawfordsville, Montgomery County, Indiana, where I was born. The same town is the setting for parts of 'A Hoosier Chronicle.' 'Lois' I think the best woman character I have done. If I were rewriting this book I should make more of her." At Chapter III he noted, regarding "the Bartlett sisters": "These women are a composite; but I have really known them."

---

*In a copy in the Indiana State Library.

1914
The Poet

THE POET | BY | MEREDITH NICHOLSON | WITH PICTURES BY FRANK-
LIN BOOTH | AND DECORATIONS BY W. A. DWIGGINS [*foregoing
within a panel of outdoor design, in sepia, including the pub-
lisher's emblem and motto*] | [*imprint, paneled and within a sepia
parallel rule box:*] BOSTON AND NEW YORK | HOUGHTON MIFFLIN
COMPANY | The Riverside Press Cambridge | 1914

[Note: All within a box formed by short sepia rules; artist's initials,
W A D, in lower left corner of the design.]

COLLATION: [1]⁴, [2–13]⁸. White wove paper. Leaf measures
7⁷⁄₁₆″ x 5⅛₆″, top edge gilt, bottom edge trimmed, fore edge untrimmed.

End paper; blank, p. [i]; list of books by the author, p. [ii]; fly title,
p. [iii]; blank, p. [iv]; title-page, p. [v]; copyright notice dated 1914,
statements: *All Rights Reserved,* and *Published October 1914,* p. [vi];
list of illustrations, p. [vii]; blank, p. [viii]; divisional half-title, *Part
One,* p. [1]; blank, p. [2]; text, pp. 3–[190] (divisional half-title, *Part
Two,* p. [95]); blank, p. [191]; imprint of the Riverside Press, p. [192];
end paper.

[Note: Text, pp. 3–(190): The Poet, Parts One and Two (untitled).]

ILLUSTRATIONS: Colored frontispiece with tissue guard, inserted as
are colored plates facing pp. 74, 110, and 188; all are by Franklin Booth,
and each bears a legend. Decorations in sepia, by W. A. Dwiggins, appear throughout the book: besides the title-page decorations there are
wreath designs on each divisional half-title, headpieces on pp. 3 and 97,
and decorative designs for the running heads.

BINDING: Light blue silk-finished mesh cloth. Front cover gilt-
stamped: THE | POET | [*floral design*] | BY | MEREDITH NICHOLSON [*all
within a floral border which is enclosed by a single rule box within
blind-stamped parallel rule box*]. Spine gilt-stamped: [*parallel rule,
blind-stamped*] | [*rule*] | [*floral border*] | THE | POET | MEREDITH | NICH-
OLSON | HOUGHTON | MIFFLIN CO. | [*floral border*] | [*rule*] | [*parallel
rule, blind-stamped*]. Back cover blank.

End papers light blue, calendered; no binder's leaf front or back.

PUBLICATION DATA: Published October 3, 1914; deposited in the Copyright Office October 5th. Earliest review noted: *The Indianapolis Star*, October 6, 1914. Price, $1.30.

NOTES: First edition bears statement on copyright page: *Published October 1914*. Grosset & Dunlap is credited in the *Cumulative Book Index* with having published an edition, but no copies have been located.

Issued on the birthday of James Whitcomb Riley, October 7, 1914, *The Poet* is usually regarded as a tribute to him. The book is fictional and not biographical; he said in April, 1932:* "The Poet in this story is only remotely James Whitcomb Riley and should not be taken as indicating the many interesting and lovable qualities that distinguish J. W. R.

"For my impressions of J. W. R. see essay in my volume, 'The Man in the Street'† also references to him in 'Old Familiar Faces.' "

He might have mentioned his other essays, articles, and poems with the same subject: "Riley in The Atlantic," a poem written in Denver, December 23, 1898, complimenting *The Atlantic Monthly* on printing Riley's verses, published in *The Indianapolis Journal*, January 1, 1899; "James Whitcomb Riley," in *The Hoosiers* (1900); address at the Indiana State Teachers' Association meeting December 28, 1905 (see *In Honor of James Whitcomb Riley*); "To James Whitcomb Riley," in *Poems* (1906); address on Riley at Manual Training High School, October 6, 1911 (see *Ephemera*); letter "To the Laird of Lockerbie Street," in *The Indianapolis Star*, October 6, 1912; tribute to him written in the first hours after his death, printed in *The Indianapolis Star*, July 24, 1916 (the reminiscences in *The Indianapolis News*, same date, are Nicholson's through an interviewer, not in his words); eulogy, in *Tributes to the Life and Memory of James Whitcomb Riley* (ca. 1916); a speech for the tenth anniversary program of the James Whitcomb Riley Hospital for Children, quoted in *The Indianapolis Star*, October 8, 1934; introduction in Jeannette Covert Nolan, *James Whitcomb Riley: Hoosier Poet* (1941); and a tribute in *The Indianapolis News*, October 6, 1945.

Nicholson's story of his first encounter with Riley was told in "Without Benefit of College," collected in *Old Familiar Faces* (1929).

---

*Inscription in a copy of the book in the Indiana State Library.
†For this essay, "James Whitcomb Riley" in *The Man in the Street* (1921) see *post* 121, with footnote of further comment.

1916

The Proof of the Pudding

THE PROOF OF THE | PUDDING | BY | MEREDITH NICHOLSON | With Illustrations | [*pen drawing*] | BOSTON AND NEW YORK | HOUGHTON MIFFLIN COMPANY | The Riverside Press Cambridge | 1916

COLLATION: [1–24]⁸. White wove paper. Leaf measures 7⁷⁄₁₆″ x 5″ (full), all edges trimmed.

End paper; fly title, p. [i]; blank, p. [ii]; frontispiece with tissue guard, inserted; title-page, p. [iii]; copyright notices with final date 1916, statements: *All Rights Reserved, Published May 1916,* and list of books by the author, p. [iv]; dedication to Carleton B. McCulloch, p. [v]; blank, p. [vi]; contents, pp. vii–[viii]; list of illustrations, p. [ix]; blank, p. [x]; text, pp. 1–[373]; imprint of the Riverside Press, p. [374]; end paper.

[Note: For text, pp. 1–(373), see *Contents.*]

ILLUSTRATIONS: Frontispiece with tissue guard, inserted as are plates facing pp. 26, 62, 66, and 372; double-page plates between pp. 44–45 and pp. 188–189; all are from drawings by C. H. Taffs. A pen drawing appears on the title-page.

BINDING: Red ribbed, and, coarse mesh cloth. Front cover gilt-stamped: THE | PROOF | OF | THE | PUDDING | BY | MEREDITH | NICHOL-SON | [*ornament, blind-stamped; all within an ornamental blind-stamped border*]. Spine gilt-stamped: [*wide rule, blind-stamped*] | THE | PROOF | OF THE | PUDDING | [*ornament, blind-stamped*] | NICHOLSON | HOUGHTON | MIFFLIN CO. | [*wide rule, blind-stamped*]. Back cover blank.

End papers white wove; no binder's leaf front or back.

PUBLICATION DATA: Published May 13, 1916; deposited in the Copyright Office May 15th. Earliest review noted: *The Indianapolis News,* May 13th. The author had copies on May 10th, known from an inscription so dated. Price, $1.35.

NOTES: First edition bears statement on copyright page: *Published May 1916.* The ribbed cloth may have been a trial binding; most copies, including one inscribed as early as May 10th*, are in the coarse mesh.

---

*In the collection of John C. Rugenstein, Indianapolis. Unfortunately both copyright deposit copies have been rebound.

A *Second Impression, May 1916*, so stated on copyright page, appeared in a different quality red mesh cloth without blind stamping on cover.

The novel was reprinted in America by Burt in 1918. It had been published in England by Hodder & Stoughton, August, 1916.

CONTENTS: The Proof of the Pudding: Chapters I–XXVII (titled); previously a serial in *The Red Book Magazine*, October, 1915–May, 1916.

1917

The Madness of May

THE | MADNESS OF MAY | BY | MEREDITH NICHOLSON | WITH ILLUS-TRATIONS BY | FREDERIC DORR STEELE | [2-*line quotation*] | —The Age of Chivalry. | NEW YORK | CHARLES SCRIBNER'S SONS | 1917

COLLATION: [1–12]⁸ (plus one unsigned leaf in first signature, and one in last). White wove paper. Leaf measures 7½" x 5⅛", fore edge untrimmed, other edges trimmed.

End paper; fly title, p. [i]; blank, p. [ii]; frontispiece with tissue guard, inserted; title-page, p. [iii]; copyright notice dated 1917, statement: *Published March, 1917*, and publishers' emblem, p. [iv]; dedication to Mrs. Charles Thomas Kountze, p. [v]; blank, p. [vi]; list of illustrations, inserted, with verso blank; half-title, p. [1]; blank, p. [2]; text, pp. 3–187 (pp. 171–172 on inserted leaf); blank, p. [188]; end paper.

[Note: For text, pp. 3–187, see *Contents*.]

ILLUSTRATIONS: Frontispiece with tissue guard, inserted as are plates facing pp. 30, 122, and 164. All are by Frederic Dorr Steele.

BINDING: Blue silk-finished mesh cloth. Front cover blind-stamped in star and crescent design; title and author's name green-stamped on a rectangular panel within a blind-stamped box: The Madness | of May | [*rule*] | Meredith Nicholson Spine bears design similar to front cover and is stamped in green on a panel with a blind-stamped rule at top and bottom: The | Madness | of | May | [*rule*] | Nicholson | [*at foot, green-stamped with blind-stamped rule at top and bottom:*] Scribners Back cover blank. Issued in a printed dust wrapper.*

---

*Not seen, but mentioned in Scribner's correspondence with the author.

End papers white calendered; no binder's leaf front or back.

PUBLICATION DATA: Published April 14, 1917; deposited in the Copyright Office April 17th. Price, $1.00.

NOTES: First edition bears statement: *Published March, 1917* (actually, the book was not on the market until the month following).

CONTENTS: The Madness of May, Chapters I–X (untitled), earlier a four-part serial in *Collier's*, March 25–April 15, 1916.

1917
A Reversible Santa Claus

A | REVERSIBLE | SANTA CLAUS [*title in red*] | BY | MEREDITH NICHOLSON | WITH ILLUSTRATIONS BY | FLORENCE H. MINARD | [*ornament in red*] | BOSTON and NEW YORK | HOUGHTON MIFFLIN COMPANY [*red*] | The Riverside Press, Cambridge | 1917
[Note: All printed in green, with exceptions noted, within an ornamental box of green and red holly-like design.]

COLLATION: [1–2]⁴, 3–12⁸, 13⁶. White wove paper. Leaf measures $7\frac{1}{2}''$ x $5\frac{3}{16}''$, all edges trimmed.

End paper; blank, p. [i]; list of books by the author, p. [ii]; fly title, p. [iii]; blank, p. [iv]; frontispiece with tissue guard, inserted; title-page, p. [v]; copyright notice dated 1917, statements: *All Rights Reserved*, and *Published October 1917*, p. [vi]; list of illustrations, p. [vii]; blank, p. [viii]; half-title, p. [1]; blank, p. [2]; text, pp. 3–[177] (with divisional leaves bearing Roman numerals between chapters); publisher's imprint, p. [178]; blank, pp. [179–180]; end paper.
[Note: For text, pp. 3–(177), see *Contents*.]

ILLUSTRATIONS: Colored frontispiece with tissue guard, inserted as are colored plates facing pp. 44, 116, and 150. Black and white head-pieces appear at the beginning of each chapter, tailpieces at end of all chapters except VI and X. All illustrations are from drawings by Florence H. Minard.

BINDING: Light blue silk-finished mesh cloth.* Front cover dark blue-stamped: A [*ornament*] REVERSIBLE | SANTA [*ornament*] CLAUS |

---

*A copy in Eagle Crest Library has binding dark red with black stamping in place of dark blue.

[*illustration, man in a snowstorm peering through a window, within a holly-like wreath, red, green, and dark blue-stamped*] | BY | MEREDITH [*ornament*] NICHOLSON   Spine dark blue-stamped: A | REVERSIBLE | SANTA CLAUS | MEREDITH | NICHOLSON | HOUGHTON | MIFFLIN CO. Back cover blank.

End papers blue plain stock printed on front in darker blue with medallions in wreaths and festoons; no binder's leaf front or back.

PUBLICATION DATA: Published October 17, 1917; deposited in the Copyright Office October 20th. Earliest review noted: *The Indianapolis Star*, November 4th. Price, $1.00.

NOTES: First edition bears statement on copyright page, *Published October 1917*.

Two states of binding: as described, and, dark red silk-finished mesh cloth with black stamping in place of dark blue; whether the latter was a trial or a remainder binding has not yet been determined. The copyright deposit copy is in the usual blue cloth.

The author said of his book in an inscription: "I suppose that I couldn't write about the folk of the underworld if I really knew anything about them!"*

CONTENTS: A Reversible Santa Claus, Chapters I–X (untitled); amplified from a short story, The Hopper, in *Collier's*, December 30, 1916.

1918

The Valley of Democracy

THE | VALLEY OF DEMOCRACY | BY | MEREDITH NICHOLSON | WITH ILLUSTRATIONS BY | WALTER TITTLE | NEW YORK | CHARLES SCRIBNER'S SONS | 1918

COLLATION: [1–18]⁸, [19]⁴. White wove paper. Leaf measures 8¼₆" x 5½", fore edge untrimmed, other edges trimmed.

End paper; fly title, p. [i]; blank, p. [ii]; frontispiece with tissue guard, inserted; title-page, p. [iii]; copyright notice with final date 1918, statement: *Published September, 1918,* and publishers' emblem, p. [iv]; dedication to the author's children, Elizabeth, Meredith, and Lionel, p. [v]; blank, p. [vi]; table of contents, p. [vii]; blank, p. [viii];

---

*In a copy owned by the Indiana State Library.

list of illustrations, pp. ix–x; half-title, p. [xi]; quotation from John H. Finley, *The French in the Heart of America*, p. [xii]; text, pp. 1–284; end paper.

[Note: For text, pp. 1–284, see *Contents*.]

ILLUSTRATIONS: Frontispiece with tissue guard, inserted as are plates facing pp. 6, 20, 66, 74, 78, 80, 100, 114, 120, 132, 142, 152, 176, 194, and 198. All are by Walter Tittle.

BINDING: Dark green ribbed cloth. Front cover gilt-stamped: THE VALLEY OF | DEMOCRACY | [*wide rule*] | Meredith Nicholson   Spine gilt-stamped: THE VALLEY | OF | DEMOCRACY | [*rule*] | Nicholson | SCRIBNERS   Back cover blank.

End papers white calendered; no binder's leaf front or back.

PUBLICATION DATA: Published September 13, 1918; deposited in the Copyright Office September 20th. Earliest review noted: *The New York Times*, September 15th. Price, $2.00.

NOTES: Four "editions" appeared in less than a year, distinguishable thus:

First Edition: *Published September, 1918* on copyright page. Font in imprint at foot of spine 5mm. high (later, 4mm.; still later, 3mm.)

Second Edition: Same as first edition except for font on binding: imprint at foot of spine 4mm. high (earlier, 5mm.)

Third Edition: Same as second edition except that copyright page bears an added statement: *Reprinted November, 1918*

Fourth Edition: Date on title-page changed to 1919. Copyright page has the added statement reading: *Reprinted November, December, 1918*.

Contains a 2–page *Author's Note to the Fourth Edition*, dated June 1, 1919

Additions to text: footnotes pp. 29, 69, 115, and 213; date, *1917*, added p. 83, 11th line from bottom

Leaf trimmed to $7\frac{7}{16}''$ x $4\frac{15}{16}''$ (earlier, $8\frac{1}{16}''$ x $5\frac{1}{2}''$)

Binding a smooth mesh cloth, front cover blank.

The fourth edition was so-termed by the publishers, implying three earlier editions; the first two show only a minor difference in binding, as above indicated.

An error on p. 220, line 5, *Inpractically* (should be two words, *In practically*), is present in all these editions.

The book was published in England by Melrose, March, 1920.

The essays in this volume supplement an earlier collection, *The Provincial American* (1912). The author wrote a prospectus probably published in advertising copy, judging from correspondence with the publishers, September–November, 1917, and explained his idea: a book to "interpret the aims and aspirations of the Middle Westerners through the people themselves. . . . The writer, himself a native Westerner, does not believe that all wisdom is centered between the Alleghenies and the Rockies . . . ."

CONTENTS: The Valley of Democracy, six chapters, earlier published as a series of articles:

CHAPTER

I   The Folks and Their Folksiness   *Scribner's Magazine,* January, 1918*

II   Types and Diversions   *Scribner's Magazine,* March, 1918

III   The Farmer of the Middle West   *Scribner's Magazine,* April, 1918

IV   Chicago   *Scribner's Magazine,* February, 1918

V   The Middle West in Politics   *Scribner's Magazine,* May, 1918

VI   The Spirit of the West   *Scribner's Magazine,* June, 1918; *The Indianapolis Star,* June 2, 1918 (part only)

1919
Lady Larkspur

LADY LARKSPUR | BY | MEREDITH NICHOLSON | [*ornament*] | NEW YORK | CHARLES SCRIBNER'S SONS | 1919

COLLATION: [1–11]⁸, [12]⁴. White wove paper. Leaf measures $6^{13}\!/_{16}''$ x $4\!/\!4''$, top edge trimmed, other edges untrimmed.

End paper; blank, p. [i]; list of books by the author, p. [ii]; fly title, p. [iii]; blank, p. [iv]; title-page, p. [v]; copyright notice dated 1919, statement: *Published March, 1919,* acknowledgment to Collier's, and

---

* Part, about Cleveland, was reprinted in *The Cleveland* (Ohio) *Press,* January 4, 1918.

publishers' emblem, p. [vi]; dedication to Bennett and Peggy Gates, p. [vii]; blank, p. [viii]; table of contents, p. [ix]; blank, p. [x]; text, pp. 1–171; blank, pp. [172–174]; end paper.

[Note: For text, pp. 1–171, see *Contents*.]

BINDING: Light blue boards, darker blue cloth shelfback. Front cover printed in dark blue: LADY | LARKSPUR | [*larkspur design*] | MEREDITH | NICHOLSON | [*stem of the larkspur design interrupted by author's name; initials,* C S; *all within a single rule box whose corners bear a loop design*]. Spine gilt-stamped: LADY | LARKSPUR | [*larkspur design*] | NICHOLSON | SCRIBNERS Back cover blank.

End papers white wove; no binder's leaf front or back.

PUBLICATION DATA: Published March 14, 1919; deposited in the Copyright Office March 20th. Earliest review noted: *The New York Times*, March 30th.* Price, $1.00.

NOTES: First edition bears statement on copyright page: *Published March, 1919*. No illustrations.

CONTENTS: Lady Larkspur, Chapters I–V (titled), earlier published as a serial in *Collier's*, October 19, 26, November 9, 16, and 23, 1918. Chapter V in the magazine entitled, His Choice (in the book entitled, Alice).

1920

Blacksheep! Blacksheep!

Blacksheep! Blacksheep! | BY | MEREDITH NICHOLSON | ILLUSTRATED BY | LESLIE L. BENSON | NEW YORK | CHARLES SCRIBNER'S SONS | 1920

COLLATION: [1–22]⁸, [23]⁴. White wove paper. Leaf measures 7$\frac{7}{16}$" (full) x 5$\frac{3}{16}$", top edge trimmed, other edges untrimmed.

End paper; fly title, p. [i]; list of books by the author, p. [ii]; frontispiece with tissue guard, inserted; title-page, p. [iii]; copyright notices with final date 1920, and statement: *Published April, 1920*, p. [iv]; dedication to Louis C. Huesmann, p. [v]; blank, p. [vi]; quotation from Richard Burton, p. [vii]; blank, p. [viii]; list of illustrations, p. [ix];

---

*Excerpts from several reviews appear in *Blacksheep! Blacksheep!* (1920), in advertisements at back of book.

blank, p. [x]; half-title, p. [1]; blank, p. [2]; text, pp. 3–346; publishers' advertisements, pp. [347–348]; blank, pp. [349–350]; end paper.

[Note: For text, pp. 3–346, see *Contents.*]

ILLUSTRATIONS: Frontispiece with tissue guard, inserted as are plates facing pp. 32, 112, and 234; all are by Leslie L. Benson.

BINDING: Red mesh cloth. Front cover black-stamped: Blacksheep! | Blacksheep! | [*row of five sheep heads, alternately cream-white and black*] | by | Meredith Nicholson   Spine black-stamped: Blacksheep! | Blacksheep! | [*ornament composed of two wide black rules separated by a wide cream-white rule*] | Nicholson | [*ornament composed of two wide black rules separated by a wide cream-white rule*] | SCRIBNERS Back cover blank. Issued in a printed dust wrapper.*

End papers white wove; no binder's leaf front or back.

PUBLICATION DATA: Published April 23, 1920; deposited in the Copyright Office April 29th. Listed in *The Publishers' Weekly,* May 1st, and, same date, in *The Indianapolis News.* Price, $1.75.

NOTES: First edition bears statement on copyright page: *Published April, 1920.*
The novel was reprinted by Burt in 1922.
Its title was borrowed from the poem by Richard Burton (see *The Indianapolis Star,* October 19, 1919).

CONTENTS: Blacksheep! Blacksheep!, Chapters *One–Seven* (untitled); previously in *Harper's Bazaar,* October, December 1919–May, 1920.†

---

*Not seen, but mentioned in Scribners' correspondence with the author. A picture from it was used on a post card announcing the book. His publishers made use of an "advertising line" supplied by the author, but it has not been seen in print: "The author of 'The House of a Thousand Candles' offers in 'Blacksheep! Blacksheep!' a tale of a thousand surprises."

†Rights were granted Publishers Autocaster Service to serialize the story in the syndicate's country weeklies, September, 1927.

1921

The Man in the Street

THE | MAN IN THE STREET | PAPERS ON AMERICAN TOPICS | BY | MEREDITH NICHOLSON | NEW YORK | CHARLES SCRIBNER'S SONS | 1921

COLLATION: [1–18]⁸. White wove paper. Leaf measures 7⁹⁄₁₆″ x 5⅛″, top edge trimmed, bottom and fore edges untrimmed.

End paper; blank, p. [1]; list of books by the author, p. [2]; fly title, p. [i]; blank, p. [ii]; title-page, p. [iii]; copyright notice dated 1921, statement: *Published September, 1921,* copyright acknowledgments, and printer's slug, p. [iv]; dedication: *To | Cornelia,* p. [v]; blank, p. [vi]; *Foreword,* dated July, 1921, pp. vii–viii; table of contents, p. [ix]; blank, p. [x]; text, pp. 1–271; blank, pp. [272–276]; end paper.
[Note: For text, pp. 1–271, see *Contents.*]

BINDING: Green mesh cloth. Front cover gilt-stamped: THE MAN IN THE | STREET | By Meredith Nicholson [*all on a blind-stamped panel which is within a blind-stamped double rule box*]. Spine gilt-stamped: THE MAN | IN THE | STREET | Meredith | Nicholson | SCRIBNERS   Back cover blank.
End papers white calendered; no binder's leaf front or back.

PUBLICATION DATA: Published September 9, 1921; deposited in the Copyright Office September 13th. Earliest review noted: *Independent and Weekly Review,* September 17th. Price, $2.00.

NOTES: First (and only) edition bears statement on copyright page: *Published September, 1921.* No illustrations.

CONTENTS: Ten essays here first collected:
Let Main Street Alone! *The New York Evening Post,* after
    March 7, 1921, but before May 12th
James Whitcomb Riley* *The Atlantic Monthly,* October, 1916

---

*"I wrote the paper on J. W. R. just after his death, for the *Atlantic Monthly.* It gives, I think, a very fair idea of the poet, whom I knew intimately for many years." These comments by the author were written in 1932 in a copy of the book in the Indiana State Library.

The Cheerful Breakfast Table*   *The Yale Review,* July, 1918

The Boulevard of Rogues   *The Atlantic Monthly,* December, 1915†

The Open Season for American Novelists [1915]   *The Atlantic Monthly,* October, 1915

The Church for Honest Sinners   *The Atlantic Monthly,* February, 1915

The Second-Rate Man in Politics [1916]   *The Atlantic Monthly,* August, 1916

The Lady of Landor Lane   *The Atlantic Monthly,* February, 1914‡

How, Then, Should Smith Vote? [1920]   *The Atlantic Monthly,* October, 1920

The Poor Old English Language   *Scribner's Magazine,* September, 1921

1922
Best Laid Schemes

BEST LAID SCHEMES | BY | MEREDITH NICHOLSON | [2-*line quotation*] | —ROBERT BURNS | NEW YORK | CHARLES SCRIBNER'S SONS | 1922

COLLATION: [1–13]⁸, [14]¹⁰. White wove paper. Leaf measures $7\frac{9}{16}''$ x $5\frac{1}{8}''$, top and bottom edges trimmed, fore edge untrimmed.

End paper; blank, p. [i]; list of books by the author, p. [ii]; fly title, p. [iii]; blank, p. [iv]; title-page, p. [v]; copyright notices with final date 1922, statements: *Printed in the United States of America* and *Published April, 1922,* and publishers' emblem, p. [vi]; dedication to Will H. Hays,§ p. [vii]; blank, p. [viii]; table of contents, p. [ix]; blank,

---

*"The 'breakfast' paper was written at the Blackstone Hotel, Chicago, in the course of a few days that I was obliged to remain there, waiting for an engagement. I consider it one of the best of my essays." Inscribed in the copy mentioned in foregoing footnote. It later appeared in *Essays by Present Day Writers,* edited by Raymond Woodbury Pence (1927).

†Later included in *Atlantic Narratives (Second Series)* edited by Charles Swain Thomas (1931).

‡"Irvington Local Color in a Nicholson Story," is the caption for a review in *The Indianapolis News,* January 26, 1914.

§For his earlier tribute to Hays see *The Indianapolis Star,* July 13, 1919.

p. [x]; half-title, p. [1]; blank, p. [2]; text, pp. 3–217; blank, p. [218]; end paper.

[Note: For text, pp. 3–217, see *Contents*.]

BINDING: Green mesh cloth. Front cover bears a lighter green-stamped panel on right-hand side and is stamped as follows: Best [*light green*] Laid [*self-cloth*] | Schemes [*first three letters and part of fourth are in light green, rest of word in self-cloth on light green panel*] | Meredith [*light green*] Nicholson [*self-cloth on light green panel*]. Spine light green-stamped: Best | Laid | Schemes | [*parallel rule*] | Nicholson | Scribners   Back cover blank. Issued in a dust wrapper.*
End papers white calendered; no binder's leaf front or back.

PUBLICATION DATA: Published April 21, 1922; deposited in the Copyright Office April 25th. Earliest review noted: *The Indianapolis News*, May 3, 1922. Price, $1.50.

NOTES: First edition bears statement on copyright page: *Published April, 1922*. No illustrations. This was Nicholson's first, and only volume of short stories.

CONTENTS: Six stories, here first collected.
The Susiness of Susan   *The Saturday Evening Post*, November 16, 1912†
The Girl with the Red Feather   *The Saturday Evening Post*, January 18, 1913
The Campbells Are Coming   *McClure's Magazine*, August, 1921
Arabella's House Party   *The Saturday Evening Post*, November 21, 1914
The Third Man   *Collier's*, May 13, 1916‡
Wrong Number   *Scribner's Magazine*, May, 1919

---

*Mentioned by Nicholson in correspondence with Scribners, but not seen.
†Nicholson wrote of this story, in an inscribed copy in the Indiana State Library: "Except for a few early efforts it is the first short story I ever wrote."
‡Later included in *My Story That I Like Best*, by Edna Ferber, *et al.* (1925), reprinted with an original foreword explaining his choice of it; see *Contributions, post* 149.

1922

Broken Barriers

BROKEN BARRIERS | BY | MEREDITH NICHOLSON | NEW YORK |
CHARLES SCRIBNER'S SONS | 1922

COLLATION: [1]⁸, [2–13]¹⁶, [14]⁸. White wove paper. Leaf measures 7½″ (full) x 5⅛″, top edge trimmed, other edges untrimmed.

End paper; blank, p. [i]; list of books by the author, p. [ii]; fly title,
p. [iii]; blank, p. [iv]; title-page, p. [v]; copyright notices with final
date 1922, statements: *Printed in the United States of America*, and
Published September, 1922, and publishers' emblem, p. [vi]; dedication to Ray Long, p. [vii]; blank, p. [viii]; half-title, p. [ix]; blank,
p. [x]; text, pp. 1–402; blank, pp. [403–406]; end paper.

[Note: For text, pp. 1–402, see *Contents*.]

BINDING: Dark blue coarse mesh cloth.* Front cover gilt-stamped:
[*wide rule*] | BROKEN | BARRIERS | MEREDITH NICHOLSON | [*wide rule*].
Spine gilt-stamped: [*wide rule*] | BROKEN | BARRIERS | [*ornament*] |
MEREDITH | NICHOLSON | SCRIBNERS | [*wide rule*]. Back cover blank.
End papers white wove; no binder's leaf front or back.

PUBLICATION DATA: Deposited in the Copyright Office September 16, 1922; published September 22nd. Earliest review noted: *The
Indianapolis News*, September 20th. Price, $2.00.

NOTES: First edition bears statement on copyright page: *Published
September, 1922*. No illustrations.

It was published in England by Hurst & Blackett, June, 1923. Burt
reprinted it in 1924.

Nicholson wrote a statement about the novel for publication in
Brentano's *Book Chat*; unlocated.†

CONTENTS: Broken Barriers, Chapters One–Fifteen (untitled); earlier a serial in *Cosmopolitan*, January–August, 1922.

---

*A border-line cloth, possibly fine-ribbed before pressed to boards.
†Discussed in correspondence with M. E. Perkins of Scribners, July 29 and
31, 1922.

1923

Honor Bright

HONOR BRIGHT | A COMEDY IN THREE ACTS | BY | MEREDITH NICH-
OLSON | AND | KENYON NICHOLSON | COPYRIGHT, 1920, BY MERE-
DITH NICHOLSON AND | KENYON NICHOLSON | COPYRIGHT, 1923, BY
SAMUEL FRENCH | CAUTION.—Professionals and amateurs are
hereby warned | that "HONOR BRIGHT," being fully protected under
the | copyright laws of the United States and Great Britain, is |
subject to a royalty and anyone presenting the play with- | out the
consent of the authors or their authorized agents | will be liable to
the penalties by law provided. Applica- | tions for the acting rights
must be made to SAMUEL | FRENCH, 28–30 West 38th Street, New
York. | [imprints separated by a vertical rule; at left:] NEW YORK |
SAMUEL FRENCH | PUBLISHER | 28–30 WEST 38TH STREET [at
right:] LONDON | SAMUEL FRENCH, LTD. | 26 SOUTHAMPTON
STREET | STRAND

COLLATION: 52 leaves, wire side-stitched. White wove paper. Leaf
measures 7⁹⁄₁₆″ x 5⅛″, bottom edge trimmed, other edges untrimmed.

Title-page, p. [1]; copyright details, p. [2]; cast of characters in production by Stuart Walker Company, Murat Theatre, Indianapolis,
August 22, 1921, p. 3; Cast Of Characters, p. [4]; text, pp. 7–105
(should be 5–103); advertisements of "Billeted," "Nothing But the
Truth," "In Walked Jimmie," and "Martha By-the-Day," p. [104].

[Note: For text, pp. 7–105 (sic), see Contents.]

ILLUSTRATIONS: Three plates inserted, opposite pp. 18, 50, and 90:
"Scene Design," "The Stage of the Murot [sic] Theatre . . .," and
"Characters in 'Honor Bright.'"

BINDING: Light brown wrappers, printed in dark brown. Front
cover reads: HONOR BRIGHT | By MEREDITH NICHOLSON | and KENYON
NICHOLSON | [decorative dragon design incorporating the statement:]
FRENCH'S STANDARD LIBRARY EDITION | SAMUEL FRENCH, 28–30 West
38th St., New York   Spine reads: HONOR BRIGHT. By Meredith Nicholson and Kenyon Nicholson. Price 75 Cents. Back cover bears advertisement of French's Standard Library Edition. Inside front wrapper

advertises "The Charm School" and "Daddy Long-Legs." Inside back wrapper advertises "Golden Days," "Come Out of the Kitchen," "His Majesty Bunker Bean," and "A Full House."

PUBLICATION DATA: Published April 18, 1923; deposited in the Copyright Office, May 25th. Price, 75¢.

NOTES: First issue with publisher's New York address 28–30 West 38th Street noted in two states:

> State 1: Last page bears advertisements of other plays (later, scene design)
> Inside front wrapper advertises "The Charm School" and "Daddy Long-Legs" (later "Golden Days," etc.); inside back wrapper advertises "Golden Days," etc. (later, "The Charm School," etc.)
> State 2: Last page bears scene design (earlier, advertisements)
> Advertisements on inside and back wrappers in reverse of earlier state (see State 1 above).

There are two corresponding states of illustrations:

> Illustrations State 1: Three plates inserted, concerned with scene design, stage plan, and characters (later, two plates, scenes from the production)
> Illustrations State 2: Two plates inserted, facing pp. 10 and 50, being from photographs of scenes in the play (earlier, three plates as above described).

The later issues with change of address to 25 West 45th Street have other differences: copyright notice on title-page reset, 9 lines instead of 8; detailed copyright notice on verso reset and given caption: "Honor Bright" | All Rights Reserved (no caption earlier); copy on front and back wrappers reset; advertisements on inner wrappers changed, inner front advertising "Pollyanna," "Martha By-the-Day," and "Seventeen," inner back advertising "Daddy Long-Legs," "To the Ladies," and "Three Live Ghosts."

First produced by Stuart Walker in Indianapolis, August 22, 1921, at the Murat Theatre, with McKay Morris, Marjorie Vonnegut, et al.

Kenyon Nicholson's play, "Tell Me Your Troubles" (1928), was based on another short story written by Meredith Nicholson.* The two

---

*Kenyon Nicholson remembers it as having been published in The Red Book Magazine "somewhere around 1926 or 1927," but the story has not been located. "We began this story together as a play, but in 1928 I moved to New York, where I finished the play alone."—Letter, March 10, 1951.

men were not related, but both were born in Crawfordsville, and the younger man gives credit to Meredith Nicholson for encouragement that led him to follow the theatre as a profession.

CONTENTS: Honor Bright, Acts I–III, written jointly with Kenyon Nicholson, based on Meredith Nicholson's story with same title earlier in *Harper's Monthly Magazine*, August, 1915.

1923

The Hope of Happiness

THE | HOPE OF HAPPINESS | BY | MEREDITH NICHOLSON | NEW YORK | CHARLES SCRIBNER'S SONS | 1923

COLLATION: [1–23]⁸. White wove paper. Leaf measures 7½″ x 5⅛″, top edge trimmed, other edges untrimmed.

End paper; blank, p. [i]; list of books by the author, p. [ii]; fly title, p. [iii]; blank, p. [iv]; title-page, p. [v]; copyright notices dated 1923, statement: *Printed in the United States of America*, statement: *Published October, 1923*, and publishers' emblem, p. [vi]; dedication to Frank Scott Corey Wicks, and quotation [Whitman's "Perfection"], p. [vii]; blank, p. [viii]; half-title, p. [ix]; blank, p. [x]; text, pp. 1–358; end paper.

[Note: For text, pp. 1–358, see *Contents*.]

BINDING: Dark blue coarse mesh cloth. Front cover gilt-stamped: [*wide rule*] | THE HOPE OF | HAPPINESS | MEREDITH NICHOLSON | [*wide rule*]. Spine gilt-stamped: [*wide rule*] | THE HOPE | OF | HAPPINESS | [*ornament*] | MEREDITH | NICHOLSON | SCRIBNERS | [*wide rule*]. Back cover blank. Issued in a pictorial, colored dust wrapper with author's picture on back.

End papers white wove; no binder's leaf front or back.

PUBLICATION DATA: Published October 5, 1923; deposited in the Copyright Office October 9th. Earliest review noted: *The Indianapolis Star*, October 21st. It was reviewed in *The* (New York) *World* before October 10th; exact date unestablished. Price, $2.00.

NOTES: First edition bears statement on copyright page: *Published October, 1923*. No illustrations.

On October 1st when the edition was ready for distribution, it was noticed that the card plate on p. [ii], the list of his books, did not include the title, *Broken Barriers*. This mistake was ordered corrected with a cancel leaf, but no such copies have been found; the order was evidently reconsidered.

The novel was reprinted by Burt in 1926.

CONTENTS: The Hope of Happiness, Chapter One—Twenty-One (untitled); previously in *Cosmopolitan*, March–October, 1923.

1925
And They Lived Happily
Ever After!

And They Lived | Happily Ever After! | By | Meredith Nicholson | New York | Charles Scribner's Sons | 1925

[Note: All within a single rule box which is within a parallel rule box; ornaments within the four corners between single and parallel rules.]

COLLATION: [1–24]⁸. White wove paper. Leaf measures 7½" (scant) x 5⅛", top edge trimmed, other edges untrimmed.

End paper; blank, p. [i]; list of books by the author, p. [ii]; fly title, p. [iii]; blank, p. [iv]; title-page, p. [v]; copyright notices dated 1925, statement: *Printed in the United States of America*, and publishers' emblem, p. [vi]; dedication to E. K. N. [Eugenie Kountze Nicholson], p. [vii]; blank, p. [viii]; half-title, p. [ix]; blank, p. [x]; text, pp. 1–369; blank, pp. [370–374]; end paper.

[Note: For text, pp. 1–369, see *Contents*.]

BINDING: Green mesh cloth. Front cover yellow-stamped: AND THEY | LIVED | HAPPILY | EVER | AFTER! | [*parallel rule*] | MEREDITH | NICHOL-SON   Spine yellow-stamped: AND THEY | LIVED | HAPPILY | EVER | AFTER! | [*parallel rule*] | NICHOLSON | SCRIBNERS   Back cover blank. Issued in a dust wrapper.*

End papers white calendered; no binder's leaf front or back.

PUBLICATION DATA: Published September 18, 1925; deposited in the Copyright Office October 14th. Earliest review noted: *The Indianapolis News*, September 18th.† Price, $2.00.

---

*Dust wrapper unlocated.

†This review quotes the author (apparently interviewed) on the origin of the story; he said it grew out of his frequent visits to the Marion County Clerk's office.

Notes: First edition as collated. No illustrations. It was reprinted by Burt in 1928. A French translation was made by Mathilde Billiads in 1927; if published, it remains unlocated.

"This novel should be read in the light of the social conditions of the period I have attempted to describe," Nicholson wrote in 1932.*

Contents: And They Lived Happily Ever After, Chapters I–XXVII (untitled); earlier a serial in *Cosmopolitan* (which became *Hearst's International* combined with *Cosmopolitan*, March, 1925), December, 1924–June, 1925.

1928

The Cavalier of Tennessee

THE CAVALIER | OF TENNESSEE | [*orange parallel rule*] | By Meredith Nicholson | [*silhouette of Andrew Jackson on his horse; vertical orange parallel rule at either side of authorship statement and silhouette*] | [*orange parallel rule*] | THE BOBBS-MERRILL COMPANY | Publishers Indianapolis

[Note: All within an orange parallel rule box which is within a box composed of printer's ornaments.]

Collation: [1–25]⁸. White wove paper. Leaf measures 7⅞" x 5⁵⁄₁₆", top edge trimmed, other edges untrimmed.

End paper; fly title, p. [1]; list of books by the author, p. [2]; title-page, p. [3]; copyright notice dated 1928, statement: *Printed in the United States of America*, and copyright acknowledgment, with final line reading: *Under the title, A Chevalier of the Cumberland.*, p. [4]; dedication to Mary Jameson Judah, and quotation from *The Chronicles of Astolat*, p. [5]; blank, p. [6]; table of contents, p. [7]; blank, p. [8]; text, pp. 11–402 (should be 9–400); end paper.

[Note: For text, pp. 11–402 (*sic*), see *Contents*.]

Illustrations: None, except decorations on title-page. For end-paper design see *Binding*.

Binding: Red coarse mesh cloth. Front cover gilt-stamped: The | Cavalier of | Tennessee | [*ornament*] | Meredith | Nicholson [*all within a blind-stamped single rule box*]. Spine gilt-stamped: The |

*In a copy inscribed for the Indiana State Library.

Cavalier of | Tennessee | [*ornament*] | Nicholson | Bobbs | Merrill
Back cover blank.

End papers ivory-colored on white, a pictorial scene in orange depicting Jackson on his horse on front portion of the end sheets; no binder's leaf front or back.

Issued in an ivory-colored dust wrapper reproducing end paper design in colors; part of the design carried on back below both text and a portrait of the author.

PUBLICATION DATA: Published July 3, 1928; deposited in the Copyright Office July 12th. Earliest review noted: *The Indianapolis News*, July 7th and listed this date in *The Publishers' Weekly*. The author had copies to inscribe as early as June 28th. Price, $2.50.

NOTES: Two states noted:

> State 1: Copyright page as described. Thus in a copy inscribed by the author June 28, 1928, for Charles C. Kryter*
>
> State 2: Copyright page bears bow and arrow device above copyright acknowledgment to International Magazine Company, Inc. (earlier, not present); same page lacks final line reading: *Under the title, A Chevalier of the Cumberland* (earlier, present).

The limited signed edition is in *State 1*. It consists of 249 numbered copies, bound in gray boards with white paper shelfback and corners, paper labels on front cover and spine; limitation leaf inserted, as is a frontispiece with tissue guard, not present in the regular edition; issued in a gilt-stamped dust wrapper of red cloth; boxed.

Burt reprinted the novel in 1929, and Grosset & Dunlap in 1939.

Nicholson had begun work on this love story of Andrew Jackson and Rachel Robards as early as November 12, 1925 (see *The Indianapolis News*, this date). In a copy inscribed in April, 1932 (inadvertently written 1923),† the author described his two years of labor to collect material toward its writing.

CONTENTS: The Cavalier of Tennessee, Chapters I–XXXII (titled); earlier published as a serial in *Hearst's International* combined with *Cosmopolitan*, January–July, 1928 (under the title: A Chevalier of the Cumberland).

---

*In Indiana Historical Society, William Henry Smith Memorial Library. Mr. Kryter was connected with the firm of Bobbs-Merrill at the time, was personally acquainted with Nicholson, and was a book collector; he had the opportunity, and surely the collector's urge, to secure a first copy. The copyright deposit copy, not received until July 12th, is in *State 2*.

†This copy, in Indiana State Library, has the copyright page in *State 2*.

1929

Old Familiar Faces

OLD | FAMILIAR | FACES | by | MEREDITH | NICHOLSON [*all within lavender decorative oval frame*] | Indianapolis | THE BOBBS-MERRILL COMPANY | Publishers

COLLATION: [1–12]⁸. White laid paper, watermarked: *Kingsley*. Leaf measures 7⁹⁄₁₆″ x 5¼″, top edge green, other edges untrimmed.

End paper; fly title, p. [1]; blank, p. [2]; title-page, p. [3]; copyright notices with final date 1929, statements: *First Edition*, and *Printed in the United States of America*, p. [4]; dedication to Charles L. Nicholson, and quotation from *The Chronicles of Tookis*, p. [5]; blank, p. [6]; quotation from a letter from Charles Lamb to William Wordsworth, p. [7]; blank, p. [8]; table of contents, p. [9]; blank, p. [10]; half-title, p. [11]; blank, p. [12]; divisional half-title, p. [13]; blank, p. [14]; text, pp. 15–189 (with divisional half-titles, versos blank, between the eight parts); blank, p. [190]; list of books by the author, p. [191]; blank, p. [192]; end paper.

[Note: For text, pp. 15–189, see *Contents*.]

ILLUSTRATIONS: None. Graduated rule and ornament on fly title, half-title, and divisional half-titles; a graduated rule appears below the title on the first page of each part; an ornament is below caption on p. [191].

BINDING: Orange and green Japanese art paper over boards, green cloth shelfback. Spine gilt-stamped: [*parallel rule*] | OLD | FAMILIAR | FACES | [*dot*] | MEREDITH | NICHOLSON | [*rule*] | [*ornament*] | [*ornament*] | [*rule*] | BOBBS | MERRILL Issued in a lavender printed dust wrapper.

End papers ivory calendered; no binder's leaf front or back.

PUBLICATION DATA: Deposited in the Copyright Office October 8, 1929. Advertised and listed in *The Publishers' Weekly*, September 21st. Earliest review noted: *The Indianapolis News*, September 28th. Date of publication recorded in Washington is October 3rd. Price, $2.50.

NOTES: *First Edition* so stated on copyright page. Two states noted: State 1: Divisional half-title, p. [117], reads: *Americans All;*

p. [173] reads: *An American Citizen* (both later corrected by cancel leaves)

State 2: Divisional half-title, p. [117], a cancel leaf tipped-in on p. [116], reads: *An American Citizen;* a cancel leaf, p. [173], tipped in on p. [172] reads: *Americans All* (both earlier in reverse and an integral part of the book).

Autographed copies of the first (and only) edition were later distributed as souvenirs of a dinner tendered to the author by his "old familiar friends of Indiana," September 6, 1933, on the eve of his departure for Paraguay: so stated in substance on a leaf tipped-in on title-page; these copies are in *State* 2. A typewritten copy of his poem, "When Friends Are Parted," from the *Washington Post* (date?), is laid in one copy, with a printed sheet, "On the Road to Paraguay," by Carleton B. McCulloch, dated September 6, 1933.

CONTENTS: Eight essays, mostly autobiographical, here first collected:

One's Grandfather   *Harper's Monthly Magazine,* December, 1923

The Oldest Case on the Calendar   *Harper's Monthly Magazine,* December, 1921

Are We a Happy People?   *Harper's Monthly Magazine,* December, 1922*

Without Benefit of College   *Good Housekeeping,* January, 1926†; *The Indianapolis News,* December 28, 1925 (part only, with caption: World's Sharp Edges Shape Man for Life's Fight without College)

An American Citizen‡ [divisional half-title in error; see foregoing *Notes*]   *Scribner's Magazine,* December, 1922

Stay in Your Own Home Town   *Collier's,* September 26, 1925§

---

*Condensed, in *Playground,* April, 1923.

†The author said of his essay: " 'Without Benefit of College' is my own story. It appeared in *Good Housekeeping*—written to order, and brought me some remarkable letters."—Statement inscribed in a copy of the book for the Indiana State Library in 1923.

‡A footnote on p. 119 advises that the subject of this paper [Lucius B. Swift] died July 3, 1929, when these pages were in the press. The first paragraph of Nicholson's tribute was quoted later in *Lucius B. Swift: A Biography,* by William Dudley Foulke (1930). It was Nicholson who delivered the main speech at a dinner honoring Swift, May 2, 1916; text of the speech was printed in *The Indianapolis Star,* May 3, 1916.

§Later in *Readings in Present Day Writers,* edited by Raymond Woodbury Pence (1933).

Should Nellie Stay at Home? *The American Legion Monthly,*
June, 1928
Americans All [divisional half-title in error; see foregoing *Notes*]
The American Legion Monthly, April, 1929 (with title: Americans Forever)

1911

James Whitcomb Riley

ADDRESS BY MEREDITH NICHOLSON AT MANUAL TRAINING | HIGH
SCHOOL, INDIANAPOLIS, OCTOBER 6, 1911

[Note: No title-page; foregoing printed at top of first page of text.]

COLLATION: 3 sheets of white wove paper, saddle-stitched with
white silk cord within wrappers, text printed in green. Leaf measures
9" x 7", all edges trimmed.

Pen portrait of James Whitcomb Riley, p. [1]; blank, p. [2]; text,
pp. [3–11]; blank, p. [12].

[Note: Text, pp. (3–11): Address at Manual Training High
School, October 6, 1911.*]

ILLUSTRATIONS: Pen portrait of Riley preceding text, and drawings
over-printed on each page of text; all in black. Parallel rule between
title and text, and illuminated initial on p. [1], in green.

BINDING: Gray mottle wrappers, slightly larger than leaf size; front
extra-wide to fold over back. Front cover gilt-lettered: James Whitcomb
Riley   Wrappers and inner sheets saddle-stitched with white silk cord.

PUBLICATION DATA: Published shortly after October 6, 1911, at the
suggestion of E. H. Kemper McComb, Principal of Manual Training
High School, for presentation to high schools and grade schools of
Indianapolis. Printed by the Cheltenham Press, Indianapolis.

NOTES: As a result of this Riley birthday talk at Manual the Principal, Mr. McComb, proposed to the Superintendent of Schools the
printing of the piece for use in the grades and high schools; it was done
by the Cheltenham Press.† The wrappers were not supplied for all

---

*Includes poem, untitled, but earlier published as "To James Whitcomb Riley"
in *Poems* (1906).
†Letter from E. H. K. McComb, August 27, 1950.

copies; most of those distributed to the Indianapolis schools were without covers, wire saddle-stitched.*

1911

Style and the Man

STYLE AND THE MAN | By | MEREDITH NICHOLSON | INDIANAPOLIS | THE BOBBS-MERRILL CO. | PUBLISHERS

COLLATION: [1–4]⁸. White calendered paper. Leaf measures 7″ x 4¼″, all edges trimmed.

End paper; fly title, p. [i]; blank, p. [ii]; title-page, p. [iii]; copyright notice dated 1911, p. [iv]; *Foreword*, p. [v]; blank, p. [vi]; half-title, p. [vii]; blank, p. [viii]; text, pp. 1–55; blank, p. [56]; end paper.

[Note: Text, pp. 1–55: Style and the Man.]

BINDING: Red ribbed cloth. Front cover gilt-stamped: THE INDIANA SOCIETY OF CHICAGO | [*rule*] | [*title on blind-stamped panel:*] STYLE AND | THE MAN | MEREDITH NICHOLSON | [*rule*] | THE BOBBS-MERRILL COMPANY   Spine blank except for a gilt-stamped rule at top and bottom. Back cover blank.

End papers white wove, *Anglo-Saxon* watermark; no binder's leaf front or back.

PUBLICATION DATA: Issued by the Indiana Society of Chicago in a set of 12 volumes by various Indiana authors, December, 1911, boxed, distributed to members at the 7th annual dinner.

NOTES: No illustrations. Only this one in the set of 12 uniformly bound volumes is by Meredith Nicholson. Later (1912) it was Vol. X in the limited edition of 100 copies of *The Hoosier Set*, bound in green ooze leather with inlaid medallion.

In the foreword the author says: "The following pages contain the notes of an address which I have delivered on various occasions." It

---

*Nicholson gave a different address before an Indianapolis high school (Manual?) judging from a manuscript copy; it begins: "Since Dr. Rice came to Indiana and told the world . . . that the schools of Indianapolis and LaPorte were the most admirable in the United States . . . ." Thus far no printing of it has been found.

was "originally a paper read before the Indianapolis Literary Club," he further stated in an inscribed copy.*

1914
A Hoosier Classic

A HOOSIER CLASSIC | By Meridith [*sic*] Nicholson | [*gilt-stamped paw-paw design*] | The Conclusion of a Response to the Toast "Hoosiers" on the Occasion of The | Fortieth Annual Banquet of the National Wholesale Druggists' Association, | Indianapolis, September Twenty-fourth, Nineteen Fourteen
[Note: All enclosed by a gilt parallel rule box.]

COLLATION: Single sheet, heavy white art paper, French folded. Leaf measures 9½" x 6¼", fore edge untrimmed.
Title-page, p. [1]; illustration, mounted, p. [2]; text, p. [3]; blank, except for gilt single rule box, p. [4].
[Note: Text, p. (3): A Hoosier Classic.]

ILLUSTRATIONS: Illustration on p. [2] consists of a photograph of a paw-paw, green on white plate paper, mounted within a gilt single rule box which is within the single rule box present on each page. Decorations appear on other pages: gilt paw-paw design and text of title-page within gilt parallel rule; illuminated initial and the gilt single rule box on third page; box only on last page.

BINDING: French fold; apparently issued without binding or sewing.†

NOTES: This is the conclusion only of Nicholson's response to the toast, "Hoosiers," at the fortieth annual banquet of the National Wholesale Druggists' Association in Indianapolis, September 24, 1914.

---

*In the Indiana State Library collection. The paper referred to is probably one presented January 7, 1907, "Style's Elusive Charm." Another Indianapolis Literary Club paper, presented April 1, 1895, "Disjecta Membra," has not been found in print; its manuscript bears fuller title: "Disjecta Membra: Being the Posthumous Manuscripts of Captain Arthur Randolph Winston, of Mississippi." His paper before the same club, "The Peter Sterling Idea," presented November 1, 1897, exists in manuscript form, in Yale University Library, bearing title, "The Hon. Peter Sterling."
†Copy examined has been bound with other pamphlets.

The entire speech has not been found printed; this concluding portion was published later in *The Indianapolis News*, May 14, 1931.

1924

On the Antietam Battlefield

ON THE ANTIETAM BATTLEFIELD | [*ornament in red*]

COLLATION: 10 leaves, wire saddle-stitched. Cream-colored laid paper, watermarked: *Roxburghe*. Leaf measures 10%₁₆″ (scant) x 8⅜″, fore edge untrimmed, other edges trimmed.

Blank, pp. [1–6]; note regarding the writing, reading, and printing of the poem, p. [7]; blank, p. [8]; title-page, p. [9]; blank, p. [10]; text, pp. [11–15]; blank, p. [16]; limitation notice with copy number stamped in red, p. [17]; blank, pp. [18–20].

[Note: Text, pp. (11–15): On the Antietam Battlefield; see *Notes*.]

ILLUSTRATIONS: None. Title-page bears an ornamental design in red.

BINDING: Cream-colored boards. Front cover bears paper label, printed in gilt within wide rule gilt box: On the | Antietam | Battlefield | By | Meredith Nicholson   Spine and back cover blank. No end papers; no binder's leaf front or back.

PUBLICATION DATA: Printed April, 1924, by Julian Wetzel for the author at the Keystone Press in Indianapolis, in an edition of 77 copies, for presentation purposes.

NOTES: The poem was written in Indianapolis in the summer of 1910 and read September 17, 1910 at the dedication of the monument erected in Antietam, Maryland, in memory of the Indiana volunteers who fell in the battle of Antietam. It was printed in *The Indianapolis News*, September 17, 1910, and in *Indiana at Antietam* (1911); see *Contributions, post* 145.*

---

*See William Herschell's article, "Two Poets 'With But a Single Thought,' " in *The Indianapolis News*, June 4, 1924, for a suggestion of its similiarity in thought to McCrae's "In Flanders Fields."

1926

The Governor's Day Off

The Governor's Day Off | By | MEREDITH NICHOLSON | A Contest Selection | Arranged By | LILIAN HOLMES STRACK | [*publisher's emblem*] | BOSTON | Walter H. Baker Company | 1926

COLLATION: 2 sheets, wire saddle-stitched. White laid paper. Leaf measures 7⅜" x 4⅞" (full), all edges trimmed.

Title-page, p. [1]; copyright notice with final date 1926 and statement: *All Rights Reserved,* above which appears: *Baker's Published Manuscript Reading, No. 15,* and below, a note of warning against infringement of copyright, p. [2]; text, pp. [3]–8.

[Note: For text, pp. (3)–8, see *Contents.*]

ILLUSTRATIONS: Headpiece at beginning, and tailpiece at end of text; a rule below running title, pp. 4–8.

BINDING: Vivid orange decorative wrappers, slightly larger than leaf size, stapled with inner sheets. Front cover printed in dark blue: The Governor's Day Off | BY | MEREDITH NICHOLSON | [*light blue:*] Baker's Manuscript Readings [*all within a light blue ornamental box*] | [*light blue decorative panel containing publisher's emblem, dark blue, in oval design of same color, and publisher's imprint in light blue on a scroll:*] WALTER H [*dot, imperfect*] BAKER COMPANY [*two dots*] BOSTON [*all within a light blue double rule box*]. Back and inside covers blank.

PUBLICATION DATA: Published February 16, 1926. Price, 50¢.

NOTES: In reducing the story, Lilian Holmes Strack did some rephrasing, but for the most part this consists of Nicholson's own words.

CONTENTS: A "contest" cutting from "The Governor's Day Off," earlier in *The Ladies' Home Journal,* March, 1919.

~~~~~~

1890

POEMS. James Whitcomb Riley; Sarah T. Bolton; Maurice Thompson; Evaleen Stein; John Clark Ridpath; Meredith Nicholson. [Indianapolis Flower Mission, 1890]

Green wrappers, embossed in imitation of morocco. Sold at the Indianapolis Flower Mission fair, November, 1890. *The Indianapolis Journal,* November 18, 1890, reported it to be an edition of 300 copies. Contains "Omar Khayyam," a poem collected in *Short Flights* (1891).

W. A. W. [Western Association Writers]. A SOUVENIR OF THE FOURTH ANNUAL CONVENTION, AT WARSAW, INDIANA: JULY 9, 10, 11, AND 12, 1889. By L. May Wheeler and Mary E. Cardwill. Richmond, Ind., M. Cullaton & Co., 1890

Contains a biographical sketch, "Benjamin Davenport House," p. 193. See *Poems of Ben. D. House* (1892) for another Nicholson tribute to House.

1892

POEMS OF BEN. D. HOUSE [edited] WITH BIOGRAPHICAL SKETCH [by Meredith Nicholson]. Indianapolis, Carlon & Hollenbeck, 1892

Flexible leather. Contains a biographical sketch of Ben. D. House, p. [1], not same as obituary in W. A. W. *Souvenir* (1890).

The Committee on Publication included Eli Lilly, Dan L. Paine, and William Fortune, as well as Nicholson. The latter says (on p. 2): "In coming to this work [of selecting the poems] the editors have been guided by a sense of what their friend, were he living, would approve." Nicholson in autograph signed himself editor on the title-page of the Indiana State Library's copy.

WESTERN ASSOCIATION WRITERS. SAYINGS AND DOINGS OF THE SIXTH GENERAL MEETING HELD AT EAGLE LAKE, WARSAW, IND.,

JULY 6 TO 10, 1891. Cincinnati, Jones Brothers Publishing Co. [1892]

Binder's title: *In-Gathering of Sketches, Essays, Poems by Western Writers.* Contains poem, "Trust," p. 257, which later appeared without title in *The Indianapolis Journal,* March 13 ,1892.

1894

THE IMPROMPTU. Indianapolis [Indianapolis Flower Mission], 1894

White wrappers. Contains "The Borderland."

1896

A NOVEMBER LEAF. [Indianapolis, Flower Mission], 1896

White pictorial wrappers. Contains a poem, "Romance," p. [10], later made proem in *The Port of Missing Men* (1907) under the title, "The Shining Road."

1897

ONCE A YEAR. [Indianapolis, Flower Mission], 1897

Colored pictorial wrappers. Contains "The Wind Patrol," later collected in *Poems* (1906); it had another appearance, in *Poets and Poetry of Indiana,* compiled by Benj. S. Parker & Enos B. Heiney (1900).

This brochure differs completely in contents from the annual of 1899 with the same title.

1898

MOTHER GOOSE FOR ALL. The Flower Mission Magazine. Edited by May Louise Shipp. [Indianapolis, Flower Mission], November, 1898

Decorative white wrappers. Contains an essay, "Flesh-Pots," p. 18.

POEMS OF AMERICAN PATRIOTISM 1776–1898. Selected by Frederic Lawrence Knowles. Boston, L. C. Page & Co. [1898]

Contains "The Old Artillerist," p. 403. The eighth impression, 1913, still contained the poem, but it was dropped in the revised edition, 1926.

SPANISH-AMERICAN WAR SONGS. A Complete Collection of Newspaper Verse during the Recent War with Spain. Compiled & edited by Sidney A. Witherbee. Detroit, Mich., Sidney A. Witherbee, 1898

Contains " 'Bless Thou the Guns,' " a poem earlier in *The Indianapolis Journal*, April 18, 1898, and later collected in *Poems* (1906).

WAR PAPERS READ BEFORE THE INDIANA COMMANDERY MILITARY ORDER OF THE LOYAL LEGION OF THE UNITED STATES. Indianapolis [Indiana] Commandery, 1898

Limited edition of 500 copies. Contains "Inherited Honors and Duties," p. [393]. The poem, "An Old Guidon," p. 395*n*, was later collected in *Poems* (1906).

A poem in tribute to Abraham Lincoln, two stanzas beginning, "Yes, this is he; | That brow all wisdom, all benignity," on p. 404, lacks acknowledgment but is probably not Nicholson's.

Nicholson later delivered a speech before the Commandery in Indianapolis at their banquet held at the time of the Indiana State Soldiers' and Sailors' Monument dedication, May 13, 1902: "What the Monument Means to Us."*

1899

ONCE A YEAR. The Flower Mission Magazine. Edited by May Louise Shipp. [Indianapolis, Flower Mission], November, 1899

Decorative tan, and, blue wrappers. Contains poems on p. [5]: "Creator Spiritus," "Moods,"† "Love's Music," and "The Valley of Vision" (the latter two collected later in *Poems* [1906]).

---

*Another speech, "Our Heritage," read before the Loyal Legion after 1902, differing in text, has been found in proof sheet form, but not in a publication.

†Another poem by the same title, but quite different in content appeared in

1900

THE FLOWER MISSION CAP & GOWN. Edited by Laurel Louisa Fletcher. [Indianapolis, Flower Mission], November, 1900

Gray wrappers printed in red and black. Contains poem, "The Winter Wind in the Rockies," p. 22, later collected in *Poems* (1906).

POETS AND POETRY OF INDIANA . . . 1800 TO 1900. Compiled and edited by Benjamin S. Parker and Enos B. Heiney. New York, Silver, Burdett & Co. [1900]

Earliest state measures 1¼" across sheets (later, 1⅛"). Earliest binding has two-color stamping on front cover and spine, and blind-stamped publishers' emblem on back cover; a later binding state has the two-color stamping, but back cover is blank; still later, one-color (green) stamping on front cover and spine, back cover blank.

Contains the following, first collected in book form (later in *Poems* [1906]): "Shadow Lines," p. 345; "The Horns," p. 345 (not p. 348 as indicated in *Index Of Authors*, p. xx), earlier in *The Century Magazine*, n. s. Vol. XXXIV, August, 1898, and *The Indianapolis Journal*, October 23, 1898; "Unmapped," p. 346, in *The Critic*, n. s. Vol. XXIX, June 18, 1898. Another poem herein, "Christmas in the Pines," p. 194, earlier in *The Catholic World*, Vol. 64, December, 1896, remained uncollected. "The Wind Patrol" had appeared in *Once a Year* (1897).

1902

INDIANA WRITERS OF POEMS AND PROSE. [Compiled by Edward Joseph Hamilton]. Chicago, Western Press Association, 1902

Contains "The Psalms in the Mountains," later collected in *Poems* (1906).*

The Indianapolis Journal, November 3, 1895, reprinted from the *Springfield Republican;* it begins: "They are the night wind speaking to the trees." In the Flower Mission brochure the poem begins: "Not always steadfast to the aims."

*Poem not found in *Century*, although acknowledgment was made to that magazine.

1903

THE HESPERIAN TREE. An Annual of the Ohio Valley—1903. Edited by John James Piatt. Columbus, O., S. F. Harriman, 1903

Gray boards, white cloth shelfback. Contains "'The Inevitable Word,'" a prose sketch, p. 98, that had a poetical counterpart in his poem, "The Inevitable Word," in *The Bookman*, August, 1903. It also includes "The Dead Archer (Maurice Thompson, Obit., Feb. 15, 1901)," p. 361, earlier in *The Indianapolis News*, February 16, 1901, and "The Spirit of Mountains," both later collected in *Poems* (1906).

1905

IN MEMORIAM MAJOR-GENERAL LEW WALLACE: THE SOLDIER [By] Capt. William A. Ketcham; THE WRITER [by] Meridith [*sic*] Nicholson; THE DIPLOMAT [by] Chaplain Daniel R. Lucas; THE CITIZEN [by] Rev. Dr. Wm. P. Kane. May 5, 1905. Published by Order of the Commandery, State of Indiana [Loyal Legion; Indianapolis, 1905]

Wrappers (missing on copy examined). Contains "Lew Wallace as an Author," p. 15 (Meredith Nicholson's name correctly spelled at end of article, erroneously on title-page). This is not the same as his chapter on Wallace in *The Hoosiers* (1900) or "Lew Wallace" in *The Reader Magazine*, April, 1905, p. [571]. Another article about Wallace, in *The Indianapolis Star*, January 9, 1910, differed, too, as did his collected tribute in "The Provincial American," in *The Atlantic Monthly*, March, 1911. His speech on the occasion of Wallace's centennial, delivered in Crawfordsville, April 10, 1927, appeared in *The Crawfordsville Journal*, on the following day.

1906

ABE MARTIN OF BROWN COUNTY, INDIANA. By Kin [Frank McKinney] Hubbard. [Indianapolis, Levey Bros.], 1906

Introduction by Nicholson, present in all three editions (second and third identified on title-page), and in the 1907 collection of Abe

Martin sayings which was also compiled from *The Indianapolis News*, but published by Bobbs-Merrill under the same title as the 1906 volume.

IN HONOR OF JAMES WHITCOMB RILEY. A Meeting of the Indiana State Teachers' Association Held in Tomlinson Hall in Indianapolis, December the Twenty-eighth, Nineteen Hundred and Five. With a Brief Sketch of the Life of James Whitcomb Riley. Indianapolis, Bobbs-Merrill [1906]

Gray wrappers over boards. *Published, April*, so stated on copyright page. D. C. Heath & Company's *Special Edition* with a half-title in place of the title-page, and limitation notice on verso of the acknowledgment leaf, text ending on p. 60, lacks the "Brief Sketch of the Life of James Whitcomb Riley," in the regular edition pp. [61] – [89]. Issued in similar bindings, but the Heath edition has title on front cover in red (in place of black) and spine is blank (regular edition bears title). Both issues contain "Address by Meredith Nicholson," p. 28.

1908

INDIANA SOCIETY OF CHICAGO. AN ACCOUNT OF THE PROCEEDINGS ON THE OCCASION OF THE FOURTH ANNUAL BANQUET. Chicago, Indiana Society of Chicago, December 11, 1908

Tan wrappers. Contains speech, "The Rise of Science in the Pawpaw District." It later appeared in *After-Dinner Speeches and How to Make Them*, speeches selected and introduction by William Allen Wood (1914).

WHO'S WHO IN AMERICA 1908–1909. [Volume 5]. Chicago, A. N. Marquis & Co. [1908]

Contains an autobiographical sketch of Meredith Nicholson, p. 1387. It appeared, with additions, in succeeding volumes through 1946–1947, Volume 24.

1911

"COME ON HOME": BEING AN INVITATION TO THE INDIANA SOCIETY OF CHICAGO BY THE COME ON HOME SOCIETY OF INDIANAPOLIS, INDIANA. Indianapolis, Come On Home Publishing Co., 1911

Brown pictorial wrappers. Contains "Hoosier Gastronomics," also published in *The Indianapolis Sun,* June 23, 1911. Nicholson, Chairman of the "Gastronomical Committee," is caricatured and given a brief biographical sketch on verso of the title-page of this brochure.

The Indiana Society of Chicago held this annual "frolic" in Indianapolis June 23 and 24, 1911.

INDIANA AT ANTIETAM: REPORT OF THE INDIANA ANTIETAM MONUMENT COMMISSION AND CEREMONIES AT THE DEDICATION OF THE MONUMENT . . . . Indianapolis, Ind. [Aetna Press], 1911

¾ morocco. Contains the poem, "On the Antietam Battlefield," p. 16, earlier in *The Indianapolis News,* September 17, 1910. It later appeared in separate form; see *ante* 137.

1912

SUGGESTIVE PLANS FOR A HISTORICAL AND EDUCATIONAL CELEBRATION IN INDIANA IN 1916. Prepared under the direction of the Indiana Centennial Celebration Commitee [*sic*], [Dr. Frank B. Wynn, Chairman], 1912

Boards, cloth shelfback (later, solid cloth). Contains "Literature," by Nicholson, p. 38.

1913

SMITH AND THE CHURCH. By Harry H. Beattys. New York, Frederick A. Stokes Co. [1913]

Copyright page bears statement, *February, 1913.* Contains an introduction by Nicholson, dated January 14, 1913, p. v. The discussion aroused by certain sermons delivered by Rev. Beattys caused this book to be published; the sermons had been inspired by Nicholson's article, "Should Smith Go to Church?," in *The Atlantic Monthly*, June, 1912. Rev. Beattys explains in his foreword: "It [Nicholson's article] represented the non-church-goer's side on the mooted question of church attendance. It suggested to me the idea that perhaps the position of the non-church-goer had not received the attention that it deserved; and I decided to take up the subject in the pulpit and try to give 'Smith' a 'square deal.'"

Nicholson's article was collected in *The Provincial American* (1912); see *Notes, ante* 108, for further comments.

1914

INDIANA SOCIETY OF CHICAGO. CATALOGUE OF BOOKS AND THE RULES OF THE LIBRARY OF THE INDIANA SOCIETY OF CHICAGO FOR THE EVENING OF DECEMBER FIFTH, 1914, CONGRESS HOTEL, CHICAGO

Wrappers. Issued on the occasion of the 10th annual dinner of the Society. Contains "Foreword" by Nicholson.

PROCEEDINGS OF THE AMERICAN ACADEMY OF ARTS AND LETTERS AND OF THE NATIONAL INSTITUTE OF ARTS AND LETTERS. Number VII: 1914. New York [American Academy of Arts & Letters, 1914]

White wrappers, front cover serving as title-page. Contains Nicholson's speech in Chicago, November 15, 1913, "The Sunny Slopes of Forty," p. 51. This had earlier been printed in part in the *Chicago Examiner*, November 16, 1913. It reappeared in Volume II of collected *Proceedings of The American Academy . . .* 1914–1921 (1922), as No. 1.

1915

LITTLE VERSES AND BIG NAMES. New York, George H. Doran Co., 1915

Contains poem, "The Call of the Children," p. 141.
"The proceeds from the sale of this book will be devoted to provid-

ing pure milk for sick babies and the maintenance of a Visiting Nurse," so reads the *Nota Bene;* notables in all walks of life had been persuaded to contribute verses to it.

1916

AN INVITATION TO YOU AND YOUR FOLKS FROM JIM AND SOME MORE OF THE HOME FOLKS. Compiled by George Ade for Indiana Historical Commission. Indianapolis, Bobbs-Merrill Co. [1916]

Wrappers. Contains "You Simply Must Come Back," p. 11.

TRIBUTES TO THE LIFE AND MEMORY OF JAMES WHITCOMB RILEY. [n.p., n.d., *ca.* 1916]

Self-wrapper. Contains a tribute to Riley as "the most unfailingly interesting person I have ever known." This had appeared in *The Hoosier* (Indiana University Writers' Club), December, 1916.

1917

SOME TORCH BEARERS IN INDIANA. By Charity Dye. Indianapolis [Hollenbeck Press, 1917]

Contains an autobiographical sketch, p. 275, reprinted from *Youth's Companion,* December 9, 1915, and copied by *The Indianapolis Star,* January 30, 1916.

The Nicholson poem, "For a Pioneer's Memorial," set to music by Corinne L. Barcus, herein p. [313], had previous publication in *Poems* (1906).

1918

AMERICA IN THE WAR. By Louis Raemaekers. New York, Century Co., 1918

Contains "The End of the Hindenburg Line," p. 16, written for this self-called "anthology of patriotic opinion."

The volume was later issued (1924) with a limitation leaf, in an edition of 250 numbered copies, by Alumni of America, in ¾ morocco.

334TH MINSTRELS. AN EVENING WITH OUR BOYS. Murat Theatre, Indianapolis, April 13, 1918

Self-wrapper. This program contains a contribution by Nicholson beginning, "Welcome and thrice welcome to the Hoosier boys . . .," p. 2.

1919

HEART OF AMERICA READERS. Meredith Nicholson, Literary Editor. A THIRD [FOURTH; FIFTH] READER. By Meredith Nicholson, Will D. Howe, and Myron T. Pritchard. New York, Chicago, etc., Charles Scribner's Sons [1919]

First issues have code letter *A* on copyright page. The only apparent contributions by Nicholson are the forewords: in the third reader, "The Flag of the Children," p. vii; fourth reader, "The Children of America," p. vii; fifth reader, "The Heart of America," p. ix.

1920

GEMS FROM INDIANA ROTARY'S LITERARY BELT. n.p., n.d. [Indianapolis, Indiana Rotary, June, 1920]

Gray boards. Contains "Tolerance," earlier in *Cosmopolitan*, April, 1920.

1921

MY MAIDEN EFFORT: BEING THE PERSONAL CONFESSIONS OF WELL-KNOWN AMERICAN AUTHORS AS TO THEIR LITERARY BEGINNINGS. With an introduction by Gelett Burgess. Garden City & Toronto, Authors' League & Doubleday, Page, 1921

First edition so stated on copyright page. Contains an autobiographical sketch, p. 181.

1922

THE STAG COOK BOOK; WRITTEN FOR MEN BY MEN. Collected and edited by C[arroll] Mac Sheridan. New York, George H. Doran Co. [1922]

Noted in two states: the earlier with cancel title-page which lacks publisher's emblem (later, title-page an integral part of the book and emblem present); both have cancel pp. vii–[viii], similar copyright page, and same binding. Contains "Wabash Valley Steak," p. 31.

1923

THE DEFINITIVE EDITION OF MARK TWAIN. New York, Gabriel Wells [1923]

Volume XII, "Life on the Mississippi," contains introduction by Meredith Nicholson, "An Appreciation," p. ix.

THE DRIFT. Published by the Junior Class, Butler College [Indianapolis], 1923

Contains "Butler," a tribute to the college written for this annual, p. [24].

1924

MY STORY THAT I LIKE BEST. By Edna Ferber, Irvin S. Cobb, Peter B. Kyne, James Oliver Curwood, Meredith Nicholson, H. C. Witwer. With an introduction by Ray Long. New York [Cosmopolitan] 1924*

Contains a two-page explanation, written for this book, of his choice of "The Third Man," a story earlier collected in Best Laid Schemes (1922) and here reprinted.

RALSTON OF INDIANA. [Indianapolis? 1924?]

White wrappers; no title-page; title above text, p. 1. Cover title:

---

*Jacob Blanck notes that the earliest located copy of this book has title-page wholly unprinted; that the third printing has, added to the plates of Nicholson and Cobb, a copyright claim in the name of Pirie MacDonald.

Samuel M. Ralston. Contains "Ralston of Indiana, by Meredith Nicholson, in the New York World," p. 3. The article had appeared in *The* (New York) *World,* December 16, 1923. A quotation on p. 1 of the brochure, from the same article, is not duplicated on the subsequent pages. This was Presidential campaign matter.

1925

FRANKLIN BOOTH. Sixty Reproductions from Original Drawings with an Appreciation by Earnest Elmo Calkins and an Introduction by Meredith Nicholson. New York, Robert Frank, 1925

Introduction by Nicholson.
Franklin Booth provided the title-page drawing for *The Provincial American* (1912), and illustrated *The Poet* (1914). The cover design of *The Port of Missing Men* (1907) bears initials, F. B.; possibly Booth's work, also.

NATIONAL EDUCATION ASSOCIATION OF THE UNITED STATES. ADDRESSES AND PROCEEDINGS OF THE SIXTY-THIRD ANNUAL MEETING HELD AT INDIANAPOLIS, INDIANA, JUNE 28–JULY 3, 1925. Volume 63. Washington, D.C., National Education Association, 1925

Contains "Culture and Brass Tacks," p. 74. This speech, delivered June 30, 1925, appeared in *The Indianapolis Star,* July 1, 1925.

"WHAT AMERICA'S MOST FAMOUS AUTHORS SAY" ABOUT NEW HOTEL SHERMAN. [Chicago, Hotel Sherman, 1925?]

Self-wrapper. Contains Nicholson's tribute, "Improved Upon Its Former Traditions," p. 10.

1926

IN APPRECIATION OF OUR NEW HOME. [Indianapolis, Chamber of Commerce, 1926]

Red wrappers. Binder's title: *Indianapolis Chamber of Commerce Activities; New Building Dedication Number 1890–1926.* Contains "To all pilgrims by land—air or water—greetings!," p. 6; signed in facsimile.

MODERN ALADDINS AND THEIR MAGIC. THE SCIENCE OF THINGS ABOUT US. By Charles E. Rush & Amy Winslow. Boston, Little, Brown, & Co., 1926

"Introduction" by Nicholson, p. [xi].

TENTH ANNIVERSARY BANQUET INDIANAPOLIS CHAPTER AMERICAN RED CROSS. A stenographic report of the banquet tendered . . . William Fortune, on July 1, 1926, commemorating his ten years of service as chairman of the chapter. [Indianapolis, 1926]

Self-wrapper; no title-page; title above text, p. 5. Cover title: *Appreciation of Civic Service.* Contains "Address of Mr. Meredith Nicholson," p. 24. Brief excerpts from the speech appeared in *The Indianapolis Star,* July 2, 1926.

1929

A BOOK OF INDIANA. THE STORY OF WHAT HAS BEEN DESCRIBED AS THE MOST TYPICALLY AMERICAN STATE IN THE AMERICAN DEMOCRACY TOLD IN TERMS OF BIOGRAPHY. Kin [Frank McKinney] Hubbard, Editor-in-Chief. Indiana Biographical Association, James O. Jones Co. [n.p.], 1929

Contains "Foreword: To the Hesitating Reader," p. 5, with signature in facsimile.

ENERGIZING PERSONALITY. By Ancil T. Brown. New York & London, McGraw-Hill Book Co. Inc., 1929

First edition so stated on title-page. Introduction by Nicholson, p. xiii.

1930

MONSOONS—PREVAILING WINDS. By Frank Richards Hall & Charles Beckman Murphy. [N. p., Lafayette, Ind.?], 1930

Green pictorial wrappers. Foreword, "A Word to the Hesitating Purchaser," by Nicholson.

PIONEER HISTORY OF ELKHART COUNTY, INDIANA, WITH SKETCHES AND STORIES. By Henry S. K. Bartholomew. [Goshen, Ind., Goshen Printery, 1930]

"Introduction" by Nicholson, p. IX.

1938

A COOKBOOK. THE STAG AT EASE. Compiled by Marian Squire. Caldwell, Idaho, Caxton Printers, 1938

Contains "Sweetbreads Nicholson," p. 107.

1941

JAMES WHITCOMB RILEY: HOOSIER POET. By Jeannette Covert Nolan. New York, Julian Messner, Inc., 1941

Regular, and special limited *Indiana Edition*. Contains an introduction by Nicholson, p. xiii.

1943

TO THE SCHOOL CHILDREN OF INDIANAPOLIS FROM MEREDITH NICHOLSON. [Indianapolis, United War Fund, 1943]

Leaflet, 4 pages, illustrated, issued in the United War Fund campaign, October 25 to November 9, 1943. The Nicholson message is a full spread over the two inside pages.

1944

CAN IT HAPPEN AGAIN? Second Printing. [Indianapolis, Clarence F. Merrell, 1944]

Self-wrapper. Contains a "Foreword to the Second Printing" by Nicholson, dated October 21, 1944, on inside front cover.

1945

WHERE DID YOU GET THAT HAT? A SYMPOSIUM. By Young E. Allison, Meredith Nicholson, William Fortune, and Harry S. New. Edited with Some Comments by J. Christian Bay. Cedar Rapids, Iowa, Torch Press, 1945

Boards, cloth shelfback. Privately printed for J. Christian Bay in an edition of 400 copies, for a Christmas greeting. Contains a letter to Young E. Allison, dated September 6, 1929, p. 39.

Periodicals Containing First Appearances

AMERICAN FOREIGN SERVICE JOURNAL
   1934: October   The Land of the Tall Poinsettia [Paraguay]*

THE AMERICAN LEGION MONTHLY
   1926: August   The Savor of Nationality*
   1927: January   The Illusion of Change*
         May   How Long Will America Last?*
   1928: March   All for One—One for All*
         June   Should Nellie Stay at Home?
         December   The Heart of American Youth*
   1929: April   Americans Forever
         June   Prosperity and Laughter*
         December   The Silver Trumpet of Romance*
   1930: May   America and Her Critics*
         December   The Girl from the River*

THE ATLANTIC MONTHLY
   1901: July   In the Great Pastures [poem]
   1902: October   Wide Margins [poem]
         December   Edward Eggleston*
   1903: August   Penalties of Precision [anonymous]†
   1904: June   Indianapolis: A City of Homes
   1908: May   The Spirit of Mischief
   1909: November   Confessions of a "Best Seller" [anonymous]
   1911: March   The Provincial American
   1912: June   Should Smith Go to Church?
         October   The Tired Business Man
   1914: February   The Lady of Landor Lane
   1915: February   The Church for Honest Sinners
         October   The Open Season for American Novelists
         December   The Boulevard of Rogues
   1916: August   The Second-Rate Man in Politics
         October   James Whitcomb Riley*
   1920: October   How, then, Should Smith Vote?

---

*Uncollected.
†Uncollected. A clipping has been found which has M. N. signed in Nicholson's hand. A later article in "The Contributors' Club" column of the issue of November, 1904, "The Tyranny of the Calendar," is probably Nicholson's, although unsigned; an excerpt is preserved among other clippings identified as his.

THE BOOKMAN
  1903: August   The Inevitable Word [poem]*
  1908: January   Concerning a Bit of Manuscript*
  1928: March   Hoosier Letters and the Ku Klux*

BOSTON EVENING TRANSCRIPT
  1889: December 26   Righteous Wrath [poem]
  1890: November 10   Where Away [poem]
  1891: April   22   At the Top of the Pillars [poem]*
  1893: October   11   Aftermath [poem]*
        May   2   West [poem]
        September 28   The Old Guidons [poem]
  1895: November 6   The Organ [poem]*

THE CATHOLIC WORLD
  1887: June   In Ether Spaces [poem]
  1889: July   Dreams [poem]
        October   Sat Est Vixesse [poem]
        November   A Rondeau of Eventide [poem]
  1890: September   Cardinal Newman [poem]
  1896: December   Christmas in the Pines [poem]*

THE CENTURY MAGAZINE
  1890: January   A Letter [poem]*
        December   On a Becalmed Sleeping Car [poem]*
  1892: January   A Parting Guest [poem]*
  1895: January   Chords [poem]
  1897: April   The Cello [poem]*
        June   Slang [poem]*
  1898: August   The Horns [poem]
        September   Orchards by the Sea [poem]
  1899: June   A Prayer of the Hill-Country [poem]
        July   Camps [poem]
  1900: September   A Shadow of the Rockies [poem]
  1904: November   God Save the State! [poem]
  1927: May   Keep off the Grass*

THE CERTIFIED PUBLIC ACCOUNTANT
  1933: February   A Bit of Old Indiana [speech at banquet of
                        American Society of Certified Public Ac-
                        countants, September 29, 1932]*

CHICAGO EXAMINER
  1913: November 16   [Speech before the American Academy of
                        Arts and Letters and the National Institute

*Uncollected.

CHICAGO EXAMINER—*continued*
>of Arts and Letters, Chicago, November 15, 1913, part only]*

THE (Chicago) INTER OCEAN
1893: September 6   A Song of Welcome [poem]†
1904: November 13   God Save the State! [poem]‡

THE CHICAGO TRIBUNE
1886: February 20   Tale of a Postage Stamp [signed W. M. N.]§
1922: June   25   The Hand on the Shoulder‡

CHILDREN's MUSEUM (Indianapolis) BULLETIN
1934: Spring   Letter [to Children's Museum]‡

THE CHURCHMAN
1895: September 28   St. Michael and All Angels' Day [poem]‡

THE CINCINNATI ENQUIRER
1925: July   19   Is Our Great National Motive Power, Curiosity, Being Educated Out of Us?‡

COLLEGE HUMOR
1928: July   Whose Business Is It [to vote]?‡

COLLIER's
1914: July   4   The Girl at the Ad Counter‡
        July   25   Meredith Nicholson's Opinion of "Bealby" [by H. G. Wells]‡
        September 26   The Last of the Kings‡
1916: January   8   Landon's Legacy‡
        February 19   The Man with the Lantern‡
        March   25,
        April   1, 8, 15   The Madness of May
        May   13   The Third Man‡
        December 30   The Hopper
1918: October   19   Lady Larkspur; Meredith Nicholson [autobiographical]‡
                    26,
        November 9, 16, 23   Lady Larkspur [continued and concluded]

---

*Uncollected; the entire speech was later published with title, "The Sunny Slopes of Forty."
†Uncollected; reprinted from *The Indianapolis News,* but not located therein. At an unestablished date (1885?) his poem, "The Pony Express," was published in this Chicago newspaper, signed *Will Meredith Nicholson.*
‡Uncollected.
§Uncollected; awarded a $10.00 prize by the *Tribune* in a short story contest. "An Eastern newspaper" is said (Banta, p. 238) to have paid him $3.00 for a poem a bit earlier and these two pieces brought him the first monetary returns for his literary efforts.

COLLIER'S—*continued*
    1925: September 26   Stay in Your Own Home Town
    1931: July   4   The Best Man Wins*

COSMOPOLITAN (see also HEARST'S INTERNATIONAL combined with COSMOPOLITAN)
    1919: May   Be a National Asset!*
          June   The Dream of the World*
          July   Buried Treasure*
          August   The Standard of Americanism*
          September   The Lesson of the Corn*
          October   The Efficiency of the Soul*
          November   The American Girl*
          December   The Star of Stars*
    1920: January   The Single Stroke*
          March   Steady, America!*
          April   Tolerance*
          May   Am I a Good Citizen?*
          June   Leadership*; As Mr. Capper Said, "We Don't Know It All"*
          July   Democracy and Laughter*
          August   The Work That Counts*
          September   The Moods of a Nation*
          October   Fooling the People*
          November   Enthusiasm*
          December   Making and Spending*
    1921: January   The Golden Age*
          February   The Crown of Defeat*
    1922: January–
          August   Broken Barriers
          November   Set a Thief to Catch a Thief*
    1923: March–
          October   The Hope of Happiness
    1924: June   The Haunted Rocking-Chair*
          December–
    1925: February   And They Lived Happily Ever After [continued in *Heart's International* combined with *Cosmopolitan, q.v.*]

THE CRAWFORDSVILLE JOURNAL
    1885: January   24   1861–1865 [poem]†
          February   7   A Bit of History [poem]†
                    14   Stricken [poem]†
          March   7   Great Salt Lake [poem]†

---

*Uncollected.
†Uncollected; signed *Will Meredith Nicholson*.

THE CRAWFORDSVILLE JOURNAL—*continued*

1885:	April	25	Light Throuhg [*sic*] Darkness [poem]*
	June	13	Fragrance [poem]*
1886:	November	20	Violin [poem]
1927:	April	11	[Speech delivered at Crawfordsville High School, April 10th, under caption:] Great Interest in 100th Birthday of Gen. Lew Wallace†

THE CRITIC

1897:	September	18	Two Greeks [poem; written in Edith Matilda Thomas' *A Winter Swallow*]†
1898:	June	18	Unmapped [poem]

THE CURRENT (Chicago)

1885:	May	9	Contentment [poem]†
	September	5	Fire-Hunting [poem]
	October	17	Faithless [poem]
	December	26	Barred [poem]
1886:	March	27	A Meeting [poem]†
	July	10	Thoreau [poem]

CURRENT LITERATURE

1907: May	The Shining Road [poem]

THE DAWN

1893: December 7	Maurice Thompson's Verse†

THE DELINEATOR

1919: November	"My Roger"†

THE DIAL

1891: February	Dieu Vous Garde [poem]

EAST AND WEST: A MONTHLY MAGAZINE OF LETTERS (New York)

1900: September	A Hopeful View of Poetry‡

EVERY WEEK

1915: May	17	The Heart Cure at Banning Farms †
1916: May	8, 15	Mr. Richard's Fiancée†

KATE FIELD'S WASHINGTON

1892: December	14	Frontier [poem]†
1894: March	21	The Sheaf of Days [poem]†

GOOD HOUSEKEEPING

1916: November	Clarissa's Baby†

---

*Uncollected; signed *Will Meredith Nicholson*.
†Uncollected.
‡Uncollected; later revised and presented as "The Future of Poetry" before the Indianapolis Literary Club, and as a Master's address at Butler University; see *The Indianapolis Journal*, June 13, 1903, for brief quotation from the latter speech.

GOOD HOUSEKEEPING—*continued*
    1917: July   A Bad Actor*
        August   Poor Butterfly*
        December   Who Killed Cock Robin?*
    1926: January   Without Benefit of College

HARPER'S BAZAAR
    1919: October,†
        December–
    1920: May   Blacksheep! Blacksheep!

HARPER'S [MONTHLY] MAGAZINE
    1897: April   Memory [poem]
    1898: June   Charm [poem]
        October   Labor and Art [poem]
    1915: August   Honor Bright
    1921: December   The Oldest Case on the Calendar
    1922: December   Are We a Happy People?
    1923: December   One's Grandfather

HEARST'S INTERNATIONAL combined with COSMOPOLITAN (see also COS-
MOPOLITAN)
    1925: March–
        June   And They Lived Happily Ever After [con-
                     tinued from *Cosmopolitan, q.v.*]
    1926: August   Finding Work for Walter*
    1928: January–
        July   A Chevalier of the Cumberland
    1930: June   Come to Kernville*
        December   Moonlight on the Susquehanna*

THE HOOSIER (Bloomington, Indiana)
    1916: December   Personal Reminiscences [of] J. W. Riley*

THE INDEPENDENT
    1894: August 16 Populistic Esthetics*
    1896: September 10 Populistic Ideals*

THE INDIANAPOLIS JOURNAL
    1885: May   10 Contentment [poem]‡
        June   28 Thy Voice [poem]§
        July   5 The Humming Bird [poem]§

---

*Uncollected.
†November, 1919, never published.
‡Uncollected; signed *Will Meredith Nicholson*. It may have been this poem
which was reprinted in "a Cincinnati newspaper" and led to James Whitcomb
Riley's first visit to Nicholson while he was working in the Wallace law office
(see Nicholson's "Without Benefit of College" for story of their meeting).
§Uncollected; signed *Will Meredith Nicholson*.

THE INDIANAPOLIS JOURNAL—*continued*

1885:	July	12	Dreams [poem]
	August	9	Glad Heart! Sweetheart! [poem]*; In the Moonlight [poem]*
		16	"Loved and Lost" [poem]*
	October	25	Actaeon [poem]*
	November	29	Estranged [poem]
1886:	January	17	Disappointment [poem]
		24	Youth [poem]*; A Discovery (according to Tommy) [poem]
	June	20	Ambition [poem]*
	July	25	Illstarred [poem]
	August	15	Recompense [poem]*; Optimistic [poem]*
	September	5	'Tis Never Night in Love's Domain [poem]†
		12	Where Love Was Not [poem]
		19	A Kind of Man [poem]
1887:	January	2	Love's Power [poem]; Transfigured [poem]
	February	13	Days of Peace and War [poem]‡
	April	17	From the East [poem]‡
	May	1	The Midas Touch [poem]‡; Half Flights [poem]
1889:	January	6	A Rhyme of Little Girls [poem]
		13	A Secret [poem]
		20	Dieu Vous Garde [poem]
	April	14	A Prince's Treasure [poem]
	July	7	A Slumber Song [poem]
	November	10	In Ether Spaces [poem]
	December	22	Greek Love Songs [poems:] The Greek Girl's Song; The Shepherd's Song
1890:	May	4	My Pumps and I [poem]‡
	June	8	Three Friends [poem]
		29	A Tragedy in Triolets [poem]‡
	July	6	In the Shadow [poem]
		13	Sonnet, Rondeau and Triolet [poems:] A Modern Puritan; In Camp Tonight‡; "Lead Kindly Light"
	August	24	A Question as to America's Culture‡
	October	26	October [poem]
1891:	August	23	"I Know a Place" [poem]‡
1892:	January	3	A Parting Guest [poem]‡

*Uncollected; signed *Will Meredith Nicholson.*

†Signed *Meredith Nicholson;* until this date his poems in *The Indianapolis Journal* and elsewhere had been signed, *"Will Meredith Nicholson."*

‡Uncollected.

THE INDIANAPOLIS JOURNAL—*continued*

1892:	March	13	[Poem on trust, untitled]*
	October	2	Alter Ego [poem]†
	December	18	Frontier [poem]†
1893:	January	22	Go, Winter [poem]†
	March	19	Harvest [poem]†
	October	15	Escheat [poem]
	December	3	Like Lost Sheep [poem]†
1894:	March	11	Alterum Nomen [poem]‡
	April	1	The Sheaf of Days [poem]†
1895:	August	8	Where Four Winds Meet [poem]
	September	29	St. Michael and All Angels' Day [poem]†
1896:	May	31	Down the Corridor (J. M. B. Obit, May 22, 1896) [poem]†
1897:	January	5	"Lighten Our Darkness" (the Rev. J. H. Ranger: Obiit Oct. 24, 1895) [poem]†
	September	26	Two Greeks [poem; written in Edith Matilda Thomas' *A Winter Swallow*]†
	December	20	[Review of Hector Fuller's *Roach & Co., Pirates*]†
1898:	January	23	A Slumber Song [poem]
	April	18	"Bless Thou the Guns" [poem]
	May	19	"First of All the New War's Slain" [poem; about Worth Bagley, Ensign]†
		29	Charm [poem]
	June	19	News [poem]
		26	Mr. [Frank L.] Stanton's Volume of Verse [*Songs of the Soil*]†
	July	3	Old Wharves [poem]†
	October	9	Labor and Art [poem]
		23	The Horns [poem]
	November	6	"An Idyl of the Wabash" [review of book by Anna Nicholas]†
1899:	January	1	Riley in the Atlantic [poem]§
	Feburary	19	How Pierre Found His Father: A Story of Vincennes†

*Uncollected; published with title, "Trust," in *Western Association Writers: Sayings and Doings of the Sixth General Meeting* (1892).

†Uncollected.

‡Uncollected; acknowledgment made to *Boston Evening Transcript* but not found therein January 1–March 10, 1894.

§Riley wrote Nicholson on September 15, 1898 (if the date is accurately transcribed in *Letters of James Whitcomb Riley*, edited by William Lyon Phelps [1930], p. 231), expressing gratitude for a "hail out of the far West" (Nicholson was living in Denver). Nicholson's footnote in Phelps explains it as referring to this poem, but it was not written until December 23, 1898, not published until January 1, 1899.

The Indianapolis Journal—*continued*

1899: February 26 Empire [poem]*

December 4 [Review of George Edward Woodberry's *Wild Eden,* under caption:] Recent Publications [unsigned]*

1902: May 14 [Speech at Indiana Commandery of the Loyal Legion banquet, at Indianapolis, May 13th, under caption:] What the Monument Means to Us*

1903: June 13 The Future of Poetry [Master's Address at Butler University, June 12th, quoted in part]*

The Indianapolis News

1885: November 19 Secrets [poem, signed *Will Meredith Nicholson*]

1886: May 28 Grape Bloom [poem, signed *Will Meredith Nicholson*]

September 2 An Idolater [poem]

1888: May 29 A Readjustment [poem]*

June 15 "Kate Greenaway" [poem]*

1889: May 30 The Battles Grandsire Missed [poem]

October 15 Sat Est Vixisse [poem]

December 16 Our Debt to the Norsemen [poem]

1890: February 8 Blind [poem]

12 The Little Boy across the Way [poem]*

15 Good Night and Pleasant Dreams [poem]

March 29 Watching the World Go By [poem]

April 5 "As You Like It" [poems:] I. Labor the Law of Life [to Charles H. Ham]*; II. Identified at Last*; III. Art's Lesson

26 To Eugene Field in London [poem]

May 10 A Hoosier Girl's Eyes [poem]*

24 The March of Lenore [poem]*

30 The Soldier Heart [poem]

June 13 [Editorial on international copyright bill, unsigned]†

July 12 When the Boss Gets Back (With Apologies to J. W. Riley) [poem]*

August 13 Newman and His Work*

November 8 Friendship's Sacrament [poem]

---

*Uncollected.

†Uncollected. From a letter of June 11, 1890, unpublished, it is known that Nicholson was asked by R. U. Johnson what publicity had been given the subject in Indiana newspapers; this was probably a response by him, one of the few editorials he was writing at the time which it is possible to trace to his pen.

The Indianapolis News—*continued*

1901:	February	16	The Dead Archer: Maurice Thompson, Obit. Feb. 15, 1901
	July	20	Felix Reville Brunot—A Biography [by Charles L. Slattery; review of]*
1902:	May	14	"What the Monument Means to Us" [speech at Indiana Commandery of the Loyal Legion banquet at Columbia Club, May 13, 1902]*
		15	A Hymn of the Monument [poem]†
1906:	May	23	[Letter to the Editor, May 22nd, under caption:] The Crapsey Verdict*
	September	29	[Self-interview, relating to *The House of a Thousand Candles,* under caption:] How Mr. Nicholson Wrote Novel‡
1907:	December	6	Days That Are No More§
1909:	January	20	[Informal talk before English Composition class of Wabash College, Crawfordsville, under caption:] Read the Bible, Says Meredith Nicholson‖
1910:	September	17	On the Antietam Battlefield [poem]*
	October	19	[Letter to Samuel M. Ralston, under caption:] Says Only Hope Is in Democratic Party*
1911:	April	12	[Speech, Purdue University, April 12th, under caption:] Nicholson at Purdue*
	December	29	[Brief tribute to Charles Dickens in introduction of his son, Alfred Tennyson Dickens, to the Indiana State Teachers' Association, under caption:] Dickens Talks to Indiana Teachers*
1913:	March	5	[Poem, untitled, beginning: "Happy the man

*Uncollected.

†Uncollected; written for dedication of the Indiana Soldiers' and Sailors' Monument. His later poem, "At the Monument," undoubtedly refers to the same memorial.

‡Uncollected; extracts quoted from an article written "for a New York paper"; earlier publication unlocated.

§Uncollected; a letter of December 5, 1907. Some years earlier, before December 1, 1901, Nicholson had written a nostalgic letter to the Editor, complaining that Indianapolis' growth had spoiled it for literary material; *The Indianapolis News,* December 18, 1901, referred to this, and quoted the *Denver Republican's* comments on it.

‖Uncollected. Nicholson spoke frequently at Wabash College. He gave an address before Phi Beta Kappa there in June, 1901; unlocated in printed form. There is also a manuscript in Yale University of an address probably delivered at Wabash, entitled, "Mental Hospitality"; context indicates that it was prepared for a graduation class. Yet another speech given in Crawfordsville, "Women Poets," exists in manuscript form.

THE INDIANAPOLIS NEWS—*continued*

			that scales the heights afar," under caption:] Poem Sent by Nicholson to the Vice-President [Thomas R. Marshall]*
1913:	May	8	[Statement in reply to Wm F. Moore, about criticism of William Jennings Bryan, under caption:] Resents Attack on Record*
	June	24	[Statement regarding declining of appointment as U. S. Minister to Portugal]*
1915:	October	8	[Tribute to Morris Ross]*
1916:	July	24	[Tribute to James Whitcomb Riley, under caption:] Death of Riley Saddens Friends*
1917:	April	20	Letting George Do It [written for the Vigilantes]*
	June	9	War Bond Best of Good Things*; The Dollars behind the Guns*
	July	3	Stand Up for Indiana*
	September	20	Whose War Is This?*
	December	18	Whose House Is Burning?*
1918:	February	8	Tribute to Billy Miller*
	August	16	What the Victory or Defeat of Germany Means to Americans*
1920:	May	12	The Spirit of Indianapolis*
1923:	November	21	Many Memories Stirred by Robert Underwood Johnson [comments on the autobiography, *Remembered Yesterdays*]*
1924:	December	23	[Speech at Cleveland Chamber of Commerce luncheon, December 23rd, under caption:] Ancient Lights*
1925:	December	28	World's Sharp Edges Shape Men for Life's Fight without College
1927:	August	19	Giants of the Diamond*
1928:	March	8,	
1929:	March	16	Shootin' 'Em and Stoppin' 'Em [Nicholson the guest writer of column conducted by W. F. F., Jr. (William F. Fox)]*
1933:	December	1	[Letter to Dr. Carleton B. McCulloch, under caption:] Nicholson Likes Paraguay Post*
1934:	December	19	[Christmas greeting, under caption:] Nicholson Hails Yuletide*
1935:	February	14	[Letter to Manual Training High School for 40th anniversary celebration]†

---

*Uncollected.

†Uncollected; praises John H. Holliday, Charles H. Ham, Charles E. Emmerich, and E. H. Kemper McComb; another excerpt from the same letter appeared in *The Indianapolis Times*, February 18, 1935, *Manual Anniversary Edition*.

THE INDIANAPOLIS NEWS—*continued*
    1936: February   5 (Supplement) Hoosier Reminisces in Far-
                            Off Caracas*
    1945: October   6 James Whitcomb Riley*

THE INDIANAPOLIS SENTINEL
    1902: June   1 [Speech for benefit of the Harrison Memorial,
                            at Indiana authors' readings, Indianapolis,
                            May 30–31st]†

THE INDIANAPOLIS STAR
    1907: February 10 The Shining Road [poem]
    1908: December 6 [Explanation of Indiana's literary greatness,
                            under caption:] Secret of Greatness of Two
                            Indiana Authors* [Nicholson's article is fol-
                            lowed by George Barr McCutcheon's]
    1910: January   9 Lew Wallace as Meredith Nicholson Knew
                            Him*
    1911: May   29 The Grandest Dream of All [sermon delivered
                            at All Souls Unitarian Church, Indian-
                            apolis, May 28th]‡
    1912: October   6 [Letter to James Whitcomb Riley, under cap-
                            tion:] Nicholson Calls Him Laird [of Lock-
                            erbie Street]*
    1913: May   5 [Open letter to Democrats of Indianapolis
                            condemning Joseph E. Bell's candidacy for
                            Mayor, under caption:] Nicholson Assails
                            Bell . . .*
                12 [Letter to the editor of the *Star*, further warn-
                            ing against Bell, under caption:] Here's the
                            Dope on Candidates*
    1916: January 30 An Autobiographical Chapter§
          May   3 [Speech at dinner honoring Lucius B. Swift,
                            May 2nd]*
          June   3 [Speech at meeting of Indianapolis Bar Asso-
                            ciation, June 2nd, under caption:] Some
                            Indiana Characters*
          July   24 [Tribute to Riley, under caption:] Death of
                            Riley Saddens Friends*

---

*Uncollected.

†Uncollected; Nicholson read his poems: "The Bugle," "To a Debutante," "Shadow Lines," "The Psalms of the Mountains." A souvenir of the occasion, *Readings by Indiana Authors in Aid of Benjamin Harrison Monument Association*, issued in pamphlet form, contains portraits of the authors, but no text.

‡Uncollected. Nicholson had delivered another address at the same church December 15, 1907, "At the Celebration of the 100th anniversary of Whittier's Birth"; manuscript in Yale University Library; not found in print.

§Uncollected; from "A Hoosier Boyhood," in *Youth's Companion, q. v.*

THE INDIANAPOLIS STAR—*continued*

1917: April	17	The Most Beautiful Thing [about French relief]*
May	6	Penrod Is Unique; He Is a Classic [tribute to Booth Tarkington]*
	7	[Speech, Lafayette Day appeal for French relief, delivered May 6th at Second Presbyterian Church, Indianapolis]*
1918: January	5	[Letter to Vice-President Thomas R. Marshall protesting, with Vigilantes, against Senator Robert M. LaFollette]*
	8	[Letter to George Seidensticker, about Indianapolis Turnverein]*
June	2	[The Spirit of the West, part only]
October	20	[Autobiographical sketch, under caption:] Meredith Nicholson†
November	10	[Christmas plea for U. S. soldiers in Europe, under caption:] If You Were a Soldier Over There and Santa Claus Forgot You . . .‡
1919: July	13	Will Hays, Head of the Republican National Committee*
1920: March	5	[Speech at Hoosier book exhibit, L. S. Ayres & Co., Indianapolis, March 4th, quoted in brief under caption:] The Development of Literature*
1923: April	22	[Greetings to Indiana League of Women Voters, 4th annual convention, under caption:] Noted Author Sees Women as Saviors in City Politics*
1924: March	3	[Speech at the negro Y. M. C. A., March 2nd, under caption:] Nicholson Pleads for Kindness and Love in Life's Code§
November	2	[Speech in campaign for State Senatorship under caption:] Nicholson Likens Party to Old Home*
December	24	[Speech, December 23rd, under caption:]

*Uncollected.

†Uncollected; from *Collier's,* October 19, 1918.

‡Uncollected. Earlier this year Nicholson mentioned his patriotic efforts in a letter, September 14, 1918, to Robert Bridges: "I'm pledged to a speaking tour for the Fourth [Liberty] Loan, and have promised the Librarians to help in their drive in November." His speeches in the drive have not been located in this or other newspapers.

§Uncollected. Nicholson later made a speech before an audience of negroes on the subject of the Ku Klux Klan, on September 8, 1924, in his campaign for State Senatorship, not found in print.

THE INDIANAPOLIS STAR—*continued*

			Nicholson Talks to Chamber of Commerce of Cleveland on "Ancient Lights"*
1925:	July	1	Culture and Brass Tacks*
	September	26	Stay in Your Own Home Town
1926:	January	5	[Speech at Indianapolis Public Library January 4th, under caption:] Nicholson Gets Up Early in Morning to Praise Library*
	September	17	[Speech at National Life Underwriters Association banquet, September 15th, under caption:] Nicholson Tells Insurance Men Writers Interpret Life*
	October	6	[Speech before Indianapolis Medical Society, October 5th, under caption:] Nicholson Slaps Public Officials and Prohibition*
1927:	June	8	"Better Hoosier Hicks," Nicholson's Motto in "Is New York a Bluff?"*
1928:	April	8	[Politics and the Citizen, under caption:] Meredith Nicholson Suggests Wrongdoing Cure*
1930:	March	11	[Wanted: A Political Emetic, under caption:] Nicholson Sees Tolerance of Bad Government as Citizenship Evil*
1932:	October	30	Yea, Wabash!*
1933:	February	15	[Speech at Century Club dinner, Indianapolis, February 14th, under caption:] Local Author May Be Envoy*
	September	7	[Speech at farewell dinner in Indianapolis, September 6th, before departure for Paraguay*; tribute to Mayor Reginald Sullivan who administered his oath as U. S. envoy to Paraguay*]
1934:	October	8	[Speech, written for 10th anniversary program of the James Whitcomb Riley Hospital for Children, read by Dr. Carleton B. McCulloch, published under caption:] Riley Travels Far*
	December	3	[The Land of the Tall Poinsettia, under caption:] Nicholson Pictures Paraguay's Charm*
1937:	January	7	[Speech before Indianapolis Bar Association, January 6th, under caption:] Nicholson Makes Peace Plea in Bar Association Address*
1942:	December	25	My Thoughts on This Christmas*

*Uncollected.

THE INDIANAPOLIS STAR—*continued*
      1943: April   19–
             November 18,
             December 23–
        1944: September 7   Without Prejudice [bi-weekly contributions
                              to the column]*
        1945: October   6   [Tribute to Riley and the James Whitcomb
                              Riley Memorial Association, under cap-
                              tion:] James Whitcomb Riley*

THE INDIANAPOLIS SUN
        1911: June   23   Hoosier Gastronomics*

THE INDIANAPOLIS TIMES
        1922: September 28   Ideals Are Gone*
        1926: November   1   [Speech, at Democratic meeting, Indianapolis,
                              October 29th, under caption:] Toll of Klan
                              in State Set Forth*
        1934: May   18   Letter [to Children's Museum, Indianapolis]*
        1935: February   18   *Manual Anniversary Edition*   [Letter to
                              Manual Training High School, for 40th
                              anniversary celebration]†
        1947: September 27   In Tune with the Times‡

THE ISHMAELITE (Indianapolis)
        1896: December   Horatio at Elsinore [poem]
        1897: January   Cuba [poem]
              May   Specialists*
        1898: January   "Lighten Our Darkness" (The Rev. J. H.
                              Ranger; Obiit Oct. 24, 1895) [poem]*
              June   A Song of Good Roads [poem]*
              August   A Rough Rider: Theodore W. Miller [poem]*
        1899: February   The Message [poem]*
              April   An April Easter [poem]

THE LADIES' HOME JOURNAL
        1918: April   Hot Biscuits and Honey*
        1919: March   The Governor's Day Off*
        1920: May   The Housewarming*

LIBRARIES
        1926: March   [Speech at Indianapolis Public Library staff
                              meeting, January 4th; part only, under cap-
                              tion:] Meredith Nicholson on the Library§

---

*Uncollected.

†Uncollected; praises Roy W. Howard; another excerpt from the same letter
appeared in *The Indianapolis News*, February 14, 1935.

‡Uncollected; reprinted December 22nd, in a Nicholson obituary.

§Uncollected; more of it was quoted in *The Indianapolis Star* and some in
The Indianapolis News, on January 5, 1926.

LIFE
    1920: December 2 Accuracy*

THE LOUISVILLE (Kentucky) POST
    1903: June   20 A Prayer of the Hill Country [poem]

MCCLURE'S MAGAZINE
    1921: January   What Would You Do?*
          August   The Campbells Are Coming

METROPOLITAN
    1917: February   Made in Mazooma*
    1919: January   Miss O'Rourke and True Romance*

MODERN ART
    1893: November   Melpomene [poem]*
    1895: January   Where Four Winds Meet [poem]; William T.
                           Walters [poem]*

MOORESVILLE (Indiana) TIMES
    1937: June   24 *Anniversary Edition* [Letter to the Editor,
                           under caption:] Jap Miller, Friend of Riley,
                           Made Brooklyn Nationally Famous*

THE NATION
    1914: April   30 Social Service by the Church Still Experi-
                           mental*

NATIONAL MONTHLY (Buffalo, N. Y.)
    1911: May   Tom Marshall of Indiana*

THE NEW ENGLAND MAGAZINE
    1893: March   Harvest*
    1898: June   Old Wharves [poem]*
          November   A Prayer [poem]
    1899: February   Heredity [poem]*
          November   The Open Doors [poem]*

NEW YORK EVENING POST
    1921: (shortly after April 5) Let Main Street Alone!

NEW YORK HERALD
    1906: September 23 Meredith Nicholson, Author of "The House
                         of a Thousand Candles," Tells the Story of
                         His Story*

*Uncollected.

THE (New York) SUN
    1898: September 25   Dialect [poem]*
          (before November 13)   New Trails [poem]*
    1899: April   9   The Earth [poem]
    1922: December 21   "U. S. in a Spiritual Twilight" [response to a
                            question regarding his article, "Are We a
                            Happy People?"]*

THE NEW YORK TIMES
    1924: October   15   [Statement in support of John W. Davis for
                            President, under caption:] Nicholson for
                            Davis*

THE (New York) WORLD
    1923: December 16   [Article on Samuel M. Ralston and Indiana
                            politics]†

THE PHI GAMMA DELTA
    1904: April   On Being an Example [about Edward Lincoln
                            Atkinson]*
    1905: November   A Virginia Impression: Washington and Lee
                            [University]*

PROGRESSIVE FARMER (Raleigh, N. C.)
    1926: August   21   Learn from Books and from People*

RATIONEWS (Marion County, Indiana, Rationing Administration)
    1943: April   7   Will You Hoard for Hitler!*

THE READER MAGAZINE
    1904: August   Simplicity [poem]
          September   One of the Least of These*
    1905: April   Lew Wallace§
          June–
          October   The House of a Thousand Candles
          November   Bellona [poem]; The House of a Thousand
                            Candles [continued]
          December   The House of a Thousand Candles [con-
                            cluded]
    1906: May   Why Send for the Doctor?; Aideen [poem]‡
          November–

---

*Uncollected.

†Uncollected; syndicated.

§Uncollected; reprinted in part in *The American Monthly Review of Reviews*,
April, 1905, under caption, "Was Lew Wallace 'an Oriental with Medieval
Tastes'?"

‡In *Poems* (1906) and in *Current Literature*, August, 1906, with correct title,
"Aileen."

THE READER MAGAZINE—*continued*
    1907: April   The Port of Missing Men
          December   The Crown of Years*

THE RED BOOK MAGAZINE
    1914: January   That Affair at Green Bay*
          December   Broken Glass*
    1915: August   Sitting Up with Susan*
          October–
    1916: May   The Proof of the Pudding
    1917: September   The Prince of Charmingville*
          November   The Guest of Honor*
    1918: April   Nothing Venture, Nothing Have*
    1921: April   Poor Dear Papa*
    1922: April   Nuttins*
    1923: January   McGillicuddy*

THE ROTARIAN
    1928: April   Politics and the Citizen*
    1930: March   Wanted: A Political Emetic*
    1933: November   Let's All Be Ourselves*
    1938: August   Politics: A Field for Young Men*

THE SATURDAY EVENING POST
    1912: November 16 The Susiness of Susan
    1913: January   18 The Girl with the Red Feather
          April   12 April's Lady*
          August   16 Registered*
          November 8 The Honorable Archie*
    1914: January   3 The Imprudence of Prudence*
          November 21 Arabella's House Party
    1917: January   Doubtful Dollars*

SCRIBNER'S MAGAZINE
    1906: August   In the Dusk [poem]*
    1917: December   The Heart of Life*
    1918: January   The Valley of Democracy, I: The Folks and
                           Their Folksiness
          February   ... II: Chicago
          March   ... III: Types and Diversions
          April   ... IV: The Farmer of the Middle West
          May   ... V: The Middle West in Politics
          June   ... VI: The Spirit of the West
    1919: May   Wrong Number
    1921: September   The Poor Old English Language
    1922: December   An American Citizen [Lucius B. Swift]

---

*Uncollected.

UNIVERSITY MAGAZINE
    1892: December   Mea Culpa [poem]; Between the Daffodil and
                          Golden Rod [poem]*

THE UNIVERSITY REVIEW
    1893: October   Escheat [poem]

THE WORLD'S WORK
    1910: January   What I Tried to Do in My Latest Book [*The
                          Lords of High Decision*]†

THE YALE REVIEW
    1918: July   The Cheerful Breakfast Table
    1924: October   The Democratic Party in 1924†

YOUTH'S COMPANION
    1915: December   9   A Hoosier Boyhood [autobiographical]†

NOTES: Clippings preserved without source or date prove that certain other pieces appeared in periodicals; list follows:

Balthasar [poem], signed *Will Meredith Nicholson*. A sonnet, based on Wallace's *Ben-Hur*, and preceded by a quotation from the book

Bryan, William Jennings. A letter regarding him, published in the *Charleston News and Courier*, according to an unidentified newspaper article, which mentions also another letter about Bryan in the *South Bend* (Indiana) *Times*; no clue to dates yet found

"I would give a good deal if I knew the answer to the question, 'How is a novel produced?'" Article published after *The House of a Thousand Candles* (1905)

Nicholson, Meredith: A Brief Story of His Life by Himself. Not same as the autobiographical article in *The Indianapolis Star*, January 30, 1916

A Tendency in Verse

Woollen, Evans. Biographical sketch from a publication with running head, *The Hoosier Democrat; ca.* August, 1927; unlocated; possibly a piece of ephemera, rather than a serial or periodical.

---

*Uncollected. Another poem, "Go, Winter," appeared in this magazine before January 22, 1893.
†Uncollected.

[JAMES] MAURICE THOMPSON

BORN: *Fairfield, Indiana, September 9, 1844*

DIED: *Crawfordsville, Indiana, February 15, 1901*

MAURICE THOMPSON is known generally as the author of *Alice of Old Vincennes*. To archery enthusiasts he is more distinguished for another reason. Skill with a bow and arrow, acquired in boyhood, became more than a personal hobby with him; he inspired others with a liking for the sport and through him it became fashionable in the United States. On June 14, 1879, *The Publishers' Weekly* commented on the fact that "Mr. Maurice Thompson was the first [in America] to call attention to the sport. By his articles in various magazines and later by his book, 'The Witchery of Archery,' he has aroused enthusiasm all over the country for the game." His brother Will deserves some credit with him, since they were inseparable companions at the time; their book, *How to Train in Archery* (1879) was a practical manual in the latter part of the nineteenth century, today it and *The Witchery of Archery* are collectors' items.

A collection of short stories about Indiana, *Hoosier Mosaics*, was his first published volume (1875). He had come back to the state of his birth after a youth spent in Georgia, and it is interesting to see how his subsequent writing reflects both backgrounds. Throughout his life he wintered in the South, spent the rest of the year in the North, at Crawfordsville, and gave both his appreciation.

Two of his early books appeared in an anonymous series: *A Tallahassee Girl* and *His Second Campaign*. There exists a statement that he signed himself at an unstated time as "An Old Trapper" and "J. Perkins Tracy," but no evidence has been found that he was connected with any publications so signed, or that he ever used any pseudonym. He dropped his first name, James, from his signature in periodicals in the spring of 1875. According to his grandniece, Wilda Thompson, Tacoma, Washington, he was named James Madison Thompson; the middle name must have been changed in his childhood.

The same year that he became literary editor of *The Independent* (1889), his dime novel, "The League of the Guadalupe" was published in *Street & Smith's New York Weekly,* evidently a youthful excursion into the field of fiction since he called it his "firstling." But, the "first stroke" he ever made at a story was "Summer Sweethearts," he told William Dean Howells in a letter of September 15, 1881, now in Harvard's Houghton Library.

The appointment as Indiana State Geologist and head of the state's Natural History Department, 1885, was the result of his intense interest in nature plus attention to politics; he was a lawyer and had served in the State Legislature in 1879. Engineering was another early test of his talents. Literature, he decided, was the field in which it was inevitable that he succeed; it was in his character to crave top place in whatever he undertook. When he had achieved a high reputation for his poems and essays and stories with their background of literature, history, sports, and nature, he still was not satisfied. So little was being paid to an author for literary labor, he complained in letters to editors.

He lived long enough to see one of his books a financial success. *Alice of Old Vincennes,* published in 1900, a short time before his death, was immediately popular. It justified his faith in himself as a writer worthy of being read, and entitled to a reward for devoting his whole time to literature; the story endeared him to future generations. The many historical novels about the Middle West which followed it indicate that he popularized this type of fiction.

Chronology of Books and Pamphlets

1875 *Hoosier Mosaics*   E. J. Hale & Son
1878 *The Witchery of Archery*   Charles Scribner's Sons
1879 *How to Train in Archery* (with Will H. Thompson)   E. I. Horsman
1882 *A Tallahassee Girl* (anonymous)   James R. Osgood and Company
1883 *His Second Campaign* (anonymous)   James R. Osgood and Company
       Songs of Fair Weather   James R. Osgood and Company
1884 *Claude's Big Trout*   (Ephemera)
1885 *At Love's Extremes*   Cassell & Company Limited
1885 *A Red-headed Family*   (Ephemera)
       By-Ways and Bird Notes   John B. Alden

1886 *The Boys' Book of Sports and Outdoor Life* The Century Co.
      A Banker of Bankersville Cassell & Company Limited
1887 *Sunshine and Song* (Ephemera)
      Sylvan Secrets John B. Alden
1888 *A Fortnight of Folly* John B. Alden
      The Story of Louisiana D Lothrop Company
1892 *Poems* Houghton, Mifflin and Company
      A Shadow of Love (Ephemera)
      Lorel Hasardour (Ephemera)
1893 *The Ethics of Literary Art* Hartford Seminary Press
      The King of Honey Island Robert Bonner's Sons
1894 *Lincoln's Grave* Stone and Kimball
1895 *The Ocala Boy: A Story of Florida* Lothrop Publishing Company
1898 *Stories of Indiana* American Book Company
      Stories of the Cherokee Hills Houghton, Mifflin and Company
1900 *My Winter Garden* The Century Co.
      Alice of Old Vincennes The Bowen-Merrill Company
1901 *Sweetheart Manette* J. B. Lippincott Company
      Rosalynde's Lovers The Bowen-Merrill Company
1928 *The Witchery of Archery (Pinehurst Edition)* The Archers Company
1934 *Genius and Morality* (Ephemera)
1935 *An Archer in the Cherokee Hills* (Ephemera)

BIOGRAPHICAL REFERENCES

Who's Who in America [Vol. I] (1899); standard biographical reference works on American authors (he is named in practically all published in the twentieth century); *Biographical Sketches of Members of the Indiana State Government* . . . 1879; L. J. Monks, *Courts and Lawyers of Indiana*, Vol. III (1916); Jacob P. Dunn, *Indiana and Indianans* (1919); Henry C. Tracy, *American Naturists* (1930); Robert P. Elmer, all his books on archery; Paul Gordon, *The New Archery* (1939); Clement C. Parker, *Compendium of Works on Archery* (1950); R. E. Banta, *American Authors and Their Books* (1949), *Hoosier Caravan* (1951); William Malone Baskervill, *Southern Writers: Biographical and Critical Studies* (1897; the Thompson study also separately published in wrappers; the manuscript and letters relating to it preserved in the Joint University Libraries, Nashville, Tennessee). The latter was the only single biography of Maurice Thompson until Otis Wheeler wrote a thesis on him, accepted at the University of Minnesota, December, 1951, and a copy is on deposit in the library there.

1875

Hoosier Mosaics

HOOSIER MOSAICS. | By MAURICE THOMPSON. | [*publishers' mono-gram*] | NEW YORK: | E. J. HALE & SON, PUBLISHERS, | MURRAY STREET. | 1875.

COLLATION: [1–3]⁶, [4]¹², [5]⁶, [6]¹², [7]⁶, [8]¹², [9]⁶, [10]¹², [11–13]⁶ (book signed as if gathered in 17 signatures: numerals 2–17 appear on p. 13 and every twelfth leaf following, and the numeral is repeated with asterisk on recto of each second leaf following, with exception of 17, where it is not repeated). White wove paper. Leaf measures 5⅞"x 4³⁄₁₆", all edges red.

End paper; blank, pp. [i–ii]; title-page, p. [1]; copyright notice dated 1875, p. [2]; dedication to his father, the Reverend Grigg Thompson, p. [3]; blank, p. [4]; table of contents, p. [5]; blank, p. [6]; text, pp. [7]–196 (conjugate of pp. 7–8 pasted under front lining paper; the conjugate of pp. 189–190 is pasted under back lining paper); blank, pp. [197–198]; end paper.

[Note: Text, pp. (7)–196: Was She a Boy?; Trout's Luck; Big Medicine; The Venus of Balhinch; The Legend of Potato Creek; Stealing a Conductor; Hoiden; The Pedagogue; An Idyl of the Rod.*]

ILLUSTRATIONS: None. An ornamental rule appears below the title of each essay, and on p. [5].

BINDING: Silk-finished mesh cloth, various colors, over flexible boards. Front cover stamped as follows: [*triple rule, in black*] | [*title in center, on gilt-stamped panel outlined in black and gilt rules, decorations at top and bottom and either side, the panel within a gilt and black ornamental design topped with a gilt-stamped jester:*] HOOSIER

---

*Two or three of the sketches were said to have first appeared in *The New York Tribune,* and when he decided to make a book it was a poet friend, Paul H. Hayne, who suggested his publishers, Hale & Son.—*The* (Indianapolis) *Saturday Herald,* August 2, 1879.

[letters of mosaic design outlined in black] | *[arrow-like ornament]* | MOSAICS *[letters of mosaic design outlined in black]* | *[triple rule in black]*. Spine gilt-stamped except for rule at top and bottom and ornaments: *[wide rule, in black]* | *[rule]* | HOOSIER *[last letter ends in a curlicue]* | MOSAICS *[first letter end in a curlicue]* | *[rule]* | *[ornament, in black]* | BY *[Y beginning and ending in short rule]* | MAURICE | THOMPSON | *[ornament, in black]* | *[rule]* | E. J. HALE & SON. | *[rule]* | *[wide rule, in black]*. Back cover blind-stamped: *[triple rule]* | *[ornament in oval design]* | *[triple rule]*.

End papers brown coated on white; no binder's leaf front or back.

PUBLICATION DATA: Listed in *The Publishers' Weekly*, September 4, 1875, deposited in the Copyright Office September 9th. Earliest review noted: *The* (Indianapolis) *Saturday Herald*, September 18th.*
Price, $1.25.

NOTES: First edition as collated. Bindings vary in color only. Poorly inked, the book has defective type present on many pages besides a few here indicated: table of contents, page references; p. 9, line 8, *with*, defective *w*; p. 63, line 6, several defects; p. 91, line 16, several of the copies examined including one deposited for copyright have a mark over or through the *H* in *He*; none of these defects appear to be evidence of later issue.

Indiana cities, identified in the book, provided background for the stories.

1878

The Witchery of Archery

THE | WITCHERY OF ARCHERY: | A COMPLETE MANUAL OF ARCHERY. | WITH MANY CHAPTERS OF ADVENTURES BY FIELD AND | FLOOD, AND AN APPENDIX CONTAINING PRACTICAL | DIRECTIONS FOR THE MANUFACTURE AND | USE OF ARCHERY IMPLEMENTS. | BY | MAURICE THOMPSON. | *[rule]* | ILLUSTRATED. | *[rule]* | NEW YORK: | CHARLES SCRIBNER'S SONS, | SUCCESSORS TO | SCRIBNER, ARMSTRONG & CO. | 1878.

COLLATION: [1]⁶, [2–17]⁸ (Sig. [7] numbered 4*; Sig. [8] num-

---

*This review evoked a reply in the next week's issue by "Naturalist, Greencastle, Ind.," defending Thompson's ornithological descriptions.

bered 5, 5* on recto of 4th leaf), [18]². White wove paper. Leaf measures 6½" (full) x 4⅞", all edges trimmed.

End paper; binder's leaf; fly title, p. [i]; blank, pp. [ii]; frontispiece, an integral part of the book; title-page, p. [iii]; copyright notice dated 1878, and imprint of Trow's Printing and Bookbinding Co., New York, p. [iv]; dedication to Will H. Thompson, p. [v]; blank, p. [vi]; table of contents, pp. [vii]–viii; list of illustrations, p. [ix]; drawing of Cupid, p. [x]; text, pp. [1]–259 (pp. [93], [141], [149], and [156] blank; note of acknowledgments to periodicals at foot of p. 259); blank, p. [260]; binder's leaf; end paper.

[Note: For text, pp. (1)–259, see *Contents*.]

ILLUSTRATIONS: Frontispiece an integral part of the book, as are all other illustrations by Will H. Low: drawing of Cupid, p. [x], and other full-page drawings on pp. [94], [142], [150], [155], [226]. Text drawings appear on pp. 233, 234, 241, and 248.

BINDING: Bluish-green mesh cloth. Front cover bears a design of bow and arrow (the bow stamped in black, the arrow in gilt) over which is black-stamped: The | WITCHERY | OF | ARCHERY [*gilt-stamped*] | BY | MAURICE THOMPSON. [*most of the letters made arrow-like*]. Spine gilt-stamped: THE | WITCHERY [W *and* R *made arrow-like*] | OF | ARCHERY [A, R, *and* Y *made arrow-like*] | [*rule*] | THOMPSON | SCRIBNERS. Back cover bears the figure of Cupid blind-stamped in center, reproduced from p. [x].

End papers brown coated on white; binder's leaf front and back, conjugates pasted under lining papers.

PUBLICATION DATA: Published July 17, 1878; deposited in the Copyright Office July 20th. Listed in *The Publishers' Weekly*, July 20th; reviewed in *Forest and Stream*, August 15th. Price, $1.50.

NOTES: First edition as collated.

The second edition: *New Edition, With A Chapter On English Archery Practice*, so stated on title-page, bears date of 1879 (the reprints later dropped date from title-page), has a preface dated February 17, 1879, pp. [vii]–viii; the added chapter, XVII, is entitled, "The English Theory and Practice of Target-shooting" (making text 269 pages, earlier, 259 pages). In back it carries an advertisement of *The Witchery of Archery* and of Cable's *Old Creole Days*. The binding is similar to the first edition, but brown, and with decorative green and black on white end papers. It was published in May, 1879, being advertised for "next week" in *The Publishers' Weekly*, May 10, 1879, and listed therein May 24th; was deposited in the Copyright Office May 22, 1879.

Both first and second editions have broken type in footnote, p. 20: *o* in *For* and *h* in *Shooting;* also, p. 190, broken 9 in folio.

The *Pinehurst Edition,* edited by Robert P. Elmer, was published by The Archers Company, Makers of Fine Bows and Arrows, Pinehurst, N. C. (1928). It contains enough revisions and additions to justify separate collation (see *post* 228).

"So long as the new moon returns in heaven, a bent, beautiful bow, so long will the fascination of Archery keep hold of the hearts of men." This sentence from the beginning of Chapter II was printed in the story of the organization of the National Archery Association with Thompson as president, in *The Crawfordsville Journal,* January 25, 1879; it has appeared in the *American Bowman Review,* official publication of the National Archery Association, since its beginning. The magazine in 1951 sponsored a junior archery shoot, planned as an annual event, and each of the 450 youngsters who finished was awarded a hand-lettered and illuminated leaflet containing the quotation. The National Archery Association had begun in 1939 the presentation of an annual "James Maurice Thompson Award," a gold medal given to the individual "who has labored most earnestly and unselfishly for the advancement of archery, especially during the preceding year."*

CONTENTS:

CHAPTER

I Prefatory Remarks

II Outline Sketch of the Practice of Archery in Hunting *Scribner's Monthly,* May, 1878 (part only, with title: Merry Days with Bow and Quiver); *Scribner's Monthly,* July, 1877 (part only, with title: Bow-shooting†)

III Some Notes on Woodpecker Shooting [introduced by a poem, untitled, later collected as "The Archer"‡] *Harper's New Monthly Magazine,* July, 1877 (part only, with title: Hunting with the Long-Bow)

IV Bow-shooting on the St. John's *Appletons' Journal,* March 11, 1876 (with title: Bow-Shots on the St. John's)

V Hare, or Rabbit Shooting *Harper's New Monthly Magazine,* July, 1877 (part only, with title: Hunting with the Long-Bow)

VI Bow-shooting with a Hermit *Appletons' Journal,* October 30, 1875

Target Archery, by Robert Elmer (1946), p. 95.
†Another part of "Bow-shooting," in *Scribner's Monthly,* was later printed in the *Pinehurst Edition* of *The Witchery of Archery* (1928), Chapter XVI.
‡Later included in *Library of Southern Literature,* Vol. XII (1910).

VII Bold Robin Hood and His Merry Clan
VIII The Mysterious Lake
  IX Shooting the Wood-Duck and His Companions *Harper's New Monthly Magazine*, July, 1877 (with title: Hunting with the Long-Bow)
   X The Death of the White Heron*
  XI The Game of Archery—Lawn Shooting and Roving *Scribner's Monthly*, May, 1878 (part only, with title: Merry Days with Bow and Quiver)
 XII The Battles of the Birds *Appletons' Journal*, February, 1878 (with title: The Battle of the Birds)
XIII Some Wing-Shots, and Other Fancy Work
 XIV Three Weeks of Savage Life *Appletons' Journal*, September 4, 1875
  XV Lady Toxophilites†
 XVI Shooting Woodcock‡ and Plover *Harper's New Monthly Magazine*, July, 1877 (with title: Hunting with the Long-Bow)
Appendix

1879

How to Train in Archery

How to Train in Archery. | [*ornamental rule*] | BEING A COMPLETE STUDY | OF THE YORK ROUND. | [*row of ornaments*] | COMPRISING | An Exhaustive Manual of Long-Range Bow Shooting | for the use of those Archers who wish to | become Contestants at the | Grand National Association Meetings. | BY | MAURICE THOMPSON, | President of the Grand National Archery Association of the United | States, Author of the "WITCHERY OF ARCHERY," etc., etc.,

---

*Reprinted in anthologies: *Poems of Wild Life*, edited by Chas. G. D. Roberts (1888); *A Library of American Literature*, edited by E. C. Stedman & E. M. Hutchinson, Vol. X (1889); and in *Library of Southern Literature*, Vol. XII (1910).

†Reprinted in *Library of Southern Literature*, Vol. XII (1910).

‡Another account of woodcock shooting appeared later in *Inter Ocean*, August 12, 1888, in a series of nature stories written by Thompson for "Our Youth's Department."

and | WILL H. THOMPSON,* | Master of the "Wabash Merry Bow-
men." | [*rule*] | PUBLISHED BY | E. I. HORSMAN, | MANUFACTURER
OF FINE ARCHERY, | New York.

[Note: All within a red single rule box with ornamental corners.]

COLLATION: [1]⁸, [2–8]⁴, [9]². White wove paper. Leaf measures
5¾″ x 4⅛″, all edges trimmed.

End paper; binder's leaf; fly title, p. [i]; blank, except for red rule
box with ornamental corners, pp. [ii–iii]; frontispiece, p. [iv]; title-page,
p. [v]; copyright notice dated 1879, and imprint of H. C. Stoothoff,
Printer, 72 John St., N. Y., p. [vi]; *Index.*, p. [1]; vignette, p. [2]; text,
pp. [3]–54; divisional half-title for advertisements, p. [55]; testimonials,
pp. [56–58]; advertisements, pp. 67–74 (should be 59–66 [67–70]);
binder's leaf; end paper.

[Note: Text, pp. (3)–54: How to Train in Archery, Chapters I–X
(titled).]

ILLUSTRATIONS: Frontispiece, and vignette, p. [2], both an integral
part of the book. Each page has a red single rule box with ornamental
corners. Each chapter has an illuminated initial. A single rule appears
below running heads, and between divisions on p. 12; rules of various
kinds are used on the pages of advertisements.

BINDING: Bright blue, brown, and, orange silk-finished mesh
cloth.† Front cover stamped in black and gilt: [*in black:*] HOW TO |
TRAIN IN [*all, with letters arrow-like, at left of a gilt-stamped target un-
der a black-stamped tree*] | [*in gilt:*] ARCHERY [*letters arrow-like, slant-
ing downward, with gilt-stamped figures at lower left*] | [*in black:*] BY
| MAURICE AND | WILL. H. | THOMPSON. [*surname slanting downward*].
Spine blank. Back cover has an ornamental design blind-stamped in
center, otherwise blank.

End papers brown coated on white; binder's leaf front and back
with conjugates pasted under the lining papers.

PUBLICATION DATA: Published June, 1879. Earliest review noted:
Forest and Stream, June 19th. Price, 50¢.

NOTES: Written jointly with Will H. Thompson.‡ First edition as

---

*Second capital *o* broken in all copies examined.
†Clement C. Parker, in a letter to the compilers, April 29, 1950, described
the first edition binding as dark brown or blue gray, so evidently the book appeared in various colors.
‡That the book was probably an advertising venture of E. I. Horsman, has
been suggested by Paul E. Klopsteg, Glenview, Illinois.

collated. Advertised in cloth and wrappers in *The Publishers' Weekly*, June 28, 1879, but no copy in wrappers yet located.*

A letter by Maurice Thompson to E. I. Horsman, dated May 10th, 1879, endorsing Horsman's Bows, appears on p. [57]; another with same date, probably the concluding paragraph of the same letter, appears on p. 71 (so numbered); it grants exclusive right to Horsman to manufacture the "Maurice Thompson Arrow."† The letter was reprinted in *The Art and Skill of Lawn Tennis*, by Benjamin Hartwick (*ca.* 1882).

The second edition, identified above title on title-page, has copyright page same as in the first edition. It is undated, but has been reported as published in 1882.‡ A "Preface to the Second Edition" appears on pp. [ii–iii], in which the authors announce addition of two chapters; the index, p. [1], adds listing of them: Chapter XI, "The Theory and Practice of Aiming," and Chapter XII, "A Record of High Scores." These extend the text, pp. [55]–79. The Thompson testimonials are on pp. [80–81], with other advertisements following, pp. [82–86]. The binding, of mustard-colored, silk-finished cloth, has gilt-stamped at lower right of front cover: REVISED | EDITION   End papers are white laid paper.

For collation of the third edition, with Will H. Thompson's revisions after the death of his co-author, see *post* 291.

1882

A Tallahassee Girl

ROUND-ROBIN SERIES | [*rule*] | A Tallahassee Girl | [*emblem and motto for Round-Robin Series*] | BOSTON | JAMES R. OSGOOD AND COMPANY | 1882

COLLATION: [1–23]⁸. White wove paper. Leaf measures 6⅝″ x 4⁷⁄₁₆″, all edges trimmed.

---

*The earliest review found, in *Forest and Stream*, June 19, 1879, describes the book as "handsomely printed and bound," gives price as fifty cents, and mentions no paper edition. Clement C. Parker, dealer in old archery books, Norristown, Pa., reported in a letter, April 24, 1950, that he has never seen it in wrappers, although over a dozen copies have passed through his hands.

†Thompson invented a method of feathering, a formula to cut the feathers to a certain length and breadth corresponding to the weight of the arrow, making their outline a parabolic curve.

‡By Clement C. Parker.

End paper; binder's leaf; title-page, p. [1]; copyright notice dated 1881, statement: *All rights reserved.*, and imprint of the Franklin Press, Boston, p. [2]; table of contents, pp. 3–4; text, pp. 5–355; blank, p. [356]; publishers' advertisements, pp. [1]–[11–12]; binder's leaf; end paper.

[Note: Text, pp. 5–355: A Tallahassee Girl, Chapters I–XXVII (titled).]

BINDING: Olive green mesh cloth. Front cover stamped as follows: [*ornament, in brown*] | ROUND-ROBIN | SERIES [*foregoing in black*] | [*ornamental design, including wheel-like emblem for Round -Robin Series, in brown*] | A | TALLAHASSEE | GIRL [*title in black*] | [*ornament, in brown*]. Spine stamped as follows: [*three ornaments, in black*] | [*five rules, in brown*] | [*gilt-stamped panel, containing ornaments and title in self-cloth:*] [*ornament*] A [*ornament*] | TALLAHASSEE | GIRL | [*parallel rule, in brown*] | [*ornamental design, in brown*] | [*five rules, in brown*] | ROUND-ROBIN | SERIES | [*publishers' emblem; foregoing in black*]. Back cover bears a brown-stamped design at upper right, a brown-stamped ornament at lower left.

End papers white wove with publishers' advertisements in red on fronts; binder's leaf front and back.

PUBLICATION DATA: Copyrighted March 20, 1882. Earliest review noted: *The Critic*, March 25th; listed in *The Publishers' Weekly*, same date. Price, $1.00.

NOTES: Published anonymously, as Vol. IX of the *Round-Robin Series*. No illustrations. See the author's letter of August 22, 1887, published in *The Critic*, September 24, 1887, for his comments on the early reception of this novel.

The book appeared without a dedication, although he had written September 15, 1881, to William Dean Howells (letter in Harvard University, Houghton Library): "I shall address 'A Tallahassee Girl' to Hon. Joseph E. Brown, Ex-Governor of Georgia and present Senator from that state, who is my friend."

Earliest end papers bear no mention of *A Tallahassee Girl* (later advertised on front free end leaf), and imprint at foot of front free end leaf reads: *James R. Osgood & Co., Boston* (later, *James R. Osgood & Company*, no place named).* Several variations occurred before

---

*The copy presented by the author to Lew Wallace (inscription undated) is in this earliest state of end papers. The story evidently failed to impress Wallace since he advised him in a letter of August, 1882, to adhere to poetry rather than novel writing. The letter is summarized in McKee, p. 204, with a comment that Thompson was yet to write his most successful book, *Alice of Old Vincennes*, a novel!

1883, when the end papers corresponded with those used for *His Second Campaign* (1883; the other Thompson book in the *Round-Robin Series*), advertising *A Tallahassee Girl* and having change in imprint on front free end leaf.

The book arrived at an eleventh edition in 1893; Houghton Mifflin (successors to Osgood & Co.) kept it in print as late as 1928.*

All copies of the first edition, as well as all reprints examined have broken type, examples as follows:

p. 57, 6th line from bottom, broken *y* in *joyfully*

p. 59, line 3, broken *k* in *smoking*

p. 66, 3rd line from bottom, *within* not aligned and first *i* broken

p. 75, line 15, broken *n* in *romance;* last line, broken *s* in *ladies*

p. 95, broken 9 in folio; last line, broken *e* in *pressing*

p. 183, broken 8 in folio.

The *Floridian*, published in Tallahassee, in 1884 carried a statement that: "It seems to be settled that Maurice Thompson is the author of 'A Tallahassee Girl,' although The Indianapolis *Journal* claims that the author is Barton D. Jones . . . The author *is* Barton D. Jones. But who is Maurice Thompson?" *The Crawfordsville Journal* on June 3, 1884, quoted the foregoing and explained Maurice Thompson to the *Floridian*. The latter's reply appeared on July 15th.

1883

His Second Campaign

ROUND-ROBIN SERIES | [*rule*] | His Second Campaign | [*emblem and motto for Round-Robin Series*] | BOSTON | JAMES R. OSGOOD AND COMPANY | 1883

COLLATION: [*]², [1–21]⁸, [22]⁴. White wove paper. Leaf measures 6⅝" x 4⁷⁄₁₆", all edges trimmed.

End paper; binder's leaf; title-page, p. [i]; copyright notice dated 1883, statement: *All rights reserved.*, and imprint of Addison C. Get-

---

*J. L. Gilder said of this book (in *The Critic*, November, 1900, p. 406) that it had sold "to the extent of one hundred thousand copies, and is still popular, though 'Alice of Old Vincennes' is likely to exceed it in popularity; the demand of the reading public today being for novels with a flavor of history." As early as February 11, 1883, the author had written to James Whitcomb Riley, in an unpublished letter now in Eagle Crest Library, that "it is having a huge run in East and South."

chell, Boston, p. [ii]; table of contents, pp. [iii]–ii (should be iv); text
pp. [1]–342; blank, pp. [343–344]; end paper.
[Note: Text pp. (1)–342: His Second Campaign, Chapters I–
XXXIV (titled).]

BINDING: Olive green mesh cloth. Front cover stamped as follows:
[*ornament, in brown*] | ROUND-ROBIN | SERIES [*series title in black*] |
[*ornamental design, including wheel-like emblem for Round-Robin
Series, in brown*] | HIS SECOND | CAMPAIGN [*title in black*] | [*ornament,
in brown*]. Spine stamped as follows: [*three ornaments, in black*] |
[*five rules, in brown*] | [*gilt-stamped panel, containing ornaments and
title in self-cloth:*] [*ornament*] HIS [*ornament*] | SECOND | CAMPAIGN |
[*parallel rule, in brown*] | [*ornamental design, in brown*] | [*five rules,
in brown*] | ROUND-ROBIN | SERIES [*series title in black*] | [*publishers'
emblem, in black*]. Back cover bears a brown-stamped design at upper
right, brown-stamped ornament at lower left.

End papers white wove, with publishers' advertisements printed in
red on fronts; binder's leaf in front, none in back.

PUBLICATION DATA: Copyrighted June 28, 1883. Listed as an anonymous publication in *The Publishers' Weekly*, June 30th. Earliest review noted: *The* (Indianapolis) *Saturday Herald*, July 7th. Price,
$1.00.

NOTES: Published anonymously as Vol. XVI of the *Round-Robin
Series*. No illustrations.

In 1891 the American Press Association reprinted the novel with
author's name present.

Thompson wrote of this work to Lew Wallace, July 15, 1884: " 'His
Second Campaign' has had a charming reception and a fine sale; but,
curiously enough, it has made ultra folk, both Northerners and South-
erners, pinch the author very sharply.

"I have been much amused behind the cover of 'anonymous,' to see
Southern critics furiously declare that the book cries down the South
and lauds the North, whilst Northern critics assault the author on account of his extreme Southern bias.

"The fact is I sketched the book on the spots it covers, drawing the
characters in their slight outlines from actual instances and personages.

"As a novel of course I do not count much on its strength, but it is
true to the life I have chosen to depict."*

---

*Letter in Wallace Papers, Indiana Historical Society.

1883

Songs of Fair Weather

Songs of Fair Weather | [*vignette of an archer*] | BY MAURICE
THOMPSON | BOSTON | JAMES R. OSGOOD AND COMPANY | 1883

COLLATION: [1]⁸, [2]⁴, 3⁸ (numbered on recto of 7th leaf), [4]⁴,
[5]⁸ (numbered 4 on recto of 3rd leaf), [6]⁴, [7]⁸ (numbered 6 on recto
of 7th leaf), [8–9]⁴ (last signature numbered 7 on recto of 3rd leaf).
White laid paper watermarked: *John Dickinson & Co.* | [*crown and
shield design*] | *JD* [*monogram*] *& Co*   Leaf measures 8$\frac{1}{16}$" x 4$\frac{7}{8}$"
(full), all edges untrimmed.

End paper; binder's leaf; title-page, p. [i]; copyright notice dated
1883, statement: *All rights reserved.*, and imprint of the University
Press, John Wilson and Son, Cambridge, p. [ii]; table of contents,
p. [iii]–iv; *Proem*, p. [1]; blank, p. [2]; text, pp. [3]–99; vignette, p.
[100]; binder's leaf; end paper.

[Note: For text, pp. (3)–99, see *Contents*.]

ILLUSTRATIONS: Title-page bears a vignette of an archer, signed
with artist's initials, *E.H.C.* Headpieces appear on pp. [iii], [1], [3].
Each poem has an illuminated initial except "Proem," p. [1], the title
of which on p. [iii], being first in table of contents, therein has its illuminated initial. Each poem has a tailpiece except those ending on pp. 4,
[26], 30, 46, 73, 75, [76], [97]; vignette on p. [100].

BINDING: White Japan vellum over beveled boards. Front cover
brown-stamped: SONGS OF FAIR WEATHER | [*vignette of an archer, re-
produced from the title-page*] | MAURICE THOMPSON   Spine brown-
stamped, reading from top to bottom: SONGS OF FAIR WEATHER   Back
cover bears a brown-stamped vignette reproduced from p. [100]. Issued
in a dust wrapper.*

End papers white laid, not same as book stock, 1$\frac{1}{8}$" (full) between
wire marks (book stock 1" [full]). Binder's leaf front and back.

PUBLICATION DATA: Copyrighted September 17, 1883. Announced
as "just published" in *The Publishers' Weekly,* September 22nd, and
reviewed in *Literary World* this date. Price, $1.50.

---

*Reported; dust wrapper not seen.

NOTES: First, and only edition as collated.

CONTENTS: All but two of the poems herein are first appearances in a Thompson book. "The Death of the White Heron" and "The Archer" had been included in *The Witchery of Archery* (1878). Later, numerous poems from *Songs of Fair Weather* were reprinted in *Poems* 1879†

Proem

A Prelude   *The Atlantic Monthly,* July, 1883; *The Crawfordsville Journal,* July 7, 1883*

A Flight Shot   *The* (Peoria, Ill.) *Saturday Evening Call,* May 3, 1879†

The Fawn   *Harper's New Monthly Magazine,* May, 1877; *The Crawfordsville Journal* and *The Indianapolis Saturday Herald,* April 21, 1877‡

The Blue Heron   *Scribner's Monthly,* May, 1875; *The Indianapolis Saturday Herald,* September 25, 1875 (with title in both: The Heron)§

The Bluebird   *Lippincott's Magazine of Popular Literature and Science,* May, 1874; *The Crawfordsville Journal,* April 7, 1877‖

The Wabash   *Lippincott's Magazine of Popular Literature and Science,* February, 1877; *Poems of Places,* edited by Henry W.

---

*"A Prelude" appeared in *Representative Poems of Living Poets,* edited by Jeanette L. Gilder (1886); in *The Golden Treasury of American Songs and Lyrics,* edited by F. L. Knowles (1898), with title, "Fertility"; in *The Home Book of Verse,* selected and arranged by Burton E. Stevenson (1912); in *The Little Book of American Poets,* 1787–1900, edited by Jessie B. Rittenhouse.

†"A Flight Shot" was reprinted in *Archer's Register,* 1883–1884 (London); was included in *Songs of Three Centuries,* edited by John Greenleaf Whittier, revised edition of 1890; also in Herringshaw's *Local and National Poets of America* (1890); in *An American Anthology,* edited by Edmund C. Stedman (1900); in *The Oxford Book of American Verse,* edited by Bliss Carman (1927); in *Lyric America, An Anthology of American Poetry,* edited by Alfred Kreymborg (1930), which book appeared also under the title, *An Anthology of American Poetry, Lyric America;* also in *The Junior Poetry Cure,* compounded by Robert Haven Schauffler (1931).

‡Frank Mayfield's parody of "The Fawn" was published in *The Crawfordsville Journal,* May 5, 1877. Thompson's poem was reprinted in *Poems of Wild Life* edited by Charles G. D. Roberts (1888).

§This poem reappeared in *Poetic and Artistic Masterpieces* (1894); and in *The Bird-Lovers Anthology,* edited by Clinton Scollard & Jessie B. Rittenhouse (1930).

‖"The Bluebird" was included in *A Library of American Literature,* edited by E. C. Stedman & E. M. Hutchinson, Vol. X (1889); in *Songs of Three Centuries,* edited by John Greenleaf Whittier (1890 revision); also in *Library of Southern Literature,* Vol. XII (1910); and in *The Bird-Lovers' Anthology,* by Clinton Scollard & Jessie B. Rittenhouse (1930).

Longfellow (1879); *The* (Indianapolis) *Saturday Herald,* May 31, 1879*

Okechobee

Dropping Corn *The Atlantic Monthly,* August, 1877†

The Morning Hills *The Atlantic Monthly,* July, 1879; *The Cambridge Book of Poetry and Song,* selected by Charlotte Fiske Bates (1882)

At the Window *The Atlantic Monthly,* April, 1873‡; *The Indianapolis Journal,* April 11, 1873

November *The Atlantic Monthly,* December, 1874§

Between the Poppy and the Rose *The Independent,* October 8, 1874; *The Indianapolis Journal,* November 12, 1874‖

Solace *Lippincott's Magazine of Popular Literature and Science,* November, 1873

Atalanta *The Atlantic Monthly,* May, 1874; *The Indianapolis Journal,* May 19, 1874¶

Ceres *Appleton's Journal,* June 6, 1874

---

*"The Wabash" was later included in *Poets and Poetry of Indiana,* edited by Benj. S. Parker & Enos B. Heiney (1900); and in *The Poetic New-World,* compiled by Lucy H. Humphrey (1910). A parody of the poem, by A. Quisenberry, appeared in *The Crawfordsville Journal,* January 27, 1877.

†"Dropping Corn" later appeared in *Patrician Rhymes,* edited by Clinton Scollard & Jessie B. Rittenhouse (1932).

‡The author said in an autobiographical letter to William M. Baskervill, March 19, 1887: "My literary life began with contributing to the Atlantic in 1873." A story about this same contribution appeared in Charles F. Smith's *Reminiscences and Sketches* (1908), p. 126: "Mr. Howells, the editor of the *Atlantic,* opening his mail one day in his office in 1873, read this to him first poem from a new poet. He was surprised and delighted, and showed it to Mr. Longfellow, who happened to be in at the time. He, too, was charmed with its simple fresh beauty and they agreed that if the author would change the word 'sapsucker' Mr. Howells would print the poem in the *Atlantic.* The change was made, the poem appeared in the *Atlantic,* and with it began Maurice Thompson's literary career. It is said, by the way, that both editor and elder poet afterwards agreed that 'sapsucker' should have stayed as Maurice Thompson wrote it." Thompson's prose article on "The Sap-Sucker," in *Appleton's Journal,* December 7, 1872, was uncollected.

§Later included in *November,* edited by Oscar F. Adams (1886).

‖"Between the Poppy and the Rose" was reprinted in *Library of Southern Literature,* Vol. XII (1910).

¶"Atalanta" was later included in *Representative Poems of Living Poets,* edited by Jeanette L. Gilder (1886); in *A Library of American Literature,* edited by E. C. Stedman & E. M. Hutchinson, Vol. X (1889); in *Poets and Poetry of Indiana,* edited by Benj. S. Parker & Enos B. Heiney (1900); in *Library of Southern Literature,* Vol. XII (1910); in *The Oxford Book of American Verse,* edited by Bliss Carman (1927); and three stanzas were quoted in Meredith Nicholson's *Rosalind at Red Gate* (1907), at the beginning of Chapter II.

Aoede   *The Atlantic Monthly*, January, 1876

Diana   *The Atlantic Monthly*, April, 1875; *The Indianapolis Journal*, March 26, 1875*

Garden Statues: I. Eros; II. Aphrodite; III. Psyche; IV. Persephone *The Atlantic Monthly*, December, 1876†

In the Haunts of Bass and Bream   *The Century Magazine*, June, 1882 (with title: In the Haunts of Bream and Bass)‡

A Morning Sail   *The* (Indianapolis) *Saturday Review*, December 3, 1881

Wild Honey   *The Atlantic Monthly*, January, 1883; *The Crawfordsville Journal*, January 27, 1883§

The Tulip

Written on a Fly-Leaf [lower case *l* in *leaf* in table of contents] of Theocritus   *Scribner's Monthly*, March, 1881 (with title: Simplicity [Written on a Fly-Leaf of Theocritus])‖

Eos

Twilight   *Living Writers of the South*, by J. W. Davidson (1869)

The Sentinel   *The Galaxy*, August, 1872

---

*"Diana" was reprinted in *Poets and Poetry of Indiana*, edited by Benj. S. Parker & Enos B. Heiney (1900); and in *Library of Southern Literature*, Vol. XII (1910).

†The group of four sonnets was included in *American Sonnets*, selected & edited by Wm. Sharp (London, 1889); the fourth alone, was printed under the title, "On a Garden Statue of Persephone," in *American Sonnets*, selected & edited by Wm. Sharp (London, 1889); the fourth, alone, was printed under the

‡Published later the same year (1883) in *Sport with Gun and Rod in American Woods and Waters*, edited by Alfred M. Mayer; title same as in *Century*. "In the Haunts of Bass and Bream" was included in several later anthologies: *Songs of Nature*, edited by John Burroughs (1901); *Three Years with the Poets*, compiled by Bertha Hazard (1904); *American Lyrics*, chosen by Edith Rickert & Jessie Paton (1912).

§"Wild Honey" appeared later in *Representative Poems of Living Poets*, edited by Jeanette L. Gilder (1886); in *The Oxford Book of American Verse*, edited by Bliss Carman (1927); and in *American Poetry, 1671–1928*, edited by Conrad Aiken (1929). The last part of it made several appearances: without title in *The Wheelman*, November, 1883, with introduction, "In a bit of verse I once tried to express my idea of the true poet . . .," this reprinted in *The* (Indianapolis) *Saturday Herald*, October 27, 1883; with title, "Poetry," in *Local and National Poets of America*, edited by Thomas W. Herringshaw (1890); and in *The Library of Literary Criticism of English and American Authors*, edited by Charles W. Moulton, Vol. 4 (1902).

‖Reprinted in *An American Anthology*, edited by Edmund C. Stedman (1900); in *The Le Gallienne Book of American Verse*, edited by Richard Le Gallienne (1925, reissued in combination with his book of English verse in 1935); in *The Oxford Book of American Verse*, edited by Bliss Carmen (1927); and in *The Book of American Poetry*, selected by Edwin Markham (1934).

At Night   *Lippincott's Magazine*, April, 1881; *The Crawfords-ville Journal*, April 9, 1881

In Exile   *The Century Magazine*, February, 1882

Before Dawn   *The Atlantic Monthly*, March, 1881; *The Craw-fordsville Journal*, February 26, 1881; *The Cambridge Book of Poetry and Song*, selected by Charlotte F. Bates (1882)

Unaware   *The Atlantic Monthly*, September, 1880*

1885

At Love's Extremes

AT LOVE'S EXTREMES | BY | MAURICE THOMPSON | Author of "A Tallahassee Girl," "His Second Campaign," | "Songs of Fair Weather," etc., etc. | [*rule*] | [*quotation, 4 lines*] | —Tennyson. | [*rule*] | NEW YORK: | CASSELL & COMPANY LIMITED | 1885

COLLATION: [1–17]⁸. White laid paper. Leaf measures 7⅜" x 4¹⁵⁄₁₆", all edges trimmed.

End paper; binder's leaf; fly title, p. [i]; blank, p. [ii]; title-page, p. [iii]; copyright notice, in name of O. M. Dunham, dated 1885, and statement, *All Rights Reserved.*, p. [iv]; table of contents, pp. [v]–vi; text, pp. [1]–266; advertisements, leaf inserted; binder's leaf; end paper.

[Note: Text, pp. (1)–266: At Love's Extremes, Chapters I–XX (titled).]

BINDING: Dark green silk-finished mesh cloth. Front cover has de-sign in self-cloth on black-stamped panel on upper portion, title in black within an ornamental gilt-stamped panel: AT LOVE'S EXTREMES | [*below it the author's name is gilt-stamped with black-stamped orna-ment at each side:*] MAURICE THOMPSON | [*black-stamped ornaments at foot*]. Spine bears similar black-stamped design, title in black within an ornamental gilt-stamped panel: AT LOVES [*sic*] | EXTREMES | [*below it the author's name is gilt-stamped:*] MAURICE | THOMPSON | [*black-stamped ornament*] | [*publisher's imprint gilt-stamped:*] CASSELL & COMPANY, | LIMITED   Back cover blind-stamped: [*ornamental border*] | [*publisher's emblem*] | [*ornamental border*].

End papers floral olive green, and, light brown, on white; binder's leaf front and back, conjugates pasted under the lining papers.

---

*"Unaware" was reprinted in *Library of Southern Literature*, Vol. XII (1910).

PUBLICATION DATA: Deposited in the Copyright Office June 8, 1885. Listed in *The Publishers' Weekly*, June 13th. Earliest review noted: *The Critic*, July 11th. Price, $1.00.

NOTES: First edition as collated. No illustrations. Binding noted in two states:

> *Binding State* 1: As described, with author's name on front cover and spine and imprint on spine gilt-stamped (later, black stamping replaced gilt in author's name and publishers' imprint)
>
> *Binding State* 2: Brown cloth similar to *Binding State* 1, with black-stamped author's name on front cover and spine, and black-stamped publishers' imprint on spine (earlier, gilt-stamped).

A second "edition" of the book was ready shortly after the first, according to a comment in the *Literary World*, July 25, 1885, p. 259. The author's own statement in a letter of November 6, 1886,* indicated that a third "edition" was issued before the latter date.

Some minor type imperfections are present in all copies examined: p. 40, next to last line; p. 94, line 8; p. 248, line 15.

The book was issued in Cassell's *Sunshine Series, No. 65*, April 18, 1891, in wrappers.

In February, 1901 it was published under the title, *Milly: At Love's Extremes*, by the New Amsterdam Book Co., New York, in cloth, and, paper.† In 1902 it was reissued by the same house in a *Red Letter Series* (paper); again, 1903, in their *Favorite Fiction Library*, No. 2.

This is perhaps the book about which *The Indianapolis Journal*, March 29, 1877, carried a statement: "Mr. J. Maurice Thompson, the Indiana poet and author, is engaged on a novel in which he designs to picture Indiana life and character"; if so, it was a long time in preparation.

Thompson wrote a letter denying that the character of "Miss Crabb" was a local study, to the editor of *The Crawfordsville Review*, published in this and in *The Crawfordsville Journal*;‡ nor, he said, was she "a particular study of any living person here or elsewhere. She is my own creation such as she is ...." See *A Banker of Bankersville, post* 199, for further comments.

---

*Letter, unpublished, addressed to R. W. Gilder, now in the New York Public Library.

†*The English Catalogue* noted this edition with the new title, published in New York, available in London, June, 1901; its listing in America was several months earlier, in *The Publishers' Weekly*, March 23, 1901.

‡*The Crawfordsville Journal*, July 4, 1885.

1885

By-Ways and Bird Notes

BY-WAYS | AND | BIRD NOTES | BY | MAURICE THOMPSON | AUTHOR OF | "AT LOVE'S EXTREMES," "HIS SECOND CAMPAIGN," "SONGS | OF FAIR WEATHER," "A TALLAHASSEE | GIRL," ETC. | NEW YORK | JOHN B. ALDEN, PUBLISHER | 1885

COLLATION: [1]–11⁸, [12]⁴. White wove paper. Leaf measures 7⁵⁄₁₆″ x 4¼″, top edge gilt, other edges trimmed.

End paper; binder's leaf; title-page, p. [1]; copyright notice dated 1885, and imprint of Trow's Printing and Bookbinding Company, New York, p. [2]; table of contents, p. [3]; blank, p. [4]; text, pp. [5]–179 (conjugate of pp. 177–178 pasted down, or excised, under back lining paper); blank, pp. [180–182]; end paper.

[Note: For text, pp. (5)–179, see *Contents*.]

BINDING: Dark blue, and, green silk-finished mesh cloth over beveled boards. Front cover gilt-stamped: BY* WAYS AND BIRD NOTES Spine gilt-stamped: BY† WAYS | AND | BIRD NOTES | [*rule*] | THOMPSON Back cover blank.

End papers olive green floral design on gray, and, tan on white; binder's leaf in front, none in back.

PUBLICATION DATA: Deposited for copyright August 12, 1885. Earliest review noted: *The Critic*, September 26th. Price, 75¢.

NOTES: First edition as collated. No illustrations. Copies with perfect folio, running head, and first line of text probably preceded those with defects therein—which persisted through the reprint edition.

The book had a second issue (probably Alden's *Ideal Edition*, listed in *The Publishers' Weekly*, June 23, 1888),‡ with same sheets, in binding uniform with *Sylvan Secrets* (1887): green cloth over boards plain,

---

*There is no hyphen here, and scarcely any space exists between BY and WAYS.

†See footnote above.

‡Contemplated as early as November 6, 1886, according to the author in a letter of that date to Gilder, of Century, his comment being that this book, "published by the so-called 'pirate' Alden is doing exceedingly well and an enlarged edition is forthcoming."—Letter in the New York Public Library. When the new edition did appear it was neither revised nor enlarged.

not beveled; top edge ungilded; front cover, hand-lettered with title and author's name, bears brown-stamped design of a palm tree and other flora along a Southern river; lettering on spine same as on first binding but for spacing, with rule a thicker one, floral design added, and imprint at foot: ALDEN The end papers are plain.

Reprinted by the United States Book Company (successors to John W. Lovell Company).*

CONTENTS: Nature stories, all first collected here with exception of "A Red-headed Family," which had earlier separate printing (see *post* 232):

In the Haunts of the Mocking-Bird *The Atlantic Monthly*, November, 1884

Tangle-Leaf Papers, I–IV *Outing* and *The Wheelman*, December, 1884–March, 1885

The Threshold of the Gods *Good Company*, Vol. 4, No. 6 [March], 1880

Browsing and Nibbling *Outing* and *The Wheelman*, October, 1884†

Out-Door Influences in Literature *The Wheelman*, November, 1883

A Fortnight in a Palace of Reeds *Good Company*, March–April, 1881

Cuckoo Notes *The Library Magazine*, July, 1885‡

Some Minor Song-Birds *The Library Magazine*, August, 1885§

Birds of the Rocks *The Library Magazine*, September, 1885

---

*Before 1892? *Book News*, April, 1892, p. 350, commenting on the book, stated that, because of the "failure of a publishing concern," it was then out of print.

†"Browsing and Nibbling" later appeared in the *Elzevir Library*, No. 300, October 1, 1887, Extra; "Cuckoo Notes" and "Minor Song-Birds" appeared in the same series as No. 302, October 8, 1887, Extra, with cover title reading, *Cuckoo Notes and Some Minor Song-Birds*.

‡*Ibid.*

§*Ibid.*

1886

The Boys' Book of Sports

THE | BOYS' BOOK OF SPORTS | AND OUTDOOR LIFE | EDITED BY | MAURICE THOMPSON | [*publisher's emblem*] | NEW-YORK: THE CENTURY CO. | 1886

COLLATION: [*]⁸, [1]–22⁸. White wove paper. Leaf measures 9⅛" x 6½", all edges trimmed.

End paper; binder's leaf; fly title, p. [i]; blank, pp. [ii–iii]; frontispiece, p. [iv]; title-page, p. [v]; copyright notice dated 1886, and imprint of the De Vinne Press, p. [vi]; *Preface* dated July, 1886, pp. [vii]–viii; table of contents, pp. [ix]–xi; *The Benefits And The Abuse Of Outdoor Sports*, pp. [xii]–xiv; divisional half-title, p. [xv]; illustration, p. [xvi]; text, pp. [1]–348; divisional half-title, p. [349]; illustration, p. [350]; *Index*, pp. [351]–352; binder's leaf; end paper.

[Note: For text, pp. (1)–348, see *Contents*.]

ILLUSTRATIONS: Frontispiece and full-page illustrations an integral part of the book. Profuse textual illustrations are present also. Various artists contributed the drawings, some of which are signed, others unsigned.

BINDING: Tan mesh cloth. Front cover decorated with sporting scenes brown-stamped, title gilt-stamped: THE [*wave rule and five dots under* HE] [*dot*] BOYS [*without apostrophe*] | BOOK [*dot*] OF [*dot*] SPORTS Spine brown-stamped except for title and imprint; title gilt-stamped within a brown-stamped box closed at bottom by three parallel rules: THE | BOYS' | BOOK | OF | SPORTS | [*boy's bust surrounded by sports' design which extends into upper box; below, it intercepts three parallel rules with row of dots between first and second rules, and extends into a lower single rule box, decorated with cattails and birds, which contains the publisher's emblem; boxed below is the gilt-stamped imprint:*] THE CENTURY CO [*period within* O]* | [*parallel rule*]. Back cover decorated with brown-stamped sporting scenes.

End papers decorative bronze and pale aquamarine, on white; binder's leaf in front and back.

PUBLICATION DATA: Copyrighted September 6, 1886. Listed in

---

*Period lacking in one copy, present in another in Indiana State Library.

The Publishers' Weekly, October 16th. Earliest reviews noted: *The Critic* and *The Literary World,* both November 27, 1886. Price, $2.50.

NOTES: First edition as collated. The presence or absence of a dot within the *o* in *Co* in imprint at foot of spine probably represents a random occurrence in the process of bindery stamping; the copyright deposit copy lacks it.

Daniel C. Beard and other writers contributed to the book. It had several reissues: 1901, 1906, and 1914.

CONTENTS: Part only by Thompson: the preface and text, pp. [1]–148, [177]–196, [241]–245, all signed; the introductory, pp. [xii]–xiv, unsigned, is probably his, also.

Preface

The Benefits and the Abuse of Outdoor Sports [*Introductory,* so specified in table of contents; probably Thompson's, though unsigned]

Marvin and His Boy Hunters, Chapters I–XXVII   *St. Nicholas,* May–October, 1884

Hints on Trap-Shooting

Fly Fishing for Black Bass   *St. Nicholas,* August, 1883

The Bow and Its Use   *St. Nicholas,* September, 1882 (with title: The Story of the Arbalist); *The Crawfordsville Journal,* September 2, 1882 (with title: Drawing the Cross-Bow)*

An Archer among the Herons

The School in the Woods   *St. Nicholas,* October, 1879

1886

A Banker of Bankersville

A | BANKER OF BANKERSVILLE | A NOVEL | BY | MAURICE THOMPSON | AUTHOR OF "AT LOVE'S EXTREMES," "HIS SECOND CAMPAIGN," | "A TALLAHASSEE GIRL," "BY-WAYS AND BIRD-NOTES," ETC., ETC. | [*rule*] | CASSELL & COMPANY, LIMITED | 739 & 741 BROADWAY, NEW YORK

COLLATION: [1–20]⁸. White laid paper. Leaf measures 7⅜" x 4¹⁵⁄₁₆", all edges trimmed.

End paper; binder's leaf; title-page, p. [1]; copyright notice, in name

---

*The story was rewritten for the book.

of O. M. Dunham, dated 1886, and imprint of W. L. Mershon & Co., Rahway, N. J., p. [2]; dedication to Honorable D. W. Voorhees, p. [3]; blank, p. [4]; text, pp. [9]–323 (should be [5]–319); blank, p. [320]; binder's leaf; end paper.

[Note: Text, pp. (9)–323 (sic): A Banker of Bankersville, (Chapters) I–XXII (untitled).*]

BINDING: Mustard-colored, and, green, mesh cloth. Front cover black-stamped: [ornaments] | [wide rule] | [ornamental panel with ornamented title on gilt-stamped design in center:] A BANKER OF | BANKERSVILLE | [wide rule] | [rule] | [ornament] | BY | MAURICE | THOMPSON | [ornaments; dots sprinkled through and around the lettering]. Spine black-stamped: [ornaments] | [wide rule] | [title, elaborated with rules and dots on gilt-stamped panel within an ornamental box:] A | BANKER | OF | BANKERSVILLE | [wide rule] | [rule] | [ornaments] | [elaborated with dots:] THOMPSON | [ornaments] | [imprint gilt-stamped:] CASSELL & COMPANY | LIMITED. Back cover blind-stamped: [ornamental rule] | [publishers' monogram] | [ornamental rule].

End papers olive green floral design on white; binder's leaf front and back.

PUBLICATION DATA: To be published "early next week," according to The Publishers' Weekly, November 6, 1886; deposited for copyright November 30th. Listed in The Publishers' Weekly, December 11th. Earliest inscription noted: December 25th. Reviewed in The Critic, February 12, 1887. Price, $1.00.

NOTES: First edition as collated. No illustrations.

Reprints: Cassell's Sunshine Series of Choice Fiction, Vol. 1, No. 28, June 8, 1889, wrappered; Street & Smith, 1900, no series identification; Street & Smith's Romance Series, No. 5, April 14, 1900; Federal Book Company, before 1905; Street & Smith's Eagle Series, No. 523, June, 1907.

It was published in England by J. & R. Maxwell, June, 1887.

The novel depicts life in an average Indiana village or city. The character, "Miss Crabb," had figured earlier in At Love's Extremes (1885). See The Critic, September 24, 1887, p. 152, for the author's own comments on these two novels and their reception.

---

*The author had sent it to Gilder for publication in The Century Magazine; his letter expressing disappointment over its rejection, October 25, 1886, is in the New York Public Library.

1887

Sylvan Secrets

SYLVAN SECRETS, | IN | BIRD-SONGS AND BOOKS. | BY | MAURICE
THOMPSON. | AUTHOR OF | "BY-WAYS AND BIRD-NOTES," "SONGS OF
FAIR | WEATHER," "THE WITCHERY OF | ARCHERY," ETC. | [*rule*]
| NEW YORK: | JOHN B. ALDEN, PUBLISHER. | 1887.

COLLATION: [1]–[8]⁸, [9]⁶. White wove paper. Leaf measures
7⁵⁄₁₆" x 4⅛", all edges trimmed.

End paper; binder's leaf; title-page, p. [1]; copyright notice dated
1887, in name of Provident Book Co., p. [2]; *Table Of Contents*, p. [3];
blank, p. [4]; *Preface*, pp. 5–10 (signed, *The Author*); text, pp. 11–
139 (author's name at foot of p. 139); blank, p. [140]; binder's leaf;
end paper.

[Note: A divisional blank page, (124), precedes last essay in the
book. For text, pp. 11–139, see *Contents*.]

BINDING: Dark green silk-finished mesh cloth. Front cover bears
brown-stamped design of a palm tree and other flora along a Southern
river, and gilt-stamped lettering: SYLVAN | SECRETS | IN BIRD SONGS AND
BOOKS [*in panel formed by river design*] | By* | MAURICE THOMPSON
Spine gilt-stamped: SYLVAN | SECRETS [*with design of a bird in flight
above the V, and two birds between the two words*] | [*brown-stamped
floral design*] | ALDEN   Back cover blank.

End papers olive green floral design on white and, plain white†;
binder's leaf front and back.

PUBLICATION DATA: Copyrighted November 29, 1887. *The English Catalogue* listed it as published in New York, December, 1887.
Price, 75¢ (however, when *The Literary World* reviewed it March 3,
1888, the price was stated as 60¢).

NOTES: First edition as collated. No illustrations. Issued in two
states of binding by Alden (not to be confused with the John A. Berry

---

*The *y* in *By* might be interpreted as a capital letter.
†A copy with floral end papers was presented by the author to Gen. & Mrs.
Lew Wallace (in Eagle Crest Library); thus, too, is the copyright deposit copy.
Another, without inscription, owned by Paul E. Klopsteg, has plain end papers.

[James] Maurice Thompson, Sylvan Secrets, *two binding states*

& Company edition of 1888, in a similar cloth, but without brown stamping):

> Binding State 1: As described. Scene on front cover shows a palm tree and flora along a river; title gilt-stamped. Copies in this binding noted with two types of end papers: green floral on white, and, all white
>
> Binding State 2: Scene on front cover is of quite different design, showing boats on a river; all but first two words of title brown-stamped (earlier, title wholly gilt-stamped). Plain white end papers.

The design on *Binding State 1* is similar to that on the second issue of an earlier Thompson book, *By-Ways and Bird Notes* (1885). *Binding State 2* may cover the issue named as *Ideal Edition* in a notice in *The Publishers' Weekly*, June 23, 1888.

Reissued, John A. Berry & Company, 1888. The International Book Company published it in the *Columbus Series* (1892?), bound with Lamb's *The Essays of Elia*.

CONTENTS: Previously "at intervals and in separate wisps in the *Atlantic*, the *Library*, and other magazines," so stated in the preface.

Sylvan Secrets

Beside the Gulf with Ruskin *The* (Chicago) *Times*, February 13, 1887; *The Library Magazine*, April, 1887

Ceryle Alcyon *The Southern Bivouac*, October, 1886

Swamp Sketches *The* (Chicago) *Times*, September 25, 1887

In the Matter of Shakespeare *The Library Magazine*, March 2, 1887

The Motif of Bird-Song *Scribner's Magazine*, September, 1887*

The Genesis of Bird-Song *The Atlantic Monthly*, May, 1886

The Anatomy of Bird-Song

Some Hyoid Hints† *The Elzevir Library*, No. 305, October 15, 1887, Extra

---

*Included later in *A Library of American Literature*, edited by E. C. Stedman & E. M. Hutchinson, Vol. X (1889).

†Read to the Indiana Academy of Science in 1887 under title, "The Secondary Functions of the Hyoid Cornua in Picus and Colaptes." Another paper, "Mineralogical Investigation in Indiana," is listed in the first volume of *Proceedings of the Indiana Academy of Science* (1891) as having been presented in 1885, but neither the report of the December 29th meeting at which the Academy was organized, nor of the earlier "field meeting," May 20th, mention a Thompson paper.

1888

A Fortnight of Folly

A FORTNIGHT OF | FOLLY. | BY MAURICE THOMPSON. | Author of "Songs of Fair Weather," "Sylvan Secrets," "A Talla- | hasse [sic] Girl," "By-Ways and Bird Notes," "A Banker of | Bankersville," "At Love's Extremes," etc. | [rule] | NEW YORK: | JOHN B. ALDEN, PUBLISHER. | 1888.

COLLATION: [1–3]⁸, 4–5⁸, [6]⁸, 7–9⁸ (4–5 and 7–9 numbered on recto of last leaf of the preceding signature). White wove paper. Leaf measures 7⁵⁄₁₆″ x 4¹⁵⁄₁₆″, all edges trimmed.

End paper; binder's leaf; title-page, p. [1]; copyright notice dated 1888, p. [2]; text, pp. 5–140 (conjugate of pp. 131–132 [sic] pasted under back lining paper*; pagination should be 3–138); blank, pp. [139–142]; end paper.

[Note: Text, pp. 5–140 (sic): A Fortnight of Folly, (Chapters) I–XXI (untitled).]

BINDING: Issued simultaneously in both cloth and wrappers. *Dark blue silk-finished mesh cloth:* Front cover gilt-stamped: A FORTNIGHT OF FOLLY | MAURICE THOMPSON   Spine gilt-stamped: A | FORTNIGHT | OF | FOLLY | [rule] | THOMPSON | ALDEN   Back cover blank.

End papers white wove, lighter weight than book stock; binder's leaf in front, its conjugate pasted under the lining paper, no binder's leaf in back.

Gray wrappers: Front cover reads: THE ELZEVIR LIBRARY | VOL. VII, NO. 345. [foregoing braced; in center:] 25 Cts. [at right, braced, on two lines:] Weekly: $10.00 a Year | July 21, 1888. | [hand-lettered on a scroll:] ELZEVIR | A Fortnight of Folly | BY | MAURICE THOMPSON. | [rule] | JOHN B. ALDEN, PUBLISHER, | The Alden Publishing Company, Proprietors. | NEW YORK and CHICAGO. [period possibly intended as comma but has imperfect tail] | 393 Pearl Street. [vertical rule] 218 Clark Street. | [rule] | Entered at the PO., N. Y., as Second-class matter. [all within a wave rule box with parallel rule and ornamental border at top and bottom, within a double rule box, within an outer decorative box]. Spine reads, from top to bottom: 345. A FORTNIGHT OF

---

*The leaf is a free blank in wrappered copies.

FOLLY, by Maurice Thompson. 25c. Back wrapper carries listing of *The Elzevir Library* continued from inside front and back wrappers.

PUBLICATION DATA: Deposited for copyright July 13, 1888. Earlier reviewed in *Literature* July 7th. Price, cloth, 50¢; wrappers, 25¢.

NOTES: First edition as collated. No illustrations. Imperfections present in all copies examined: in folios on pp. 9, 58 (8 imperfect), 73, 79 (7 lacking), 103, 116 (6 lacking); inking poor on many pages of text besides. Issued simultaneously in cloth, and, wrappers; title-page, copyright page, and text same in both.

Reprints: John A. Berry & Company, 1888; Alden's reissue with 1889 date on title-page; Street & Smith, 1902. In the latter edition it bore Thompson's title, but had additions: "The Tale of a Sculptor" by Hugh Conway, and "Carriston's Gift" (not by Thompson).

1888

(Published 1889?)

The Story of Louisiana

THE STORY OF THE STATES | [*rule*] | THE STORY OF LOUISIANA | BY | MAURICE THOMPSON | [*emblem, a seal of the state of Louisiana*] | Illustrations by L J Bridgman | BOSTON | D LOTHROP COMPANY | FRANKLIN AND HAWLEY STREETS

COLLATION: One unsigned leaf, [1–21]^8. White wove paper. Leaf measures 8$\frac{3}{16}$″ (full) x 5$\frac{1}{2}$″, all edges trimmed.

End paper; fly title, with verso blank, inserted, but figured in the pagination as pp. [1–2]; frontispiece with tissue guard, inserted; title-page, p. [3]; copyright notice dated 1888, and imprint of Berwick & Smith, Boston, p. [4]; *Preface*, signature at end in facsimile, pp. [5–6]; table of contents, pp. [7–8]; list of illustrations, p. [9]; blank, p. [10]; text, pp. 11–301; blank, p. [302]; chronological story, pp. 303–324; *The Peoples' Covenant*, pp. 325–329; list of books relating to Louisiana, pp. 330–332; index, pp. 333–337; advertisements of *The Story of the States*, pp. [338–341]; blank, pp. [342–344]; end paper.

[Note: The pagination includes not only the fly title inserted in front, and numerous full-page illustrations which are an integral part of the book, but also three inserted plates; see *Illustrations*. Text, pp. 11–301: The Story of Louisiana, Chapters I–XII (titled); followed by data not Thompson's.]

ILLUSTRATIONS: Frontispiece with tissue guard, inserted as are three plates figured in the pagination: pp. [105–106], [151–152], and [277–278]; other full-page plates, with versos blank, are an integral part of the book. All are by L. J. Bridgman. A folding map of Louisiana is tipped in on p. 303. Each chapter is introduced with an illuminated initial accompanied by an illustration.

BINDING: Light brown mesh cloth. Front cover bears brown-stamped design of three radiant stars, the center one gilt-stamped above an eagle perched on an olive branch over shield of the United States, elaborated with ribbons and rules, incorporating title gilt-stamped in semi-circular arrangement: [ornament, gilt] THE [dot] STORY [dot] OF [tilde-like line over each O] [dot] THE [dot] STATES [ornament, gilt] | [the following brown-stamped below the design:] THE STORY OF [tilde-like line over each O] | LOUISIANA | [ornament] | MAURICE THOMPSON [the whole within a triple rule box, the center rule wider than the outer ones]. Spine brown-stamped except for series title and book title: [triple rule, center rule wider than others] | [series title embossed:] THE STORY [tilde-like line over O] | OF THE | STATES | [triple rule, center rule wider than others] | [radiant star ornament] | [title blind-stamped:] THE STORY [tilde-like line over O] | OF | LOUISIANA | [ornament] | MAURICE THOMPSON | [ornament] | LOTHROP | [triple rule, center rule wider]. Back cover blank.

End papers white calendered; no binder's leaf front or back.

PUBLICATION DATA: Deposited for copyright January 10, 1889. It had been noted in The Publishers' Weekly, December 1, 1888, as "just ready," but did not receive regular listing until January 19, 1889. Earliest review noted: The Critic, March 2nd. Price, $1.50.

NOTES: First edition as collated. This was third in the series, The Story of the States, edited by Elbridge S. Brooks.

The review in The Critic, March 2, 1889, approved the choice of the poet for the writing of this history, while mentioning numerous typographical errors. Thompson, replying in the same magazine, March 23rd, that he did not read the proofs, added that he "wrote no part of the book except that which appears in large type—namely the preface and story proper." His writing, therefore, stops at p. 301.

1892

Poems

POEMS | BY | MAURICE THOMPSON | [*publishers' emblem*] | BOSTON
AND NEW YORK | HOUGHTON, MIFFLIN AND COMPANY | The River-
side Press, Cambridge | 1892

COLLATION: [1–14]⁸. White laid paper. Leaf measures 7¾″ x 5″,
top edge gilt, other edges untrimmed.

End paper; binder's leaf; title-page, p. [i]; copyright notice dated
1892, statement: *All rights reserved.*, and imprint of the Riverside
Press and H. O. Houghton & Co., p. [ii]; dedication: *To My Wife*,
p. [iii]; proem beginning, "Songs of a mocking-bird," p. [iv]; table of
contents, pp. [v]–vii; blank, p. [viii]; text, pp. 1–216; binder's leaf; end
paper.

[Note: For text, pp. 1–216, see *Contents*.]

BINDING: Green silk-finished mesh cloth. Front cover gilt-stamped
with title and author's name in ornamental design within gilt frame:
[*ornament*] | POEMS | BY MAURICE | THOMPSON | [*ornament; all within
a single rule box*]. Spine gilt-stamped: POEMS | MAURICE | THOMPSON
| HOUGHTON | MIFFLIN [*dot*] & [*dot*] CO   Back cover blank.

End papers dark red on white; binder's leaf, slightly heavier than
book stock, front and back.

PUBLICATION DATA: Deposited for copyright February 12, 1892.
Noted as "ready today" in *The Publishers' Weekly*, February 13th, and
listed in issue of February 20th. Earliest review noted: *The Independent*, April 7th. Price, $1.50.

NOTES: First, and only edition as collated. No illustrations.

Charles Forster Smith, in his *Reminiscences and Sketches* (1908),
p. 135, said: "When the new volume of 'Poems' was coming out, he
[Thompson] wrote me: 'The first copy is for my wife, the next for you
and Baskervill.' "

CONTENTS: Numerous poems herein had earlier publication in
Songs of Fair Weather (1883), but the following are first appearances
in a Thompson book:*

---

*Thompson, when asked which one of his own poems he liked best, answered:

[Proem]

In Captivity   *The Independent*, April 4, 1889 (with title: A Song of the Mocking-Bird [In Captivity])

To an English Nightingale   *The Century Magazine*, August, 1884 (with title: A Song of the Mocking-Bird [Dedicated to an English Nightingale])*

To an English Skylark   *The Century Magazine*, September, 1886 (with title: A Song of the Mocking-Bird [Dedicated to an English Sky-Lark])

Before Sunrise   *The Century Magazine*, February, 1888 (with title: A Song of the Mocking-Bird [Before Sunrise])

To Provence

To Sappho   *The Independent*, August 25, 1887 (with title: The Song of the Mocking-Bird [To Sappho])

An Early Bluebird [hyphenated in table of contents: *Blue-Bird*] *The Independent*, April 1, 1886†

Ho, for the Kankakee! [*Ho! for the Kankakee* in table of contents] *The Manhattan*, May, 1884; *The* (Indianapolis) *Saturday Herald*, April 19, 1884‡

Spring's Torch-Bearer   *The Independent*, April 30, 1891

The Assault   *The Indianapolis News*, March 12, 1891 (untitled); *The Critic*, March 7, 1891§

Ode—Spring

Lazing   *The Indianapolis Journal*, May 2, 1874

To a Wild Flower   *Lippincott's Magazine of Literature and Science*, June, 1874

A Breath of Morn   *The Independent*, August 27, 1891

Seven Gold Reeds   *Harper's New Monthly Magazine*, March, 1885; *The Indianapolis Journal*, February 21, 1885

The Orphic Legacy   *The Independent*, November 29, 1883

Pan in the Orchard   *The Indianapolis Journal*, October 23, 1891

"My 'Songs of a Mocking-Bird' which are the first four pieces in my latest volume of poems published by Houghton, Mifflin & Co., Boston."—*The Dawn*, December 7, 1893, p. 7.

*Part, entitled, "Song of the Mocking Bird" was reprinted in *The Indianapolis Journal*, October 13, 1895.

†Included in *An American Anthology*, edited by Edmund C. Stedman (1900), and *Library of Southern Literature*, Vol. XII (1910). Title in manuscript, "An Early Blue Bird."

‡Criticism of the poem, "Ho, for the Kankakee!," appeared in *The* (Indianapolis) *Saturday Herald*, April 26 and May 3; Thompson's reply was published May 10, 1884, under caption, "About 'Tarns.'"

§Reprinted in *America*, April 2, 1891.

Out of the South   *The Independent,* August 7, 1890*

A Creole Slave-Song   *The Independent,* May 14, 1885†

A Morning Prayer   *The Independent,* September 13, 1888

Full-fledged   *The Independent,* December 11, 1884

The Final Thought   *The Independent,* December 16, 1886

Nectar and Ambrosia   *The Independent,* January 10, 1884; *The Crawfordsville Journal,* January 26, 1884‡

A Dream of Romance   *The Independent,* May 28, 1891

To a Realist   *The Independent,* November 22, 1888

America§

An Address   *The American Magazine,* October, 1887; *The Indianapolis Journal,* September 27, 1887 (with title in both: Rebel or Loyalist?)||

An Incident of War   *The Independent,* May 26, 1887¶

To the South   *The Independent,* September 11, 1884; *The Indianapolis Journal,* September 21, 1884

Our Legend   *The American Magazine,* August, 1887; *The Terre Haute Express,* July 17, 1887

A Taunt   *The Atlantic Monthly,* September, 1885

Morning Dew   *The Independent,* May 8, 1884

Old Rochon

A Study for the Critics   *Lippincott's Magazine of Popular Literature and Science,* September, 1874

The Gold-Bird   *The Independent,* May 14, 1874

The Kingfisher   *Harper's New Monthly Magazine,* May 1874; *The Indianapolis Journal,* April 21, 1874

Farewell   *Lippincott's Magazine of Popular Literature and Science,* December, 1874£

---

*Later included in *Library of Southern Literature,* Vol. XII (1910).

†"A Creole Slave-Song" appeared in *An American Anthology,* edited by Edmund C. Stedman (1900).

‡"Nectar and Ambrosia" was later included in *Library of Southern Literature,* Vol. XII (1910).

§Last two stanzas were reprinted in *The Indianapolis Star,* December 26, 1915.

||Part of this "Address" by an ex-Confederate soldier to the Grand Army of the Republic was quoted in *Reminiscences and Sketches,* by Charles Forster Smith (1908), p. 115, and the second part in *The Indianapolis Star,* December 26, 1915.

¶Later included in *Ballads of American Bravery,* edited by Clinton Scollard (1900).

£"Farewell" appeared later in *A Treasury of American Verse,* by Walter Larned (1897).

1893

The King of Honey Island

THE | KING OF HONEY ISLAND. | A Novel. | BY | MAURICE THOMP-
SON, | Author of "Mordbank," "The Fighting at Point Rose," "A
| Tallahassee Girl," "His Second Campaign," | "Hoosier Mosaics,"
etc. | WITH ILLUSTRATIONS BY H. M. EATON. | NEW YORK: | ROBERT
BONNER'S SONS, | 1893.

COLLATION: [1–22]⁸. White wove paper. Leaf measures 7¾" x
5½", all edges trimmed.

End paper; blank, pp. [1–2]; fly title, p. [3]; blank, p. [4]; frontispiece with tissue guard, inserted; title-page, p. [5]; copyright notice
with final date 1893, and statement: (*All rights reserved.*), p. [6]; text,
pp. 7–343; publishers' advertisements, pp. [344–350]; blank, pp. [351–
352]; end paper.

[Note: For text, pp. 7–343, see *Contents*.]

ILLUSTRATIONS: Frontispiece with tissue guard, inserted as are
plates facing pp. 38, 66, and 92; all are by H. M. Eaton. The chapters
bear decorative headpieces with the exception of Chapters XII, XIII,
XIX, XX, XXI, XXIII, XXIV, XXVI, XXVII, XXVIII, XXX, which
follow preceding chapter with only a decorative rule between. Chapter I has an illuminated initial.

BINDING: Light blue silk-finished mesh cloth. Front cover gilt-
stamped: KING | OF | HONEY | ISLAND [*title within a dark blue and gilt-
stamped decorative panel*]. Spine gilt-stamped: THE | KING OF | HONEY
| ISLAND [*title within a gilt-stamped panel*] | MAURICE | THOMPSON |
ROBERT BONNER'S | SONS   Back cover blank.

End papers tan flowered and screened on white. No binder's leaf,
front or back.

[Note: Issued simultaneously in cloth, and, wrappers; see *post* 209.]

PUBLICATION DATA: Copyrighted March 3, 1893. Listed in *The
Publishers' Weekly*, March 11th. Price, cloth, $1.00*; paper, 50¢.

NOTES: First edition as collated. The cloth copies bear no mention

*Listed in *The Publishers' Weekly*, March 21, 1893, at $1.00; advertised in
same, March 25th, at $1.50.

of a "series" or "library" as do the wrapped ones: *The Choice Series* and *Ledger Library*. All were deposited for copyright the same day. For description of the paper editions see below.

A "new issue" by George D. Hurst was published in *The Ambrosial Library for Every-Day Reading* [No. 2], in 1895.

The book was reprinted by G. W. Dillingham Co., New York, 1896, bound in gray cloth, white-stamped; two issues noted: copyright page with, and without imprint of the Press of the New York Ledger. Illustrations in the former are tinted orange, and the plate that appeared facing p. 66 in the first edition here faces p. 32. Illustrations in those lacking the imprint are untinted. Dillingham also issued the book in red cloth, leaf trimmed to 7¼″ x 4⅞″; type shows wear; probably the "New Edition" listed in *The Publishers' Weekly*, March 2, 1901.

Street & Smith published it in a paper edition, August 8, 1904; again, as No. 508 in *The Eagle Series*, February 19, 1907, in colored, pictorial white wrappers.

In England it was published by J. Henderson in the *Anglo-American Library*, August, 1893.

CONTENTS: The King of Honey Island, Chapters I–XXX (titled), earlier a serial in *The New York Ledger*, September 3–December 3, 1892.

1893
The King of Honey Island
(Bonner's Choice Series No. 79)

THE | KING OF HONEY ISLAND. | A Novel. | BY | MAURICE THOMPSON, | Author of "Mordbank," "The Fighting at Point Rose," "A | Tallahassee Girl," "His Second Campaign," | "Hoosier Mosaics," etc. | WITH ILLUSTRATIONS BY H. M. EATON. | NEW YORK: | ROBERT BONNER'S SONS, | PUBLISHERS. | [*rule*] | THE CHOICE SERIES: ISSUED SEMI-MONTHLY. SUBSCRIPTION PRICE, TWELVE DOLLARS PER ANNUM. NO. 79, | FEBRUARY 15, 1893. ENTERED AT THE NEW YORK, N. Y., POST OFFICE AS SECOND CLASS MAIL MATTER.

PAGINATION: Advertisements, pp. [1–2]; fly title, p. [3]; blank, p. [4]; title-page, p. [5]; copyright notice with final date 1893, and statement, (*All rights reserved.*), p. [6]; text, pp. 7–343; advertisements, pp. [344–352].

[Note: For text, pp. 7–343, see *ante* 209.]

BINDING: White wrappers. Front cover printed in sepia and red: The King of | Honey Island [*title in red*] | By Maurice Thompson, | Author of "The Fighting at Point Rose," etc. | ILLUSTRATED BY H. M. EATON. [*in red*] | [*illustration, signed, boxed*] | NEW YORK: | ROBERT BONNER'S SONS, [*in red*] | PUBLISHERS. Spine missing in only copy located, which is rebound with wrappers present. Back cover bears list, in sepia, of *The Choice Series*, including this title as No. 79. Inside front cover bears advertisement in sepia of *Zina's Awaking;* inside back, of *Beatrix Rohan.*

NOTES: No illustrations. Issued simultaneously with the cloth-bound copies (see *ante* 208). It appeared at the same time, too, as *Bonner's Ledger Library*, No. 79, the title-page differing only in the series name; wrappers same except for advertisements: the back cover advertises Pears' soap; inside front lists the *Ledger Library*, including this title as No. 79; inside back lists *The Popular Series*. In all three the text is the same, as are advertisements on pp. [344–351]. In both wrappered issues the same advertisements appear on leaf preceding fly title.

1893

The Ethics of Literary Art

THE | ETHICS OF LITERARY ART | THE CAREW LECTURES | FOR 1893 | HARTFORD THEOLOGICAL SEMINARY | BY | MAURICE THOMPSON | Author of "A Tallahassee Girl," "Sylvan Secrets," | "Songs of Fair Weather," "Poems," etc. | [*ornament*] | HARTFORD, CONN. | Hartford Seminary Press | 1893

COLLATION: [1]–11^4, one unsigned leaf. White wove paper. Leaf measures 7$\frac{5}{16}$" x 5$\frac{1}{8}$", top edge gilt, other edges trimmed.

End paper; binder's leaf; fly title, p. [1]; blank, p. [2]; title-page, p. [3]; copyright notice dated 1893, and imprint of the Case, Lockwood & Brainard Co., p. [4]; *Author's Note* (so identified in running head) signed *M.T.* and dated August, 1893, pp. [5]–6; text, pp. [7]–89 (p. 89 on inserted leaf, with publisher's list on verso); binder's leaf; end paper.

[Note: For text, pp. (7)–89, see *Contents.*]

ILLUSTRATIONS: None. An ornament appears above text on p. [5], and an illuminated initial on p. [7].

BINDING: Dark blue silk-finished mesh cloth. Front cover blind-stamped: The Ethics of Literary Art | Maurice Thompson [*all within a blind-stamped single rule box*]. Spine bears a paper label printed as follows: THE ETHICS | OF | LITERARY ART | [*ornament*] | THOMPSON Back cover blank.

End papers white pebbled; binder's leaves of book stock, conjugates pasted under lining papers, front and back.

PUBLICATION DATA: Listed in *The Publishers' Weekly*, November 11, 1893. Deposited in the Copyright Office November 23rd. Price, $1.00.

[Note: Silver Burdett Company acted as consignees of the book not publishers of it.]

NOTES: First edition as collated. Thompson explained in the "Author's Note": "The matter of the following pages was delivered in three lectures, and it will not be hard for the reader to find the lines of division. A different plan might have been followed had my purpose originally been a book. Still I have not felt it necessary to recast any part of the work, and in arbitrarily dividing my discussion into three parts, it came easy to make Conception, Composition, and Expression stand, in the order named, as themes for successive treatment."

The subject of these talks delivered May 15, 16, and 17, 1893, in the Carew course at the Hartford Theological Seminary, was described in an advance notice in *The Hartford Times*, May 13, 1893, as "The Moral Principles Characteristic of True Literary Art." Only one lecture, the first, appeared in print before book publication. The second lecture, "The Ethics of Composition," was reviewed in both the *Hartford Courant* and *Times*, May 17th; the third and last, "The Ethics of Expression," was briefly reviewed in the *Hartford Courant*, May 18th; his own words not quoted.

CONTENTS: The Ethics of Literary Art, in three untitled and unnumbered parts; first part, (pp. [7]–37), earlier in *The Hartford Seminary Record*, June, 1893 (with title: The Ethics of Conception). The second part (second lecture) ends and last part begins on p. 65.*

---

*Part of the second lecture (pp. 48–56) appeared later with title, "The Romance of Composition," in *Library of Southern Literature*, Vol. XII (1910). Extracts from the whole, being Thompson's comments on Shelley, Lord Byron, Scott, and Wordsworth, were included in *The Library of Literary Criticism of English and American Authors*, edited by Charles W. Moulton, Vols. 4 and 5 (1902).

1894
Lincoln's Grave

LINCOLN'S | GRAVE [*foregoing in red*] | BY | MAURICE | THOMPSON | [*publishers' emblem, fan-shaped,* * *intercepting date:*] 18 [*point of the emblem*] 94 | CAMBRIDGE | AND CHICAGO | [*the following in red:*] STONE | AND | KIMBALL

[Note: All boxed within a floral panel which is within a decorative box. The panel bears artist's initials at lower right: *G. H.* (George H. Hallowell).]

COLLATION: [1]⁸ (plus one unsigned leaf), [2-5]⁴. White laid paper. Leaf measures 6¹³⁄₁₆" x 4⅜", top edge gilt, other edges untrimmed.

End paper; binder's sheet; fly title, p. [i]; blank, p. [ii]; title-page, inserted, its verso bearing copyright notice dated 1894; limitation notice, p. [iii]; blank, p. [iv]; dedication to Phi Beta Kappa of Harvard College, p. [v]; blank, p. [vi]; proem, dated 1893, p. [vii]; blank, p. [viii]; three words in Greek, p. [ix]; blank, p. [x]; text, pp. [1-36]; colophon of John Wilson & Son, University Press, p. [37]; blank, p. [38]; binder's sheet; end paper.

[Note: Not paginated. For text, pp. (1-36), see *Contents.*]

BINDING: Vellum, brown silk ties. Front and back covers blank. Spine gilt-stamped, reading from bottom to top: STONE & KIMBALL   A POEM BY MAURICE THOMPSON

End papers same as book stock; binder's sheet front and back.

Also, "secondary bindings"† of orange buckram, and, gray boards with paper label on spine. See *Notes* for description of large paper copies.

PUBLICATION DATA: Copyrighted February 19, 1894 (colophon gives date of printing as January, 1894). Listed in *The Publishers' Weekly*, April 21, 1894. Earliest review noted: *The Indianapolis News*, June 27, 1894. Price of limited edition of 450 copies, $1.25; large paper edition of 50 copies, $3.50.

---

*"Publishers Devices, No. 2"; see *A History of Stone & Kimball and Herbert S. Stone & Co.*, by Sidney Kramer (1940), p. 194.

†Kramer No. 10, pp. 201-202.

NOTES: Issued in a limited edition of 450 copies as collated. Also, simultaneously, a large paper edition (leaf 8¼" x 5⅛"), limited to 50 numbered copies, bound in vellum, spine gilt-stamped, was issued in a marbled paper slipcase.

No illustrations. Besides the orange buckram binding on the limited edition there was another "secondary binding" of gray boards with white paper shelfback located in two states: spine gilt-stamped,* and, with a leather label. Title-page is an insert in all copies, bearing publishers' address as Cambridge and Chicago (none found with "Cambridge imprint only," as erroneously described in *Merle Johnson's American First Editions* [1942]).

CONTENTS: Lincoln's Grave, Stanzas I–XXXVI. Read before Phi Beta Kappa of Harvard College, June, 1893. Part of the poem, Stanzas XVII–XX, earlier appeared in *The Indianapolis News,* July 5, 1893, and in *The Dawn* (Indianapolis High School, now Shortridge), December 7, 1893.†

---

*A copy, No. 2 of the gray boards with white paper shelfback, gilt-stamped, inscribed to General Lewis Wallace, May 23, 1894, is in the Eagle Crest Library.

†Selections from the poem have been frequently reprinted. A review of the book in *The Independent,* July 19, 1894, quoted the opening lines and four stanzas; one stanza was printed in *The Dial,* February 1, 1895. It appeared in the following anthologies: part, with title, "At Lincoln's Grave," in *Poets and Poetry of Indiana,* edited by Benj. S. Parker & Enos B. Heiney (1900); part, "A Prophecy," in *An American Anthology,* edited by Edmund C. Stedman (1900); part in *The Library of Literary Criticism of English and American Authors,* edited by Charles W. Moulton, Vol. 6 (1904); *Lincoln's Birthday* (*Our American Holiday Series*) edited by Robert H. Schauffler (1909); part in *The Poetic New-World* by L. H. Humphrey (1910); part, with title, "At Lincoln's Grave," in *The Praise of Lincoln,* by A. Dallas Williams (1911); part, with title, "Lincoln," in *Pieces for Every Day the Schools Celebrate,* by Norma H. Deming & Katharine I. Bemis (1921; 1922; 1931; 1939); part, with title, "He Is Not Dead," in *Poems for Special Days and Occasions,* compiled by Thomas C. Clark (1930); part, with title, "At Lincoln's Grave," in *Great Americans as Seen by the Poets,* by Burton E. Stevenson (1933).

1895
The Ocala Boy

THE OCALA BOY | A STORY OF FLORIDA TOWN | AND FOREST | BY | MAURICE THOMPSON | AUTHOR OF "A TALLAHASSEE GIRL," "THE COLN'S GRAVE," ETC. | [*rule*] | WITH ILLUSTRATIONS BY E. W. STORY OF LOUI- | SIANA," "BY WAYS AND BIRD NOTES," "AT | LIN-KEMBLE | [*rule*] | BOSTON | LOTHROP PUBLISHING COMPANY | 1895

COLLATION: [1–14]⁸. White wove paper. Leaf measures 7¹⁄₁₆" x 4¾", all edges trimmed.

End paper; blank, pp. [1–4]; frontispiece with tissue guard, inserted; title-page, p. [5]; copyright notice dated 1895, statement: *All rights reserved.*, and imprint of C. J. Peters & Son, Boston, p. [6]; table of contents, p.[7]; blank, p. [8]; half-title, p. [9]; blank, p. [10]; text, pp. 9–225 (should be 11–227; four of the plates are figured in the pagination); blank, pp. [228–232]; end paper.*

[Note: Text, pp. 9–225 (*sic*): The Ocala Boy, Chapters I–XI (titled).]

ILLUSTRATIONS: Frontispiece with tissue guard, inserted as are plates facing pp. 16, 78, 110, 138, and 182; all are by Edward Windsor Kemble; the latter four are figured in the pagination.

BINDING: Gray, red, and, light green mesh cloth; also, dark green with red cloth imposed upon the upper portion. The front cover bears black-stamped on the upper portion a design of two boys holding between them a shield which bears the title: THE | OCALA | BOY | [*below the shield the author's name:*] MAURICE THOMPSON [*all within a double rule box*]. Spine black-stamped on the upper portion: THE | OCALA | BOY | THOMPSON | [*decorative design*] | [*at foot, black-stamped:*] LOTHROP Back cover blank.

End papers white wove; no binder's leaf front or back.

PUBLICATION DATA: Deposited in the Copyright Office, October 7, 1895. Noted in *The Publishers' Weekly*, September 7, 1895: "Will publish next week"; advertised in same, September 14th: "Will issue at once", and on October 5th described as "just published." Earliest review noted: *The Independent*, November 7, 1895. Price, $1.00.

---

*Also noted with last leaf of last signature used as lining paper.

NOTES: First edition as collated. Priority in bindings unestablished. One copy, in solid color binding,* has been noted with no end paper in back but last leaf of last signature used as lining paper; the copyright deposit copy has the true end paper; is bound in solid color.

Type imperfections in folios *87* and *141;* same in all copies.

1898

Stories of Indiana

STORIES OF INDIANA | BY | MAURICE THOMPSON | [*publisher's emblem*] | NEW YORK [*ornament formed of four dots*] CINCINNATI [*ornament formed of four dots*] CHICAGO | AMERICAN BOOK COMPANY | 1898

COLLATION: [1]–19⁸. White calendered paper. Leaf measures 7⁵⁄₁₆″ x 5¹⁄₁₆″, all edges trimmed.

End paper; binder's leaf; title-page, p. [1]; copyright notice dated 1898, title, and symbol, *E. P. 1*, p. [2]; *Preface*, pp. 3–4; table of contents, pp. 5–6; text, pp. 7–296; publisher's advertisements, pp. [297–304]; binder's leaf; end paper.

[Note: Text, pp. 7–296: The Very First Inhabitants; The First Human Inhabitants; Traits and Habits of Wild Indians; Early Explorers; Early French Life in Indiana Pontiac (dash before *Pontiac* in table of contents); Clarke's Capture of Fort (*Ft.* in table of contents) Vincennes, and Other Incidents; Tecumseh—The Prophet—Tippecanoe; A Daring Man—Narrow Escapes; An Itinerant Pioneer Preacher; Flatboat Days; A Great Man's Boyhood and Youth; Black and White; A Genial Hermit; The Romance of New Harmony; A Distinguished Oddity; Frontier Pests and Afflictions; Characteristic Incidents and Anecdotes; The Period of Canals and Plank Roads; The Birth and Growth of Free Public Schools; A Raid into Indiana; Richard Jordan Gatling; The Writers of Indiana; The Latest Developments in Indiana.]

ILLUSTRATIONS: Text illustrations throughout the book. Ornamental rule below book title on p. 7.

BINDING: Gray mesh cloth. Front cover dark blue-stamped: [*ornament*] STORIES [*ornament*] OF [*ornament*] | [*ornament*] INDIANA [*ornament*] | [*foregoing has an ornamental design on each side, joined by a*

*In Indiana State Library.

chain of bell-like ornaments from which hangs a wreath of similar de-sign enclosing the author's name:] THOMPSON [*all within a single rule box*]. Spine dark blue-stamped: [*wide decorative border*] | STORIES | OF | INDIANA | [*narrow ornamental border*] | THOMPSON | [*rule*] | AMERICAN | BOOK | COMPANY   Back cover bears dark blue-stamped sil-houette of the state of Indiana within a wreath formed of bell-like orna-ments; all within a single rule box.

End papers white wove; binder's leaf front and back.

PUBLICATION DATA: Deposited for copyright June 21, 1898. Listed in *The Publishers' Weekly*, July 2, 1898. Earliest review noted: *The Indianapolis News*, November 2, 1898. Price, 60¢.

NOTES: First edition bears symbol on copyright page, E. P. 1

The broken 8 in folio, p. 81, was not remedied until within the sixth edition; some of the copies with E. P. 6 on copyright page contain its replacement.

The gathering of material for this book led to the writing of *Alice of Old Vincennes,* according to Lee Burns (see *post* 225). The appearance of William H. English, *Conquest of the Country Northwest of the River Ohio,* in 1896, may have given Thompson historical background for both these books.

1898

Stories of the Cherokee Hills

STORIES OF | THE CHEROKEE HILLS | BY | MAURICE THOMPSON | [*publishers' emblem*] | BOSTON AND NEW YORK | HOUGHTON, MIFF-LIN AND COMPANY | The Riverside Press, Cambridge | 1898

COLLATION: [1]⁴, [2–17]⁸. White laid paper. Leaf measures 7⁵⁄₁₆″ x 4⅞″, all edges trimmed.

End paper; binder's leaf; blank, p. [i]; list of books by the author, p. [ii]; frontispiece with tissue guard, inserted; title-page, p. [iii]; copy-right notice dated 1898, p. [iv]; table of contents, p. [v]; blank, p. [vi]; list of illustrations, p. [vii]; blank, p. [viii]; text, pp. [1]–255; pub-lishers' imprint, p. [256]; binder's leaf; end paper.

[Note: For text, pp. (1)–255, see *Contents.*]

ILLUSTRATIONS: Frontispiece with tissue guard, inserted as are plates facing pp. 48, 102, 116, 134, 160, 166, 178. All are in black and white, drawn by Edward Windsor Kemble.

BINDING: Light green mesh cloth. Front cover bears an elaborate floral design stamped in dark green, white, and gilt, including a center panel within which is gilt-stamped: STORIES | OF THE [*dark green and gilt-stamped leaf ornament on each side of foregoing two lines; rule under O's*] | CHEROKEE HILLS [*rule under* O] | MAURICE THOMPSON Spine gilt-stamped: STORIES [*rule under* O] | OF THE | CHEROKEE [*rule under* O] | HILLS | [*floral design stamped in dark green, white, and gilt*] | M [*dot*] THOMPSON | HOUGHTON | MIFFLIN [*dot*] & [*dot*] CO. Back cover blank.

End papers similar to, slightly heavier than book stock; binder's leaf front and back.

PUBLICATION DATA: Deposited in the Copyright Office October 4, 1898. Advertised in *The Publishers' Weekly*, October 1st for October 8th publication; listed October 15th. Price, $1.50.

NOTES: First edition as collated. Reissued by Houghton, Mifflin with date, 1900 on the title-page.

The short stories in this collection were drawn from Thompson's own boyhood experiences in the South, his life in the Confederate Army, and his observations of the South immediately after the Civil War. He discussed them in 1890 in unpublished letters to R. W. Gilder of *Century*, preserved in the New York Public Library.

CONTENTS: The first story, written for the book, is in the nature of a lengthy foreword.

Color-Line Jocundities
Ben and Judas   *The Century Magazine*, October, 1889
Hodson's Hide-Out   *The Century Magazine*, March, 1885*
Rudgis and Grim   *The Century Magazine*, July, 1892†
A Race Romance   *The Century Magazine*, April, 1891
A Dusky Genius   *The Century Magazine*, April, 1890‡

---

*Described in the magazine as "A transcript from Sand Mountain." *The Indianapolis News*, April 10, 1885, carried a Thompson story, uncollected, entitled, "A Sand Mountain Wedding." Possibly more with the same background appeared under other titles, in other newspapers.

The author had trouble himself with the spelling of "Hodson": in a letter to R. W. Gilder, October 25, 1886, he referred to "Hodkin's Hide-out" and, on November 6th, to "Hodgson's Hide-out" (letters in the New York Public Library).

†Included in *Best Things from American Literature*, edited by Irving Bacheller (1899).

‡"A Dusky Genius" impressed many readers as factual, which it was not; it brought Thompson more letters than any story he ever wrote, he said, April 22, 1890, in a letter to R. W. Gilder, in the New York Public Library.

The Balance of Power   *Harper's* [Monthly] *Magazine, April,* 1895*

1900

My Winter Garden

My Winter Garden | A NATURE-LOVER UNDER | SOUTHERN SKIES | [*ornament*] | BY | MAURICE THOMPSON | [*publisher's emblem*] | New York | The Century Co. | 1900

COLLATION: [*]⁸, 1–19⁸. White laid paper. Leaf measures 7⅝″ x 5¼″, top edge gilt, other edges untrimmed.

End paper; blank, pp. [i–ii] (leaf pasted under the lining paper, its conjugate the half-title); fly title, p. [iii]; blank, p. [iv]; title-page, p. [v]; copyright notice dated 1900, and imprint of the De Vinne Press, p. [vi]; dedication to his wife, Alice Lee, p. vii; blank, p. [viii]; *Preface*, pp. ix–xii; table of contents, p. xiii; blank, p. [xiv]; half-title, p. [xv]; blank, p. [xvi]; text, pp. 1–302 (conjugate of pp. 289–290 pasted under back lining paper); end paper.

[Note: For text, pp. 1–302, see *Contents*.]

ILLUSTRATIONS: Colored frontispiece by Frank Hill, with tissue guard, inserted.

BINDING: Gray silk-finished mesh cloth. Front cover bears a design of intertwined trees stamped in dark green, gilt, and pale pink, below which is gilt-stamped: My | Winter Garden | Maurice Thompson [*all within a gilt-stamped single rule box*]. Spine is gilt-stamped: My | Winter | Garden [*tail of the initial extends under the word*] | Maurice | Thompson | The | Century | Co [*wave rule under* o]. Back cover blank.

End papers same as book stock; no binder's leaf front or back.

PUBLICATION DATA: Deposited in the Copyright Office September 17, 1900. Listed in *The Publishers' Weekly,* November 10th. Price, $1.50.

---

*Later collected in *Southern Lights and Shadows*, edited by William Dean Howells & Henry Mills Alden (1907). The story includes "De Sassafras Bloom" and other negro songs, untitled, which may, or may not be original Thompson poems; one of them appeared as "Plantation Song" in *The Indianapolis Journal*, March 31, 1895, ascribed to him.

NOTES: First edition as collated. Reissued with date 1902 on the title-page.

CONTENTS: A group of essays here first collected. Two of them have not been found in any earlier printings; they may have been part of the manuscript of "Toxophilus in Arcadia," a long article which *The Century Magazine* published, greatly cut down, as "In the Woods with the Bow," herein collected; see *post* 248*n*.*

My Winter Garden | An Idyl of the Gulf Coast   *The Century Magazine*, November 1900 (with title: My Midwinter Garden)†

Paradise Circle

Where the Mocking-Bird Sings [in running title *bird* (not *Bird*)]
   Cosmopolitan, December 1892

A Poet of the Poor   *The Independent*, December 15, 1892

Shrike-Notes | With a Buffon Interlude   *The Independent*, May 26, 1898 (part, with title: Recent Shrike-Notes)

The Touch of Inspiration   *The Independent*, February 5, 1891

A Marsh-Land Incident [in running title *land* (not *Land*)]   *The Independent*, January 27, 1898

Art and Money   *The Independent*, December 14, 1899

Return to Nature   *The Independent*, June 10, 1897 (with title: To Return to Nature)

By a Woodland Spring   *The Independent*, June 13, 1895

A Swamp Beauty   *The Independent*, March 1, 1900

In the Woods with the Bow   *The Century Magazine*, August 1900

Under a Dogwood with Montaigne‡   *The Independent*, April 21, 1898 (part, with title: Montaigne the Provincial Belletrist); March 31, 1898 (part, with title: Montaigne in His Study); December 9, 1897 (part, with title: Montaigne's Literary Recipe); March 10, 1898 (part, with title: Montaigne's Philosophy); February 10, 1898 (part, with title: Montaigne's Materials)

---

*"Archery Excerpts" from *My Winter Garden*, selected by H. H. McChesney, were later published in *The Archery Review*, August-September, 1932.

†Written for *Century*, designed as a "fit initial chapter for the little book we have discussed . . ." Letter to R. W. Gilder, January 4, 1900. This, with other letters to Gilder on the subject, is in the New York Public Library.

‡Thompson had written an essay on Montaigne, published in *The Chap-Book*, May 1, 1895, under the title, "Nuts from Perigord"; it is not contained in *My Winter Garden*.

1900

Alice of Old Vincennes

Alice of Old Vincennes [red] | by | Maurice Thompson | ILLUS-
TRATIONS BY | F. C. YOHN | INDIANAPOLIS | THE BOWEN-MERRILL
COMPANY | PUBLISHERS

COLLATION: [1]⁴ (plus two unsigned leaves), [2–28]⁸. White laid
paper, ⅞" (scant) between wire marks. Leaf measures 7⁷⁄₁₆" x 4¹⁵⁄₁₆",
all edges trimmed.

Blank, pp. [i–ii] (leaf used as lining paper, its conjugate the half-
title); fly title, p. [iii]; blank, p. [iv]; frontispiece with tissue guard, inserted; title-page, p. [v]; copyright notice dated 1900, statement: *All
Rights Reserved,* and imprint of Braunworth, Munn & Barber, p. [vi];
dedication to *M. Placide Valcour, M.D., Ph. D., LL. D.,* dated July,
1900, inserted; table of contents, inserted; half-title, p. [vii]; blank, p.
[viii]; text, pp. 1–419; blank, p. [420]; divisional half-title: *A List Of
Publications Of* | *The Bowen-Merrill Co.,* p. [421]; notice, boxed, of
one quarter million copies of *When Knighthood Was in Flower,* p.
[422]; advertisements, pp. [423–432]; end paper.
[Note: Text, pp. 1–419: Alice of Old Vincennes, Chapters I–
XXIII (titled).*]

ILLUSTRATIONS: Colored frontispiece with tissue guard, inserted
as are black and white plates facing pp. 10, 44, 130, 236, and 374; all
are by F. C. Yohn.

BINDING: Light blue, and, green mesh cloth. Front cover bears a
panel stamped in gilt, light tan, blue, and light green, depicting a fort
[Sackville], below which is gilt-stamped: ALICE OF OLD | VINCENNES |
[the following brown-stamped:] by MAURICE THOMPSON [*all within a
bright blue parallel rule box*]. Spine gilt-stamped: ALICE | of | OLD |
VINCENNES | [*rule*] | MAURICE | THOMPSON | [*design in gilt and brown*

---

*Part of Chapter I was reprinted in *Library of Southern Literature,* Vol. XII
(1910), with title, "Under the Cherry Tree." A selection from Chapter XX appeared in *New Pieces That Will Take Prizes,* by Harriet Blackstone (1926), as
"Alice's Flag."

of a crossed sword and tomahawk] | BOWEN- | MERRILL Back cover blank.*

No end paper in front; in back, of laid paper 1¼" between wire marks (book stock, ⅞"); no binder's leaf front or back (for variants, see *Notes* below).

PUBLICATION DATA: Deposited for copyright September 24, 1900. Advance copies were available as early as September 5th. Earliest reviews noted: *The Independent*, October 18th; *The Indianapolis Press*, October 23rd; and *The Critic*, October, 1900. *The Crawfordsville Journal*, September 14th, carried a notice of it, from an advance copy. Price, $1.50.

NOTES: The first issue consisted of copies called "advance" by the author, "special" by the publishers, but so many were distributed that have the running head in bold-faced capitals that collation as a first edition, first issue, has seemed indicated (some hastily bound and badly cracked copies have defied signature detection and appear to be truly "advance," not a trade issue). A change in the running head was made before the *Acknowledgment* was added to verso of last page of text:

> State 1: Running head in bold-faced capitals (later, light-faced upper and lower case)
>
> Verso of last page of text blank (later, bears *Acknowledgment*)
>
> Sigs. [1]⁴ (plus two unsigned leaves, carrying dedication and table of contents), [2–28]⁸ (later, [1–28]⁸); advertisements in back followed by end paper (later, final signature has two blank leaves following advertisements)
>
> Book stock laid paper with ⅞" (scant) between wire marks (later, ¾")
>
> Leaf measures 7⅟₁₆" x 4¹⁵⁄₁₆" (later, 7⅜" x 4⅞")
>
> Folio present on first page of text (later, dropped)
>
> Divisional half-title, p. [421], reads: *A List Of Publications* . . . (later, *A List Of Recent Fiction* . . .)
>
> P. [428], listing of Riley's *The Golden Year* complete (later, *Year* imperfect)
>
> State 2: Running heads in upper and lower case (earlier, all capitals)

---

*The dust wrapper on the first-state copy in the Indiana State Library originally must have accompanied a later issue, since it reprints newspaper comments based on review copies.

Verso of last page of text blank as in *State* 1

First signature gathered in 8 (plus one unsigned leaf; the title-page being an insert); end paper and binder's leaf present in front followed by one blank leaf (earlier, no free blank before fly title, first leaf being used as lining paper); advertisements in back followed by two blank leaves before end paper (earlier, end paper follows advertisements)

Book stock same as, or similar to *State* 1

Leaf measures 7⅜" x 4⅞" (earlier, 7⁷⁄₁₆" x 4¹⁵⁄₁₆")

Folio present on first page of text as in *State* 1

Divisional half-title, p. [421], same as in *State* 1

P. [428], listing of Riley's *The Golden Year* has *Year* imperfect (earlier, perfect)

State 3: Same as *State* 2, but *Acknowledgment* present on verso of last page of text (earlier, page blank), and advertisements changed as well as the divisional half-title which now reads: *A List Of Recent Fiction* . . . (earlier, *A List Of Publications* . . .); pp. [423–429] advertise a separate book on each page (earlier, many titles in an alphabetical catalogue); leaf advertising *The Redemption of David Corson* and *Sweepers of the Sea* still present, but on pp. [423–424] (earlier, [431–432])

State 4: Same as *State* 3, but book stock is laid paper with ¾" between wire marks (earlier, ⅞" [scant])

State 5: Same as *State* 4, but folio dropped from first page of text, and leaf trimmed to 7⅜" x 4¾".

A copy, probably later, advertises a book first published in 1901, George Horton's *Like Another Helen,* and has other changes within the last signature. Because the final gathering was a separate publishers' catalogue, many variations in advertisements were possible within any issue. The absence of folio on first page of text is a point identifying a copy as definitely *State* 5 or later; a change within advertisements beyond above mention indicates probably later than *State* 5.

An advance copy with points of earliest issue, lacking illustrations, bears the following letter from the author tipped in*:

"Dear Mr. Greene:

"My new novel 'Alice of Old Vincennes' is just coming from the press, and I send you the advance copy as a little token of my vast and

---

*In the Crawfordsville Public Library.

never ending determination to bore my friends with my writings. I hope that you'll like the story for its loyalty to Indiana and the great West, if not for the interest that I tried to put into the dramatic action.

"Yours most sincerely

"Maurice Thompson

"5 September 1900."

Another copy* is stamped on lining paper, first free leaf, and title-page: *Salesman's Sample Copy,* and bears a printed slip pasted on the lining paper which reads: *This Special Copy Of | Alice Of Old Vin-cennes | Sent In Advance Of Publication | Is Printed With The | Compliments Of | The Author And Publishers.* It is similar to the copy collated.

The folio on first page of text, dropped during one or more print-ings, was replaced before 1904, since plates used by Grosset & Dunlap contain it.

Type defects are present even in the earliest state. To name just one of many examples: in table of contents, second *I* in *II* broken. Late is-sues show wear in type from the many reprintings.

Various states of illustrations have the following probable sequence:

Illustrations State 1: Frontispiece colored, other plates black and white. Thus in copies in *States* 1 and 2 of text

Illustrations State 2: Frontispiece in black and white as are other plates.† Thus in copies in *States* 2 and 3 of text

Illustrations State 3: Frontispiece in color, other plates in ivory and sepia tint. Thus in copies in *States* 3 and 4 of text. Since the tinted plates continued to be used in later issues, these copies appear to follow *Illustra-tions State* 2, even though the frontis-piece is as in *Illustrations State* 1. In-scriptions show that *Illustrations States* 1, 2, and 3 were all available before Christmas, 1900

Illustrations State 4: Frontispiece in ivory and sepia tint as are other plates. Thus in *States* 4 and 5 of text.

---

*In Eagle Crest Library.

†All such copies thus far examined that are also in *State* 2 of text have calen-dered end papers, not the white laid with 1⅜6″ between wire marks as in copy collated.

The color of binding (blue, and, green) is not a point of precedence; both colors occur on copies of the first issue. A variation in stamping, however, makes two binding states:

Binding State 1: On front cover between foot of title and top of author's name, space measures 3″ (later, 2¾″). Thus on earliest copies, text in States 1 and 2

Binding State 2: On front cover between foot of title and top of author's name, space measures 2¾″ (earlier, 3″). Thus on copies with text States 3 and later, Illustrations States 3 and 4.

End-paper variations are numerous in the earliest state of the book, due probably to the fact that many copies were hastily assembled for salesmen's use (some even bound without illustrations). Whether lacking altogether in front, or present and of book stock, or laid paper, or calendered paper, in all issues they are the binder's addition, not the printer's and a poor guide to sequence of issue, hence omitted from further discussion here.

That the book was immediately popular is known from the review in *The Independent*, October 18, 1900: "Already, the publishers inform us, the demand far exceeds the supply." On October 28th the author wrote his brother, Will H., about the success of the book: "I stand amazed."*

Bobbs-Merrill published a limp leather edition in 1902 and kept the book in print as late as 1928. Grosset & Dunlap issued it in 1904 and made reprints available until 1941, sales having dropped between 1938 and 1941 to not more than 2,000 copies per year, but in all, the book sold for them "well over the 150,000 mark."†

In England, Cassell issued it in July, 1901. The American edition was being distributed in Great Britain as early as November, 1900, judging by a listing in the *English Catalogue*.

Thompson wrote no plays, but that he had conceived his "Alice" in such form "The Lounger" tells in a contemporary review in *The Critic*, October, 1900: "Mr. Thompson had an idea of making a play of this subject [Vincennes at the time of Clark's conquest of the Wabash Valley] and was working on it when he received a letter from the publishers . . . asking him if he would not write a novel laying his scene in the very place where the scene of his play was laid. He at once

---

*Holograph letter in collection of Will's son, General Maurice Thompson, Tacoma, Washington.

†The *Vincennes Sun-Commercial*, February 18, 1947, quotes these figures as supplied by Grosset & Dunlap, Inc.

set aside the play and went to work on the novel." *Current Literature,* April, 1901, p. 490, further discusses the origin of the novel. *The Book-man,* March, 1901, contains a facsimile of the first page of the original manuscript, together with comment.

A dramatization by E. E. Rose was produced a year after the book's appearance (see *The Indianapolis News,* February 15, 1901, for advance statements about it, and, later, October 22, 1901, for an account of the first performance, October 21, 1901, at the Euclid Avenue Theater, Cleveland, Ohio, under direction of Charles Frohman; criticism of it appears in Lewis C. Strang, *Players and Plays of the Last Quarter Century* [1902], Vol. II, p. 244).* A printed script of the Rose dramatization, bound in covers like the book and with frontispiece an illustration from a scene in the production, has been reported, but not examined.

Lee Burns, of Indianapolis, writing March 1, 1950,† says: "It may be worth recording that Maurice Thompson did not write his story of 'Alice of Old Vincennes' and then try to find a publisher for it. Instead, the suggestion that he write a historical novel was made to him by me as a representative of The Bowen-Merrill Company.

"At that time this company had published 'When Knighthood Was in Flower,' which had been a best-seller month after month and we were in search of another book to take its place. Knowing that Mr. Thompson had made some studies of early Indiana history in preparing his little book for school children entitled, 'Stories of Indiana,' I wrote to him asking if he would not like to write for us a historical novel. He accepted this idea with enthusiasm. The result was 'Alice of Old Vincennes.'

"Mr. Thompson spent some time going through the old books and manuscripts in the Cathedral Library in Vincennes to further his research and enrich the novel's background."

The book inspired a composition by E. C. Keithly, "Alice of Old Vincennes (I Love You)," sheet music published by Frank K. Root & Co., 1914. Thompson's title, if no more, possibly suggested another song, "The Hoosier Girl I Loved in Old Vincennes," dedicated to the memory of Paul Dresser by M. M. Redding and Charles H. Roth, 1910.

The history woven into Thompson's romance has led to many attempts to identify persons and places. "Alice," it has been claimed, was actually Mary Shannon, but since the latter was only four years old when Fort Sackville was captured by George Rogers Clark, it is un-

---

*A typewritten prompt book is preserved in the New York Public Library.
†In a letter addressed to the compilers.

likely that she was the belle of Vincennes portrayed by our author. He probably gave his heroine the name in tribute to his wife. The dedication, purporting to explain the origin of the story, may, or may not be a bit of fiction, the "Roussillon letter" referred to not having been found. Mary Hannah Krout suggested in an article, in *The Independent*, February 21, 1901, Vol. 53, p. 416, that his home, Sherwood Place, which had belonged to a member of the Du Bois family who moved to Crawfordsville from Vincennes, "may have had some influence in shaping the author's latest and most successful work." The centennial issue of *The Western Sun*, Vincennes, July 4, 1904, mentioned the "ancient cottage of Gaspard Roussillon of 1779" as "legendary" and the home of "Alice" as "alleged." The historical effects of the book were brought out in the Clark Memorial issue of the *Vincennes Sun-Commerical*, June 14, 1936, which carried an article captioned, "Alice of Thompson's Immortal Story Awoke Nation to History Here," claiming that the book's publication aroused the people of Vincennes to the importance of the community's background, the result being much published material on its history. The same newspaper, on July 2, 1950, in its historical section memorializing the Indiana Territory Sesquicentennial, relegated it to the place of fiction by omitting mention of it except in a reference to Will C. Conrad's article, "Alice of Old Vincennes Lives Again," in the *Milwaukee Journal*, June 27, 1950.

1901

Sweetheart Manette

SWEETHEART | MANETTE | BY MAURICE THOMPSON | AUTHOR OF | "ALICE OF OLD VINCENNES," ETC. | WITH A FRONTISPIECE BY | EMLEN MC CONNELL | [*publisher's emblem*] | PHILADELPHIA AND LONDON | J. B. LIPPINCOTT COMPANY | 1901

COLLATION: [1]–16⁸, 17². White laid paper. Leaf measures 7$\frac{5}{16}$" x 4¾" (full), all edges trimmed.

End paper; fly title, p. [1]; blank, p. [2]; frontispiece, inserted; title-page, p. [3]; copyright notices with final date 1901, and publisher's imprint, p. [4]; text, pp. 5–259; blank, p. [260]; end paper.

[Note: For text, pp. 5–259, see *Contents*.]

ILLUSTRATIONS: Frontispiece by Emlen McConnell, with legend quoted from p. 199.

BINDING: Blue, and, tan (rose beige) mesh cloth. Front cover red-stamped: SWEETHEART | MANETTE | [*design of Cupid, hearts, and dart, gilt and red-stamped*] | MAURICE | THOMPSON Spine red-stamped: SWEET- | HEART | MANETTE | [*two hearts pierced by a dart*] | LIPPIN-COTT Back cover blank.

End papers white wove; no binder's leaf front or back.

PUBLICATION DATA: Deposited in the Copyright Office February 26, 1901. Advertised in *The Publishers' Weekly*, March 2, 1901, as "just published." Earliest review noted: *The Independent*, April 4th. Price, $1.25.

NOTES: First edition as collated. Sheets of the original magazine publication were bound with printed title-page for this story, and deposited in the Copyright Office, July 19, 1894. The second edition is so stated on the fly title.

It was listed in the *English Catalogue* as a MacQueen publication, October, 1901.

Lippincott's Series of Select Novels, issued in wrappers, included it in 1904.

CONTENTS: Sweetheart Manette, earlier in *Lippincott's Monthly Magazine*, August, 1894.

1901

Rosalynde's Lovers

Rosalynde's [*red, outlined in black*] | Lovers [*red, outlined in black*] | [*red heart, outlined in black on each side of a pictorial design joined to an outer panel by bead-like ornaments*] | by | Maurice Thompson | With Drawings by | G. Alden Peirson | Indianapolis: | The Bowen-Merrill Company | Publishers

[Note: All within a decorative panel.]

COLLATION: [1–18]⁸. White wove paper. Leaf measures 7$\frac{7}{16}$" x 4$\frac{7}{8}$", top edge gilt, other edges untrimmed.

End paper; blank, pp. [i–iv]; fly title, p. [v]; blank, pp. [vi–vii]; frontispiece, p. [viii]; title-page, p. [ix]; copyright notices dated 1901, and imprint of Braunworth & Co., Brooklyn, N. Y., p. [x]; decoration, p. [xi]; blank, p. [xii]; list of illustrations, pp. [xiii–xiv]; decoration, p. [xv]; blank, p. [xvi]; text, pp. 1–246; illustration, p. [247]; blank,

p. [248]; text concluded, p. [249]; blank, pp. [250–254]; end paper. [Note: For text, pp. 1–(249), see *Contents*.]

ILLUSTRATIONS: Frontispiece and 10 full-page plates, facing pp. 10, 30, 40, 50, 140, 162, 168, 194, 222 (not 221 as listed on p. [x]), and 246; all an integral part of the book but not figured in the pagination. All drawings are by G. Alden Peirson. Fly title is decorated and has title in red, outlined in black; decorations appear also on title-page and p. [xi]. The list of illustrations has a headpiece and tailpiece as does each chapter. A double rule appears below the running head.

BINDING: Gray coarse mesh cloth. Front cover green-stamped: Rosalynde's | Lovers | [*green-stamped panel within which is mounted a colored scene signed:* Peirson. 1901] | Maurice Thompson   Spine gilt-stamped: Rosalynde's | Lovers | by | Maurice | Thompson | [*ornamental design*] | Bowen- | -Merrill   Back cover blind-stamped: Rosalynde's | Lovers
End papers decorative light green and brown design on white; no binder's leaf front or back.

PUBLICATION DATA: Listed in *The Publishers' Weekly*, October 5, 1901. Deposited in the Copyright Office October 12th. Earliest review noted: *The Indianapolis News*, November 4th. Price, $1.50.

NOTES: First edition as collated.
Reprinted by New York Book Company after 1912, but before 1917.

CONTENTS: Rosalynde's Lovers: Chapters One to Twenty-One (untitled; hyphen omitted in last chapter); previously in *Lippincott's Monthly Magazine*, March, 1901.

1928

The Witchery of Archery
(Pinehurst Edition)

The | Witchery | of | Archery | By | J. MAURICE THOMPSON | With an added chapter by | WILL H. THOMPSON | Edited by | ROBERT P. ELMER, M. D. | Pinehurst Edition | Published by | The Archers Company | Makers of Fine Bows and Arrows | Pinehurst, North Carolina
[Note: All within a double rule box.]

COLLATION: [1–8]⁸, [9]¹⁰, [10–18]⁸. White wove paper. Leaf measures 7⅜″ x 4¹⁵⁄₁₆″, all edges trimmed.

End paper; fly title, p. [i]; blank, p. [ii]; frontispiece, inserted; title-page, p. [iii]; publisher's trademark and registry statement, and copyright notice dated 1928, p. [iv]; dedication to Will H. Thompson, p. [v]; blank, p. [vi]; table of contents, p. vii; blank, p. [viii]; publisher's notice: *To Maurice And Will Thompson*, p. [ix]; blank, p. [x]; editor's introduction dated January 1, 1928, pp. xi–xxvii; blank, p. [xxviii]; *Mental Images Of Maurice And Will Thompson*, by Samuel G. McMeen, pp. xxix–xxx; text, pp. 1–259; blank, pp. [260–262]; end paper. [Note: For text, pp. 1–259, see *Contents*.]

ILLUSTRATIONS: Frontispiece, photograph of Maurice Thompson, inserted as is photograph of Will Thompson facing p. 234.

BINDING: Tan ribbed cloth. Front cover black-stamped: The | Witchery | of | Archery | J. MAURICE THOMPSON | [*illustration of a hunter shooting a deer stamped within a rectangular panel*] | The Archers Company   Spine black-stamped: The | Witchery | of | Archery | [*rule*] | Thompson | The | Archers | Company   Back cover blank. End papers white calendered; no binder's leaf front or back.

PUBLICATION DATA: Published May 24, 1928. Deposited in the Copyright Office January 31, 1929. Price, cloth, $2.00; limited edition, leather, $5.00.

NOTES: First trade edition as collated. Issued also in a limited edition; leather-bound. Most of the text had appeared earlier, in 1878 and 1879 (see *ante* 180–183). The 1879 edition added only one chapter, but this 1928 edition was so revised that it can be considered a new book. The check-list of Thompson's published works in the introduction notes *The Witchery of Archery* as published in 1877; should be 1878.

CONTENTS: Preliminary matter not by Maurice Thompson: publisher's notice, editor's introduction, and tribute by Samuel G. McMeen; the last chapter is by Will H. Thompson, "Deep in the Okefinokee."* Chapters I–VI are as in earlier editions of *The Witchery of Archery*; Chapters VII–IX were earlier Chapters VIII–X, and X–XII were earlier XII–XIV; XIII earlier XVI; omitted here are chapters VII and XI of the earlier editions, as also XVII of the 1879 edition, and the

---

*It was this account of a trip through the swamplands of southeastern Georgia made by the Thompson brothers in 1866 that led two archers in 1949 to take the same journey; their story is told in *The Bowhunter*, March, 1951.

appendix of the earlier editions.* Chapter XIV herein, "The Fawn," was earlier in *Songs of Fair Weather* (1883). Chapter XV, "An Archer among the Herons," was earlier in *The Boys' Book of Sports and Outdoor Life* (1886). The chapter consisting of Maurice Thompson material not previously collected is:

CHAPTER

XVI   The Bow as a Hunting Weapon   *Scribner's Monthly*, July, 1877 (with title: Bow-Shooting); *Sport with Gun and Rod in American Waters*, edited by Alfred M. Mayer (1883), *q. v.*

---

*Doctor Elmer, in his introduction, says, "True to my professional training as a surgeon I have cut out the appendix."

First Editions—Ephemera

1884
Claude's Big Trout

CLAUDE'S BIG TROUT | BY | MAURICE THOMPSON | [*fishhook and fly design*] | BOSTON | D. LOTHROP AND COMPANY | FRANKLIN AND HAWLEY STREETS

COLLATION: 32 leaves, side-stitched. White wove paper. Leaf measures $6^{15}/_{16}''$ x $4\frac{5}{8}''$, all edges trimmed.

Title-page, p. [1]; copyright notice dated 1884, p. [2]; text, pp. [3–56]; publisher's advertisements, pp. [57–64].

[Note: The pagination supplied includes the plates; see *Illustrations*. For text, pp. (3–56), see *Contents*.]

ILLUSTRATIONS: Full-page drawings, pp. [5], [13], [31],* [39], and [45]; the plates, with their versos blank, are here considered an integral part of the book, since they are on its stock and are side-stitched with all the other leaves. A tailpiece appears at end of first story, and text illustrations on p. [17] and within the story, "Green Pants and a Will."

BINDING: Gray mesh cloth. Front cover has a red-stamped water-lily design, its stamens gilt-stamped, and a river scene, above which, at right, is gilt-stamped: Claude's [*ornament*] | Trout   Spine and back cover blank.

End papers white wove; no binder's leaf front or back.

PUBLICATION DATA: Published 1884, according to copyright notice in the book (copyright deposit copies unlocated).

NOTES: Binder's title: *Claude's Trout*. Copy collated has following advertisements: *"Pansy" Books*, p. [57]; *Recent and Choice Books for S. S. Libraries*, p. [58]; *Margaret Sidney's Books*, p. [59]; *The Yensie Walton Books*, p. [60]; *Works of Julia A. Eastman*, p. [61]; *Books by*

---

*Within the portion that has pages jumbled in copy collated (see *Contents*); a correctly-assembled copy may have had illustrations in another arrangement.

Popular Authors, p. [62]; *Marie Oliver's Stories*, p. [63]; *Books of the Celebrated Prize Series*, p. [64].

This was evidently one of Lothrop's many "series" of illustrated books listed in *The Publishers' Weekly* without individual titles named.

CONTENTS: Claude's Big Trout; A True Bit of History*; Green Pants and a Will [*a* capitalized in running head]; Behind the Barn [*t* in *the* capitalized in running head]; Jonathans Fourth of July [*Jonathan's* in running head]. These stories had been published earlier in *Our Young Folks at Home* (1881).†

1885

A Red-headed Family

THE ELZEVIR LIBRARY. | No. 149. Vol. IV. [*in center, two lines high:*] 2 Cents. [*period squared; at right, on two lines:*] Weekly, $5.00 a Year. | April 2, 1885. | [*rule*] | [Entered at the Post-Office, New York, as Second-Class Mail Matter.] | A Red-Headed Family. [*hyphen doubled, period diamond-shaped*] | BY | MAURICE THOMPSON. | [*rule*] | PUBLISHER'S NOTICE. [*period squared*] | The present issue of THE ELZEVIR LIBRARY shows the form in | which it will hereafter appear. We are confident our readers will be pleased | with the change. | The delightful paper from MAURICE THOMPSON, which forms the | contents of this number, appeared as a contribution to *The Library Magazine* | for April, 1885. It represents fairly the high standard of the literature em- | bodied in that periodical, and also the unexampled smallness of its cost. | Reckoning by the space occupied, it requires more than 240 such contribu- | tions to fill the 1,152 pages of that magazine which, during the year, are given | for the subscription price of only $1.50. See the "TRIAL TRIP" | offer on another page. | [*rule*] | NEW YORK: | JOHN B. [*period squared*] ALDEN, PUBLISHER, | 393 Pearl St., P. O. Box 1227.

---

*In the book collated, Indiana State Library copy, the leaves of this story and the one following are in wrong order.

†Later reprinted in *Story Time* (1888), and in *Good Cheer for 1892* (1891).

[Note: Foregoing printed on front cover; no title-page.]

COLLATION: 6 sheets, saddle-stitched. White laid paper. Leaf measures 7⅛″ x 4⅛″ (scant), all edges trimmed.

Text, pp. [5]–21 (with figure 2 at foot of p. 17, and commendations of *The Library Magazine* at foot of p. 21; no preliminary matter, so should be paginated [1]–17); advertisements, pp. [18–24].

[Note: For text, pp. (5)–21 (*sic*), see *Contents*.]

BINDING: Terra cotta, and, pale green, wrappers, trimmed to leaf size. Front cover serves as title-page; described above. Back wrapper advertises *The Intellectual Life* by Philip Gilbert Hamerton. Inside front wrapper offers "Fair Terms to Buyers," "New Club Terms," and advertises *"Chinese Gordon."* Inside back wrapper advertises Guizot's *History of France.*

PUBLICATION DATA: Published April 2, 1885, according to statement on front wrapper. Price, 2¢.

NOTES: Reprinted from *The Library Magazine*, April, 1885; no preliminary pages present in any of the four copies examined,* but in all, the verso of the first page is numbered 6. No illustrations. No. 149 of *The Elzevir Library* series.

"A Red-headed Family" appeared later, August of the same year, in Thompson's *By-Ways and Bird Notes* (1885).

CONTENTS: A Red-headed Family; earlier in *The Library Magazine*, April, 1885.†

1887

Sunshine and Song

SUNSHINE AND SONG, | OR | SOUTHERN LITERATURE. | [*rule*] | DELIVERED BEFORE | VANDERBILT UNIVERSITY, | December 16, 1886. | [*rule*] | BY MAURICE THOMPSON, | Author of "Hoosier Mosaics," "Witchery of Archery," "A Tallahassee Girl," | "His Second Campaign," "Songs of Fair Weather," "By-Ways | and Bird-Notes," "Banker of Bankersville," etc., etc. | [*rule*] | NASHVILLE, TENN.: | CUMBERLAND PRESBYTERIAN PUBLISHING HOUSE. | 1887.

---

*Two in Indiana State Library, two in Eagle Crest Library.
†It was republished in *The Southern Bivouac*, June, 1885.

COLLATION: 4 sheets, wire side-stitched. White laid paper. Leaf measures 9½" x 6⅜6" (full), all edges trimmed.

Title-page, p. [1]; blank, p. [2]; text, pp. [3]–16.

[Note: Text, pp. (3)–16: Sunshine and Song, or Southern Literature.]

BINDING: Green wrappers, trimmed to leaf size. Front cover reproduces the title-page. Back wrapper bears descriptive notes and notices of Vanderbilt University. Inside wrappers blank.

PUBLICATION DATA: Published January, 1887.

NOTES: No illustrations. This address, third in a series of four, was delivered before Vanderbilt University, December 16, 1886, and published in *The* (Nashville, Tenn.) *Daily American,* December 17, 1886. *The Critic,* January 8, 1887, p. 22, printed a brief extract from the address. The pamphlet received a brief notice in the same magazine, July 23, 1887.

His opening lecture, "At the Threshold," delivered December 14, 1886, appeared in *The* (Nashville) *Daily American,* December 15, 1886. His second, "Disembodied Genius," was published the day after delivery in the same newspaper, on December 16th. The third lecture was apparently the only one printed in pamphlet form. His fourth and last, "The Suggestions of Nature," delivered December 17th, was published in *The* (Nashville) *Daily American,* December 18, 1886.

See *Reminiscences and Sketches,* by Charles Forster Smith (1908), pp. 123–124, for account of the reason why Thompson was chosen as Vanderbilt's first lecturer in this series, and the story of his reception there.

1892

A Shadow of Love

Volume I March 26 1892 Number 3 | TWO TALES [*in red*] | A Shadow of Love | Maurice Thompson | Jule's Light | Frances A Doughty | Published Every Saturday | By the Two Tales Publishing Company | 8 Beacon Street Boston Mass | Price Ten Cents | Four Dollars a Year

[Note: Foregoing printed on front wrapper; no title-page.]

COLLATION: 5 sheets, wire saddle-stitched through wrappers. White laid paper. Leaf measures 9⁷⁄₁₆" x 6⁵⁄₁₆", all edges trimmed.

Text, pp. [47]–64; advertisements, pp. [65–66].
[Note: Text, pp. [47]–56: A Shadow of Love (remainder not Thompson's).]

BINDING: White wrappers printed on book stock and wire saddle-stitched with the book sheets. Back and inside wrappers bear advertisements.

PUBLICATION DATA: Published March 26, 1892. Price, 10¢.

NOTES: No illustrations. A border line publication, here considered an ephemeral brochure rather than a periodical. The first volume of *Two Tales* was collected under the title, *The Story Teller, Number I: The Red-Letter Library*, published by W. B. Clarke & Co. [1892]; it contains this Thompson story on p. 47. If another number of *The Story Teller* appeared, it may have included the subsequent "Lorel Hasardour," but it is not recorded.

1892

Lorel Hasardour

Volume IV Number 40 | TWO TALES [*in red*] | Lorel Hasardour | Maurice Thompson | The Court at Big G Ranch | Thomas P Montfort | December 10 1892 | Price Ten Cents—Four Dollars a Year | Published Every Saturday | By the Two Tales Publishing Company | 8 Beacon Street Boston Mass
[Note: Foregoing printed on front wrapper; no title-page.]

COLLATION: 7 sheets, wire saddle-stitched through wrappers. White laid paper. Leaf measures 9⁷⁄₁₆″ x 6½″, all edges trimmed.
Text, pp. [1]–28.
[Note: Text, pp. (1)–13: Lorel Hasardour (remainder not Thompson's).]

BINDING: White wrappers, printed on book stock and wire saddle-stitched with the book sheets. Back and inside wrappers bear advertisements.

PUBLICATION DATA: Published December 10, 1892. Price, 10¢.

NOTES: No illustrations.

1934
Genius and Morality

GENIUS AND MORALITY | A curious but sincere appreciation of Poe: The Man, | in A letter written by Maurice Thompson forty- | seven years ago, and now printed for a few friends | by the American Autograph Shop. Christmas 1934.

COLLATION: Single sheet of cream-white wove paper, folded. Leaf measures 10″ x 7″ (full), fore edge untrimmed, other edges trimmed. Title-page, p. [1]; text, pp. [2–3]; blank, p. [4].
[Note: For text, pp. (2–3), see *Contents*.]

PUBLICATION DATA: Printed for Guido and Eleanore Bruno, Ridley Park, Pa., for use as a Christmas greeting, 1934.

NOTES: The leaflet had neither illustrations nor binding. Distributed in a mailing envelope.

CONTENTS: A letter to a Mr. Hoyt, dated March 21, 1887, Crawfordsville, Indiana, in reply to his letter of March 18th, relating to Thompson's article on Poe, "Genius and Enthusiasm," in *The Independent*, March 17, 1887.

1935
An Archer in the Cherokee Hills

AN ARCHER | IN | THE CHEROKEE | HILLS | [ornament] | by | MAURICE THOMPSON | [ornament] | Reprinted from | The Atlantic Monthly, April, 1897 | by permission

COLLATION: [1–5]⁴. White wove, Stoneridge cover paper. Leaf measures 7¾″ x 5⅝″, all edges trimmed.
End paper; blank, pp. [1–2]; fly title, p. [3]; blank, p. [4]; title-page, p. [5]; blank, p. [6]; text, pp. Seven–[38]; limitation notice, p. [39]; blank, p. [40]; end paper.
[Note: For text, pp. Seven–(38), see *Contents*.]

ILLUSTRATIONS: None. An ornamental rule appears under title on first page of text.

BINDING: Black silk cloth with gilt floral design, shelfback of terra cotta, silk-finished mesh cloth. Front, and, back cover blank. Spine gilt-stamped, reading from top to bottom: [*ornament*] AN ARCHER IN THE CHEROKEE HILLS [*ornament*].

End papers similar to, less heavy than book stock; no binder's leaf front or back.

PUBLICATION DATA: Privately printed, *ca.* 1935, by Walther Buchen, of Chicago, in an edition of 25 numbered copies.

NOTES: The book was printed for Buchen by J. M. Bundscho, Inc., Chicago, with an enlargement in the photoengraving process of about 30 per cent from the original magazine printing. Mr. Buchen recalls it as done in 1935, and explains: "I published this article in book form because my bow-and-arrow hunting companion, Captain Cassius Styles, had told me about the article in the *Atlantic* and how delightfully it was written. At the time, we were hunting mountain lion with the bow and arrow in the coast ranges of Oregon."* When Buchen returned and read the article he thought that it would interest his archery friends and also others of his associates appreciative of good writing about hunting.

CONTENTS: An Archer in the Cherokee Hills, earlier in *The Atlantic Monthly*, April, 1897.†

---

*Letter, Walther Buchen, May 8, 1950.
†Reprinted in *Ye Sylvan Archer*, December, 1932, Vol. 6, No. 8.

1869

THE LIVING WRITERS OF THE SOUTH. By James Wood Davidson. New York, Carleton; London, S. Low, Son & Co., MDCCCLXIX

Contains a prose sketch, "Geometry of Thought," p. 562, and three poems: "An Allegory," p. 558, "In Love," p. 561, and "Twilight," p. 560, the latter only collected, in *Songs of Fair Weather* (1883). Also contains a critical and biographical sketch of Thompson.

1879

THE ARCHER'S REGISTER: A YEAR BOOK OF FACTS FOR 1878–79. Edited by J[ames] Sharpe. Shrewsbury, Adnitt & Naunton, 1879

Contains "Archery in the United States," p. [9], with editorial comments. Thompson contributed also to the volume of the following year; see *post* 240.

BREVIER LEGISLATIVE REPORTS EMBRACING SHORT-HAND SKETCHES OF THE JOURNALS AND DEBATES OF THE GENERAL ASSEMBLY OF THE STATE OF INDIANA, REGULAR AND SPECIAL SESSIONS OF 1879. By C. E. & W. H. Drapier, Reporters. Volumes 17 & 18. Indianapolis, W. H. Drapier, 1879

Contains digests of Thompson's remarks in the House of Representatives of the Indiana State Legislature during his term of office (January 9th to March 31, 1879); his own words are quoted only once, in Vol. 17, p. 97, in explanation of a vote.

The four bills which he introduced (109, 110, 578, 581) did not appear in print, nor did they become law. H. R. 109, "to create the Forty-second Judicial Circuit and providing for the appointment of judge and prosecutor, etc." was mentioned in *The Indianapolis Journal*, January 15, 1879. H. R. 110, an act to amend an act prohibiting supreme, circuit, or other judges, clerks of criminal courts, justices of the peace, auditors, treasurers, sheriffs, and their deputies from practicing law, except as permitted in this Act (*Brevier Legislative Reports*, Vol. 17, p. 24), was reported in *The Indianapolis Journal*, January 15th and March 3, 1879, latter a statement that the bill had been ordered engrossed. H. R. 581, a bill to amend section one of an act providing for voluntary assignments (*Brevier Legislative Reports*, Vol. 17, p. 154), was passed by the House and ordered engrossed (*The Indianapolis Journal*, March 27, 1879), but died in the Senate.

Thompson's remarks about a bill relating to fees and salaries, introduced by Osborn of Elkhart, were reviewed, but not directly quoted, in *The Indianapolis Journal*, February 15, 1879; the *Brevier Legislative Reports*, p. 148, merely state: "Mr. Thompson spoke at length in favor of a bill fixing the salaries of county officers."

The Journal of the House of Representatives of the State of Indiana, during the Fifty-first Session of the General Assembly (1879), briefly notes the four bills introduced by Thompson, but does not quote any of his speeches.

CHRISTMAS SNOWFLAKES. Illustrated Poems by Favorite American Authors. [Edited by Mrs. Ella (Farman) Pratt.] Boston, D. Lothrop & Co. [1879]

Contains a poem, "Waking Up a Bear," later in a compilation by Ernest Ingersoll, *Bear Stories* (1884).*

POEMS OF PLACES. AMERICA: WESTERN STATES. Edited by Henry W. Longfellow. Boston, Houghton, Osgood, & Co.; Cambridge, Riverside Press, 1879

Binder's title: *Poems of America*. Volume 29 of the *Poems of Places* series. Contains "The Wabash," p. 250. The poem was earlier published in *Lippincott's Magazine of Popular Literature and Science*, February, 1877. A parody signed A. Quisenberry, appeared in *The Crawfordsville Journal*, January 27, 1877. The poem itself, without title, was included in a review of Longfellow's anthology, in *The* (Indianapolis) *Saturday Herald*, May 31, 1879. It was first collected in *Songs of Fair Weather* (1883) and reprinted in *Poems* (1892). For appearance in anthologies later, see *ante* 191*n*.

SCRAP-BOOK RECITATION SERIES, NO. 1. Edited by Henry M. Soper. Chicago, T. S. Denison & Co. [1879]

---

*Latter reported by Jacob Blanck; not seen.

Green pictorial wrappers. Contains "The Doom of Claudius and Cynthia," p. 105, earlier in *Scribner's Monthly*, February, 1879. It was included later, abridged, in *One Hundred Choice Selections*, No. 22, compiled by Phineas Garrett (1883; reprinted 1911). It reappeared in *Standard Recitations by Best Authors*, No. 17, compiled by Frances P. Sullivan (September, 1887); in *The New Century Speaker for School and College*, by Henry A. Frink (1898); and in *The Speaker's Garland*, Vol. 6 (1909).

1880

THE ARCHER'S REGISTER: A YEAR BOOK OF FACTS FOR 1879–80. Edited by J[ames] Sharpe. Shrewsbury, Adnitt & Naunton, 1880

Contains "A Review of Archery in America during the Season of 1879," p. 178.

1881

OUR YOUNG FOLKS AT HOME. ILLUSTRATED PROSE STORIES. By American Authors and Artists. Boston, D. Lothrop & Co. [1881]

Contains "Claude's Big Trout," later a separate book (see *ante* 231). The story also made later appearances in *Story Time*, a Lothrop publication of 1888, and in their *Good Cheer for 1892*.

1882

THE CAMBRIDGE BOOK OF POETRY AND SONG. Selected from English and American Authors by Charlotte Fiske Bates. New York & Boston, Thomas Y. Crowell & Co. [1882]

Contains "The Morning Hills," p. 853, and "Before Dawn," p. 854. Both poems were collected in *Songs of Fair Weather* (1883).

1883

SPORT WITH GUN AND ROD IN AMERICAN WOODS AND WATERS. Edited by Alfred M. Mayer. New York, Century Co. [1883]

Issued in one volume in cloth, and, leather; also in two volumes in cloth, and, leather.

Contains "Bow-shooting," p. 854, earlier in *Scribner's Monthly*, July, 1877; later, a part of it not previously collected appeared in the *Pinehurst Edition* of *The Witchery of Archery* (1928), Chapter XVI (a different portion had been included in the first and second editions of *The Witchery of Archery*, Chapter II). "In the Haunts of Bream and Bass," p. 396, was earlier collected in *Songs of Fair Weather* (1883), *q.v.*

1886

AUGUST. Edited by Oscar Fay Adams. Boston, D. Lothrop & Co. [1886]

Separate volume in a series, *Through the Year with the Poets*, edited by Oscar Fay Adams. Contains "The Humming Bird," p. 95, earlier in *Lippincott's Magazine of Popular Literature & Science*, July, 1873. This is an uncollected poem, not the one that appeared with same title in *The Bird-Lover's Anthology* (1930), collected as "The Assault," *q.v.*

INDIANA DEPARTMENT OF GEOLOGY AND NATURAL HISTORY. FIFTEENTH ANNUAL REPORT [for 1885 and 1886]. By Maurice Thompson, State Geologist. Indianapolis [Wm. B. Burford], 1886

Contains the following by Maurice Thompson: "Preface," p. [5]; "Compendium of Geology and Mineralogy of Indiana," p. [10]; "Indiana Building Stone," p. [26]; "The Clays of Indiana," p. [34]; "Indiana Chalk Beds," p. [41]; "Glacial Deposits of Indiana," p. [44]; "A Terminal Moraine in Central Indiana," p. [57]; "Geographical Botany," p. [242]; "Fossil Mammals of the Post-Pliocene in Indiana," p. [283]; "Natural Gas," p. [314]. His brief letter of transmittal, addressed to Isaac P. Gray, Governor, November 5, 1886, appears in front matter.

Comments on this first report of Thompson as State Geologist, with quotations from the contents, appeared later in "A Century of Geology in Indiana," by W. S. Blatchley, in *Proceedings of the Indiana Academy of Science 1916*, p. 155.

THIRTY-FIFTH ANNUAL REPORT OF THE INDIANA STATE BOARD OF AGRICULTURE, Vol. XXVII, 1885, including the Proceedings of the Annual Meeting, 1886. Indianapolis [Wm. B. Burford], 1886

Contains "Some Song-Birds of Indiana," p. 247.

1887

THE TRIBUNE BOOK OF OPEN-AIR SPORTS. Prepared by the New York Tribune with the aid of acknowledged experts; edited by Henry Hall. New York, Tribune Association, 1887

Contains "Archery," p. 7. The whole of the second chapter is Thompson's.*

1888

ARBOR DAY. Edited & compiled by Robert W. Furnas. Lincoln, Neb., State Journal Co., 1888

Contains a letter dated April 8, 1888, to H. L. Wood, editor of the *Nebraska City Daily Press*, p. 108. Thompson had been requested, among others, to write a letter for the Arbor Day edition of the *Press*, April 22, 1888,* honoring the founder of the day, Hon. J. Sterling Morton; his response, on account of illness, was brief.

INDIANA DEPARTMENT OF GEOLOGY AND NATURAL HISTORY. SIX-TEENTH ANNUAL REPORT [for 1887 and 1888]. By Maurice Thompson, State Geologist; edited by S. S. Gorby. Indianapolis [Wm. B. Burford, Printer], 1889

Contains the following by Maurice Thompson: "Introductory," p. [11]; "Drift Beds of Indiana," p. [20]; "The Wabash Arch," p. [41]; "Gold, Silver and Precious Stones," p. [87]; "The Formation of Soils and Other Superficial Deposits," p. [93]; "Preliminary Sketch of the Characteristic Plants of the Kankakee Region," p. [155]; "Preliminary Sketch of the Aquatic and Shore Birds of the Kankakee Region," p. [162].

Comments on, and quotations from this second report of Thomp-

---

*Not seen. Reported by C. N. Hickman, letter of March 12, 1951.
*This issue not located; file in Nebraska City destroyed by fire.

son's appeared later in an article, "A Century of Geology in Indiana," by W. S. Blatchley, in *Proceedings of the Indiana Academy of Science 1916*, p. 157.

WHAT AMERICAN AUTHORS THINK ABOUT INTERNATIONAL COPY-RIGHT. New York, American Copyright League, 1888

Contains Thompson's statement, a single paragraph, on p. 9.
At a meeting of western literary men and women in Indianapolis on July 1, 1886, Thompson had discussed the subject and a resultant resolution, unsigned but possibly written by him, appeared in *The Indianapolis Journal* on July 2nd. The group organized with Thompson as president; it was later known as the Western Association of Writers (see *post*, 244).
An article by him, "International Copyright," appeared in *America*, December 25, 1890.

1890

AMERICAN SONNETS. Selected & edited by T. W. Higginson & E. H. Bigelow. Boston & New York, Houghton, Mifflin & Co.; Cambridge, Riverside Press, 1890

Contains "A Green Heron," p. 224, earlier in *Scribner's Monthly*, July, 1878, under caption, "Wabash Bubbles, III," and reprinted in *The Crawfordsville Journal*, June 29, 1878. Also contains "On a Garden Statue of Persephone," collected earlier in *Songs of Fair Weather* (1883), under caption, "Garden Statues." A second edition of the anthology was published in 1891.

MY FIRST VOYAGE. By Maurice Thompson, and Other Stories by Noted Authors. With pictures. Boston, D. Lothrop [1890]

Contains story (true?) of his youthful adventure in Bay St. Louis, "My First Voyage," p. 17. The other stories in the book, unsigned, are not Thompson's.
Probably issued in boards; only copy located is rebound.*

POEMS. James Whitcomb Riley; Sarah T. Bolton; Maurice

---

*In the New York Public Library.

Thompson; Evaleen Stein; John Clark Ridpath; Meredith Nicholson. [Indianapolis Flower Mission, 1890]

Green wrappers, embossed in imitation of morocco. Sold at the Indianapolis Flower Mission Fair, November, 1890. *The Indianapolis Journal*, November 18, 1890, reported it to be an edition of 300 copies. Contains "E Pluribus Unum," later collected in Thompson's *Poems* (1892) with title, "Our Legend."

For a later Flower Mission brochure with Thompson contribution see *post* 249.

w. a. w. [Western Association of Writers]. A SOUVENIR OF THE FOURTH ANNUAL CONVENTION, AT WARSAW, INDIANA: JULY 9, 10, 11, AND 12, 1889. By L. May Wheeler & Mary E. Cardwill. Richmond, Ind., M. Cullaton & Co., 1890

Contains extracts from a speech by Thompson at the third (second annual) convention, June 29, 1887, quoted in Mary E. Cardwill's "Historical Sketch," p. 14. These are not the same portions as were quoted in *The Indianapolis Journal*, June 30, 1887, or in *The Literary World*, July 23, 1887. The latter concerned Tolstoi; it led to editorial discussion and a reply on August 20th.

His subject, development of good American literature, was discussed by him more fully in subsequent articles in *The Independent*.

Certain comments on William Dean Howells in his speech provoked an editorial attack in *The Literary World*, September 3, 1887. He defended his stand in an interview published in *The Indianapolis Journal*, September 18, 1887, "A Literary Controversy."

The group when first assembled, June 30, 1886, in Indianapolis, in response to an invitation (not Thompson's) to writers, "especially to the writers of the Wabash valley and the adjacent States,"* was called the "Convention of Western Writers." At the second convention, October 5th of the same year, the name adopted was "American Association of Writers." Thompson's speech on this occasion was printed in *The Indianapolis Journal*, October 6, 1886, and in *The Critic*, October 16, 1886; a brief comment by him on the second day, October 6th, was reported in *The Indianapolis Sentinel*, October 7, 1886. He was the Association's first president and served until June, 1888.† In addressing

---

*The invitation was published in the *Current* (Chicago), April 3, 1886.

†*The* (Indianapolis) *Saturday Herald*, February 26, 1887, quoted a single sentence from his letter of instructions to the secretary for a committee meeting on February 19th which he was not able to attend.

both the second convention, October, 1886, and this third (second annual), June 29, 1887, he referred to the "Association of American Writers," but before the latter meeting adjourned the name was changed to the "Western Association of Writers"; his speech was printed in *The Indianapolis Journal* and *Sentinel*, June 30, 1887.

The other two "souvenirs" in book form do not contain Thompson contributions: *W. A. W. Souvenir No. 2, Proceedings of the Fifth Annual Convention ... 1890* (1891), and *Sayings and Doings of the Sixth General Meeting ... 1891* (1892).

1891

ELEVEN POSSIBLE CASES. [By] Frank R. Stockton, Joaquin Miller, ... Maurice Thompson .... New York, Cassell [1891]

Among the eleven stories by as many authors is Thompson's "The Mystic Krewe," p. 92, copyright on which was taken out by Franklin Files, April 29, 1891.

INDIANA DEPARTMENT OF GEOLOGY AND NATURAL RESOURCES. SEVENTEENTH ANNUAL REPORT [for 1889–1891]. By S. S. Gorby, State Geologist. Indianapolis [Wm. B. Burford], 1892 [*i.e.*, 1891]

Contains "A Report upon the Various Stones Used for Building Purposes, and Found in Indiana," p. [18]; the lengthy report that follows, pp. [19]–113, was prepared by Thompson and A. C. Benedict. Thompson's name is signed to the section, "Indiana Building Stone," pp. [19]–55. "The Quarrying Industry in Indiana," pp. [56]–65, is unsigned but probably written by Thompson from data supplied by Benedict; the latter compiled the statistics, "Quarries in Indiana," pp. [66]–113. The book also contains "Geological and Natural History Report of Carroll County," by Thompson, p. [171].

Thompson had resigned as state geologist in December, 1888, but continued to act as chief assistant to Gorby. Comments on the above reports appeared later in "A Century of Geology in Indiana," by W. S. Blatchley, in *Proceedings of the Indiana Academy of Science 1916*, p. 162.

TALES OF THE NEW YORK STORY CLUB. FORTY COMPLETE STORIES BY KIPLING, STEVENSON, DAUDET, HAWTHORNE, MAURICE THOMPSON, EDITH SESSIONS TUPPER, MARY H. CATHERWOOD, M. QUAD,

AND OTHERS, BEING "ROMANCE" LIBRARY NO. 1. New York, Romance Publishing Co., 1891

Contains "For Isobel," p. 185, earlier in *The New York Ledger,* October 4, 1890. It reappeared in *Romance, Volume I: Sixty Complete Stories by Eminent Writers* (1891).

1895

HOW TO STUDY HISTORY, LITERATURE, THE FINE ARTS. By Albert Bushnell Hart, Maurice Thompson, Charles M. Fairbanks. Meadville, Pa., Flood & Vincent, 1895

Wayside Course Series, No. 2. Contains "How to Study Literature," p. 21, earlier in *The Chautauquan,* November, 1893.
Evidently issued in wrappers, since priced at only 20¢ (copy located has been rebound).

'THE TIME HAS COME', THE WALRUS SAID, 'TO TALK OF MANY THINGS;' [*punctuation sic*]. [East Aurora, N. Y., Roycroft Printing Shop, 1895]

Self-wrapper, pictorial design on front. This brochure of eight pages contains responses of those invited who could not come to a dinner held by the Society of the Philistines in honor of Stephen Crane, December 19, 1895 (see *Stephen Crane: A Bibliography*, by Ames W. Williams & Vincent Starrett [1948], pp. 153–154). Maurice Thompson's reply appears as the second item on the first page of text and reads: "It would give me great pleasure to sit over against Stephen Crane for an eating bout. Lately he made the gooseflesh wiggle on me—he is a fiendish warrior.* Eat, drink and be merry! for tomorrow the critics will be abroad."
The Thompson letter was reprinted in *The Roycroft Quarterly,* May, 1896, p. 7.

1896

ESSAYS FROM THE CHAP-BOOK: BEING A MISCELLANY OF CURIOUS AND INTERESTING TALES, HISTORIES, ETC.; NEWLY COMPOSED BY

---

*Evidently Thompson had been reading Crane's *The Red Badge of Courage.*

MANY CELEBRATED WRITERS AND VERY DELIGHTFUL TO READ. Chicago, Herbert S. Stone & Co., 1896

Kramer No. 119. Contains three essays by Thompson: "Is the New Woman New?," p. 223; "The Return of the Girl," p. 239; "The Art of Saying Nothing Well," p. 253. The first named had appeared in *The Chap-Book* on October 1, 1895; the second, March 15, 1896; the third, July 1, 1896.

See *New Stories from the Chap-Book* (1898) for another Thompson contribution. Nothing by him had appeared in the first of the three compilations from *The Chap-Book, i.e., Stories from the Chap-Book* (1896).

1897

STANDARD RECITATIONS BY BEST AUTHORS. No. 46. Compiled by Frances P. Sullivan. New York, M. J. Ivers & Co., December, 1897

Pictorial white wrappers. Contains "The Ballad of Chickamauga [September 19, 20, 1863]," p. 14. The poem was earlier in *The Century Magazine*, September, 1895, and in *The* (Chicago) *Inter Ocean*, September 9, 1895. It was reprinted in *Poems of American History*, collected and edited by Burton E. Stevenson (1908; 1922), and in his collection entitled, *My Country* (1932).

1898

NEW STORIES FROM THE CHAP-BOOK: BEING A MISCELLANY OF CURIOUS AND INTERESTING TALES, HISTORIES, ETC.; NEWLY COMPOSED BY MANY CELEBRATED WRITERS AND VERY DELIGHTFUL TO READ. Chicago, Herbert S. Stone & Co., 1898

Kramer No. 168. Contains "Gil Horne's Bergonzi," p. 191, earlier in *The Chap-Book*, March 1, 1898. Duffield reprinted the book in 1906.

For another compilation from *The Chap-Book* with contributions by Thompson see *Essays from the Chap-Book* (1896).

SPANISH-AMERICAN WAR SONGS. A Complete Collection of Newspaper Verse during the Recent War with Spain. Compiled &

edited by Sidney A. Witherbee. Detroit, Mich., Sidney A. Witherbee, 1898

Contains a poem, "A Song of the New," p. 869, earlier in *The Independent*, July 21, 1898, and in *The Indianapolis Journal*, July 24th.

1899

WHO'S WHO IN AMERICA [1899–1900]. [Vol. I] Chicago, A. N. Marquis & Co. [1899]

Contains an autobiographical sketch of Maurice Thompson, p. 725.*

1900

AN AMERICAN ANTHOLOGY, 1787–1900: SELECTIONS ILLUSTRATING THE EDITOR'S CRITICAL REVIEW OF AMERICAN POETRY IN THE NINETEENTH CENTURY. Edited by Edmund Clarence Stedman. 2 volumes. Cambridge, Riverside Press, 1900

Boards. Issued in an edition of 300 numbered and signed copies: "Author's Autograph Copy" on limitation leaf. Volume II contains a poem, "The Lion's Cub," p. 483, addressed earlier in *The Independent*, December 29, 1898, "To the United States Senate," and in *The Indianapolis News*, same date; *The Indianapolis Journal* published it the day following.

The anthology appeared also in a one-volume, trade edition, with Houghton Mifflin's imprint added.

BALLADS OF AMERICAN BRAVERY. The Silver Series of English and

---

*It is here that he lists, among things authored, *Toxophilus in Arcadia*, of which no record of publication has been found. His letters to *Century*, now in the New York Public Library, shed some light. On October 12, 1899, he mentioned that he had, in his drawer, a book of "sylvan archery papers of a wide range." He probably drew on this manuscript, as well as the refreshment of an early spring "saunter" through the Carolina hills, when he wrote the long article which *The Century Magazine* published August 1900, as "In the Woods with the Bow." When he sent the manuscript, April 2, 1900, he wrote: ". . . I offer two titles. I rather prefer 'Toxophilus in Arcadia'; but choose ye."

American Classics. Edited by Clinton Scollard. New York, Boston, & Chicago, Silver, Burdett, & Co. [1900]

Contains "The Ballad of a Little Fun," p. 131, earlier in *The Century Magazine*, June, 1895. A note on p. 223 of the book describes it as relating an adventure that befell a Confederate scouting party near Hogan's Ford during the Civil War.

THE FLOWER MISSION CAP & GOWN. Edited by Laurel Louisa Fletcher. [Indianapolis, Flower Mission], November, 1900

Gray wrappers, printed in red and black. Contains a poem, "Opulence."

For an earlier Flower Mission brochure with contribution, see *Poems* (1890).

THE HESPERIAN TREE. An annual of the Ohio Valley—1900. Edited by John James Piatt. Cincinnati, O., George C. Shaw, 1900

Gray boards, white cloth shelfback. Contains a poem, "Migration," p. 156, also a prose sketch, "A Touch of Nature," p. 408; both were written especially for this volume.

Issued later with imprint of John Scott & Co., North Bend, O., with undated preface, bound in white cloth.

The two contributions were printed separately by W. E. Taylor, Harrison, Ohio, with copyright in name of John James Piatt, dated 1906, under the title, *A Touch of Nature;* title-page bears two imprints: John Scott & Co., North Bend, O., and The Western Literary Press, Cincinnati; the decorative front cover bears series title: *The Swallow-flight Series.*

1900?

WHEN KNIGHTHOOD WAS IN FLOWER. By Edwin Caskoden [Charles Major]. Indianapolis, Bowen-Merrill Co. [1898]

The first edition, published 1898, contains no contribution by Thompson, but some of the issues probably published 1900 and later include, after the text, his article, "The Author and the Book," from *The Saturday Evening Post*, December 30, 1899. In the magazine it was entitled, "Charles Major, Lawyer and Romancer."

1901

THE CHRISTMAS GARLAND: A Miscellany of Verses, Stories and Essays by Well-Known Authors. Chicago, Herbert S. Stone & Co., 1901

Issued in a limited edition bound in white padded silk and in a popular edition bound in white vellum cloth (according to Sidney Kramer, *A History of Stone & Kimball and Herbert S. Stone & Co.* [1940], p. 342). No copy located. Thompson was named as a contributor in *The Publishers' Weekly* advertisement of the book, September 28, 1901.

1902

INDIANA WRITERS OF POEMS AND PROSE. [Compiled by Edward Joseph Hamilton]. Chicago, Western Press Association, 1902

Contains "Beyond the Limit," a poem previously in *The Century Magazine*, November, 1892.

1904, 1905

THE LIBRARY OF LITERARY CRITICISM OF ENGLISH AND AMERICAN AUTHORS. Edited by Charles Wells Moulton. Volumes VII, VIII. Buffalo, N. Y., Moulton Publishing Co., 1904, 1905

Volume VII contains, p. 206, a phrase about George Eliot, from "The Domain of Romance," in *The Forum*, November, 1889. It contains also two extracts about Paul Hamilton Hayne, one on pp. 591–592, from "The Last Literary Cavalier," in *The Critic*, April, 1901; the other, on p. 593, quoted from an article in *Literature*, September 22, 1888. Also, on p. 711, there is an extract from "Browning as a Poet," in *America*, January 2, 1890.

Volume VIII contains, p. 38, a selection from Thompson's letter regarding James Russell Lowell, published in *The Critic*, February 23, 1889.

Other criticisms by Thompson, in Volumes IV, V, and VI of the set, were earlier collected.

1907

WESTERN FRONTIER STORIES. Retold from St. Nicholas. New York, Century, 1907

Contains "A Prairie Home," p. 73, earlier in *St. Nicholas*, September, 1891.

1923

ST. NICHOLAS BOOK OF VERSE. Edited by Mary Budd Skinner & Joseph Osmun Skinner. New York, Century, 1923

Contains poems, "In the Clover" p. 186, earlier in *St. Nicholas*, July, 1891; and "The Ballad of Berry Brown," p. 329, earlier in *St. Nicholas*, February, 1899, and in *The Indianapolis Journal*, January 30, 1899.

1926?

HUNTING-STORIES RETOLD FROM ST. NICHOLAS. New York & London, Century [n.d., (1926?)]

Contains "Watching for an Otter," p. 106, earlier in *St. Nicholas*, December, 1879 (see *post* 279n for the author's comment on the story).

Periodicals Containing First Appearances

AMERICA (Chicago)

1888:	April	21	Alienism and Patriotism in American Literature*
	September	6	Rush's Still House*
1889:	July	4	Literary Loyalty*; Fatal Leisure†
		11	Balzac, Sainte-Beuve, and the Realists*
		18	The Editorial Decision*
		25	Literature and the College*
	August	1	What Is a Drama?*
		8	The Art of Suggestion*
		15	The Alien Taint in Criticism*
		22	The Wordsworthian Influence*
		29	Adventures with Editors*
	September	5	Women in Novels*
		12	One of Our True Poets [Edgar Fawcett]*
		19	Holding the Mirror*
		26	The Editorial Influence*
	October	3	The Point of Hesitancy*
		10	Walt Whitman's True Value*
		17	Must the Review Be Abolished?*
		24	The Lees of Old Wine*
		31	Daudet's "Artists' Wives"*
	November	7	Materialism and Criticism*
		14	The Big Bow-Wow*
		21	Faded Flowers*
		28	Reserve and Understatement*
	December	5	The Limit of the Short Story*
		12	The American Bouquet*
		19	Cacoethes Scribendi‡
		26	The Touch of Genius*
1890:	January	2	Browning as a Poet*
		9	More about the Short Story*
		16	A Literary Execution*
		23	Une Flute D'Ebene*
		30	The Romance of New Orleans*

*Uncollected.

†Uncollected; it was announced that Thompson began with this issue to furnish the leading article to *America's* column captioned, "Literature," to "make the department reflect more nearly western views upon current literary topics."

‡Uncollected; reprinted in *The Independent*, September 24, 1896.

AMERICA (Chicago)—*continued*

February   6   The Closing of an Epoch*
13   The Best Novels*
20   Improvement in Blue-Stockings*
27   The Book-Making Disease*
March   6   Spring Notes*
13   Christian Criticism*
20   The Provincial Poet*
27   The Benefit of Change*
April   3   Feeding the Brain*
10   The Price of Excellence*
17   Barriers against Universality*
24   The Basis of Art*
May   1   Off-Hand Criticism*
15   Authorship and Common Sense*
29   The Vote on Copyright*
June   12   Another Provincial View*
26   Portraits of Authors*
July   3   The First Novel*
17   Literary Gambling*
31   The Novels that Shakespeare Read*
August   14   Some Notes on Romance-History*
28   A Winter Ritual for Writers*
September   11   The American "Forty"*
18   A Little Question of Soil*
25   Machine-made Appreciation*
October   2   Are Authors Men?*
16   Cadmean Bucket-Shops*
30   Editors and Short-Story Writers*
November   6   A Hint to Chicago*
27   The Urban Influence*
December   11   Literature and the Exposition*
25   International Copyright*
1891: January   8   Miss [Emily] Dickinson's Poems*
15   Heroes and Heroines in Fiction*
29   Literary Hysteria*
February   12   The Low Tide in Poetry*
26   The Badge of Genius*
March   12   Notes of the Creole Coast*
26   "Style Is the Man Himself"*
April   9   Theodore De Banville*
23   The Golden Inspiration*
May   7   The Poet and the Specialist*
14   Personal and Literary*
21   A Plethora of Ink*

*Uncollected.

AMERICA (Chicago)—*continued*

1891: June	4	A Touch of June*
	18	The Nude in Fiction*
July	2	The Birth of Art*
	9	Independence Day†
	16	Sylvan Study*
September	17	A Realistic Critic*

AMERICAN MAGAZINE

1887: August		Our Legend [E Pluribus Unum; poem]
October		Rebel or Loyalist? [poem]

APPLETON'S JOURNAL

1872: February	10	The Pockets of North Georgia*
December	7	The Sap-Sucker*
1873: April	19	The Long-Bow*
June	21	The Sunfish*
September	20	Tallulah Falls*
1874: June	6	Ceres: A Vision of the Day [poem]
1875: June	26	The Island of Song*
September	4	Three Weeks of Savage Life
October	30	Bow-Shooting with a Hermit
1876: March	11	Bow-Shots on the St. John's
December		Some of Our Game-Birds*
1877: April		A Naked Babe [poem]*
1878: February		The Battle of the Birds

THE ATLANTIC MONTHLY

1873: April	At the Window [poem]
1874: May	Atalanta [poem]
December	November [poem]
1875: April	Diana [poem]
1876: January	Aoede [poem]
December	Garden Statues: I. Eros; II. Aphrodite; III. Psyche; IV. Persephone
1877: August	Dropping Corn [poem]
1879: July	The Morning Hills [poem]
1880: September	Unaware [poem]
1881: March	Before Dawn [poem]
1883: January	Wild Honey [poem]
July	A Prelude [poem]
1884: November	In the Haunts of the Mocking-Bird
1885: September	A Taunt [poem]
1886: May	The Genesis of Bird-Song

---

*Uncollected.

†Published in *The Independent*, same date, under the title, "The Day We Celebrate."

The Atlantic Monthly—*continued*

1894:	March	The Sapphic Secret*
1896:	April	An Archer's Sojourn in the Okefinokee†
1897:	April	An Archer in the Cherokee Hills‡
1900:	June	An Archer on the Kankakee§

Badminton Magazine (London)

1896:	February	An Archer's Outing‖

Book News

1887:	September– November	Studies of Prominent Novelists, No. 1: Count Tolstoi; No. 2: Alphonse Daudet; No. 3: William Dean Howells¶
1888:	January– March	Studies of Prominent Novelists, No. 4: Thomas Hardy; No. 5: Nathaniel Hawthorne; No. 6: General Lew Wallace£

The Boston Post

1900:	June	7	Literature and Life**

The Century Magazine

1882:	February	In Exile [poem]
	June	In the Haunts of Bream and Bass
1884:	August	A Song of the Mocking-Bird (Dedicated to an English Nightingale) [poem]
1885:	March	Hodson's Hide-Out
1886:	September	A Song of the Mocking-Bird (Dedicated to an English Sky-Lark) [poem]
1888:	February	A Song of the Mocking-Bird (Before Sunrise) [poem]
1889:	October	Ben and Judas
1890:	April	A Dusky Genius
	December	A Pair of Old Boys¶
1891:	April	A Race Romance

---

*Uncollected; see also, "Again 'The Sapphic Secret' " in *The Critic*, March 31, 1894, a reply to criticism.

†Uncollected; reprinted in *Ye Sylvan Archer*, September, 1932.

‡Uncollected; reprinted in *Ye Sylvan Archer*, December, 1932.

§Uncollected; reprinted in *Ye Sylvan Archer*, October–November, 1932.

‖Uncollected; reprinted in *Ye Sylvan Archer*, November, 1928–March, 1929 (Vol. 2 Nos. 4–6).

¶Uncollected.

£Uncollected. Thompson's defense of Wallace against the charge of amateurism (No. 6 of this series) was printed in *The Indianapolis Journal*, March 11, 1888.

**Uncollected; quoting part of his Commencement Day address at Boston University, June 6, 1900; delivered also at Wabash College, June 9, 1900, and printed in part in *The Crawfordsville Journal*, June 16, 1900.

THE CENTURY MAGAZINE—*continued*

1892:	May	Love's Horizon [poem]*
	July	Rudgis and Grim
	November	Beyond the Limit [poem]*
1893:	June	An Impossibility [poem]*
1895:	June	Ballad of a Little Fun [poem]*
	September	The Ballad of Chicamauga [poem]*
1897:	July	The Defense by Resurrection*
1900:	August	In the Woods with the Bow
	November	My Midwinter Garden

THE CHAP-BOOK

1895:	May	1	Nuts from Perigord*
	September	15	[Letter on essay writing, to editor of department of "Notes"]*
	October	1	Is the New Woman New?*
1896:	March	15	The Return of the Girl*
	July	1	The Art of Saying Nothing Well*
1897:	January	1	The Rustic Muse*
	February	15	From the Critic's Point of View*
	May	1	Literary Greens*
	August	1	Walt Whitman and the Critics*
		15	The Personal Note*
	October	1	Ram's-Horns and Duffers*
1898:	March	1	Gil Horne's Bergonzi*

THE CHAUTAUQUAN

1887:	February	The Western Literary Outlook*
1888:	February	Winter Sports and Pastimes*
	March	Riding and Driving*
	April	Walking*
	May	Bicycling and Tricycling*
	June	Archery, Tennis, and Croquet*
1890:	January	Zenobia*
	February	The Poetry of the Civil War*
1891:	October	The Theory of Fiction-Making*
1892:	January	Richter, a Painter of Picturesque Portraits*
	June	Poetry since Pope*
	October	The Romance and the Novel*
1893:	November	How to Study Literature*
1894:	May	The Limit of Athletics for Brain Workers*
1896:	June	Contemporary American Authors*
1897:	July	An Inexpensive Summer Outing*
	August	What We Gain in the Bicycle*
	September	Common Sense on the Wheel*

---

*Uncollected.

(Chicago) CURRENT (see CURRENT)

THE (Chicago) INTER OCEAN

1880:	December	25	Christmas Tide [poem]*
1888:	August	12	Woodcock Shooting*
1889:	January	1	An Inglorious Genius†
	December	22	The Best Christmas Gift*
1890:	May	18	Curious Habits of the Green Heron*
	July	13	The Flight of the Hawk*
	August	10	Habits of Mocking Birds*
		24	Curious Habits of the Woodcock*
1891:	November	1	How a Boy Outwitted John A. Murrell*
	December	6	The Strange Adventures of John Shadden*
1892:	February	14	The Wild Boy of Wallahee*
1893:	June	11	The Humming Bird‡
	November	19	A Pearl River Silhouette*
1895:	March	17	A Lucky Shot*
		24	High-Water Friendship*
	April	14	Shooting by Eye-Light*
		21	Swamp Duck Shooting§
		28	Turkey Shooting*
	May	19	Kildee Shooting*
		26	Among the Woodcocks‖
	June	2	Bagging a Wild Goose¶
		9	After Gray Rabbits*
		16	A Close Call*
		23	Twin Boys and Bears*
	July	14	A Wildcat at Home*
		28	A Panther and a Boy*
	August	4	Robbers' Strategy*
		11	Grouse on the Ausable*
	September	9	The Ballad of Chickaumauga [poem]*

---

*Uncollected.

†Uncollected; in the *Weekly Inter Ocean,* appearing at this time on Tuesday in addition to the daily issue. Most of the Thompson stories were features of the Sunday issues; this is his only first-published item in the Tuesday *Weekly.* His article of December 22, 1889, was reprinted in the *Weekly* of the Tuesday following.

‡Uncollected; a factual nature story (not his earlier poem). Copyrighted June 12, 1893, under the title, "How a Humming Bird Builds Its Nest."

§Uncollected. Copyrighted April 15, 1895, under the title, "From the Note-book of an Archer. Duck Shooting in the Swamp."

‖Uncollected. Copyrighted May 20, 1895, under the title, "Archers among the Woodcocks. Hunting Shy Birds with Bow and Arrows."

¶Uncollected. Copyrighted May 27, 1895, under the title, "How an Archer Bags a Wildgoose . . ."

THE (Chicago) INTER OCEAN—*continued*

1895:	September	22	Humpback Sam*
		29	At New Orleans*
	October	20	Besieged by a Hog*
		27	Winter Wolves*
	November	10	An Awful Night*
		17	A Boy's Strategy; an Incident of Count D'Estaing's Siege of Savannah*
		24	At the Stake; A Boy's Experience with the Creek Indians*
1896:	January	19	Mark Spears with the Warring Creeks in Georgia*
		26	In the Storm*
	March	1	A Woodland Battle*
	May	10	A Boy's Grim Patience*
		31	The Girl Detective*
	June	7	Bettie's Prisoner*
	August	2	A Forest Mystery*
	September	6	The Mysterious Twin*
		13	Backwoods Luck*
		27	A Boy with a Will*
	October	25	The Trap*
	November	8	Dancing Ghosts*
1897:	May	23	A Strange Rescue: The Turkey Killer's Story of an Adventure*

THE (Chicago) TIMES

1881:	April	9	A Confirmed Smoker: The Mysterious Smoke that Rises from the Depths of an Unpenetrated Swamp*
1886:	November	21	Southern Song and Story*
	December	12	Genius in Science and Literature: A Lay Sermon*
1887:	January	2	A Hummock Eden*
		30	Inherited Habit in Birds*
	February	13	Beside the Gulf with Ruskin
1887:	March	20	A Chat about Chaucer*
		27	A Snipe Shooting Idyl*
	April	24	The Man of the Marsh*
	May	1	Terre aux Boeufs*
		15	The End of Desire*
		29	The English Point of View*
	July	10	Sappho, the Queen of Song*
		31	Three Miles below Mobile*

---

*Uncollected.

THE (Chicago) TIMES—*continued*
  1887: August   14   Realism and Criticism*
              28   Chickamauga†
        September 25   Swamp Sketches

THE COSMOPOLITAN
  1892: June   A Woodland Mood†
        December   Where the Mocking Bird Sings
  1896: January   A Jocund Feud†
        September   The Neighborhood Rooster†; William Wet-
                          more Story†
  1898: November   The Tragedies of the Kohinoor†
  1900: March   The Man on the High Horse†
        April   Will Imagination Run Dry?†

THE CRAWFORDSVILLE JOURNAL
  1875: January   16   A Winter Song [poem]†
        May   1   The Song-Wind [poem]†
        August   21   A Dream of Fair Weather [poem]†
  1876: November 25   Justice [poem]†; The Lawyer [poem†; both
                        read at the dedication of the courthouse at
                        Crawfordsville, November 20, 1876]
  1877: April   7   The Blue-Bird [poem]
  1878: June   29   A Green Heron [poem]†; A Paw-Paw
                        [poem]‡
        December 28   Temptation [poem]†
  1879: May   17   In Santford's Pocket§
  1881: February   26   Before Dawn [poem]
        May   21   A Sweetheart [poem]†
        June   25   [Speech, representing citizens of Crawfords-
                        ville, in tribute to Henry S. Lane]†
  1882: September   2   Drawing the Cross-Bow‖
        December 30   Coeur de Leon [poem]†
  1883: January   27   Wild Honey [poem]
        July   7   A Prelude [poem]
  1884: January   26   Nectar and Ambrosia [poem]

---

*Uncollected; for response to this article, see *The Literary World,* September 3, 1887.

†Uncollected.

‡Uncollected; with a criticism of his "ode to the paw-paw," reprinted from *The* (Indianapolis) *Saturday Herald.*

§Uncollected; stated to be from the "last number" of the *Quincy Modern Argo,* and a manuscript of it in the Eagle Crest Library bears note that it was written for *Modern Argo,* but periodical as yet unlocated.

‖Reprinted from *St. Nicholas,* September, 1882, where it appeared under title, "The Story of the Arbalist"; collected under title, "The Bow and Its Use," *q. v.*

THE CRAWFORDSVILLE JOURNAL—*continued*

1885: April   11   At the Window [poem]
      July   4   A Health to Indiana [poem; read in lieu of
                      speech on "Our State"]*; [letter to editor of
                      The Crawfordsville Review, about "Miss
                      Crabb" in *At Love's Extremes*]*
1887: May   28   A Memory [poem]*
1889: December   28   [Statement that his most acceptable Christmas
                      gift came at the age of 14: a long flint-lock
                      rifle]*
1895: May   17   A Morning Stroll in Indiana†

THE CRAWFORDSVILLE REVIEW

1885: June   10   A Plea for the Present*

THE CRITIC

1884: January   12   Plantation Music*
                 26   Sketching for Literary Purposes*
      February   16   "Cash Down," or a Percentage?*
      August   30   [Tribute to Oliver Wendell Holmes]*
      September   6   The Limit of Expression*
1885: June   27   A Plea for the Present*
1886: April   17   [Letter to a friend, December 28, 1884, un-
                      der caption:] Swamp-Notes*
      July   10   [Speech at Woman's Club of Indianapolis
                      meeting, June, 1886, under caption:] The
                      Analysts Analyzed*
      August   28   [Letter about "The Analysts Analyzed," dated
                      August 9, 1886]*
      October   16   [Speech before the American Association of
                      Writers, Indianapolis, October 5, 1886;
                      part only, under caption:] The Association
                      of American Writers‡
1887: August   13   Literary Perfume*
      September 24   Thorns in the Novelist's Chair*; [letter re-
                      garding *A Banker of Bankersville* and *A
                      Tallahassee Girl*]*
      October   8   "Prof. Gustavi" [comment on Gosse's letter to
                      The Critic, September 15th]*
1888: March   24   [Novel writing, article about]*
      December   1   America's Poet*

---

*Uncollected.

†Uncollected; part of article, "A Stroll in Indiana with a British Critic,"
post 268.

‡Uncollected; Thompson's name for the Association differed slightly from the
one adopted by them. The same speech was reported in part in *The Indianapolis
Journal,* October 6, 1886.

THE CRITIC—*continued*

    1889: February 23 [Letter concerning James Russell Lowell, dated February 15, 1889]*

          March   23 [Letter concerning *The Story of Louisiana*]*

          August   10 [Letter favoring tulip tree as national flower, under caption:] The National Flower Controversy*

                     31 "Genius in Women" [lecture delivered at Chautauqua, Monteagle, Tennessee]*

    1891: March   7 The Assault [poem]

          April   11 Poetry *versus* Botany*

          December 19 [Letter to *The Critic re* Andrew Lang]*

    1892: July   23 A Sylvan Call [includes untitled poem beginning, "In a wildwood there came to me"]*

    1893: January 28 Theocritus, Weatherly and Kipling*

          November 25 Impressions of the [Chicago] World's Fair*

    1894: March   31 Again "The Sapphic Secret"†

    1895: October 12 Authors Who Ride*

    1896: April   11 Food for the Gods*

    1898: January   1 The Bird in Literature‡

          December   The Poetry of James Whitcomb Riley§

    1899: March   [Letter about error in "The Poetry of James Whitcomb Riley"]*

    1901: April   The Last Literary Cavalier [Paul Hamilton Hayne]*

THE CURRENT (Chicago)

    1884: February 16 The Question of International Copyright*

          October   18 Novels and Novels*

THE DAWN (Indianapolis High School, No. 1)

    1893: December 7 [Poem, addressed to High School Boys and Girls, beginning: "So, when I fall like some old tree"]‖; Lincoln's Grave [poem,

---

*Uncollected.

†Uncollected; a reply to John Burrough's criticism of "The Sapphic Secret" in *The Atlantic Monthly*, March, 1894; Burrough's article had appeared in *The Critic*, March 17, 1894.

‡Uncollected; this article was criticised by "W. P. M." in the issue of January 29, 1898, p. 76.

§Uncollected. For Riley's comments on the review, written January 20, 1899, see *The Letters of James Whitcomb Riley*, edited by William Lyon Phelps (1930), p. 234.

‖Uncollected; the issue contains also much reprinted material by and about Thompson. "An Anecdote," p. 19, is probably from one of his earlier published articles on Southern literature. "If I Were a Boy Again," two paragraphs, autobiographical, is reprinted from *The Indianapolis News*, November 27, 1886.

THE DAWN (Indianapolis High School, No. 1)—*continued*
   1893: December 7   part only]; "If I Were a Boy Again"*

THE EARLHAMITE
   1877: April   March [poem]*

THE EPOCH
   1888: July   27 [Letter to the Editor, July 23, 1888, about "E. C. S.," author of an article in *Literature*, July 7, 1888]*

FOREST AND STREAM
   1880: February 19 [Letter] To the Officers and Members of the National Archery Association of the United States, January 26, 1880*

THE FORUM
   1889: November   The Domain of Romance*

THE GALAXY
   1872: August   The Sentinel [poem]
   1876: August   An After-Thought [poem]*

GOOD COMPANY
   1880: [March]   The Threshold of the Gods
       May (?)   Archery as It Is†
       September   An Idyl of the Longbow*
   1881: March–April A Fortnight in the Palace of Reeds
       August   North Georgia Notes*
       September   A Floridian Fancy*

HARPER'S [MONTHLY] MAGAZINE
   1874: May   The Kingfisher [poem]
   1875: September   A Dream of Fair Weather [poem]*
   1877: May   The Fawn [poem]
       July   Hunting with the Long-Bow
       August   Pan-Fish Angling*
   1884: January   Ensnared [poem]*
   1885: March   Seven Gold Reeds [poem]
   1895: April   The Balance of Power

HARPER'S YOUNG PEOPLE
   1886: July   20, 27 Archery for Girls and Boys*

THE HARTFORD SEMINARY RECORD
   1893: June   The Ethics of Conception

THE (ILLUSTRATED) INDIANA WEEKLY
   1900: June   23 [Speech before Phi Beta Kappa, Wabash College; part only]‡

---

*Uncollected.

†Uncollected; in Vol. 5, No. 8, month unstated (May?).

‡Uncollected; this speech, delivered June 9th, was earlier his Commencement Day address at Boston University, June 6th; see "Literature and Life," *ante* 255.

The Independent
1874: May   14   The Gold-Bird [poem]
       October   8   Between the Poppy and the Rose
1875: January   14   The Snow Bird [poem]*
1876: January   27   Poe and Baudelaire: The Question of Their
                          Sanity*
1883: November 29   The Orphic Legacy [poem]
1884: January   10   Nectar and Ambrosia [poem]
       February   21   Some Notes on Southern Literature*
       May   8   The Morning Dew [poem]
                   15,
       June   12,
       July   24,
       August   21   Some Notes on Southern Literature*
       September 11   To the South [poem]
       October   9   The Tendency of Art in Fiction*
       November 27   Some Notes on Southern Literature*
       December 11   Full-fledged [poem]
                   18   The Word and the Phrase†
1885: February   12   The Picturesque in Poetry*
       March   19   Matter and Style*
       May   14   A Creole Slave-Song [poem]
       July   9   Day-Break [poem, printed with a letter to
                          Henry C. Bowen, June 24, 1885]‡
                   23   Critics and Criticism*
       September 24   Concerning Enthusiasm*
       December 17   Science and Poetry*
1886: January   21   Between Showers at Bay St. Louis*
       April   1   An Early Blue-Bird [poem]
       May   6   Zoro*
                   20   Alphonse Daudet's "Tartarin sur les Alpes"*
       August   19   Precious Titles*
       September 16   The Critics and Russian Novels*
       November 18   Water or Wine§
1886: December   2   Colors from Keats*
                   16   The Final Thought [poem]
1887: February   3   Handicapped Critics*
       March   17   Genius and Enthusiasm‖

*Uncollected.

†Uncollected; reprinted in *The Library Magazine*, January, 1885.

‡Both uncollected. The poem, without accompanying letter, was printed in *The Indianapolis Journal*, July 5, 1885, as "The Daybreak."

§Uncollected; printed also in *The Library Magazine*, November, 1886, whether later or earlier than in *The Independent* is not yet established.

‖Uncollected. When Thompson sent autobiographical data to William M.

THE INDEPENDENT—*continued*

1887:	April	21	"Truth" in Fiction*
	May	12	In a Creole Book-Stall*
		26	An Incident of War [poem]
	June	30	Passion in Poetry and Fiction*
	August	25	The Song of the Mocking-Bird (To Sappho) [poem]
	September	1	The Spirit of Specialism*
	October	13	Realistic Christianity*
	November	10	R. W. Gilder's Poems*
	December	8	The Literary Lesson of Archery*
1888:	January	12	Greek as a Fertilizer*
	March	8	Literary Sincerity*
	April	12	Founded on a Rock*
	May	24	Cant and Criticism*
	July	5	Mr. Howells's Poetry*
	August	30	Daudet's Latest Novel*
	September	13	A Morning Prayer [poem]
	November	1	To-morrow's Poetry*
		22	To a Realist [poem]
		29	A Provincial View*
1889:	January	17	Concerning a Good Style*
	February	28	Halcyon Notes*
	April	4	A Song of the Mocking-Bird (In Captivity) [poem]
		25	Washington: His Place in History*
	May	23	Poets and Portraits*
	June	27	How Bony Grew Rich*
	July	18	Who Is to Blame?*
	September	12	Art for Mankind's Sake*
	October	3	Women and Men in Literature*
	November	7	Christianity and Poverty*
	December	26	Science and Inspiration*
1890:	January	30	The Banjo and the Britannica†
	March	6	The Limit of Criticism*
		27	A Study in Black*
	April	17	A Plea for the Rich*

Baskervill, in a letter March 19, 1887, now in Joint University Libraries, Nashville, Tennessee, he commented on the episode in "Genius and Enthusiasm" of a young soldier cutting down a telegraph pole under fire, saying: ". . . I was that boy!"

*Uncollected.

†Uncollected. E. H. Kemper McComb, of Indianapolis, recalls a magazine article by Will H. Thompson on banjo-playing, not located, but this article by his brother Maurice contained the germ of it, he believes.

The Independent—*continued*

1890:	May	8	The Gulf-Coast Country*
	July	3	Are We a Nation of Thieves?*
		10	A Hint to Critics*
	August	7	Out of the South [poem]
		28	The Point of Aim*
	September	4	Sedgwick's Life and Letters [review, unsigned]†
		18	The Elizabethan Novelists [review of *The English in the Time of Shakespeare* by J. J. Jusserand, unsigned]*
	October	2	A Certain Condescension in Natives*
		30	American Humor*
	November	27	Art and Responsibility*
1891:	February	5	The Touch of Inspiration
		26	The New Influence of Religious Journals*
	March	26	Sentimentality *vs.* the Law*
	April	16	The Intellectual Future of the Negro‡

---

*Uncollected.

†Uncollected; this review and the one of September 18, 1890, are known to be Thompson's by reason of an unpublished letter to Kingsley Twining, July 19, 1890 (in Eagle Crest Library), mentioning that he was at work on them. Similarly, those of June 18, 1891, May 7th and June 4, 1896, are identified as his by letters to Herbert Ward, June 10, 1891, and March 16, 1896. The review of Kipling's *Stalky & Co.*, published November 9, 1899, was surely his, judging by a letter to Ward, October 24, 1899. Other reviews of Kipling's books earlier in the year may, or may not have been his. It had been announced in *The Independent* of October 3, 1889, that, with the first of October, Maurice Thompson became "associated with the editorial corps" and "his best work and his continuous work will appear from week to week, beginning with the next issue, in the columns of our book department." Unfortunately the book reviews are unsigned. Otis Wheeler, St. Paul, Minnesota, writing a thesis on Thompson in the spring of 1951, suggests that the following are his, identified by inference: "Montague Chamberlain's *Popular Handbook of Ornithology of the United States and Canada*," January 7, 1892; "Thomas Nelson Page: *The Old South*," September 1, 1892; "Walt Whitman's Eulogists," March 15, 1894; "Brander Matthews: *An Introduction to the Study of American Literature*," May 7, 1896; "Joel Chandler Harris: *Sister Jane*," February 4, 1897; "Andrew J. George: *From Chaucer to Arnold*," December 15, 1898; "Booth Tarkington: *The Gentleman from Indiana*," January 4, 1900; "Theocritus Again" (review of translation of "Sycillian Idyls" by Marion Miller), February 8, 1900; "Caroline Brown: *Knights in Fustian*," June 7, 1900; "Olive Thorne Miller: *First Book of Birds*," September 13, 1900; editorial, "A Nature Note in French Poetry," October 4, 1900, p. 2404. Proof of his authorship of these is as yet unobtained.

‡Uncollected; the article evoked considerable criticism and the author felt he was misunderstood, so he followed it with "Pure or Mixed," June 11th, and "A Noble Negro," July 16th.

THE INDEPENDENT—*continued*

1891:	April	30	Spring's Torch-Bearer [poem]
	May	7	Virility in Fiction*
		28	A Dream of Romance [poem]
	June	11	Pure or Mixed*
		18	*Ryle's Open Gate,* by Susan Teackle [review unsigned]†
		25	Appreciation and Discrimination*
	July	9	The Day We Celebrate [poem, for 4th of July celebration, Roseland Park, with a letter addressed to Mr. (Henry C.) Bowen]‡
		16	A Noble Negro*
		30	What Is Criticism?*
	August	13	Where the Fault Lies*
		27	A Breath of Morn [poem]
	September	17	Time's Winnowing*
	October	8	Poetry and Money§
	November	19	Literary Mendicity*
	December	3	Some Plain Words*
		17	Scattered Stitches*
		31	Literary Cant [about Jane Austen]*
1892:	January	21	A Voodoo Prophecy [poem]*
	February	4	Cleanliness and Sanity*
		18	Literary Fashions*
	March	10	Sixty-Seven Letters on a Dry Subject [about Jane Austen: responses to "Literary Cant"]*
	April	7	Estimates at Second Hand*
		21	Mr. Fawcett's Latest, Verses [review of *Songs of Doubt and Dream* by Edgar Fawcett; unsigned]‖
	May	19	Current American Poetry¶

---

*Uncollected.

†Uncollected; known to be Thompson's through an unpublished letter to Ward, June 10, 1891, in Yale University Library.

‡Both poem and letter uncollected; Thompson's subject was announced as "An American Boy"; the poem appeared on the same date, July 9th, in *America*, under the title, "Independence Day."

§Uncollected; concerns Andrew Lang; Maurice Thompson's article was stimulated by an editorial of Slason Thompson's, and, in turn, evoked a reply in *The Critic*, December 5, 1891, p. 323, from "The Lounger."

‖This book review, unsigned is known to be Thompson's from a letter to Herbert Ward, February 29, 1892, offering to extend his notice of the book; he made it a lengthy review. The letter is in Eagle Crest Library.

¶"Current American Poetry" was an article which, seeming to belittle British poets, aroused some attacks in British periodicals, referred to by "The Lounger" in *The Critic*, November 5, 1892, p. 252.

908 East Main Street
Crawfordsville
Indiana

My dear Dr. Twining —

By all means send
me the *Life & Letters* of Dr. Sedgwick,
if you would like to have me notice
it. It will please me to do it,
and anything else you wish.

I am making a leader of some
length on Jusserand's "*The Novel in
the time of Shakespeare*". There
are very few books in hand
worth noticing at all, not more
than a half-dozen.

Wishing you a great bag-full
of ozone. Sincerely and truly yours

Maurice Thompson

19 July 1890

Letter from Maurice Thompson to the editor of THE INDEPENDENT,
about his book reviews therein

THE INDEPENDENT—*continued*

1892:	June	23	For One Evening Only*
		30	Aloof [poem]*
	July	28	Literary Reciprocity*
	September	8	A Pipe Solo [poem]*
		15	The Plea for the Pot-Boilers*
	November	3	Literary Half-Acres*
	December	15	A Poet of the Poor
1893:	January	19	The Pierian Freshness*
	February	2	The Charm of Song [poem]*
	March	16	Sex and Genius*
	April	27	Running from Grippe*
	May	11	Love's Voyage [poem]†
		25	Anacreontea*
	July	13	The Bloom of the World [poem, captioned:] The Fourth of July‡
	August	24	Buffon and the Birds*
	September	7	[*The Prince of India*, review unsigned, under caption:] General Wallace's New Book§
		14	Thalysia; The Song of Lycidas; The Song of Simichidas [poems, dedicated to Prof. C. F. Smith, Vanderbilt University, under caption:] The Golden Pastoral*
	October	12	The Test of Originality*
		26	Phonographic American French*
	November	16	A Bit of Realism*
	December	7	The Lyric Muse*
		14	Honey, Pure and Adulterated*
		28	Beyond the Mist [poem]*
1894:	January	4	The Melic Charm*
		18	A Beautiful Assassin*
	February	15	Hand in Hand [poem]*
	March	29	Literature and Ignorance*
	April	19	Beside Running Water*
		26	The First Spring Outing*

---

*Uncollected.

†"Love's Voyage" was printed in London in *Sylvia's Journal*, August, 1893 (*Sylvia's Annual*, 1893).

‡Uncollected. An error in printing remained uncorrected in spite of the author's plea of July 15, 1893 (letter in Eagle Crest Library): "How upon the green, fourth of July earth did you folk come to change my phrase, 'a fight and a frolic' into 'a fight and a colic'? It's the absurdest and most comical exchange of words that I ever knew of! Won't you be good enough to make the poor amend of correction in the next issue of the Independent? Don't hurt the printer."

§Identified as Thompson's on the clipping in the collection from Wallace's Study, now in Eagle Crest Library.

THE INDEPENDENT—*continued*

1894:	May	10	Avian Athletics*
		31	Booming the Britons*
	June	21	A Christian Silhouet of 1812*
	July	26	André Chénier*
	August	16	Miller-Boy's Song [poem]*
		23	Southern Bird-Superstitions*
		30	Fiction and Moral Lessons*
	September	20	Verbal Adumbrations*
	October	11	An Original Grotesque*
	November	1	The Ethical Discrimination*
		15	Two Lyrics in One†
		29	Evening Song [poem]*
	December	27	On Being Independent*
1895:	January	10	A Halcyon Note*
		24	Budding Poets*
	February	21	Summer Song*; Winter Song* [poems, under caption:] Two Songs
		28	A Siren's Whisper*
	March	28	Gryllus Grilled*
	April	18	A Leaf from a Fly-Book*
	May	9	A Stroll in Indiana with a British Critic [Edmund Gosse]*
		23	A Man and a Bird*
		30	Bragget and Bird-Bolts*
	June	13	By a Woodland Spring
		27	Beside a Brook with Izaak [Walton]*
	July	11	Toxophilus on the Kankakee*
		25	The Fletcher's Art*
	August	1	Heyday! [poem]*
		15	A Bit of Advice*
		29	The Art of Being Provincial*
	October	17	Speaking of the Weather*
	November	14	A Bird in the Bush*
		21	Balzac's Romances*
		28	A New Edition of [Gilbert] White's *Selborne**
	December	5	For Cuba*
		12	Alexander Dumas, the Younger*
		26	A Winter Walk*
1896:	January	16	The Bird of Optimism*
	February	6	An Instance of Good Roads*
		13	A New Edition of Poe's Works*

---

*Uncollected.

†Uncollected; Maurice's story of his brother Will's poem, "The High Tide at Gettysburg."

THE INDEPENDENT—*continued*

1896:	February	20	The Turning of the Tide*
	March	19	Mullet, Mocking Birds and Montaigne*
	April	16	Some Faded Notes*
		23	Budding Time*
	May	14	Observe the Lily*
		28	Down in the Wilderness [poem]*
	June	4	Summer-Time Recreation*; *The Exploits of Brigadier Gèrard* by A. Conan Doyle [review, unsigned]†
	July	16	Burns [poem]*
		23	An Instance of Bird Study*
	August	13	Geology as a Summer Pastime*
		27	All on a Summer's Eve*
	September	3	From Sherwood to Chattahoochee*
	October	8	A Trio [poem]*
		29	When Papaws Are Ripe*
	December	10	Handmade Literature*
1897:	January	28	A Winter Atom*
	February	11	A Leaf from an Old Book*
	March	18	Heron Sketches*
	April	8	The Heresy of the Gad*
	May	20	Meadow Music*
	June	3	Summer Reading [unsigned]‡
		10	To Return to Nature
		24	Fame and Popularity*
	July	15	Foot-Notes for an Old-Time Southern Book*
		22	A Midsummer Scorch*
	August	12	Exquisite*
		19	What Is Prose Style?*
		26	Some Interrogatories*
	September	9	A Trencher-Memory of Old Days*
		23	The First Sign of Autumn*
	October	21	A Contribution to Pure Ignorance*
		28	Surrender [poem]*
	November	18	Novels and Morals*
	December	9	Montaigne's Literary Recipe
1898:	January	20	Southward Away [poem]*
		27	A Marsh-Land Incident
	February	10	Montaigne's Materials
		17	A Word to Southern Tourists*

---

*Uncollected.

†Uncollected; known to be Thompson's from a letter to Herbert Ward, March 16, 1896, in Eagle Crest Library.

‡Uncollected; written at request of H. Ward, according to a letter of May 15, 1897, in Eagle Crest Library.

THE INDEPENDENT—*continued*

1898: March   10   Montaigne's Philosophy
                 24   Stranded [poem]*
                 31   Montaigne in His Study*
      April   21   Montaigne, the Provincial Belletrist
      May   26   Recent Shrike-Notes
      June   2   An Afternoon Outing*
                 16   A Summer Jaunt Southward*
      July   21   A Song of the New*
      August   18   A Midsummer Shade*
                 25   Epitaph [poem]*
      September   1   Vigorous Men, a Vigorous Nation*
                  8   Our Vanishing Birds*
                 15   The Lesson of Fiction*
                 29   Athanatos [poem]*
      October   20   An Old Southern Humorist*
      November   3   The Touch of Magic*
                 17   A Southern Pioneer Poet*
      December   8   Criticism by the Rule of Darwin*
                 15   The Return of Romance*
                 29   The Lion's Cub [poem]*
1899: January   26   The Source of Originality*
      February   9   It Shall Never Come Down [poem]†
      March   2   The New Poetry*
                 16   Our Earliest Spring Bird*
                 23   A Song in Season [poem]*
      April   20   The Flagship [poem]*
      May   25   A Pied Piper of Walnut Creek*
      June   1   Loafing-Day [poem]‡
      July   20   A Hoosier Triangle*
      August   10   A Strike of the Bass*
                 31   A Winter Forecast*
      September 14   The Literary Market*
      October   5   A Ballad of Harvest Time [poem]*
                 19   On the Prairie's Edge*
      November   9   Bewildered Critics*; *Stalky & Co.*, by Rud-
                        yard Kipling [review, unsigned]§
                 23   The Revolt of the Illiterates*
      December   7   Our Winter Cardinal*

*Uncollected.
†Uncollected; also in the February, 1899, issue of *The Indianian*, without acknowledgment to *The Independent*, but probably reprinted from it.
‡Uncollected; reprinted in *The* (Illustrated) *Indiana Weekly*, July 15, 1899.
§Uncollected; known to be Thompson's from a letter to Ward, October 24, 1899 (in Eagle Crest Library); reviews of Kipling books in issues of July 6th and 13th, and October 19, 1899, possibly his also.

THE INDEPENDENT—*continued*

1899:	December	14	Art and Money
		21	Bird Books*
1900:	January	25	The Magnetic Story*
	February	8	Some Floridian Pigmies*
	March	1	A Swamp Beauty
		15	The Faculty of Flight*
	April	19	Writing the Record*
	May	3	An Idle Day*
		17	The Prospect in Fiction*
		31	A Stranger in Tuscaloosa*
	June	7	Breezy Books for Summer†
	August	9	The Critics and the Romancers*
		23	Shall This Thing Be?*
	September	13	About the Purple Grackle*
	October	18	The Badge of Originality*
	November	22	A Literary Journey*
1901:	February	21	Sappho's Apple [poem]‡
	March	28§	Jere Jones's Ride*
	May	2	The Golden-Wings' Home*
		30	The Meeting of the Veterans*
	June	6	Rocked in the Wind's Cradle*

THE INDIANAPOLIS JOURNAL

1873:	April	11	At the Window [poem]
		21	The Meadow-Lark [poem]*
		25	The Secret [poem]*
1874:	April	10	Closed Up [poem]*
		21	The Kingfisher [poem]
	May	2	Lazing [poem]
		19	Atalanta [poem]
	July	4	The Chatelaine (From the French of J. De Ressiginer) [poem, signed *J. M. T.*]*
		18	A Mediaeval Romance [poem]*
	October	24	[Review of William Dean Howells, *Poems*, under caption:] A Western Poet*
	November	12	Between the Poppy and the Rose [poem]
		14	[Review of Paul Hamilton Hayne, *Legends and Lyrics*, under caption:] A Southern Poet*

---

*Uncollected.

†Uncollected. The article that follows, a review of Caroline V. Krout's *Knights in Fustian*, unsigned, is possibly Thompson's also.

‡Uncollected; Thompson's last poem, which was reprinted in the March 7, 1901, issue; also in the memorial issue of *The Phi Gamma Delta*, February, 1901.

§In the issue of March 14th there appeared a collection of "Literary Judgments by the late Maurice Thompson," taken from his past contributions to *The Independent*.

THE INDIANAPOLIS JOURNAL—*continued*

1874: December 5   [Review of Wallace, *A Fair God,* under caption:] A Western Novelist*

               12   [Review of Charles Warren Stoddard, *South Sea Idyls*]*

               24   [Review of Thomas Bailey Aldrich, *Cloth of Gold and Other Poems*]*

1875: March   26   Diana [poem]

       May   29   [Review of Paul H. Hayne, *The Mountain of the Lovers*]*

       June   12   [Review of *The Odd Trump*]*

       December 28   The New Evangel [poem, unsigned]*

1877: August   13, 18, 22, 25, 28–30   Summer Saunterings [letters from Michigan]*

       November 27   Looking Southward [poem]*

       December 12   Alternative: A Song of Love*

1881: April   9   At Night [poem]

1884: September 21   To the South [poem]

1885: February 21   Seven Gold Reeds [poem]

       July   5   The Daybreak [poem]*

       November 29   The New Troubadours (Avignon, 1879) [poem]*

1886: August   29   Loup-Garon: A Story of the Gulf Swamp*

       October   6   [Speech before the American Association of Writers, Indianapolis, October 5, 1886; part only, under caption:] The Writers of the West†

1887: April   26   Geology of the Gas Field*

       May   3   Drilling for Natural Gas‡

                6   What Scientists Think‡

       June   30   [Speech, before American Association of Writers, Indianapolis, June 29, 1887, part only with caption:] What Some Writers Think*

       September 27   Rebel or Loyaltist? [poem]

               28   [Letter regarding *A Banker of Bankersville* and *A Tallahassee Girl*]§

---

*Uncollected.

†Uncollected; Thompson addressed the group as "Association of American Writers"; its name adopted at this second convention was The American Association of Writers; later, The Western Association of Writers. This same speech was reported in part in *The Critic,* October 16, 1886.

‡Uncollected, and, by inference, an interview, but his statements are quoted at length, and surely either from a stenographic report, or from manuscript, or interviewer's copy proofread by Thompson (highly technical).

§Uncollected; earlier in *The Critic,* September 24, 1887.

THE INDIANAPOLIS JOURNAL—*continued*

1888: March   11   A Study of [Lew] Wallace's Literary Character*

1889: March   3, 10, 17, 24, 31   The Lily of Rochon: A Legend of Bay St. Louis*

September 19   Thompson's Dime Novel [about "The League of the Guadalupe," *q.v.*]*

November 17   A True Story of Shipwreck†

1890: January   12, 19, 26   The Rose of Chatham: A True Story of the Siege of Savannah in 1779*

1891: March   15   A Certain Good Man*

June   14   The Thompson-Riley Coincidence [on similarity of lines in his and James Whitcomb Riley's poems]*

July   5   The Day We Celebrate [poem]‡

October   23   Pan in the Orchard [poem]

1895: March   31   Plantation Song [poem]§

August   4   Heydey! [poem]*

December 7   For Cuba [poem]*

1896: February 13   [Letter of regrets, to Loyal Legion, Indiana Commandery celebration, Indianapolis, February 12th; letter read by Lew Wallace]*

October   25   A Trio [poem]*

1897: May   30   Down in the Wilderness [poem]*

November 7   Surrender [poem]‖

1898: January   23   Southward Away [poem]*

April   3   Stranded [poem]*

May   1   The Stroke of Ruin*

June   21   [Letter, June 20, 1898, favoring acquisition of Cuba and other Spanish possessions, under caption:] Colonial Dependencies*

27   [Letter, June 25, 1898, favoring acquisitions; further arguments under caption:] The Governing of Cuba*; [editorial regarding acquisition of Cuba and other Spanish pos-

---

*Uncollected.

†Uncollected. Also in *The* (Chicago) *Inter Ocean,* same date, with title, "A Story of Shipwreck."

‡Uncollected; also in *The Independent,* July 9, 1891; the introductory letter, published with the poem in *The Independent,* is not included here; for further comments see ante 266n.

§Part of "The Balance of Power," later collected in *Stories of the Cherokee Hills* (1898), *q.v.*

‖Uncollected; printed later, December 5th, in the same newspaper, under the title, "Into Light."

THE INDIANAPOLIS JOURNAL—*continued*

1898:	June	27	sessions, under caption:] Mr. Thompson's Second Letter*
	July	6	Next Political Issue*
		24	A Song of the New [poem]*
	September	5	[Letter, September 3, 1898, urging acceptance of Republican policy, under caption:] No Longer a Democrat*
1899:	January	2	The True Imperialism*
		30	The Ballad of Berry Brown [poem]*
	February	12	It Shall Never Come Down*
		17	Weaklings to the Rear*
		22	[Speech before Indiana Commandery, Loyal Legion, February 21, 1899, under caption:] A Night for Expansion*
	March	24	A Song in Season [poem]*
	April	27	[Speech before Contemporary Club, Indianapolis, April 26, 1899, under caption:] Literature of Old South*; Mr. Thompson on Georgia Lynching*
	June	5	Loafing Day [poem]*

THE INDIANAPOLIS NEWS

1885:	April	10	A Sand Mountain Wedding†
	July	24, 25	Old Rook; a Tale of the Georgia Mountains†
1886:	November	27	If I Were a Boy Again*
1890:	January	12, 19, 26	The Rose of Chatham: A True Story of the Siege of Savannah in 1779*
	March	15	The Story of Thomas Cushaw*
		22	On Guns and Their Use‡
	April	5	How to Use a Rifle*
		12	Use of the Scatter Gun§
1891:	March	12	[The Assault (poem)]
1893:	July	5	[Lincoln's Grave (poem), part only, under caption:] Maurice Thompson on Lincoln
1898:	October	8	A Boy against a Fleet‖
	December	29	The Lion's Cub [poem]*
1899:	June	30	The Flagship [poem]*

---

*Uncollected.

†Uncollected; syndicated by S. S. McClure.

‡Uncollected; appeared a day later in The (Chicago) Inter Ocean with title, "Guns and Their Use."

§Uncollected; appeared a day later in The (Chicago) Inter Ocean with title, "How to Handle a Shotgun."

‖Uncollected; later in The (Chicago) Inter Ocean, October 16, 1898, with title, "A Boy and a Fleet."

THE INDIANAPOLIS NEWS—*continued*

1900: June   20   A Breath of Morn [poem]

THE (Indianapolis) SATURDAY HERALD

1875: September 25   The Heron [poem]; Picus [poem]*

         October   16   Home [poem]*

1877: April   21   The Fawn [poem]

1879: May   31   [The Wabash, (poem) without title, under caption:] Talk About Books, "Poems of Places"

1880: February   21   Phases*

                 28   [Letter] To the . . . National Archery Association, January 26, 1880*

         May   8   Afternoon [poem]*

         December 25,

1881: January   1 8, 15, 22, 29   Familiar Talks on Literature and Art, Numbers I–VI†

         December   3   A Cavalry Reminiscence: To Major J. W. Gordon [poem]*

1882: August   19   The Dreamer [poem]*

1883: August   18   A "Modern Instance" of Criticism [review of W. D. Howells' *A Modern Instance* and comments on Henry James]‡

         October   13   A Woman's Reason [review of W. D. Howells' book]*

1884: January   12   Genius and Virility*

         April   19   Ho for the Kankakee (A Sportsman's Song) [poem]

         May   10   About "Tarns"§

THE (Indianapolis) SATURDAY REVIEW

1881: December   3   A Morning Sail [poem]

THE INDIANAPOLIS STAR

1915: December 26   [Poem, addressed to High School boys and girls, beginning: "So, when I fall like some old tree," under caption:] The Centennial Story: For the Children of Montgomery County‖

---

*Uncollected.

†Uncollected; No. III is on "Western Literature and Art."

‡Uncollected; Howells is said to have written this book while staying at Thompson's house in Crawfordsville (see *The Literary World*, November 4, 1882).

§Uncollected; a response to criticism of the use of "tarns" in "Ho for the Kankakee."

‖Uncollected; facsimile of the manuscript of an original verse, published in *The Dawn, q.v.*

THE INTER OCEAN (see: THE [Chicago] INTER OCEAN)

THE ISHMAELITE (Indianapolis)
    1897: July   Poe and His Art*
    1898: September   Easy Questions Hard to Answer*

THE KOKOMO (Indiana) TRIBUNE
    1879: December 27 A Winter Reverie [poem]*

LAFAYETTE (Indiana) COURIER
    1886: June   9 [Speech, Purdue University, June 8th]*

THE LIBRARY MAGAZINE
    1885: April   A Red-headed Family
         July   Cuckoo Notes
         August   Some Minor Song-Birds
         September   Birds of the Rocks
    1886: March   2 In the Matter of Shakespeare
         November   Mind, Memory and Migration of Birds*
    1887: April   Beside the Gulf with Ruskin

LIPPINCOTT'S [MONTHLY] MAGAZINE OF POPULAR LITERATURE AND SCIENCE
    1873: July   The Humming-Bird [poem]†
         November   Solace [poem]
    1874: May   The Bluebird [poem]
         June   To a Wild Flower [poem]
         September   A Study for the Critics [poem]
         December   Farewell [poem]
    1875: May   The Song-Wind [poem]*
    1876: April   Sonnet [poem beginning: "I saw a garden-bed
                        on which there grew"]*
         June   Blooming [poem]*
         July   At the Last [poem]*
         October   A Butterfly [poem]*
    1877: February   The Wabash [poem]
    1881: April   At Night [poem]
         June   A Sweetheart [poem]*
         September   The Haunts of the Grayling*
         October   Grand Traverse Bay*
    1883: December   To a Mocking-Bird [poem]*
    1885: August   A Forest Beauty*
    1889: October   Banzou Jean*

---

*Uncollected.

†Uncollected. Thompson wrote a factual nature story, published under same title in The (Chicago) Sunday Inter Ocean, Illustrated Supplement, June 11, 1893, describing the building of a humming bird's nest. The Bird Lover's Anthology (1930) gave title, "The Humming Bird," to his poem collected as "The Assault."

LIPPINCOTT'S [MONTHLY] MAGAZINE OF POPULAR LITERATURE AND
SCIENCE—*continued*
    1892: June   Smithers*
    1894: August   Sweetheart Manette
    1895: August   A Friend to the Devil*
    1896: May   Resaca*
    1899: August   The Court of Judge Lynch*
          September A Sunday Eclogue*
    1901: March   Rosalynde's Lovers

LITERARY LIFE (Cleveland)
    1886: May   Tests of Originality in Art*
          August   The Risks of Authorship*

THE LITERARY WORLD
    1887: July   23   [Speech before American Association of
                       Writers, June 29, 1887; part only under
                       caption:] Two Opinions of Tolstoi*
          August 20   Tolstoi [reply to editorial criticism in issue
                       of July 23rd]*

LITERATURE, AN ILLUSTRATED WEEKLY MAGAZINE
    1888: February 25 Some Notes on Creole Literature*
          April   28,
          May   5   The Sixth Sense in Literature [Papers I and
                       II]*
          June   2   Beside Ben-Hur [about Lew and Susan Wal-
                       lace]*
          September 22 Paul Hamilton Hayne*

LIVING AGE
    1892: July   2   Pan in the Orchard [poem]

THE MANHATTAN
    1884: May   Ho! For the Kankakee! (A Sportsman's Song)

THE (Nashville, Tennessee) DAILY AMERICAN
    1886: December 15 At the Threshold*
                 16 Disembodied Genius*
                 17 Sunshine and Song*
                 18 The Suggestions of Nature*

THE NEW YORK LEDGER
    1890: April   26 The Fate of Louis Capdau*
          October   4 For Isobel*
          December 6 Love and Rapiers*
    1891: March   14 A Certain Good Man*
    1892: January 16 A Legend of Bayou Galère*

---

*Uncollected.

THE NEW YORK LEDGER—*continued*

  1892: April   9 Mordbank: A True Story of Early Days in Georgia*
     June   11 The Fighting at Point Rose*
     August 6 The Lost Count de Lisle*
     September 3–
     November 12 The King of Honey Island
          19 A Woman's Way: A Sketch from Early Frontier Life in Georgia*; The King of Honey Island (continued)
          26,
     December 3 The King of Honey Island (concluded)

NEW YORK WEEKLY (see STREET & SMITH's NEW YORK WEEKLY)

NORTH AMERICAN REVIEW
  1889: July   Foreign Influence on American Fiction*

OUTING
  1884: January–
     July   Summer Sweethearts (Chapters I–XXV)*
     October   Browsing and Nibbling
     December–
  1885: March   Tangle-Leaf Papers, I–IV
     November Katie Winterbud*
  1897: April   Woodland Archery*
  1900: November Confessions of an Ancient Poacher*

THE (Peoria, Illinois) SATURDAY EVENING CALL
  (Before March 16, 1878) The Blue Bird†
  1879: May   3 A Flight Shot [poem]
  1881: December 24 Seed*

THE PHI GAMMA DELTA
  1922: November An Acadian Conspiracy (Theocritus Epigram V) [poem]‡

ST. NICHOLAS
  1879: October   The School in the Woods
     December Watching for an Otter*
  1882: September The Story of the Arbalist
     October   A Picus and His Pots*

---

*Uncollected.

†Uncollected; prose, not his poem, "The Bluebird." Reprinted in *The Crawfordsville Journal,* March 16, 1878, with acknowledgment to the Peoria *Call.* Issues of this latter, of date sought, not located.

‡Uncollected; a nonsense jingle.

St. Nicholas—*continued*

1883: May–
    July   The Story of Robin Hood*
    August   Fly-Fishing for Black Bass

1884: May–
    October   Marvin and His Boy Hunters

1891: July   In the Clover [poem]*
    September   A Prairie Home†

1892: September   Alexander Wilson [poem, with brief biographical sketch]*

1893: May   Springtime Holiday [poem]*
    October   The Orchard on the Hill [poem]*

1899: February   The Ballad of Berry Brown [poem]*

The Saturday Evening Post

1898: December 17 Young Men the Strength of the Nation*

1899: January 7 The Literary Fascination*
    February 4 The Lightheartedness of Americans*
    March   4 Our Nation Must Lead or Lose*
              11 The Passing of Old-Time Oratory*
    April   1 The True Success in Literature*
              15 At the Threshold of a New Age*
              29 The Inspiration of a Walk*
    June   10 The Uppermost Success*
              17 The Golden Rule of Exercise*
    July   1 The New Dietary Theory*
              8 Education and Discontent*
              15 The New Outlook for Young Men*
              22 The Man with the Hoe*
              29 Horsehoe Statesmanship*
    August 5 Having a Good Time*
              12 The New Diplomacy*
              19 Pessimism in Politics*
    September 2 The Revival of the Historical Romance*
              9 The Capacity for Work*
              23 The Stroke of Genius*
              30 The Right Sort of Vagabond*
    October 7 The Measure of Success*
              21 The Hysterical Citizen*
              28 The War against the Classics*
    November 25 The Falsehood of Extremes*

---

*Uncollected.

†Along with his manuscript, the author submitted some drawings as a suggestion for illustrations, and wrote to the editor of St. *Nicholas:* "The story has the merit of being true as to the main incidents, and it has been favorably criticized by my own little boy and girl!"

THE SATURDAY EVENING POST—*continued*

1899: December   2   The Bosses of the World*
              16   Chocking the Chariot of Destiny*
              23   The Book and the Fireside*
              30   Charles Major, Lawyer and Romancer*
1900: January   6   The Man and the Bird*
              20   Educational Buttresses*
     February   3   Geography from a Car Window*
              17   The Hat and the Home*
              24   Those Who Take Early and Hold Long*
     March   3   The Curse of Wings*
              10   American Crudity*
              17   Variegated Monotony*
              24   The Business and Art of Living*
              31   Getting Acquainted with Life*
     April   7   The Quadrennial Furore*
              28   Going with the Current*
     June   2   The Acrobat in Politics*
               9   The Spice of Workaday Life*
              30   Mixing Business and Sentiment*
     July   7   The Absurd Statesman with a Literal Mind*
              14   The Jolly Joker of the Nations*
              28   The Fiend of Industry*
     August   11   New Chances for the Historian*
              18   The Revealing Anecdote*
              25   Dyspepsia on Record*
     September 15   New Words for New-Century-Thoughts*
     October   20   The Bacillus of Printer's Ink*
     November   3   Making Dry Facts Attractive*
              17   What We Like to Read*

SCOTT'S MONTHLY MAGAZINE†

1866: October   Tennyson's Poems*
1867: February   Leibnitz*
     April   Italy and the Arts*
     July   Longfellow—Flower de Luce*
     December—
1868: January (joint issue)   Imaginative Romance*
     February   F. O. Ticknor—Other Poets and "The Poet"*;
                     A Song [poem]*
     March   Invenustus*
     April   The Rose of Sharon [poem]*
     September   Ad Cynthiam Retrospiciens [poem]*

---

*Uncollected.

†"James Maurice Thompson" was the signature with his contributions to this magazine.

Scott's Monthly Magazine—*continued*
  1869: February–
        October   The Mill of God. A Prose Idyll*
        November   My Fleet [poem]*

Scribner's Magazine
  1887: September   The Motif of Bird-Song

Scribner's Monthly
  1874: November   The Great South*
  1875: February   Picus*
        May   The Heron [poem]
  1877: July   Bow-Shooting
  1878: May   Merry Days with Bow and Quiver
        July   Wabash Bubbles, Parts I–V: A Paw-Paw; A
                         Sandpiper; A Green Heron; A Frog; An
                         Owl [poems all]†
        September   Glimpses of Western Farm Life*
  1879: February   The Doom of Claudius and Cynthia*
  1881: March   Simplicity (Written on a Fly-Leaf of Theoc-
                         ritus) [poem]

The Southern Bivouac (Louisville)
  1885: July   Our Brookside Birds*
  1886: May   A Memory: May, 1864 [poem]*
        October   Ceryle Alcyon

Street & Smith's New York Weekly: A Journal of Useful Knowledge, Romance, Amusement, etc. (running title: The New York
  Weekly)
  1889: September 28–
        December 21   The League of the Guadalupe (Chapters I–
                         XXXVII)‡

The Terre Haute Express
  1887: July   17   Our Legend—E Pluribus Unum

The (Terre Haute) Saturday Evening Mail
  1875: July   3   Beauty (Imitated from the French of Chas.
                         Baudelaire) [poem]§

Things and Thoughts
  1901: November–
        December (joint issue)   Prayer [poem]*

---

*Uncollected.
  †All uncollected; "A Paw-Paw" and "A Green Heron" had separate newspaper
appearances.
  ‡Uncollected. Thompson called it a novel, and his "firstling"; see *The Indianapolis Journal*, September 19, 1889, p. 4, for his account of it.
  §Uncollected; reprinted in *The* (Indianapolis) *Saturday Herald*, July 10,
1875, and in *The Crawfordsville Journal*, July 17, 1875.

THE WHEELMAN (see also OUTING; called for a time OUTING and THE
   WHEELMAN)
      1883: November   Out-Door Influences in Literature [including
                         a poem* beginning, "He is a poet strong and
                         true"]

NOTES: No verse or prose by Thompson in *The New York Tribune,* 1871, has been located, although the *Dictionary of American
Biography* mentions that he contributed to it. The list that follows is a
record of titles known to have been published in periodicals which are
unidentified; all are uncollected:

   Archery Today. Copyrighted by the author August 12, 1893, accord-
      ing to Copyright Office records
   Content [poem]. Unidentified periodical clipping in Blair Taylor
      Scrapbook, Montgomery County Historical Society
   [Frost, Robert] Comments by Thompson on Frost's poem, "My Butter-
      fly," were probably published soon after its appearance on Novem-
      ber 8, 1894. Frost said: "I had two copies of Twilight printed and
      bound by a job printer in Lawrence Mass. in 1894 probably out of
      pride in what Bliss Carman and Maurice Thompson had said about
      the poem in it called My Butterfly . . ." The foregoing was in-
      scribed February 1, 1940, in Earle J. Bernheimer's copy of *Twilight,*
      the inscription being reproduced in facsimile in the Parke-Bernet
      Galleries Catalogue No. 1027 (1950). It is, of course, possible that
      Carman's and Thompson's expressions regarding it were contained
      in unpublished letters, but the latter's literary opinions were being
      widely published at this time in periodicals
   Grouse Shooting. Copyrighted by the author October 14, 1887
   Hare Hunting. Copyrighted by the author December 24, 1887
   Hunting with a Bow and Arrow: Wildwood Archery. Copyrighted
      (syndicated?) by S. S. McClure October 5, 1891
   In a Well. Copyrighted by the author June 29, 1896
   In Love's Hands. Copyrighted July 17, 1889, by Franklin File; pub-
      lished before September 21, 1889 (noted as a previous publication
      in announcement on that date of his "League of the Guadalupe");
      probably in some weekly of the dime novel variety
   A Legend of the Satilla. Copyrighted (syndicated?) by S. S. McClure
      December 31, 1886
   [Letter] To Lew Wallace, October 17, 1877, inviting the Montgomery
      Guards' rifle team to a match with his long-bow team. Probably

---

*The poem is the last part of "Wild Honey" earlier collected in *Songs of Fair
Weather* (1883), and later printed separately under title, "Poetry" (see *ante*
192*n*).

printed in a Crawfordsville newspaper; clipping in Wallace Papers unidentified

Mark and the Panther. A Sketch of Old Days in the Pearl River County. Copyrighted (syndicated?) by S. S. McClure February 26, 1892

Squirrel Shooting. Copyrighted by the author December 16, 1887

The Téche Terror. Copyrighted by The Authors' Alliance December 26, 1891; deposited January 12, 1892

Tornado. Copyrighted by The Authors' Alliance January 28, 1892

When My Dream Comes On [poem]. Two notes were penciled on the manuscript in Yale University Library: "Published February 8, 1890," and: "Story & Verse for issue of Sept. 17"

Wood Duck Shooting: Down-Stream after Wary Ducks, in Early Morning. Copyrighted by the author October 4, 1887

WILL HENRY THOMPSON

BORN: *Calhoun, Georgia, March 10, 1846*

DIED: *Seattle, Washington, August 10, 1918*

WILL HENRY THOMPSON was less a literary man, more a practical lawyer with a reputation in the state of Washington as an orator. The fact that he left little as an author to fill a bookshelf is not important in the light of the quality of a few poems he wrote that have proved enduring. Also, his published work in the field of archery with his brother Maurice will keep his name from being overlooked in American literature. Will was five times champion archer of America. In *Forest and Stream* his articles and letters were being published before he became editor of the Archery Department in July, 1879. He collaborated with Maurice in writing *How to Train in Archery* (1879) and revised the book in 1905, after his brother's death.

The trip to Seattle in 1889 that led to his moving his family there and settling for the rest of his life put space between the two brothers who had been inseparable companions since their boyhood in Georgia. Both had the same education under private tutors and guides in outdoor activities; both fought in the Civil War on the Confederate side; came afterwards to Crawfordsville, married sisters there, worked close together.

It was in Crawfordsville that Will wrote his most famous piece, "The High Tide at Gettysburg." The history of the poem is an interesting one, as told by the author in *The* (New York) *Sun*, September 19, 1915, and by Maurice Thompson in *The Independent*, November 15, 1894. After he submitted it to *The Century Magazine* the editor, Richard Watson Gilder, wrote him and suggested that it be made to show that the South "was not lost but saved by the result of the great battle." The poem was published July, 1888; he had changed a line in the sixth stanza and added the last four as "a solemn comment on the meaning and result of the colossal conflict."

Another poem, "The Bond of Blood," had both magazine and anthology printings. A third one, usually spoken of with the others and with as high regard, bears the title, "Together against the Stream." Curiously, it seems to have been overlooked in poetical anthologies, but it appeared in *The Century Magazine,* September, 1895. Since no collection of his poems was published, these are not mentioned in the list of his works that follows.

CHRONOLOGY OF BOOKS AND PAMPHLETS

1879   *How to Train in Archery* (with Maurice Thompson)   E. I. Horsman

1901   *McKinley Memorial Address*   (Ephemera)

1905   *How to Train in Archery (Revised Edition)*   E. I. Horsman

1907   *Memorial Address, B. P. O. E.*   (Ephemera)

1912   *Abraham Lincoln: An Address*   (Ephemera)

1913   *"Abraham Lincoln": Memorial Address*   (Ephemera)

BIOGRAPHICAL REFERENCES

Who's Who in America (1906–1916); *National Cyclopaedia of American Biography,* Vol. 11; Meredith Nicholson, *The Hoosiers* (1900; 1915); Jacob P. Dunn, *Indiana and Indianans* (1919); Frank Moody Mills, *Early Days in a College Town* (1924); W. J. Burke & Will D. Howe, *American Authors and Books 1640–1940* (1943); R. E. Banta, *Indiana Authors and Their Books* (1949), *Hoosier Caravan* (1951); archery books listed under Maurice Thompson biographical references; newspapers obituaries, *Seattle Post-Intelligencer* and *Seattle Times,* August 11, 1918; biographical sketch by his granddaughter, Wilda Thompson, Tacoma, Washington (unpublished), and her letters 1951–1952 (unpublished).

~~~~~~

1879

How to Train in Archery

How to Train in Archery. | [*ornamental rule*] | BEING A COMPLETE STUDY | OF THE YORK ROUND. | [*row of ornaments*] | COMPRISING | An Exhaustive Manual of Long-Range Bow Shooting | for the use of those Archers who wish to | become Contestants at the | Grand National Association Meetings. | BY | MAURICE THOMPSON, | President of the Grand National Archery Association of the United | States, Author of the "WITCHERY OF ARCHERY," etc., etc., and | WILL H. THOMPSON,* | Master of the "Wabash Merry Bowmen." | [*rule*] | PUBLISHED BY | E. I. HORSMAN, | MANUFACTURER OF FINE ARCHERY, | New York.

[Note: All within a red single rule box with ornamental corners.]

COLLATION: [1]⁸, [2–8]⁴, [9]². White wove paper. Leaf measures 5¾" x 4⅛", all edges trimmed.

End paper; binder's leaf; fly title, p. [i]; blank, except for red rule box with ornamental corners, pp. [ii–iii]; frontispiece, p. [iv]; title-page, p. [v]; copyright notice dated 1879, and imprint of H. C. Stoothoff, Printer, 72 John St., N. Y., p. [vi]; *Index.*, p. [1]; vignette, p. [2]; text, pp. [3]–54; divisional half-title for advertisements, p. [55]; testimonials, pp. [56–58]; advertisements, pp. 67–74 (should be 59–66 [67–70]); binder's leaf; end paper.

[Note: Text, pp. (3)–54: How to Train in Archery, Chapters I–X (titled).]

ILLUSTRATIONS: Frontispiece, and vignette, p. [2], both an integral part of the book. Each page has a red single rule box with ornamental corners. Each chapter has an illuminated initial. A single rule appears below running heads, and between divisions on p. 12; rules of various kinds are used on the pages of advertisements.

---

*Second capital *o* broken in all copies examined.

BINDING: Bright blue, brown, and, orange silk-finished mesh cloth.* Front cover stamped in black and gilt: [*in black:*] HOW TO | TRAIN IN [*all, with letters arrow-like, at left of a gilt-stamped target under a black-stamped tree*] | [*in gilt:*] ARCHERY [*letters arrow-like, slanting downward, with gilt-stamped figures at lower left*] | [*in black:*] BY | MAURICE AND | WILL. H. | THOMPSON. [*surname slanting downward*]. Spine blank. Back cover has an ornamental design blind-stamped in center, otherwise blank.

End papers brown coated on white; binder's leaf front and back with conjugates pasted under the lining papers.

PUBLICATION DATA: Earliest review noted: *Forest and Stream,* June 19, 1879. Price, 50¢.

NOTES: Written jointly with Maurice Thompson.† First edition as collated. Advertised as in cloth and wrappers in *The Publishers' Weekly,* June 28, 1879, but no copy in wrappers yet located.‡

A testimonial by Will H. Thompson to the merits of E. I. Horsman's bows and arrows, dated March 17, 1879, appears on the verso of the divisional half-title for advertisements in back; it was included in Horsman's advertisement in *Forest and Stream,* April 10, 1879, p. 196. The second edition is so identified on title-page; see *ante* 185. For the third edition, revised by Will Thompson in 1905, see *post* 291.

Will H. Thompson apparently did not contribute to his brother's earlier manual, *The Witchery of Archery* (1878), but a story by him appeared as an added chapter in its revision, *Pinehurst Edition* (1928); see *Contributions, post* 299.

Maurice Thompson, in his writings on archery, told innumerable stories of adventures with his brother while hunting with the bow and arrow.

---

*Clement C. Parker, in a letter to the compilers, April 29, 1950, described the first edition binding as dark brown or blue gray, so evidently the book appeared in various colors.

†That the book was probably an advertising venture of E. I. Horsman, has been suggested by Paul E. Klopsteg, Glenview, Illinois.

‡Clement C. Parker, dealer in old archery books, Norristown, Pa., reported in a letter to the compilers, April 24, 1950, that he has never seen it in wrappers, although over a dozen copies have passed through his hands. The earliest review found, in *Forest and Stream,* June 19, 1879, describes the book as "handsomely printed and bound," gives price as fifty cents, and mentions no paper edition.

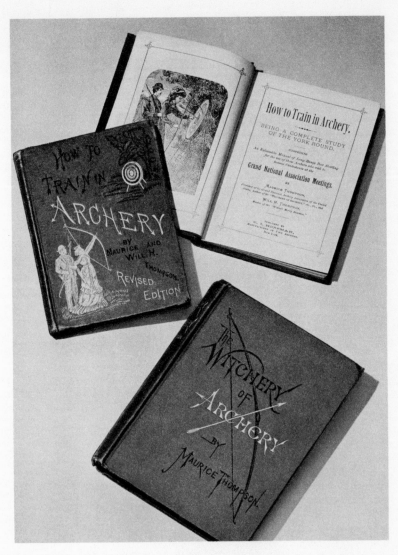

*Archery books: one by both Thompsons, the other by Maurice,
but dedicated to his brother Will*

1905
How to Train in Archery
(Revised Edition)

REVISED EDITION. | [*rule*] | How to Train in Archery [*ornament*] | [*double rule*] | BEING A COMPLETE STUDY | OF THE YORK ROUND. | [*double rule*] | COMPRISING | An Exhaustive Manual of Long-Range Bow Shooting for the use of those | Archers who wish to become Contestants at the | GRAND NATIONAL ASSOCIATION MEETINGS. | BY | MAURICE THOMPSON, | President of the Grand National Archery Association of the United States, | Author of the "WITCHERY OF ARCHERY," etc., etc., and | WILL H. THOMPSON, | Master of the "Wabash Merry Bowmen." | [*rule*] | Revised, 1905, by | WILL H. THOMPSON. | [*rule*] | Copyright by E. I. HORSMAN CO., 1905. | [*ornament*] | PUBLISHED BY | E. I. HORSMAN CO., | NEW YORK.

COLLATION: 48 leaves. White calendered paper. Leaf measures 5¾" x 4⁷⁄₁₆", all edges trimmed.

Blank, p. [1]; portrait of Maurice Thompson, p. [2]; fly title, p. [3]; portrait of Will H. Thompson, p. [4]; title-page, p. [5]; *Preface* by Will H. Thompson, dated Seattle, July 25th, 1905, pp. [6–7]; illustration, p. [8]; *Index*, p. [9]; blank, p. [10]; text, pp. 11–79; illustrations, pp. [80–81]; testimonials, pp. 82–84; advertisements, pp. 85–95; blank, p. [96].

[Note: Text, pp. 11–79; How to Train in Archery, Chapters I–XII (titled).]

ILLUSTRATIONS: Two portraits, from photographs of the authors, precede title-page. The brochure is profusely illustrated with full-page plates from photographs of many archers, singly or in groups. All are an integral part of the book and figured in the pagination.

BINDING: Gray paper, coated, over boards. Front cover printed as follows: Revised edition, 1905 | How to train in | [*illustration showing two men with bows and arrows near an archery target*] | Archery | By Maurice and Will H. Thompson | Price 50 cents | [*all within single rule box*]. Spine and back cover blank.

PUBLICATION DATA: Deposited in the Copyright Office August 23, 1905. Price, 50¢.

NOTES: *Revised Edition* so stated on title-page and front cover. The earlier editions were written by Maurice and Will H. Thompson jointly; for collation of the first edition (1879) and description of the second, see *ante*, 289 and 185. This revision of their book was done by Will alone, after Maurice's death in 1901, hence here considered a new work by him. The changes are as follows:

Illustrations and decorations of the first edition omitted; numerous new illustrations from photographs added

New title-page, bearing copyright notice (on verso in first edition)

Preface, 2 pages, by Will H. Thompson added (but *Prefatory Remarks,* Chapter I, retained)

Chapter II, p. 16, third paragraph from bottom has an added last sentence; p. 17, single-sentence paragraph added, beginning, *So rapid . . .*; p. 19, description of the *Columbia Round* lacks three paragraphs (second, third, and fifth in first edition), and has one added paragraph beginning, *This round has been adopted . . .*

Chapter III, p. 23, last paragraph reworded; p. 24 and first three paragraphs of p. 25 all added

Chapter VII ends, . . . *very rapid rotary motion;* lacks remainder of first edition text

Chapter VIII lacks first paragraph of first edition text

Chapter IX, p. 51, third paragraph reworded; lacks two paragraphs about snakewood and self-snakewood bows (on p. 49 of first edition)

New advertisements, pp. 85–95, with an illustration replacing the earlier divisional half-title; no advertisement of *The Witchery of Archery;* testimonials to Horsman's bows and arrows by Will H. and Maurice Thompson present as earlier, but in reverse order.

~~~~~~

1901

McKinley Memorial Address

A Study in Patriotism [*printer's ornaments*] | w. g. hartranft |
SUPERINTENDENT OF SCHOOLS, KING COUNTY

COLLATION: Pamphlet, 8 leaves, wire saddle-stitched. White calendered paper. Leaf measures 6" x 3^{15}⁄$_{16}$", all edges trimmed.

Title-page, p. [1]; imprint, with parallel rule above and below: *Seattle:* | *Trade Register Press* | 1901., p. [2]; text, pp. [3]–16.

[Note: For text, pp. (3)–16, see *Contents*.]

BINDING: White wrappers. Front cover bears a 2-line quotation: "*A country of the people, by the people and for the people."—Lincoln.* within box-like rule arrangement; below it an oval portrait of the author and the following within rules forming box-like arrangement: MCKINLEY MEMORIAL ADDRESS | HON. WILL H. THOMPSON | Sept. 19, 1901, at Seattle, Wash. On inside front cover is printed a message signed by W. G. Hartranft: "Dear Teachers: | [*three rules with ornament*] | The following oration by | Will H. Thompson, | is to be used as a | reading lesson for sixth, seventh and | eighth grades . . . ." Back wrapper blank.

CONTENTS: McKinley Memorial Address. Delivered at public funeral ceremonies in Seattle, Washington, September 19, 1901. It was published in the *Seattle Post-Intelligencer* on September 20th.

1907

Memorial Address, B.P.O.E.

Memorial Address | DELIVERED BY | Hon. Will H. Thompson | of Seattle | [*elk head vignette*] UNDER AUSPICES OF | Bellingham

Lodge No. 194 | B. P. O. E. | Bellingham, Washington | [*rule*] |
[*ornament*] Beck's Opera House. December 1, 1907 [*ornament*] |
[*rule*]

COLLATION: Pamphlet, 6 leaves, wire saddle-stitched. White wove
paper. Leaf measures 7¹¹⁄₁₆″ x 4¾″, all edges trimmed.
   Title-page, p. [1]; blank, p. [2]; text, pp. [3–11]; blank, p. [12].
   [Note: Text, pp. (3–11), Memorial address, Bellingham, Washington, December 1, 1907.]

BINDING: White wrappers, slightly heavier than book stock. Front
cover printed identically with title-page. Back cover bears imprint:
Union | Printing Co. | Bellingham   Inside covers blank.

NOTES: Thompson was not a member of the Elks, but was invited
to be present as speaker at the memorial services for members who had
died during the year.

1909
Turning Love's Calendar

Turning Love's Calendar | [*poem, dated at foot:*] January 1, 1909

   Printed in brown on a single sheet of heavy tan paper, with initial
in red, within ornamental red border. Sheet measures 9″ x 5½″
(scant), all edges trimmed.
   The author's name does not appear except at foot in autograph. His
granddaughter, Wilda Thompson, explains the item as follows:
   "From date and context of the poem it seems certain this item was
privately printed by the author and sent as 'thank-you' greeting to the
many persons who contributed to the 'Archer's Register' which Mr.
Thompson received as a Christmas present on Christmas, 1908. This
'Archer's Register' is a loose-leaf album of manuscript material on post-
card size paper, which was compiled by his friends, Mr. and Mrs. J. M.
Challiss of Atchison, Kansas. They solicited pictures, reminiscences,
anecdotes, etc., from dozens of Mr. Thompson's friends and archery
associates all over the country, and assembled them on a wooden base
which resembles the ordinary loose-sheet desk calendar. Each sheet is
dated to form a complete calendar for the year 1909."*

---

*Letter, November 20, 1951.

1912

Abraham Lincoln

ABRAHAM LINCOLN | AN ADDRESS BY | WILL H. THOMPSON | [*rule*] | [*text follows, within quotation marks*]

Printed with caption title above text, on 6 leaves of white wove paper, 8⅞" x 6⅛". The only copies located are in the Henry E. Huntington Library and Art Gallery, and the private collection of the granddaughter, Wilda Thompson. The former carries, on a binding supplied by a former owner, the date, 1911, which is in error, as context shows it to be a 1912 address.*

Without imprint or title-page, or explanatory introduction this remains a mystery as to place of delivery, though obviously a Lincoln's Birthday speech.† It is similar in text to his address delivered in 1913 before the Washington State Legislature (described below). On p. 5, line 10 begins: "It is 103 years ago tonight ... ," whereas p. 14, line 15 of the 1913 address begins: "It is 104 years ago today ...." Another difference in time bears witness to this as presented in 1912.

As early as February 12, 1908, Thompson was delivering a Lincoln's Birthday address before the Tacoma Bar Association; printed in full in the *Tacoma Ledger*, February 16, 1908. He repeated it the following year, polished and revised, in the Tacoma Armory, under sponsorship of the Boosters Club, the text given in *The Tacoma Ledger* the next day. The latter is essentially the same as the 1912–1913 addresses.

1913

Lincoln Memorial Address

"Abraham Lincoln" | [*double rule*] | Memorial Address delivered by Mr. Will | H. Thompson before a Joint Session of | the Senate

---

*So reported by Leslie E. Bliss, in letters of January 27, and November 20, 1951.

†Neither the Seattle Public Library nor State of Washington Law Library found report of a Will H. Thompson address in 1912, either in the Seattle newspapers of February 12 or 13, or in the bar association annual report for 1912.

and House of Representatives | of the Thirteenth Legislature of the State | of Washington, held in the House Chamber | at Olympia, Wednesday, February the | Twelfth, Nineteen Hundred and Thirteen | [double rule] | Published by Authority of the Thirteenth Legislature

COLLATION: Pamphlet, 12 leaves, wire saddle-stitched. Leaf measures 8¾" x 6⅟₁₆", fore edge untrimmed, other edges trimmed.

Title-page, p. [1]; *Press Of* | *Frank M. Lamborn, Public Printer* | *Olympia, Wash.*, p. [2]; notice from Senator George Piper, p. [3]; *Senate Concurrent Resolution No. Ten*, p. [4]; history of the resolution, p. [5]; blank, p. [6]; text, pp. 7–24.

BINDING: White linen-finished wrappers. Front cover reads: Abraham Lincoln | [double rule] | Memorial Address by | Will H. Thompson | [double rule]. Back and inside covers blank. A transparent sheet, alligator-finished, is used as dust jacket, saddle-stitched through the pamphlet with light blue silk thread.

[Note: Dr. Robert P. Elmer, in his introduction to the *Pinehurst Edition* of *The Witchery of Archery* (1928) speaks of a copy sent him by the author, "bound in white and gold." Shortly before his death he tried to locate it, but was unsuccessful.]

PUBLICATION DATA: One thousand copies were ordered printed by the Washington State Legislature, 1913.

NOTES: In the *Washington State Bar Association Report of Proceedings of the 35th Annual Convention* (1923), p. 119, the address was reprinted "at the request of many of our members."

For an earlier, almost identical speech, see *ante* 295.

First Editions — Contributions

1886

INDIANA DEPARTMENT OF GEOLOGY AND NATURAL HISTORY. FIF-
TEENTH ANNUAL REPORT [for 1886]. By Maurice Thompson, State
Geologist. Indianapolis [Wm. B. Burford], 1886

Contains the following by Will H. Thompson: "A Geological
Survey of Clinton County," p. [154]; "Marshall County," p. [177];
"Maxinkuckee," p. [182]; "A Geological Survey of Starke County,"
p. [221].

1888

INDIANA DEPARTMENT OF GEOLOGY AND NATURAL HISTORY. SIX-
TEENTH ANNUAL REPORT [for 1887 and 1888]. Maurice Thomp-
son, State Geologist. Edited by S. S. Gorby. Indianapolis [Wm. B.
Burford], 1889

Contains the following by Will H. Thompson: "Fossils and Their
Value," p. [54]; "Outline Sketch of the Most Valuable Minerals of
Indiana," p. [77]; "Partial Report of Survey of the Western Division,
Including Sketches of Pulaski and White Counties," p. [131].
Comments on the reports and brief quotations from them appeared
later in "A Century of Geology in Indiana," by W. S. Blatchley, in
Proceedings of the Indiana Academy of Science 1916, pp. 158–159.

1890

OPEN SESAME! POETRY AND PROSE FOR SCHOOL-DAYS. Edited by
Blanche Wilder Bellamy & Maud Wilder Goodwin. Volume III.
Boston, New York, etc., Ginn & Co. [1890]

Contains the poem, "The High Tide at Gettysburg," p. 158, first published in *The Century Magazine*, July, 1888, Thompson's most famous piece of writing. The first draft contained nine stanzas. In *The* (New York) *Sun*, September 19, 1915, the author gave its literary history, describing it as an attempt to portray the most notable and picturesque achievement of the Confederate arms, the charge of Pickett's division at Gettysburg. He sent the manuscript to *The Century Magazine*. In reply the editor, Richard Watson Gilder, suggested that he add another stanza to the effect that "the South was not lost but saved by the result of the great battle. Thereafter I rewrote the poem, changing the first line of the sixth stanza to its present form and added the last four stanzas. . . . The Confederacy was lost . . . and it seemed necessary that something be said of the lesson taught by the great conflict . . . and I attempted to make the concluding stanzas a solemn comment upon the meaning and result of the colossal conflict shadowed forth in the preceding stanzas."

An early manuscript with the title, "The High Tide," in the possession of Miss Wilda Thompson, Tacoma, Washington, is an eleven-stanza version, with a revision of the final one, showing how much effort it cost before the poem evolved into its published state.

Maurice Thompson gave his own recollection and views on it in "Two Lyrics in One," in *The Independent*, November 15, 1894; the author himself in *The* (New York) *Sun*, above quoted.

"The High Tide at Gettysburg" had innumerable appearances in later anthologies and periodicals. In 1915 there was a separate printing in circular form, a single sheet folded in three, with note by Byron Phelps, Seattle.

1900

AN AMERICAN ANTHOLOGY, 1787–1900: SELECTIONS ILLUSTRATING THE EDITOR'S CRITICAL REVIEW OF AMERICAN POETRY IN THE NINETEENTH CENTURY. Edited by Edmund Clarence Stedman. 2 volumes. Cambridge, Riverside Press, 1900

Boards. Issued in an edition of 300 numbered and signed copies: "Author's Autograph Copy" on limitation leaf. Vol. II contains a poem, "Come Love or Death," p. 509, earlier in *The Century Magazine*, April, 1892.

The anthology appeared also in a one-volume, trade edition, with Houghton Mifflin's imprint added.

BALLADS OF AMERICAN BRAVERY. The Silver Series of English and American Classics. Edited by Clinton Scollard. New York, Boston, & Chicago, Silver, Burdett & Co. [1900]

Contains "The Bond of Blood," p. 138, a poem earlier in *The Century*, March, 1899. It appeared in 1900 in *Poets and Poetry of Indiana*, edited by Benj. S. Parker & Enos B. Heiney (Scollard's *Ballads of American Bravery* had been copyrighted June 30th, the Parker & Heiney volume not copyrighted until October 27th).

PROCEEDINGS OF THE WASHINGTON STATE BAR ASSOCIATION, TWELFTH ANNUAL SESSION. Held at the City of Seattle, July 10, 11, 12, and 13, 1900. Olympia, Wash., Record Publishing Co., 1900

Gray wrappers. Contains his address, "The Status of Our Newly Acquired Territory [Philippine Islands]," p. 90. His response to discussion of it appears on p. 21. Comments by him on other lawyers' papers read during the session are on pp. 42 and 57.

1906

WHO'S WHO IN AMERICA 1906–1907. Chicago, A. N. Marquis & Co. [1906]

Contains an autobiographical sketch of Will H. Thompson, p. 1777. It appeared, with some additions, in succeeding volumes through 1916, Volume IX.

1928

THE WITCHERY OF ARCHERY. By J. Maurice Thompson. With an added chapter by Will H. Thompson. Edited by Robert P. Elmer, M.D. Pinehurst Edition. Archers Co., Pinehurst, N.C. [1928]

Earlier editions, 1878 and 1879, were dedicated to Will H. Thompson by his brother. This *Pinehurst Edition* includes, as Chapter XVII, "Deep in the Okefinokee Swamp," written by Will, and earlier published in longer form in *Forest and Stream*, May and June, 1915. See *ante* 229n for a modern retracing by others of the Thompson journey herein described.

Periodicals Containing First Appearances

THE ARCHERY REVIEW

1932: October   [Letter to J. M. Challiss, May 27, 1911,* included in article by Challiss, "Will H. Thompson, the Great"; another letter to same, August 28, 1911]*

1933: February   Down Stranger Creek: February 15, 1908 [poem]†

June   [Letters to L. L. Peddinghaus, December 16, 1878, February 20, 1879, and May 4, 1880; all are about archery; included in article by Eugene Conner, "Fragments from the '80's"]*

July   [Letter to L. L. Peddinghaus, May 27, 1880; also one of June 14, 1880, captioned "As to That Point of Aim"; both are about archery; included in article by Eugene Conner, continued from the June issue]*

THE CENTURY MAGAZINE

1888: July   The High Tide at Gettysburg [poem]*
1892: April   Come Love or Death [poem]*
1895: September   Together against the Stream [poem]‡
1897: February   The Death-Dream of Armenia [poem]*
1899: March   The Bond of Blood [poem]*

CHICAGO HERALD

1915: April   26   To an Old Archer Friend (E. B. W[eston])*

THE CRAWFORDSVILLE JOURNAL

1881: October   1   Will H. Thompson's Tribute [to President Garfield, September 25th]*

December 31   Spes [poem]*

FOREST AND STREAM

1878: September 19   Archery Ranges and Bows [signed *Archer*]§
October   17   Archery [letter to the Editor, signed *Archer*]§

---

*Uncollected.

†Uncollected; "poem contributed from private correspondence, by J. M. Challiss."

‡Uncollected. Issued also in separate, pamphlet form; reported but not seen.

§Uncollected. No signed articles by him appeared until March, 1879, but an editorial on January 30, 1879 speaks of him as having "already supplied our col-

FOREST AND STREAM—*continued*

	December 12	How to Draw the Bow [letter to the Editor, December 2, 1878, signed *Archer*]*
1879: March	20	The Archer's Chief Enemy—The Wind†
April	10	American Bows‡; [letter in Horsman's advertisement, endorsing bows]
May	8	Rifled Arrows‡
July	24	National Meeting of American Archers‡
	31	Things to Be Remembered in Archery Practice§
August	7	[Letter, July 28, 1879, captioned:] Highland Park Archery Club‡
	14	The Fables of Archery‡
	21	National Archery Association Tournament [signed *Archer*]‡
September 11		American *vs.* English Bows‡
October	9	What Sort of an Arrow Should Be Used?‖ What Is the Utmost Flight of an Arrow?¶
November 20		Hunting with the Bow‡
December 11		The Days and Places of Archery‡; Archery in the Winter‡
	18	Where and When Shall the Second Grand National Meeting Be Held?‡
1880: January	15	A Retrospect of the Archery Season of 1879‡
February	12	Private Practice Club‡
	19	Shall We Change Our System of Scoring?‡
April	15	Private Practice Club, March Scores‡
May	27	Private Practice Club, April Scores£
June	10	The Grand National Archery Meeting‡
August	19	Private Practice Club, June Scores‡
September	2, 9	Private Practice Club, Annual Report for the Season Ending June 30th‡
October	28	Private Practice Club, August Scores‡

---

umns largely"; these writings from Crawfordsville by "Archer" are surely the earlier large supply referred to.

*Uncollected; reprinted in *The Archery Review*, June, 1933.

†Uncollected; first article in *Forest and Stream* to be signed Will H. Thompson; earlier contributions signed "Archer."

‡Uncollected.

§Uncollected. This issue, July 31st, announces that the Archery Department is now under the supervision of Mr. Will H. Thompson.

‖Uncollected; reprinted in *The Archery Review*, August, 1933.

¶Uncollected; reprinted in *The Archery Review*, July, 1933. A comment on the article appeared in *Forest and Stream*, October 30, 1879.

£Uncollected; reprinted in *The Archery Review*, July, 1933.

FOREST AND STREAM—*continued*

1915: March		What a Good Bow Has Done and Will Do*
	April	Some Old-Time Rifles and Rifle Shooting*
	May	To an Old Archer Friend (E. B. W[eston])†; Deep in the Okefinokee Swamp
	June	Deep in the Okefinokee Swamp [concluded]

THE INDEPENDENT

1915: June　　7　Yew Bow and Clothyard Shaft‡

THE INDIANAPOLIS JOURNAL

1873: August　11　Erotic [poem]*
1897: February　2　The Death Dream of Armenia [poem]*

THE (New York) SUN

1915: September 19　[Editorial on "The High Tide at Gettysburg"]*

PORT ANGELES (Washington) EVENING NEWS

1916: June　　15　[Speech, Flag Day Address at Port Angeles, June 14th]*

RICHMOND (Virginia) TIMES-DISPATCH

1935: October　　6　The Mother of Edgar [Elizabeth Arnold Poe] [poem]*

SCOTT'S MONTHLY MAGAZINE

1867: December		The Silent Army [poem]*
1869: January		To James Maurice T . . . . [poem addressed to his brother]*
	March	"There Is No God but God" [poem]*
	May	A Dream [poem]*
	June	The Bowman [poem]§
	November	My Fleet [poem]*

SEATTLE (Washington) POST-INTELLIGENCER

1899: September　3　The Voyage [poem]‖
1901: September 20　[Address at memorial services for President McKinley, at Seattle, September 19th]*

SEATTLE (Washington) TELEGRAPH

1894: October　16　[Speech introducing Lew Wallace, who was

---

*Uncollected.

†Uncollected; also in *The Literary Digest*, May 15, 1915.

‡Uncollected; reprinted in *The Archery Review*, October, 1933.

§Uncollected. Later, without title, in "Deep in the Okefinokee Swamp," *Forest and Stream*, June, 1915; not included in *Pinehurst Edition* of *The Witchery of Archery* (1928).

‖Uncollected. The voyage was an excursion to get Seattle's totem pole.

SEATTLE (Washington) TELEGRAPH—*continued*
    1894: October   16   lecturing on Turkey and the Turks in
                                      Seattle, October 15th]*

TACOMA (Washington) LEDGER
    1908: February   16   [An address on Abraham Lincoln delivered
                                        February 12th before the Tacoma Bar As-
                                        sociation]*

*Uncollected.

LEW[IS] WALLACE

BORN: *Brookville, Indiana, April 10, 1827*

DIED: *Crawfordsville, Indiana, February 15, 1905*

LEW WALLACE and *Ben-Hur*: these were names of fame to successive generations of Americans in whose minds the two, the author and his work, have been inextricably associated. His hero of the chariot race placed in the most dramatic era of all history, appearing in novel form (1880), extravaganza play (1899), and motion picture (1925), thrilled for repeated decades a national and international reading and play-loving public, the young and their elders alike. *Ben-Hur* finally proved its adjustability to changing times and tastes by becoming a television drama in the year 1952.

Wallace's two other novels, *The Fair God* (1873) and *The Prince of India* (1893), were popular in their day; the sequel to the latter which he planned but never wrote was to bring "The Prince" (The Wandering Jew) to America with Christopher Columbus. He ventured, too, in other fields of art. His ambitions as playwright remained unfruitful: "Commodus" was published, not produced; "Our English Cousin" and "No. 120" were neither published nor brought to production. Credit for the success of the dramatized form of *Ben-Hur* probably belongs largely to another writer, although the story was his and he helped in making it a play. A ballad written during the Civil War, "The Stolen Stars," was published as a piece of sheet music, seldom remembered today. A long narrative poem, "The Wooing of Malkatoon," became a book, but did not add distinction to his name; nor did his story, "The Boyhood of Christ." His drawings, some of which were used as illustrations in his wife's books, show that he had ability in that direction and might have become an artist of note. Numerous originals are preserved in the Indiana Historical Society, William Henry Smith Memorial Library.

The man, Lewis (usually known as Lew) Wallace, expressed himself in all his pursuits with some of the verve and color with which he endowed his tale of the Jewish prince. His enthusiasm for action, love of the heroic, appreciation of temporal and spiritual conquests: these are clearly visible both in his writings and the events of his life. It is not surprising that he engaged in warfare, was governor of a turbulent Territory, and became United States Minister to Turkey. His father, David Wallace, had served a while as lieutenant-governor, then governor of the state of Indiana, so Lew Wallace's youth was largely spent in Indianapolis. An erratic education, mostly derived from his own reading and as a lackadaisical apprentice in the law, ended abruptly at the age of nineteen when he raised a company of volunteers, was elected its second lieutenant, and marched off to the Mexican War (1846–1847). His own words tell of this period, contemporary letters having been published in the *Indiana State Journal* and *Indiana State Sentinel;* further comments appear in his *Autobiography* (1906).

This early experience of war and of Mexico foreshadowed much of Wallace's later life. He had then his first taste of the exoticism of a foreign world. He became the soldier that he remained the rest of his life, although his military career brought many disappointments. Ready at the outbreak of the Civil War with a unit from Crawfordsville known as the Montgomery Guards, drilled and dressed in Zouave fashion, he was appointed Adjutant General of Indiana and, after a quick and effective job of organizing Governor Morton's first troops, became the colonel of the Eleventh Indiana Volunteer Regiment. A major general at the age of thirty-four, he commanded a division at the bloody Battle of Shiloh, but became a victim of the following characteristic disputes and recriminations, and was relieved. Except for being placed in charge of the defense of Cincinnati in September, 1862, and once again at Monocacy where General Early was effectively detained in his strike toward Washington, General Wallace was never given command of any other unit in the field. He suffered until his death in 1905 from the blame for the inability of his division to reach the field of battle on the first day of Shiloh. The *Autobiography,* his only literary treatment of contemporary American life, was primarily a vehicle for discussion of the episode; he died before he finished it, but his wife, with the help of Mary Hannah Krout, brought it to publication.

The bibliographical story of Wallace's career as governor of the Territory of New Mexico is told herein under "Ephemera," in connection with his first *Proclamation* (1878), *Report* (1879), and *Message* (1880). It was as a military man that he received the appointment, to quell the Lincoln County war; it was as an author that he spent his spare time there, completing the writing of *Ben-Hur*.

His *Life of Gen. Ben Harrison* (1888), published in two forms and later revised only slightly for the second Harrison Presidential campaign in 1892, was too hastily written to be considered a literary work, but it represents his interest in politics. He was a familiar figure as speaker at Republican Party political rallies.

On the public platform he had had practice during the Civil War, talking at citizens' mass meetings to secure recruits for the Union Army; afterwards, appearing before groups of war veterans. He also delivered lectures throughout the country on "Mexico and the Mexicans" and "Turkey and the Turks."

Perhaps the many-sided features of Lew Wallace show best through our section called, "Contributions." This includes a guide to his printed papers that relate to Turkey, letters to the American Secretary of State during his service as Minister to that country, 1881–1885. It was during this period that he visited the Holy Land; delved, too, into Oriental literature and gathered material for the writing of *The Prince of India*. His appointment had come through his authorship: President Garfield read and admired *Ben-Hur*, and asked for another book to follow it. Lonesome for home at Crawfordsville, Wallace refused the Sultan's offer of a post as Inspector-General of the Ottoman Army and spent the rest of his life close to the Indiana city of his choice.

If there were any doubt as to Susan Wallace's place in his literary as well as personal life, his tributes to her in his *Autobiography* make clear his acceptance of her as critic. The book quotes a letter to her from Santa Fe, December 4, 1879: "A poet . . . asked me, confidentially, if my wife had not helped me in writing the *Fair God* and my new book [*Ben-Hur*]. I told him yes—that I never put away a chapter as finished without first reading it to you to get your criticism. In many instances I had great help in that way. He came in evidently thinking you were joint author." With the help of his

Susan, a tendency toward grandiloquence was kept in check, and the vitality and integrity that were Lew Wallace's great assets became reflected in his works.

CHRONOLOGY OF BOOKS AND PAMPHLETS

1873   *The Fair God*   James R. Osgood and Company
1875   *General Wallace's Military Record*   (Ephemera)
1876   *Commodus*
1879   *Report of the Governor of New Mexico*   (Ephemera)
1880   *Message of Governor Lewis Wallace*   (Ephemera)
      Ben-Hur   Harper & Brothers
1888   *Life of Gen. Ben Harrison*   Hubbard Brothers
      The Democratic Party and the Solid South   (Ephemera)
1889   (*i.e.,* 1888)   *The Boyhood of Christ*   Harper & Brothers
1892   *Life and Public Services of Hon. Benj. Harrison*   (reissue of
      Life of Gen. Ben Harrison [1888], q.v.)
1893   *The Prince of India*   Harper & Brothers
1898   (*i.e.,* 1897)   *The Wooing of Malkatoon* [and] *Commodus*
      (latter earlier issued separately [1876], q.v.)
1899   *The First Christmas*   Harper & Brothers
1901   *An Ideal Indiana Soldier: James R. Ross*   (Ephemera)
1903   *Address . . . at the Dedication of Indiana's Monuments on the
      Battlefield of Shiloh*   (Ephemera)
1906   *Lew Wallace: An Autobiography*   Harper & Brothers

BIOGRAPHICAL REFERENCES

Who's Who in America, Vols. 1–3; standard encyclopedias and biographical reference works on American authors (he is named in almost all); Louis C. Schaedler, *Lew Wallace: Middle-Class Novelist* (1941; thesis deposited in Duke University Library); Irving McKee, *"Ben-Hur" Wallace* (1947; all the items in the bibliography in this book-length biography were checked for bibliographical clues; many of the references are to background material); R. E. Banta, *Indiana Authors and Their Books* (1949); Wallace Papers, Eagle Crest Library, and Indiana Historical Society, William Henry Smith Memorial Library.

~~~~~~

1873

The Fair God

THE FAIR GOD; | OR, | THE LAST OF THE 'TZINS. | A Tale of the Conquest of Mexico. | BY | LEW. WALLACE. | [*quotation, 4 lines, from Draper*, Int. Development of Europe] | [*publishers' emblem*] | BOSTON: | JAMES R. OSGOOD AND COMPANY, | LATE TICKNOR & FIELDS, AND FIELDS, OSGOOD, & CO. | 1873.

COLLATION: 1–25^{12} (numbered on recto of 8th leaf. Number repeated on each 12th leaf with an asterisk, except Sigs. 4 and 9. Lettered besides, on 8th and 4th leaves alternately of Sigs. 1–25 except Sig. 8 which is not lettered on its 4th leaf. Lettered on 12th leaves alternately of Sigs. 2–24 except Sig. 4 which bears neither letter nor numeral on its 12th leaf). White wove paper. Leaf measures 7$\frac{7}{16}$" x 4$\frac{13}{16}$", all edges trimmed.

End paper; binder's leaf; title-page, p. [i]; copyright notice dated 1873, and imprint of the University Press: Welch, Bigelow, & Co., Cambridge, p. [ii]; *Note By The Author* dated August 8, 1873, pp. [iii]–iv; table of contents, pp. [v]–vii; blank, p. [viii]; half-title, p. [ix]; blank, p. [x]; *Introductory*, pp. [xi]–xiv; text, pp. 1–586 (with printers' imprint at foot of p. 586); binder's leaf; end paper.

[Note: Text, pp. 1–586: The Fair God, Books One–Seven.]

BINDING: Various colors: brown, maroon, and, green mesh cloth over beveled boards. Front cover bears gilt-stamped ornamental design in the center. Spine gilt-stamped: THE | FAIR GOD | [*rule*] | LEW WALLACE | [*ornament*] | [*publishers' emblem*]. Back cover same as front except that design is blind-stamped.

End papers brown coated on white; binder's leaf front and back.

PUBLICATION DATA: Entered for copyright July 9, 1873. Published September 6, 1873, but not deposited in the Copyright Office until

November 8th.* Reviewed in *The Literary World,* September (*i.e.,* August), 1873.† Price, $2.00.

NOTES: First edition as collated. No illustrations. It appeared in two states thus distinguishable:

> *State* 1: Paper stock thin, bulking book to 1″ across sheets (later, 1¼″ [full])
>
> > Bound in cloth over beveled boards (later, plain boards); stamping as described (later, rules added)
>
> *State* 2: Paper stock heavier, bulking book to 1¼″ (full), (earlier, 1″)
>
> > Bound in cloth over plain boards (earlier beveled); front and back covers have design boxed within a blind-stamped parallel rule which is within a blind-stamped wide single rule; spine has triple gilt rule top and bottom (earlier, these rules all lacking).

That the change in binding accompanied the change in book stock is indicated by a letter from the publisher, B. H. Ticknor, September 24, 1873, addressed to the author: "We have got out a new edition of Guatamo [*The Fair God*] which is thicker and I think handsomer than the first."‡ The "new edition" was put on the market in September, soon after distribution of the earlier copies; it was advertised (with a review from the *New York Tribune*) in the *Boston Evening Transcript,* September 24, 1873.

Before the end of 1874 this historical novel is reported to have undergone four printings; "more than seven thousand copies were disposed of the first year."§ In 1888 it had reached its 38th "edition"; an 1892 reissue is identified as "One Hundred and First Thousand." In 1898 the Riverside Press issued it with illustrations by Eric Pape‖ in

---

*B. H. Ticknor wrote the author on August 28, 1873: ". . . We propose to gratify an impatient public by getting out the book next Saturday, Sept. 6th. The copy I mail herewith is a proof copy and the lettering is too large; it will be corrected in the edition. The five bound copies on your list will be sent on Tuesday." —Letter in Wallace Papers.

†This review, by Samuel Crocker, was used to advertise the book, 500 copies being reported by the publishers, August 25, 1873, as being made ready to distribute to the trade and press.—Letter in Wallace Papers. See McKee, pp. 125–126, for summaries of contemporary reviews. Maurice Thompson's review entitled, "A Western Novelist," was in *The Indianapolis Journal,* December 5, 1874.

‡This letter and the book sent Wallace by Ticknor on September 24th (a copy in *State* 2) are now in Eagle Crest Library.

§McKee, p. 126.

‖For the designs the artist went to Mexico, "gathering inspiration upon the very scene of the story."—*The Publishers' Weekly,* November 19, 1898.

two volumes: cloth, and, de luxe edition in ooze leather limited to 250 copies. A "new edition" in one volume with the Pape illustrations appeared in 1905. In May of 1908 Harpers made arrangements to include this in a collected edition of Lew Wallace's works to be sold by subscription. In 1928 a "holiday edition" was issued in two volumes.

Grosset & Dunlap distributed their reprint edition in 1908.

In 1941 *The Fair God* was still selling "with an all-time total of 217,000 copies to its credit."*

In Great Britain the novel appeared in Warne's *Crown Library,* No. 16, 1887. A piracy was reported† as being sold in India in 1889. A British edition was issued by Ward & Locke in 1890; by the Walter Scott Publishing Company in June, 1895; another, by Ward Locke & Co., Ltd., *ca.* November, 1909, as *The Pansy Series,* No. 42.

A Spanish translation is said to have been published in Buenos Aires, *ca.* 1888.‡ A Swedish translation was projected by Mrs. N. S. Moore in 1887, to follow her translation of *Ben Hur;* it is not known whether or not this was completed and published.

The author was disappointed in his hope that Richard Mansfield would want it adapted for him on the stage; the latter wrote April 30, 1902, explaining its unsuitability (letter in Wallace Papers). A dramatization was written by Ira B. Goodrich, Jr., in 1904; typewritten copies were deposited in the Copyright Office March 14, 1905; it did not reach production; nor did Owen Davis' plan, to dramatize it in 1921 for Lee Shubert to produce, come to maturity.§

A motion picture project by the Selig Company in 1913 was dropped on account of Mexican troubles.

The early manuscript title was "The Last of the 'Tzins"; its story is told in *Lew Wallace: An Autobiography* (1906), Vol. I, pp. 88–91; Vol. II, pp. 887–[894]; see also McKee, pp. 10, 122. A charge of plagiarism (that his book had received help from W. W. Fosdick's *Malmistic, the Toltec, and the Cavaliers of the Cross*) was published in the Franklin (Ind.) *Herald* and answered in various newspapers (see *The Indianapolis Sentinel,* November 2, 1873, p. 6); this provoked a reply from Wallace in the form of a letter to the *Cincinnati Commercial,* November 10, 1873, published therein on November 11th. He did not consider it even a "literary coincidence."

---

*McKee, p. 126.

†In an article in the *New York Mail and Express,* July 10, 1889.

‡McKee, p. 127n. Correspondence regarding the translation (in 1887) in Wallace Papers, Indiana Historical Society.

§Negotiations with the author's son appear in correspondence preserved in the Eagle Crest Library.

1876

Commodus

COMMODUS | AN HISTORICAL PLAY | BY | LEW. WALLACE.

COLLATION: 34 leaves, sewn within wrappers. White wove paper. Leaf measures 8¹⁵⁄₁₆″ x 6″, all edges trimmed.

Title-page, p. [1]; copyright notice dated 1876, p. [2]; *Persons Represented*, p. [3]; blank, p. [4]; text. pp. [5]–65; blank, pp. [66–68].

[Note: Text, pp. (5)–65: Commodus.]

BINDING: Sewn within bluish gray wrappers, trimmed to leaf size. Front wrapper bears title within a double rule box: COMMODUS   Back and inside wrappers blank.

PUBLICATION DATA: Privately published by the author. Deposited in the Copyright Office June 20, 1876.

NOTES: Place of publication not stated; probably Crawfordsville. No illustrations. A copy in the Library of Congress has a slip pasted over the original copyright notice, which is also dated 1876 but claims entry in the Office of the Librarian of Congress at Washington, not in the Clerk's Office of the District of Indiana as originally printed; it also has an errata slip inserted between pp. [4–5].

The work was revised and reissued in wrappers later the same year, with dedication to S[amuel] R. Crocker on an inserted leaf between pp. [2–3]. Act III, Scene 2, of this reworked version was printed in *The Sword and the Pen* (Boston), December 13, 1881,* under the caption, "Scene from an Unpublished Play." The play had another reprinting, January, 1889, in *Harper's New Monthly Magazine. The Indianapolis Journal*, January 6, 1889, published some "quotable lines" therefrom, including the poem, "Sleep."

Commodus was republished in 1898 [*i.e.*, 1897] with *The Wooing of Malkatoon, q.v.*

It remained "closet drama" (see McKee, pp. 130–131) and failed to satisfy the author's hopes for it. ". . . I am determined to write a suc-

---

*Referred to by Wallace in a letter to Benjamin H. Ticknor, as a "little sheet to be sold for the benefit of the 'Soldiers' Home Bazaar'"; letter quoted in *Glimpses of Authors* by Caroline Ticknor (1922), p. 101; see p. 103 in the same book for another letter regarding the play.

cessful play if it takes the remainder of my life," he wrote his son Henry, January 16, 1883.* His ambition was in a sense realized through his supervision of William Young's dramatic arrangement of "Ben-Hur."

1880

Ben-Hur

BEN-HUR | A TALE OF THE CHRIST | BY | LEW. WALLACE | AUTHOR OF "THE FAIR GOD" | "Learn of the philosophers always to look for natural causes in all extraor- | dinary events; and when such natural causes are wanting, recur to God" | COUNT DE GABALIS | NEW YORK | HARPER & BROTHERS, FRANKLIN SQUARE | 1880

COLLATION: [1]–35⁸, [36]². White wove paper. Leaf measures 6⅝"x 4⅝" (scant), all edges trimmed.

End paper; binder's leaf; title-page, p. [1]; copyright notice dated 1880, and statement: *All rights reserved.*, p. [2]; dedication, *To | The Wife Of My Youth*, p. [3]; quotations from Richter and Milton, p. [4]; text, pp. [5]–552; publishers' advertisements, pp. [1]–12; binder's leaf; end paper.

[Note: Text, pp. (5)–552: Ben-Hur: A Tale of the Christ.†]

BINDING: Cadet blue (light blue-gray) silk-finished mesh cloth. Front cover bears a floral design stamped in red, blue, green, and black; this intercepts a black horizontal single rule above and below the title

---

*Letter in the Wallace Papers. Wallace's other unproduced plays, "Our English Cousin" (McKee, p. 129) and "No. 120" (alternate manuscript titles: "An American Duchess" and "the New American Industry"; see McKee, p. 263) were also unpublished.

†Three songs included in the novel were later issued with musical settings (see *Ben-Hur Music, post* 333-4); two of them appeared without music: "Kapila" in *Poets and Poetry of Indiana,* edited by Benj. S. Parker & Enos B. Heiney (1900); "Song [Wake Not]" in the same, also in *An American Anthology,* 2 vols., edited by E. C. Stedman (1900). About these songs Wallace had written his wife on July 29, 1880: "The poor little verses in the 'Ben-Hur' will be credited to you; of that I feel very certain; yet if you can stand the imputation I can."—Letter in Wallace Papers.

There is a "Table Blessing" in Elizabeth Hough Sechrist's *Merry Meet Again* (1941), quoted from the end of Chapter II. For reprints of certain prose sections see *post* 325-6.

and author's name, the rules being joined to a vertical one at right and extending, except for break at hinges, across spine and back cover; in the panel thus formed on the front there is black-stamped: BEN-HUR | A TALE OF THE CHRIST | [rule] | LEW. WALLACE Spine has colored floral decorations stamped at top and bottom, similar to those on front cover, intercepting the above-mentioned black rules; in the panel thus formed is black-stamped: BEN-HUR | A TALE OF | THE CHRIST | [rule] | WALLACE Back cover bears colored stamping of a floral bouquet in a black-stamped urn; an upper horizontal rule, continued from front cover and spine except for break at hinges and interception by the floral bouquet, is joined to a vertical rule at left which connects with a short horizontal one below an imprint: HARPERS. [rule below all but initial letter]; another horizontal rule, continued from front cover and spine except for break at hinges, is intercepted by the urn.

End papers gray calendered; binder's leaf front and back.

PUBLICATION DATA: Copyrighted October 12, 1880; published November 12th.* It was reviewed in *The New York Times,* November 14, 1880, as "printed and in hands of book dealers"; this review was reprinted in *The Crawfordsville Journal,* November 20, 1880. Price, $1.50 For size of edition see *post* 318.

NOTES: First edition as collated, with date, 1880, on the title-page (later, in 1881,† date dropped). No illustrations. The dedication reads: *To | The Wife Of My Youth* (the words, *Who Still Abides With Me* were added in 1884,‡ after the issuance of many printings). Mrs Wallace herself was responsible for the original phrase as well as for its revision. The author wrote to Alexander Hill, January 27, 1899: "When Ben Hur was finished I told my wife it was to be dedicated to her, and that she must furnish the inscription. She wrote: 'To the Wife of My Youth.' The book became popular. Then I began to receive letters of sympathy and inquiries as to when and of what poor Mrs. Wallace died. I laughed at first, but the condolences multiplied until finally I told the good woman that, having got me into the trouble, she must now get me out, which she did by adding the words, 'who still abides with me.' The device was perfect."§

---

*Publishers' statement, letter to the author, November 13, 1880. The earliest autographed copy noted bears author's inscription dated November 17, 1880; in the Indiana Historical Society, William Henry Smith Memorial Library.

†A copy with the date dropped was presented by Mrs. Wallace to her sister, Helen E. Blair, Christmas, 1881; in collection of F. Bates Johnson, Indianapolis.

‡Date of the addition established by the publishers' statement in a letter to Mrs. Wallace, December 5, 1884; letter in the Eagle Crest Library.

§Wallace's letter, here quoted, appeared both in facsimile and transcription in

Lew Wallace's BEN-HUR *in flower-stamped cloth and in later undecorated bindings; all first edition copies*

To quote his wife's own words in the letter of instructions for the addition, November 24, 1884, it was ordered because of the "inquiries of correspondents as to the *number* of *wives* Gen. Wallace has had."*

At the time of change in dedication a table of contents was added, extending the book to 560 pages (earlier, 552 pages).

The first edition appeared in at least three states of binding:

> *Binding State* 1: Cadet blue cloth, stamped with colored floral decorations, over unbeveled boards
>
> *Binding State* 2: Drab, grayish mesh cloth (probably a poorly-dyed brown) over beveled boards
>
> *Binding State* 3: Similar to *Binding State* 2, but pebbled cloth.

The third state of binding occurs also on an issue with date dropped from title-page, known to have appeared in 1881 (the copy presented to Helen E. Blair is thus bound; see *ante* 316n).

The change to second-state binding, plain cloth over beveled boards, of nondescript color that has been described as gray, but might better be called drab, was made immediately after publication as established by a letter from Harpers to Wallace, November 13, 1880: "We published 'Ben-Hur' yesterday as you will see from the enclosed advt. When your previous letter reached us *it was too late to make any change in the style of binding—but we have ordered bound a dozen copies in plain cloth* . . . [italics supplied]."†

There is a legend that Mrs. Wallace thought the elaborate flower design on pale cloth inappropriate to the book. The story has been told in reverse: she is said to have protested against the plain binding, whereupon the publishers used a floral one; this is contrary to fact.‡ Her own statement shows that she considered the floral decoration a sign of earliest binding, for she wrote Harpers on January 3, 1885, in answer to a question about the first edition: ". . . I incline to the belief that the volume seen was one of the first issue of *Ben-Hur*, which

---

The Cincinnati Times-Star, but the clipping preserved in the Wallace Papers, now in Eagle Crest Library, lacks date. The letter was reprinted in *The Phi Gamma Delta*, April, 1936, Vol. 58, No. 6.

*This letter of hers to Harpers was reproduced in Ida M. Tarbell, *All in the Day's Work: An Autobiography* (1939).

†The letter mentions that they had "also ordered to be bound in full morocco, as requested, ten copies" of the book.

‡David A. Randall and John T. Winterich were evidently misled by a belief that the book was published in December. They saw in Eagle Crest Library a copy in plain cloth sent to Benson J. Lossing December 20, 1880, by Susan E. Wallace, and they described it as an "*A* binding" (preceding the flowered cloth) in an article in *The Publishers' Weekly*, February 15, 1941, p. 860. The Wallace-Harper correspondence and an earlier inscribed copy have come to light since that time.

would explain the *gay binding*."* The italics are ours, for by no stretch of the imagination could the grayed greenish-brown (drab) plain cloth covers be called "gay."

A meticulous interest in the matter of binding is exhibited by her later correspondence with the publishers. On January 10, 1887, she wrote: "I enclose a small sample of muslin† from the Warne & Co. edition of *Ben-Hur* (London). Gen. Wallace would like the new edition like it. The quality and color [green?] of the muslin are unusually fine, as you will notice, if you have the volume. The *twill* makes it look more finished than the familiar brown muslin." The "brown muslin" she calls "familiar" was not the drab cloth of the Lossing copy, December, 1880, nor the pebbled cloth of similar nondescript color over beveled boards, found on a copy‡ inscribed for Mary Hannah Krout, June 17, 1881, but was undoubtedly the brown over unbeveled boards used in 1886 (possibly a little earlier) to bind the sheets with date dropped from title-page, a cloth which appeared also on copies with the change in dedication, and continued to be used for some years with constancy in color, but not in shade. In March of 1887 she approved a dark blue cover for the new edition, with the comment that "the dark green of Warne & Co's copy is very pretty but with the star is not a suitable background."§

An excerpt from an undated proof sheet, evidently copy for the circular, *Harpers Literary Gossip,* gives the publishers' description, captioned, "How the First 'Ben-Hur' Was Bound": "Inquiries have reached the Harpers concerning the binding of the first edition of *Ben-Hur,* which appeared in 1880. The first edition was issued in a series which the Harpers were then publishing.‖ It was in 16mo form, bound in cadet-blue cloth, and decorated with clusters of flowers in red, blue, and green on the front cover and a vase of flowers in the same colors on the back cover. The lettering on the cover is black."¶

Whether or not its statement as to the size of the first edition and the impression that followed is correct, a notice in *The Daily New Mexican,* December 22, 1880, is interesting: "The first edition of 'Ben Hur' has been exhausted, the entire 5,000 copies composing the edi-

---

*The word "gay" is distinct in the letter preserved in the Eagle Crest Library; it does not have an "r" that would make it "gray."

†Mrs. Wallace's letter is in Eagle Crest Library, but the sample mentioned has been lost.

‡In Indiana Historical Society, William Henry Smith Memorial Library.

§Correspondence in the Eagle Crest Library.

‖Series included *Mary Anerley* by R. D. Blackmore, and *George Bailey* by Oliver Oldboy, according to John T. Winterich and David A. Randall.

¶Excerpt in Eagle Crest Library.

GEN. WALLACE'S
NEW NOVEL.
BEN-HUR. A Tale of the Christ. By Lew.
Wallace, Author of "The Fair God."
16mo, Cloth, $1.50.

"General Wallace is an original and powerful writer.
* * * It is a work of a superior order and it will have
a wonderful fascination among a multitude of readers."

NKLIN SQUARE, NEW YORK.

Nov. 13/80.

General Lew Wallace,

Dear Sir:

Your favor of
the 10" inst. is at hand.
We published
"Ben Hur" yesterday, as
you will see from the
enclosed ad't.

When your previous
letter reached us it
was too late to make
any change in the
style of binding — but

Harpers' letter to Wallace, November 13, 1880, relating to
BEN-HUR *bindings*

we have ordered bound
a dozen copies in plain
cloth, following your
suggestions as to lettering &c.
Shall we send you these,
when ready?

We have also
ordered to be bound,
in full morocco, as requested,
ten copies of "Ben Hur," which
we will forward to you
shortly.

We remain,
Yours very truly,
Harper & Brothers
per H.S.K.

tion having been sold. The publishers, Harper Bros., will begin to issue the 2nd edition of 5,000 copies immediately. . . . And the author smiles." The newspaper was published in Santa Fe and Wallace was still there at the time this appeared, so he may have supplied the figures to the newspaper (he left for Washington on the 26th).

When the date was dropped from the title-page in 1881 there was at first no change in either dedication or advertisements in back. Before addition to the dedication, late in 1884, at least one issue appeared with new advertisements. In earliest state of advertisements the 12-page catalogue, *Some Popular Novels . . .*, has opening paragraph beginning: *The Novels in this list which are not otherwise designated are in Octavo . . .* (later, *The Octavo Paper Novels in this list may be obtained in half-binding . . .*). The list itself starts with *Black's A Daughter of Heth* (later, *Baker's . . . Carter Quarterman*); it ends, p. 12, with *Waverley Novels* (later, with *Woolson's Anne* and *For the Major*); other changes within the list. A further alteration in advertisements was made in 1886 or earlier, but none in 1887 in the copies bound in dark blue, front cover decorated with a radiant star, crescent, and rosary. Subsequent issues had changes in both advertising matter and binding; the text remained unrevised. The lack of date on title-page is enough to establish them all as late copies.

The following list of editions and reprints is probably incomplete, but is indicative of their extent through 1950; the copyright expired in 1936. Adaptations for the stage are here omitted (discussed *post* 326):

> Harpers:
> 1880, first edition, as described
> 1881–1887, original edition reissued, undated for several years, in a variety of bindings as above reviewed
> 1888, *New Edition*, cloth, half-seal, half-calf, three-quarter russia, and, three-quarter crushed levant
> 1891, *Garfield Edition* (MDCCCXCII on title-page, but available November, 1891), illustrated with profuse drawings by William Martin Johnson, and photogravures; issued in a Gladstone box, orange silk cloth; also, *De Luxe Garfield Edition*, limited to 350 numbered copies; later (1902) the *Garfield Edition* was advertised as available in three-quarter calf, three-quarter levant, and, "white and purple [cloth?]." Harpers in 1893 issued a pamphlet prepared by Paul Van Dyke, entitled, *A Referendum for the Illustrations in the Garfield Edition of General Lew Wallace's Novel "Ben-Hur"*

1899, recopyrighted, cheaper edition, bearing this date on title-page

1901, an edition bearing this date on title-page, in one, and, two volumes, latter with drawings reproduced from *Garfield Edition,* but lacking its photogravures; also, *Players' Edition,* illustrated with scenes and characters from the play; reissued 1904

1902–1906, one, and, two-volume (illustrated) editions advertised in a variety of bindings, among them the *Players' Edition* with change of date to 1904*

1908, *Wallace Memorial Edition,* copyrighted this date

1922, *New Large Type Edition,* with recopyright date†

1925, *Large Type Photoplay Edition* (the motion picture was first shown December 30, 1925; see *post* 329); this is probably Grosset & Dunlap's, not Harpers' edition, part of Sears, Roebuck & Co's "million copies," for which Grosset & Dunlap put on a large selling campaign, in 1925, distributing free leaflets to school children, of "The Chariot Race"

1928, *Boys' Ben-Hur,* abridged edition with illustrations by Ralph D. Dunkelberger; code letters on copyright page, M–C (December, 1928) probably the earliest of several issues

1929, reprint without illustrations, still bearing 1922 copyright date, but with symbol, C–D

1930, *Modern Classics,* text for schools, edited by Mabel A. Bessey

1932, *Boys' Ben-Hur* reprinted (earlier edition 1928)

Reprints in America, other than Harpers:

Sears, Roebuck & Co.:

1913, special edition of a million copies, the first cheap edition in the United States; later the same year they arranged for marketing the edition also through Grosset & Dunlap, but the latter firm's imprint did not appear until 1926

Grosset & Dunlap:

1926, "part of an edition of one million copies ..." (by July of this year Sears, Roebuck & Co. and Grosset & Dunlap had together disposed of 611,511 copies); probably pre-

---

The Phi Gamma Delta this year in the February issue quoted a statement from *The* (New York) *Sun* that there had been 110 "editions" of *Ben-Hur.*

†A reprint of this edition, in a small quantity, was planned by Harpers in December, 1942; no copies have been located.

ceded their reprint of Harpers' *Photoplay Edition* the
same year
1935, *New Edition*
1941, *Books of Distinction*
Modern Library:
1933, *The Modern Library*, No. 139
Consolidated Book Publishers
1936, edition unnamed
Fountain Press
1949, *World's Greatest Literature*
Webster Publishing Company
1949, *Everyreader Series*, adapted by William Kottmeyer.

Ben-Hur was made a book for the blind. In 1887, in Louisville, 25
copies were done in embossed letters for the American Association of
Instructors for the Blind.* It was later one of the first novels to be put
into Braille (1925), and in 1946 was made a Talking Book for the
blind.

In 1934 Bell Syndicate included *Ben-Hur* in its series of condensa-
tions of "best sellers from 1875–1933," published in Sunday newspapers.

British editions, following the original Harpers issued with sheets of
the American edition, appeared in great numbers, among them the following:

Sampson, Low:
1881, edition unnamed in the *English Catalogue*, issued by
Low (later, Sampson Low); 1888, *New Edition*; 1900, *New
Edition*; 1924, *Cheap Edition*; 1936, *Cheap Edition*
Warne:
1884, *Star Series*†; 1887; 1888, *"Crown" Library Edition*;
1924, edition unnamed in the *English Catalogue*; 1927
(October), *Complete Edition*, and (December), edition unnamed, but probably another printing of the same
Rose Publishing Company, Toronto:
1887, the first Canadian edition
Nisbet & Co.:
1887, edition unnamed
Walter Scott Publishing Co.:
1887; 1923, *Carnarvon Series*

---

*The copy presented to the author is now in Eagle Crest Library: 4 volumes,
bound in three-quarter morocco.
†Mrs. Wallace admired the binding (see *ante* 318), but Lew Wallace objected

Ward, Lock & Co.:

    1887, *Lily Series* [No. 18]; 1889(?), *The World Library of Standard Books.** Previous to 1911 the *English Catalogue* listed only one edition of *Ben-Hur* from this publishing house, but it is known† that the firm issued at least three more prior to November, 1909: *The Windsor Library*, No. 120, *The Pansy Series*, No. 41, and *The Royal Series*, No. 22. Later editions: 1911, *World Library*; 1921, *New Edition*; 1927, *Popular Edition*; 1931, *Cheap Edition*; 1936, *Prize Library*

Routledge:

    1895, *New Edition*; 1905, *New Edition*

Partridge:

    1895, edition unnamed in the *English Catalogue*; 1910, *New Edition*

King:

    1895, *New Edition*

Nimmo:

    1895, edition unnamed in the *English Catalogue*

Sunday School Union:

    1895, *Endeavor Library*

Simpkin:

    1895, *Evening Hour Library*

The Masterpiece Library:

    1896, *Penny Popular Novels*, No. 7, undated, but published *ca.* January, 1896

Pearson:

    1901, *New Edition*

Chatto & Windus:

    1906, edition unnamed in the *English Catalogue*; 1912, *Popular Edition*

Collins:

    1914, *Illustrated Pocket Classics*; 1930, *Canterbury Classics*; 1935, *Albany Classics*; *ca.* 1939, *Illustrated School Classics*

Blackie:

    1914, *New Edition*; 1915, *Standard Library*; 1923, *New Edi-*

---

to the edition with its new preface and with other changes not authorized by him (see report in *The Indianapolis Journal*, August 18, 1885).

*This edition is known to have been available in Canada in October, 1889. The same year a piracy of *Ben-Hur* (publisher?) was being sold in India, according to an article in the *New York Mail & Express*, July 10, 1889. In 1895 there was a Canadian piracy; publisher unknown to us.

†From advertisements in *The Pansy Series* of *The Fair God* (1909).

tion; 1934, *Library of Famous Books;* 1939, *Library of Famous Books, Cheaper Edition*

Chapman & Dodd:
> 1922, *Cheap Edition*

Hayes:
> 1923, *Cheap Edition*

Readers' Library:
> 1927, *Readers' Library*

Bell & Sons:
> 1927, a school edition adapted by E. D'Oyley

Hamilton:
> 1930, *Sundial Popular Library*

Strang:
> 1931, *Herbert Strang's Library*

Marshall, Morgan & Scott:
> 1933, *Cheap Edition.*

The translations of *Ben-Hur* were numerous.* A few are here noted:

Arabic:
> Translated by Rev. Cornelius V. A. Van Dyke, published at Cairo, 1896, and at Beirut, 1897, by the Press of the Board of Foreign Missions of the Presbyterian Church

Bohemian:
> Translations unlocated, but three persons had asked for permission to translate in 1887, and the language is listed by McKee† as one in which the story appeared

Bulgarian:
> Translation rights for part of book were granted Ivan Vaptzaroff, January, 1923

Burmese:
> Translation rights for an abridged edition were granted B. M. Jones, November, 1930

Czechoslovakian:
> In 3 volumes, undated (before 1930); in 2 volumes, 1948, translated by A. Filo

---

*The total surely is much more than the small number located by the compilers, but probably not as great as indicated by Frank Moody Mills in his reminiscences, *Early Days in a College Town* (1924), p. 42, when he speaks of seeing in Wallace's Study "sixty-four copies of 'Ben-Hur' translated in as many languages." The sixty-four possibly included some of the many American and British editions.

†McKee, p. 174.

Danish:

A "second Danish edition" was announced in the *Davenport* (Iowa) *Democrat*, February 4, 1894, as published in Copenhagen at the time of first publication of a Danish edition of *The Prince of India,* further details lacking. Folkets-Bogsamburg (?), *Popular Library,* August, 1899; not located, but referred to in private correspondence*

Dutch:

Translation published in Rotterdam by D. Bolle, undated

Finnish:

Before 1930

Flemish:

Before 1930

French:

A translation mentioned in *The Indianapolis Journal,* September 23, 1888. Another, by Fred Zohn and G. Secretan, was approved by Wallace December 14, 1895 (published?). A translation by Maurice Strauss is known to have appeared *ca.* May, 1902,† and another by R. D'Humières and J. L. de Janasz in *Libraire Delagrave,* Paris, 1918; another, by Ph. Magoyer, Paris, 1929

German:

A translation by Rev. Bonaventure Hammer, O. F. M., of St. Boniface Roman Catholic Church, Lafayette, Indiana, authorized by Lew Wallace, underwent numerous printings from the serialization in *Roman-Bibliothek* and the book appearance in Leipzig in 2 volumes (1888), to a popular edition in one volume, and to a finely illustrated one issued first in parts in 1894; the 25th edition was reached in 1900. Harpers published in New York a German translation by "H. W. S. [Henry W. Seibert]," 1895. An unauthorized translation appeared in Germany before 1900. J. Cassirer's translation was published in Berlin in 1909. The *Tauchnitz Edition, Collection of British and American Authors,* 2 volumes (Vol. II is No. 2502 in the series) in English, but published in Germany, had appeared in 1888

Greek:

Before 1930

---

*In Eagle Crest Library.
†According to a letter from the translator, in Eagle Crest Library; book unlocated.

Hungarian:
> Translation received in this country by Harpers in 1930, not seen; one listed as a 1933 publication, Budapest, in *Index Translationum*

Italian:
> Translation in 1887 by Rev. Monti.* Father Hammer's German version was translated into Italian by Alfonso M. Galea and published at Modena in 1895. Later, there appeared an Italian translation by Prof. Henry Salvadori.† A translation by H. Mildmay and Gastone Cavalieri was published at Milano, 1922. One by Giovanni Zacchin, Milano, 1938.

Norwegian:
> Part published serially in a Minneapolis newspaper, *Foedrelandet og. Emigranten,* in 1890; stopped by action of Harpers. A book publication appeared before 1930 (not seen); one done by Rune Berkeland in 1948

Polish:
> By Jonas Montvila, Chicago, 1912. A translation was published later, 1938, in Warsaw

Russian:
> A translation published in Beketova, 1908

Spanish:
> By A. A. Barberan, Barcelona, undated; possibly the Spanish translation referred to in *The Indianapolis Journal,* September 23, 1888, as "now in progress." A Spanish translation by Hugo Reichenbuch was listed in *Index Translationum* as published in Leipzig, 1932

Swedish:
> A translation by Mrs. N. S. Moore was projected in 1887; published? A Swedish edition appeared in Stockholm in 1927.

Translations into Portuguese, Turkish, and Oriental languages have also been claimed for the work; as yet unlocated.

Separate printings were made by Harpers of two incidents from *Ben-Hur:*
> *The First Christmas: From "Ben-Hur."* New York, Harper & Brothers, 1899. Only the preface is original writing; the con-

---

*Published? A letter to Harpers from William H. Elder, April 4, 1887, now in Eagle Crest Library, mentions the translation.

†This, with modifications in the interests of piety, brought the translator the blessings of Pope Leo XIII.—*Lew Wallace: An Autobiography,* Vol. II (1906), p. 942.

tents proper consist of Book One of *Ben-Hur* (see *post* 347). Reissued with 1902 on title-page

The Chariot-Race: From Ben-Hur. Illustrated by Sigismond Ivanowski. New York, Harper & Brothers, 1908. *Published October, 1908* on copyright page; earliest binding stamped in color and gilt; later stamped in black only. Contains extracts from *Ben-Hur,* but no original writing. Reprinted 1922 by Owen Publishing Company in their *Instructor Literature Series,* No. 307 and 307C, in wrappers and limp cloth covers.

Extracts of the above, the story of the chariot race, have made appearance in school readers, periodicals, and collections of literature too numerous to itemize here. Of his account of the birth of Jesus Christ besides the separate, *The First Christmas,* extracts were published in anthologies of elocutionary nature, under various titles, "The Angel and the Shepherds," "The Crucifixion," etc. "Ben-Hur and Iras," adapted from Book VIII, was another extract, offered as dialogue for public speaking.

A Christmas brochure published by George R. Lockwood & Son (1886), *Seekers After "The Light" from "Ben-Hur,"* consists of brief extracts from the book with illustrative etchings by "F. M."; several states, earliest probably without etcher's initials.

Wallace's story of the three Magi was included in a book by W. D. Mahan in 1884: *Archaeological Writings of the Sanhedrin and Talmuds of the Jews, Taken from the Ancient Parchments and Scrolls at Constantinople and the Vatican at Rome,** without acknowledgment to Wallace, but instead claimed to be from a manuscript discovered by Mahan in Constantinople. Wallace discussed its plagiaristic nature in a letter published in *Harper's Weekly,* June 23, 1888, p. 447. Further details appear in *Lew Wallace: An Autobiography,* Vol. II (1906), p. 942.

In the field of drama "Ben-Hur" appeared in many forms. Henry M. Soper's *Scrap Book Recitation Series,* No. 5 included an adaptation, "The Chariot Race," before May, 1887. A dramatic reading by Zara McCosh, Salem, Ohio, with twenty tableaux, was reported at this time in a number of newspapers. Ellen K. Bradford prepared and published her *Selections from Ben-Hur Adapted for Reading with Tableaux* (1887), and *Directions for Preparatory Work and Materials Needed for Producing the "Ben Hur" Tableaux* (1888), reissued as *Directions*

---

*"This work is considered a forgery . . .," the Library of Congress records show; in cataloguing its later publication in *The Archko Volume* and *The Archko Library* they note it to be "generally regarded as spurious."

for Producing Ben Hur Tableaux (1889). None of these was sanctioned by the author.

The first authorized public performance occurred in Crawfordsville on December 17 and 18, 1888, at the old Music Hall, a benefit for the First Methodist Church. "The programme is taken from Ben Hur and will comprise readings and recitations in character, besides tableaux from the most thrilling portions of the work. The cast is taken from the best amateur talent," so read an advance notice in *The Crawfordsville Journal*, November 24, 1888. Presented under the direction of David W. Cox and O'Neal Watson, its success encouraged Cox to organize a company which gave other performances in Crawfordsville, on March 7, 1889, and November 3, 1890. In August of 1890 it was a feature at Chautauqua. Printed, it took the form of a 38-page brochure issued in wrappers, copyrighted October 24, 1890: *Ben-Hur, In Tableaux And Pantomime, Arranged By Thr* [sic] *Author For Messrs.* [*Walter C.*] *Clark &* [*David W.*] *Cox*; with letter of authorization, April 2, 1889, on title-page, reissued by Harpers with 1891 date on title-page, and title reading: *Ben-Hur In Dramatic Tableaux And Pantomime.*

Wallace himself gave a reading from his novel, for a Press Club benefit in Indianapolis, June 21, 1893. A souvenir booklet of the occasion appeared under the title, *Readings by Indiana Authors*; a description of it was given in *The Indianapolis Journal*, June 22, 1893.

In 1896, there was advertised in London and Washington, D. C., an unauthorized spectacle: "Riley Brothers' 'Ben-Hur' in the Magic Lantern; 72 Pictures . . . with Special Reading."* A prospectus in pamphlet form is said to have been published by the Rileys (not our Indiana family!) purporting to be copyrighted in Great Britain and the United States, entitled, *The Stereoptican Illustrator of Ben-Hur.* The "Special Reading," without imprint, was apparently published also.†

An undated scenario, of a "Pyro-Spectacular Dramatization of General Lew Wallace's Great Work [Ben-Hur]" by Frank Oakes Rose, General Stage Director, The Pain Pyro-Spectacle Company, New York, has been preserved in typescript.‡

The most famous stage presentation of "Ben-Hur" was William Young's arrangement made under Wallace's supervision. It opened in New York at the Broadway Theatre, November 29, 1899, produced by Marc Klaw and Abraham Erlanger. A scenario of it, without imprint, dated 1899 (copyrighted November 2nd), entitled, *Lew Wallace's*

---

*This annoyed Wallace; the correspondence with Harpers on the subject is in Eagle Crest Library.

†Information from Harpers-Wallace correspondence.

‡In Eagle Crest Library.

Ben-Hur: A Play Arranged For The Stage By William Young, consisting of 116 pages, was issued in wrappers.

The *Souvenir Album* (so named on cover) of the William Young drama bears title: *Klaw & Erlanger's Production of Gen. Lew Wallace's "Ben-Hur," dramatized by William Young*, and gives other information: staged by Ben Teal, vocal and instrumental music composed by Edgar Stillman Kelley, business direction [by] Joseph Brooks, illustrations from flash-light photographs by Joseph Byron; published New York & Chicago [1900]; its sheets, unpaged, together with pictorial colored front wrapper and decorated sepia back wrapper, are tied with ribbon. It contains the score of the musical theme on the first page, but consists mostly of plates, sepia scenes from the play, with descriptive letter-press on tissue guards.

In 1902 the score was published in New York by Towers & Curran, thus entitled: *Words and Music of Klaw & Erlanger's Production of Gen. Lew Wallace's Ben-Hur, by Edgar Stillman Kelley*; it was edited by Charles Feleky (see *post* 331).

An interview with Lew Wallace about the play, published in *The Illustrated Indiana Weekly*, July 22, 1899, was forerunner of considerable publicity that appeared in newspapers before the November opening. The author's own comments after attending the first performance were published in the form of a letter addressed to the Editor, in *The* (New York) *World*, November 30, 1899, p. 12.

The "Secret of That Thrilling Ben-Hur Race Explained," with diagram of the stage apparatus for horses, chariots, and moving cyclorama background, was told in the *New York Journal*, December 1, 1899, and the "Stage Effects in Ben-Hur" were further discussed in the *Scientific American*, August 25, 1900. When the play was to be produced in England there was only one theatre possessed of the stage facilities required, the Drury Lane; it opened there on April 3, 1902.

"The Most Successful Play Ever Produced," "Ben-Hur" was thus described in an article by Glenmore Davis in *The Green Book*, January, 1914. Before final production in April, 1920, and dissolution in 1921 of Klaw and Erlanger's contract (see *Variety*, April 15, 1921, for a summary of the matter), the play had toured the British Empire (see McKee, pp. 175–186). When the twenty-fifth hundredth performance occurred in New York at the Academy of Music, in the season 1906–1907, Klaw and Erlanger presented a copy of the novel to every woman attending.* William S. Hart told in his memoirs, *My Life East and West* (1929), how he played "Messala."

---

*McKee, p. 183.

A one-reel motion picture by Kalem, with Herman Rottjer as Ben-Hur, in 1907 had opened the battle for cinema production. McKee, pp. 186–188, tells the photoplay history in some detail. The Metro-Goldwyn production, two years in the making, with Ramon Navarro as Ben-Hur and Francis X. Bushman as Messala, opened Christmas week, 1925, in New York. Abraham L. Erlanger's story of Ben-Hur on stage and film was quoted in *The Crawfordsville Journal*, February 6, 1926, at the time of showing there.

A radio adaption was presented by Hallmark Playhouse on CBS network, April 10, 1952.

For a brief account of "Ben-Hur" in its musical settings see *post* 331–334.

At time of publication *Ben-Hur* received slight attention. The publishers gave it a one-line listing among "New Novels" in their advertisements in *The Publishers' Weekly* on November 13, 1880, and in the Christmas number that followed. On December 4, 1880, in the "Weekly Record of New Publications" it was briefly reviewed. By June 24, 1881, the book had sold to the extent of 4,187 copies only, but by the middle of November, 1884, sales had totaled almost forty thousand; on December 14, 1889, the total was 390,938; by February, 1902, 719,343 copies of the various editions had been sold or given away for review purposes.* Harpers reported in March, 1941† that the total sale was near two and a half million.

Maurice Thompson had described it in 1898 as a "wonderfully popular novel which, next to 'Uncle Tom's Cabin' has had the greatest sales of any romance ever written by an American."‡ Irving McKee, in his *"Ben-Hur" Wallace* (1947), devoting a chapter to the book, has provided a summary of contemporary criticism, as well as the story of the book's subsequent popularity.

All accounts of Wallace after 1880 identify him primarily as the "author of *Ben-Hur*." The book led President Garfield to select its author for Ministry to Turkey, which in turn caused Wallace to write *The Prince of India*. Joseph Henry Harper in his books, *The House of Harper* (1912) and *I Remember* (1934), told how it impressed the publishers. "How 'Ben-Hur' Came to the Harpers" was another account of it from this angle, published in *Harper's Literary Gossip*, February 23, 1905. Elizabeth Rider Montgomery, in *The Story behind*

---

*Reports from Harpers to Mrs. Lew Wallace; correspondence in Eagle Crest Library.

†To Louis C. Schaedler, whose Master's thesis, *Lew Wallace: Middle-Class Novelist* (1941), is deposited in Duke University Library.

‡*Stories of Indiana* by Thompson (1898), pp. 277–278.

Great Books (1946), gave it consideration as "The Book That Converted Its Author." In this same year, 1946, *Ben-Hur* was included by the Grolier Club in an exhibit of one hundred "books that influenced America."

The "Governor's Palace" in Santa Fe, now housing the New Mexico Historical Society, with its museum, bears note of the fact that Wallace wrote much of *Ben-Hur* therein, while he was governor of that Territory (see *The Ben Hur Room, post* 382). The beech tree in Crawfordsville, under which part of the manuscript took shape, was preserved after its destruction in 1907 in the form of some leaves distributed in a circular issued by the Supreme Tribe Ben-Hur (*post* 393).

The latter, a Legal Reserve Fraternal Life Insurance society in Crawfordsville, founded 1894, known since 1929 as the Ben-Hur Life Association, issued a bulletin, *The Chariot*, 1895–1910. A Ben-Hur scholarship established by them, discontinued after being in effect a few years, is recorded in a pamphlet entitled, *Ben-Hur Scholarships: A Memorial in Honor of David W. Gerard, Founder of the Supreme Tribe of Ben-Hur* (1920). "The only connection this society has had with Lew Wallace is that the name Ben Hur was adapted from his famous book with his written permission."*

Poems by a "Ben Hur: Of Whitley" (not Wallace), written from Columbia City, Indiana, appeared for a while in *The* (Chicago) *Inter Ocean*; noted especially January 5, 12, 26, and 29, 1889.

Wallace appears to have been silent regarding a book, *Esther:† A Sequel to Ben-Hur; or, The Lost Epistles of the First and Second Centuries*, translated (!) by J. O. A. Clark (1892); in his introduction the writer claims that "the gifted author of 'Ben-Hur' did not have access to these newly discovered records. . . ."

A list of novels inspired by Ben-Hur is given in McKee, p. 175.

The innumerable uses of the name "Ben-Hur" need not be described here, beyond mentioning the "Ben-Hur" bicycles manufactured by the Central Cycle Manufacturing Company of Indianapolis, *ca.* 1895, which can be considered of some bibliographical interest because of the firm's printing of J. H. Cody's *Ben-Hur March* (*post* 332), with the "Ben-Hur Tandem" depicted on the inside wrapper.

There often appeared in print words of the author regarding his "Ben-Hur" ("Judah" was its early manuscript title). When Meredith Nicholson interviewed him soon after a contract for publication had

---

*Letter, R. B. McCain, Secretary, January 15, 1951.

†The wife of "Ben-Hur" in the Wallace novel, was named Esther in memory of the author's mother, according to *Harper's Bazaar*, March 26, 1887.

been signed with Harpers on May 7, 1880, Wallace gave him a lengthy written statement about the novel. This was printed in *The Crawfordsville Journal*, May 22, 1880, also in Nicholson's article, "Lew Wallace as an Author," published by the Indiana Commandery of the Loyal Legion in a brochure entitled, *In Memoriam, Major-General Lew Wallace . . . May 5, 1905*.

"How I Came to Write Ben-Hur," Wallace's article in the *Youth's Companion*, February 2, 1893, has been frequently quoted. He gave a lecture on the same subject in San Francisco, October 29, 1894. In the preface to *The First Christmas* (1902) he again told of the origin of the story. His autobiography, p. 949, contains a letter regarding the work, addressed to Paul Hamilton Hayne, January 19, 1881, and Mc-Kee quotes from it, p. 167.

He usually gave credit to Robert G. Ingersoll for the development and even for the inception of "Ben-Hur," through a talk on agnosticism that crystallized his own Christian belief, but there is reason to believe, from a letter to Agnes Wallace, November 27, 1874, published in Mc-Kee, p. 165, that he had the story under way at least two years before he met Ingersoll. That Wallace recognized the book as his greatest literary achievement is indicated in a letter to his wife, of January 28, 1887 (unpublished, in the Wallace Papers): ". . . I am looking to you and Ben-Hur to keep me unforgotten after the end of life."

Ben-Hur Music

The musical score of "Ben-Hur," Klaw and Erlanger's production (see *ante* 327 for further details), contains songs from Wallace's book, set to music by Edgar Stillman Kelley. The same songs inspired other compositions: "The Lament (Egyptian)," which had appeared in the original edition of *Ben-Hur* (1880) on p. 281, beginning, "I sigh as I sing for the story land"; "Kapila," p. 298; and "The Song," p. 111, beginning, "Wake not, but hear me, love!"* The following is a list of the musical selections:

BEN-HUR [words and music of Klaw & Erlanger's production of Gen. Lew Wallace's "Ben-Hur"]. Composer: Edgar Stillman Kelley. Edited by Charles Feleky. New York, Towers & Curran, 1902. Prel-

---

*See *Lew Wallace: An Autobiography*, Vol. II (1906), p. 934, for his story of the writing of this "Song."

ude and Acts I–VI, music with words, pp. 1–93.† Pictorial colored wrappers, back blank. See SONG OF IRAS (described under THE LAMENT) for appearance of pp. 61–65 in earlier sheet music form. See also SACRED CHORUSES FROM BEN-HUR, for another separate printing of Kelley's compositions.

BEN-HUR MARCH. Composer: J. H. Cody. Arranged by Chas. W. A. Ball. Indianapolis, n.d. Distributed with compliments of the Central Cycle Mfg. Co., Indianapolis, makers of Ben-Hur Bicycles. Dedicated to L. M. Wainwright, president of the firm. Music without words, pp. [3]–5. Pictorial colored wrappers, advertisements on back and inside front.

BEN HUR CHARIOT RACE MARCH: see CHARIOT RACE OR BEN HUR MARCH

THE CHARIOT RACE. Composer: Richard J. Carpenter. Denver, Colo., Denver Music Co., 1895. Music without words, *Entrance March of the Charioteers*, pp. 2–3: arrangements for 1st mandolin, 2nd mandolin, and 1st guitar. Dedicated to General Lew Wallace. Contains a quotation from Ben-Hur: *"The race was on; the souls of the racers were in it; over them bent the myriads."*—Ben-Hur (1880), p. 362.

CHARIOT RACE OR BEN HUR MARCH [cover title; inside title:] BEN HUR CHARIOT RACE MARCH. Composer: E. T. Paull. New York, E. T. Paull Music Co., 1894. Music without words, pp. 3–7. Pictorial colored cover with statement: *Played By Sousa's Band*; advertisements of the "Edition Paull" on back cover, and Paull's compositions on inside front cover. Also, an edition published by the Richmond (Va.) Music Co., 1894; front cover lacks statement about Sousa's band; back cover and inside front blank. No plate number in either, but a statement in both at foot of pp. 4–7: *Ben-Hur etc. – 5.*

Also, same march with a descriptive song, a poem by H. A. Freeman, published 1899 by E. T. Paull Music Co. Words with music, pp. 2–9. Issued with front cover same as the New York, 1894, piece, including statement about Sousa's band, back bearing selections dated 1898.

EGYPTIAN SONG (THE LAMENT); see THE LAMENT

FROM THE ORIENT [general title for three songs composed by E. R. Kroeger: KAPILA, WAKE NOT, and THE LAMENT; *q.v.*]

I SIGH AS I SING; see THE LAMENT

---

†For comments, see "The Music of Ben-Hur," by Elizabeth Reynolds, in *Music*, October, 1901.

KAPILA.* Composer: E. R. Kroeger. St. Louis, Kunkel Bros., 1886. From *Ben-Hur* (1880), p. 298. Words with music, pp. 3–5; Plate No. 893–3. Front wrapper bears general title: *From the Orient,* also dedication to Gen. Lew Wallace, and a decorative box in gilt and blue; back wrapper advertises Kunkel's *Royal Edition;* inside wrappers blank. Laid in pink wrappers which bear publishers' catalogue on inside front and back.

THE LAMENT.† Composer: E. R. Kroeger. St. Louis, Kunkel Bros., 1886. From *Ben-Hur* (1880), p. 281. Words with music, pp. 3–5; Plate No. 856–3; statement at foot of p. 4: *This piece is one of five that appeared in* Kunkel's Musical Review *for Oct. 1886.* See KAPILA for description of wrappers.

Also, EGYPTIAN SONG (THE LAMENT); inside title: I SIGH AS I SING. Composer: Leandro Campanari. Cincinnati, John Church Co., 1893. Words, p. [1]; music with words, pp. 2–7; Plate No. 9680–7–L. Pictorial colored wrappers, advertisement of new songs by Campanari on back, inside front and back blank.

Also, THE LAMENT. Composer: Victor Kemp. New York, Edward Schuberth & Co., 1900. Words with music, pp. 3–6; *E. S. & Co.* 3473 at foot of each page. Decorative wrappers printed in brown, *Select Parlor Songs* on back, inside front and back blank.

Also, SONG OF IRAS. Composer: Edgar Stillman Kelley. Cincinnati, John Church Co., 1900. Words with music, pp. 2–7; Plate No. 13349–6. Pictorial wrappers, front printed in brown, back blank.‡ The composition later appeared in the score of BEN-HUR, Klaw and Erlanger's production, Towers & Curran publication (1902), pp. 61–65.

SACRED CHORUSES FROM BEN-HUR. Composer: Edgar Stillman Kelley. N.p., n.d. Pp. [1]–29, words beginning on p. 2: "The vision of Isaiah . . . ." Tan printed wrappers. See BEN-HUR for the printing of the complete Kelley score.

SERENADE§

---

*A musical composition of "Kapila" by Henry Pettit is referred to in correspondence, July 31, 1899, now in Eagle Crest Library (published?).

†The same poem, set to music by Herbert Sparling, in form of an incomplete manuscript, undated, is in the Eagle Crest Library.

‡Copy in Eagle Crest Library was inscribed by the composer to Gen. Lew Wallace, April, 1900.

§A composition by F. E. Sawyer, 1898, is recorded in the Music Collection of the Library of Congress, but not seen; its title, "Serenade (from *Ben-Hur*)." Probably "Tirzah's Serenade" ("Wake Not, But Hear Me, Love").

SLUMBER SONG; see WAKE NOT, BUT HEAR ME, LOVE

SONG OF IRAS; see THE LAMENT

THE SONG OF TIRZAH; see WAKE NOT, BUT HEAR ME, LOVE

TIRZAH'S SERENADE; see WAKE NOT, BUT HEAR ME, LOVE

WAKE NOT, BUT HEAR ME, LOVE. Composer: George L. Osgood. Boston, Oliver Ditson & Co., 1886. From *Ben-Hur* (1880), p. 111. Words with music, pp. 3–5; Plate No. 51819–3. Decorative wrappers, back and inside front blank.

Also, WAKE NOT. Composer: E. R. Kroeger. St. Louis, Kunkel Bros., 1887. Words with music, pp. 3–5; Plate No. 427–3. One of three companion pieces, "From the Orient"; see KAPILA for description of wrappers.

Also, TIRZAH'S SERENADE.* Composer: Annie M. Lyon. Chicago, Geo. E. Marshall & Co., 1888. Words with muisc, pp. [3]–5. Decorative wrappers, back and inside front blank.

Also, WAKE NOT, BUT HEAR ME, LOVE! Composer: Harry G. Martin. Baltimore, Otto Sutro & Co., 1888. Words with music, pp. 3–5. Decorative wrappers, back and inside front blank.

Also, WAKE NOT, BUT HEAR ME, LOVE! Composer: Lillian L. Bissell. Boston, Oliver Ditson Co., 1895. Words with music, pp. 2–5; Plate No. 105–58603–4. Decorative wrappers, *Delightful Songs* advertised on back.

Also, THE SONG OF TIRZAH.† Composer: C. E. Merrifield; arranged by H. D. Beissenherz. Indianapolis, C. E. Merrifield, 1897. Words with music, pp. [2–3]. Pictorial wrappers printed in green, back blank.

Also, WAKE NOT, BUT HEAR ME, LOVE! (SLUMBER SONG). Composer: Pierre Mellarde (pseudonym of R. Price, Halesworth, Suffolk, England). London, Weekes & Co., n.d. Words, "Slumber Song," p. [1]; music with words, pp. 2–5; Plate No. W. 5622. Decorative wrappers, compositions by "Mellarde" advertised on back, inside front blank.

---

*Another musical setting of "Tirzah's Serenade," by *Rhys ap Rhys,* a manuscript undated, is in Eagle Crest Library.

†This title was set to music by Henry Pettit, mentioned July 31, 1899 in correspondence now in Eagle Crest Library (published?).

1888

Life of Gen. Ben Harrison

(Combined with Townsend's Life of Levi P. Morton)

LIFE OF | GEN. BEN HARRISON. | BY | GEN. LEW WALLACE, | Author of "BEN HUR." | ALSO, | LIFE OF HON. LEVI P. MORTON. | BY | GEORGE ALFRED TOWNSEND. | (GATH.) | [*rule*] | FULLY ILLUSTRATED. | [*rule*] | HUBBARD BROTHERS, PUBLISHERS, | PHILADELPHIA, CHICAGO, KANSAS CITY; | GUERNSEY PUBLISHING CO., Boston; JAS. MORRIS & CO., Cincinnati; | PERRY PUBLISHING CO., Denver; A. L. BANCROFT & CO., | San Francisco.

COLLATION: [1]–21^8, 22^6, one unsigned sheet, 23–36^8, 37^2. White wove paper. Leaf measures 7$\frac{5}{16}$" x 7$\frac{7}{8}$", all edges trimmed.

End paper; blank, pp. [1–2]*; frontispiece with tissue guard, inserted; title-page, p. [3]; copyright notice dated 1888, p. [4]; *Preface* dated August 6, 1888, pp. 5–6; table of contents, pp. 7–12; list of illustrations, pp. 13–14; divisional half-title, p. 15; blank, p. [16]; text, pp. 17–348; divisional half-title, p. 349; blank, p. [350]; *Hon. Levi P. Morton*, by George Alfred Townsend, pp. 351–438; *Our Former Presidents*, pp. 439–542; divisional half-title, p. 543; quotation from James A. Garfield, p. 544; citizens' handbook (so-named in table of contents), pp. 545–578; blank, pp. [579–580]*; end paper.

[Note: Text, pp. 17–348: Life of Gen. Ben Harrison, Chapters I–V (titled). The remainder of the book is not by Wallace, but consists of a biography of Levi P. Morton by George Alfred Townsend, followed by biographies of former Presidents, and by a *Citizen's Handbook Of Valuable Facts For Campaign Work* (so named on divisional half-title, p. 543).†]

ILLUSTRATIONS: Frontispiece with tissue guard, inserted as are 25 plates, pp. [25], [27], [31], [39], [45], [79], [183], [189], [197], [203], [213], [225], [231], [239], [247], [271], [273], [349], [351],

---

*Pasted under lining paper in copies bound in partial morocco, and, partial russia leather.

†A rebound copy of the book, in the New York Public Library, is catalogued under the title, *Presidential Campaign Lives*.

[401], [439], [457], [533],* [545], [561]. The list of illustrations describes them as facing these pages, and thus gives erroneous references.

BINDING: Gray mesh cloth.† Front cover gilt-stamped: LIVES | OF | [black-stamped on gilt-stamped panel:] HARRISON | AND | MORTON [all the foregoing within a black-stamped design suggesting flowers growing over a fence]. Spine gilt-stamped within similar black-stamped design: LIVES | OF | [black-stamped on gilt-stamped panel:] HARRISON | AND | MORTON Back cover blank.

End papers blue with floral design, on white; no binder's leaf, front or back.

PUBLICATION DATA: Published September 1, 1888 (The Indianapolis Journal, this date, carries an advertisement of this volume of combined biographies as "just issued"‡). Deposited in the Copyright Office, September 4, 1888. Price, $2.00 (subscription price of cloth-bound copies; half morocco, $2.50, and half russia, $3.00).

NOTES: Two different editions (this combination and the separate "life" of Harrison) were published simultaneously; see post 338–340. The separate has been found only with Hubbard Brothers' imprint; the combination bears that of various publishing agencies in addition to Hubbard; also, original title-page excised and a new one inserted, i.e., Union Book Co., Indianapolis, and Winter & Co., Springfield, Mass.

A life of Hon. Whitelaw Reid replaced that of Levi P. Morton in a later edition, 1892, with copyright in name of J. Beale; Murat Halstead was co-author in place of George Alfred Townsend. The text of Harrison's biography was here extended to include accounts of his career as successful candidate for President, and nominee for second term; the revisions and extensions were slight.

This 1892 edition appeared with various imprints and at least two variant titles. The issue with imprint of the Edgewood Publishing Co. (n.d.) is entitled: Life And Public Services | Of | Hon. Benjamin Harrison | President Of The U. S. | With a Concise Biographical Sketch | Of | Hon. Whitelaw Reid | Ex-Minister To France [title-page continues with each author's name and identification, and summary of the

*A copy bound in ¾ (called "half") leather has the plate facing p. 533.

†Also, "half-morocco and half-russia" bindings with front cover stamping similar to the separate volume; spine with gilt ornamentation, lettered: HARRISON | AND | MORTON | WALLACE

‡Other newspapers published reviews at this tme, the earliest noted being a clipping, identified by hand as from a Poughkeepsie, New York, newspaper, August 29, 1888, which indicates distribution of the book as a few days before September, but this paper describes the separate edition (see post 338).

added articles]. Issues with imprint of the Franklin Publishing Co., Savannah, Ga., and J. K. Hastings, Boston, bear same title. A slightly different one was used by the Victory Publishing Co., Cincinnati: *Life And Public Services* | [rule] *Of* [rule] | *Benjamin Harrison* | *President Of The U. S.* | *With a Choice Biographical Sketch* | [rule] *Of* [rule] | *Hon. Whitelaw Reid,* | *Ex-Minister To France* [title-page continues with differences, very minor, from the Edgewood issue].

The Edgewood copies are in two states of binding: one similar in gilt-stamped design and lettering to the earlier separate life of Harrison (see *post* 338); the other has title on cover and spine within wreath of wheat-like design as on Victory Publishing Company's edition.

Wallace is said to have contributed 15,000 words to his hastily assembled biography; the other 50,000 were either Harrison's own words or those of others, "from the record."* He prepared the book in Indianapolis, at the home of his sister-in-law, Mrs. A. H. Blair, who lived near General Harrison.† In a biographical sketch of his father, a manuscript in his hand among the Wallace Papers, there is mention of David Wallace's having known William Henry Harrison, and of the fact that his sons, William and Lewis "were warm advocates of the election of Benjamin Harrison . . . . In 1892 they were equally faithful. The good relation between the families seems to have become a thing of heredity." Lew Wallace's campaign speech, October 23, 1888, was published under the title, *The Democratic Party and the Solid South, q.v.* Mary Hannah Krout, in her reports to *The* (Chicago) *Inter Ocean,* July–November, 1888 (see *ante* 39), particularly on August 26th and November 30th, made reference to Wallace's friendship with Harrison. The same newspaper, August 12, 1889, carried a story of Wallace's campaign efforts, and on June 3, 1892, published an interview under the caption, "General Lew Wallace on the Political Situation: Outspoken for Harrison." On June 22, 1832, Harrison wrote Wallace thanking him for "years of devoted service" (letter in the Wallace Papers).

---

*Figures from McKee, p. 231.
†According to a contemporary newspaper account; clipping in Montgomery County Historical Society, in a scrapbook presented by Blair Taylor.

1888

Life of Gen. Ben Harrison

LIFE | OF | GEN. BEN HARRISON. | BY | LEW WALLACE, | AUTHOR OF "BEN HUR," "FAIR GOD," ETC. | [rule] | ILLUSTRATED. | [rule] | HUBBARD BROTHERS, PUBLISHERS, | PHILADELPHIA, CHICAGO, KANSAS CITY, A. L. BANCROFT & CO., | SAN FRANCISCO, CAL.

COLLATION: [1]⁶ (plus a cancel leaf), 2–22⁸. White wove paper. Leaf measures 7⅜″ x 4⅞″, all edges trimmed.

End paper; binder's leaf; frontispiece with tissue guard, inserted; title-page, p. [1]; copyright notice dated 1888, p. [2]; *Publishers' Preface*, pp. [iii]–iv (cancel leaf); *Preface* by the author dated August 6, 1888, pp. 5–6; table of contents, pp. 7–9; blank, p. [10] (leaf following, conjugate of pp. [iii]–iv, excised, hence no pp. 11–12); list of illustrations, p. 13; blank, p. [14]; half-title, p. 15; blank, p. [16]; text, pp. 17–348; blank, pp. [349–350] (conjugate of pp. 337–338 pasted under the lining paper); end paper.

[Note: Text, pp. 17–348: Life of Gen. Ben Harrison, Chapters I–V (titled).]

ILLUSTRATIONS: Frontispiece portrait with tissue guard, inserted as are plates facing pp. 26 (not 27 as stated in list of illustrations), 30 (not 31), 38 (not 39), 44 (not 45), 78 (not 79), 272 (not 273), and 344 (not 349). Rule below caption pp. [iii], 5, 7, and 13; rule above and below copyright notice p. [2], above and below half-title, p. 15.

BINDING: Dark blue mesh cloth over beveled boards. Front cover gilt-stamped: LIFE | OF | BEN HARRISON | by the Author of [*branch-like design below* Life *intercepted by the first two letters in* Harrison *and* b *in* by] | BEN HUR* Spine gilt-stamped: [rule] | LIFE | of | HARRISON [*title intercepts a branch-like design*] | [rule] | WALLACE | [rule]. Back cover blank.

End papers orange, floral design, on white; binder's leaf in front, none in back.

---

*In 1888 hundreds knew Lew Wallace as the author of *Ben-Hur* to one who knew him as a political or military figure, it has been suggested by James Ford Rhodes in *The History of the United States from Hayes to McKinley* (1919), p. 320, hence the publishers' indirect identification of the author of this biography on the front cover; *Wallace* appears on spine.

PUBLICATION DATA: See *Notes*.

NOTES: This *Life of Gen. Ben Harrison* presents some bibliographical problems. It appeared both separately, in the volume above-described, and in combination with George Alfred Townsend's "Life of Hon. Levi P. Morton." Which volume was first on the market? The plan, certainly, was for the combined biographies of Harrison and Morton, the nominees for Presidency of the United States and Vice-Presidency. A title-page mailed to the Copyright Office, July 5, 1888, is that of the combination volume, as were the books deposited there September 4th, and the earliest advertisement located, a bookseller's, in *The Indianapolis Journal*, September 1, 1888, announces the book with combination title as "just issued." Again, it is the only issue mentioned in the first *Publishers' Weekly* listing, September 22nd. On the other hand contemporary reviews as early as August 29th gave the single title with statement of the book's length as 348 pages. Both, then, were ready by September 1st.

The fact that Wallace had contracted with Hubbard Brothers, Philadelphia, to write a campaign life of General Harrison, was subject of an editorial in *The Crawfordsville Journal*, July 7, 1888, where it was announced for publication about August 1st.* *The Indianapolis Journal*, August 6, 1888, quoted extracts from the unpublished book and mentioned that it would probably be ready by the 15th of August. That it was the end of August or first day of September before it reached the public is indicated by the September 1st advertisement. Wallace's autobiography (completed after his death) merely states that *"The Life of Harrison"* was published as a campaign document in 1888.†

The volume containing the separate Harrison biography shows signs of hasty adaptation from the combined biographies, with a new title-page and reset table of contents and list of illustrations, but from half-title to p. 348 the sheets are the same. This is as one would expect;

---

*On July 9, 1888, Robert A. Reid of J. A. and R. A. Reid, Publishers, Providence, R. I., wrote Harrison that they had a biography of him "largely in type now"; they wanted him to recommend a friend to check it. "We shall publish several editions both by subscriptions and for sale through the country." Evidently Harrison stopped it, for no record has been located except the letter above-quoted, in *Benjamin Harrison Papers*, Vol. 33, No. 6990–6992.

†George Alfred Townsend, author of the Morton biography, reported a conversation with Wallace regarding the latter's terms of consent when asked by the publisher to write the campaign life of Harrison, not mentioning his own connection with the enterprise. The report was published over Townsend's pseudonym, "Gath," as a "Boston letter" in the *Cincinnati Enquirer*, reprinted in *The Indianapolis Journal*, August 6, 1888.

the curious circumstance is that the separate contains a "Publisher's Preface," a cancel leaf whose wording proves it intended for the Harrison-Morton combine, but only to be found in the separate edition. For the combination volume and further notes, see *ante* 335–337.

1889
(Published 1888)
The Boyhood of Christ

THE [*yellow outlined in black within yellow floral design*] | BOY-HOOD | OF | CHRIST [*yellow, outlined in black*] | BY | LEW WALLACE | Author of "Ben Hur" and "The Fair God" | ILLUSTRATED [*yellow*] | NEW YORK | HARPER & BROTHERS FRANKLIN SQUARE. [*yellow*] | 1889

COLLATION: [*]^2, [1]–9^4. White heavy wove paper, calendered. Leaf measures 10½" (full) x 8", all edges gilt.

End paper; binder's leaf; fly title, p. [1] (its conjugate the title-page); blank, p. [2]; frontispiece with tissue guard, inserted; title-page, p. [3]; copyright notice dated 1888, and statement: *All rights reserved*, p. [4]; dedication, to *The Soul Of My Mother* ..., p. [5]; blank, p. [6]; *Preface* dated June, 1888, p. [7]; blank, p. [8]; list of illustrations, p. [9]; blank, p. [10]; quotation, p. [11]; blank, p. [12]; text, pp. [15]–101 (should be [13]–99); blank, pp. [100–102]; binder's leaf; end paper.

[Note: Inserted plates are figured in the pagination; see *Illustrations*. For text see *Contents*.]

ILLUSTRATIONS: Frontispiece with printed tissue guard, inserted; thirteen plates with printed tissue guards are inserted, but figured in the pagination; they are engravings from various artists. Dedication within single rule box; rule below running head on each page of text; illuminated initial, p. [15].

BINDING: Smooth dark blue leather. Front cover gilt-stamped; lettered within ornamental design of scrolls and thorns: THE BOYHOOD OF CHRIST | BY | LEW WALLACE [*all elaborately boxed*]. Spine gilt-stamped: [*ornamental border, similar to box design on front cover*] | [*ornamental parallel rule box containing the author's name:*] LEW | WALLACE | [*ornamental parallel rule box containing:*] [*floral ornament*] | [*rule*] |

THE | BOYHOOD | OF | CHRIST | [*ornament*] | [*parallel rule box containing:*] HARPER | BROTHERS | [*ornamental border*]. Back cover gilt-stamped with star in upper right, design of a cross, shepherd's crook, flowers, and scroll at left; all boxed as on front cover.

End papers same as book stock; binder's leaf front and back.

PUBLICATION DATA: Deposited in the Copyright Office, November 17, 1888. Listed in *The Publisher's Weekly*, December 1, 1888. Price, $3.50. "More than 10,000 copies were sold."*

NOTES: First edition as collated.† The same publishers reissued it with date changed to 1893, to 1900, to 1901; then with date dropped from title-page. Their "new edition" appeared in 1909.

A cheaper edition, for the British market, was issued by James R. Osgood, McIlvaine & Co., London, November, 1892.

It has been suggested that Wallace's mouthpiece in the book, "Uncle Midas," was a self-portrait.‡

CONTENTS: The Boyhood of Christ, previously in *Harper's* [*Monthly*] *Magazine*, December, 1886.

1893

The Prince of India

THE PRINCE OF INDIA | OR | WHY CONSTANTINOPLE FELL | BY | LEW WALLACE | AUTHOR OF "BEN-HUR" "THE BOYHOOD OF CHRIST" | "THE FAIR GOD" ETC., ETC. | [*quotation, 8 lines*] | LONGFELLOW | VOL. I. [II.] | NEW YORK | HARPER & BROTHERS PUBLISHERS | 1893

COLLATION: Vol. I: [1]–[3]–32⁸ (signed on fifth leaf); Vol. II: [1]–35⁸, 36⁴, 37⁸ (signed on first leaf). White wove paper. Leaf measures 6⅝″ x 4⅝″, all edges trimmed.

Vol. I: End paper; blank, pp. [1–2]; title-page, p. [i]; copyright notice dated 1893, and statement: *All rights reserved.*, p. [ii]; table of contents, pp. [iii]–v; blank, p. [vi]; divisional half-title, p. [1]; blank, p. [2]; text, pp. [3]–502; blank, pp. [503–504]; end paper.

Vol. II: End paper; title-page, p. [i]; copyright notice dated 1893,

---

*McKee, p. 224.

†No copy located with 1888 date on title-page, erroneously noted in *Merle Johnson's American First Editions* (1942).

‡McKee, p. 223.

and statement: *All rights reserved.*, p. [ii]; table of contents, pp. [iii]–v; blank, p. [vi]; divisional half-title, p. [1]; blank, p. [2]; text, pp. [3]–578; end paper.

[Note: Text, Vol. I, pp. [3]–502; Vol. II, [3]–578: The Prince of India, Books I–VI (titled).]

Binding: Blue coarse mesh cloth. Front cover bears a red-stamped rosary* hooked over a silver-stamped crescent, a silver-stamped star being within the crescent, and looped around a red-stamped cross formée, the crucifix blind-stamped; bears book title gilt-stamped: THE | PRINCE | OF | INDIA   Spine gilt-stamped: THE | PRINCE | OF | INDIA | [*rule*] | WALLACE | I. [II.] | HARPERS   Back cover blank.

End papers white laid; no binder's leaf front or back.

[Note: For comment on other bindings see *Publication Data*.]

Publication Data: Deposited in the Copyright Office August 26, 1893 (there are two earlier records in the Copyright Office of title registration: February 7 and May 18, 1893). A review in *The Independent*, September 7, 1893, was written by Maurice Thompson,† but is unsigned. Price, cloth, $2.50 (advertised at $1.90 by an Indianapolis bookstore); half-leather $4.00; ¾ leather, $5.00; ¾ calf, $6.00. A binding of ¾ crushed Levant, $8.00, boxed, was mentioned in October advertisements.

Notes: First edition as collated. No illustrations. No dedication.‡ The second issue had a dedication added, to David Wallace, the author's father, and had numerous corrections:

> State 1: No dedication
> Volume I:
> > Page 62, line 4, *tints* (later, *tents*)
> > Page 89, 1st line, *your* (later, *thy*)
> > Page [123], 4th line from bottom, no comma after *wonderful* or *rare* (later, commas added)
> > Page 126, 132, 204, *Gul Bahar* (later, hyphenated)

---

*No copy of the first edition has been located with rosary other than red-stamped, though *Merle Johnson's American First Editions*, revised by Jacob Blanck (1942), by its mention of the color as a mark of "probable first cloth binding," intimates that another color was used.

†According to a note on a clipping in the Wallace Papers, Eagle Crest Library.

‡Wallace wanted to dedicate this novel to Abdul-Hamid II, Sultan of Turkey, and requested permission through the Turkish Minister, January, 1893 (see McKee, p. 239); no acknowledgment of the request arrived, so the book was let come from the press without dedication. The second edition had one present, to David Wallace.

Page 165, Hilarion's letter dated *3d June, 1452* (later, 20th April, 1451)

Page 170, line 23, *Kameses* (later, *Kamares*)

Page 349, lines 23–24, *Bible in Hebrew, copied from* (later, *Bible, copied in part from*)

Page 356, line 17, *this* (later, *his*)

Page 369, end of second paragraph, *Porphyrogentes* (later, *Porphyrogeniti*)

Page 405, passage relating to Father Theophilus (regarded as abrupt, so considerably altered, but using same amount of space)

Page 458, last line, *from the Son* (later, *from the Father*)

Page 459, line 2, first word *Son* (later, *Father*)

Page 486, 7th line from bottom, *passengers* (later, *passenger*)

Page 490, line 21, noumia (later, noumiae; italics, all issues)

Volume II:*

Page 4, line 4, *Princess's* (later, *Princess'*)

Page 12, 8th line from bottom, *Irene* (later, *Irenè*)

Page 85, 86, 94, 105, 106 (twice), 107, 109, 164, 171, 173, *Gul Bahar* (later hyphenated)

Page 183, 1st paragraph, line 3, *early in the morning* (later, *early in the second morning*)

Page 190, line 12, *o* in *to* not aligned (later corrected)

Page 197, line 14, *sat* (later, *set*)

Page 204, line 13, *epxlored* (later, *explored*)

Page 275, 3rd line from bottom, *A* (later, *At*, and 2 lines reset)

Page 328, 2nd paragraph, *leavened* (later, *unleavened*)

Page 350, line 10, *noumias* (later, *noumiae*)

Page 363, line 12, *Magesty* (later, *Majesty*)

Page 403, line 16, *Asometon* (later, *Asomaton*)

Page 424, line 22, *Cerco Portae* (later, *Cercoporta*)

Page 454, line 14, *ire* (later, *fire*)

---

*Some bad type in this volume, notably on pp. 156, 294, 336, and 505, is found in many of the first issue copies, even the earliest ones, inscribed by the author.

Page 499, 4th line from bottom, *house led* (later, *houseled*)

State 2: Dedication present, dated May 20, 1893
Date on title-page, as in *State* 1
Corrections within text, as above indicated.

The second issue was in press September 29, 1893, very soon after first publication. Some copies of the book were offered by the Bowen-Merrill bookstore, December, 1893, as an *Author's Autograph Edition*, with added portrait and autograph.

For use in a "second edition" Wallace suggested, December, 1893, a reproduction of his ink drawing of the city of Constantinople, the one he had used as his first step in writing the story,* but the idea was evidently rejected; it did not appear.

A resume of about 350 words was written by Wallace for Harpers to send to European publishers; he mailed a manuscript copy to them on March 4, 1893, and it probably was printed as a circular or letter, but no copy has been located.

The author had made an early suggestion, March, 1893, that a one-volume edition be published by Harpers.† None appeared until 1911, and Grosset & Dunlap reprinted it. Sears, Roebuck & Company issued their cheap edition in 1913. Harpers republished the book in 1921.

A German translation by E. Albert Witte was published by F. E. Fehsenfeld, Freiburg, Germany, in 1894, unauthorized. A Danish translation was reported in the Davenport, Iowa, *Democrat*, February 4, 1894.

Wallace's own account of the book's origin as written at President Garfield's urging when he appointed him Minister to Turkey (he did gather his material there and begin writing September, 1886, soon after the end of his service) was printed in *Harper's Weekly*, August 19, 1893, and frequently requoted in magazines and newspapers. Earlier, *The Louisville Courier Journal*, May 26, 1887, carried the story told by T. M. Nichol: "'Ben Hur' Did It. How General Lew Wallace Was Given the Turkish Mission." An unpublished letter from the author to Whitelaw Reid, March 27, 1891, in the Wallace Papers, shows that he had hoped to be invited back to Constantinople by the Sultan of Turkey to finish the writing of his book without taking office or entering service, civil or military.

Accounts of the book's reception are to be found in McKee, pp.

---

*Correspondence in Eagle Crest Library.
†*Ibid.*

242–245. During the six months following publication 100,000 copies were sold.*

Lew Wallace's conception of the Wandering Jew was explained by him in an introduction written for a new edition of *Salathiel;* it differed from George Croly's (see *Tarry Thou Till I Come, post* 392).

A mention of the emerald which was woven into Wallace's story appears in Edwin A. Grosvenor's *Constantinople* (1895), Vol. 2, p. 730: of its deposit in the Seraglio's Hazneh (Treasure House). Wallace wrote the introduction for Grosvenor's historical work.

A "Prince of India March," by C. R. Hodge, dedicated to Lew Wallace, was published in Indianapolis by N. W. Bryant & Company, 1895; it consisted of music for the piano without words.

"The Prince of India," dramatized by J. I. C. Clarke in 1904 and produced by Klaw & Erlanger, was first played at the Colonial Theatre in Chicago, February 5, 1906.† It opened in New York on September 24th of the same year; came to Indianapolis January 14, 1907.

The novel that Wallace had outlined in his mind as a sequel was never written; the plan was that the Wandering Jew ("The Prince of India") "should go from Constantinople to the Court of Spain, and sail with Columbus in search of a new world . . ." ‡

1898

(Published 1897)

The Wooing of Malkatoon

The Wooing | of Malkatoon [*foregoing in red*] | [*rule*] | Commodus [*red*] | By Lew. Wallace | ILLUSTRATIONS BY | Du Mond & Weguelin | [*publishers' emblem*] | [*rule*] | NEW YORK AND LONDON | HARPER & BROTHERS PUBLISHERS [*red*] | 1898
[Note: The foregoing is within double rule box.]

COLLATION: [*]⁴, [1]–[6]–10⁸, 11⁶. White laid paper, watermarked with publishers' emblem. Leaf measures 8¾" x 5⅞" (full), top edge gilt, other edges untrimmed.

---

*Lew Wallace: *An Autobiography,* Vol. II (1906), p. 1000. See also *The Publishers' Weekly,* January 27, 1894, p. 165, for story of the book's popularity.

†The play's manuscript bears date May, 1904, not 1894 as stated by McKee, p. 272.

‡*Lew Wallace: An Autobiography,* Vol. II (1906), p. 1002.

End paper; blank, pp. [i–ii]; frontispiece with tissue guard, inserted; title-page, p. [iii]; copyright notices with final date 1897, and statement: *All rights reserved.*, p. [iv]; table of contents, p. [v]; blank, p. [vi]; list of illustrations, p. [vii]; blank, p. [viii]; divisional half-title, p. [1]; blank, p. [2]; text, pp. 3–[80]; divisional half-title, p. [81]; blank, p. [82]; text, pp. 83–[168]; list of books by Wallace, p. [169]; blank, pp. [170–172]; end paper.

[Note: Text, pp. 3–(80): The Wooing of Malkatoon; pp. 83–(168): Commodus.]

ILLUSTRATIONS: Frontispiece with tissue guard, inserted. Also inserted are full-page plates facing pp. 4, 12, 20, 58, 74, 98, 114, 120, 132, 156, 166; done by Frank Vincent Du Mond and John Remhard Weguelin.

BINDING: Light green silk-finished mesh cloth. Title gilt-stamped within a mosaic design stamped in dark green, orange, and silver*: THE WOOING | OF | MALKATOON | [*rule*] | COMMODUS [*the double O's interlinked, all O's underlined; the mosaic forms a panel within which is gilt-stamped:*] LEW. WALLACE   Spine bears decorations similar to front cover, the title, author's name, and publishers' imprint gilt-stamped within panels formed by silver mosaics: [*mosaic design, stamped in dark green, orange, and silver*] | THE WOOING | OF | MALKATOON | [*rule*] | COMMODUS [*all double O's interlinked, all O's underlined*] | [*mosaic design, stamped in dark green, orange, and silver*] | LEW. | WALLACE | [*mosaic rule in silver*] | [*mosaic ornament stamped in dark green and orange*] HARPERS [*mosaic ornament stamped in dark green and orange*] | [*mosaic rule in silver*]. Back cover blank except for mosaic box stamped in dark green, orange, and silver.

End papers same as book stock; no binder's leaf front or back.

PUBLICATION DATA: Deposited in the Copyright Office November 24, 1897. Published December, 1897.† Earliest review noted: *Harper's New Monthly Magazine*, December 1897, Supplement 2, and *The Indianapolis Journal*, January 3, 1898. Price, $2.50.

NOTES: First printing of *The Wooing of Malkatoon* in book form; *Commodus* had appeared earlier in separate pamphlet form (*ante* 314). A later issue (December, 1898?) has leaf trimmed to 8½" x 5⅝",

---

*The copyright deposit copies have the design in silver, but lack other colored stamping; evidently sent in advance of publication.

†Wallace asked the publishers, on December 16th, for "a couple of the volumes (Malkatoon) in choisest [*sic*] binding, one of them to be sent to the Sultan of Turkey."—Correspondence, in Eagle Crest Library.

all edges trimmed, top ungilded. It is bound in similar cloth but stamped in orange instead of gilt, and white instead of silver; back cover blank.

A page of the manuscript (p. 47, lines 1537–1571), was printed in facsimile in *Our Day*, February, 1898, p. 59.

On May 2, 1898, The Missouri School for the Blind, St. Louis, wrote Wallace, asking permission to reprint the poem in Braille.

1899
The First Christmas

[*Parallel rule*] | THE FIRST | CHRISTMAS | FROM "BEN-HUR" | [*parallel rule*] | By Lew. Wallace | [*parallel rule*] | [*publishers' emblem*] | [*parallel rule*] | NEW YORK AND LONDON | HARPER & BROTHERS | [*parallel rule*] | MDCCCXCIX | [*parallel rule*]

[Note: Text of title-page and publishers' emblem in blue; the black rules are supplemented by a vertical one at each side which makes the whole appear boxed.]

COLLATION: A–I⁸ (plus one inserted sheet of plate paper in first signature; all lettered on recto of fifth leaf), [J]⁴. White laid paper. Leaf measures 6¼" (full) x 3¼", top edge blue, other edges untrimmed.

End paper; acknowledgment of story as part of *Ben-Hur* with new introduction, verso blank; frontispiece, inserted; title-page, with verso bearing copyright notice with final date 1899, and statement: *All rights reserved.*, (on plate paper, its conjugate the acknowledgment leaf that follows end paper); dedication: *To All The | Sunday-School Scholars | In The World*, p. [i]; blank, p. [ii]; *Preface*, pp. v–ix (should be iii–vii); blank, p. [viii]; text, pp. 1–[140]; list of *Little Books by Famous Writers*, p. [141]; blank, pp. [142–144]; end paper.

[Note: For text, see *Contents*.]

ILLUSTRATIONS: Frontispiece from a photograph of Jerusalem, inserted.

BINDING: Teal blue silk-finished mesh cloth. Front cover silver-stamped: The | First |Christmas [m *ends in a curlicue which forms an ornament below*] | Lew | Wallace [*double l intertwined at top, first l ending in a curlicue which forms an ornament below; all appears within an ornamental border which is within a single rule box*]. Spine silver-stamped: The | First | Christ- | mas [*s ends in a curlicue which forms an ornament below*] | Wallace | Harpers   Back cover same as front.

End papers same as book stock; no binder's leaf front or back.

PUBLICATION DATA: Published October 10, 1899; deposited in the Copyright Office, November 18th. Price, 50¢.

NOTES: Part of a series of ten *Little Books by Famous Authors,* uniformly bound; this is the only Lew Wallace title.

Harpers reissued it in 1902 with illustrations from drawings by William Martin Johnson and from photographs.

The other excerpt from *Ben-Hur* published by Harpers as a separate book, in 1908, *The Chariot-Race,* contained no original writing (see *ante* 326).

CONTENTS: Only the preface, five pages, is original writing*; the text, pp. 1–[140], is from *Ben-Hur* (1880), Book One.

1906
Autobiography

LEW WALLACE | AN AUTOBIOGRAPHY | ILLUSTRATED | VOL. I [II] | [*publishers' emblem*] | NEW YORK AND LONDON | HARPER & BROTHERS PUBLISHERS | MCMVI

COLLATION: Vol. I: One unsigned sheet, 1–32⁸. Vol. II: [1]–34⁸ (Sig. 2 in this second volume numbered 33 on recto of fourth leaf, 3 numbered 34, 14 numbered 45, 33 numbered 64, 34 numbered 65). White wove paper. Leaf in Vol. 1 measures 8¼₆″ x 5⅜″; in Vol. II, 8⅛″ x 5⅜″; in both, top edge gilt, other edges untrimmed.

Vol. I: End paper; title-page, p. [i]; copyright notice dated 1906, statements: *All rights reserved.*, and *Published October, 1906.*, p. [ii]; table of contents, pp. iii–[x]; list of illustrations, p. [xi]; blank, p. [xii]; half-title, p. [xiii]; blank, p. [xiv]; text, pp. 1–[502]; end paper.

Vol. II: End paper; title-page, p. [i]; copyright notice dated 1906,

---

*Wallace's own account of the origin of *Ben-Hur,* herein told, is commented on by McKee, p. 167*n*, as not corresponding with evidence in an unpublished letter to Agnes Wallace (quoted on p. 165), that the plot of the story had progressed beyond the "First Christmas" as early as November, 1874.

statements: *All rights reserved.*, and *Published October, 1906.*, p. [ii]; table of contents, pp. iii–vii; blank, p. [viii]; list of illustrations, p. [ix]; blank, p. [x]; half-title, p. [xi]; blank, p. [xii]; text, pp. 503–[1003]; blank, p. [1004]; index, pp. 1005–[1028]; blank, pp. [1029–1034]; end paper.

[Note: For text, pp. 1–(1003), see *Contents.*]

ILLUSTRATIONS: Vol. I: Frontispiece with tissue guard, inserted as are illustrations facing pp. 8, 208, and 436. Sketches by Wallace appear on pp. 15 and 20. Within the text are some maps, diagrams, etc.

Vol. II: Frontispiece with tissue guard, inserted as are illustrations facing pp. 884, 968, and 992. Text includes maps, diagrams, etc.

BINDING: Dark blue ribbed cloth. Front cover gilt-stamped: LEW WALLACE | AN | AUTOBIOGRAPHY   Spine gilt-stamped: LEW | WALLACE | AN | AUTOBIOGRAPHY | VOL. I. [II.] | HARPERS   Back cover blank.

End papers white wove; no binder's leaf front or back.

PUBLICATION DATA: Deposited in the Copyright Office October 25, 1906. Earliest review noted: *The Indianapolis News*, October 24, 1906. Price, $5.00.

NOTES: First edition as collated; bears statement on copyright page of each volume: *Published October, 1906.* A limited edition of 250 numbered copies was issued in boards with cloth shelfback, paper labels on spine, with a photogravure portrait of Wallace in first volume and his autograph, thus explained: "This being a posthumous publication, the autographs have been cut from various letters and checks supplied by Mrs. Wallace."

The book appeared in 1916 in light blue mesh cloth, black-stamped, with leaf trimmed to 8″ x 5¾₆″; all edges are trimmed and top ungilded.

Susan E. Wallace's statement regarding the completion of the autobiography appears in Vol. II, p. 796: "And here the Autobiography ends. What follows must be a plain record of facts without attempt at polish or effect.

"Whatever merit it may have belongs to my friend, Mary H. Krout, whose careful work has made this continuation possible."

Excerpts from the autobiography have been frequently quoted in histories of the Mexican and Civil Wars.

CONTENTS: An Autobiography: Vol. I [Chapters] I–LV; Vol. II, LVI–LXXIV, concluding with the statement by Susan E. Wallace on p. 796. Wallace wrote his memoirs to July, 1864, only; the book continues with Part II which consists mostly of reports and letters by Lew

Wallace, but selected by Mrs. Wallace and Mary H. Krout. The letter to members of the Board of (Florida) State Canvassers, January 19, 1877, printed on p. 908, had earlier publication in the Tallahassee *Sentinel,* and was reprinted in *The Crawfordsville Journal,* February 3, 1877, as well as in other newspapers (see *post* 399 for uncollected contributions to *The Indianapolis Journal* and *New York Tribune,* 1876, and *The Cincinnati Commerical,* 1877, which are contemporary accounts by Wallace of the Hayes' electoral vote count; see also *post* 373 for his testimony before the Potter Committee in 1878). On p. 926, there appears a selection without title, earlier in *Youth's Companion,* February 2, 1893, as "How I Came to Write Ben-Hur"; and, on p. 991, his address to Cadets at the United States Military Academy, earlier in *Harper's Weekly,* June 23, 1894, and in newspapers of the period.*
The letter from Wallace to his son, Henry, February 14, 1885, about his gift of a dog to the Sultan of Turkey, in Vol. II, Part II, p. 979, is acknowledged as printed in *The Ladies' Home Journal,* but unlocated therein. His letter to President Porfirio Diaz of Mexico, August 15, 1889, published in Vol. II, Part II, pp. 843, 862, had appeared in *The* (Chicago) *Inter Ocean,* August 27, 1889; his letter to the editor of the *Cincinnati Commercial,* March 23, 1870, denying ownership of Mexican bonds, appeared contemporaneously in that newspaper.

Part of his speech of July 4, 1866, Vol. II, p. 860, had earlier appearances in print (see *post* 370).

A selection from the *Autobiography,* Vol. I, p. 254, appeared in *Werner's Readings and Recitations,* No. 45, *Lincoln Celebrations, Part I* (1910), "Lew Wallace at the Lincoln-Douglas Debate."

---

*Clippings examined lack identification.

~~~~~~

1861
Civil War broadside

WAR! WAR!! | [*double rule*] | ONE HUNDRED VOLUNTEERS | WANTED. | [*double rule*] | The President of the United States having called | out the Militia to the number of 7[5?],000, and Six Regiments be- ing re- | quired from Indiana for | IMMEDIATE SERVICE, | An oppor- tunity is now offered to Volunteer in DEFENSE OF THE | UNION AND THE GOVERNMENT. Those who are willing to de- | fend the Stars and Stripes will call at the | GUARDS' ARMORY | In Crawfordsville, where the books are now open. Rally to the Flag | of our Country! | ("LOCOMOTIVE" JOB PRINT—CRAWFORDSVILLE.) Lew Wallace.

Printed in bold face, with squared commas and periods, on one side only of a sheet of white wove paper, 14¾" x 10⅞" (scant). The numeral after the seven in the number of thousands called for to enlist is torn out in the only copy located, preserved in a frame in the Wallace Study, Crawfordsville, but 75,000 was the total required.

This is only one of the handbills sent out by Wallace immediately after President Lincoln's proclamation of a need for troops to put down the rebellion. One that is phrased similarly is reproduced in McKee, p. 34. They are part of the "productive work" which Lew Wallace be- gan in his office as adjutant general of Indiana on Monday morning, April 15, 1861.

For published orders and letters issued by Wallace in April, 1861, see (Indiana) *State Sentinel* and *The Indianapolis Journal*, in the section beginning *post* 399.

351

1863

The Stolen Stars

THE | [*row of 11 stars*] | STOLEN STARS. | [*6 stars*] OR [*6 stars*] | Good old Father Washington. [*row of 11 stars*] | [*rule dividing a shield, on which foregoing is printed; the following, below, over stripes:*] WRITTEN BY | GEN. LEW. WALLACE. | MUSIC ADAPTED & ARRANGED BY | R. HASTINGS. | [*below the shield and within a star:*] 3 | Published. | Cincinnati. A. C. PETERS & BRO: — J. L. PETERS & BRO: St. Louis. | 3639

[Note: Printed on the cover, on an inlaid panel measuring 10⅞″ x 7¹⁵⁄₁₆″.]

COLLATION: A single sheet folded to make 4 pages, with a leaf loosely inserted. White wove paper. Leaf measures 13¹⁵⁄₁₆″ x 10¾″, all edges trimmed.

Front cover, p. [1]; blank, p. [2]; text: words, and music, pp. 3–4 (acknowledgement to Harper & Bros., plate number 3639.4, and copyright notice dated 1863, at foot of p. 3; brief title and plate number at foot of p. 4); words, with statement at foot regarding origin of the ballad, brief title, and plate number, p. 5; blank, p. [6].

[Note: For text, pp. 3–5, see Contents.]

ILLUSTRATIONS: Front cover decorated with a patriotic shield design.

NOTES: The note at foot of p. 5 describes the origin of this piece of sheet music: "At a dinner, at which were present Major-General Lewis Wallace, Thomas Buchanan Reed [Read], and James E. Murdoch, a conversation sprung up respecting ballads for soldiers. The General maintained that hardly one had been written suited for the camp. It was agreed that each of them should write one. The above is that by General Wallace."

The verses without music appeared as a broadside, with red and green decorations, issued for the Great Western Sanitary Fair in Cincinnati, which opened December 21, 1863, and continued through the holidays. Another separate reprint has been reported as issued in Nashville, 1863.*

---

*McKee, p. 281.

CONTENTS: The Stolen Stars, earlier a poem in *Harper's Weekly*, August 22, 1863.

1875

Military Record

GENERAL WALLACE'S | MILITARY RECORD. | [*decorative rule*] | The Badeau Libel—Full and Complete Vindica- | tion over the Signature of General Grant. | [*text, double-columned*]
[Note: Caption title; no title-page.]

COLLATION: Pamphlet, 8 pages, unbound. White wove paper. Leaf measures 9¼" x 5½", edges untrimmed.
Title and text, p. [1]; text, continued, pp. 2–8.
[For text, pp. (1)–8, see *Contents*.]

NOTES: Issued without binding, folded. Two copies were filed as 6198, A. G. O., 1875, Enclosure 2, in the War Office, with a letter of December 7, 1875, transmitting them (for more details see *post* 376, [*U. S. War Department*] *Correspondence, Etc., on the Subject of the Records of the Rebellion, and Exhibiting the Rules Governing the Same* [1883]). With the copies of the Wallace *Military Record* was filed, too, Col. Charles Whittlesey's pamphlet entitled, *General Wallace's Division—Battle of Shiloh—Was It Tardy?* (1875).

Wallace prepared this piece as a response to criticism in Col. Adam Badeau's "Life of Grant" in *The Chicago Tribune*, December 25, 1867,* and to General Grant's suggestion that he publish the letters exonerating his conduct of April 6, 1862, at the battle of Pittsburg Landing.

That Badeau's *Life of Grant* seemed to him to be unjust is further apparent from a newspaper account (published *ca.* 1884, but the clipping in the Wallace Papers lacks identification except for a note: "J. H. Woodard's Enquirer Letter") quoting marginal comments written by him in a copy of the book located at the time in Washington; the copy has not yet come to light, however.

For Wallace's story of the battle and its aftermath see also his *Autobiography*, pp. 459–580; his report in *The War of the Rebellion*,

---

*The Badeau biography was evidently syndicated and published in many newspapers at this time.

Series I, Vol. X, Part 1 (1884), p. 169; the *Address of Gen. Lew Wallace at the Dedication of Indiana's Monuments on the Battlefield of Shiloh* (1903); and his article, "My Own Account of the First Day at Shiloh" in *Appleton's Booklovers Magazine,* January, 1906.

Benson J. Lossing's *Pictorial History of the Civil War in the United States of America,* 3 volumes (1866–1868), contains many references to Wallace, and Vol. 2 (1868), p. 262n, prints part of a letter written by him to Lossing, describing the movement of the army up the river.

CONTENTS: Letter to General U. S. Grant, February 29, 1868. The other letters that constitute the text are written to and about him, from Col. James R. Ross, Col. J. A. Strickland, Brig.-Gen. G. F. McGinnis, Col. Fred. Knefler, Capt. Ad. Ware, Jr., and Brig.-Gen. John M. Thayer, concluding with General Grant's letter of March 10, 1868. These letters were all published in a newspaper (*The Chicago Tribune?*), but the clipping examined lacks identification and date; necessarily after June 24, 1868, the date of the latest letter in the group.

1878

New Mexico

Proclamation by the Governor. | [*double rule*] | [*text*]

Single sheet of white wove paper, 10″ x 8″, all edges trimmed. Printed on one side only, double-columned. Text at left in English, dated at end: *Done at the city of Santa | Fé, this 13th day of November, A* [no period] *D. 1878.* | *Lewis Wallace,* [name in upper case] | *By the Governor,* | *W. G. Ritch,* | *Secretary.* Repeated in Spanish at right.

This is a proclamation declaring that "the disorders lately prevalent in Lincoln County . . . have been happily brought to an end," and extending amnesty to residents and to Army officers in the county. It appeared in the *Rocky Mountain Sentinel* (Santa Fe), November 14, 1878, and in other newspapers of the region (in the *Mesilla Independent* as late as November 23, 1878).

The Weekly New Mexican (Santa Fe), November 23, 1878, published his proclamation designating November 28th as a day for Thanksgiving to God.

It was President Rutherford B. Hayes, not Governor Wallace, who had issued the proclamation warning all citizens against participating in the "Lincoln County War," published in *The Weekly New Mexican*, October 12, 1878. Some years later Wallace's letters to President Hayes from New Mexico were published in *The New England Quarterly*, March, 1942 (see *post* 413).

Wallace's request of October 26, 1878, to General Hatch to dispatch troops to Fort Stanton was possibly published in the *Rocky Mountain Sentinel* or other regional newspapers, not yet located. It exists in manuscript form in the Wallace Papers. His letter to the same, December 7, 1878, requesting removal of Lieut. Col. N. A. M. Dudley, appeared in *The Mesilla News*, March 22, 1879, and in *The Western-ers Brand Book* (1949); see *post* 397.

A letter from Wallace to "Billy the Kid [William H. Bonney]," March 15, 1879, was first published in *Pat F. Garrett's Authentic Life of Billy the Kid*, edited by Maurice G. Fulton (1927), in facsimile, facing p. 116, and transcribed, p. 123.

On March 19, 1879, Wallace offered a reward of $1,000 for capture of two men, Evans and Campbell, who escaped from Fort Stanton, according to a handwritten order (manuscript, a letter, in Wallace Papers) to Capt. Juan Patron; probably not published.

The Denver Tribune in the spring of 1879 (April 9th?) evidently printed a charge that Wallace had reported New Mexico to be overrun by thieves and murderers, and he in reply asserted that he referred only to conditions in Lincoln County, but this not yet located. Wallace referred to the matter as having received widespread publicity, in a letter to Schurz, May 5, 1879.*

The Mesilla (New Mexico) *News*, May 17, 1879, published "Wallace's Orders While in Command at Fort Stanton," about Lincoln County troubles, addressed to U. S. Army officials. The captain of the Post, on May 21, 1879, sent a letter of apology to the Governor for these letters having come into the hands of the newspaper and been made public.†

Wallace's testimony during five days on the witness stand in the trial of Colonel Dudley, May, 1879, was referred to but not published in *The Mesilla News*, May 24, 1879.

Dispatches from Wallace, at Santa Fe, September 17, 1879 (two so-dated) and September 20th, about Indian troubles, addressed to S. M. Ashenfelter, Silver City, New Mexico, appeared in the Santa Fe *Weekly New Mexican*, September 20, 1879.

---

*Letter in Wallace Papers.
†*Ibid.*

For Wallace's "Report of the Governor of New Mexico," September 23, 1879, see *post* 359.

A speech delivered at Silver City near the end of October, 1879, calling for troops to exterminate roving Apaches is mentioned in McKee*; possibly quoted in a contemporary newspaper, more likely unpublished or only briefly reviewed.

The "Governor's Message to the Legislative Assembly of New Mexico," January 8, 1880, appeared in *The Weekly New Mexican*, January 10, 1880, also in pamphlet form with English, and, Spanish text (see *post* 360).

Two telegrams from Wallace to Carl Schurz, January 16 and 19, 1880, about Indian troubles, were published in a regional newspaper (New Mexico? Colorado?) on February 5, 1880.†

Wallace's reward notice of December 13, 1880, for the capture of William H. Bonney (Billy the Kid) was mentioned in *The Daily New Mexican* (Santa Fe), December 14, 1880, printed in the *Las Vegas Gazette*, December 24, 1880; offer renewed and printed May 4, 1881, in *The Daily New Mexican*.‡

His letter to Frederick W. Pitkin, Governor of Colorado, May 28, 1881, about outlaws operating on the border line between Colorado and the Territory of New Mexico, appeared in *The Daily New Mexican*, May 29, 1881.

The New Mexican period is described (in slight detail only) in *Lew Wallace: An Autobiography* (1906), Vol. II, pp. 912–925, mainly in letters quoted. The only mention here of Billy the Kid is in Susan's words, in her letter to their son, Henry L. Wallace, May 11, 1879 (p. 921). A sensational story in *The* (New York) *World*, June 8, 1902, had claimed contents to be copied and compiled for the Sunday *World Magazine* "from the advance sheets of Gen. Wallace's book [autobiography]," and was captioned: "General Lew Wallace Writes a Romance of 'Billy the Kid' Most Famous Bandit of the Plains." If true, the fact remains that no such manuscript was preserved in the Wallace Papers, nor was any part of it included in the *Autobiography* published four years later. The *World* story has been frequently quoted in accounts of Wallace and Bonney, to large extent in McKee's *"Ben-Hur" Wallace* (1947). In the article Wallace is quoted as saying that a letter from

---

*McKee, p. 157.
†Unidentified clipping in Wallace Papers.
‡Was the renewal published in April, 1881, after Bonney's break from jail? The Santa Fe Publishing Company, which printed both the daily and weekly *New Mexican*, billed Wallace for an "advt (1 in) Reward for 'Kid'" on April 26 (the bill, receipted May 20, 1881, is in the Wallace Papers).

him to Bonney, with a narrative of the circumstances connected with it, was given "to the paper published in the town [where Bonney was jailed]. It was duly printed and upon its appearance a copy was sent to 'Billy' in his cell." This would have been March of 1881, but no such publication has been found. The letter from him to Bonney, referred to, is probably the one of March 15, 1879, which, with Bonney's reply, appeared in facsimile in Maurice Garland Fulton's edition of *Pat F. Garrett's Authentic Life of Billy the Kid* (1927); again in Henry F. Hoyt's *A Frontier Doctor* (1929).*

A facsimile of the death warrant of William H. Bonney (Billy the Kid), May 30, 1881, written in Wallace's hand, addressed to the Sheriff of Lincoln County, New Mexico, was published in *Frontier Fighter: The Autobiography of George W. Coe* . . . (1934); see *post* 396.

A letter about his writing "Ben-Hur" in the Governor's Palace at Santa Fe, addressed to A. J. Wissler, May 6, 1890, appeared in a broadside, *The Ben Hur Room* (*post* 382).

About Lew Wallace's term as Governor of New Mexico little appears in histories of the state. The contemporary newspapers, scattered now through many states and libraries,† contained spirited attacks on, and some justifications of Wallace in his attempts to bring law and order into the Territory. It is interesting to note that as early as November 21, 1878 (Wallace had arrived in Santa Fe on September 30th), the *Rocky Mountain Sentinel* (Santa Fe) gave a review of his administration, and this was copied in other newspapers, among them *The Crawfordsville Journal*, November 30, 1878. *The Rocky Mountain Sentinel*, very soon thereafter, evidently published more about him, for Wallace wrote to Col. N. A. M. Dudley, November 30, 1878, saying that he was enclosing a half-sheet (probably that day's issue of the *Sentinel* or one quite recent to it‡): "Your reports furnished me a perfect answer to the gentlemen in the Territory who are fighting my confirmation on the ground that my proclamation is false and Lincoln County not pacified." While not his own communications, he is believed to have assembled the reports and sent them to the newspaper. Certain letters published by Colonel Dudley in *The New Mexican*, December 14, 1878, complaining of a clause in the November 13th proclamation,

---

*Erna Fergusson, in *Murder & Mystery in New Mexico* (1948), p. 70, quotes from a letter written by Wallace about "The Kid," a letter unlocated.

†A search of them was made in our behalf by Maurice G. Fulton, Roswell, New Mexico. His comments and findings beyond the scope of this bibliography are filed with the Wallace Papers.

‡Letter in Wallace Papers. An undated clipping of the *Rocky Mountain Sentinel* with the Dudley reports has been preserved in the Hayes Memorial Library, Fremont, Ohio.

provoked a letter of reply from Wallace on December 16, 1878, in which he said that they made it "important for me to answer publicly." Whether or not an answer was published is as yet unknown.

The newspapers of the region and period mostly attacked Wallace's policies as he attempted to bring the Santa Fe Ring under the law. *The Rocky Mountain Sentinel* and *Albuquerque Review* appear to have been the only ones independent or favorable to Wallace.*

A body of literature devoted to the legends of Billy the Kid has grown to considerable bulk. J. C. Dykes' brief " 'Billy the Kid' Bibliographic Check List" which appeared as appendix in his reprint (1946) of the first known publication (1881) devoted wholly to this outlaw, a list published also in the *Southwestern Historical Quarterly*, Vol. 49, April, 1946, pp. 644–648, has grown to book size: *Billy the Kid: The Bibliography of the Legend*, by J. C. Dykes, a forthcoming (1952) publication of the University of New Mexico Press. Its manuscript reveals a definitive list of 428 items reviewed and correlated. Beginning with five forerunners (concerned with another "Billy the Kid") and the dime novel by "Don Jernando" published about six weeks after the killing of Bonney, the bibliography leads one through a chronological description of anthologies, magazine articles, verse, bibliographies, biographies and narratives, histories, novels and short stories, juveniles, comics, motion pictures, plays, phonograph records, and sheet music. In many of the items Wallace figures somewhat. One pamphlet of reminiscences, by Colonel Jack M. Potter, *Cattle Trails of the Old West* (1935), is noted as crediting him with saving the cattle industry of New Mexico by stopping the Lincoln County War; Potter, to honor him, named one of his lead steers "Lew Wallace." Another sidelight might be mentioned here: the production of a play, Philip Stevenson's "Sure Fire, Episodes in the Life of Billy the Kid," unpublished but presented in 1931 at the Santa Fe Fiesta and again in Santa Fe in 1934 at a teachers' convention; General and Mrs. Lew Wallace both figured as characters in the play.

Was Wallace given the appointment as governor partly because of the publicity aroused by an article in the *Cincinnati Commercial* in August, 1877, further elaborated by a reporter in *The Indianapolis Journal*, August 28, 1877? It outlined his plan for fighting Indians with their own methods to replace the "present style," which he is said to

---

*An interesting document in the Wallace Papers is a pocket notebook with information about the various newspapers' attitudes, prepared for him by Judge Frank Warner Angel, before he took office, since it was to him that Wallace went in the beginning for information that would help him avoid mistakes; the book also contains notes on persons with whom Wallace would be involved.

have regarded as "both inhuman and absurd," and may have influenced Hayes, already wanting to reward Wallace for his work in the electoral vote count in Louisiana and Florida (see *ante* 350).

Susan Wallace's summary of their life in New Mexico is revealed in her edited portion of *Lew Wallace: An Autobiography* (1906), Vol. II, pp. 912–925. Her book about New Mexico, *The Land of the Pueblos* (1888), contains a descriptive account of the region and its people, but is not an account of his administration. It does, however, include a drawing by him of the ancient Governors' Palace in Santa Fe.

New Mexico has not forgotten Lew Wallace. A *Guide to the Museum of New Mexico in the Palace of the Governors, Santa Fe* (1915) told the story of his writing the final chapters of "Ben-Hur" while occupying a room there; recent guide books are still calling public attention to their Territorial Governor's literary activities.

1879
New Mexico: Report of the Governor

REPORT | of the | Governor of New Mexico | Made to the | SECRETARY OF THE INTERIOR | For | The Year 1879 | WASHINGTON | Government Printing Office | 1879

COLLATION: Pamphlet, 5 leaves, saddle-stitched. White wove paper. Leaf measures 9″ x 5⅞″. Title-page, p. [1]; blank, p. [2]; text, pp. [3]–10.

[Note: Text, pp. (3)–10: Report . . . to the Secretary of the Interior.]

BINDING: Light green wrappers; front reads same as title-page, but has a decorative rule added above imprint. Back and inside covers blank.*

NOTES: This report, dated September 23, 1879, appeared also in the *U. S. House Executive Documents*, 46th Congress, 2nd Session, Ex. Doc. 1, Part 5: *Report of the Secretary of the Interior* . . . (1879), p. [447]. It was published also in a collection of regional reports, wrap-

---

*Description of this pamphlet is from correspondence with the New Mexico Law Library, Santa Fe, where a copy is located.

pered: *Reports of the Governors of Arizona, Dakota, Idaho, Montana, New Mexico, Utah and Washington Territories, Made to the Secretary of the Interior for the Year 1879* (1879), p. [39].

1880

New Mexico: Message of the Governor

MESSAGE | [*rule*]OF [*rule*] | Governor Lewis Wallace | [*rule*] TO THE [*rule*] | LEGISLATIVE ASSEMBLY | [*rule*] OF [*rule*] | New Mexico | Twenty-fourth session. | [*Territorial emblem*] | SANTA FE, N. M. | [*rule*] | 1880.

[Note: All within a parallel rule box on front cover, which serves as title-page.]

COLLATION: 4 leaves, stitched within light salmon-colored wrappers. No title-page. The "Governor's Message" occupies p. [1]–8. Not seen, but information from the copy in the Ritch Collection, Huntington Library and Art Museum.

NOTES: Also published in Spanish: *Mensaje del Gob. Lewis Wallace a la Asemblea de Nuevo Mejico; Sesion Vigesima Cuarta* (1880), 8 pages, in wrappers.

It appeared also in a volume entitled: *1880. Territory of New Mexico. Governor's Message and Journals of the Council and House of the Twenty-fourth Session of the Legislative Assembly*, issued in gray wrappers, containing three separately paginated reports: the Council Journal, House Journal, and Governor's Message; latter only is by Wallace.

The text made its original appearance in the *Weekly New Mexican*, Santa Fe, January 10, 1880. The message was delivered January 8th. It is briefly summarized in *Lew Wallace: An Autobiography*, Vol. II (1906), p. 916; also in McKee, pp. 157–158, with a quotation of two sentences from it. Widespread publication was evidently given it contemporaneously; *The Crawfordsville Journal*, February 28, 1880, reprinted it in part from the *Denver Tribune*.

1888

The Democratic Party and the Solid South

SPEECH | [rule] OF [rule] | GEN. LEW. WALLACE | [rule] ON [rule] | The Democratic Party and the Solid South | [rule] | Delivered on occasion of a Rally called by the Ben Hur Re- | publican Club at Whitlock, Montgomery County, Indiana, Octo- | ber 23, 1888. | [rule] | CRAWFORDSVILLE JOURNAL PRINT, | 1888.

COLLATION: 8 leaves, side-stitched. White wove paper. Leaf measures 9⅛" x 6³⁄₁₆", all edges trimmed.
Title-page, p. [1]; blank, p. [2]; text, pp. [3]–15; blank, p. [16].
[Note: For text, pp. (3)–15, see Contents.]

ILLUSTRATIONS: None. A rule appears below title on first page of text.

BINDING: Brown wrappers. Front cover reads: [double rule] | GEN. LEW. WALLACE | [rule] ON [rule] | The Democratic Party and the Solid South. | [double rule]. Back and inside wrappers blank. Leaves side-stitched and tipped in covers.

NOTES: For a story of this speech, in behalf of Benjamin Harrison, see Lew Wallace: An Autobiography, Vol. II (1906), p. 990.* The (Chicago) Inter Ocean reported it as delivered at Wingate, but the city's name had been changed to Whitlock in July, 1884. His Life of Gen. Ben Harrison (1888), ante 335, was written for the Presidential campaign. A later biographical sketch of Harrison in brief was written by him for Living Leaders of the World (1889), q.v.

Mary Hannah Krout, in her accounts of the Harrison campaign written for The (Chicago) Inter Ocean, frequently mentioned Wallace's efforts in Harrison's behalf. That he wanted no position in President Harrison's Cabinet was indicated in her article of November 30, 1888; his own statement to that effect appeared in The Crawfordsville Journal of January 12, 1889.

---

*McKee, pp. 230–232, discusses Harrison-Wallace connections, before, during, and after this period.

CONTENTS: The Democratic Party and the Solid South; a speech published in *The* (Chicago) *Inter Ocean,* October 24, 1888, under caption: "Hitting the Bourbons Hard," and reprinted in the Sunday issue, October 28th.

1901

James R. Ross: An Ideal Indiana Soldier

AN IDEAL INDIANA SOLDIER. | [*rule*] | JAMES R. ROSS, | Brevet Lieutenant Colonel and A.D.C., U.S.V. Colonel Second Regiment | Indiana National Guard. | DIED IN INDIANAPOLIS, OCTOBER 27, 1900. | [*rule*] | A TRIBUTE TO HIS MEMORY | BY | MAJOR GENERAL LEW WALLACE. | [*rule*] | Published by the Indiana Commandery of the Military Order of the Loyal | Legion and Colonel Harry B. Smith, Second Regiment | Indiana National Guard. | INDIANAPOLIS, OCTOBER 27, 1901.

COLLATION: 4 leaves, wire saddle-stitched. White calendered paper. Leaf measures 8⅜₆" x 5¹¹⁄₁₆", all edges trimmed.

Title-page, p. [1]; *The Official Register,* p. [2]; text, pp. [3–7]; blank, p. [8].

[Note: Text, pp. (3–7), Wallace's tribute to his friend, James R. Ross.]

BINDING: None; self-wrapper.

NOTES: This tribute appeared in *The Indianapolis News,* October 26, 1901, under the caption, "An Indiana Soldier—Maj. James R. Ross." Part of it was reprinted in a biographical sketch of Ross in *Commemorative Biographical Record of Prominent and Representative Men of Indianapolis and Vicinity,* J. H. Beers & Co. (1908), p. 1053.

Wallace's letter of endorsement of Ross as candidate for Sheriff of Marion County, in 1886, was probably published in Indianapolis newspapers of that year, as yet unlocated.

1903
Shiloh Address

ADDRESS | OF | GEN. LEW WALLACE | AT THE | DEDICATION OF INDI-
ANA'S MONUMENTS | ON THE BATTLEFIELD OF SHILOH, | TENNES-
SEE, APRIL 6, 1903. | [*ornament*] | News-Review Print, | Craw-
fordsville, | Indiana.

COLLATION: 10 leaves, wire saddle-stitched. White laid paper. Leaf
measures 6⅝" x 4⅜" (scant), all edges trimmed.

Title-page, p. [1]; blank, p. [2]; text, pp. 3–19; blank, p. [20].

[Note: Text, pp. 3–19, Wallace's speech on the occasion above-
named.]

ILLUSTRATIONS: None. A rule appears below the running title on
each page, and each paragraph bears a symbol at beginning.

BINDING: Gray, and, green wrappers, trimmed to leaf size. Front
cover reads: SHILOH | ADDRESS | BY | GEN. LEW WALLACE. Back and in-
side wrappers blank.

PUBLICATION DATA: Printed for private distribution; a copy has
been noted with inscription dated July 29, 1903.*

NOTES: Part of this address appeared in *The Indianapolis Sentinel*,
April 7, 1903, quoted in an article by H. G. Brown, captioned, "Gen.
Wallace Attacks Grant." The whole speech was published in the same
newspaper on April 10th. It aroused a great deal of discussion in print.
The facsimile of one page of Wallace's manuscript (second paragraph
in the brochure above-described) appeared under the caption, "Gen.
Wallace Did Not Criticise Gen. Grant in His Shiloh Speech," in *The
Indianapolis News*, May 8, 1903. The address was included in *Indiana
at Shiloh*, compiled by John W. Coons (1904).

Earlier, Wallace wrote from Constantinople to the Eleventh Indiana Regiment a letter which was read at a soldiers' reunion in Tipton,
Indiana, September 19, 1883, regarding Grant's exoneration of him;
letter printed in part in a contemporary newspaper (clipping unidentified). For more of Wallace's statements about Shiloh, the battle of
Pittsburg Landing, and his procedure on April 6, 1862, see *General
Wallace's Military Record, ante* 353.

---

*In Eagle Crest Library.

First Editions — Contributions

~~~~~~

1857

JOURNAL OF THE SENATE OF INDIANA, DURING THE THIRTY-NINTH
SESSION OF THE GENERAL ASSEMBLY, COMMENCING THURSDAY,
JANUARY 8, 1857. Indianapolis, Joseph J. Bingham, 1857

Contains reports by Wallace, pp. 124, 141, 539, 603, 616, 746; protests by him, pp. 237 and 480; resolutions, pp. 34 (two resolutions), 101, 108 (two), 131, 153, 176, 423, 671, 675, 702; Joint Resolution No. 8, p. 606. Motions made by him are referred to on pp. 5, 6, 7, 9, 25, 82, 90, 98, 121, 166, 180, 181, 204, 205, 229, 237, 239, 274, 294, 302, 318 (two), 356 (two), 357, 367, 370, 378 (two), 379, 404, 414, 484, 491, 492, 493, 519, 553, 558, 621, 637, 638 (two), 640 (two), 684, 686 (request to be excused from voting), 743, 748, 749, 806, 818, 820. He introduced Senate bills Nos. 32, 41, 60, 72, 94, 99, 100, 104, 117 (named on pp. 134, 161, 280, 316, 337, 370, 384, 422).

There was no volume of *Brevier Legislative Reports* of 1857.

Wallace served also as State Senator from Montgomery county during the called session of the General Assembly in 1858 and the fortieth regular session, 1859; see *Journal of the Indiana State Senate*, these dates, also *The Legislative Sentinel* (1858) and *Brevier Legislative Reports* (1859).

1858

THE LEGISLATIVE SENTINEL: CONTAINING THE PROCEEDINGS AND
DEBATES OF THE SPECIAL SESSION OF THE GENERAL ASSEMBLY OF
THE STATE OF INDIANA, CONVENED . . . NOVEMBER, 1858. Reported
by W. H. Drapier and A. E. Drapier. Indianapolis, Bingham &
Doughty, 1858

Bound in book form but headings make it appear to be a periodical, beginning, Vol. 1, No. 1, November 26, 1858; catalogued in Indiana State Library as *Brevier Legislative Reports, Vol. 1*. Gives daily stenographic reports, quoting Wallace's own words on pp. 8, 11, 20, 22, 25, 26, 27, 28, 29, 43, 44, 70, 86, 87, 122,* 126, 142, 156. Digests of his motions, reports, and resolutions, or reference to him, appear on the above pages and on pp. 21,† 35, 36, 45, 65, 71, 72, 73, 95, 121, 123, 127, 128, 134, 135, 141, 149, 154, 155, 157, 159, 162, 163, 164, 166, 167, 170, 177, 178, 179, 185, 186, and 189.

See also, *Journal of the Indiana State Senate* (1858). For his earlier contributions as Legislator see *Journal of the Senate of Indiana* (1857); for later ones see *Journal of the Indiana State Senate* and *Brevier Legislative Reports*, both for 1859.

JOURNAL OF THE INDIANA STATE SENATE, DURING THE CALLED SESSION OF THE GENERAL ASSEMBLY, COMMENCING SATURDAY, NOVEMBER 20, 1858. Indianapolis, Joseph J. Bingham, 1858

Contains reports by Wallace, pp. 10, 199, 250, and 329; on p. 14 his own words requesting excuse from voting; resolutions, pp. 11, 14, 70, 103, 185, 241, 272, 300; Joint Resolutions Nos. 1 and 3, pp. 43 and 107. Motions made by him are referred to on pp. 10, 14, 33, 36, 38, 39, 45, 72, 124, 128, 192, 200, 211, 224, 243 (not 246 as indexed), 309, 311, 327 (not 329, which contains a report above-mentioned), 331 (not 332), 355. He introduced four bills: Nos. 4,‡ 10, 23, 91§ (pp. 30, 33, 65, 187).

The first volume of *Brevier Legislative Reports*, entitled, *The Legislative Sentinel* (1858), quotes Wallace at greater length.

Wallace had served as Legislator in 1857 (see *Journal of the Senate of Indiana*, that year); for his later contributions see *Journal of the Senate of Indiana* (1859) and *Brevier Legislative Reports* (1859).

---

*Wallace's speech presenting his Bill No. 91 to the Indiana State Senate is here quoted. It preceded his Bill No. 2 presented in the following session, on January 11, 1859 (*post* 366n), which also related to the choosing of United States Senators.

†Mentions his introduction of Senate Bill No. 4, on November 23, 1858, relating to divorce; see *An Autobiography* (1906) Vol. I., p. 251, for the author's account of it.

‡See foregoing footnote for account of this bill.

§Senate Bill No. 91 relates to choosing of U. S. Senators, introduced December 13, 1858; similar to his Senate Bill No. 2 introduced in the 1859 session, on January 11th.

1859

BREVIER LEGISLATIVE REPORTS: EMBRACING SHORT-HAND
SKETCHES OF THE JOURNALS AND DEBATES OF THE GENERAL ASSEM-
BLY OF THE STATE OF INDIANA, CONVENED IN REGULAR SESSION ON
THE 6TH DAY OF JANUARY, 1859. Reported by Ariel & W. H. Dra-
pier. Indianapolis, Daily Indiana State Sentinel, 1859

Volume II of the *Brevier Legislative Reports* (for contributions to
the preceding volume see *The Legislative Sentinel* [1858]). Contains
digests of numerous motions by Wallace; quotes provisions of a Senate
bill (No. 2) introduced by him, January 11, 1859*, p. 20; quotes a
committee report, p. 21, and remarks on recommitment of a bill (not
his), p. 211; resolutions offered by him, pp. 38 and 186. His resolution
(joint) on the admission of Kansas to statehood January 31, 1859 is
quoted on p. 81; his hour-long speech of February 1st, urging adoption,
is briefly described, not quoted, on p. 112. He is mentioned on p. 4;
other mentions, and motions described (including a few quoted), on
pp. 20, 21, 27, 33, 38, 41, 42, 63, 70, 75, 80, 81, 86, 102, 103, 105, 111,
112, 124, 138, 140, 141, 149, 186, 192, 211.
See also *Journal of the Indiana State Senate* (1859).

JOURNAL OF THE INDIANA STATE SENATE, DURING THE FORTIETH
SESSION OF THE GENERAL ASSEMBLY, COMMENCING THURSDAY,
JANUARY 6, 1859. Indianapolis, John C. Walker, 1859

Contains reports by Wallace, pp. 26, 46, 213, 223, 336, 440, and
515; resolutions, pp. 52, 129, 155, 292, 305, 415, and 527. Motions
made by him are referred to on pp. 12, 38, 52, 53, 54, 56, 60, 93, 111,
112, 128, 155, 159, 160, 172, 175, 177, 211, 254, 291, 299, 300, 303,
304, 305, 306, 312 (not 310 as indexed), 314, 336, 345 (not 344), 347,
348, 365, 385, 411, 418, 421, 446, 456, 464, 501, 528, 529, 530, 546,

---

*The title of this bill, "An Act to regulate the choosing of United States Sena-
tors by the General Assembly . . ." was noted by Wallace in his *Autobiography*
(1906), Vol. I, p. 252, followed by the story of its origin. It resulted from his
hearing a debate between Abraham Lincoln and Stephen A. Douglas. A similar
bill had been introduced by him in the Special Session of 1858, on December 13th (Bill No. 91; see *ante* 365n). This is evidently the one referred to by
Charles Zimmerman in his article, "The Republican Party in Indiana," *Indiana Magazine of History*, December, 1917, Vol. XIII, No. 4, p. 366.

578, and 591. A letter to Caleb Mills, January 10, 1859, jointly signed by nine senators, including Wallace, appears on p. 254. Joint Resolutions Nos. 9 and 10, introduced by him, are mentioned on pp. 305 and 344. He introduced Senate bills Nos. 2,* 20, 46, 100, 119, 140, and 149 (pp. 42, 145, 150, 219, 242, 302, and 410), none of which became law. See also, *Brevier Legislative Reports* (1859).

1862

[United States] EXECUTIVE DOCUMENTS OF THE SENATE OF THE UNITED STATES, FOR THE SECOND SESSION OF THE THIRTY-SEVENTH CONGRESS, 1861–'62 [Volume XXXIX; Washington, D. C., Government Printing Office, 1862]

Vol. 6, No. 66, in the collected volumes of Executive Documents for this session; captioned: "Letter of the Secretary of War, transmitting . . . the reports of officers in command in relation to the recent battles at Pittsburg Landing." Report No. 6 herein, p. 17, is Wallace's, dated April 12, 1862, and addressed to Captain John A. Rawlins, p. 17. It appeared also in *The Indianapolis Journal*, April 26, 1862, and later in *The War of the Rebellion*, Series I, Volume X, Part I (1884).

1863

REPORT OF THE ADJUTANT GENERAL OF THE STATE OF INDIANA. TO THE GOVERNOR. Indianapolis, Joseph J. Bingham, State Printer, 1863

Contains Lewis [*sic*] Wallace's instructions as Adjutant General of the state, "General Orders, No 1," April 15, 1861, p. 7, accompanying Governor Oliver P. Morton's proclamation of April 16th, announcing the besiegment of Fort Sumter, and calling for the organization of six regiments; the same appeared in *The Indianapolis Daily Journal* and *Daily State Sentinel* (Indianapolis), April 16, 1861.

These newspaper issues, the same day, published his letter of April 15th, calling for the organization of a "Zouave Regiment."

Proclamations appeared all over the state, over the names of Wallace and Morton; a typical one by Wallace, calling for one hundred

---

*See *ante* 366n (*Brevier Legislative Reports* [1859]) for account of this bill.

volunteers in Crawfordsville, was reprinted in *"Ben-Hur" Wallace* by Irving McKee (1947), p. 34; see also *ante* 351.

A letter of April 17th, addressed by him to ladies of Indianapolis, probably from the Adjutant General's Office since it consisted of a plea for help in the war effort, appeared in the *Daily State Sentinel*, April 18th.

His "General Orders, No. 2," April 20th, not included in the *Report of the Adjutant General*, were published in the *Daily State Sentinel*, April 22nd.

His letter to Oliver P. Morton, April 23rd, in resignation from his office as Adjutant General, appeared in both *The Indianapolis Daily Journal* and *Daily State Sentinel*, April 25th. He served only from the 15th to 26th of April, 1861, resigning to become colonel of the 11th Regiment, Indiana Volunteers.

For his later Civil War reports and letters see *post* 399.

1865

THE ASSASSINATION OF PRESIDENT LINCOLN AND THE TRIAL OF THE CONSPIRATORS . . . Compiled and arranged by Benn Pitman. New York & Cincinnati, Moore, Wilstach & Baldwin, 1865

Wallace was a member of the Military Commission that conducted the trial. Brief comments by him in court, May 27th and May 25th, appear on pp. 134 and 135, respectively.

1868

PICTORIAL HISTORY OF THE CIVIL WAR IN THE UNITED STATES OF AMERICA. By Benson J. Lossing. 3 volumes. Hartford, T. Belknap, 1868

Vol. II contains excerpt from a letter to the author, regarding the movements of the army up the river, near Pittsburg Landing, p. 262*n*. See *Shiloh Address*, *ante* 363, for account of Wallace's other writings about the Battle of Shiloh.

The work contains numerous accounts of Wallace's career in the Civil War, and quotations from his official reports in the *War of the Rebellion* series.

[United States] THE EXECUTIVE DOCUMENTS OF THE HOUSE OF REPRESENTATIVES, FOR THE FIRST SESSION OF THE FORTIETH CONGRESS, 1867. Washington, D. C., Government Printing Office, 1868

Document No. 33, *United States, European, and West Virginia Land and Mining Company and Mexico*, p. 48, contains a letter from General Wallace to Matias Romero, August 31, 1865,* about Mexican bonds, which is listed as Document No. 25 of those sent by the Mexican Legation to the Department of State of the United States; and another letter, p. 156, also to Romero, dated April 12, 1867, (Document No. 157 from the Mexican Legation). The latter is a lengthy statement by Wallace of his knowledge of the negotiation between General J. M. J. Carvajal and Daniel Woodhouse. It is followed by General Carvajal's account of the enterprise and Wallace's connection with it.

The first document in this Executive Document No. 33, p. 18, a letter by Romero, April 26, 1865, mentions General Wallace's sympathy for "our cause" and describes the occasion of his first meeting with General Carvajal. The letter from Romero to William H. Seward, Secretary of State, which accompanied the documents, contains a paragraph, on p. 3, expressing gratitude toward Wallace.

A pamphlet printing Woodhouse's petition to the Congress of the United States, referred to by Wallace in his letter of April 12, 1867, has not yet been located. Wallace says: "The contract which Mr. Woodhouse appends to his very absurd petition to the United States Congress is of my draughting [done at the request of General Carvajal, in New York]."

For other Wallace-Mexican matters see *post* 371.

[United States] EXECUTIVE DOCUMENTS PRINTED BY ORDER OF THE HOUSE OF REPRESENTATIVES DURING THE SECOND SESSION OF THE FORTIETH CONGRESS, 1867–'68. 20 volumes. Washington, D. C., Government Printing Office, 1868

---

*It was in the spring of 1865, while Wallace waited in Washington for a report on a manuscript he had submitted to a commission there, that he saw Romero "once in a while" and acquired "great interest in Mexican affairs" (*Autobiography*, p. 859). His manuscript was a skirmish book, on military tactics, which he revised later in the summer and fall, during progress of the Henry Wirz trial (see *post* 370; and *Autobiography*, p. 857). It was finally rejected, and remained unpublished.

Only Volume 8, Ex. Doc. No. 23, *Trial of Henry Wirz*, has Wallace contributions. He was President of the special military commission which heard the trial of the man responsible for conditions in the Andersonville Prison, beginning August 23, 1865, dissolved, November 6th. This documentary report contains many comments and questions "by the President": pp. 32, 73, 75, 80, 81, 150, 211, 231, 267, 268, 269, 294, 307, 412, 413, 414, 424, 425, 431, 432, 441, 442, 443, 481, 495, 496, 501, 512, 520, 526, 529, 530, 531, 532, 533, 534, 535, 536, 541, 568, 580, 589, 596, 608, 614, 618, 646, 652, 680, 683, 690, 691, 693, 694, 695, 698, 701, and 702. The final "Findings and Sentence," pp. 805–808, is signed, Lew Wallace.

1869

INDIANA IN THE WAR OF THE REBELLION. Official Report of W. H. H. Terrell, Adjutant General. Indianapolis, Douglass & Conner, 1869

Identical, except for title-page, with Vol. I (1869) of *Report of the Adjutant General of the State of Indiana* [W. H. H. Terrell], 8 volumes (1865–1869), published by Alexander H. Conner. The first volume did not appear until last, after all troops had been mustered out. The second part of the volume, "Statistics and Documents," separately paginated, contains, p. 175, Wallace's speech of July 4, 1866, at Indianapolis, when he presented to Governor Morton the scarred battle flags borne by the Indiana regiments and batteries during the Civil War. The speech had appeared in *The Indianapolis* (Daily) *Herald*, July 6, 1866. It was later published in part in William Henry Smith, *The History of the State of Indiana* ... Vol. 1 (1897), and in full in *Modern Eloquence*, Vol. 9 (1900); in the latter under the title, "Return of the Flags." The concluding part was printed in *Lew Wallace: An Autobiography*, Vol. 2 (1906), and part was included in *Proceedings in Statuary Hall upon the Unveiling of the Statue of General Wallace* (1910).

THE SOLDIER OF INDIANA IN THE WAR FOR THE UNION. [By Catherine Merrill]. Indianapolis, Merrill & Co., 1869

Second volume of this anonymous Civil War history. Contains, p. 7, Major-General Wallace's "Proclamation" upon taking command of Cincinnati, Newport, and Covington, September, 1862. The proclamation was publicized in the regional newspapers on September 2nd: *Cincinnati Gazette, Commercial, et al.*; later it appeared in *The War of the Rebellion,* Series 1, Vol. LII, Part 1 (1898), p. 277, and in *Lew Wallace: An Autobiography,* Vol. II (1906), p. 607. Contains, also, his farewell instructions "To the People of Cincinnati, Newport and Covington," publicized in the Sunday, September 14, 1862 newspapers and in those of the following day: *Cincinnati Enquirer,* September 14th, *Cincinnati Gazette,* September 15th, *et al.* Both first and last proclamations were included in an article, "The Siege of Cincinnati," by T. B. Read, in the *Atlantic Monthly,* February, 1863.

The City of Cincinnati, on October 18, 1862, gave formal thanks to Wallace for his services, in a letter and resolutions, published in *Lew Wallace: An Autobiography,* Vol. II (1906), p. 624. The local newspapers were full of accounts of his activities during the period of his command of the Kentucky forces, September 2–18, and published many of his orders, general and special (see *post* 402).

If any of the proclamations and orders were printed and distributed in broadside form, none have yet been brought to light.

Both Lew and Susan Wallace contributed data for Miss Merrill's work,* and references to him appear throughout it. The first volume contains nothing identified as by Wallace. The description of him as Colonel of the colorful Zouave regiment, Eleventh Indiana, on p. 61, is reprinted in McKee, p. 36.

1872

AMERICAN AND MEXICAN COMMISSION. HERMAN STURM VERSUS THE REPUBLIC OF MEXICO. Indianapolis, J. G. Doughty, 1872

Contains "Deposition of Major General Lewis Wallace," May 9, 1870, p. 278: No. 408 of the papers and documents relating to the claim of Herman Sturm *versus* Republic of Mexico (Claim No. 676). On p. 271 Wallace is mentioned in the "Deposition of William Francis Elston," but not quoted.

Sturm's earlier publication, *The Republic of Mexico and Its Amer-*

---

*Wallace's long letter of June 9, 1866, to Miss Merrill, consisting of his account of the Cincinnati proceedings, is in the Indiana Historical Society, William Henry Smith Memorial Library; it is the basis for pp. 7–13 in the Merrill book.

ican Creditors (1869), had no contributions by Wallace among the many allusions to him.

Wallace's plea on Sturm's behalf to President Díaz, in the form of a letter of August 15, 1889, was published in *The* (Chicago) *Daily Inter Ocean*, August 27, 1889, and in *Lew Wallace: An Autobiography*, Vol. II (1906), pp. 843, 862.

His claim against Mexico (Docket No. 425), presented in 1869, is listed, but not published in the U. S., 44th Congress, 2d Session, *Senate Ex. Doc. No. 31: Claims on the Part of the Citizens of the United States, and Mexico under the Convention of July 4, 1868, between the United States and Mexico* (1877).*

Certain letters of his relating to Mexican affairs appeared in the 40th Congress, 1st Session, *Executive Documents of the House of Representatives* (*ante* 369). See also Chapter VIII in McKee's *"Ben-Hur" Wallace* (1947) for extracts from some letters written during his "Mexican Mission" which have not been found elsewhere in print. His reply to attacks in the Democratic press during the political campaign of 1870, denying that he owned Mexican bonds or was connected with a Mexican ring, was published in *The Cincinnati Commercial*, March [24?], 1870, and in his *Autobiography*, Vol. II (1906), p. 887; earlier he discussed the subject in an uncollected letter to A. C. Sands, September 23, 1869, preserved in the form of an unidentified newspaper excerpt.†

For his early experiences in Mexico, 1846–1847, see *Indiana in the Mexican War*, compiled by Oran Perry (1908), *post* 393; also his letters printed in *Indiana State Journal*, 1846–1847, and in the *Indiana State Sentinel*, 1847 (see *post* 406).

See *Lew Wallace: An Autobiography*, Vol. II (1906), pp. 812–[846], 859, 862–887, for his own report of his post-Civil-War efforts to keep Confederates from gaining hold in Mexico; it includes contemporary letters. A lengthy letter of June 15, 1865, about the danger of conspiracy, addressed to Colonel ─ ─, was published in an unidentified newspaper.‡

Dealing, too, with Mexico were his articles, "The Mines of Santa Eulalia, Chihuahua" and "A Buffalo Hunt in Northern Mexico," *q.v.*

---

*A manuscript copy of his claim, Edw. Thornton, Washington, Umpire, dated September 2, 1875, is in the Indiana Historical Society, William Henry Smith Memorial Library; the claim was paid in part in 1882 (McKee, p. 113).

†In the Wallace Papers.

‡Clipping preserved in the Wallace Papers. After his death there appeared a pamphlet, *The Benevolent Raid of General Lew Wallace; How Mexico Was Saved in 1864* . . . , compiled by A. W. Barber (1914), its dramatic story of a man identified as Wallace on a secret mission interesting, but not substantiated.

Wallace composed a lecture on "Mexico and the Mexicans" and delivered it first on June 16, 1868, at Waveland, Indiana. It has not been found in print, although he gave the talk frequently in Indiana (see *post* 390*n*).

In 1875 he added readings from *The Fair God*, called his lecture "An Hour with the Mexicans," and delivered it on tour under auspices of James Redpath's Lyceum. Major J. B. Pond told of Wallace's platform career in *Eccentricities of Genius* (1900), p. 465, and McKee, pp. 131 and 224, discussed both this and his other, later lecture, "Turkey and the Turks."

A SOUVENIR OF THE ANCHOR LINE AGENTS EXCURSION ON THE STEAMER CALIFORNIA, AUGUST 14, 1872. New York, D. Appleton & Co. [1872]

Pictorial wrappers. Contains his speech in response to a toast to the Army and Navy at the banquet on board the Anchor Line Steamer California, off New York, p. 11.

1879

[United States] PRESIDENTIAL ELECTION INVESTIGATION. TESTIMONY TAKEN BY THE SELECT COMMITTEE ON ALLEGED FRAUDS IN THE PRESIDENTIAL ELECTION OF 1876. House of Representatives, 45th Congress, 3rd Session, Misc. Doc. No. 31, Vol. 1. Washington, D. C., Government Printing Office, 1879

Contains Wallace's testimony, p. 509, regarding his part in the electoral vote count in Florida, given before the Potter Committee, June 28, 1878. It appeared also in *The Indianapolis Journal*, June 29, 1878. See *ante* 350 for note of other accounts by him of the count in New Orleans and Tallahassee.

1880

A BIOGRAPHICAL HISTORY OF EMINENT AND SELF-MADE MEN OF THE STATE OF INDIANA. 2 volumes. Cincinnati, O., Western Biographical Publishing Co., 1880

Binder's title: *Representative Men of Indiana.* Vol. II, 8th District, contains a biographical sketch of Peter S. Kennedy, p. 27, unsigned but by Wallace, who practiced law at the same bar with Kennedy for many years. The sketch was identified as his in *Biographical Sketches and Review of the Bench and Bar of Indiana* (binder's title: *Bench and Bar of Indiana*), by Charles W. Taylor (1895), p. 783, where it was reprinted with some additions.

THE WAR OF THE REBELLION: A COMPILATION OF THE OFFICIAL RECORDS OF THE UNION AND CONFEDERATE ARMIES. Series I, Volume II. Washington, Government Printing Office, 1880

Contains report of the descent of Union troops on Romney, W. Va., June 14, 1861, p. 123; report on battle at Frankfort, W. Va., in letter to Gen. Geo. B. McClellan, June 27, 1861, p. 134; report of battle on Patterson's Creek, W. Va., June 27, 1861, p. 134. Also contains letter to Major-Gen. Robert Patterson, June 11, 1861, p. 676; letters to Major F. J. Porter, June 15, 1861, p. 689, and June 18, 1861, p. 704.

1882

[Turkey]. PAPERS RELATING TO THE FOREIGN RELATIONS OF THE UNITED STATES, TRANSMITTED TO CONGRESS ... December 5, 1881. House of Representatives, 47th Congress, 1st Session, Ex. Doc. 1, Part 1. Washington, D. C., Government Printing Office, 1882

Contains letters from Wallace soon after assuming office as Minister Resident to Turkey, dated from Constantinople, addressed to James G. Blaine, Secretary of State: No. 9 (Doc. No. 724), September 19, 1881, p. 1188; No. 22 (Doc. No. 725), October 26th, p. 1189, plus Inclosure, to Assim Pacha [sic], October 22nd, p. 1190.

THE WAR OF THE REBELLION: A COMPILATION OF THE OFFICIAL RECORDS OF THE UNION AND CONFEDERATE ARMIES. Series I, Volume VII. Washington, Government Printing Office, 1882

Contains report of the expedition (December 28–31, 1861) to Camp Beauregard and Viola, Ky., dated January 1, 1862, p. 66; also, report of the siege and capture of Fort Donelson, Tenn. (February 12–16, 1862), dated February 20, 1862, p. 236.

1883

SPORT WITH GUN AND ROD IN AMERICAN WOODS AND WATERS.
Edited by Alfred M. Mayer. New York, Century [1883]

Issued in one volume in both cloth, and, leather; also in two volumes in cloth, and, leather. Contains "A Buffalo Hunt in Northern Mexico," p. [101], with an illustration by Wallace, also illustrations by others from sketches by him; earlier in Scribner's Monthly, March, 1879.

[Turkey]. PAPERS RELATING TO THE FOREIGN RELATIONS OF THE UNITED STATES, TRANSMITTED TO CONGRESS ... December 4, 1882. House of Representatives, 47th Congress, 2nd Session, Ex. Doc. 1. Washington, D. C., Government Printing Office, 1883

Contains letters, 1881–1882, from Constantinople during Wallace's service as Minister to Turkey, addressed to James G. Blaine until January 13, 1882, when they were addressed to Frederick T. Frelinghuysen: No. 30 (Doc. No. 300), November 22, 1881, p. 491, plus Inclosure 2, to Assim Pacha [sic], November 17th, p. 493; No. 33 (Doc. No. 301), November 23rd, p. 494; No. 45 (Doc. No. 302), December 20th, p. 495, plus Inclosure, to Lord Dufferin, December 17th, p. 496. The letters that follow are addressed to Frederick T. Frelinghuysen: No. 56 (Doc. No. 305), January 13, 1882, p. 499, plus Inclosure 2, to Assim Pasha, January 11th, p. 500; No. 62 (Doc. No. 306), February 1st, p. 501; No. 71 (Doc. No. 308), March 13th, p. 502; No. 72 (Doc. No. 309), March 20th, plus Inclosure 1, to Earl Dufferin, March 18th, p. 503; No. 74 (Doc. No. 310), March 21st, Extract, plus Inclosure, to Assim Pasha, March 8th, p. 504; No. 90 (Doc. No. 312), April 21st, Extract, p. 505; No. 96 (Doc. No. 315), June 6th, p. 508, plus Inclosure 2, to Sayd [sic] Pasha, June 5th, p. 509; No. 98 (Doc. No. 316), June 9th, Extract, p. 509, plus Inclosure 4, to Said Pasha, June 7th, p. 514; No. 107 (Doc. No. 319), July 11th, Extract, p. 516, plus Inclosure 2, to Said Pasha, June 13th, p. 518; No. 129 (Doc. No. 321), September 30th, p. 522.

[U. S. War Department]. CORRESPONDENCE, ETC., ON THE SUB-
JECT OF THE RECORDS OF THE REBELLION, AND EXHIBITING THE
RULES GOVERNING THE SAME

Unbound; 5 leaves, wire side-stitched. Contains, p. 4, Wallace's
letter to Hon. Robert T. Lincoln, from Florence, October 28, 1883,
asking that search be made for the pamphlet, *General Wallace's Military Record, q.v.*, and that publication of the volume of Official Records
of the War of the Rebellion with reports of Shiloh be deferred until
Grant's exoneration of him and other papers could be included. The
reply from Robert Todd Lincoln that concludes the pamphlet indicates
that the volume was already in the press and that, anyway, the material
was not by rule acceptable for governmental publication.

1884

[Turkey]. PAPERS RELATING TO THE FOREIGN RELATIONS OF THE
UNITED STATES, TRANSMITTED TO CONGRESS ... December 4, 1883.
House of Representatives, 48th Congress, 1st Session, Ex. Doc. 1,
Part 1. Washington, D. C., Government Printing Office, 1884

Contains letters from Constantinople during Wallace's service as
Minister to Turkey, 1882–1883 addressed to Frederick T. Frelinghuysen, Secretary of State: No. 126 (Doc. No. 518), September 28, 1882,
p. 809, plus Inclosure 3, to Said Pasha, September 25th, p. 811; No.
134 (Doc. No. 519), October 15th, *Extract*, p. 812; No. 158 (Doc. No.
524), December 25th, *Extract*, p. 817; No. 159 (Doc. No. 525), January 1, 1883, *Extract*, p. 819, plus Inclosure 2, December 27, 1882, to
Aarifi Pasha, p. 820; No. 160 (Doc. No. 526), January 3, 1883, p. 821;
plus Inclosure, to Aarifi Pasha, January 2nd, p. 822; No. 166 (Doc.
No. 528), January 18th, p. 824, plus Inclosure 3, to Aarifi Pasha,
January 14th, p. 827; No. 168 (Doc. No. 529), January 25th, plus
Inclosure 1, to Aarifi Pasha, p. 828; No. 169 (Doc. No. 530), Jan-
uary 25th, p. 829, plus Inclosure 3, to Aarifi Pasha, p. 830; No. 175
(Doc. No. 534), February 13th, plus Inclosure 2, to Aarifi Pasha, Feb-
ruary 10th, p. 833; No. 178 (Doc. No. 535), February 20th, *Extract*,
p. 834; No. 189 (Doc. No. 538), March 14th, *Extract*, p. 836; No. 205
(Doc. No. 539), April 12th, *Extract*, p. 837, plus Inclosure 2, to Aarifi
Pasha, p. 838; No. 211 (Doc. No. 540), May 1st, plus Inclosure, to
Aarifi Pasha, April 23rd, p. 839; No. 218 (Doc. No. 542), May 15th,
plus Inclosure 2, to Rev. Mr. Pettibone, May 11th, p. 840; No. 219

(Doc. No. 543), May 19th, *Extract*, plus Inclosure 2, to Aarifi Pasha, p. 841; No. 220 (Doc. No. 544), May 22nd, p. 842; No. 222 (Doc. No. 545), May 23rd, *Extract*, p. 843; No. 225 (Doc. No. 546), May 29th, p. 844; No. 227 (Doc. No. 547), June 4th, *Extract*, plus Inclosure 1, to Munir Bey, May 31st, and Inclosure 2, *Memorandum*, p. 845; No. 229 (Doc. No. 548), June 8th, *Extract*, plus Inclosure, to Aarifi Pasha, June 6th, p. 848; No. 233 (Doc. No. 549), June 13th, p. 849; No. 234 (Doc. No. 553), June 18th, p. 850, plus Inclosure 3, to Aarifi Pasha, June 13th, p. 853; No. 235 (Doc. No. 554), June 19th, *Extract*, p. 853, plus Inclosure 5, to Aarifi Pasha, May 26th, p. 863; No. 241 (Doc. No. 556), June 30th, *Extract*, p. 865; No. 243 (Doc. No. 557), July 10th, *Extract*, p. 865; No. 245 (Doc. No. 559), July 12th, plus Inclosure 1, to Aarifi Pasha, July 9th, p. 867; No. 251 (Doc. No. 560), July 20th, *Extract*, p. 870; No. 255 (Doc. No. 561), July 26th, plus Inclosure 1, to Aarifi Pasha, p. 871; No. 258 (Doc. No. 563), July 31st, p. 874, plus Inclosure 2, to Aarifi Pasha, July 30th, p. 875; No. 262 (Doc. No. 565), August 10th, *Extract*, p. 877; No. 264 (Doc. No. 566), August 14th, p. 878; No. 266 (Doc. No. 567), August 14th, p. 878; No. 267 (Doc. No. 568), August 22nd, *Extract*, plus Inclosure 2, to Aarifi Pasha, August 21st, p. 879; No. 272 (Doc. No. 570), September 7th, *Extract*, p. 881, plus Inclosure 2, to Aarifi Pasha, September 6th, p. 882; No. 274 (Doc. No. 571), September 12th, *Extract*, p. 882, plus Inclosure 5, to Aarifi Pasha, September 10th, p. 885; No. 275 (Doc. No. 572), September 14th, plus Inclosure 1, to Hugh W. Wyndham, September 12th, p. 886; No. 283 (Doc. No. 573), October 3rd, p. 887; No. 287 (Doc. No. 574), October 15th, p. 887.

THE WAR OF THE REBELLION: A COMPILATION OF THE OFFICIAL RECORDS OF THE UNION AND CONFEDERATE ARMIES. Series I, Volume X, Part I. Washington, Government Printing Office, 1884

Contains report of operations about Crump's Landing (March 9–13), dated March 13, 1862, p. 9; report of the expedition toward Purdy, Tenn., March 13, 1862, p. 9; report of the skirmish on the Purdy Road, near Adamsville, Tenn., April 1, 1862, p. 78. Also contains letter to Major-Gen. H. W. Halleck, March 14, 1863, p. 174; letters to Hon. E. M. Stanton, July 18, 1863, p. 188, and September 16, 1863, p. 190.

His report of the battle of Shiloh, Tenn. (Pittsburg Landing, April 6–7, 1862), dated April 12, 1862 on p. 169, had earlier publication in a U. S. Senate Executive Document (*ante* 367).

—————————, Part II

Contains letter to Capt. [C. T.] Hotchkiss, May 3, 1862, p. 158; letter to John A. Rawlins, April 4, 1862, p. 90.

1885

[Turkey]. PAPERS RELATING TO THE FOREIGN RELATIONS OF THE UNITES STATES, TRANSMITTED TO CONGRESS . . . December 1, 1884. House of Representatives, 48th Congress, 2nd Session, Ex. Doc. 1, Part 1. Washington, D. C., Government Printing Office, 1885

Contains letters from Constantinople during Wallace's service as Minister to Turkey, 1884, addressed to Frederick T. Frelinghuysen: No. 315 (Doc. No. 414), January 24, 1884, p. 535, plus Inclosure 2, to Aarifi Pasha, p. 536; No. 317 (Doc. No. 415), January 25th, p. 537, plus Inclosure, to Aarifi Pasha, January 24th, p. 538; No. 318 (Doc. No. 416), January 26th, *Extract*, p. 539, plus Inclosure 4, to Aarifi Pasha, January 25th, p. 541; No. 322 (Doc. No. 417), February 6th, *Extract*, p. 542; No. 327 (Doc. No. 418), February 14th, p. 543, plus Inclosure 1, to G. H. Heap, January 4th, *Extract*, p. 543; No. 337 (Doc. No. 420), February 28th, *Extract*, p. 544, plus Inclosure 2, to Aarifi Pasha, February 27th, p. 546; No. 340 (Doc. No. 422), March 1st, p. 548; No. 350 (Doc. No. 423), March 12th, p. 549, plus Inclosure 2, to Aarifi Pasha, p. 550; No. 353 (Doc. No. 424), March 22nd, p. 550; No. 357 (Doc. No. 428), March 28th, p. 556, plus Inclosure, to Aarifi Pasha, March 27th, p. 557; No. 358 (Doc. No. 429), March 28th, *Extract*, p. 557, plus Inclosure, to Aarifi Pasha, March 24th, p. 558; No. 362 (Doc. No. 430), April 4th, *Extract*, p. 558; No. 374 (Doc. No. 432), April 16th, *Extract*, p. 561; No. 378 (Doc. No. 433), April 21st, *Extract*, p. 562; No. 381 (Doc. No. 434), April 25th, *Extract*, p. 563.

1886

[Loyal Legion]. PROCEEDINGS OF THE THIRD ANNUAL DINNER OF THE OHIO COMMANDERY OF THE MILITARY ORDER OF THE LOYAL LEGION OF THE UNITED STATES, GIVEN AT THE BURNET HOUSE, CINCINNATI, O., FEBRUARY 10, 1886. Written and arranged by A. H. Mattox, Recorder. Cincinnati, H. C. Sherick, 1886

Gray printed wrappers. Contains speech, "'The Teachings and Results of the War,'" p. 114. It appeared "in substance" in *The Cincinnati Commercial Gazette*, February 11, 1886.

THE SLING OF DAVID, AND OTHER POEMS. By Rev. Alfred Kummer. New York, Hurst & Co. [1886]

Contains "Introduction" by Wallace, dated September 10, 1886, on p. [5], written for the author who was pastor of the Methodist Church in Crawfordsville, Indiana.

[Turkey]. PAPERS RELATING TO THE FOREIGN RELATIONS OF THE UNITED STATES, TRANSMITTED TO CONGRESS . . . December 8, 1885. House of Representatives, 48th Congress, 1st Session, Ex. Doc. 1, Part 1. Washington, D. C., Government Printing Office, 1886

Contains letters from Constantinople during Wallace's service as Minister to Turkey, 1885,* addressed to Frederick T. Frelinghuysen, Secretary of State (until April 3, 1885, when they were addressed to T. F. Bayard): No. 460 (Doc. No. 631), January 8th, 1885, p. 825; No. 461 (Doc. No. 633), January 13th, p. 827; No. 466 (Doc. No. 635), January 24th, p. 829, plus Inclosure, to Assim Pasha, January 9th, p. 830; No. 467 (Doc. No. 636), January 24th, p. 831; No. 468 (Doc. No. 638), January 30th, p. 832, plus Inclosure, to Moustapha Pasha, January 27th, p. 833; No. 471 (Doc. No. 640), February 6th, p. 834, plus Inclosure 3, to G. H. Heap, January 27th, p. 836, and Inclosure 4, to Moustapha Pasha, February 1st, p. 837; No. 475 (Doc. No. 641), February 12th, p. 838, plus Inclosure 2, to Rev. Dr. Eddy, February 10th, p. 839; No. 476 (Doc. Nov. 642), February 23rd, p. 839; No. 477 (Doc. No. 643), February 24th, p. 840; No. 479 (Doc. No. 646), February 28th, p. 841, plus Inclosure, to Assim Pasha, February 27th, p. 842; No. 480 (Doc. No. 647), February 28th, plus Inclosure, to Assim Pasha, p. 842. The letters that follow are addressed to T. F. Bayard: No. 487 (Doc. No. 650), April 3rd, p. 844, plus Inclosure, to Mr. Barnum, March 28th, p. 845; No. 490 (Doc. No. 651), April 6th, p. 845; No. 491 (Doc. No. 652), April 9th, *Extract*, p. 846.

*Wallace's friendly relations with the Sultan of Turkey continued after he ceased to be Minister there; his letter of January 14, 1890, declining an offer of service from the Sultan, appeared in his *Autobiography*, Vol. II (1906), p. 996.

THE WAR OF THE REBELLION: A COMPILATION OF THE OFFICIAL RECORDS OF THE UNION AND CONFEDERATE ARMIES. Series I, Volume XVI, Part I. Washington, Government Printing Office, 1886

Contains Wallace's report as president of the commission which investigated and reported (*ca.* April 15, 1863) on operations of the army under command of Gen. D. C. Buell: "Opinion of the Commission," p. 8; this appears also in *Lew Wallace: An Autobiography,* Vol. II (1906), p. 646. Contains also his report on the action at Big Hill, Ky. (August 23, 1862), August 24, 1862, p. 884.

——————, Part II

Contains letters to Gen. Horatio G. Wright, September 12, 1862, p. 511, and September 17, 1862, p. 525.

1887

BATTLES AND LEADERS OF THE CIVIL WAR. Edited by Robert Underwood Johnson & Clarence Clough Buel. 4 volumes. New York, Century Co. [1887–1889]

Volume I only contains contributions by Wallace: "The Capture of Fort Donelson [battles of February 12–16, 1862]," p. 398, earlier in *The Century Magazine,* December, 1884 (not same as his report of the event in *The War of the Rebellion* . . ., Ser. 1, Vol. VII, p. 236); later in *Amateurs at War: The American Soldier in Action,* edited by Ben Ames Williams (1943), under the title, "Unconditional Surrender." It also contains a letter to General Grant, September 16, 1884, p. 610.

His report of the Romney engagement [June 12, 1861], p. 128n, had earlier appeared in *The War of the Rebellion* . . ., Ser. 1, Vol. II (1880), p. 123.

THE WAR OF THE REBELLION: A COMPILATION OF THE OFFICIAL RECORDS OF THE UNION AND CONFEDERATE ARMIES. Series I, Volume XVII, Part II. Washington, Government Printing Office, 1887

Contains letter to Capt. C. T. Hotchkiss, June 18, 1862, p. 14.

1889

LIVING LEADERS OF THE WORLD. Prepared by an Able Corps of Distinguished Authors, Such as Lew Wallace . . . . Chicago & St. Louis, Hubbard Bros. [1889]

Contains "Benjamin Harrison," p. 19, a biographical sketch for which acknowledgment is made to Lew Wallace in the preface. It embodies some of the material in his *Life of Gen. Ben Harrison* (1888), but so revised as to constitute original writing.

[Loyal Legion] HISTORY OF THE ORGANIZATION OF THE INDIANA COMMANDERY OF THE MILITARY ORDER OF THE LOYAL LEGION OF THE UNITED STATES, AND THE INAUGURATION BANQUET GIVEN AT THE BATES HOUSE, INDIANAPOLIS, INDIANA, DECEMBER 19, 1888. Indianapolis, Baker & Randolph, 1889

Wrappers?* Contains address of welcome by Lew Wallace, Commander, p. 13, published earlier in *The Indianapolis Journal*, December 20, 1888.

[United States Military Academy] REPORT OF THE BOARD OF VISITORS TO THE UNITED STATES MILITARY ACADEMY, MADE TO THE SECRETARY OF WAR, FOR THE YEAR 1889. Washington, Government Printing Office, 1889

Contains Wallace's paper, p. 12, addressed to the Board of Visitors, recommending extension of the West Point system to the whole army, with certain suggested changes in education. The last page of text, 116, captioned "Miscellaneous" is signed by Lew Wallace and others; it reads as if wholly written by him.

THE WAR OF THE REBELLION: A COMPILATION OF THE OFFICIAL RECORDS OF THE UNION AND CONFEDERATE ARMIES. Series I, Volume XXIII, Part I. Washington, Government Printing Office, 1889

Contains letter to Gen. Jeremiah T. Boyle, July 12, 1863, p. 732.

---

*Missing from copy examined.

1890

THE ART OF AUTHORSHIP: LITERARY REMINISCENCES, METHODS OF WORK, AND ADVICE TO YOUNG BEGINNERS PERSONALLY CONTRIBUTED BY LEADING AUTHORS OF THE DAY. Compiled and edited by George Bainton. London, James Clarke & Co., 1890

Published also in New York, by Appleton, 1890, from plates of the London edition. Contains portion of a letter, p. 65, commenting on *Plutarch's Lives*, written in 1887 to the editor, Rev. George Bainton, at Coventry. Part of the final sentence was reprinted in *"Ben-Hur" Wallace*, by Irving McKee (1947), p. 228.

BEN-HUR, IN TABLEAUX AND PANTOMIME. Arranged by the* Author for Messrs. Clark & Cox. [n.p.,1890]

Printed wrappers, light tan, and, gray. Bears statement at foot of title-page, addressed to Messrs. [Walter C.] Clark & [David Wilson] Cox, April 2, 1889, beginning: "This is to certify that you are the only persons authorized by the Messrs. Harper & Brothers and myself, to give exhibitions from my book, "Ben-Hur."

Before 1889, various churches were using for benefit shows Ellen K. Bradford's "Selections from Ben-Hur Adapted for Reading with Tableaux," but Wallace "did not sanction its publication."† On January 12, 1889, *The Crawfordsville Journal* carried an announcement that "D. W. Cox and two associates, whose names are for the present withheld, have completed arrangements and closed a contract with Gen. Wallace for the exclusive privilege of using Ben Hur in spectacular. Gen. Wallace is to write the libretto . . . ." The first presentation of this authorized production occurred March 7, 1889 in Crawfordsville, in Music Hall. See *Ben-Hur, Notes, ante* 327, for its subsequent development.

The pamphlet was reissued in New York by Harpers, 1891.

THE BEN HUR ROOM [in the old Governors' Palace at Santa Fe]. [n.p., n.d., 1890?]

Single sheet, printed on one side only, containing a letter to A. J.

---

*Typographical error appears on title-page: *thr.*
†McKee, p. 175.

Wissler from Wallace, May 6, 1890, about his having written the sixth, seventh, and eighth books of "Ben-Hur" while occupying a room in the Governor's Palace, now a historical museum.

Two printings preserved among Wallace Papers,* both undated.

When Wallace was appointed Governor of New Mexico, Maurice Thompson, in an unpublished letter† of September 4, 1878, congratulated him, but urged him to continue his literary work and produce a second book. It happened so; Wallace used his hours outside of duty to complete "Ben-Hur."

MINUTES OF THE THIRTY-NINTH ANNUAL SESSION OF THE NORTH-WEST INDIANA CONFERENCE OF THE METHODIST EPISCOPAL CHURCH HELD AT CRAWFORDSVILLE, IND., OCT. 1–6, 1890. Attica, Ind., Attica Book & Job Print, 1890

Contains Wallace's "Address of Welcome," delivered October 1st, on p. 26. The speech was first printed in *The Crawfordsville Journal*, October 4, 1890.

THE WAR OF THE REBELLION: A COMPILATION OF THE OFFICIAL RECORDS OF THE UNION AND CONFEDERATE ARMIES. Series I, Volume XXX, Part III. Washington, Government Printing Office, 1890

Contains letter to Hon. E. M. Stanton, September 21, 1863, p. 760.

—————————, Part IV

Contains letter to Hon. E. M. Stanton, October 3, 1863, p. 57.

1891

THE WAR OF THE REBELLION: A COMPILATION OF THE OFFICIAL RECORDS OF THE UNION AND CONFEDERATE ARMIES. Series I, Volume XXXIII. Washington, Government Printing Office, 1891

Contains Wallace's orders assuming command of Middle Department (8th Army Corps), at Baltimore, Maryland, on March 22, 1864,

---

*In Indiana Historical Society, William Henry Smith Memorial Library.
†*Ibid.*

p. 717; earlier in *The* (Baltimore) *Sun*, March 22, 1864. Also contains letter to Hon. E. M. Stanton, April 16, 1864, p. 884; letter to Col. E. D. Townsend, April 28, 1864, p. 1008. For Wallace's orders and letters while in Baltimore see *post* ooo–ooo.

————, Volume XXXVI, Part II

Contains letters to Major-Gen. H. W. Halleck, May 13, 1864, p. 738, and May 16, 1864, p. 830; letter to Hon. E. M. Stanton, May 15, 1864, p. 802; letter to Col. E. D. Townsend, May 15, 1864, p. 801.

————, Part III

Contains letter to Major-Gen. H. W. Halleck, June 5, 1864, p. 634.

————, Volume XXXVII, Part I

Contains report of operations in the Shenandoah Valley, Maryland, and Pennsylvania, being an informal report of the Battle of the Monocacy, dated July 10, 1864, p. 191, and full report dated August, 1864, p. 193. Also contains letter to Commissioner of Police, City of Baltimore, May 5, 1864, p. 391; letters to Major-Gen. H. W. Halleck, May 16, 1864, p. 472, June 5, p. 596, and June 9, 1864, p. 617; letters to Hon. E. M. Stanton, May 14, 1864, p. 458, and May 17, 1864, p. 483; letters to Col. E. D. Townsend, May 3, 1864, and April 2, 1865, p. 200; letter to Gen. E. B. Tyler, May 5, 1864, p. 392.

1892

SONGS OF A LIFE-TIME. By Sarah T. Bolton. Edited by John Clark Ridpath. Indianapolis, Bowen-Merrill Co., 1892

Contains an introduction by Lew Wallace, p. xi. The same introduction reappeared in *Paddle Your Own Canoe and Other Poems* by Sarah T. Bolton (1897).

1893

[Loyal Legion] 10TH ANNUAL DINNER OHIO COMMANDERY, MILITARY ORDER OF THE LOYAL LEGION OF THE UNITED STATES. Grand Hotel, Cincinnati, May 3rd, 1893. [Cincinnati, 1893]

Pictorial cream-colored wrappers, front cover serving as title-page. Contains speech in response to the first toast, "The Siege of Cincinnati," (in program called "The Defense of Cincinnati"), p. 9. For an earlier speech, February 10, 1886, see *Proceedings of the Third Annual Dinner of the Ohio Commandery of the Military Order of the Loyal Legion* (1886).

For his address of welcome at the Indiana Commandery's banquet, December 19, 1888, see *History of the Organization of the* _____, *ante* 381. The Indiana Commandery later gave him a loving cup; his speech of acceptance was printed in *The Loving-Cup Presentation* ... (1898); see *post* 388.

SCENES FROM EVERY LAND. With an introduction by General Lew Wallace. Edited by Thomas Lowell Knox. Springfield, O., Mast, Crowell, & Kirkpatrick; New York, Bryan, Taylor, & Co., 1893

"Introduction," p. v, signed in facsimile.

THE WAR OF THE REBELLION: A COMPILATION OF THE OFFICIAL RECORDS OF THE UNION AND CONFEDERATE ARMIES. Series I, Volume XLIII, Part I. Washington, Government Printing Office, 1893

Contains letter to Hon. C. A. Dana, August 30, 1864, p. 969; letter to Lieut.-Col. James W. Forsyth, August 19, 1864, p. 854; letter to Hon. E. M. Stanton, August 11, 1864, p. 773; letter to Col. E. D. Townsend, August 9, 1864, p. 750; letters to Major [Thomas M.] Vincent, August 11, 1864, p. 773.

_____, Part II

Contains letter to Col. [T. S.] Bowers, December 10, 1864, p. 775; letters to Major-Gen. H. W. Halleck, September 29, 1864, p. 216, October 1, p. 256, October 7, p. 317, and November 12, 1864, p. 616; letter to Lieut.-Col. S. B. Lawrence, October 4, 1864, p. 279; letter to Hon. E. M. Stanton, December 11, 1864, p. 777; letter to Brig.-Gen. [John D.] Stevenson, September 26, 1864, p. 184; letters to Col. E. D. Townsend, October 18, 1864, p. 409, October 21, p. 657, October 27, p. 479, October 28, p. 484, and October 29, 1864, p. 492; letter to Brig.-Gen. [E. B.] Tyler, September 14, 1864, p. 88; letter to Lieut.-Col. T. M. Vincent, November 18, 1864, p. 644.

1894

FAMOUS PAINTINGS OF THE WORLD. A COLLECTION OF PHOTO-
GRAPHIC REPRODUCTIONS OF GREAT MODERN MASTERPIECES . . . .
Under the Editorial Supervision of John Clark Ridpath & George
J. Bryan. New York, Fine Art Publishing Co., 1894

Binder's title: *Art Portfolio*. Cloth covers, tied with cord. Wallace's
four-page introduction has the last two paragraphs in facsimile.

The book reappeared in 1900 under the title, *Gems of Modern Art:
A Collection of Photographic Reproductions of Great Modern Paint-
ings* . . ., without editors' names, published in New York by Knight &
Brown, with the same introduction by Wallace.

THE WAR OF THE REBELLION: A COMPILATION OF THE OFFICIAL
RECORDS OF THE UNION AND CONFEDERATE ARMIES. Series I, Volume XLVI, Part III. Washington, Government Printing Office,
1894

Contains General Orders, No. 85, April 19, 1865, p. 843. Also con-
tains letter to Lieut.-Col. T. S. Bowers, June 6, 1865, p. 1261; letter to
Hon. A. W. Bradford, April 19, 1865, p. 843; letter to Brig.-Gen. W. A.
Nichols, May 3, 1865, p. 1080; letters to Hon. E. M. Stanton, April 23,
1865, p. 915, and April 24, 1865, p. 936; letter to Brig.-Gen. E. D.
Townsend, April 19, 1865, p. 842.

1895

CONSTANTINOPLE. By Edwin A. Grosvenor. 2 volumes. Boston,
Roberts Brothers, 1895

Also, London, 1895. Volume I contains "Introduction" by Lew
Wallace, p. [xi]. This introduction was reprinted in *The Book Buyer*,
December, 1895. Both volumes contain references to Wallace.

Another edition was published, 1900, by Little, Brown, & Company.

In October, 1900, Wallace wrote a eulogy of Grosvenor for the
Amherst Juniors' *Olio*; see *post* 391.

THE WAR OF THE REBELLION: A COMPILATION OF THE OFFICIAL
RECORDS OF THE UNION AND CONFEDERATE ARMIES. Series I, Volume XLVI, Part II. Washington, Government Printing Office,
1895

Evidently published later than Part III of the same series and volume which was dated 1894. Contains General Orders, No. 3, January 5, 1865, p. 51. Also contains letter to Major-Gen. [C. C.] Augur, January 5, 1865, p. 48; letters to Gen. U. S. Grant, January 8, p. 73, January 11, p. 103, and January 27, 1865, p. 279; letters to Major-Gen. P. H. Sheridan, January 4, 1865, p. 38, January 5, p. 51, January 17, p. 168, January 18, p. 176, January 20, p. 190, and January 30, 1865, p. 310.

1896

THE STORY OF AMERICAN HEROISM; THRILLING NARRATIVES OF PERSONAL ADVENTURES DURING THE GREAT CIVIL WAR. As Told by the Medal Winners and Roll of Honor Men. Chicago & New York, Werner, 1896

¾ morocco. Contains "The Story of a Flag" (battle flag of the 17th Virginia Cavalry, C. S. A.), p. 523. In Lew Wallace: An Autobiography, Vol. 2 (1906), pp. 806–807, the author describes appearance of the flag, but his account of it herein otherwise is in different words.

The book was reissued by J. W. Jones, Springfield, O., 1897, with cancel title-page.

THE WAR OF THE REBELLION: A COMPILATION OF THE OFFICIAL
RECORDS OF THE UNION AND CONFEDERATE ARMIES. Series I, Volume XLVIII, Part I. Washington, Government Printing Office,
1896

Contains letter to Col. [Christian T.] Christensen, February 25, 1865, p. 973; letters to Lieut.-Gen. U. S. Grant, January 14, 1865, p. 512, February 22, p. 937, March 14, 1865, p. 1166, and p. 1276; letter to Brig.-Gen. J. E. Slaughter, March 10, 1865, p. 1280; letter to Brig.-Gen. J. E. Slaughter and Col. J. S. Ford, March 12, 1865, p. 1280.

—————————, Part II

Contains letter to Col. J. S. Ford, March 24, 1865, p. 459; letters to Lieut.-Gen. U. S. Grant, April 18, 1865, p. 457, April 19, p. 122, and May 16, 1865, p. 457; letter to Brig.-Gen. J. M. Hawes, March 30, 1865, p. 460; letter to Major-Gen. S. A. Hurlbut, April 6, 1865, p. 37, letter to Brig.-Gen. J. E. Slaughter, March 17, 1865, p. 458; letter to Brig.-Gen. J. E. Slaughter and Col. J. S. Ford, April 6, 1865, p. 462; letters to Major-Gen. [J. G.] Walker, March 30, 1865, p. 460, and April 2, 1865, p. 462.

1897

THE WAR OF THE REBELLION: A COMPILATION OF THE OFFICIAL RECORDS OF THE UNION AND CONFEDERATE ARMIES. Series I, Volume LI, Part I. Washington, Government Printing Office, 1897

Contains letter to Lieut.-Col. [Lynde] Catlin, July 8, 1864, p. 1174; letter to Comdg. Officer Detach. Sixth Army Corps, Plane No. 1, July 9, 1864, p. 1177; letters to Gen. [James B.] Ricketts, July 9, 1864, p. 1176, and July 10, 1864, p. 1177.

1898

ALONG THE BOSPHORUS AND OTHER SKETCHES. By Susan E. Wallace (Mrs. Lew Wallace). Chicago & New York, Rand, McNally & Co., 1898

Contains an unacknowledged contribution by Lew Wallace, Chapter XI, "Letter from Dresden," giving impressions of the Sistine Madonna, printed in quotation marks. It is dated December, 1884, and Mrs. Wallace was not in Europe at the time, but her husband was there; moreover, there is a statement in Irving McKee, "Ben-Hur" Wallace (1947), p. 214, that: "At Dresden he [Lew Wallace] painstakingly compared Raphael's 'Madonna' with Murillo's."

[Loyal Legion] THE LOVING-CUP PRESENTATION TO MAJOR-GENERAL LEW WALLACE BY THE INDIANA COMMANDERY OF THE MILITARY ORDER OF THE LOYAL LEGION, December 16, 1898. Indianapolis, Sentinel Printing Co. [1898]

Green wrappers, with cover title, *The Wallace Souvenir, M.O.L. L.U.S.*

Contains Wallace's speech in response to the presentation of the loving-cup. Printed at his expense, to be sent to "every Companion," according to a printed slip laid in the brochure. The speech was quoted in *The Indianapolis Journal,* December 17, 1898.

THE WAR OF THE REBELLION: A COMPILATION OF THE OFFICIAL RECORDS OF THE UNION AND CONFEDERATE ARMIES. Series I, Volume LII, Part I. Washington, Government Printing Office, 1898

Contains General Orders, No. 1, Hdqrs. U. S. Volunteer Forces, Sunman, July 15, 1863, p. 412; report of Morgan's Raid in Kentucky, Indiana and Ohio, July 27, 1863, p. 68; report of troops at North Vernon, July 13, 1863, p. 407. Also contains letter to Col. [J. H.] Burkham, July 12, 1863, p. 406; letter to Commanding Officer of Twelfth Kentucky Cavalry, July 13, 1863, p. 410; letter to Capt. John A. Duble, September 2, 1862, p. 279; letter to Col. [Lawrence S.] Shuler, July 12, 1863, p. 406; eleven letters to Gen. [O. B.] Willcox, July 12, 1863, p. 400–406; three letters to same, July 13, 1863, p. 407–408; two letters: July 14, 1863, p. 410, and July 15, 1863, p. 412.

The proclamation on taking command of Cincinnati, Covington and Newport, September 2, 1862, herein p. 277, had previously appeared in *The Soldier of Indiana in the War for the Union* [by Catherine Merrill, Vol. II] (1869); later in *Lew Wallace: An Autobiography,* Vol. II (1906).

1899

PHI GAMMA DELTA [*menu*] 51st Convention Banquet, Hotel Beckel, Dayton, Ohio, October 20th, 1899

A souvenir booklet without title-page, designed by Harry Weidner of the DePauw chapter,* printed by Dreka, Philadelphia, issued in decorative lavender wrappers tied with purple silk cord. Contains a facsimile of Wallace's letter to the fraternity, captioned, "Greeting." The message appeared the following day in *The Dayton* (Ohio) *Jour-*

---

*"The Fifty-first Ekklesia," *The Phi Gamma Delta,* December, 1899, Vol. XXII, No. 1, p. 16, gives designing details.

nal, October 21, 1899,* and, in facsimile, in *The Phi Gamma Delta,* December 1899, Vol. XXII, No. 1, p. [14].

A mounted photograph of Wallace precedes his letter, which was read on the occasion by John Clark Ridpath, toastmaster.

Wallace was president of the national Phi Gamma Delta from 1898 to 1900. According to accounts in *The Phi Gamma Delta,* February and May, 1933, he had been initiated into the fraternity during an evening's visit to Lambda Chapter, DePauw University, January 10, 1868.† In 1898 the Psi Chapter at Wabash College claimed him.

On March 16, 1900, the fraternity had a "Phi Gamma Delta Night at Ben Hur," Broadway Theatre, New York, and Wallace was expected to be present. His telegram of regrets to the committee was published in *The Phi Gamma Delta,* March, 1900. It was reported that the Wallace telegram "was copied and handed to every member of the party"; it is unlocated in such form.

THE WAR OF THE REBELLION: A COMPILATION OF THE OFFICIAL RECORDS OF THE UNION AND CONFEDERATE ARMIES. Series II, Volume IV. Washington, Government Printing Office, 1899

Contains letters to Hon. E. M. Stanton, September 26, 1862, p. 563, September 29, p. 572, and October 28, 1862, p. 661; letters to Gen. L. Thomas, September 22, 1862, p. 546, and September 28, 1862, p. 569.

—————————, Volume VII

Contains letter to Col. E. D. Townsend, April 15, 1864, p. 56.

—————————, Volume VIII

Contains letter to Brig.-Gen. [W. A.] Nichols, April 26, 1865, p. 515; letter to Brig.-Gen. E. D. Townsend, April 23, 1865, p. 505.

—————————, Series III, Volume I

Contains letter to Hon. H. S. Lane, April 6, 1861, p. 65; letter to Abraham Lincoln by Wallace, *et al.,* May 21, 1861, p. 220.

---

*The Dayton Public Library has a microfilm copy of this newspaper, their file having been destroyed in the 1913 flood; they also have the afternoon paper, *Dayton Daily News,* of the same date, October 21, 1899, containing the letter and a description of the souvenir menu.

†He had lectured that same evening at the University on "Mexico and the Mexicans"; see *ante* 373.

WHO'S WHO, 1899. Edited by Douglas Sladen. London, Adam & Charles Black, 1899

Contains a brief autobiographical sketch, p. 952, written with the help of Mrs. Wallace,* summarizing his life and works, and concluding with a note of his recreations; it continued through Volume III (1905) with no changes except additions in details of his Civil War service.

WHO'S WHO IN AMERICA [1899–1900]. [Vol. I]. Chicago, A. N. Marquis & Co. [1899]

Contains an autobiographical sketch of Lew Wallace, p. 761. It continued to appear through Volume III.

1900(?)

THE AMHERST OLIO, 1900. Published by the Juniors, Class of 1902. Philadelphia, Elliott Press [1900? 1901?]

Contains eulogy, "Professor Edwin Augustus Grosvenor," dated October 19, 1900, p. 5.
Probably issued late in the winter of 1900, but possibly early in 1901; exact date unestablished.

1900

THE HOME OF BEN HUR. A Series of Photographs . . . by T[homas] B. Nicholson, with Marginal Illustrations . . . by Fred N. Vance. Crawfordsville, Ind., Lacey & Nicholson, 1900

Cream-colored pictorial wrappers. Contains a letter of Wallace's, in facsimile, dated July 4th, 1899, authorizing the brochure. A brief biographical sketch by J. A. Green precedes the photographic content.

---

*McKee, p. 222.

THE WAR OF THE REBELLION: A COMPILATION OF THE OFFICIAL
RECORDS OF THE UNION AND CONFEDERATE ARMIES. Series III,
Volume IV. Washington, Government Printing Office, 1900

Contains letter to Hon. Edward Bates, May 30, 1864, p. 413; letters
to Hon. E. M. Stanton, May 18, 1864, p. 392, and June 14, 1864,
p. 432.
A later communication, a telegram to Stanton, July 11, 1864, not
published in these official records, appeared in *The Indianapolis Journal*, January 22, 1886, p. 5.

1901

INDIANA AT CHICKAMAUGA: 1863–1900. REPORT OF INDIANA COM-
MISSIONERS CHICKAMAUGA NATIONAL MILITARY PARK. Indianapolis, Wm. B. Burford, 1901

Contains Wallace's speech prepared for the dedication of Chickamauga Park, September 19, 1895, p. 104. It appeared in *The Indianapolis Journal* on the day of the ceremonies with a statement that the
length of the program did not permit its delivery.

TARRY THOU TILL I COME OR SALATHIEL, THE WANDERING JEW. By
George Croly. New York & London, Funk & Wagnalls Co., 1901

A new edition of Croly's *Salathiel, the Wandering Jew* (first published in 1827), containing "Introductory Letter [to the publishers]
from General Lewis Wallace," dated September 1, 1900, p. v; signature
at end in facsimile. With Croly the wandering Jew was a young man;
". . . with me he was the Prince of India," said Wallace.
This book with its Wallace contribution went through many editions; Grosset & Dunlap reprinted it "from 16th edn., January, 1902."

1902

THE INDIANAPOLIS NEWS SOUVENIR. DEDICATION CEREMONIES AND
HISTORY, INDIANA SOLDIERS' AND SAILORS' MONUMENT. [Indianapolis, The Indianapolis News, 1902]

Blue-gray wrappers printed in blue. Contains "Address by Presiding Officer, Maj.-Gen'l Lew Wallace" on May 15, 1902 [not paginated]. The first page of the speech appeared in facsimile in *The Indianapolis News*, the same day, and the entire speech appeared in *The Indianapolis Journal*, May 16, 1902.

1907(?)

THE SUPREME TRIBE BEN-HUR: A FRATERNAL BENEFICIAL SOCIETY, HOME OFFICE, CRAWFORDSVILLE, INDIANA [circular, n.d., printed in Crawfordsville after March, 1907]

Single sheet of stiff white calendered paper, 7" x 6⅛" (full), folded to make four pages. Contains a letter in facsimile, certifying that O'Neal Watson had the "privilege of taking all the leaves he wanted from the beech tree under which Ben-Hur was for the most part written." At side of the letter, between slits made evidently for insertion of one of the leaves, is printed: "The beech tree was destroyed March, 1907." On another page is a picture of Lew Wallace in his study; the fourth page shows the office building of the fraternal society (for further notes about the "Supreme Tribe" see *ante* 330).

1908

INDIANA IN THE MEXICAN WAR. Compiled by Oran Perry, Adjutant General. Indianapolis, Wm. B. Burford, 1908

Contains, on p. 127, a letter to his father, David Wallace, December 19, 1846, earlier in the *Indiana State Journal*, January 22, 1847. Also contains a letter, on p. 149, addressed to "Friend Chapman," March 12, 1847, published in the *Indiana State Sentinel*, April 10, 1847.

Another contemporary letter written from Mexico, not included in Perry, appeared in the *Indiana State Journal*, August 26, 1846, and was later quoted in brief in R. C. Buley's "Indiana in the Mexican War," *The Indiana Magazine of History*, September, 1919, p. 278n. Wallace's letter read at the organization meeting of the Indiana Association of Mexican War Veterans was published in *The Indianapolis Journal*, May 28, 1874, and in *Lew Wallace: An Autobiography*, Vol. II (1906), p. 895. For his detailed account of Mexican War experiences, see *Lew Wallace: An Autobiography*, Vol. I (1906), Chapters X–XX, pp. 101–196 (referred to in Perry, with an extract on p. 57). McKee devoted a chapter to Wallace's "Marching to Mexico."

See *Contributions, ante* 371, for other notes on Wallace and Mexican affairs.

1909

THE TIPPECANOE BATTLE-FIELD MONUMENT. A HISTORY OF THE ASSOCIATION FORMED TO PROMOTE THE ENTERPRISE . . . AND THE CEREMONIES AT THE DEDICATION OF THE MONUMENT. Compiled by Alva O. Reser. Indianapolis, Wm. B. Burford, 1909

Contains, on p. 75, "Address by Gen. Lew Wallace (Delivered at Tippecanoe Battle-ground, Sunday, June 20, 1899)."

Wallace is said* to have delivered a speech at the Tippecanoe battleground, September 28, 1870, in connection with his Congressional campaign, which has not been found in print.

1919

A GOLDEN AGE OF AUTHORS: A PUBLISHER'S RECOLLECTION. By William Webster Ellsworth. Boston, Houghton Mifflin Co., Cambridge, Riverside Press, 1919

Contains a letter to William Webster Ellsworth, dated July 6, 1895, p. 185. Questioned for purpose of listing in *The Century Cyclopedia of Names*, Wallace herein explained that "*Lew.*, being an abbreviation or nickname derived from school associates" was "continued for convenience." Within the letter there is a period after "Lew," but in his signature it is left out! *The Century Cyclopedia of Names* omitted any mention of the abbreviation; carried his name as Lewis.

In his own books the period in the abbreviation is present on the title-pages except in the case of *The Life of Gen. Ben Harrison* (1888), *The Boyhood of Christ* (1889), and the posthumous *Autobiography* (1906). In none of his books did his surname appear in full.

---

*McKee, p. 121.

1922

GLIMPSES OF AUTHORS. By Caroline Ticknor. Boston & New York, Houghton Mifflin Company; Cambridge, Riverside Press, 1922

Contains letters to Benjamin Holt Ticknor, pp. 101, 103, and 106: the one of October, 1881, concerning "Commodus"; another, December, 1881, on the same subject; the third, January, 1885, relates to a manuscript unnamed, but possibly the same play.

1927

PAT F. GARRETT'S AUTHENTIC LIFE OF BILLY THE KID. Edited by Maurice Garland Fulton. New York, Macmillan Co., 1927

Binder's title: *The Authentic Life of Billy the Kid, the Noted Desperado, by Pat. F. Garrett, Sheriff of Lincoln County, N. Mex., Edited by Maurice G. Fulton.* Contains facsimile of Wallace's letter to Billy the Kid, March 15, 1879, facing p. 116, and transcript on p. 123, together with Bonney's reply of March 20th and comments by the editor, pp. 123–126. The correspondence was again reproduced, in *A Frontier Doctor*, by Henry F. Hoyt (1929).

An interview with Wallace about Billy the Kid is quoted in part on p. 197. The interview was first published as a feature in *The* (New York) *World*, June 8, 1902. In the newspaper the article is introduced thus: "From advance sheets of Gen. Wallace's book the following account of this strange rendezvous has been copied and compiled for the Sunday World Magazine." If true, no copy in Wallace's hand has been preserved among his papers. The published autobiography contains only one mention of Billy the Kid, and that a comment by Susan Wallace in a letter to her son, Henry (Vol. II, p. 921).

For further details about Wallace as Governor of New Mexico, see *ante* 354.

1929

HISTORY OF MARYLAND: PROVINCE AND STATE. By Matthew Page
Andrews. Garden City, N. Y., Doubleday, Doran & Company,
Inc., 1929

Contains, p. 555, portions of two orders by "General Lewis Wallace" as commander of the Eighth Army Corps, Middle Department,
Maryland. One, No. 112, part of his military system to protect emancipated negroes through establishment (November 9, 1864) of a Freedmen's Bureau, directed that the building of the Maryland Club be
seized and renamed "Freedmen's Rest," and further arranged for its
maintenance; it appeared earlier in *The* (Baltimore) *Sun,* November 10, 1864. The other, issued before November 9th, related to confiscation of all property held by rebel sympathizers.* The orders were
suspended by direction of President Lincoln (see *The Diary of Edward
Bates,* edited by Howard K. Beale [1933], pp. 376, 379, for comments
not by Wallace).

For other orders not in this volume, particularly those concerning
subsequent affairs of the Freedmen's Bureau, see *Periodicals, Contributions, post* 399–401.

1934

FRONTIER FIGHTER. THE AUTOBIOGRAPHY OF GEORGE W. COE WHO
FOUGHT AND RODE WITH BILLY THE KID. As related to Nan Hillary
Harrison. Boston & New York, Houghton Mifflin; Cambridge,
Riverside Press, 1934

Contains, between pp. 154 and 155, a facsimile of the death warrant of William H. Bonney (Billy the Kid) in Wallace's hand, signed
and dated May 30, 1881, addressed "To the Sheriff of Lincoln County,
New Mexico, Greeting." References to Wallace appear on pp. 144 and
152.

Second edition issued in 1951.

The *New Mexico Historical Review,* Vol. 23, April 1948, p. 154,
carried a reference to the fact that the death warrant had been found

---

*The latter order, which is said to have appeared earlier, was not found in
Baltimore newspapers.

in the office of the Secretary of State of New Mexico in Santa Fe in December, 1947, but Maurice G. Fulton reports that he had found it there *circa* 1930, and its use in this book proves its availability in the '30's.

1947

"BEN-HUR" WALLACE: THE LIFE OF GENERAL LEW WALLACE. By Irving McKee. Berkeley & Los Angeles, University of California Press, 1947

Contains quotations from Lew Wallace's letters and remarks, not clearly identified as to source, some otherwise unpublished, some traceable to earlier publications. This is the only book-length biography of Wallace, frequently referred to herein as "McKee."

1949

THE WESTERNERS BRAND BOOK. Los Angeles Corrall, 1949

Contains a letter, p. 211, from Wallace to General Hatch, Commander of the Department of New Mexico, December 7, 1878, requesting that Lieut. Col. N. A. M. Dudley be removed; included in a paper by P. J. Rasch, "A Note on N. A. M. Dudley." On the same page there is quoted an opinion of Dudley from Wallace's private notebook. Although the latter is attributed to Wallace it is more likely Frank Angel's (see *ante* 358*n*).

The Wallace letter to Hatch was printed in *The Mesilla* (N. M.) *News*, March 22, 1879.

NOTES: *Drawings by Wallace were used to illustrate two of his wife's books.*

GINEVRA OR THE OLD OAK CHEST: A CHRISTMAS STORY. By Susan E. Wallace. With illustrations by General Lew Wallace. New York, Worthington Co., 1887 [*i.e.*, 1886]. *Frontispiece and plates facing pp. 8,* [18], [24], *38,* [42], *and* [44] *are by Wallace**

THE LAND OF THE PUEBLOS. By Susan E. Wallace. With illustrations. New York, John B. Alden, 1888. *Two illustrations from*

---

*One of the illustrations, a drawing of a castle, was later reproduced in *The Literary News*, February, 1887, p. 36.

drawings by Wallace: frontispiece and plate facing p. 14. Part of his article, "The Mines of Santa Eulalia," *q.v.*, was woven into Chapter XVII, pp. 166–167.

Note: *The Literary World,* November 4, 1882, p. 374, carried a statement that Wallace is "said to be furnishing sketches from Constantinople for an Eastern illustrated newspaper." True? If so, where published? Possibly a plan of Wallace's that did not materialize. Furthermore, on June 7, 1885, in an unpublished letter to Mrs. Wallace, from Rome, he mentioned that his time was occupied with "the Christmas article for Harpers which I am bent on taking home complete and ready for submission. My spare time is given to the galleries, *looking for illustrations* [italics supplied]."* This, too, was an unfulfilled project (McKee, p. 216).

A collection of Wallace drawings is in the Indiana Historical Society, William Henry Smith Memorial Library; the author's great-grandson, Lew Wallace III, also owns some fine examples of his work.

---

*Letter in Indiana Historical Society, William Henry Smith Memorial Library, Wallace Scrapbooks.

Periodicals Containing First Appearances

~~~~~~

APPLETON'S BOOKLOVERS MAGAZINE
1906: January   My Own Account of the First Day at Shiloh*

ATLANTIC MONTHLY
1863: February   Proclamation [of Martial Law in Cincinnati,
            Newport, and Covington]†; To the People
            of Cincinnati, Newport and Covington
            [congratulations on defense of cities and
            farewell instructions; both proclamations
            included in article, "The Siege of Cincin-
            nati" by T. B. Read]†

(Baltimore, Maryland) AMERICAN and COMMERCIAL ADVERTISER
1864: April 18 Headquarters, Middle Department, Baltimore,
         Special Orders No. 97, April 16th]‡
      19 [Speech at opening of Maryland State Fair,
         April 18th: opening remarks and Lincoln's
         reply]†
   May 19 [Order for discontinuance of the (Baltimore)
         Evening Transcript, May 18th, addressed
         to C. W. Tayleure]†
  1865: January 31 Headquarters, Middle Department, Balti-
         more, General Orders No. 18, January 30th
         [abolishing Freedmen's Bureau]§
   February 1 [Letter to J. M. Frazier, January 28th, about
         freedmen's affairs]†; [letter to Col. W. E.
         W. Ross, December 23, 1864, about Freed-
         men's Bureau]†
   April 20 Headquarters Middle Department, Baltimore,

---

*Uncollected; first printing of a letter to General James Grant Wilson in the
90's, when the latter was doing a "Life of Grant."
†Uncollected.
‡Uncollected. See *The* (Baltimore) *Sun*, for earlier orders and communications. His speech at the Maryland Institute, at a meeting called by the Unconditional Union State Central Committee, has been found only in the form of an
unidentified clipping in the Wallace Papers; it was delivered April 1st, probably
in a Sunday paper, April 3rd.
§Uncollected. See *The* (Baltimore) *Sun* for publication of General Orders
No. 112 on November 10, 1864, which laid plans for a Freedmen's bureau, but
hereby was cancelled.

(Baltimore, Maryland) AMERICAN AND COMMERCIAL ADVERTISER
—*continued*

General Orders No. 85, April 19th [announcing resumption of command of Middle Department]*

21 Order of Procession [to escort Lincoln's body to the rotunda of the Exchange]†; [circular, addressed to clergymen of Baltimore, relating to their loyalty]†

26 [Letter to Rev. J. J. Bullock, April 22nd, relating to loyalty]‡

May 2 [Extract from Special Orders No. 103, April 29th, about removal of restrictions on steamer trade and travel to the west coast of Maryland]†

THE (Baltimore, Maryland) SUN

1864: March 22 Headquarters, Middle Department, Baltimore, General Orders No. 16, March 22nd [on assuming command of Middle Department]§

April 2 [Letter to Gov. A. W. Bradford, March 30th, about pending Constitutional Election]†

July 19 Circular, July 18th [expressing appreciation of services of loyal citizens of Baltimore in recent invasion]†

November 10 Headquarters, Middle Department, Baltimore,

---

*Uncollected. General Orders No. 86, April 19th, about gray uniforms, found as an unidentified clipping in the Wallace Papers, was not located in this newspaper or in *The Sun*.

†Uncollected.

‡Uncollected. See *The* (Baltimore) *Sun*, May 2, 1865, for more letters on the subject.

§Uncollected. After this date there appeared many orders "by command of Major General Wallace," signed by other officers; probably in his words, but here omitted: General Orders No. 17 (published March 28th); Special Orders No. 79 (published March 30th); General Orders No. 19 (published April 4th), General Orders No. 51 and 53 (published July 15th); Special Order No. 17 (published July 21st); General Order No. 57 (published July 23rd); Special Order No. 182 (published July 26th); General Orders No. 115 (published November 26th). His letter to the editor of the (Baltimore) *Evening Post*, September 30th, suppressing its publication, was likewise signed "By command of . . . ." Throughout the months of October, November, and December his name is mentioned in connection with trials conducted by the Military Commission, but he did not sign the reports. On April 26, 1865, the *Sun* published General Orders No. 87, "by command of" Wallace, and on the 27th more about the same; his General Orders 91, 92 and 93 are mentioned but not quoted in the issue of May 1st.

THE (Baltimore, Maryland) SUN—*continued*

General Orders No. 112, November 9th [regarding Freedmen's Bureau]*

1865: May   2 [Letter to Mayor John Lee Chapman, May 1st, about vindication of certain clergymen from charges of disloyalty]†; [letter to Rev. John A. Williams, April 27th, inviting him to submit to oath of allegiance]†

BOOKLOVERS MAGAZINE
See: APPLETON'S BOOKLOVERS MAGAZINE

THE BOSTON ADVERTISER

1886: October 20 [Speech in Boston, October 19th, opening series of historical war lectures, under caption:] The Third Division, Army of the Tennessee at Pittsburg Landing]‡

THE CENTURY MAGAZINE

1884: December   The Capture of Fort Donelson, February 12–16, 1862†

1901: September   How I Saved Ben: A Skit§

THE CHICAGO EVENING POST

1905: February 27 [Letters to Lyon & Healy October 4 and December 4, 1904, and February 15, 1905, *re* violins, under caption:] Author Violin Lover†

THE (Chicago) INTER OCEAN

1888: October 24 [Speech, at Wingate (Whitlock), Ind., October 23rd, at rally of the "Ben Hur" Harrison Club, under caption:] Hitting the Bourbons Hard†

1889: August 27 [Letter to President Diaz, of Mexico, August 15th, under caption:] A Page of Secret Business†

1897: May 16 [Lecture, Chicago, February, 1895, quoted in part, under caption:] What Lew Wallace Thought of the Sultan‖

---

*Uncollected. His communication of December 23rd, about postponement of action on the Freedmen's Bureau, has not been located except in form of an unidentified clipping in the Wallace Papers.

†Uncollected.

‡Uncollected; reprinted and commented on in many papers; *The Indianapolis Journal*, November 6, 1886, quoted parts of both speech and criticism under caption, "Grant and Lew Wallace."

§Uncollected; two letters to R. U. Johnson of *Century* regarding this story are in the manuscript collection of the New York Public Library.

‖Uncollected; lecture not found earlier reported; possibly a portion of his frequently delivered speech, "Turkey and the Turks."

THE (Chicago) INTER OCEAN—*continued*

1898: May   5   [Letter to Col. P. A. Hoffman, Detroit, May 4th, under caption:] Lew Wallace Disappointed; Veteran of Two Wars Cannot Go to War with Spain*

CINCINNATI COMMERCIAL

1863: February   24   [Speech at Union Mass Meeting, Cincinnati, February 23rd]*

     March   20   [Letter to Editors, March 19th, in defense of Gen. Edward O. C. Ord]*

1869: September 27   [Letter to A. C. Sands, September 23rd, captioned:] The Mexican Bonds*

1870: March   26   [Letter to the Editor, March 23rd, denying ownership of Mexican bonds, under caption:] Card from General Wallace*

1873: November 11   [Letter to the Editor, about *The Fair God*]*

1877: January   3   [Letter (telegram) to Gov. Edward F. Noyes, about the electoral vote count for Hayes]†

THE CINCINNATI COMMERCIAL GAZETTE

1886: January   26   [Letter to the Editor, January 23rd, about Shiloh]*

     February   11   [Speech before Loyal Legion, Ohio Commandery, Cincinnati, February 10th]*

1889: (before January 12)   [Statement about not wanting any position in Pres. Harrison's Cabinet]‡

CINCINNATI ENQUIRER

1862: September 14   To the People of Cincinnati, Newport and Covington [congratulations on defense of cities and farewell instructions]§

CINCINNATI GAZETTE

1862: August   1   [Speech, Citizens' Union mass meeting, Cincinnati, July 31st]*

     September   2   Proclamation [declaring Martial Law in Cincinnati, Covington, and Newport]

            3   Headquarters, U. S. Forces, Cincinnati, General Orders Nos. 2* and 4*; Special Order [to teachers in public schools*; all dated September 2nd]

---

*Uncollected.

†Uncollected. Wallace's testimony in the questioning of Noyes about the electoral vote count was published in a newspaper, also; the clipping examined lacks identification and date.

‡Uncollected; reprinted in *The Crawfordsville Journal*, January 12, 1889.

§Uncollected; published the following day in the *Cincinnati Gazette*.

CINCINNATI GAZETTE—*continued*

1862: September   4   Headquarters, U. S. Forces, Cincinnati, General Orders No. 5*; Special Order of September 3rd*; Circular [appointing surgeon for Second Ward]*; Order [to railway employees to remain at work]*; Order [re exemptions in Commissary Department]*

  5   Headquarters, U. S. Forces, Cincinnati [notice of staff appointments]*; Special Orders Nos. 7*, 12*, 13*, and 14* [plus one extending exemptions]*; Office Provost Marshal, Special Orders Nos. 1* and 4*

  6   Headquarters, U. S. Forces, Cincinnati, Circular [notice regarding T. Buchanan Read]*; Proclamation [re market supplies, military protection to farmers and market men]*

  8   Headquarters, U. S. Forces, Cincinnati, Special Order of September 6th [about market provisions]*; [Letters (2) to George Hatch, Mayor, September 5th]*; Special Order No. 37*

10   Medical Director's Office, General Order No. 9*; Headquarters, U. S. Forces, Covington, General Order of September 10th*

17   [Speech to riflemen in camp near Fort Mitchell, September 16th]*

1863: March   25   [Speech at reception for Major-General A. E. Burnside, Cincinnati, March 24th]*

1874: June   20   [Letter to the Editor, June 18th, captioned:] Decidedly Not a Candidate [for Congress]*

THE CRAWFORDSVILLE JOURNAL

1867: August   1   [Letter to editor of *The Chicago Tribune*]†

1868: December   10   A Card [announcing resumption of law practice in Crawfordsville, dated December 7th]*

1869: June   10   Resolution of Thanks [to those aiding in Memorial Day services, signed by Wallace, *et al.*]*

24   [Letter to Calvin M. Cheney *re* construction of I. C. & D. railroad]*

---

*Uncollected.

†Uncollected; not found in *The Chicago Tribune;* only clue to date of first publication is an editorial statement: "Letter written prior to the publication of Mr. Seward's dispatch concerning the arrest of Santa Anna."

THE CRAWFORDSVILLE JOURNAL—*continued*

1875: May   8   [Speech at laying of the corner stone of the Crawfordsville Court House, May 6th]*

1876: October   21   [Letter to Gen. W. T. Sherman, October 19th: brief greetings from Society of the Eleventh Indiana Regiment]†

1877: December 29   [Report of committee to establish a reading room, under caption:] Murphy Notes†

1878: August   24   [Address to the Republicans of the 9th Cong. Dist., Ind., Montgomery County, under caption:] Address of the Anti-Orth Club†

1880: May   22   [Statement about *Ben Hur*, written for his interviewer, Meredith Nicholson]†

October   23   [Speech, to Montgomery Guards, October 18th]†

1882: May   6   Letter to Lord Dufferin, March 3rd [expressing relief that the Queen's life was spared in an attempt upon it]†

1885: September   5   [Letter to Col. L. W. Winchester, August 1st, under caption:] Gen. Lew Wallace and the New York Seventh [to march together in Grant's funeral]†

1886: January   9   [Letter to Hadji Ali, Second Chamberlain to the Sultan of Turkey, May 19, 1885, acknowledging gifts from the Sultan]†

1889: September 21   [Statement about Imogene Brown's picture, "Beautiful Theano at the School of Pythagoras"]†

1890: October   4   [Speech welcoming North-West Indiana Conference, Methodist Episcopal Church, October 1, 1890]†

1905: February 20   [Letter to Charles B. Landis, February 12th, *re* autographing of a copy of *Ben-Hur* for J. J. Insley]†

THE CRAWFORDSVILLE REVIEW

1856:[?]   22   [Speech, at Crawfordsville, on presenting a pitcher to Mr. Voorhees from the Old Liners of Montgomery County]‡

---

*Uncollected. The issue of the 22nd might have contained his speech in greeting to Knights of Pythias, May 20, 1875, at Crawfordsville, found only in the form of an unidentified clipping in the Wallace Papers.

†Uncollected.

‡Uncollected. Clipping preserved in the Wallace Papers lacks month date.

THE CRAWFORDSVILLE REVIEW—*continued*
    1877: July   28 [Dispatches (2) to Lieut. I. C. Elston,
                            July 27th, ordering Montgomery Guards to
                            Indianapolis to prevent a riot in connection
                            with a railroad strike]*

THE CRITIC
    1895: February   2 [Reply to newspaper men who represented
                            him as desiring establishment of a "College
                            of Immortals" in America]†

THE DAILY NEW MEXICAN (Santa Fe)
    1881: March   6 [Commutation, as Governor of the Territory
                            of New Mexico, of the sentence of John J.
                            Webb, March 5th, addressed:] To Whom
                            It May Concern‡

          May   1 [Death warrant for Frank C. Clark, dated
                            April 30th, addressed:] To the Sheriff of
                            Dona Ana County, New Mexico [simul-
                            taneous death warrant for Santos Barela
                            mentioned but not quoted because sim-
                            ilarly worded]‡

                       4 [Reward offer for capture of William Bonney,
                            captioned:] Billy the Kid, $500 Reward‡

                      29 [Letter to Frederick W. Pitkin, Governor of
                            Colorado, May 28th]‡

DAYTON (Ohio) JOURNAL
    1899: October   21 [Letter to Phi Gamma Delta Society, written
                            for an annual convention, under caption:]
                            Phi Gams§

THE EVANSVILLE (Indiana) JOURNAL
    1861: August   15 [Address to his men, August 14th, on learning
                            of Gen. Lyon's death, under caption:] The
                            Indiana Zouaves‡

    1862: August   14 [Speech at Evansville, August 12th, recruiting
                            for Civil War]‖

---

*Uncollected. Later this year Wallace's letter of October 18th to Maurice
Thompson, replying to an invitation to a match between his long-bow team and
the Montgomery Guards' rifle team, was published in one of the Crawfordsville
newspapers; not located; clipping in Wallace Papers.
    †Uncollected; "taken from Washington *Post*." In an earlier issue of *The Critic*,
May 12, 1894, there appeared a story that Wallace had his friend, General Black,
introduce a bill in Congress, to provide for a National Academy of twenty-five
immortals; it led to considerable publicity.
    ‡Uncollected.
    §Uncollected; information from a microfilm copy in the Dayton Public Library.
    ‖Uncollected; similar to other speeches on Union loyalty delivered summer of
1862.

HARPER'S [MONTHLY] MAGAZINE
1867: November   The Mines of Santa Eulalia, Chihuahua*
1886: December   The Boyhood of Christ
1888: January   Lines Addressed to the Lady Who Bandaged My Cut Finger—An Afterthought [poem]†
1889: January   Commodus: A Play
1897: December   The Wooing of Malkatoon

HARPER'S WEEKLY
1863: August   22   The Stolen Stars‡
1888: June   23   [Letter, re W. D. Mahan's archaeological "translation," under caption:] "Ben-Hur" and "Ben-Eli"§
1894: June   23   Address to the Cadets at the United States Naval Academy‖

INDIANA MAGAZINE OF HISTORY
1919: September   [Letter to Indiana State Journal, July 26, 1846, about Mexican War; part only, in article, "Indiana in the Mexican War" by R. C. Buley]‡

INDIANA STATE JOURNAL (Indianapolis)
1844: December   4–
1845: January   14   Indiana Legislature, House of Representatives [daily reports, unsigned]¶
1846: August   26   [Letter to the Editor, July 26th, about the Mexican War]‡

---

*Uncollected. Mrs. Wallace later quoted from p. 698 of this article, without making acknowledgment, in her story, "The Miners," included as "Old Miners," Chapter XVII in The Land of the Pueblos (1888). Letters from Wallace to his wife from Chihuahua, October 5th and November 11th, 1866, appeared in his autobiography, Vol. II, pp. 881, 885.

†Uncollected. A manuscript was listed in a book auction catalogue as bearing title, "An Afterthought."

‡Uncollected.

§Uncollected; see Ben-Hur, Notes, ante 326.

‖Collected in his Autobiography (1906). It had appeared in print some time in 1899, in The (New York) World, known from a clipping in the Wallace Papers which, however, lacks the exact date.

¶Uncollected; see Lew Wallace: An Autobiography (1906), Vol. I, p. 96, for Wallace's statement that he daily reported for the Journal the proceedings of the House during this 29th session (he did not make the reports in later years although so indicated in Courts and Lawyers of Indiana, by L. J. Monks, Logan Esarey, & Ernest V. Shockley [1916], Vol. III, p. 1292); the issue of December 4, 1844, is known to carry a report, and it has to be assumed, on the strength of his own statement, that subsequent issues through the closing on January 13, 1845 (reported the next morning) published his reports, but they have not been located.

INDIANA STATE JOURNAL (Indianapolis)—*continued*
1847: January   22   [Letter to David Wallace, December 19, 1846, about the Mexican War]*

INDIANA STATE SENTINEL (Indianapolis)
1847: April   10   [Letter to "Friend Chapman," March 12th, about the Mexican War]*
1858: January   18   [Letter to Mr. Brigham, January 14th, containing resolution concerning the Kansas-Nebraska bill]*
1860: July   10   [Letter to J. J. Bingham, July 7th, under caption:] A Challenge to the Military Companies of Indiana [invitation to contest for a purse to be given the best drilled, on September 20th]*
1861: April   18   [Letter to ladies of Indianapolis, April 17th, appealing for help in Civil War effort]*
                 22   Adjutant General's Office, General Orders No. 2, April 20th†
                 26   Regimental Orders, 11th Regiment Indiana Volunteers, Indianapolis, April 24th: General Orders No. 1*

INDIANAPOLIS HERALD
1866: July   6   [Speech, July 4, 1866]‡

THE INDIANAPOLIS JOURNAL
1861: April   16   Adjutant General's Office, General Orders No. 1, April 15th§; [Letter to the Editor, April 15th, under caption:] A Zouave Regiment‖
                 25   [Letter to Oliver P. Morton, April 23rd, resigning from office of Adjutant General]¶
      June   17   Special Dispatch from Col. Lew Wallace, Cumberland, Md., June 16th, addressed to the Editor£
                 24   [Letter to Maj. Gen. Patterson, June 14th,

---

*Uncollected.

†Uncollected; his April 15th General Orders No. 1 appeared in both *Indianapolis Daily Journal* and the *State Sentinel,* on April 16, 1861.

‡Part only collected; see *ante* 370.

§Uncollected; printed in the *Daily State Sentinel* (Indianapolis), same date. General Orders, No. 2, appeared in the latter newspaper on April 22nd.

‖Uncollected; printed in the *Daily State Sentinel* (Indianapolis), same date, without caption, addressed to J. J. Bingham, Publisher.

¶Uncollected; printed in *Daily State Sentinel* (Indianapolis), same date.

£Uncollected; comments on the contents appeared in the issue of June 18th under caption, "A Rebel Major in Limbo."

THE INDIANAPOLIS JOURNAL—*continued*

		under caption:] Official Report of the Affair at Romney]*
1862: April	26	The Battle of Shiloh: Official Report of Major General Lew Wallace, April 12th [letter addressed to Capt. John A. Rawlins]*
1874: May	28	[Letter to Indiana Association of Mexican War Veterans, May 26th]
1875: October	4	[Invitation, October 1st, to 11th Indiana Infantry (Zouaves) to a reunion at Terre Haute, October 19th]*
1876: November	17	[Statement from New Orleans, about electoral vote count in Hayes campaign, November 16th, signed by Wallace among many others, captioned:] Reply to the Republicans . . .*; [special telegram, November 16th, about the New Orleans electoral vote, signed by Wallace and two others, captioned:] Meeting of the Returning Board . . . Democratic Majority Vanishing*
	18	[Telegram from New Orleans, about electoral vote count in Hayes campaign, November 17th, signed by Wallace and two others, captioned:] Proof of Intimidation in Louisiana Accumulating*
	22	[Telegram from Tallahassee, about electoral vote count in Hayes campaign, November 20th, captioned:] Florida*
December	29, 2, 4, 7	[Telegrams and letters from Tallahassee, about electoral vote count]†
1877: May	31	[Speech at New Albany, Memorial Day, May 30th, under caption:] In God's Acres*
June	9	[Speech at Butler University, Commencement exercises, June 8th, under caption:] Beginning Life*
July	28	[Order to Montgomery Guards, July 27th, to assemble and come to Indianapolis]*
October	20	[Speech, 11th Indiana Regiment, annual reunion, Indianapolis, October 19th, part only]*
November	2	[Telegram to Morton family expressing sym-

---

*Uncollected.

†Uncollected; see *The New York Tribune* and the *Tallahassee Sentinel* for subsequent contributions on the subject.

THE INDIANAPOLIS JOURNAL—*continued*

pathy from Montgomery Guards for loss by death of Oliver P. Morton]*

1877: November 3   General Orders of Chief Marshal [for Morton's funeral procession]*

5   Orders from the Chief Marshal [for Morton's funeral procession]†

16   Address to the People of Indiana [prospectus, Morton Memorial Association]‡

1883: May   9   [Letter to a Crawfordsville friend, from Constantinople]*

September 20   [Letter to Eleventh Indiana Regiment, August 17th, about battle of Pittsburg Landing]*

1886: January   22   [Telegram to Hon. E. M. Stanton, July 11, 1864]*

1887: October   20   [Speech, 11th Indiana Regiment annual reunion, October 19, 1887; part only quoted]*

December 27   Lines Addressed to the Lady Who Bandaged My Cut Finger—An Afterthought [poem]*

1888: December 20   [Speech of welcome at the Loyal Legion banquet, December 19th, under caption:] Companions of the Legion§

1890: August   22   [Speech at American Association for the Advancement of Science reception, August 21st, in Indianapolis, under caption:] Numerous Scientific Topics*

1891: July   5   [Speech before Indiana Commandery of the Loyal Legion, July 4th, in Indianapolis, under caption:] The Virtue of Patriotism*

November 25   [Telegram to Maj. M. G. McLain, under caption:] Gov. [Alvin P.] Hovey Honored in Death‖

---

*Uncollected.

†Uncollected; not same as "General Orders . . ." also in this issue, reprinted from November 3rd.

‡Uncollected. It was these plans of Wallace's in combination with a group of interested citizens which nearly a quarter of a century later, and after many revisions, materialized in the Indiana Soldiers' and Sailors' Monument, Indianapolis. At its dedication Wallace made a speech; see *The Indianapolis Journal*, May 16, 1902.

§Uncollected. Wallace was made Commander of the Indiana Commandery and Councilman of the national Loyal Legion in 1889; his speech at the 1889 assembly (second annual) of the Indiana Commandery is given in digest in McKee, p. 234.

‖Uncollected; reprinted in *The Crawfordsville Journal*, November 28, 1891.

THE INDIANAPOLIS JOURNAL—*continued*

1892: March   5   [Letter to Republican State Central Committee of Indiana, John K. Gowdy, chairman,
March 4th, declining offer of delegation to
the national convention]*

1894: July   8   [Notice to Old Montgomery Guards to organize Companies A and B, one a Home
Guard, other subject to military call]*

1895: September 19   [Speech, prepared for dedication of Chickamauga Park, September 19th]*

1896: February 13   [Speech introducing James Whitcomb Riley
at Loyal Legion, Indiana Commandery cel-
ebration in Indianapolis, February 12th]*

1896: May   31   [Speech, Memorial Day, 1896, at Crown Hill
Cemetery, Indianapolis, under caption:]
Gen. Wallace's Oration†

December 3   [Letter to the Editor, December 2nd, about
not seeking Senatorship or any office, elec-
tive or appointive]*

1897: December 28–29   [Speeches (2) at biennial Republican
Conference, December 27th and 28th]*

1898: February 13   [Speech at Indiana Republican League reception, Lafayette, February 11th, under cap-
tion:] Indiana Republicans‡

14   [Speech at Lincoln Day banquet, Lebanon,
February 12th, under caption:] Why Lincoln Was Sad§

April   17   [Statement to the Editor: "In view of the cer-
tainty of war with Spain I to-day tendered
the national government my services in the
field . . .," under caption:] Tenders His
Services for War and Withdraws from
Senatorial Race‖

---

*Uncollected.

†Uncollected; speech repeated in Louisville the year following and printed
again, in *Louisville Courier-Journal*, June 1, 1897. McKee (p. 235) is surely in
error in stating that Wallace had delivered the address in 1892 at Crown Hill
Cemetery, since Wallace was not mentioned in newspapers in connection with
the program of the occasion; a downpour of rain prevented ceremonies planned
that year.

‡Uncollected. Very few of the many speeches made by Wallace for the Republican Party in various campaigns have been found printed.

§Uncollected; quoted later in *The* (Chicago) *Inter Ocean*, February 20, 1898,
under caption: "Challenged to Duel: General Lew Wallace Invited to the Field
of Honor; George E. Oaks Angry, Denies Truth of a Story about General
McClellan."

‖Uncollected; printed again in *The Indianapolis Star*, February 17, 1905, in

THE INDIANAPOLIS JOURNAL—*continued*

1898: December 17 [Speech at Loyal Legion Meeting, Indianapolis, December 16th, under caption:] Gave Him a Loving Cup*

1902: May   16 [Speech at dedication of the Indiana Soldiers' and Sailors' Monument, Indianapolis, May 15th, under caption:] General Wallace Presides†

THE INDIANPOLIS NEWS

1894: October 21 [Speech at reunion of the 11th Indiana Regiment, October 20th]*

1897: December 16 [Speech, extemporaneous, to officers of Indiana National Guard, predicting a war with Japan in which America would "thrash them"; brief quotations]‡

1898: April   23 [Letter to the Editor, April 22nd, answering an article of April 21st, under caption:] General Lew Wallace; He Simply Wants to Serve His Country§

November 21 [Letter *re* candidacy for U. S. Senate]*

1901: February 15 Gen. Lew Wallace's Tribute to Maurice Thompson*

October 26 An Indiana Soldier—Maj. James R. Ross*

THE INDIANAPOLIS PRESS

1900: March 20 [Letter to Editor, March 19th, under caption:] Gen. Lew Wallace Offers a Sixteenth Amendment to the Constitution‖

THE INDIANAPOLIS SENTINEL

1899: February 23 [Speech before Indiana Historical Society, February 22nd, under caption:] Gen. Wallace Defends*

1902: June   1 [Speech for Harrison Memorial, Indiana Authors' Readings, Indianapolis, May 30 and 31]¶

---

facsimile, under caption: "Tenders Services at Age of Seventy."

*Uncollected.

†Uncollected; first complete printing of the speech; a facsimile of the first page of the address had appeared in *The Indianapolis News*, May 15, 1902.

‡Uncollected; possibly an interview rather than contribution.

§Uncollected. The *News* published Wallace's offer of services in the Spanish-American War on April 18th, *The Indianapolis Journal* a day earlier.

‖Uncollected; text printed twice in this issue.

¶Uncollected; the speech, which included a tribute to Maurice Thompson, was introductory to his reading of part of "Ben-Hur"; an interview before the program gave comments by him on the Harrison Memorial, possibly not his own words.

THE INDIANAPOLIS SENTINEL—*continued*
>   1903: April   10   [Shiloh address, under caption:] Gen. Lew
>   Wallace's Address Delivered at Shiloh,
>   April 6*

THE INDIANAPOLIS STAR
>   1905: February   20   [Letters to Cong. Chas. B. Landis *re* fish pond,
>   under caption:] Among Last Notes of Lew
>   Wallace†
>   1910: January   9   [Letter written when he was Minister to Tur-
>   key, unaddressed and undated, part only]†;
>   [letter to Susan E. Wallace from Constan-
>   tinople, March 3, 1885, part only]†
>   1919: October   12   [Fragment from an unidentified manuscript
>   in facsimile, included in an unsigned article
>   captioned:] The Author of Ben-Hur as a
>   Friend Knew Him†

THE INTER OCEAN (see THE [Chicago] INTER OCEAN)

LAS VEGAS (New Mexico) GAZETTE
>   1880: December   24   [Reward notice for capture of William H.
>   Bonney (Billy the Kid)]†

LEVANT HERALD (Constantinople)
>   1881: September   28   [Speech at meeting of sympathy over Presi-
>   dent Garfield's death, September 27th, in
>   Constantinople]‡

THE MARIETTA (Ohio) REGISTER
>   1877: September   4   [Speech at Soldiers' Reunion, Marietta, Sep-
>   tember 4th]§

THE MESILLA (New Mexico) INDEPENDENT‖
>   1879: Vol. 2, No. 47 (*ca.* February)   [Reply to charges of *The Me-
>   silla News* that he was involved in cattle-
>   stealing and a partisan in the McQueen-
>   Murphy War; being a statement given a
>   reporter for the *Rocky Mountain Sentinel*]¶

A souvenir of the occasion, *Readings by Indiana Authors in Aid of Benjamin Harrison Monument Association,* issued in pamphlet form, contains portraits of the authors, but no text.

*Uncollected; see *Ephemera, ante,* 363, for the address in a pamphlet. See *The Indianapolis News,* May 8, 1903, for facsimile of one page of the manuscript.

†Uncollected.

‡Uncollected. Not seen, but reported and quoted in part in *The Crawfordsville Journal,* October 29, 1881.

§Uncollected; repeated in weekly issue on September 7th.

‖Also called *The Mesilla Valley Independent.*

¶Uncollected; probably reprinted from the *Rocky Mountain Sentinel,* as yet unlocated.

THE MESILLA (New Mexico) NEWS
 1879: March   22   [Letter to Col. Edward Hatch, December 7,
                              1878, about Col. N. A. M. Dudley]*
          May   17   [Letters to U. S. Army officials at Fort Stan-
                              ton, Lincoln County, N. M., March and
                              April, 1879, captioned:] Wallace's Orders
                              While in Command at Fort Stanton*

THE NEW ENGLAND QUARTERLY
 1942: March   [Letter to President Rutherford B. Hayes, No-
                              vember 28, 1878, about New Mexican af-
                              fairs]*; [letter to same, September 22,
                              1880, about leaving New Mexico to visit
                              Indiana for campaign purposes]*; [letter to
                              same, November 20, 1880, accompanying
                              gift of a copy of Ben-Hur]*

NEW MEXICAN (see DAILY NEW MEXICAN and WEEKLY NEW MEXICAN)

THE NEW YORK PRESS
 1882: November 25   [Letter of orders to Lieut. Dan Macaulay, In-
                              dependent Zouaves, April 16, 1861]*

THE NEW YORK TRIBUNE†
 1876: December 28   The New Count in Florida*

THE (New York) WORLD
 1899: November 30   [Letter to the Editor, about Klaw & Erlanger's
                              production of "Ben-Hur"]*

THE NORTH AMERICAN REVIEW
 1901: December   Prevention of Presidential Assassinations*

OHIO STATE JOURNAL
 1862: September 22   Headquarters Paroled Forces, Columbus,
                              Ohio, September 22nd, General Orders
                              Nos. 2 & 3*

OMAHA TRIBUNE & REPUBLICAN
 1872: (after August 30) [Letter to the Editor, August 30th, de-
                              fending General Grant's conduct at the
                              battles of Donelson and Shiloh]‡

---

*Uncollected.
 †In a periodical clipping which lacks full identification, a letter of Wallace's
appeared addressed to the editor of The Tribune (probably the New York newspaper), dated September 16 (probably 1879), replying to "R's" letter of September 5th which was a published criticism of his Civil War actions.
 ‡Uncollected; reprinted in The Indianapolis Journal, September 12, 1872; no
file of the Omaha paper located.

THE PHI GAMMA DELTA [QUARTERLY]

    1898: October   [Letter to E. L. Mattern, September 13th, regretting inability to attend Ekklesia]*

    1900: March   [Telegram to Phi Gamma Delta's Committee for "Phi Gamma Delta Night at Ben Hur"]†

    1901: February   The Tribute of General Wallace [to Maurice Thompson]‡

    1905: April   [Letter to Phi Gamma Delta, Sigma Mu Chapter, Syracuse University, August 29, 1901]§

    1936: April   [Letter to Alexander Hill, regarding dedication of *Ben Hur*]§

THE (Rochester, N. Y.) ADVERTISER

    1887: February 22 [Speech, "Turkey and the Turks," quoted "in substance"]‖

THE ROCKY MOUNTAIN SENTINEL (Santa Fe)¶

    1878: November 14 [Proclamation of the Governor, November 13th, extending amnesty to army officers and residents of Lincoln County, Territory of New Mexico]£

THE SANTA FE NEW MEXICAN (see THE DAILY NEW MEXICAN and THE WEEKLY NEW MEXICAN)

SCRIBNER'S MONTHLY

    1879: March   A Buffalo Hunt in Northern Mexico§

SOUTH BEND TRIBUNE

    1898: March   16 [Speech at South Bend, March 15th, in tribute to Schuyler Colfax]§

TALLAHASSEE (Florida) SENTINEL

    1877: (between January 19
          and February 3)   [Letter to members of (Florida) Board of State Canvassers, January 19th]**

---

*Uncollected. See *Contributions, ante* 389, for his letter to the 1899 Ekklesia.

†Uncollected; evidently printed, too, as a broadside for distribution to members present on the occasion, from context on p. 133.

‡Uncollected; same as in *The Indianapolis News*, February 15, 1901.

§Uncollected.

‖Uncollected. The lecture has not been found printed anywhere in its entirety. It was first delivered in Crawfordsville, April, 1886, then given on tour in many cities in 1886–1887, again October, 1894, in Seattle, Washington, when Will H. Thompson introduced his fellow townsman.

¶It was probably this newspaper, or one of the Denver papers that, on February 5, 1880, printed Wallace's telegrams of January 16th and 19th, about Indian troubles addressed to Carl Schurz; clipping lacks identification.

£Uncollected; issued in broadside form (see *ante* 354).

**No file of *Tallahassee Sentinel* of January–February, 1877 yet located. Collected in *Lew Wallace: An Autobiography, q.v.*

THE WABASH (Wabash College, Crawfordsville)
    1903: February   The Spirit of '62 [Speech, June 17, 1902, at
                          Wabash, for dedication of Civil War tab-
                          let]*

WASHINGTON (D. C.) CHRONICLE
    1866: [before May 17]   [Letter to Judge Jno. A. Bingham, March
                          31st, about reorganization of the Army]†

WASHINGTON (D. C.) POST
    1895: (January?)   [On "College of Immortals"]‡

THE WEEKLY NEW MEXICAN (Santa Fe)
    1878: November 23   Thanksgiving Proclamation*
    1879: September 20   [Dispatches to S. M. Ashenfelter, under cap-
                          tion:] More Indian Outrages§
    1880: January   10   The Governor's Message to the Legislative As-
                          sembly of New Mexico, January 8th*

YOUTH'S COMPANION
    1893: February   2   How I Came to Write Ben-Hur

Unidentified Periodical Contributions:

Civil War orders, reports, letters, and speeches; all uncollected:
    Order, February 28, 1862, congratulating soldiers of the First Di-
    vision
    Letter to Alderman Holden, Shimp, and Hoyt, April 3 [1862?],
    "read at the great Union meeting held in Chicago on Friday
    evening [April 4th]"
    Official Report of the Battle of Pittsburgh Landing (Shiloh),
    April 12, 1862
    Letter to Crawfordsville Committee, S. C. Wilson, J. P. Campbell,
    and John Lee, May 8, 1862, in thanks for "an elegant sword"
    given him by friends in Montgomery County [probably in a
    Crawfordsville newspaper, not available]
    Speech in Washington, D. C., June, 1862, when serenaded at the
    National Hotel by a number of Indianians; he urged that negroes
    be freed and armed
    Speeches, summer and autumn, 1862, at various Union mass meet-
    ings in Indiana, on military missions; see Cincinnati Gazette,
    August 1, 1862, for substance of his message

---

*Uncollected.
†Uncollected; reprinted from the Washington Chronicle in The Crawfords-
ville Journal, May 17, 1866.
‡Uncollected; reprinted in The Critic, February 2, 1895.
§Uncollected; in another newspaper, unidentified, captioned: "Our Indian
Troubles."

Speech, in a "hospitable and beautiful" city, on subject of Lincoln's Emancipation Proclamation of January 1, 1863

Letter to General Grant, February 29, 1868, justifying his conduct on April 6, 1862, at the battle of Pittsburg Landing, written after reading Badeau's "Life of General Grant" which was syndicated and published in newspapers all over the country; from context published after June 24, 1868

Hayes campaign; uncollected:

Speech at a Republican Convention, August 22, 1876, about Hayes; Wallace's own words quoted at length in some newspaper of August 28th.

SUSAN ARNOLD ELSTON WALLACE
(MRS. LEW WALLACE)

BORN: *Crawfordsville, Indiana, December 25, 1830*

DIED: *Crawfordsville, Indiana, October 1, 1907*

SUSAN ARNOLD ELSTON WALLACE, daughter of Isaac C. and Maria E. Aiken Elston, was born at Crawfordsville, Indiana, December 25, 1830; received an education in Crawfordsville and Poughkeepsie, New York; married Lew Wallace in 1852; died in her native city on October 1, 1907. She would be satisfied with this brief summary of her life, for she was content to remain in the shadow of her husband's colorful career. It was a true marriage: she helped him at every turn; he appreciated and counseled her. She kept all his letters to her as important to posterity, and destroyed her own; contributed comparatively little as a published writer although Lew Wallace and her friends thought she had great talent. It was her pleasure to encourage other writers. To Mary Hannah Krout, a protegée for many years, she entrusted the editing of her husband's autobiography. Perhaps her place in the literary field was that of consultant, and it may be that Lew Wallace's success as an author was due in large measure to her criticism and his respect for it.

The theme of her writing was home and friends, travel, and Christianity. Her attitudes were thoroughly feminine at all times. Some poems were written and published before she was thirty, but most of her literary efforts came after she was fifty. The first book was a plan to ward off homesickness while living in Constantinople, in 1881. The six volumes of writing wholly hers that appeared between 1883 and 1903 include a very slight Christmas story based on an Italian legend; the rest are essays, fact mixed with fiction, with a background of her travels with her husband in Europe, the Orient, the Holy Land, and the Territory of New Mexico, which she visited during his governorship. A biographical study of Susan Wallace as a woman who came into the Southwest at an early date and wrote about it is being undertaken by Miss Mabel Major, of Fort Worth, Texas.

Her poems were never collected. Her last piece of writing, as far as is known, was a story submitted March, 1904, to *The Century Magazine* but unpublished: "The End of the Rainbow. An Old,

419

Old Story," which she described in a letter to the editor (letter now in the New York Public Library's manuscript collection) as "an Eastern tale adapted from the 'Arabian Nights,'" designed to be as "Oriental as musk and fantastic as possible." It was probably an attempt to entertain Lew Wallace in his long, last illness.

A biographical summary of her as writer, done by Lew Wallace, not published, but preserved in the Indiana State Library in photostat from the original manuscript, adds to the tribute he paid her in his *Autobiography*, Volume II (1906), pp. 206–212. With her equipment of mind and heart and facility in expressing her ideas Susan Wallace could have been a more famous author; she preferred to be known as Mrs. Lew Wallace. Many have described her as an excellent wife and mother, hostess and friend, a charming and good woman.

CHRONOLOGY OF BOOKS

1883   *The Storied Sea*   James R. Osgood and Company
1887 (*i.e.*, 1886)   *Ginèvra; or, The Old Oak Chest, A Christmas Story*   Worthington Co.
1888   *The Land of the Pueblos*   John B. Alden
    The Repose in Egypt   John B. Alden
1898   *Along the Bosphorus and Other Sketches*   Rand, McNally & Co.
1903   *The City of the King; What the Child Jesus Saw and Heard*   The Bobbs-Merrill Company

BIOGRAPHICAL REFERENCES

Who's Who in America, Vols. 1–4; Frances E. Willard & Mary A. Livermore, *A Woman of the Century* (1893), *American Women* (1897); Irving McKee, *"Ben-Hur" Wallace* (1947); R. E. Banta, *Indiana Authors and Their Books* (1949); Wallace Papers, Indiana Historical Society, William Henry Smith Memorial Library.

1883

The Storied Sea

THE STORIED SEA [*red*] | BY | SUSAN E. WALLACE | [*publishers' emblem*] | BOSTON [*red*] | JAMES R. OSGOOD AND COMPANY | 1883 [*red*]
[Note: The foregoing, with red ornament in each corner, is within a single rule box, within a red rule box.]

COLLATION: One unsigned leaf, [1]⁶, 2⁴ (signed on recto of 3rd leaf), 3–[6]–[11]–15⁸ (numbered signatures from 3–15 are signed on recto of 7th leaf), [16]⁴. White wove paper. Leaf measures 5¹⁵⁄₁₆″ x 4⅛″, all edges orange.

End paper; binder's leaf; title-page, inserted, with verso bearing copyright notice dated 1883, statement: *All rights reserved.*, and imprint of the University Press, John Wilson and Son, Cambridge; half-title, p. [i]; quotation from Charles Kingsley's *Prose Idylls*: a description of the Mediterranean Sea, p. [ii]; *Preface*, dated May 1, 1883, pp. [iii]–v; blank, p. [vi]; table of contents, pp. [vii]–viii; text, pp. [9]–233 (imprint of University Press at foot of p. 233); blank, pp. [234–236]; binder's leaf; end paper.
[Note: For text, pp. (9)–233, see *Contents*.]

ILLUSTRATIONS: None. Headpieces appear on pp. [iii], [vii], and at beginning of each chapter; an ornamental rule is below caption on pp. [iii], [vii], and [9].

BINDING: Light green, and, brown mesh cloth. Front cover brown-stamped: [*rule*] | [*gilt-stamped cable intercepting a border of dots within double rule, also intercepting O in line below*] | [*dot*] THE [*dot*] STORIED [*dot*] | [*dot*] SEA [*dot*] | [*gilt-stamped seal, outlined in dark brown, containing ship design in center and row of dots bordering the following circular design, all gilt:*] BY [*dot*] SUSAN [*dot*] E [*dot*] WALLACE [*dot*] [*the seal intercepts an ornamental arrangement of rules and dots, center wave-like; the gilt-stamped cable continues to a bottom rule after intercepting a border of dots within a double rule*] |

[*rule*]. Spine brown-stamped: [*border of dots within double rule*] |
[*the following four lines on gilt-stamped panel:*] [*ornament*] THE [*ornament*] | [*ornament*] STO- [*ornamental hyphen*] | RIED [*ornament*] |
[*ornament*] SEA [*ornament*] | [*ornamental arrangement of rules and dots, center wave-like*] | SUSAN [*dot*] E | WALLACE | [*row of dots intercepted by first* L *in* WALLACE *above*] | [*publishers' emblem within ornamental design*]. Back cover blank.

End papers olive-green floral design on white, two different patterns noted; binder's leaf front and back, same as book stock, their conjugates pasted under lining papers.

PUBLICATION DATA: Deposited in the Copyright Office September 17, 1883. Earliest review noted: *Boston Evening Transcript*, September 14, 1883. Price, $1.00.

NOTES: First edition as collated. Bindings vary in color, and end papers in design, without precedence. All copies examined have p. 15, line 21, *Niarara* for *Niagara*.

The book reappeared with Harpers' imprint on title-page, dated 1890, and is probably the *Travel Sketches* listed in the *Cumulative Book Index* (1902), since no book of hers by this title has been found elsewhere recorded.

This was Mrs. Wallace's first book. She had already chosen its name when she wrote her son from Constantinople on November 7, 1881, about her undertaking: "... I have collected material for a long series of letters from the Mediterranean countries and shall gather in the rough much more as I journey along ... It is such a long and painstaking work I hesitate to plunge in, still I do not want to be idle and unless I busy myself I am homesick and miserable."* Two other books grew out of her travels in Europe, Asia, and Africa in company with her husband, then Minister to Turkey: *The Repose in Egypt* (1888) and *Along the Bosphorus* (1898).

CONTENTS: All but the "Postscript" earlier published as a series in *The Independent*:

CHAPTER

I   On the Sea   *The Independent*, May 11, 1882 (with title: The Storied Sea)

II The Man of Destiny [Napoleon]   *The Independent*, May 25, 1882

III Among the Brigands   *The Independent*, July 27, 1882 (with title: The Storied Sea)

---

*Letter in the Wallace Papers.

IV In and about Tunis *The Independent*, August 10, 1882
    (with title: The Storied Sea)
V   A Day in Carthage *The Independent*, August 24, 1882
VI About the Arabs *The Independent*, September 7, 1882
VII Doing a Little Shopping *The Independent*, September 14, 1882
VIII, IX, X The Light of the Harem (in three parts; Part II
    contains "Gazzel; or, Love Song," translated from the
    Arabic) *The Independent*, September 21, 28, and October 5, 1882
XI Byron *The Independent*, November 2, 1882
XII Classic Funerals *The Independent*, November 16, 1882
XIII, XIV The American Girl: An Interlude (in two parts)
    The Independent, November 30, and December 14, 1882
XV Something About Homer *The Independent*, March 1, 1883
XVI, XVII About Smyrna (in two parts) *The Independent*, December 21, 1882, and January 4, 1883
XVIII Postscript

1887

(Published 1886)

Ginèvra

GINÈVRA | OR | THE OLD OAK CHEST | A CHRISTMAS STORY | BY |
SUSAN E. WALLACE | WITH ILLUSTRATIONS BY | GENERAL LEW WAL-
LACE | [*ornamental rule*] | NEW YORK | WORTHINGTON CO., 747
BROADWAY | 1887

COLLATION: [1–2]⁸, one cancel leaf, [3]⁶, [4]⁸. White plate paper.
Leaf measures 8⅜″ x 6¾″, all edges trimmed.

End paper; frontispiece, inserted; title-page, p. [1]; copyright notice
dated 1886, p. [2]; dedication to *My Beloved Nieces* ..., dated Christmas, 1886, p. [3]; blank, p. [4]; introduction, p. [5]; blank, p. [6]; text,
pp. [7]–46 (pp. 33–34 on cancel leaf); divisional half-title, p. [47];
blank, p. [48]; poem: *The Mistletoe Bough*, pp. [49]–51; blank, p.
[52]; divisional half-title, p. [53]; portrait of Samuel Rogers, p. [54];

poem by Samuel Rogers, pp. [55]–60; vignette, p. [61]; blank, p. [62]; end paper.

[Note: For text, see *Notes*.]

ILLUSTRATIONS: Frontispiece inserted, as are plates facing pp. 8, [18],* [24], 38, [42], and [44]; all by Lew Wallace. The introduction, four chapters, and conclusion all bear illuminated initial and tailpiece by Lew Wallace. The portrait of Samuel Rogers, p. [54], and vignette, p. [61], are an integral part of the book; these are not by Wallace.

BINDING: Pictorial colored boards. Front cover elaborately colored and decorated on gilt background, title and other lettering printed over, at the side of and below a picture of a young girl: GINEVRA | A CHRIST-MAS STORY | BY | SUSAN E. WALLACE | ILLUSTRATED [*printed vertically*] | BY | GEN. LEW. WALLACE | WORTHINGTON CO. 747 BROADWAY N. Y.† Spine has decorations continued from front cover. Back cover bears a continuation of the decorations and an illustration.

PUBLICATION DATA: Copyrighted September 29, 1886. It had been advertised in *The Publishers' Weekly*, July 10, 1886. Earliest review noted: *The Critic*, December 4, 1886. Price, $1.25.

NOTES: The main portion of the book, Susan Wallace's prose version of an old Italian legend given an English setting, is followed by Thomas Bayly's poem, "The Mistletoe Bough" (although no author's name is signed to it), and Samuel Rogers' "Ginevra." She drew on both poems for her Christmas story and added romantic episodes; included, too, a poem, "Prince Edward's Song," p. 22, beginning, "In blinding snow, as wild winds blow," perhaps not hers.

The Wallace content, "Ginevra; or, The Old Oak Chest," was published before the book in *The Independent*, December 18, 1884.

1888

The Land of the Pueblos

THE LAND OF THE | PUEBLOS. | BY | SUSAN E. WALLACE. | Author of "The Storied Sea," "Ginevra," etc. | [*rule*] | WITH ILLUSTRATIONS. | [*rule*] | NEW YORK: | JOHN B. ALDEN, PUBLISHER. | 1888.

---

*Facing p. 20 in the Indiana State Library copy.
†Imprint faint; no comma visible before or after street address.

Susan E. Wallace's six books

COLLATION: [1]–12 [13–14]–[16]–18⁸ (all signed signatures have numeral on recto of second leaf). White laid paper. Leaf measures 7⁵⁄₁₆″ x 4⅞″, all edges trimmed.

End paper; binder's leaf; frontispiece with tissue guard, inserted; title-page, p. [i]; copyright notice in name of the Provident Book Co. dated 1888, p. [ii]; blank, p. [1]; table of contents, p. [2]; list of illustrations, p. [3]; blank, p. [4]; *Introduction*, dated March, 1888, pp. 5–6; text, pp. 7–285; blank, p. [286]; binder's leaf; end paper.

[Note: For text, pp. 7–285, see *Contents*.]

ILLUSTRATIONS: Frontispiece with tissue guard, inserted as are plates facing pp. 14, 44, 46, 130, 132, 154, 200, 234, 238, 244, and 246. The frontispiece and plate facing p. 14 are from sketches by General Lew Wallace.

BINDING: Olive-green, blue-green, brown, and, mustard-colored mesh cloth. Front cover bears an illustration of a Mexican scene with title and author's name gilt-stamped: THE | LAND [L *ornamented*] OF THE [*article slightly lowered, not aligned*] | PUEBLOS | SUSAN E. WAL-LACE   Spine black-stamped: [*triple wave rule*] | [*ornamental design*] | [*double wave rule*] | [*the following gilt-stamped:*] [*four dots*] | The | LAND OF | The | PUEBLOS | [*ornamental rule*] | WALLACE | [*ornament*] ALDEN [*ornament*] | [*black-stamped double wave rule*]. Back cover blank.

End papers same as book stock. Binder's leaf front and back, conjugates pasted under lining papers.

PUBLICATION DATA: Deposited in the Copyright Office, June 20, 1888. Earliest review noted: *Avalanche* (Memphis, Tenn.), June 29, 1888. An extract from the book appeared in *Literature*, June 2, 1888, so copies may have been ready early in the month. Price, 75 cents.

NOTES: First edition as collated. No priority in color of binding.

Reprinted by John A. Berry & Co., 1888, with copyright in name of Susan E. Wallace. Nims & Knight issued an 1889 edition. Alden reissued it with date 1890 on title-page. George D. Hurst published a reprint in 1895 as No. 3 in *The Ambrosial Library*.

Mrs. Wallace joined her husband in New Mexico at the end of January, 1879, and stayed until October of that year, sharing for a short time his life as Governor of that territory; part of a letter to one of her sisters describing their adventures is printed in Irving McKee, *"Ben-Hur" Wallace: The Life of General Lew Wallace* (1947), p. 153, in a chapter which contains many references to Susan Wallace.

A letter from her to her son, Henry L. Wallace, May 11, 1879, from Fort Stanton, describes her impressions of life in New Mexico and quotes the threats of "Billy the Kid" (letter published in *Lew Wallace: An Autobiography*, Vol. II [1906], p. 920).

Her book, *The Land of the Pueblos*, is full of history and description of the region, but does not deal with contemporary politics.

CONTENTS: A series of letters written from Sante Fe, earlier published in *The Independent*, *The Atlantic Monthly*, *The New York Tribune*,* and several "in a certain magazine which died young," so stated in the introduction.†

CHAPTER

I   The Journey   *The Independent*, January 22, 1880 (with title: To the Land of the Pueblos)

II   Historic   *The Atlantic Monthly*, August, 1880 (with title: Among the Pueblos); *The Denver News*, July, 1880 (part only)‡

III   Laws and Customs   *Good Company*, May, 1881 (with title: Among the Pueblos)

IV   The City of the Pueblos   *The Independent*, February 26, 1880§

V   Mexican Cottages   *The Independent*, March 4, 1880 (with title: The City of the Pueblos)

VI, VII, VIII, IX   To the Turquois [*sic*] Mines [(*Continued*) present, within parentheses, on pp. 93 and 101; word, continued, not present on p. 80 although indicated in table of contents] *The Independent*, July 1, 8, 22, and 29, 1880

X   Among the Archives—Things New and Old   *The Independent*, January 6, 1881 ‖

XI   Among the Archives—A Love Letter   *The Independent*, February 10, 1881

---

*Whitelaw Reid wrote to Lew Wallace September 25, 1878: "Why don't you try your hand at occasional letters for us yourself? There will be no trouble about concealing the authorship—if you thought that important—and I fancy before you have been there very long you will want some method of amusement." —Letter in Wallace Papers. There is no record that he accepted the invitation, but the acknowledgment indicates that his wife did.

†The "certain magazine which died young," probably *Good Company*.

‡Lew Wallace, in a letter to his wife, July 29, 1880, commented on the fact that the "opening paragraphs" were copied in *The Denver News*; letter in Wallace Papers, Indiana Historical Society.

§Another article with the same title, in *The Independent*, February 12, 1880, was not included in this book.

‖An article with the same title, in *The Independent*, January 20, 1881, was not included in this book.

XII, XIII,* XIV Among the Archives (Continued) [lower case c and no parentheses in table of contents] *The Independent,* February 24, March 17, and April 7, 1881

XV The Jornada Del Muerto *The Independent,* January 27, 1881

XVI Something about the Apache *The Independent,* June 11 and 18, 1885 (with title in latter: Victorio, the Apache Chief)

XVII Old Miners *The Independent,* May 26, 1881 (with title: The Miners)†

XVIII The New Miners *The Independent,* June 30, 1881 (with title: The Land of the Pueblos)

XIX The Honest Miner *The Independent,* July 21, 1881 (with title: Among the Archives—Things New and Old)

XX The Assayers *The Independent,* August 4, 1881

XXI The Ruby Silver Mine—A True Story *The Independent,* September 8, 1881

XXII The Ruby Silver Mine—Continued [lower case c in table of contents] *The Independent,* September 15, 1881

XXIII Mine Experience *Good Company,* January, 1881

XXIV The Ruins of Montezuma's Palace

XXV To the Casas Grandes

XXVI A Frontier Idyl‡

XXVII The Pimos *Good Company,* June, 1881

---

*Most of Chapter XIII appeared later in *Literature,* June 2, 1888, with title, "Religion of the Pueblos."

†In her description of the Mexican miner, pp. 166–167, the author quotes from Lew Wallace's article, "The Mines of Santa Eulalia," in *Harper's New Monthly Magazine,* November, 1867, p. 698.

‡The three chapters XXIV–XXVI may have been the portion published in *The New York Tribune,* between 1879 and 1888, but not yet located therein.

1888

The Repose in Egypt

THE | REPOSE IN EGYPT | A MEDLEY | BY | SUSAN E. WALLACE | AU-
THOR OF "THE LAND OF THE PUEBLOS," "THE STORIED SEA," | "GIN-
EVRA," ETC. | [*rule*] | WITH ILLUSTRATIONS | [*rule*] | NEW YORK |
JOHN B. ALDEN, PUBLISHER | 1888

COLLATION: [1–12]¹⁶ (plus one unsigned leaf in first signature; signatures numbered 2–24 on recto of 1st and 9th leaf as for gathering in
8's), [13]⁴ (numbered 25). White wove paper. Leaf measures 7⅚₆″
x 4⅞″ (full), top edge gilt, other edges trimmed.

End paper; binder's leaf; frontispiece with tissue guard, inserted;
title-page, p. [1]; copyright notice dated 1888, p. [2]; dedication: *To* |
The two dear friends with whom I learned that | *travel is the saddest of*
pleasures. | *S. E. W.* | *Crawfordsville, Ind* | *October, 1888.,* p. [3];
blank, p. [4]; table of contents, pp. [5–6]; list of illustrations, verso
blank, inserted*; *Preface,* p. [7]; blank, p. [8]; text, pp. 9–259; blank,
p. [260]; divisional half-title, p. [261]; blank, p. [262]; text, pp. 263–
391; blank, p. [392]; binder's leaf; end paper.

[Note: For text, pp. 9–391, see *Contents*.]

ILLUSTRATIONS: Frontispiece with tissue guard, inserted as are
plates facing pp. 32, 38, 52, 60, 64, 68, 76, 80, 96, 110, 168, 176, 178,
180, 196, and 206.

BINDING: Dark green, and, pumpkin-colored mesh cloth. Front
cover gilt-stamped: THE REPOSE IN EGYPT | [*rule*]. Spine gilt-stamped:
THE | REPOSE | IN | EGYPT | [*rule*] | WALLACE | ALDEN Back cover
blank.

End papers white wove; binder's leaf front and back, conjugates
pasted under lining papers.

PUBLICATION DATA: Deposited in the Copyright Office November 23, 1888. Earliest review noted: *The* (New York) *Sun,* November 18, 1888. Price, $1.00.

NOTES: First edition as collated. Title-page, *With Illustrations,* has

---

*List present in earliest inscribed copies, one, "Thanksgiving, 1888," in pos-
session of Lew Wallace, III; another, "Christmas, 1888," in Eagle Crest Library.

broken capital *h* in *With* in all copies; copyright page has poor type also. Some copies lack list of illustrations.

Nims & Knight published an edition in 1889. Alden reissued it in 1891. Two Hurst reprints have been noted, besides their issue which was No. 4 of *The Ambrosial Library*, 1895: one with imprint of George D. Hurst on spine; the other with imprint of Hurst & Co. on spine; both undated.

CONTENTS: In the preface the author makes acknowledgment to "the father of the nameless magazine which died young . . .,* the respective editors of *The Independent, Advance, Congregationalist, Youth's Companion, Christian Advocate,* Bacheller Syndicate, *Frank Leslie's Magazine,* and *Sunday-School Times."*

CHAPTER
I   The Burden of Egypt
II   The Landing
III   Suez and Sinai   *Advance,* January 14, 1886 (with title: Egypt and Sinai)
IV   Crossing the Red Sea   *Advance,* March 4, 1886
V   Alexandria
VI   Obelisks [in two separated parts, both captioned, *VI;* first relates to Alexandria, second to Constantinople] *The Independent,* January 28, 1886 (part with title: Alexandria Obelisks, under caption: About Egypt), and February 4, 1886 (part, with title: The Obelisks of Alexandria)
VII   Cleopatra
VIII   To Cairo   *Advance,* August 5, 1886 (with title: About Egypt)
IX   The Rise of the Nile
X   At Heliopolis   *The Christian Advocate,* August 9 and 16, 1888
XI   The Flight into Egypt   *The Independent,* December 17 and 24, 1885
XII   The Return of the Holy Carpet   *The Christian Advocate,* March 17 and 24, 1887 (with title: Cairo; the Return of the Holy Carpet)
XIII   The Pilgrimage to Mecca
XIV   Mecca, the Sacred City   *The Indianapolis Journal,* July 31, 1887 (with title: The Sacred City of Mecca)

---

*The "nameless magazine" remains in obscurity, with its "father" not yet identified.

XV   Pilgrimage   *The Congregationalist,* April 21, 1887 (with
      title: A Pilgrimage to Mecca)
XVI   The Repose
XVII Poetry and Music of the Arabs   *Literature,* April 7 and
      14, 1888
XVIII The First Cinderella: A Tale of the Red Pyramid   *Frank
      Leslie's Popular Monthly,* August, 1887
XIX   In the Isle of the Lily: The Story of the Three Kings [run-
      ning title: The Story of the Three Kings]
XX   In the Isle of the Lily: Thalia's Story [running title:
      Thalia's Story]
XXI   Still in the Isle of the Lily: The Antiquary's Story [run-
      ning title: The Antiquary's Story]
XXII Conclusion
Along the Bosphorus [with divisional half-title]*
   Two Voyages up the Bosphorus
      I   The First Voyage: [comma in place of colon in table of
          contents] 1390 B. C. *The Independent,* April 17 and
          May 8, 1884 (with title: Sailing up the Bosphorus:
          Voyage First—Before Christ, 1390)
      II The Second Voyage, A. D. [comma after D. in table of
          contents] 1884   *The Independent,* June 12 and July 3,
          1884 (with title: Voyage Second—After Christ, 1884)
   One Woman: A True Romance [Chapter III in table of con-
      tents]   *The Independent,* August 20, 27, September 3, 10,
      and 17, 1885†
   In the Harem [Chapter IV in table of contents]
   Wedding Customs in the East [Chapter V in table of contents]
      Sunday School Times, March 17, 1888
   At Yildiz Palace [Chapter VI in table of contents]

---

*See *Along the Bosphorus* (1898), Chapter I, for travel sketches with same
title, differing in content.

†The identity of "one woman" is hidden by the author under the name, "Lady
Ellen," but Mrs. Burton in *The Independent,* September 24, 1885, p. 17, iden-
tifies her as Lady Ellenborough.

1898

Along the Bosphorus

ALONG THE BOSPHORUS | AND OTHER SKETCHES | BY | SUSAN E. WAL-
LACE | (MRS. LEW WALLACE), | AUTHOR OF "GINERVA [*sic*], OR THE
OLD OAK CHEST," "THE STORIED | SEA" "THE LAND OF THE PUEB-
LOS," "THE | REPOSE IN EGYPT." | [*publishers' emblem*] | CHICAGO
AND NEW YORK | RAND, MCNALLY & CO., PUBLISHERS, | 1898.

COLLATION: [1]–24⁸ (plus one unsigned leaf in first signature),
25⁴. White laid paper. Leaf measures 7⅝″ x 5⁵⁄₁₆″, top edge gilt, other
edges untrimmed.

End paper; fly title, p. [i]; blank, p. [ii]; frontispiece with tissue
guard, inserted; title-page, p. [iii]; copyright notice dated 1898, p. [iv];
table of contents, p. [v]; blank, p. [vi]; *Introductory* dated July 24,
1881, pp. [1]–4; acknowledgements, on inserted leaf, with verso blank;
text, pp. 5–383 (with conjugate of pp. 7–8 pasted under lining paper);
blank, p. [384]; end paper.

[Note: For text, pp. 5–383, see *Contents*.]

ILLUSTRATIONS: Frontispiece in sepia with tissue guard printed in
red, inserted as are illustrations with tissue guards printed in red facing
pp. 6, 9, 16, 28, 36, 48, 54, 60, 66, 82, 91, 119, 122, [128], [238], 256,
280, 296, 311, 322, 334, 350, and 383.

BINDING: Light blue, silk-finished mesh cloth. Front cover gilt-
stamped: ALONG THE BOSPHORUS [*dot in each* O] | [*scene along the
Bosphorus, with gilt crescent, stamped in gilt, green, and red; within
which is gilt-stamped:*] SUSAN | [*crescent-like ornament*] E [*crescent-
like ornament*] | WALLACE [*crescent-like ornament*]. Spine gilt-
stamped: ALONG THE | BOSPHORUS | [*oriental scene stamped in gilt,
green, and red, intercepted by author's name:*] WALLACE | [*at foot:*]
RAND, | MCNALLY & CO. Back cover bears a green-stamped oriental scene,
and, at lower left, a floral design stamped in red, green, and gilt.

End papers similar to, slightly heavier than book stock; no binder's
leaf front or back.

PUBLICATION DATA: Deposited in the Copyright Office October 31,
1898. Listed in *The Publishers' Weekly*, November 19, 1898. Price,
$1.50.

NOTES: First edition as collated. The sheets appeared in a later binding of blue coarse mesh cloth with white stamping in place of gilt, imprint on spine occupying 3 lines (earlier, 2 lines), and back cover blank; leaf trimmed to 7⅜″ x 4⅞″ (earlier, 7⁹⁄₁₆″ [full] x 5¼″), top edge ungilded.

A British edition published by Unwin is listed as appearing August, 1898.

Two chapters in this book are not Susan Wallace's (see *Contents*).

An earlier work, *The Repose in Egypt* (1888), included a section, "Along the Bosphorus," but the stories are not the same in the two books.

CONTENTS: The author makes acknowledgments as follows: "My thanks are with the Messrs. Harper, through whose courtesy I am allowed to reprint The Tower of Many Stories. Also, I acknowledge my debt to The Independent and to the respective editors of the Sunday School Times, Frank Leslie's Magazine, Youth's Companion, Bacheller Syndicate, McClure Syndicate, Bok Syndicate, and The Arena, for permission to gather together these scattered Autumn leaves."

Chapter III, "A Trip to Hebron," is not by Mrs. Wallace, but by Mrs. Henry S. Lane. Chapter XI, about the Sistine Madonna, entitled, "Letter from Dresden" and dated December, 1884, is Lew Wallace's though unsigned.*

CHAPTER

I　Along the Bosphorus

The Mohammedan Sunday　*The Indianapolis Journal*, April 27, 1890 (part, with title: A Peep at Turkish Royalty); *The Indianapolis Journal*, June 15, 1890 (part, with title: Summer on the Bosphorus)

Feast of Bairam

Buying a Dog

Under the Cypresses　*The* (?) *Sunday Herald* (end of March, 1888?; with title: Oriental Cemeteries)†

Seraglio Point

Throne Room

Imperial Treasury

---

*See McKee, p. 214: "At Dresden he [Lew Wallace] painstakingly compared Raphael's 'Madonna' with Murillo's." Mrs. Wallace was not in Dresden at this time.

†A clipping in the Wallace Papers states, "Written for The Sunday Herald"; possibly the article copyrighted March 29, 1888, under the title, "Large Turkish Cemeteries," by the New York Syndicate Bureau. Mrs. Wallace wrote an earlier article on a similar subject, "In a Turkish Cemetery," *q.v.*

II Lepers and Leprosy [*Leprousy* in table of contents] in the East *Sunday School Times,* January 5, 1889

IV* Gypsies I Have Seen

V Housekeeping in Turkey

VI At Bethlehem†

VII In the Tower of Many Stories
The Little Princes
Sir Walter Raleigh *The Independent,* August 2, 1883 (part, with title: Two Days in Westminster Abbey); *Harper's Round Table,* December 24, 1895
Lady Arabella Stuart
The Earl of Essex and His Ring *Harper's Round Table,* July 7, 1896
Henry the Eighth *Harper's Round Table,* May 5 and 12, 1896
Last Letter of Anne Boleyn to Henry Eighth [this subtitle not in table of contents] *Harper's Round Table,* May 12, 1896
The Virgin Queen Imprisoned *Harper's Round Table,* May 12, 1896 (with title: Henry the Eighth)

VIII A Fair Client's Story‡ *Frank Leslie's Popular Monthly,* February, 1886

IX William Wetmore Story [with subtitles not in table of contents:]
A Memory *The Cosmopolitan,* September, 1896
Letter of Mrs. Story [Emelyn (Mrs. W. W. Story), to Mrs. Wallace] *The Cosmopolitan,* September, 1896
Letter of W. W. Story

X Among the Palace-Galleries of Florence—Madonnas—Raphael [co-titles omitted in table of contents where hyphen after *Palace* is also omitted]

XII§ A Reminiscence [of General William T. Sherman at West Point in 1890]

XIII About Books‖

---

*Chapter III is by Mrs. Henry S. Lane, hence omitted here.

†Later included in *The City of the King* (1903).

‡"Founded on a client's story told me about the year 1870 by John M. Butler," so written in copy presented by the author to Joanna M. Lane [Mrs. Henry S. Lane], November, 1898, in the Indiana State Library.

§Chapter XI is a quotation of Lew Wallace's letter, December, 1884, though his name does not appear; hence omitted here.

‖Chapter XIII is by Susan Wallace, but acknowledged as "From Edward Bok"; probably from the series of "Literary Leaves" syndicated by him *ca.* 1886–1891,

XIV   Florence Nightingale*
XV   Two Days in Westminster Abbey†
      Introductory
      Historic   *The Independent,* May 24, 1883 (with title:
      Two Days in Westminster Abbey, I)
      Andre and Mary, Queen of Scots [this subtitle brief in
      table of contents: *Andre*]   *The Independent,* June 21,
      1883 (part, with title: Two Days in Westminster Ab-
      bey, II)
      Mary, Queen of Scots [no comma in table of contents]
      The Independent, June 21, 1883 (part, with title: Two
      Days in Westminster Abbey, II)
      Queen Elizabeth   *The Independent,* July 5, 1883 (part,
      with title: Two Days in Westminster Abbey, III)
      Catharine De Valois   *The Independent,* July 5, 1883
      (part, with title: Two Days in Westminster Abbey, III)
      Anne Boleyn   *The Independent,* August 2, 1883 (with
      title: Two Days in Westminster Abbey)
      The Chair of State   *The Independent,* September 20
      and 27, 1883 (with title in both: Two Days in West-
      minster Abbey)
      Poets' Corner   *The Independent,* October 4 and 18, 1883
      (with title in both: Two Days in Westminster Abbey)
XVI   The Chain of the Last Slave of Maryland   *The Arena,* Au-
      gust, 1892 (with title: The Chain of the Last Slave. An
      Incident of the War of the Rebellion)‡

---

and subscribed to by *The Philadelphia Times,* among other newspapers. The
chapter was reprinted in *The Crawfordsville Journal,* October 1, 1912: "Mrs.
Lew Wallace Discusses Her Favorite Book, 'Pilgrim's Progress.'"

*This sketch of Florence Nightingale by Susan Wallace was reprinted in *The
Indianapolis Star,* August 17, 1910.

†The author wrote a cousin on October 9, 1881 (letter in Wallace Papers) that
she had just forwarded "a very careful description of Westminster Abbey" to
Good Company. That magazine ceased publication with the issue of September,
1881.

‡Lossing's *Pictorial History of the Civil War in the United States of America,*
Vol. 3 (1868), p. 346n, carries a summary of the part that General Wallace
played in the final abolishment of slavery in Maryland, by removing the chains
of Margaret Toogood.

1903

The City of the King

The City of the King [blue] | What the Child Jesus | Saw and Heard | By Mrs. Lew Wallace | Author of | The Storied Sea, The Land of the Pueblos | The Repose in Egypt, Along the Bosphorus | With Illustrations | Indianapolis | The Bobbs-Merrill Company | Publishers

COLLATION: [1-6]⁸ (plus one unsigned leaf in first signature). White laid paper. Leaf measures 9⁵⁄₁₆″ x 6″, top edge gilt,* other edges untrimmed.

End paper; fly title, p. [1]; blank, p. [2]; frontispiece with tissue guard, inserted; title-page inserted, but figured in the pagination as p. [3]; copyright notice dated 1903, *October*, acknowledgements to Rand, McNally & Company, the *New York Journal,* and the *Ladies' Home Journal,* and imprint of Braunworth & Co., Brooklyn, N. Y., p. [4]; dedication, *To All Them That Love | His Appearing,* p. [5]; blank, p. [6]; half-title with quotation, p. [7]; blank, p. [8]; text, pp. 9–34; divisional half-title with quotations, p. [35]; blank, p. [36]; text, pp. 37–85; blank, p. [86]; divisional half-title with quotation from Phillips Brooks, p. [87]; blank, p. [88]; text, pp. 89–97; blank, p. [98]; end paper.

[Note: For text, pp. 9–97, see *Contents.*]

ILLUSTRATIONS: Frontispiece with tissue guard, inserted as are plates facing pp. 10, 20, 28, 38, 46, 56, 60, 70, 76, 84, and 92; all are from photographs of the Holy Land, in dark sepia.

BINDING: Gray coarse mesh cloth. Front cover gilt-stamped: a star's descending rays intercepted by the title and author's name: THE CITY OF THE KING [red-stamped, gilt-outlined] | MRS. LEW WALLACE Spine gilt-stamped: THE | CITY | OF | THE | KING | [radiant star] | WALLACE | BOBBS | MERRILL Back cover blank.

End papers same as book stock; no binder's leaf front or back.

PUBLICATION DATA: Deposited in the Copyright Office October 19, 1903. Earliest review noted: *Bookseller, Newsdealer & Stationer* (New York), November 15, 1903. Price, $1.00.

---

*The copyright deposit copy lacks gilding.

NOTES: First edition bears statement, *October,* on copyright page.

CONTENTS: The last of the three stories in the book, "At Bethlehem" had appeared in *Along the Bosphorus* (1898), hence acknowledgment to Rand, McNally & Co.; the others are first collected here:

What the Child Jesus Saw and Heard* *The New York Journal,* April 7, 1901

Jerusalem as It Now Is *The Ladies' Home Journal,* December, 1900 (with title: Jerusalem as We See It Today)

---

*A sheet of advertising copy sent to the literary editors of newspapers on March 28, 1904, contains an extract from the essay, pp. 33–34, captioned: "Why We Color Eggs at Easter."

First Editions—Contributions

~~~~~~

1860

THE POETS AND POETRY OF THE WEST: WITH BIOGRAPHICAL AND CRITICAL NOTICES. By William T. Coggeshall. Columbus, [O.], Follett, Foster & Co., 1860

Contains two poems: "The Patter of Little Feet," p. 614, and "The Singing Tree," p. 615; both were early published anonymously in the *Cincinnati Daily Gazette,* April 17th and September 20, 1858. "The Patter of Little Feet" appeared also in *Harper's New Monthly Magazine,* February, 1859, in column, "Editor's Drawer." It had later publication in anthologies: *Poets and Poetry of Indiana,* compiled and edited by Benj. S. Parker & Enos B. Heiney (1900), and in *Laurel Leaves for Little Folks,* edited by Mary E. Phillips (1903).

In this book Susan E. Wallace's name is given as Sarah E. Wallace. The biographical notice is very brief.

1864

SOLDIERS' AND SAILORS' PATRIOTIC SONGS. New York, Loyal Publication Society, 1864

Gray wrappers. Publication No. 49. Contains "Banner-Song of the Indiana Eleventh," p. 11 (without music; to be sung to the air of "Flag of Our Union").

1896

A NOVEMBER LEAF. [Indianapolis, Indianapolis Flower Mission], 1896

White pictorial wrappers. Contains a brief essay, "Women in the Orient," p. [9].

1899

WHO'S WHO IN AMERICA (1899–1900). Chicago, A. N. Marquis & Co. [1899]

Contains an autobiographical sketch of Susan Wallace, p. 762. It appeared in succeeding volumes, with slight additions, through Volume IV, 1906–1907.

1900

POETS AND POETRY OF INDIANA . . . 1800 TO 1900. Compiled & edited by Benjamin S. Parker & Enos B. Heiney. New York, Boston & Chicago, Silver, Burdett & Co. [1900]

Earliest state measures $1\frac{1}{4}''$ across sheets (later, $1\frac{1}{8}''$). Earliest binding has two-color stamping on front cover and spine, and blind-stamped publishers' emblem on back cover; a later binding state has the two-color stamping, but back cover is blank; still later, one color (green) stamping on front cover and spine, back cover blank.

Contains "My Song," p. 233, earlier in *The Independent*, (date?) and in *The Crawfordsville Journal*, January 13, 1870. "The Patter of Little Feet," p. 9, had previous publication in an anthology (see *ante* 437).

The paragraph about her on p. 462 is very brief and contains no part of the biographical sketch which Lew Wallace had written *ca.* 1874, and which, apparently, the Wallaces submitted to Parker, together with copies of her poems and a newspaper account of her, when this anthology was in preparation.*

---

*From Jethro W. Parker, son of Benjamin S. Parker, the Indiana State Library secured a photostat copy of the 4–page Lew Wallace holograph biography of Susan, also of Parker's notes indicating that it needed to be abbreviated and brought up to date. McKee quotes a single sentence from the Wallace manuscript, p. 128.

1906

LEW WALLACE: AN AUTOBIOGRAPHY. 2 volumes. New York & London, Harper & Bros., MCMVI

Brought to publication by Susan E. Wallace after the death of Lew Wallace. She gives credit for the editorial work in Vol. II, Part II, pp. 799–[1003], to Mary H. Krout. Her acknowledgment to Miss Krout appears on p. 796 of Vol. II, her initials, *S.E.W.*, at the end of the final page of text.

A letter from Mrs. Wallace to her son, Henry, and others to unnamed persons appear in Vol. II, pp. 912, 913, 920; they relate to the New Mexican period.

One verse, 8 lines, from "A Song of Songs," written for Lew Wallace, is printed in Vol. I, p. 212. The song, "Three Dreams," p. 210, is probably not hers; a manuscript copy is in the Wallace Papers, but unsigned.

1910?

CHILD-LIFE ABROAD. THE LIBRARY SERIES FOR YOUNG PEOPLE AND THEIR LEADERS. W.C. T. U. [1910?]

Wrappers. Said to consist of sketches by Susan Wallace, Mary C. Ninde, Sho Nemoto. Unlocated.

1939

ALL IN THE DAY'S WORK: AN AUTOBIOGRAPHY. By Ida M. Tarbell. New York, Macmillan, 1939

Contains a letter, p. 71, from Susan E. Wallace to Harpers, November 24, 1884, in which she requests a change in the dedication of *Ben-Hur* (see *ante* 317). The transcript is from the letter laid in a copy of *Ben-Hur*, in the possession of Marjorie Wiggin Prescott in 1939.

1947

"BEN-HUR" WALLACE: THE LIFE OF GENERAL LEW WALLACE. By Irving McKee. Berkeley & Los Angeles, University of California Press, 1947

Contains letters from Mrs. Lew Wallace to her family, pp. 152, 153, relating to "Billy the Kid" and other New Mexican experiences. Other letters appear on pp. 191, 193, 229: to Joanna Lane, July 3, 1881; to Henry Wallace, July 31, 1881; to Mrs. Edwin A. Grosvenor, May, 1885, and June, 1888. Excerpts from other letters are too brief to require mention here. The book is full of biographical data on Susan Wallace.

Periodicals Containing First Appearances

ADVANCE
    1886: January   14   Egypt and Sinai
           March   4   Crossing the Red Sea
           August   5   About Egypt

THE ARENA
    1892: August   The Chain of the Last Slave. An Incident of
                        the War of the Rebellion

THE ATLANTIC MONTHLY
    1879: June   Archery [poem]*
    1880: August   Among the Pueblos

THE CHRISTIAN ADVOCATE
    1887: March   17, 24   Cairo, the Return of the Holy Carpet
    1888: August   9, 16   At Heliopolis

CINCINNATI DAILY GAZETTE
    1858: April   17   The Patter of Little Feet [poem, unsigned]*
           September 20   The Singing Tree [poem, unsigned]*
    1859: June   14   Sitting in Sunshine [poem, signed *Ellen
                        Paige]*

THE CONGREGATIONALIST
    1887: April   21   A Pilgrimage to Mecca

THE COSMOPOLITAN
    1896: September   William Wetmore Story

THE CRAWFORDSVILLE JOURNAL
    1868: December 24   Christmas Song for Children [poem]†
    1870: January   13   My Song [poem]*
    1871: December 14   What Parepa Sang [poem]*
    1878:‡ May   18   The Angel of the House*
    1879: May   31   Archery [poem]*
    1881: February 26   Prescience [poem]*

---

*Uncollected.

†Uncollected; reprinted in *The Independent*, December 8, 1881, and in later newspapers with title, "A Leaf from the Christmas Tree."

‡Between 1871 and 1875 this *Journal* may have contained contributions by Mrs. Wallace; unfortunately there is a gap in the file in the Crawfordsville Recorder's Office.

THE CRAWFORDSVILLE JOURNAL—*continued*

1883: April   21   [Woman's place]*
1886: November 27   Souvenir [cross] to Be Sold [for benefit of the
                        Methodist church]†
1887: February 23   Letter to the Editor [about Lew Wallace's
                        mother]†

THE DAWN (Indianapolis High School No. 1)

1893: December   7   Under the Ice and Snow. A Love Song
                        [poem]‡

GOOD COMPANY

1881: May   Among the Pueblos
      June   The Pimos: The Land of the Pueblos

HARPER'S [MONTHLY] MAGAZINE

1859: February   The Patter of Little Feet [poem unsigned]§
1867: November   Another Weak-minded Woman: A Confes-
                        sion‖

HARPER'S ROUND TABLE

1895: December 24   Sir Walter Raleigh [captioned:] In the Tower
                        of Many Stories
1896: May   5, 12   Henry The Eighth [captioned:] In the
                        Tower of Many Stories
      July   7   The Earl of Essex and His Ring [captioned:]
                        In the Tower of Many Stories

THE INDEPENDENT

1880: January   22   To the Land of the Pueblos
      February   5   The Palace of the Pueblos†
                 12,† 26,
      March   4   The City of the Pueblos
      July   1, 8, 22, 29   To the Turquoise Mines
1881: January   6, 20,† 27,
      February   10   The Land of the Pueblos
                 17   Prescience [poem]†
                 24,
      March   17,
      April   7,

---

*Uncollected; from *Harper's Magazine*, November, 1867, part of article, "An-
other Weak-minded Woman."
†Uncollected.
‡Uncollected; earlier in *The New York Tribune*, date unknown, and re-
printed in *The Crawfordsville Journal*, November 20, 1875, with title, "A Love
Song."
§Uncollected. This is a poem frequently reprinted and usually chosen for
mention in accounts of Susan Wallace.
‖Uncollected; reply to "A Weak-minded Woman," in issue of July, 1867,
p. 259.

THE INDEPENDENT—*continued*

1881: May   26,
      June   30,
      July   21,
      August   4,
      September 8, 15   The Land of the Pueblos
      December   8   A Leaf from the Christmas Tree [poem]*
1882: May   11, 25,
      July   27,
      August   10, 24,
      September 7, 14, 21, 28,
      October   5,
      November   2, 16, 30,
      December   14, 21,
1883: January   4   The Storied Sea
      March   1   Something about Homer
      May   24,
      June   21,
      July   5,
      August   2,
      September 20, 27,
      October   4, 18   Two Days in Westminster Abbey
1884: April   17,
      May   8   Sailing up the Bosphorus: Voyage First—Before Christ, 1390
      June   12,
      July   3   Sailing up the Bosphorus: Voyage Second—After Christ, 1884
      December   18   Ginevra; or, The Old Oak Chest
1885: June   11   Something about the Apache
                 18   Victorio, the Apache Chief
      August   20, 27,
      September 3, 10, 17   One Woman [Lady Ellenborough†]
      December   17, 24   The Flight into Egypt
1886: January   28   Alexandria Obelisks [under caption:] About Egypt
      February   4   The Obelisks of Alexandria
1890: July   1, 8, 22, 29   To the Turquoise Mines [under caption:] The Land of the Pueblos

THE INDIANAPOLIS JOURNAL
1861: June   18   The Indian Giver [poem]*

---

*Uncollected.
†Unnamed in Mrs. Wallace's story, but identified and an account of her life given by Mrs. Burton in *The Independent*, September 24, 1885, p. 17.

THE INDIANAPOLIS JOURNAL—*continued*

1870: August	2	Letter from Niagara: A Day among the Turtle Doves*
1871: May	12, 30	On Writing for the Papers [letters, second headed No. Two]†
1873: May	31	*Supplement* The Wife of General [E. R. S.] Canby‡
1876: June	22	A Centennial Letter [from] Philadelphia, June 20th†
July	11	Centennial Correspondence [from Philadelphia, July 8th]†
1877: September	19	A Letter to Every Good Woman, September 17th§
1885: May	31	Miss [Mary H.] Krout's New Comedy [review of "A Man in the House"]†
1887: July	31	The Sacred City of Mecca
1890: April	27	A Peep at Turkish Royalty
June	15	Summer on the Bosphorus
1901: October	20	A Last Farewell and Tender Tribute [to Maurice Thompson] from an Old Friend†
1903: December	28	On the We-a Trail [review of the book by Caroline Brown (Caroline V. Krout)]†

THE INDIANAPOLIS STAR

1926: March	28	Letter to Rose Blair Marsh, May, 1895 [under caption:] Sincerity and Simplicity Marked Life of Susan Arnold Wallace†

THE JANESVILLE (Wisconsin) GAZETTE

1886: March	25	[Letter to Elizabeth P. H. Little, March 16, 1886, relating to *Ben-Hur*]‖

THE LADIES' HOME JOURNAL

1899: February	The Murder of the Modern Innocents [on modern education]¶

---

*Uncollected. Another letter of this period was published in *The Indianapolis Journal*, known from clippings in the Wallace Scrapbooks: "At West Point" (July, 1870 written in, but not found in July issues).

†Uncollected.

‡Uncollected; this is a tribute to General Canby, as well as to his wife; he had died on April 11th.

§Uncollected; reprinted under caption, "Communion Wine," in *The Crawfordsville Journal*, September 29, 1877.

‖Uncollected. She tells herein that "Geikie's Life of Christ was the reference book, after the Bible, in the writing of Ben-Hur."

¶Uncollected; later in *The New Haven Union*, April 20, 1899, with title,

The Ladies' Home Journal—*continued*
1900: December   Jerusalem as We See It Today

Frank Leslie's Popular Monthly
1886: February   A Fair Client's Story
1887: August   The First Cinderalla: A Tale of the Red Pyra-
                      mid

Literature, an Illustrated Weekly Magazine (New York)
1888: April   7, 14   Poetry and Music of the Arabs

The Locket
1874: (month?)   [Letter to the Editor, signed *W*, with subscrip-
                      tion to the periodical]*

The New Haven Union
1899: April   20   Is Slaying Thousands [on modern education]†

The (New York) Evening Post
1870: September 14   Letter from New York†

The New York Journal
1901: April   7   What the Child Jesus Saw and Heard

The Oskaloosa (Iowa) Times
1886: April   26   In a Turkish Cemetery‡

The Pioneer
(1871: August)   With a Wine Cup: To Mrs. Commodore
                      Worden [poem]§

Pittsburgh (Pennsylvania) Dispatch
1881: December 11   In Turkish Harems‖

"Is Slaying Thousands." Susan Wallace received a letter from Henry K. Sienkiewicz approving her article and she sent it to the editor of *The Indianapolis
Journal* where it was printed with no mention of her name, but introduced by
the statement (hers?): "Now that schools are opening there comes a message
across the seas from the author of 'Quo Vadis.'" The clippings in the Wallace
Papers bear no date; show that the Sienkiewicz letter was widely copied. For an-
other response to her article see the Rochester (New York) *Post Express, post*
446.
*Uncollected. A clipping, lacking date other than year, is in the Wallace Scrap-
books.
†Uncollected.
‡Uncollected. Was this revised for an article copyrighted by the New York
Syndicate Bureau, March 29, 1888: "Large Turkish Cemeteries"?
§Uncollected; clipping bears printed identification, "For the Pioneer," and
"August, 1871" is written in; preserved in the Wallace Papers. Later, the same
poem was revised to accompany a tin wedding gift to Mr. and Mrs. William
Breeden, from Santa Fe, June 11, 1879, and published without title in an un-
identified newspaper; of this, too, a clipping is present in a Wallace Scrapbook.
‖Uncollected; also in *The Galveston* (Texas) *News*, December 25 [1881?],

ROCHESTER (New York) POST-EXPRESS
1899: February (18?)   [Letter to the Editor, February 17th, thank-
                         ing Mrs. Caroline Mason for writing in ap-
                         proval of her "Murder of the Innocents"
                         article]*

SAXBY'S TRAVELER'S MAGAZINE
1905: May   [Announcement of death of Lew Wallace]†

STREET & SMITH'S NEW YORK WEEKLY
1869: April   1   The Silver Book [poem]*

SUNDAY SCHOOL TIMES
1888: March   17   Wedding Customs in the East
1889: January   5   Lepers and Leprosy in the East

THE WASHINGTON (D. C.) CHRONICLE
1867: January   20   To Zayde Bancroft—With a Shell [poem]*

THE YOUTH'S COMPANION
1882: November 23   Indian Archery*

Unidentified Periodical Contributions
[Note: Clippings found in Krout and Wallace Papers; all uncol-
lected]:

Among Turkish Royalty   In *The Argus* (place? date?)
In the Tent [poem]. Written during the Civil War‡
[Letter to the Editor of the *Journal*, with her poem, signed *Santa
Claus*, Baltimore, 1864, under caption:] Santa Claus to Henry
Lane Wallace, with a Flag
My Song [poem]. Published in a magazine (*The Independent?*) as
well as in *The Crawfordsville Journal*, January 13, 1870
The Tomb of Mohammed.

[Note: The *Home Journal* an unlocated newspaper, contained her
poem, "A New Year's Gift," published January, 1868.]

"In the Turkish Harems"; not same as an article, "An Imperial Harem" "written
for the [Indianapolis?] Sunday Star," date unestablished.
*Uncollected.
†Uncollected. This statement was sent February 15, 1905, in the form of a
printed letter, to publishing houses, and probably to many newspapers and individuals. The copy in the Manuscript Collection of the New York Public Library,
originally sent to R. U. Johnson, of Century, bears no signature, but this magazine attributes the announcement to Mrs. Wallace.
‡See *The* (Indianapolis) *Saturday Herald*, August 2, 1879, for Maurice
Thompson's opinion of this poem, quoted from an interview in the *Cincinnati
Gazette*.

GENERAL INDEX

General Index

Abe Martin of Brown County, 143
About Egypt, 429
About "Tarns," 206n
About Smyrna, 423
About the Arabs, 423
About the Purple Grackle, 271
About Work, 57
Absurd Statesman with a Literal Mind, The, 280
Acadian Conspiracy, An, 278
Accuracy, 169
Acrobat in Politics, The, 280
Actaeon, 160
Ad Cynthiam Retrospiciens, 280
Adams, Oscar Fay, 191n, 241
Address [by an ex-Confederate soldier], An, 207
Address by Meredith Nicholson at Manual Training High School, 134–135
Address of Gen. Lew Wallace at the Dedication of Indiana's Monuments, on the Battlefield of Shiloh, 363
Address to the Cadets, 406
Ade, George, 47n, 147
Advance, 68, 441
Adventures with Editors, 252
Aeode, 192
After Breakfast Chat, 66
After-Dinner Speeches, 144
After Gray Rabbits, 257
After-Thought, An, 262
After Work, 62
Aftermath, 155
Afternoon, 275
Afterthought, An, 406n
Again "The Sapphic Secret," 255n, 261
Aideen, 94
Aiken, Conrad, 192n
Aileen, 94
Albuquerque Review, 358
Alden, Henry Mills, 218n
Aldrich, Thomas Bailey, 272

Alexandria Obelisks, 429
Alice of Old Vincennes, 176, 220–226
Alice of Old Vincennes (I Love You), 225
Alice's Visit to the Hawaiian Islands, 26–27
Alien Taint in Criticism, The, 252
Alienism and Patriotism, 252
All for One—One for All, 154
All in the Day's Work, 317n, 439
All on a Summer's Eve, 269
All Souls Unitarian Church, 165
Allegory, An, 238
Allison, Young E., 153
Along the Bosphorus, 430, 432; (book), 388, 422, 431–434
Aloof, 267
Already, 67
Alter Ego, 161
Alternative: A Song of Love, 272
Alterum Nomen, 161
Am I a Good Citizen?, 157
Amateurs at War, 380
Ambition, 160
America (by M. Thompson), 207
America (magazine), 39, 206n, 252
America and Her Critics, 154
America in the War, 147
American Academy of Arts & Letters, 146
American and Mexican Commission, 371–373
American Anthology, An, 190n, 192n, 206n, 207n, 213n, 248, 298, 315n
American Association of Writers, 244, 260
American Booksellers Association, 106
American Bouquet, The, 252
American Bowman Review, 182
American Bows, 301
American Boy, An, 266n
American Citizen, An, 132
American Consulate in China, An, 39
American Consulates and Embassies, 39n

American Crudity, 280
American Duchess, An, 315n
American Education of Chinese Girls, 39
American Foreign Service Journal, 154
American "Forty," The, 253
American Girl, The, 157, 423
American Heathen, 63
American Humor, 265
American Legion Monthly, The, 154
American Lyrics, 192n
American Magazine, 254
American Monthly Review of Reviews, 170n
American Poetry, 192n
American Red Cross, 151
American Sonnets (by Higginson & Bigelow), 192n, 243; (by W. Sharp), 192n
American vs. English Bows, 301
American Woman at a Chinese Feast, An, 61
American Women Millionaires, 66
Americans All, 133
Americans Forever, 133
America's Poet, 260
Amherst Olio, 391
Among the Archives, 426, 427
Among the Pueblos, 426
Among the Woodcocks, 257
Among Turkish Royalty, 446
Anacreontea, 267
Analysts Analyzed, The, 260
Anatomy of Bird-Song, The, 201
Anchor Line, 373
Ancient Lights, 164, 167
And They Lived Happily Ever After!, 129; (book), 128–129
Andersonville Prison, 370
Andrews, Matthew Page, 396
Anecdote, An, 261n
Angel, Frank Warner, 358n, 397
Angel of the House, The, 441
Another Provincial View, 253
Another Weak-minded Woman, 442
Answer, The, 67
Anthology of American Poetry, 190n
Antietam, 137, 145
Antiquary's Story, The, 430
Apart, 62
Aphrodite, 192
Appleton's Booklovers Magazine, 399

Appleton's Journal, 254
Appreciation and Discrimination, 266
April, 66
April Easter, An, 92
April's Lady, 171
Arabella's House Party, 123
Arbor Day, 242
Archaeological Writings of the Sanhedrin, 326
Archer (pseud.), 300, 301
Archer, The, 182, 190
Archer among the Herons, An, 198, 230
Archer in the Cherokee Hills, The, 237; (brochure), 236–237
Archer on the Kankakee, An, 255
Archers among the Woodcocks, 257n
Archer's Chief Enemy, The, 301
Archer's Outing, An, 255
Archer's Register, The, 190n, 238, 240; (album), 294
Archer's Sojourn in the Okefinokee, An, 255
Archery, 175, 180–185, 189, 190, 198, 219, 228–230, 236–237, 238, 240, 242, 254, 255, 256, 257n, 262, 264, 275, 278, 281, 282, 287, 289, 290, 291, 292, 299, 300, 301, 302, 441, 446
Archery (by S. E. Wallace), 441
Archery as It Is, 262
Archery Excerpts, 219n
Archery for Girls and Boys, 262
Archery in the United States, 238
Archery in the Winter, 301
Archery Ranges and Bows, 300
Archery Review, The, 219n, 300, 301n
Archery, Tennis, and Croquet, 256
Archery Today, 282
Archibald Kenshaw, 12
Are Authors Men?, 253
Are We a Happy People?, 132, 170
Are We a Nation of Thieves?, 265
Arena, The, 94n, 441
Argus, The, 446
Armstrong, Le Roy (pseud.), 56
Around the Home, 43
Art and Money, 219
Art and Responsibility, 265
Art and Skill of Lawn Tennis, The, 185

Art for Mankind's Sake, 264
Art of Authorship, The, 382
Art of Being Provincial, The, 268
Art of Saying Nothing Well, 247
Art of Suggestion, The, 252
Art's Lesson, 77
As Mr. Capper Said, "We Don't Know It All," 157
Ashenfelter, S.M., 355
Asphodel, 92
Assassination of President Lincoln, 368
Assault, The, 206, 241
Assayers, The, 427
Associate on Her Travels, The, 58
Association of American Writers, 245, 260
At Bethlehem, 433, 436
At Heliopolis, 429
At Last, 50
At Lincoln's Grave, 213n
At Love's Extremes, 193–194
At New Orleans, 258
At Night, 193
At Parting, 66
At the Celebration of the 100th Anniversary of Whittier's Birth, 165n
At the Last, 276
At the Mansion House, 61
At the Monument, 94
At the Stake, 258
At the Threshold, 234
At the Threshold of a New Age, 279
At the Top of the Pillars, 155
At the Window, 191
At West Point, 444n
At Yildiz Palace, 430
Atalanta, 191
Athanatos, 270
Athens of Indiana, vii, 62
Atkinson, Edward Lincoln, 170
Atlantic Monthly, The, 154, 191n, 254–255, 399, 441
Atlantic Narratives (Second Series), 122n
August, 241
Aunt Polly, 63
Austen, Jane, 266
Australia, 49, 65, 66
Authentic Life of Billy the Kid, 355, 395
Author and the Book, The, 249

Authors Who Ride, 261
Authorship and Common Sense, 253
Autobiographical Chapter, An, 165
Avian Athletics, 286
Awful Night, An, 258
Ayres, L. S., & Co., 166

Bacheller, Irving, 217n
Bacillus of Printer's Ink, The, 280
Backwoods Luck, 258
Badeau's Life of Grant, 353
Badge of Genius, The, 253
Badge of Originality, The, 271
Badminton Magazine, 255
Bagging a Wild Goose, 257
Bagley, Worth, 161
Bainton, George, 382
Balance of Power, The, 218
Balhinch Christmas, A, 62
Ballad of a Little Fun, The, 249, 256
Ballad of Berry Brown, The, 251
Ballad of Chickamauga, The 247
Ballad of Harvest Time, A, 270
Ballads of American Bravery, 207n, 248, 299
Balthasar, 172
Baltimore American & Commercial Advertiser, 399–400
Baltimore, (Civil War, Middle Department), 383, 384, 396, 399, 400, 401
Baltimore Evening Post, 400n
Baltimore Evening Transcript, 399
(Baltimore) Sun, The, 384, 399n, 400–401
Balzac, Sainte-Beuve, and the Realists, 252
Balzac's Romances, 268
Bancroft, Zayde, 446
Banjo and the Britannica, The, 264
Banker of Bankersville, A, 198–199
Banner-Song of the Indiana Eleventh, 437
Banta, R. E., 6n, 80n, 156n
Banzou, Jean, 276
Barber, A. W., 372n
Barcus, Corinne, L., 93n, 147
Barela, Santos, 405
Barred, 78
Barriers against Universality, 253
Basis of Art, The, 253
Baskervill, William M., 264n

Bates, Charlotte Fiske, 240
Battle of the Birds, The, 183
Battles and Leaders of the Civil War,
    380
Battles Grandsire Missed, The, 78
Baudelaire, 263, 281
Bay, J. Christian, 153
Bay St. Louis, 263, 273
Bayard, T. F., 379
Bayly, Thomas, 424
Be a National Asset!, 157
Beach, 67*n*
Beacon Lights of Patriotism, 36
Bealby, 156
Bear Stories, 239
Beattys, Harry H., 145
Beautiful Assassin, A, 267
Beautiful Songs Unsung, 57
Beauty, 281
Beethoven, 59, 60
Before Dawn, 193
Before Sunrise, 206
Before the Fire, 78
Behind the Barn, 232
Bell, Joseph E., 165
Bellona, 93
Bemis, Katharine I., 213*n*
Ben and Judas, 217
Ben-Hur, 172, 307, 309, 315–334,
    348, 357, 382, 383, 391, 393, 397,
    404, 411, 412, 413, 414, 439, 444
Ben-Hur drama, 326–329, 413, 414
Ben-Hur, extracts from, 325–326
Ben-Hur, in Tableaux and Panto-
    mime, 382
Ben-Hur music, 331–334
Ben-Hur reprints, 319–323
Ben-Hur Room, 357, 359, 382–383
Ben-Hur, stories about, 329–331
Ben-Hur translations, 323–325
"*Ben-Hur*" Wallace, 329, 356, 368,
    372, 397, 425, 440
Bench and Bar of Indiana, 374
Benefit of Change, The, 253
Benefits and the Abuse of Outdoor
    Sports, The, 198
Benevolent Raid, The, 372*n*
Bennett, F. I., 8
Benson, Leslie L., 119
Beside a Brook with Izaak, 268
Beside Ben-Hur, 277
Beside Running Water, 267

Beside the Gulf with Ruskin, 201
Besieged by a Hog, 258
Bess, 64
Best Christmas Gift, The, 257
Best Laid Schemes, 122–123
Best Man Wins, The, 157
Best Novels, The, 253
Best Things from American Litera-
    ture, 217*n*
"Better Hoosier Hicks," 167
Bettie's Prisoner, 258
Between Showers at Bay St. Louis,
    263
Between the Daffodil and Golden Rod,
    171
Between the Poppy and the Rose, 191
Bewildered Critics, 270
Beyond, 57
Beyond the Limit, 250
Beyond the Mist, 267
Bicycling and Tricycling, 256
Biddy, 64
Big Bow-Wow, The, 252
Big Medicine, 179
Bigelow, E. H., 192*n*, 243
Billy the Kid, 355, 356, 357, 358, 395,
    396
Bingham, J. J., 407
Bingham, Jno. A., 415
Biographical History of Eminent and
    Self-Made Men, 373
Biographical Sketches and Review,
    374
Birch, Reginald, 104
Bird Books, 271
Bird in Literature, The, 261
Bird in the Bush, A, 268
Bird-Lovers Anthology, The, 190*n*,
    241
Bird of Optimism, The, 268
Birds of the Rocks, 196
Birth of Art, The, 254
Bishop, Bernice Pauahi, 32, 33
Bishop, Charles R., 32, 33
Bit of Advice, A, 268
Bit of History, A, 157
Bit of Old Indiana, 155
Bit of Realism, A, 267
Blacksheep! Blacksheep!, 120; (book),
    119–120
Blackstone, Harriet, 220*n*
Blaine, James G., 374, 375

Blair, Anna Elston, 59
Blair, Dodie, 58
Blanck, Jacob, 149n
Blatchley, W. S., 241, 243, 245, 297
"Bless Thou the Guns," 93, 141
Blind, 79
Blind Boys, The, 94
Bliss, Leslie E., 295n
Bloom of the World, The, 267
Blooming, 276
Blue Bird, The, 278
Blue Heron, The, 190
Bluebird, The, 190, 278n
Bok, Edward, 433n
Bold Robin, 8
Boleyn, Anne, 433
Bolton, Sarah T., 384
Bond of Blood, The, 287, 299
Bonney, William H., 355, 356, 357, 358, 395, 396
Book and the Fireside, The, 280
Book Chat, 124
Book-making Disease, The, 253
Book News, 255
Book of American Poetry, The, 192n
Book of Indiana, A, 151
Booklovers Magazine, 399
Bookman, The, 97, 155
Booming the Britons, 268
Booth, Franklin, 107, 111, 150
Borderland, The, 140
Bosphorus, 430, 432
Bosses of the World, The, 280
Boston Advertiser, The, 401
Boston Evening Transcript, 39, 155, 161n
Boston Letter, 59
Boston Post, The, 255
Boston University, 255n, 262n
Boulevard of Rogues, The, 122
Bounty of a Queen, 25
Bow and Its Use, The, 198
Bow as a Hunting Weapon, The, 230
Bow-shooting, 182, 230, 241
Bow-shooting with a Hermit, 182
Bow-Shots on the St. John's, 182
Bowen, Henry C., 263
Bowhunter, The, 229
Bowman, The, 302
Boxer Rebellion, 65n
Boy against a Fleet, A, 274
Boy and a Fleet, A, 274n

Boy with a Will, A, 258
Boyhood of Christ, The, 307; (book), 340-341
Boys and Girls, 63
Boys' Book of Sports, 197-198
Boy's Grim Patience, A, 258
Boy's Strategy, A, 258
B.P.O.E., 293, 294
Bragget and Bird-Bolts, 268
Brandon's Beat, 65
Brannigan, 12
Breath of Morn, A, 206
Breeden, Mr. & Mrs. William, 445n
Breezy Books for Summer, 271
Brevier Legislative Reports, 238-239, 364, 366
Bridges, Robert, 166n
Bridgman, L. J., 203, 204
Brigham, 407
Broken Barriers, 124; (book), 124
Broken Glass, 171
Brown, Ancil T., 151
Brown, Caroline (pseud.), [1]-12
Brown, H. G., 363
Brown, Imogene, 404
Brown, Joseph E., 186
Brown, Ryland Thomas, 12
Browning as a Poet, 250
Browsing and Nibbling, 196
Bruno, Guido & Eleanore, 236
Brunot, Felix Reville, 163
Bryan, George J., 386
Bryan, William Jennings, 164, 172
Buchen, Walther, 237
Budding Time, 269
Budding Poets, 268
Buell, Clarence Clough, 380
Buell, D.C., 380
Buffalo Hunt in Northern Mexico, A, 414
Buffon and the Birds, 267
Bugle, The, 165n
Buley, R. C., 393, 406
Buried Treasure, 157
Burns, Lee, 216, 225
Burns, Robert, 269
Burnside, A. E., 403
Burroughs, John, 192
Burton, Richard, 119, 120
Business and Art of Living, The, 280
Butler College [University], 149, 162
Butterfly, A, 276

By a Woodland Spring, 219
By Rail to Peking, 39
By Sheridan's Grave, 78
By-Ways and Bird Notes, 195–196, 201
Byron, 423

Cabinet Talk, 40
Cacoethes Scribendi, 252
Cadmean Bucket-Shops, 253
Cairo, 429
Call of the Children, The, 146
Cambridge Book of Poetry & Song, The, 240
Campbell, 355
Campbells Are Coming, The, 123
Camps, 93
Can It Happen Again?, 152
Canby, General & Mrs. E. R. S., 444
Cant and Criticism, 264
Capacity for Work, The, 279
Card, A, 403
Cardwill, Mary E., 139, 244
Carman, Bliss, 190n, 191n, 192n
Carrington, Henry Beebee, vii, 36
Casas Grandes, 427
"Cash Down," or a Percentage?, 260
Catherwood, Mary Hartwell, 40, 60
Catholic World, The, 155
Cavalier of Tennessee, The, 130; (book), 129–130
Cavalry Reminiscence, A, 275
Cello, The, 155
Centennial Letter, A, 444
Centennial Story, The, 275
Century Club, 167
Century Cyclopedia of Names, 394
Century Magazine, The, 92n, 142n, 155, 255–256, 300, 401, 419
Century of Geology in Indiana, A, 241, 243, 245, 297
Ceres, 191
Certain Condescension in Natives, A, 265
Certain Good Man, A, 273, 277
Certified Public Accountant, The, 155
Ceryle Alcyon, 201
Chain of the Last Slave, The, 434
Challiss, J. M., 300
Challiss, Mr. & Mrs. J. M., 294
Chamberlain, Montague, 265n
Chap-Book, The, 93n, 247, 256

Chapman, 393
Chapter on Shirks, A, 63
Chariot-Race, The, 326
Charleston News and Courier, 172
Charm, 92
Charm of Song, The, 267
Chat about Chaucer, A, 258
Chatelaine, The, 271
Chautauqua, 261
Chautauquan, The, 39, 256
Checking the Chariot of Destiny, 280
Cheerful Breakfast Table, The, 122
Cheney, Calvin M., 403
Chénier, André, 268
Chevalier of the Cumberland, A, 130
Chicago, 118
Chicago Evening Post, The, 401
Chicago Examiner, 155
Chicago Herald, 300
(Chicago) Inter Ocean, 16, 39–56, 156, 257–258, 337, 401–402
(Chicago) Interior, 56
Chicago Letter, 59
Chicago, Special Correspondence, 62
(Chicago) Times, The, 258–259
(Chicago) Times-Herald, The, 56
Chicago Tribune, The, 156, 354, 403
Chicago Working Women, 59
Chickamauga, 247, 259, 392
Child Life: A Collection of Poems, 36
Child-Life Abroad, 439
Childhood Land, 57, 64
Children, 63
Children of America, The, 148
Children's Museum Bulletin, 156
Children's Museum, Indianapolis, 156, 168
Children's Wishes, The, 67
China, 28, 29, 39, 64
Chinese Paradise, A, 21
Chisholm, Cornelia, 62
Chords, 92
Christian Advocate, The, 441
Christian Criticism, 253
Christian Silhouet of 1812, A, 268
Christianity and Poverty, 264
Christmas, 41, 61, 142, 155, 164, 167, 239, 250, 257, 260, 325, 331, 347, 348, 397, 423, 424, 441, 443, 446
Christmas Bells, 41, 61
Christmas Garland, The, 250
Christmas in the Pines, 142, 155

Christmas Snowflakes, 239
Christmas Song for Children, 441
Christmas Tide, 257
Christy, Howard Chandler, 87
Church for Honest Sinners, The, 122
Churchman, The, 156
Cincinnati, 57, 156, 308, 358, 371, 384, 389, 399, 402, 403
Cincinnati Commercial, 358, 372, 402
Cincinnati Commercial-Gazette, The, 402
Cincinnati Enquirer, The, 156, 371, 402
Cincinnati Gazette, 57, 371, 402–403, 441
City of the King, The, 433n, 435–436
City of the Pueblos, The, 426
Civil War, 58, 63, 351, 352, 353, 354, 367, 368, 370, 371, 374, 376, 377, 380, 381, 383, 384, 385, 386, 387, 388, 389, 390, 392, 399, 400, 401, 402, 405, 407, 408, 413, 415, 416, 434, 446
Civil War (poem by M.H. Krout), 58, 63
Clarissa's Baby, 158
Clark, Frank C., 405
Clark, J.O.A., 330
Clark, Thomas Curtis, 93n, 213n
Clark, Walter C., 327, 382
Classic Funerals, 423
Claude's Big Trout, 232; (book), 231–232
Clay, John Cecil, 84
Clays of Indiana, 241
Cleanliness and Sanity, 266
Clemens, S.L., 149
Cleopatra, 429
Cleveland Press, The, 118n
Clod, The, 64
Close Call, A, 257
Closed Up, 271
Closing of an Epoch, The, 253
Coe, George W., 357, 396
Coeur de Leon, 259
Coggeshall, William T., 437
Coign of Vantage, The, 68
Colfax, Schuyler, 414
College Humor, 156
College of Immortals, 405, 415
Collier's, 156
Colonial Staple, A, 67

Color from Keats, 263
Color-Line Jocundities, 217
Columbus, Ohio, 413
Come Love or Death, 298
"Come On Home," 145
Come to Kernville, 159
Commemorative Biographical Record, 362
Commodus, 307, 314–315, 345–347, 395
Common Grievance, A, 63
Common Sense on the Wheel, 256
Communion Wine, 444n
Compendium of Geology and Mineralogy of Indiana, 241
Concerning a Bit of Manuscript, 155
Concerning a Good Style, 264
Concerning Enthusiasm, 263
Concerning Rest, 63
Confessions of a "Best-Seller," 90, 109
Confessions of an Ancient Poacher, 278
Confirmed Smoker, A, 258
Congregationalist, The, 441
Conner, Eugene, 300
Constantinople, 345, 386
Consummation, The, 65
Contemporary American Authors, 256
Content, 282
Contentment, 158, 159
Contribution to Pure Ignorance, A, 269
Convention of Western Writers, 244
Cookbook, A: The Stag at Ease, 152
Coons, John W., 363
Cornelia Chisholm, 62
Correspondence, etc., on the Subject of the Records of the Rebellion, 376
Cosmopolitan, The, 12, 157, 259, 441
Coulter, John Merle, viii
Country Homes, 63
Course of True Love, The, 39
Court of Judge Lynch, The, 277
Courts and Lawyers of Indiana, 406n
Covington Journal, The, 68
Cow, The, 67
Cox, David W., 327, 382
Crane, Stephen, 246
Crapsey Verdict, The, 163
Crawfordsville, 61, 62, 81, 110, 259, 351, 404, 409, 415

Crawfordsville Alley, A, 62n
Crawfordsville Girls, 58
Crawfordsville Journal, The, 15, 57,
    67, 68, 157–158, 243, 259–260,
    281n, 300, 357, 360, 402n, 403–
    404, 409n, 412n, 434n, 441–442,
    444n
Crawfordsville Letter, 61
Crawfordsville Review, The, 68, 194,
    260, 404–405
Creator Spiritus, 141
Creole Slave-Song, A, 207
Critic, The, 158, 204, 260–261, 266n,
    272n, 405
Criticism by the Rule of Darwin, 270
Critics and Criticism, 263
Critics and Russian Novels, The, 263
Critics and the Romancers, The, 271
Crocker, Samuel R., 314
Crocus, The, 67
Croly, George, 345, 392
Crown Jewels, The, 21
Crown of Defeat, The, 157
Crown of Years, The, 171
Cuba, 93, 268, 273
Cuckoo Notes, 196
Cuckoo Notes and Some Minor Song-
    Birds, 196n
Culture and Brass Tacks, 150
Curious Habits of the Green Heron,
    257
Curious Habits of the Woodcock, 257
Current, The, 60, 158, 261
Current American Poetry, 266
Curse of Wings, The, 280
Customs of Hawaii, 22n
Customs of Oxford, 26

Daily Nebraskan, The, 60
Daily New Mexican, The, 356, 405
Dancing Ghosts, 258
Daudet, 252, 255, 263, 264
Davidson, James Wood, 238
Davis, John W., 170
Dawn, The, 158, 206n, 261–262, 442
Day-Break, 263
Day in Carthage, A, 423
Day We Celebrate, The, 254n, 266,
    273
Daybreak, The, 263
Days and Places of Archery, The, 301
Days of Peace and War, 160

Days That Are No More, 163
Dayton Daily News, 390n
Dayton Journal, The, 389, 405
De Sassafras Bloom, 218n
Dead, 67
Dead Archer, The, 93, 143
Dead in May, 39, 61
Dead Painter, The, 57
Death-Dream of Armenia, The, 300,
    302
Death of the White Heron, The, 183,
    190
De Banville, Theodore, 253
Deep in the Okefinokee, 229, 299
Defense by Resurrection, The, 256
Defense of Cincinnati, The, 385
Definitive Edition of Mark Twain,
    149
Delineator, The, 158
Deming, Norma H., 213n
Democracy and Laughter, 157
Democratic Party, 163
Democratic Party and the Solid South,
    The, 337, 361–362
Democratic Party in 1924, The, 172
Denver, 45, 60
Denver News, The, 426n
Denver Times, The, 60, 66n
Denver Tribune, The, 355, 360
Departed Days, 68
Departure of Summer, The, 65n
De Pauw University, 390
Dependence, 78
Derelict, 93
Dial, The, 77n, 158, 213n
Dialect, 170
Diana, 192
Diaz, Porfirio, 350, 401
Dickens, Alfred Tennyson, 163
Dickens, Charles, 163
Dickinson, Anna (pseud.), 15
Dickinson, Emily, 253
Died, 67
Dieu Vous Garde, 77
Dionis of the White Veil, 9
Disappointment, 76
Discipline, 44
Discovery, A, 78
Disembodied Genius, 234
Disjecta Membra, 136n
Dodie Blair, 58
Doing a Little Shopping, 423

Dole, Mr. & Mrs. Sanford Ballard, 56
Dollars behind the Guns, The, 164
Domain of Romance, The, 250, 262
Doom of Claudius and Cynthia, 240
Doubt, 59, 67
Doubtful Dollars, 171
Doughty Page, The, 9
Doves of Honolulu, The, 65
Down in New Zealand, 67
Down in the Wilderness, 269, 273
Down Stranger Creek, 300
Down-Stream after Wary Ducks, 283
Down the Aisles, 78
Down the Corridor, 161
Doyle, A. Conan, 269
Drapier, W.H. & A.E., 364
Drawing the Cross-Bow, 198
Dream, A, 302
Dream of Fair Weather, A, 259, 262
Dream of Romance, A, 207
Dream of the World, The, 157
Dreamer, The, 275
Dreams, 77
Dress and Its Associations, 63
Drift, The, 149
Drift Beds of Indiana, 242
Dropping Corn, 191
Duck Shooting, 257n
Dudley, N.A.M., 355, 357, 397
Dufferin, Lord, 375, 404
Dumas, Alexander, the Younger, 268
Dunn, Jacob P., 10
Dumont, Julia L., 80
Dusky Genius, A, 217
Dwiggins, W.A., 111
Dye, Charity, 93n, 147
Dying Year, The, 67
Dykes, J.C., 358
Dyspepsia on Record, 280

E Pluribus Unum, 244
Earl of Essex and His Ring, The, 433
Earlhamite, The, 262
Early Bluebird, An, 206
Early Days in a College Town, 38
Earth, The, 93
Earth's Moods of Might, 93n
East and West, 158
Easter Miracle, The, 41
Easter Praise, 56
Easy Questions Hard to Answer, 276
Eaton, H.M., 208

Editorial Decision, The, 252
Editorial Influence, The, 252
Editors and Short-Story Writers, 253
Education and Discontent, 279
Educational Buttresses, 280
Educational Fallacy, An, 65
Efficiency of the Soul, The, 157
Eggleston, Edward, 81, 109, 154
Egypt, 429
Egypt and Sinai, 429
1861–1865, 157
86th Indiana Battle Flag, The, 57
Elder, Bowman, 102
Eleven Possible Cases, 245
Eleventh Hour, The, 17, 68
Eleventh Indiana Regiment, 58, 363,
    368, 371, 404, 408, 409, 411, 437
Eliot, George, 250
Elizabethan Novelists, The, 265
Ellenborough, Lady, 430n
Ellsworth, William Webster, 394
Elmer, Robert P., 228, 229n
Elston, I.C., 405
Elston, W.F., 59
Elves' Work, The, 64
Elzevir Library, 196n, 201, 202, 203,
    232, 233
Emmerich, Charles E., 164n
Empire, 162
Empty Nest, The, 67
End of Desire, The, 258
End of the Hindenburg Line, 147
End of the Rainbow, The, 419
Energizing Personality, 151
England in August, 24
English at Home, The, 39
English Housekeeping, 61
English Point of View, The, 258
Ensnared, 262
Enthusiasm, 157
Eos, 192
Epitaph, 270
Epoch, The, 262
Equal Suffrage Societies, 63
Eros, 192
Erotic, 302
Escheat, 92
Essays by Present Day Writers, 122n,
    132n
Essays from the Chap-Book, 246
Essays of Elia, The, 201
Esther, 330

Estimates at Second Hand, 266
Estranged, 76
Ethical Discrimination, The, 268
Ethics of Composition, The, 211
Ethics of Conception, The, 211n
Ethics of Expression, The, 211
Ethics of Literary Art, The, 210–211
Evans, 355
Evansville Journal, The, 405
Evelyn Claire, 67
Evening of Jubilee, 26
Evening Promise, An, 39
Evening Song, 268
Every Week, 158
Experience and the Calendar, 109
Exquisite, 269

Fables of Archery, The, 301
Face in the Fire, The, 68
Faculty of Flight, The, 271
Faded Flowers, 252
Fair Client's Story, A, 433
Fair God, The, 307, 309, 311–313, 373
Fair Indiana, 38
Fair Samoa Recalled, 61
Faith, 62
Faithless, 77
Falsehood of Extremes, The, 279
Fame and Popularity, 269
Familiar Talks on Literature and Art, 275
Famous Paintings of the World, 386
Fancy, A, 79
Farewell, 207
Farm and Home, The, 42
Farmer of the Middle West, The, 118
Fatal Leisure, 252
Fate of Louis Capdau, 277
Fawcett, Edgar, 252, 266
Fawn, The, 190, 229
Feast in the Forest, The, 9, 12
Feeding the Brain, 253
Fergusson, Erna, 357n
Ferns, 39
Fertility, 190n
Fiction and Moral Lessons, 268
Field, Eugene, 78
Field, Kate, 158
Fiend of Industry, The, 280
Fifth Reader, A, 148
Fighting at Point Rose, The, 278

Final Thought, The, 207
Finding Work for Walter, 159
Fire-hunting, 78
First Christmas, The, 325, 331, 347–348
First Cinderella, The, 430
First Novel, The, 253
"First of All the New War's Slain," 161
First Sign of Autumn, The, 269
First Spring Outing, The, 267
Fisher, Harrison, 81
Flag of the Children, The, 148
Flagg, James Montgomery, 100, 101
Flagship, The, 270, 274
Flesh-Pots, 140
Fletcher, Laurel Louisa, 142, 249
Fletcher's Art, The, 268
Flight into Egypt, The, 429
Flight of the Hawk, The, 257
Flight Shot, A, 190
Florida, 350, 373, 408, 413
Floridian, The, 187
Floridian Fancy, A, 262
Flower, Lucy L., 49n
Flower Mission Cap & Gown, The, 142, 249
Flute D'Ebene, Une, 252
Fly Fishing for Black Bass, 198
Folks and Their Folksiness, The, 118
Food for the Gods, 261
Fooling the People, 157
Foot-Notes for an Old-Time Southern Book, 269
For a New Year's Morn, 77
For a Pioneer's Memorial, 93, 147
For Cuba, 268, 273
For Isobel, 246
For One Evening Only, 267
For the Veterans, 61
Foreign Influence on American Fiction, 278
Forest and Stream, 262, 300–302
Forest Beauty, A, 276
Forest Mystery, A, 258
Formation of Soils, The, 242
Fort Donelson, 375, 380, 401, 413
Fort Mitchell, 403
Fort Stanton, 355
Fortnight in a Palace of Reeds, A, 196
Fortnight of Folly, A, 202–203
Fortune, Russell, 77

Fortune, William, 151
Forum, The, 262
Fosdick, W.W., 313
Fossil Mammals of the Post-Pliocene, 241
Fossils and Their Value, 297
Foulke, William Dudley, 132*n*
Founded on a Rock, 264
Four Knights, The, 63
Fourth in Indiana, The, 61
Fourth of July, The, 61, 254*n*, 266, 267
Fourth Reader, A, 148
Fox, William F., Jr., 164
Fragrance, 158
Freedmen's Bureau, 396, 399, 401
Frelinghuysen, Frederick T., 375, 376, 378, 379
Fresh London Notes, 21
Friend to the Devil, A, 277
Friendship's Sacrament, 78
Frink, Henry A., 240
Frog, A, 281
From Bethlehem to Calvary, 93
From Chicago, 62
From Chicago to Mackinaw, 65
From My Windows, 57
From Sherwood to Chattahoochee, 269
From the Campus, 38
From the Critic's Point of View, 256
From the East, 160
From the Notebook of an Archer, 257*n*
Frontier, 161
Frontier Doctor, A, 357, 395
Frontier Fighter, 357, 396–397
Frontier Idyl, A, 427
Frost, Robert, 282
Full-fledged, 207
Fuller, Hector, 161
Fulton, Maurice G., 355, 357, 395
Furnas, Robert W., 242
Future of Poetry, The, 158*n*, 162

Galaxy, The, 262
Galveston News, The, 445*n*
A Game of Piquet, 6*n*
Garden Statues, 192, 243
Garfield, President James A., 300, 412
Garrett, Pat F., Authentic Life of Billy the Kid, 355, 395
Garrett, Phineas, 240

Garrison, Gertrude, 58
Gazzel; or, Love Song, 423
Gems from Indiana Rotary's Literary Belt, 148
Gems of Modern Art, 386
Genesis of Bird-Song, The, 201
Genius and Enthusiasm, 236, 263, 264*n*
Genius and Morality, 236
Genius and Virility, 275
Genius in Science and Literature, 258
"Genius in Women," 261
Geographical Botany, 241
Geography from a Car Window, 280
Geological and Natural History Report of Carroll County, 245
Geological Survey of Clinton County, A, 297
Geological Survey of Starke County, A, 297
Geology as a Summer Pastime, 269
Geometry of Thought, 238
George, Andrew J., 265*n*
George o'Green and Robin Hood, 9, 12
Georgia, 254, 262, 274, 278
Gérome's Statue, 93
Getting Acquainted with Life, 280
Ghost at Christmas, The, 59
Giants of the Diamond, 164
Gibson, Louis C., 78
Gil Horne's Bergonzi, 247
Gilder, Jeanette L., 190*n*, 191*n*, 192*n*
Gilder, R.W. 195*n*, 199*n*, 217, 219*n*, 264, 298
Ginevra; or, The Old Oak Chest, 424; (book), 397, 423–424
Girl at the Ad Counter, The, 156
Girl Detective, The, 258
Girl from the River, The, 154
Girl with the Red Feather, The, 123
Glacial Deposits of Indiana, 241
Glad Heart! Sweetheart!, 160
Glimpse of Spring, A, 58
Glimpses of Authors, 314*n*
Glimpses of Western Farm Life, 281
Go, Winter, 161, 172*n*
God Save the Republic, 49*n*
God Save the State!, 92
Going with the Current, 280
Gold-Bird, The, 207
Gold Hunters of Indiana, 56

Gold, Silver and Precious Stones, 242
Golden Age, The, 157
Golden Age of Authors, A, 394
Golden Inspiration, The, 253
Golden Pastoral, The, 267
Golden Rule of Exercise, The, 279
Golden Treasury of American Songs, 190n
Golden-Wings' Home, The, 271
Good Cheer for 1892, 232n
Good Company, 60, 262, 426n, 434n, 442
Good Housekeeping, 158–159
Good Night and Pleasant Dreams, 78
Goodrich, Ira B., Jr., 313
Gordon, J.W., 275
Gosse, Edmund, 268
Governor's Day Off, The, 138, 168; (pamphlet), 138
Gowdy, John K., 410
Grace Chimes, 91
Grand National Archery Meeting, The, 301
Grand Traverse Bay, 276
Grandest Dream of All, The, 165
Grant, U.S., 353, 363, 387, 399n, 401n, 404, 413
Grape Bloom, 77
Grasshopper's Song, The, 68
Gray, Isaac P., 241
Great, The, 57
Great Americans as Seen by the Poets, 213n
Great Salt Lake, 157
Great South, The, 281
Great Western Sanitary Fair, 352
Greek as a Fertilizer, 264
Greek Girl's Song, The, 77
Greek Love Songs, 77
Green Heron, A, 243
Green Pants and a Will, 232
Greene, 222
Grosse, E.M., 29
Grosvenor, Edwin A., 345, 386, 391
Grosvenor, Mrs. Edwin A., 440
Grouse on the Ausable, 257
Grouse Shooting, 282
Grown Old, 66
Gryllus Grilled, 268
Guarding Shadows, 77
Guest of Honor, The, 171

Guide to the Museum of New Mexico, 359
Gulf Coast Country, The, 265
Guns and Their Use, 274n

Habits of Mocking Birds, 257
Halcyon Note, A, 268
Halcyon Notes, 264
Half Flights, 78
Hall, Anna E., 59
Hall, Annie Rachel, 59n
Hall, Frank Richards, 151
Hall, Henry, 242
Halstead, Murat, 336
Ham, Charles H., 78, 162, 164n
Hamilton, Edward Joseph, 142, 250
Hand in Hand, 267
Hand on the Shoulder, The, 156
Handicapped Critics, 263
Happy the man that scales the heights afar, 163
Harbert, Elizabeth Boynton, 65
Harding, George C., 59
Hardy, Thomas, 255
Hare Hunting, 282
Harper's Bazaar, 159
Harper's [Monthly] Magazine, 159, 262, 314, 406, 442
Harper's Round Table, 442
Harper's Weekly, 60, 406
Harper's Young People, 262
Harris, Joel Chandler, 265n
Harrison, Benjamin, 39, 40, 43, 44, 309, 335, 336, 337, 338, 339, 340, 361, 381, 402, 411
Harrison, William Henry, 337
Hartford Seminary Record, The, 262
Hartford Theological Seminary, 210, 211
Hartwick, Benjamin, 185
Harvard College, 213
Harvest, 169
Hastings, R., 352
Hat and the Home, The, 280
Hatch, General, 355, 397
Haunted Rocking-Chair, The, 157
Haunts of the Grayling, The, 276
Having a Good Time, 279
Hawaii, 19, 20, 21, 22, 23, 29, 30, 31, 32, 33, 39, 46, 48, 49n, 50, 56, 61
Hawaii and a Revolution, 19–23
Hawaiian Farm, A, 21

Hawaiian Gardens, 39n
Hawaiian Politics, 20
Hawaiians at Home, 20
Hawthorne, Nathaniel, 255
Hay, John, 54
Hayes, Rutherford B., 350, 354, 359, 402, 408, 413, 416
Hayne, Paul Hamilton, 77, 179n, 250, 271, 272, 277
Hays, Will H., 122, 166
Hazard, Bertha, 192n
He Is Not Dead, 213n
Health to Indiana, A, 260
Hearst's International, 159
Heart Cure at Banning Farms, The, 158
Heart of America, The, 148
Heart of America Readers, 148
Heart of American Youth, The, 154
Heart of Life, The, 171
Heart of the Bugle, The, 93
"Heartache," 78
Heiney, Enos B., 37, 140, 142, 191n, 192n, 213n, 299, 315n, 437, 438
Helpless Girls, 67
Henley's Gay Scene, 25
Henry the Eighth, 433
Heredity, 169
Heresy of the Gad, The, 269
Heroes and Heroines in Fiction, 253
Heron, The, 190
Heron Sketches, 269
Herringshaw, Thomas W., 190n, 192n
Hesperian Tree, The, 143, 249
Heyday!, 268, 273
Higginson, T.W., 192n, 243
High Tide at Gettysburg, The, 268n, 287, 298
High-Water Friendship, 257
Higher Light, The, 66n
Highland Park Archery Club, 301
Hill, Alexander, 316
Hill, Frank, 218
Hint to Chicago, A, 253
Hint to Critics, A, 265
Hints on Trap-shooting, 198
His Second Campaign, 187–188
History of Maryland, 396
History of the Organization of the Indiana Commandery . . . Loyal Legion, 381

Hitting the Bourbons Hard, 362
Ho, for the Kankakee, 206
Hodson's [Hodgson's or Hodkin's] Hide-Out, 217
Hoffman, P.A., 402
Hoiden, 179
Holden, Alderman, 415
Holding the Mirror, 252
Holland, E.M., 89
Holliday, John H., 164n
Holmes, Oliver Wendell, 260
Home, 275
Home, The, 40, 41, 42, 43, 44
Home Book of Verse, The, 190n
Home Circle, 43, 44, 45, 46, 47, 48, 49, 54
Home-coming, The, 65
Home Department, 43
Home Journal, 68, 446
Home-Maker, The, 60
Home of a Princess, 21
Home of Ben Hur, The, 391
Homer, 423
Honey, Pure and Adulterated, 267
Honolulu, 20, 30, 31, 65
Honor Bright, 127; (book), 125–127
Honorable Archie, The, 171
Hoof-Marks in the Sod, 93n
Hoosier, The, 159
Hoosier Almanack and Family Magazine, The, 11, 38
Hoosier Athens, The, 62
Hoosier Boyhood, A, 165n, 172
Hoosier Caravan, 6n, 80n
Hoosier Chronicle, A, 105–107, 110
Hoosier Classic, A, 136
Hoosier Delegates, 45
Hoosier Democrat, The, 172
Hoosier Gastronomics, 145, 168
Hoosier Girl I Loved in Old Vincennes, The, 225
Hoosier Girl's Eyes, A, 162
Hoosier Letters and the Ku Klux, 155
Hoosier Mosaics, 179–180
Hoosier Reminisces in Far-Off Caracas, 165
Hoosier Triangle, A, 270
Hoosiers, 136
Hoosiers, The, 79–81
Hope of Happiness, The, 128; (book), 127–128
Hopeful View of Poetry, A, 158

Hopper, The, 116
Horatio at Elsinore, 94
Horns, The, 93, 142
Horseshoe Statesmanship, 279
Horsman, E.I., 185, 290
Hosmer, Harriet, 48
Hot Biscuits and Honey, 168
Hot Days in London, 25
Hotel Sherman, 150
Hour with the Mexicans, An, 373
House, Benjamin Davenport, 58, 139
House of a Thousand Candles, The, 87–90, 163, 169
House of Peers, The, 24
Housewarming, The, 168
Hovey, Alvin P., 409
How a Boy Outwitted John A. Murrell, 257
How a Humming Bird Builds Its Nest, 257n
How an Archer Bags a Wildgoose, 257n
How Bony Grew Rich, 264
How I Came to Write Ben Hur, 331, 350
How I Saved Ben, 401
How Long Will America Last?, 154
How Pierre Found His Father, 161
How, Then, Should Smith Vote?, 122
How to Draw the Bow, 301
How to Handle a Shotgun, 274n
How to Study History, Literature, the Fine Arts, 246
How to Study Literature, 246
How to Train in Archery, 183–185, 289–292
How to Use a Rifle, 274
Howard, Roy W., 168n
Howells, William Dean, 186, 191n, 218n, 244, 255, 264, 271, 275
Hoyt, 236
Hoyt, Henry F., 357, 395
Hubbard, Kin [Frank McKinney], 143, 151
Huesmann, Louis C., 119, 120
Humming Bird, The, (by M. Nicholson), 159; (by M. Thompson, poem), 241, (prose), 257
Hummock Eden, A, 258
Humpback Sam, 258
Humphrey, Lucy H., 191n, 213n
Hunting Shy Birds, 257n

Hunting Stories Retold from St. Nicholas, 251
Hunting with a Bow and Arrow, 282
Hunting with the Bow, 301
Hunting with the Long-Bow, 182, 183
Hutchinson, E.M., 183n, 190n, 191n, 201n
Hymn of the Monument, A, 163
Hysterical Citizen, The, 279

"I Know a Place," 160
"I would give a good deal if I knew the answer," 172
Ideal Indiana Soldier, An, 362
Ideals Are Gone, 168
Identified at Last, 162
Idle Day, An, 271
Idler, An, 64
Idolater, An, 76
Idyl of the Longbow, An, 262
Idyl of the Rod, An, 179
Idyl of the Wabash, An, 161
If I Were a Boy Again, 261n, 262
If You Were a Soldier Over There and Santa Claus Forgot You, 166
Ill-starred, 77
Illinois Woman's Exposition Board, 48
Illinois Women's Press Association, 42
Illusion of Change, The, 154
(Illustrated) Indiana Weekly, The, 262, 270n
Imaginative Romance, 280
Imperial Harem, An, 446n
Impossibility, An, 256
Impression of the World's Fair, 261
Impromptu, The, 140
Improvement in Blue-Stockings, 253
Imprudence of Prudence, The, 171
In a Creole Book-Stall, 264
In a Day, 63
In a Great Prison, 25
In a Turkish Cemetery, 432n, 445
In a Well, 282
In a wildwood there came to me, 261
In an Early Day, 12
In Appreciation of Our New Home, 150
In April, 40
In Camp Tonight, 160
In Captivity, 206
In Convalescence, 67
In Crawford's Woods, 38, 67

In Ether Spaces, 76
In Exile, 193
In-Gathering of Sketches, Essays, Poems by Western Writers, 140
In Halcyon Hilo, 21
In Honor of James Whitcomb Riley, 144
In Lincoln Street, 59
In Love, 238
In Love's Hands, 282
In Memoriam Major-General Lew Wallace, 143
In Regal Quarters, 21
In Santford's Pocket, 259
In the Clover, 251
In the Dusk, 171
In the East and West, 62
In the Great Pastures, 92
In the Harem, 430
In the Haunts of Bass and Bream, 192
In the Haunts of Bream and Bass, 192, 241
In the Haunts of the Mocking-Bird, 196
In the Hilo Swim, 21
In the Isle of the Lily, 430
In the Matter of Shakespeare, 201
In the Moonlight, 160
In the Shadow, 77
In the South Seas, 22
In the Storm, 258
In the Street, 94
In the Tent, 446
In the Tower of Many Stories, 433
In the Woods with the Bow, 219
In Tune with the Times, 168
In Turkish Harems, 445
"In Winter I Was Born," 78, 91
Incident of War, An, 207
Independence Day, 254, 266n
Independent, The, 60–61, 159, 175, 252, 263–271, 302, 430n, 442–443
Indian Archery, 446
Indian Giver, The, 443
Indiana Academy of Science, 201n, 241, 243, 245, 297
Indiana: Adjutant General's Report, 367
Indiana and Indianans, 10n
Indiana Association Mexican War Veterans, 393
Indiana at Antietam, 145

Indiana at Chickamauga, 392
Indiana at Shiloh, 363
Indiana Athens, The, 61
Indiana authors, 6n, 80n, 156n, 165, 327, 411
Indiana Authors and Their Books, 6n, 80n, 156n
Indiana Authors' Readings, 165, 327, 411
Indiana: Brevier Legislative Reports, 364
Indiana Building Stone, 241, 245
Indiana Centennial Celebration, 145
Indiana Chalk Beds, 241
Indiana Democracy, 40
Indiana Department of Geology . . . Report, 241, 242, 245, 297
Indiana Historical Society, 411
Indiana in the Mexican War, 372, 393–394
Indiana in the War of the Rebellion, 370
Indiana: Journal of the Senate, 364, 365, 366
Indiana League of Women Voters, 166
Indiana: Legislative Sentinel, 364
Indiana Legislature, 40, 238, 406
Indiana Magazine of History, 12, 393, 406
Indiana Poetry, 76n, 92n
Indiana Politics, 43
Indiana Republican League, 410
Indiana Rotary, 148
Indiana School Journal, The, 61
Indiana Society of Chicago, 11, 135, 144, 145, 146
Indiana Soldier, An, 362
Indiana Soldiers and Sailors Monument, 163n, 392, 409n
Indiana State Board of Agriculture, 241–242
Indiana State Council of Defense, 67
Indiana State Journal, 406–407
Indiana State Legislature, 40, 238, 406
Indiana State Sentinel, 407
Indiana State Teachers' Association, 144, 163
Indiana Weekly, 262, 270n
Indiana Writers of Poems and Prose, 142, 250
Indianapolis, 40, 63, 85n, 109, 164

Indianapolis: A City of Homes, 109
Indianapolis Bar Association, 165
Indianapolis Chamber of Commerce, 150
Indianapolis Flower Mission, 139, 140, 141, 142, 244
Indianapolis Herald, 407
Indianapolis Journal, The, 61, 159–162, 243, 244, 271–274, 302, 314, 358, 407–411, 413n, 443–444
Indianapolis Literary Club, 136, 158n
Indianapolis News, The, 12, 61, 90n, 162–165, 274–275, 411, 414n
Indianapolis News Souvenir, The, 392
Indianapolis Press, The, 61, 411
Indianapolis Saturday Herald, The, 61–63, 179n, 192n, 206n, 244, 275, 281n
Indianapolis Saturday Review, 61n, 63, 239, 275
Indianapolis Sentinel, The, 165, 244, 411–412
Indianapolis Star, The, 63, 103, 165–168, 207n, 275, 410n, 412, 434n, 444
Indianapolis Sun, The, 168
Indianapolis Times, The, 168
Indianapolis Turnverein, 166
Indiana's Future Poet, 42
Indianian, The, 270n
Inevitable Word, The, 143, 155
Inexpensive Summer Outing, An, 256
Ingersoll, Ernest, 239
Inglorious Genius, An, 257
Inherited Habit in Birds, 258
Inherited Honors and Duties, 141
Insley, J.J., 404
Inspiration of a Walk, The, 279
Instance of Bird Study, An, 269
Instance of Good Roads, An, 268
Intellectual Future of the Negro, The, 265
Inter Ocean, The, (see Chicago Inter Ocean)
Interior, The, 56
International copyright, 162, 243, 261
Into Light, 273n
Into Mischief, 68
Invenustus, 280
Invitation to You and Your Folks, An, 147
Invocation—To the Seasons, 76

Ireland, 54, 93
Is New York a Bluff?, 167
Is Our Great National Motive Power, Curiosity, Being Educated Out of Us?, 156
Is Slaying Thousands, 445n
Is the New Woman New?, 247
Ishmaelite, The, 168, 276
Island of Song, The, 254
It Shall Never Come Down, 270, 274
Italy and the Arts, 280

Jack's Half-Holiday, 56, 63
Jackson, Andrew, 129, 130
James, Henry, 275
Jameson, Dr. Leander Starr, 26
Janesville Gazette, The, 444
Jere Jones's Ride, 271
Jerusalem as It Now Is [as We See It Today], 436
Jessie's Guest, 62
Jock o'Nimble Heels, 9
Jocund Feud, A, 259
John and Jonathan, 25, 26
John Bull at Home, 25
Johnson, Robert Underwood, 162n, 164, 380, 401n
Johnson, William Martin, 319, 348
Jolly Joker of the Nations, 280
Jonathan's Fourth of July, 232
Jornada Del Muerto, The, 427
Joslin, Mrs, N.S., 61n
Jottings, 49, 50, 51
Journal of the Senate of Indiana, (1857), 364; (1858), 365; (1859), 366
Judah, 330
Judah, Mary Jameson, 129
Junior Poetry Cure, The, 190n
Jusserand, J.J., 265
Justice, 259
Justice as Administered in . . . English Courts, 25

Kalakaua's Palace, 21
Kapila, 315n, 333
Karl, Mynheer Heinrich, (pseud.), 58
Kate Field's Washington, 158
"Kate Greenaway," 162
Katie Winterbud, 278
Keats, 263
Keep Off the Grass, 155

Keithly, E.C., 225
Keller, Arthur I., 97, 98, 102
Kemble, Edward Windsor, 214, 216
Kennedy, Madam, 68
Kennedy, Mary Hannah, (pseud.), 65n
Kennedy, Peter S., 374
Khayyam, (see Omar Khayyam)
Kildee Shooting, 257
Kind of Man, A, 78
King of Honey Island, The, 209; (book), 208–210
Kingfisher, The, 207
King's Road, The, 65
Kipling, Rudyard, 261, 265n
Klepper, Max, 6
Knights in Fustian, 5
Knights of Pythias, 404n
Knowles, Frederic L., 141, 190n
Knox, Thomas Lowell, 385
Kokomo Saturday Tribune, 63, 65n, 276
Kountze, Herman, 94
Kountze, Mrs. Charles Thomas, 114
Kreymborg, Alfred, 190n
Krout, Caroline Virginia, [1]–12, 81, 444
Krout, Mary Hannah, [13]–68, 81, 226, 308, 337, 349, 350, 444
Krout, Mary Hannah, letters to: Editor, Evening Post, 68; Ladies and Gentlemen of Crawfordsville, 58; J. E. Le Rossignol, 60
Krout, Mary Hannah, speeches: Banquet for candidates for Trustees of Illinois State University, 49n; D.A.R., 59; Illinois Woman's Republican Committee, 49n; Republican Women's Rally, 49; Woman's Reading Club of Terre Haute, 59
Krout, Robert Kennedy, 17, 19
Ku Klux Klan, 166n, 168
Kummer, Alfred, 379
Kunse, Luella G., 61

La Maison des Milles Flambeaux, 89
Labor and Art, 94
Labor the Law of Life, 162
Ladies' Home Journal, The, 350, 444–445
Ladies Repository, The, 64

Lady Larkspur, 119; (book), 118–119
Lady of Landor Lane, The, 122
Lafayette Courier, 276
La Follette, Robert M., 166
Lamb, Charles, 201
Land of the Pueblos, The, 427; (book), 359, 397, 424–427
Land of the Swallow, The, 62
Land of the Tall Poinsettia, The, 154, 167
Landis, Charles B., 404, 412
Landon's Legacy, 156
Lane, Henry S., 259
Lane, Mrs. Henry S., 432, 433n, 440
Lang, Andrew, 261, 266n
Langtry, Lily, 56
Lanier, Sidney, 77
Large Turkish Cemeteries, 432n, 445n
Lark, The, 60, 61
Larned, Walter, 207n
Last Farewell and Tender Tribute, A, 444
Last Letter of Anne Boleyn, 433
Last Literary Cavalier, The, 250
Last of the Kings, The, 156
Last of the 'Tzins, The, 313
Last Prayer, The, 61
Las Vegas Gazette, 356, 412
Late London Notes, 25
Laurel Leaves for Little Folks, 37, 437
Law of Life, The, 78
Lawrence, Austin, 39n
Lawyer, The, 259
Lazing, 206
"Lead, Kindly Light," 77, 91
Leadership, 157
Leaf from a Fly-Book, A, 268
Leaf from the Christmas Tree, A, 441, 443
League of the Guadalupe, The, 273, 281
Learn from Books and from People, 170
Lee, Alice, (Mrs. Maurice Thompson), 58, 205, 218
Lees of Old Wine, The, 252
Legend of Bayou Galère, A, 277
Legend of Potato Creek, The, 179
Legend of the Satilla, A, 282
Legislative Sentinel, The, 364
Leibnitz, 280
Leighton, Lord, 24

Lepers and Leprosy in the East, 433
Lepers and Molakai, 21
Le Rossignol, J.E., 60
Leslie's Popular Monthly, 445
Lesson of Fiction, The, 270
Lesson of the Corn, The, 157
Let Main Street Alone!, 121
Let's All Be Ourselves, 171
Letter, A, 155
Letter from Dresden, 388, 432
Letter from Niagara, 444
Letter of Mrs. Story, 433
Letter to Every Good Woman, A, 444
Letters of James Whitcomb Riley, 161n
Letting George Do It, 164
Levant Herald, 412
Library Magazine, The, 263n, 276
Library of American Literature, A, 183n, 190n, 191n, 201n
Library of Literary Criticism, 192n, 211n, 213n, 250
Library of Southern Literature, 182n, 183n, 190n, 191n, 192n, 193n, 206n, 207n, 211n, 220n
Life, 64; (magazine), 169
Life and Public Services of [Hon.] Benjamin Harrison, 336, 337
Life in Honolulu, 20
Life of Gen. Ben Harrison, 309, 335–340
Light of the Harem, The, 423
Light through Darkness, 158
"Lighten Our Darkness," 161, 168
Lightheartedness of Americans, 279
Like Lost Sheep, 161
Lilly, J. K., viii
Lily of Rochon, The, 273
Limit of Athletics, 256
Limit of Criticism, The, 264
Limit of Expression, The, 260
Limit of the Short Story, The, 252
Lincoln, Abraham, 141, 212, 213, 295, 296, 368, 399, 400, 410, 416
Lincoln Memorial Address, 295–296
Lincoln, Robert Todd, 376
Lincoln County, N.M., 354, 355, 357, 396
Lincoln-Douglas Debate, 350, 366n
Lincoln's Birthday, 213n
Lincoln's Emancipation Proclamation, 416

Lincoln's Grave, 213; (book), 212–213
Lines Addressed to the Lady Who Bandaged My Cut Finger, 406, 409
Lion's Cub, The, 248
Lippincott's Magazine of Popular Literature and Science, 64, 276–277
Literary Cant, 266
Literary Controversy, A, 244
Literary Execution, A, 252
Literary Fascination, The, 279
Literary Fashions, 266
Literary Gambling, 253
Literary Greens, 256
Literary Half-Acres, 267
Literary Hysteria, 253
Literary Journey, A, 271
Literary Judgments, 271
Literary Lesson of Archery, The, 264
Literary Life, 277
Literary Loyalty, 252
Literary Market, The, 270
Literary Mendicity, 266
Literary News, The, 397
Literary Perfume, 260
Literary Reciprocity, 267
Literary Redemption of Indiana, The, 12
Literary Sincerity, 264
Literary World, The, 277, 398
Literature, 145; (magazine), 64, 262, 277, 427n, 445
Literature and Ignorance, 267
Literature and Life, 255, 262
Literature and the College, 252
Literature and the Exposition, 253
Little, Elizabeth P.H., 444
Little Acorn, The, 64
Little Book of American Poets, The, 190n
Little Boy across the Way, The, 162
Little Brown Hands, 36, 57n, 65, 66
Little Brown Jug at Kildare, The, 100–102
Little Children Fed, 26
Little Dinner, A, 64
Little, Old Cradle, The, 57, 64
Little Purple Heartsease, 64
Little Question of Soil, A, 253
Little Ruth, 57
Little Verses and Big Names, 146

Living Age, 277
Living Leaders of the World, 381
Living Writers of the South, The, 238
Loafing-Day, 270, 274
Local & National Poets of America, 190n, 192n
Locket, The, 445
London, 21, 23–26, 51, 52, 53, 54, 55, 56, 68
London in Mourning, 25
London's Big Show, 26
Long, Ray, 124
Long-Bow, The, 254
Long Live the King, 39, 61
Longfellow, H.W., 191n, 239, 280
Looker On in London, A, 23–26
Looking Southward, 272
Lords of High Decision, 102–103
Lorel Hasardour, 235
Lossing, Benson J., 354, 368, 434n
Lost Count de Lisle, The, 278
Lost Lamb, The, 64
Louisiana, 203, 204, 408
Louisville Courier-Journal, 410n
Louisville Exposition, The, 59
Louisville Post, The, 169
Loup-Garon: A Story of the Gulf Swamp, 272
Love and Rapiers, 277
Love Song, A, 442n
"Loved and Lost," 160
Lovely Island Lake, 43
Love's Horizon, 256
Love's Midas Touch, 76
Love's Music, 92, 141
Love's Power, 78
Love's Voyage, 267
Loving Cup Presentation, The, 388–389
Low Tide in Poetry, The, 253
Lowell, James Russell, 250
Loyal Legion, Indiana Commandery, 141, 143, 362, 381, 388, 409, 410
Loyal Legion, Ohio Commandery, 381, 384
Lucas, Harriet M., 94
Lucky Shot, A, 257
Lullaby, 64
Luther's Choral, 36, 63
Lydie Darrah, 60, 63
Lyon & Healy, 401
Lyon, General, 405

Lyric America, 190n
Lyric Muse, The, 267

Macauley, Dan, 413
McChesney, H.H., 219n
McClellan, General, 410n
McClure's Magazine, 169
McComb, E.H.K., 134, 164n, 264
McConnell, Emlen, 226
McCulloch, Carleton B., 132, 164, 167
McGillicuddy, 171
Machine-made Appreciation, 253
McKee, Irving, 329, 356, 360, 361, 371, 372, 397, 398, 409, 410n, 425, 440
McKinley Memorial Address, 293
McLain, M.G., 409
McLaughlin, M. Louise, 36
Maclure, William, 81
McMeen, Samuel G., 229
Made in Mazooma, 169
Madness of May, The, 115; (book), 114–115
Magnetic Story, The, 271
Mahan, W.D., 326
Major, Charles, 249
Major, Mabel, 419
Making and Spending, 157
Making Dry Facts Attractive, 280
Main Chance, The, 81–84
Man and a Bird, A, 268
Man and the Bird, The, 280
Man in the House, A, 16, 444
Man in the Street, The, 121–122
Man of Destiny, The, 422
Man of the Marsh, The, 258
Man on the High Horse, The, 259
Man with the Hoe, The, 279
Man with the Lantern, The, 156
Manhattan, The, 277
Manila, 59
Manual Training High School, 134, 164, 168
Manuscript fragment, 412
March, 262
March of Lenore, The, 162
Marietta Register, The, 412
Marjorie, 94
Mark and the Panther, 283
Mark Spears with the Warring Creeks, 258
Markham, Edwin, 192n

Marsh, Rose Blair, 444
Marsh-Land Incident, A, 219
Marshall, Thomas Ryan, 61, 104, 164, 166, 169
Marshall County, 297
Marvin and His Boy Hunters, 198
Maryland, 396, 399, 400, 401, 434
Marys, The, 35
Mason, Caroline, 446
Massingberd, Mrs. E. L., 54
Masters of Men, 93n
Materialism and Criticism, 252
Matter and Style, 263
Matter of History, A, 50
Mattern, E.L., 414
Matthews, Brander, 265n
Maxinkuckee, 297
Maybrick, Florence Holbrook, 55, 64
Mayer, Alfred M., 192n, 240, 375
Mayfield, Frank, 190n
Mea Culpa, 93
Meadow-Lark, The, 271
Meadow Music, 269
Measure of Success, The, 279
Mecca, 429
Mediaeval Romance, A, 271
Meeting, A, 158
Meeting of the Veterans, The, 271
Melbourne, 49
Melic Charm, The, 267
Melpomene, 169
Memoirs of Hon. Bernice Pauahi Bishop, The, 32–33
Memorial Address: B.P.O.E., 293–294
Memorial Address: Lincoln, 295, 296
Memorial Address: McKinley, 293
Memorial Day poem, 58
Memory, 93
Memory, A, 260
Memory, A: May, 1864, 281
Men and Women, 12
Mensaje del Gob. Lewis Wallace, 360
Mental Hospitality, 163n
Meredith, George, 51
Meredith, William Morton, 75
Merrell, Clarence F., 152
Merrill, Catherine, 80, 370, 371
Merry Days with Bow and Quiver, 182, 183
Merry Meet Again, 315n
Message, The, 168
Mesilla Independent, 354, 412

Mesilla News, The, 355, 397, 412, 413
Mesilla Valley Independent, The, 412n
Metropolitan, 169
Mexican bonds, 350, 369, 372, 402
Mexican War, 308, 393
Mexico, 308, 309, 369, 371, 372, 373, 390n, 393, 427
Mexico and the Mexicans, 309, 373, 390n
Michigan, 272
Mid-West Quarterly, 60
Midsummer Scorch, A, 269
Midsummer Shade, A, 270
Midas Touch, The, 160
Middle West in Politics, The, 118
Middleton, George, 90
Migration, 249
Mikels, Rose M.R., 93n
Military Order of the Loyal Legion, 141, 143, 362, 378, 381, 384, 388
Military Record: General Wallace's, 353–354
Military tactics, 369n
Mill of the God, The, 281
Miller, Billy, 164
Miller, Jap, 169
Miller, Marion, 265n
Miller, Olive Thorne, 265n
Miller, Theodore W., 168
Miller-Boy's Song, 268
Mills, Caleb, 79, 80, 367
Mills, Frank Moody, 38
Milly: At Love's Extremes, 194
Minard, Florence H., 115
Mind, Memory and Migration of Birds, 276
Mine Experience, 427
Mineralogical Investigation in Indiana, 201n
Miners, The, 427
Mines of Santa Eulalia, 372, 406, 427n
Minor Trials, 63
Minutes of the . . . M.E. Church, 383
Miriam: At a Concert, 94
Miss Dickinson's Poems, 253
Miss O'Rourke and True Romance, 169
Mission Schools in China, 39
Missions in China, 64

Mr. Jiggers' Toothpick, 62
Mr. Richard's Fiancée, 158
Mistletoe Bough, The, 424
Mrs. J. (pseud.), 62
Mixing Business and Sentiment, 280
Modern Aladdins & Their Magic, 151
Modern Argo, 259n
Modern Art, 169
Modern Eloquence, 370
Modern Puritan, A, 78
Mohammed, 446
Monocacy, 308
Monon Route, The, 58
Monsoons—Prevailing Winds, 151
Montaigne, 219, 269, 270
Montezuma's Palace, 427
Montgomery Guards, 282, 308, 404,
    405, 408, 409, 410
Moods, 141
Moods of a Nation, The, 157
Moonlight on the Susquehanna, 159
Moore, William F., 164
Mooresville Times, 169
Moral Qualifications, 63
Mordbank, 278
More about the Short Story, 252
Morning Dew, 207
Morning Hills, The, 191
Morning Prayer, A, 207
Morning Sail, A, 192
Morning Stroll in Indiana, A, 260
Morton, Levi P., 335, 339
Morton, J. Sterling, 242
Morton, Oliver P., 367, 368, 370, 407,
    409
Morton Memorial Association, 409
Most Beautiful Thing, The, 166
Mother Earth's House-cleaning, 64
Mother Goose for All, 140
Mother of Edgar, The, 302
Motif of Bird-Song, The, 201
Moulton, Charles W., 192n, 211n,
    213n, 250
Mud Pies, 57, 64
Mullet, Mocking Birds and Mon-
    taigne, 269
Munsey's Magazine, 64
Murder & Mystery in New Mexico,
    357
Murder of the Modern Innocents,
    The, 444, 446
Murphy, Charles Beckman, 151

Murphy Notes, 404
Must Annex Hawaii, 21
Must the Review Be Abolished?, 252
My Butterfly, 282
My Castle in the Air, 57
My Country, 247
My First Voyage, 243
My Fleet, 302
My Friend, 61
My Lady of the Golden Heart, 77
My Maiden Effort, 148
My Own Account of the First Day
    at Shiloh, 354, 399
My Paddle Gleamed, 76
My Pumps and I, 160
"My Roger," 158
My Ship, 57
My Song, 438, 446
My Story That I Like Best, 123n, 149
My Thought, 63
My Thoughts on This Christmas, 167
My Valentine, 68
My Winter Garden, 219; (book),
    218–219
Mysterious Twin, The, 258
Mystic Krewe, The, 245

Naked Babe, A, 254
Napoleon, 422
Nashville Daily American, The, 277
Nation, The, 169
National Archery Association, 182,
    262, 275, 301
National Education Association, 150
National Institute of Arts & Letters,
    146
National Meeting of American Arch-
    ers, 301
National Monthly, 169
National Wholesale Druggists' Asso-
    ciation, 136
Nation's Dead, The, 58
Natural Gas, 241
Nature Note in French Poetry, A,
    265n
Nebraska City Daily Press, 242
Nebraskan, The, (see Daily Nebras-
    kan)
Nectar and Ambrosia, 207
Neighborhood Rooster, The, 259
Neighbors, Old and New, 63
Nethersole, Olga, 68

New American Industry, 315n
New Century Speaker, The, 240
New Chances for the Historian, 280
New Dietary Theory, The, 279
New Diplomacy, The, 279
New England, 59
New England Magazine, The, 169
New England Quarterly, The, 355, 413
New Evangel, The, 272
New Haven Union, The, 444n, 445
New Influence of Religious Journals, The, 265
New Mexican, The, 354, 355, 356, 357, 405, 415
New Mexico: Territory of, 308, 309, 354–360, 396, 397, 405, 425
New Orleans, 252, 258
New Outlook for Young Men, The, 279
New Pieces That Will Take Prizes, 220n
New Poetry, The, 270
New Stories from the Chap-Book, 247
New Trails, 170
New Troubadours, The, 272
New Words for New-Century-Thoughts, 280
New Year's Collect, 93
New Year's Gift, A, 446
New York, 59
New York Evening Post, The, 169, 445
New York Herald, 169
New York Journal & Advertiser, 64, 445
New York Ledger, The, 277–278
New York Press, The, 413
(New York) Sun, The, 16, 170, 298, 302
New York Times, The, 170
New York Tribune, 57n, 64, 179n, 282, 413, 427n
New York Weekly, 281, 446
(New York) World, The, 170, 356, 413
New Zealand, 48, 67
New Zealand and Its Resources, 39
New Zealand Cities and Government, 39
Newman, Cardinal, 77, 162
Newman and His Work, 162

News, 93
Next Political Issue, 274
Nicholas, Anna, 161
Nicholson, Charles L., 131
Nicholson, Edward Willis, 85
Nicholson, Elizabeth, 116
Nicholson, Eugenie Kountze, 82, 128
Nicholson, Kenyon, 125
Nicholson, Lionel, 116
Nicholson, Margaret, 87
Nicholson, Meredith, 42, 60, [69]–172, 404
Nicholson, Meredith: A Brief Story of His Life, 172
Nicholson, Meredith: American Man of Letters, 92n
Nicholson, Meredith, autobiographical, 147, 148, 156, 165, 166, 172
Nicholson, Meredith, letters to:
    Young E. Allison, 153; Robert Bridges, 166n; Children's Museum, 156, 168; Democrats, 165; Editor, Indianapolis News, 163n; Editor, Indianapolis Star, 165; J. K. Lilly, viii; Manual Training High School, 164, 168; Samuel M. Ralston, 163; James Whitcomb Riley, 165; George Seidensticker, 166
Nicholson, Meredith, speeches:
    American Academy of Arts & Letters, 146; American Red Cross, 151; American Society of Certified Public Accountants, 155; Century Club dinner, 167; Cleveland Chamber of Commerce, 164, 167; Crawfordsville High School, 158; Democratic meeting, 168; Harrison Memorial, 165; Indiana Society of Chicago, 144; Indiana State Teachers' Association, 144; Indianapolis Bar Association, 165, 167; Indianapolis Medical Society, 167; Indianapolis Public Library, 167, 168; James Whitcomb Riley Hospital for Children, 167; L. S. Ayres & Co., 166; Lafayette Day, 166; Loyal Legion, Indiana Commandery, 162; Lucius B. Swift dinner, 165; National Life Underwriters Association, 167; Negro Y.M.C.A., 166; Manual Training

High School, 134; Phi Beta Kappa, 163n; Purdue University, 163; State Senatorial campaign, 166
Nicholson, Meredith, Jr., 116
Nicholson, Thomas B., 391
Nicholson, Walter, 67
Nicholson, Will Meredith, 76, 77, 78, 79, 156n, 157n, 158n, 159n, 160n, 172
Nightingale, Florence, 434
No War with America, 26
Noble Negro, A, 265n, 266
Nolan, Jeannette Covert, 152
North American Review, The, 278, 413
North Georgia Notes, 262
North Western Farmer, The, 65
Northwest Indiana Conference, M.E. Church, 383
Noted Women of Hawaii, 61
Notes of the Creole Coast, 253
Nothing Venture, Nothing Have, 171
Novel writing, 260
Novels and Morals, 269
Novels and Novels, 261
Novels That Shakespeare Read, The, 253
November (by Maurice Thompson), 191; (book by O. F. Adams), 191n
November Day, A, 57
November Leaf, A, 140, 437
Noyes, Edward F., 402
Nude in Fiction, The, 254
No. 120, 315n
Nuts from Perigord, 219n, 256
Nuttins, 171

O Soul, be strong!, 68
Oaks, George E., 410n
Obelisks of Alexandria, 429
Observe the Lily, 269
Ocala Boy, The, 214–215
October (by M. H. Krout), 57, 65; (by M. Nicholson), 78
Odd Trump, The, 272
Odds and Ends, 60
Ode—Spring, 206
Off-Hand Criticism, 253
Offield, Ben, (pseud.), 61, 62, 63n
Ohio State Journal, 413
Okechobee, 191
Old Artillerist, The, 141

Old Familiar Faces, 77n, 131–133
Old Glory Down, 21
Old Guidon, An, 93, 141
Old Guidons, The, 93
Old Homestead, The, 61
Old Liners, Montgomery County, 404
Old Rochon, 207
Old Rook, 274
Old Southern Humorist, An, 270
Old Stone House, The, 68
Old Trapper, An, 175
Old Wharves, 161, 169
Oldest Case on the Calendar, The, 132
Omaha, 84, 85
Omaha Tribune & Republican, 413
Omar Khayyam, 78, 139
On a Becalmed Sleeping Car, 155
On a Garden Statue of Persephone, 243
On Being an Example, 170
On Being Independent, 268
On Guns and Their Use, 274
On the Antietam Battlefield, 137, 145, 163
On the Mediterranean, 77
On the Prairie's Edge, 270
On the Road to Paraguay, 132
On the We-a Trail, 6, 444
On Writing for the Papers, 444
Once a Year (1897), 140; (1899), 141
Once at Battle Eve, 36
One Hundred Choice Selections, 240
One of Our True Poets, 252
One of the Least of These, 170
One Woman, 430
One's Grandfather, 132
Only a Meadow Mist, 25
Open Doors, The, 169
Open Season for American Novelists, The, 122
Open Sesame!, 297
Opportunity, 65
Optimistic, 160
Opulence, 249
Orchard on the Hill, The, 279
Orchards by the Sea, 93
Ord, O. C., 402
Organ, The, 155
Oriental Cemeteries, 432
Original Grotesque, An, 268
Orphic Legacy, The, 206

Orth, 404
Oskaloosa Times, 445
Ostrich Farms, An, 21
Otherwise Phyllis, 109–110
Our Alley, 62
Our Brookside Birds, 281
Our Day, 347
Our Debt to the Norsemen, 79
Our Earliest Spring Bird, 270
Our English Cousin, 307, 315n
Our Hawaii Letter, 21
Our Heritage, 141n
Our Indian Troubles, 415n
Our Legend, 207, 244
Our Nation Must Lead or Lose, 279
Our Vanishing Birds, 270
Our Winter Cardinal, 270
Our Young Folks, 65
Our Young Folks at Home, 240
Out-Door Influences in Literature, 196, 282
Out in the Street, 57, 64
Out of the Depths, 61n
Out of the South, 207
Outing, 12, 278, 282
Outline Sketch of the Most Valuable Minerals of Indiana, 297
Outsider, The, 42
Outward Bound, 39
Overland Monthly, The, 65
Owen, Robert Dale, 81
Owl, An, 281
Oxford Book of American Verse, 190n, 191n, 192n

Pacific Royalty, 21
Paddle Your Own Canoe, 384
Page, Thomas Nelson, 265n
Paige, Ellen (pseud.), 441
Pair of Old Boys, A, 255
Palace of the Pueblos, The, 442
Pan-Fish Angling, 262
Pan in the Orchard, 206
Panther and a Boy, A, 257
Pape, Eric, 312, 313
Paradise Circle, 219
Paraguay, 132, 154, 167
Paris, 53, 54
Parker, Benj. S., 37, 140, 142, 191n, 192n, 213n, 299, 315n, 437, 438
Partial Report of Survey of the Western Division, 297

Parting Guest, A, 155, 160
Passing of Old-Time Oratory, The, 279
Passion in Poetry and Fiction, 264
Pathfinders, The, 12
Patient Workers, 68
Paton, Jessie, 192n
Patrician Rhymes, 191n
Patron, Juan, 355
Patter of Little Feet, The, 437
Pauahi, Bernice, 32, 33
Paw-Paw, A, 259, 281
Peabody, Mrs. James H., 60
Pearl River Silhouette, A, 257
Pedagogue, The, 179
Peddinghaus, L. L., 300
Peep at Turkish Royalty, A, 432
Peirson, G. Alden, 227, 228
Penalties of Precision, 154
Pence, Raymond Woodbury, 122n, 132n
Penrod Is Unique, 166
Peoria Saturday Evening Call, 16, 65, 278
Perfect, The, 67
Perry, Oran, 372, 393
Perry's Expedition to Japan, 67
Persephone, 192, 243
Personal and Literary, 253
Personal Note, The, 256
Personal Reminiscences of Lew Wallace, 60, 159
Pessimism in Politics, 279
Peter Sterling Idea, The, 136n
Phases, 275
Phelps, Byron, 298
Phelps, William Lyon, 161n
Phi Beta Kappa, 212, 262
Phi Gamma Delta banquet menu, 389
Phi Gamma Delta fraternity, 389, 390, 414
Phi Gamma Delta magazine, 60n, 170, 271n, 278, 317n, 389, 390, 414
Philippine Islands, 299
Philistines, 246
Phillips, C. Coles, 104
Phillips, Mary E., 37, 437
Phonographic American French, 267
Piatt, John James, 143, 249
Pictorical History of the Civil War, 368, 434n
Picturesque Honolulu, 29

Picturesque in Poetry, The, 263
Picus, 275, 281
Picus and His Pots, A, 278
Pieces for Every Day, 213n
Pied Piper of Walnut Creek, A, 270
Pierian Freshness, The, 267
Pilgrimage to Mecca, 429, 430
Pilgrim's Progress, 434
Pimos, The, 427
Pioneer, The, 445
Pioneers, The, 12
Pipe Solo, A, 267
Pitkin, Frederick W., 356
Pittsburg Landing, 353, 354, 363, 367, 368, 377, 401, 409, 415
Pittsburgh Dispatch, 445
Plaint of the Country Editor, The, 58
Plantation Music, 260
Plantation Song, 218n
Platters and Pipkins, 33–34
Playground, 132n
Plea for the Pot-Boilers, The, 267
Plea for the Present, A, 260
Plea for the Rich, A, 264
Plethora of Ink, A, 253
Pockets of North Georgia, The, 254
Poe, Edgar Allan, 236, 263, 268, 276, 302
Poe, Elizabeth Arnold, 302
Poe and Baudelaire, 263
Poe and His Art, 276
Poem on Spring, The, 41
Poems (by Nicholson), 90–94; (by M. Thompson), 205–207
Poems for Special Days, 213n
Poems (Indianapolis Flower Mission), 139, 243
Poems of America, 239
Poems of American History, 247
Poems of American Patriotism, 141
Poems of Ben. D. House, 139
Poems of Places, 239
Poems of Wild Life, 183n, 190n
Poet, The, 111–112
Poet and the Specialist, The, 253
Poet of the Poor, A, 219
Poetic & Artistic Masterpieces, 190n
Poetic New-World, The, 191n, 213n
Poetry, 192n
Poetry and Money, 266
Poetry and Music of the Arabs, 430

Poetry of James Whitcomb Riley, The, 261
Poetry of the Civil War, The, 256
Poetry of Today, 93n
Poetry since Pope, 256
Poetry *versus* Botany, 261
Poets and Poetry of Indiana, 37, 140, 142, 191n, 213n, 299, 315n, 437, 438
Poets and Poetry of the West, The, 437
Poets and Portraits, 264
"Poets of Indiana, The," 59
Point of Aim, The, 265
Point of Hesitancy, The, 252
Pointers for Women, 68
Policy of Infamy, A, 50
Politics: A Field for Young Men, 171
Politics and the Citizen, 167, 171
Pond, J. B., 373
Pony Express, The, 156n
Poor Dear Papa, 171
Poor Old English Language, The, 122
Popular Taste, 63
Populistic Esthetics, 159
Populistic Ideals, 159
Port Angeles Evening News, 302
Port of Missing Men, The, 97; (book), 94–97
Portraits of Authors, 253
Portugal, 164
Potter Committee, 350, 373
Prairie City, The, 59
Prairie Home, A, 251, 279
Praise of Lincoln, The, 213n
Pratt, Ella Farman, 239
Prayer, 281
Prayer of the Hill-Country, A, 92
Precious Titles, 263
Preliminary Sketch of the Aquatic and Shore Birds, 242
Preliminary Sketch of the Characteristic Plants of the Kankakee Region, 242
Prelude, A, 190
Premonition, 61
Prescience, 441, 442
Presidential Campaign Lives, 335n
Presidential Election Investigation, 373
Prevention of Presidential Assassinations, 413

Price of Excellence, The, 253
Prince Edward's Song, 424
Prince of Charmingville, The, 171
Prince of India, The, 307, 309, 341–345, 392
Prince of Painters, 24
Prince's Treasure, A, 77
Princess Perizade, The, 58
Private Practice Club, 301
Proceedings in Statuary Hall, 370
Proceedings of the American Academy of Arts & Letters, 146
Proceedings of the Indiana Academy of Science, 201n, 241, 243, 245, 297
Proceedings of the Third Annual Dinner, Ohio Commandery Military Order, Loyal Legion, 378
Proceedings of the Washington State Bar Association, 299
"Prof. Gustave," 260
Professional Women, 63
Professor Emeritus, 60, 61
Progressive Farmer, 170
Prologue, A, 63
Promised Land, The, 57, 68
Proof of the Pudding, The, 114; (book), 113–114
Prophecy, A, 213n
Prose and Poetry of Today, 94n
Prospect in Fiction, The, 271
Prosperity and Laughter, 154
Provincial American, The, 109; (book), 107–109
Provincial Capital, A, 109
Provincial Poet, The, 253
Provincial View, A, 264
Psalms in [of] the Mountains, The, 92, 142, 165n
Psyche, 192
Pueblos, 424, 425, 426, 427
Pullman Laid Bare, 49
Purdue University, 276
Pure or Mixed, 265n, 266

Quadrennial Furore, The, 280
Quarrying Industry in Indiana, The, 245
Queen Dowager, A, 21
Question as to America's Culture, A, 160

Question of International Copyright, The, 261
Quincy Modern Argo, 259n
Quisenberry, A., 191n, 239

Race Romance, A, 217
Raemaekers, Louis, 147
Raleigh, Sir Walter, 433
Ralston, Samuel M., 149–150, 163, 170
Ralston of Indiana, 149
Ram's-Horns and Duffers, 256
Ranger, J. H., 161, 168
Rasch, P. J., 397
Rationews, 170
Rawlins, John A., 367
Read, T. B., 371, 403
Reader Magazine, The, 65, 170–171
Readings by Indiana Authors, 165–327
Readings by Indiana Authors in Aid of Benjamin Harrison Monument, 411, 412n
Readjustment, A, 162
Realism and Criticism, 259
Realistic Christianity, 264
Realistic Critic, A, 254
Rear Admiral Charles Wilkes, 67
Rebel Major in Limbo, A, 407n
Rebel or Loyalist?, 207
Recent Shrike-Notes, 219
Recompense, 160
Red Book Magazine, The, 171
Red-headed Family, A, 196; (pamphlet), 232–233
Red-Letter Library, The, 235
Referendum for the Illustrations in . . . "Ben Hur," A, 319
Registered, 171
Reid, Dorothy Davenport, 90
Reid, Robert A., 339
Reid, Whitelaw, 336, 426n
Religion of the Pueblos, 427n
Remembered Yesterdays, 164
Reminiscence, A, 433
Reminiscences and Sketches, 191n, 205, 207n, 234
Reminiscences of Mrs. Mary S. Rice, 31–32
Report of the Adjutant General of Indiana, 367, 370
Report of the Board of Visitors to the U.S. Military Academy, 381

Report of the Governor of New Mexico, 359–360
Report upon the Various Stones Used for Building, 245
Repose in Egypt, The, 422, 428, 432
Representative Men of Indiana, 374
Representative Poems of Living Poets, 190n, 191n, 192n
Republican Conference, 410
Republican Convention, 416
Republican State Central Committee, 410
Resaca, 277
Reserve and Understatement, 252
Resolution of Thanks, 403
Retrospect of the Archery Season of 1879, A, 301
Return of Romance, The, 270
Return of the Flags, 370
Return of the Girl, The, 247
Return of the Holy Carpet, The, 429
Return to Nature, 219
Revealing Anecdote, The, 280
Reversible Santa Claus, A, 116; (book), 115–116
Review of Archery in America, A, 240
Revival of the Historical Romance, The, 279
Revolt of the Illiterates, The, 270
Rhyme of Little Girls, A, 78
Richmond Times-Dispatch, 302
Richter, a Painter of Picturesque Portraits, 256
Rickert, Edith, 192n
Riding and Driving, 256
Rifled Arrows, 301
Right Sort of Vagabond, The, 279
Righteous Wrath, 77
Rice, Mrs. Mary S., 31, 32
Richardson, Jane, 15
Ridpath, John Clark, 386, 390
Rights of Women, The, 57
Riley, James Whitcomb, 12, 76, 81, 91, 112, 121, 134, 144, 147, 152, 154, 159, 161, 162, 164, 165, 167, 168, 187n, 261, 273, 410
Riley, James Whitcomb: Hoosier Poet, 152
Riley in the Atlantic, 161
Ripley, Emily Meigs, 42
Rise of Science in the Paw-Paw District, 144

Risks of Authorship, The, 277
Rittenhouse, Jessie B., 190n, 191n
Roach & Co., Pirates, 161
Road to Happiness, The, 77
Roars of John Bull, 56
Robbers' Strategy, 257
Roberts, Chas. G.D., 183n, 190n
Robin Hood, 8, 9, 278
Robin Hood's Pennyworth, 9
Robinette, Edward, 102
Rochester Advertiser, The, 414
Rochester Post-Express, 446
Rocked in the Wind's Cradle, 271
Rocky Mountain Sentinel, The, 354, 355, 357, 358, 412, 414
Rogers, Samuel, 423, 424
Romance, 140; (book), 246
Romance and the Novel, The, 256
Romance of Composition, The, 211n
Romance of Dollard, The, 40
Romance of New Orleans, The, 252
Rondeau of Eventide, 77
Rosalind at Red Gate, 97–100, 191n
Rosalynde's Lovers, 228; (book), 227–228
Rose, Edward E., 96, 225
Rose of Chatham, The, 273, 274
Rose of Sharon, The, 280
Ross, James R., 362
Ross, Morris, 164
Rotarian, The, 171
Rough Rider, A, 168
Round Robin Hood's Barn, 9
Round Robin Series, 185, 186, 187, 188
Royal Emissaries Return, 21
Roycroft Quarterly, The, 246
Ruby Silver Mine, The, 427
Rudgis and Grim, 217
Ruin, 78
Running from Grippe, 267
Rush, Charles E., 151
Rush's Still House, 252
Rustic Muse, The, 256

Sacred City of Mecca, The, 429
Sailing up the Bosphorus, 430
St. Louis Notes, 58
St. Michael and All Angels' Day, 156, 161
St. Nicholas, 12, 251, 278–279
St. Nicholas Book of Verse, 251

St. Paul Letter, 59
Sainte Beuve, 252
Salathiel, 392
Samoa, 61, 63
Sand Mountain Wedding, A, 217n
Sanders, Mrs. Jean, 74
Sandpiper, A, 281
Sands, A.C., 372, 402
Sansberry, Charles T., 7
Santa Claus to Henry Lane Wallace, 446
Santa Fe, 354, 355, 356, 357, 358, 359, 382
Sap-Sucker, The, 254
Sapphic Secret, The, 255, 261
Sappho, the Queen of Song, 258
Sappho's Apple, 271
Sapsucker, 191n
Sat Est Vixesse, 76
Saturday Evening Post, The, 171, 279–280
Savor of Nationality, The, 154
Saxby's Traveler's Magazine, 446
Say, Thomas, 81
Scattered Stitches, 266
Scearce, Robert and Richard, 8
Scene from an Unpublished Play, 314
Scenes from Every Land, 385
Schauffler, Robert Haven, 190n, 213n
School in the Woods, The, 198
Schurz, Carl, 355, 356
Science and Inspiration, 264
Science and Poetry, 263
Scollard, Clinton, 190n, 191n, 207n, 249, 299
Scottish Sketches, 24
Scott's Monthly Magazine, 280–281, 302
Scrap-Book Recitations, 239
Scribner's Magazine, 171, 281
Scribner's Monthly, 281, 414
Season Suggestive of Thanksgiving, The, 48
Seattle, 287, 293, 295n, 302, 303
Seattle Post-Intelligencer, 302
Seattle Telegraph, 302
Sechrist, Elizabeth Hough, 315n
Second-Rate Man in Politics, The, 122
Secondary Functions of the Hyoid Cornua, The, 201n
Secret, A, 76
Secret, The, 271

Secret of [Indiana's literary] Greatness, 165
Secrets, 79
Sedgwick's Life and Letters, 265
Seed, 278
Seekers After "The Light," 326
Seidensticker, George, 166
Senatorial race, 410
Sentimentality vs., the Law, 265
Sentinel, The, 192
Set a Thief to Catch a Thief, 157
Seven Gold Reeds, 206
Sex and Genius, 267
Shadow Lines, 92, 142, 165n
Shadow of Love, A, 234–235
Shadow of the Rockies, A, 92
Shakespeare, 253
Shall This Thing Be?, 271
Shall We Change Our System of Scoring?, 301
Sham, 63
Sharp, William, 192n
Sharpe, James, 238, 240
"She Gathers Roses," 94
She Stood Amazed, 26
Sheaf of Days, The, 161
Shepherds, The, 48
Shepherd's Song, The, 77
Sheridan, 78
Sheridan, C. Mac, 149
Sherman, Wm. T., 404, 433
Shiloh, 93, 308, 353, 354, 363, 367, 368, 376, 377, 399n, 413, 415
Shining Road, The, 97, 140
Shootin' 'Em and Stoppin' 'Em, 164
Shooting by Eye-Light, 257
Short Flights, 75–79
Should Nellie Stay at Home?, 133
Should Smith Go to Church?, 108, 109, 146
Shoup, Grace, 93n
Shrike-Notes, 219
Sick Boy, The, 68
Siege of Cincinnati, The, 371, 384
Siege of the Seven Suitors, The, 104
Sienkiewicz, Henry K, 445n
Sights in New York, 59
Silent Army, The, 302
"Silent Majority, The," 63
Silver Book, The, 446
Silver Trumpet of Romance, The, 154

Simplicity (by M. Nicholson), 92;
(by M. Thompson), 192
Singer, The, 58, 60
Singing Tree, The, 437
Single Stroke, The, 157
Siren's Whisper, A, 268
Sitting in Sunshine, 441
Sitting Up with Susan, 171
Sixth Sense in Literature, The, 277
Sixty Complete Stories, 246
Sixty-Seven Letters on a Dry Subject, 266
Sketching for Literary Purposes, 260
Skirmish book, 369n
Slang, 155
Slattery, Charles L., 163
Sleep, 314
Sling of David, The, 379
Slumber Song, A, 78
Smith, Charles Forster, 191n, 205, 207n, 234, 267
Smith, William Henry, 370
Smith and the Church, 145
Smithers, 277
Smyrna, 423
Snipe Shooting Idyl, A, 258
Snow Bird, The, 263
So, when I fall like some old tree, 261, 275
Social Service by the Church Still Experimental, 169
Society of the Philistines, 246
Solace, 191
Soldier Heart, The, 77
Soldier of Indiana, The, 370
Soldiers' and Sailors' Patriotic Songs, 437
Some Faded Notes, 269
Some Floridian Pigmies, 271
Some Hints to Young . . . Gentlemen, 68
Some Hyoid Hints, 201
Some Indianapolis Women, 63
Some Interrogatories, 269
Some Minor Song-Birds, 196
Some Notes on Creole Literature, 277
Some Notes on Romance-History, 253
Some Notes on Southern Literature, 263
Some of Our Game-Birds, 254
Some Old Fashions, 63
Some Old-Time Rifles, 302

Some Plain Words, 266
Some Song-Birds of Indiana, 242
Some Torch Bearers in Indiana, 93n, 147
Something about Homer, 423
Song, 76
Song, A, 280
Song in Season, A, 270, 274
Song of Birds, A, 65
Song of Good Roads, A, 168
Song of Lycidas, The, 267
Song of Simichidas, The, 267
Song of Songs, A, 439
Song of the Mocking-Bird, A, 206
Song of the New, A, 248
Song [Wake Not], 315n
Song-Wind, The, 259, 276
Songs and Words, 77
Songs of a Life-Time, 384
Songs of a mocking bird, 205
Songs of Fair Weather, 189–193, 205
Songs of Nature, 192n
Songs of the Soil, 161
Songs of the Wayside, 16
Songs of Three Centuries, 190n
Sonnet ("I saw a garden-bed . . ."), 276
Soper, Henry M., 239, 326
Sorosis, 68
Sorrow, A, 62
Soul, The, 68
Source of Originality, The, 270
South Bend Times, 172
South Bend Tribune, 414
South Pacific, 48
Southern Bird-Superstitions, 268
Southern Bivouac, The, 233n, 281
Southern literature, 182n, 183n, 190n, 191n, 192n, 193n, 206n, 207n, 211n, 220n, 263, 274
Southern Pioneer Poet, A, 270
Southward Away, 269, 273
Souvenir of the Anchor Line Agents, 373
Souvenir to Be Sold, 442
Sower, The, 64
Spain, 402, 410
Spanish-American War Songs, 141, 247
Speaker's Garland, The, 240
Speaking of the Weather, 268
Specialists, 168

"Sphere," 57
Spes, 300
Spice of Workaday Life, The, 280
Spirit of Indianapolis, The, 164
Spirit of Mischief, The, 109
Spirit of Mountains, The, 92, 143
Spirit of '62, The, 415
Spirit of Specialism, The, 264
Spirit of the West, The, 118
Spirits Four, 65
Sport with Gun and Rod, 192n, 240–241, 375
Spring Ledge, a Bird Paradise, 61
Spring Notes, 253
Springfield Republican, 142n
Spring's Torch-Bearer, 206
Springtime Holiday, 279
Squire, Marian, 152
Squirrel Shooting, 283
Stag at Ease, The, 152
Stag Cook Book, The, 149
Stand Up for Indiana, 164
Standard of Americanism, The, 157
Standard Recitations by Best Authors, 240, 247
Stanton, E.M., 409
Stanton, Frank L., 161
Star of Stars, The, 157
Status of Our Newly Acquired Territory, The, 299
Stay in Your Own Home Town, 132
Steady, America!, 157
Stealing a Conductor, 179
Stedman, E.C., 183n, 190n, 191n, 192n, 201n, 206n, 207n, 213n, 248, 298, 315n
Steele, Frederic Dorr, 114
Steele, Theodore C., 78
Sterling, Peter, 136n
Stevenson, Burton E., 190n, 213n, 247
Stevenson, Philip, 358
Stevenson, Robert Louis, 63
Still in the Isle of the Lily, 430
Stockholm, 55
Stoddard, Charles Warren, 272
Stolen Stars, The, 307, 352–353
Storied Sea, The, 422, 423; (book), 421–423
Stories of Indiana, 215, 225
Stories of the Cherokee Hills, 216–218
Story, Emelyn (Mrs. W.W.), 433

Story, William Wetmore, 259, 433
Story of a Flag, The, 387
Story of American Heroism, The, 387
Story of Louisiana, The, 203–204
Story of Robin Hood, The, 279
Story of the Arbalist, The, 198
Story of the Bloody Shirt, The, 62
Story of the Three Kings, The, 430
Story of Thomas Cushaw, The, 274
Story Teller, The, 235
Story Time, 232n
Strack, Lilian Holmes, 138
Stranded, 270, 273
Strange Adventures of John Shadden, The, 257
Strange Rescue, A, 258
Stranger in Tuscaloosa, A, 271
Street & Smith's New York Weekly, 281, 446
Stricken, 157
Strike of the Bass, A, 270
Striving, 76
Stroke of Genius, The, 279
Stroke of Ruin, The, 273
Stroll in Indiana with a British Critic, A, 260n, 268
Stubble, 37, 64
Studies of Prominent Novelists, 255
Study for the Critics, A, 207
Study in Black, A, 264
Study of Wallace's Literary Character, 273
Sturm, Herman, 371
Style and the Man, 135–136
"Style Is the Man Himself," 253
Styles, Cassius, 237
Style's Elusive Charm, 136n
Success, 12
Suggestions of Nature, The, 234
Suggestive Plans for a Historical and Educational Celebration, 145
Sullivan, Frances P., 240, 247
Sullivan, Reginald, 167
Summer Jaunt Southward, A, 270
Summer on the Bosphorus, 432
Summer Reading, 269
Summer Saunterings, 272
Summer Song, 268
Summer-Time Recreation, 269
Summer Sweethearts, 176
Sunbeams, 57
Sunday Eclogue, A, 277

Sunday School Times, 446
Sunfish, The, 254
Sunny Slopes of Forty, The, 146
Sunset, 77
Sunshine and Song, 234; (pamphlet), 233–234
Supplication, 48
Support the New Government, 21
Supreme Tribe Ben-Hur, 330, 393
Surrender, 269, 273
Susiness of Susan, The, 123
Swallows at Sunset, 66
Swamp Beauty, A, 219
Swamp Duck Shooting, 257
Swamp-Notes, 260
Swamp Sketches, 201
Sweet, Ada C., 45
Sweetbreads Nicholson, 152
Sweetheart, A, 259, 276
Sweetheart Manette, 227; (book), 226–227
Sweetheart Time, 77
Swift, Lucius B., 132n, 165
Switzerland, 53
Sword and the Pen, The, 314
Sydney, 49
Sydney Mail, 65
Sydney Morning Herald, 66
Sylvan Call, A, 261
Sylvan Secrets, 201; (book), 200–201
Sylvan Study, 254
Sylvia's Annual [Journal], 267n

Table Blessing, 315n
Tacoma Bar Association, 303
Tacoma Ledger, 295, 303
Taffs, C.H., 113
Tale of a Postage Stamp, 156
Tales of the New York Story Club, 245
Tallahassee, 350, 373, 408
Tallahassee Girl, A, 185–187
Tallahassee Sentinel, 414
Tallula Falls, 254
Tangle-Leaf Papers, 196
Tantalus, 30
Tarbell, Ida M., 317n, 439
Tarkington, Booth, 166, 265n
Tarry Thou Till I Come, 345, 392
Taunt, A, 207
Taylor, Aletha Mae, 76n, 92n
Taylor, Charles W., 374

Taylor, Harold, 59
Teachings and Results of the War, The, 379
Teackle, Susan, 266
Téche Terror, The, 283
Tell Me Your Troubles, 126
"Tell Us a Story," 57, 64
Temptation, 259
Tenant, A, 93
Tendency in Verse, A, 172
Tendency of Art in Fiction, The, 263
Tennyson's Poems, 280
Tenth Anniversary Banquet Indianapolis Chapter American Red Cross, 151
Terminal Moraine in Central Indiana, A, 241
Terre aux Boeufs, 258
Terre Haute, 59
Terre Haute Daily News, 67
Terre Haute Express, The, 66, 67, 281
Terre Haute Gazette, The, 16
Terre Haute Saturday Evening Mail, 66, 281
Terrell, W.H.H., 370
Test of Originality, The, 267
Tests of Originality in Art, 277
Thalia's Story, 430
Thalysia, 267
Thanksgiving, 42
Thanksgiving proclamation, 354
That Affair at Green Bay, 171
Theocritus, Weatherly and Kipling, 261
Theory of Fiction-making, The, 256
There Is a God, 57
"There Is No God but God," 302
They Breathe Easier, 40
Things and Thoughts, 281
Things to be Remembered in Archery Practice, 301
Third Man, The, 123, 149
Third Reader, A, 148
Thomas, Charles Swain, 122n
Thomas, Edith Matilda, 158, 161
Thompson, James Madison, 175
Thompson, [James] Maurice, 5n, 7, 12, 40, 60, 81, 93, 143, 158, 173–283, 289, 290, 291, 292, 297, 302, 329, 383, 411, 414, 444, 446n

Thompson, [James] Maurice, at Home, 60
Thompson, [James] Maurice, book reviews, 265, 266, 267, 268, 269, 270, 271, 272, 275
Thompson, [James] Maurice, letter to a friend, 260
Thompson, [James] Maurice, letters to:
William M. Baskervill, 191n, 263n, 264n; Henry C. Bowen, 263, 266; Editor, The Chap-Book, 256; Editor, Crawfordsville Review, 194, 260; The Critic, 186, 260, 261; Editor, The Epoch, 262; R. W. Gilder, 195n, 199n, 217, 219n; Isaac P. Gray, 241; Mr. Greene, 222–223; E. I. Horsman, 185; Wm. Dean Howells, 186; Mr. Hoyt, 236; Indianapolis Journal, 273, 274; Loyal Legion, 273; National Archery Association, 262, 275; James Whitcomb Riley, 187n; Will H. Thompson, 224; Kingsley Twining, 265n; Lew Wallace, 188, 282, 383; Herbert Ward, 265n, 266n, 269n; H. L. Wood, 242
Thompson, [James] Maurice, speeches:
American Association Writers, 244; Boston University, 262n; Contemporary Club, 274; Henry S. Lane tribute, 259; Loyal Legion, 274; Phi Beta Kappa, 262; Purdue University, 276; Wabash College, 262; Woman's Club, Indianapolis, 260
Thompson, Mrs. Maurice (Alice Lee), 58, 205, 218
Thompson, Slason, 266n
Thompson, Wilda, 288, 294
Thompson, Will H., 60, 181, 184, 224, 229, 264n, 268n, [285]–303, 414n
Thompson, Will H., letters to:
J. M. Challiss, 300; Editor, Forest and Stream, 300, 301; E. I. Horsman, 290; L. L. Peddinghaus, 300
Thompson, Will H., speeches:
Flag Day, 302; introducing Lew Wallace, 302–303; Lincoln Memorial, 295, 296, 303; McKinley Memorial, 293
Thompson-Riley Coincidence, The, 273
Thoreau, 79
Thorns in a Novelist's Chair, 260
Those Who Take Early and Hold Long, 280
Three Dreams, 439
Three Friends, 77
334th Minstrels, 148
Three Miles below Mobile, 258
Three Weeks of Savage Life, 183
Three Years with the Poets, 192n
Threshold of the Gods, The, 196
Through the Windows, 68
Thy Voice, 159
Ticknor, Benjamin H., 314n, 395
Ticknor, Caroline, 314n, 395
Ticknor, F.O., 280
"Time Has Come, The," 246
Time's Winnowing, 266
Tippecanoe Battle-Field Monument, 394
Tired Business Man, The, 109
'Tis Never Night in Love's Domain, 76
Tittle, Walter, 116, 117
To a Debutante, 92, 165n
To a Mocking Bird, 276
To a Realist, 207
To a Wild Flower, 206
To All Gentle Book Men, 106n
To an English Nightingale, 206
To an Old Archer Friend, 300, 302
To Benefit Other Lands, 65n
To-day, 64
To Eugene Field in [London] England, 78
To James Maurice T., 302
To James Whitcomb Riley, 91, 134n
To Mrs. Maurice Thompson, 58
To Olga Nethersole, 68
To Provence, 206
To Return to Nature, 219
To St. Louis and Back, 58
To Sappho, 206
To the Land of the Pueblos, 426
To the Marys, 35
To the School Children of Indianapolis, 152
To the Seasons (Invocation), 76, 91

To the South, 207
To the Turquoise Mines, 426
To the United States Senate, 248
To the Wild Goose, 65
To Zayde Bancroft, 446
Together against the Stream, 287, 300
Tolerance, 148, 157
Tolstoi, 244, 255
Tomb of Mohammed, 446
To-morrow's Poetry, 264
Topics of the Town, 58
Tornado, 283
Touch of Genius, The, 252
Touch of Inspiration, The, 219
Touch of June, A, 258
Touch of Magic, The, 270
Touch of Nature, A, 249; (book), 249
Tower of Many Stories, 432, 433
Townsend, George Alfred, 335, 339
Toxophilus in Arcadia, 219
Toxophilus on the Kankakee, 268
Tracy, J. Perkins, 175
Tragedies of the Kohinoor, The, (by
    C.V. Krout), 12; (by M. Thomp-
    son), 259
Tragedy in Triolets, A, 160
Transfigured, 78
Trap, The, 258
Travel Sketches, 422
Treasury of American Verse, A, 207n
Trencher-Memory of Old Days, A,
    269
Trials of the President Elect, 40
Tribune, The, 413n
Tribune Book of Open Air Sports, The
    242
Tributes to the Life & Memory of
    James Whitcomb Riley, 147
Trio, A, 269, 273
Troubadour, 92
Trout's Luck, 179
True Bit of History, A, 232
True Imperialism, The, 274
True Story of Shipwreck, A, 273
True Success in Literature, The, 279
Trust, 140
"Truth" in Fiction, 264
Turkey, 303, 308, 309, 342n, 344,
    346n, 350, 373, 374, 375, 376,
    377, 378, 379, 401n, 404, 412,
    414, 422, 432, 433, 445, 446

Turkey and the Turks, 303, 309, 373,
    401n, 414
Turkey Shooting, 257
Turkish cemeteries, 432
Turning Love's Calendar, 294
Turning of the Tide, The, 269
Tusitala: Teller of Tales, 65
Twain, Mark, 149
Twilight (by M.H. Krout), 67; (by
    M. Thompson), 192, 238; (by
    Robert Frost), 282
Twin Boys and Bears, 257
Twining, Kingsley, 265n
Two Country Towns, 63
Two Days in Westminster Abbey,
    433, 434
Two Famous Roads, 50
Two Girls in China, 28-29
Two Greeks, 158, 161
Two Lyrics in One, 268, 298
Two Poet Brothers, 60
Two Tales, 235
Two Voyages up the Bosphorus, 430
Tyndall, John, 93
Types and Diversions, 118
Tyranny of the Calendar, The, 154n

Unaware, 193
Uncle Riley's Funeral, 63
Unconditional Surrender, 380
Under a Dogwood with Montaigne,
    219
Under the Cherry Tree, 220n
Under the Ice and Snow, 442
Under the Shadow of Tyburn-Tree,
    12
Underwood, Clarence F., 94, 95
Une Flute D'Ebene, 252
Union mass meetings, 402, 415
United States and Hawaii, The, 39
United States: Executive Documents
    of the House of Representatives,
    40th Cong., 369-370
United States House Executive Docu-
    ments, 46th Cong., 359
United States Military Academy, 350,
    381
United States Naval Academy, 406
United States Naval Institute Pro-
    ceedings, 67
United States: Presidential Election
    Investigation, 373

United States Senate: *Executive Documents*, 367
United States War Department, 353, 376
United War Fund, 152
University Magazine, 172
University Review, The, 172
Unmapped, 93, 142
Unwritten Letter, An, 77
Uppermost Success, The, 279
Urban Influence, The, 253
"U.S. in a Spiritual Twilight," 170
Use of the Scatter Gun, 274

Valcour, M. Placide, 220
Vallance, Zona, 60
Valley of Democracy, The, 108, 116–118
Valley of Vision, The, 92, 141
Vanderbilt University, 234
Van Dyke, Paul, 319
Variegated Monotony, 280
Venus of Balhinch, The, 179
Verbal Adumbrations, 268
Victorio, the Apache Chief, 427
Vigilantes, 164, 166
Vigorous Men, a Vigorous Nation, 270
Viking, 78
Vincennes, 161
Violin, 79
Violin: letters about, 401
Virginia Impression, A, 170
Virility in Fiction, 266
Visiting a Volcano, 21
Voices of Children, 94
Voodoo Prophecy, A, 266
Voorhees, 404
Voorhees, D.W., 199
Vote on Copyright, The, 253
Voyage, The, 302
Voyage First, 430; Second—After Christ, 430

Wabash, The, (poem) 190, 239; (magazine), 415
Wabash and Co-education, 59
Wabash Arch, The, 242
Wabash Bubbles, 243
Wabash College, 38, 59, 67, 163, 167, 255n, 262, 390, 415
Wabash (Ind.) schools, 59
Wabash Magazine, The, 67

Wabash Valley Steak, 149
Wages of Sin, The, 63
Waking Up a Bear, 239
Walking, 256
Wallace, David, 342, 393
Wallace, Henry Lane, 350, 356, 446
Wallace, Lew[is], 8, 12, 37, 38, 39n, 40, 44, 45, 57, 60, 61, 64, 81, 143, 158, 159n, 165, 170, 172, 186n, 255, 267, 272, 273, 277, 282, 302, [305]–416, 419, 420, 423, 424, 425, 432, 434, 438, 446
Wallace, Lew, abbreviation, 394
Wallace, Lew, *Autobiography*, 38, 308, 326, 348–350, 353, 356, 359, 360, 361, 365n, 366n, 369n, 371, 372, 379n, 387, 389, 393, 406n, 420, 426, 439
Wallace, Lew, illustrations by, 307, 397–398, 423, 424, 425
Wallace, Lew, letters:
"Ben-Hur" Wallace, 397; Civil War, Cincinnati command, 402, 403; Civil War, Indiana Adjutant General's, 407; Civil War, Middle Department, 399, 400, 401; Civil War, Official Records, 374, 377, 378, 380, 381, 383, 384, 385, 386, 387, 388, 389, 390, 392, 408; congratulating soldiers of First Division, 415; Hayes electoral vote, 408; Mexican War, 393, 406, 407; from Turkey, 412
Wallace, Lew, letters to:
S. M. Ashenfelter, 355; Baltimore Police Commissioner, 384; T.F. Bayard, 379; Billy the Kid, 355, 357, 395; J. J. Bingham, 407; Jno. A. Bingham, 415; Jas G. Blaine, 374, 375; William H. Bonney, 355, 357, 395; Mr. Brigham, 407; Chapman, 393; Calvin M. Cheney, 403; Editor, *Chicago Tribune*, 403; Editor, *Cincinnati Commercial*, 313n, 350, 402; Editor, *Cincinnati Gazette*, 403; Colonel (unidentified), 372; Porfirio Diaz, 350, 372, 401; N.A.M. Dudley, 357–358; Lord Dufferin, 404; William W. Ellsworth, 394; Florida State Canvassers, 350; F. T. Frelinghuysen, 375, 376,

378; friend in Crawfordsville, 409; U.S. Grant, 354, 387, 416; *Harper's Weekly*, 326; General Hatch, 355, 397; Rutherford B. Hayes, 355, 413; Paul H. Hayne, 331; Alexander Hill, 316, 317n; P. A. Hoffman, 402; Holden, Shimp & Hoyt, 415; Independent Zouaves, 413; Indiana Association Mexican War Veterans, 393; Editor, *Indiana State Journal*, 406; Editor, *Indianapolis Journal*, 407, 410; Indianapolis ladies, 407; Editor, *Indianapolis News*, 411; Editor, *Indianapolis Press*, 411; R. U. Johnson, 401n; Charles B. Landis, 404, 412; Robert Todd Lincoln, 376; Benson J. Lossing, 354; Lyon & Healy, 401; M. G. McLain, 409; E. L. Mattern, 414; Catherine Merrill, 371n; Caleb Mills, 367; Oliver P. Morton, 368, 407; Editor, New York *World*, 328; Thomas B. Nicholson, 391; Edward F. Noyes, 402; Editor, *Omaha Tribune*, 413; Paroled Forces, Columbus, 413; Juan Patron, 355; Phi Gamma Delta, 60n, 170, 271n, 278, 317n, 389, 390, 414; Frederick W. Pitkin, 356; Publishers of *Tarry Thou Till I Come*, 392; John A. Rawlins, 367; Whitelaw Reid, 344; Republican State Central Committee, 410; *Rocky Mountain Sentinel*, 355; Matias Romero, 369; A. C. Sands, 372, 402; Carl Schurz, 355, 356; W. T. Sherman, 404; Supreme Tribe Ben-Hur, 393; Maurice Thompson, 186n, 405n; Benjamin H. Ticknor, 314n, 395; Sultan of Turkey's Chamberlain, 404; Agnes Wallace, 331, 348; David Wallace, 393; Henry Lane Wallace, 350; Susan E. Wallace, 309, 315n, 331, 398, 406n, 412, 426n; Wilson, Campbell & Lee, 415; L. W. Winchester, 404; A. J. Wissler, 357, 382

Wallace Lew, Orders, Civil War (see *War of the Rebellion;* see also 370, 396)

Wallace, Lew, speeches: American Association Advancement of Science, 409; Anchor Line banquet, 373; "Ben Hur" Harrison Club, 361, 362, 401; A.E. Burnside reception, 403; Butler University, 408; Chickamauga Park, 392; Civil War recruiting, 405; Schuyler Colfax tribute, 414; Constantinople, 412; Crawfordsville Court House, 404; 11th Indiana Regiment, 408, 409, 411; Fort Mitchell, 403; Harrison Memorial, 411; historical war lecture, 401; Indiana Historical Society, 411; Indiana National Guard, 411; Indiana Republicans, 410; Indiana Soldiers and Sailors Monument dedication, 393, 411; Indiana Zouaves, 405; Indianians at Washington National Hotel, 415; July 4, 1866, 350, 370; Knights of Pythias, 404n; Lincoln Day banquet, 410; Loyal Legion, 379, 381, 384, 389, 409, 410, 411; Maryland State Fair, 399; Memorial Day, 408, 410; Methodist Episcopal Church conference, 383; Mexico and the Mexicans, 309, 373, 390n; Montgomery County Old Liners, 404; Montgomery Guards, 404; Republican Convention, for Hayes, 416; Republicans of Montgomery County, 404; Shiloh, 363; Silver City, 356; Soldiers' Reunion, Marietta, 412; Tippecanoe Battleground, 394; Turkey and the Turks, 303, 309, 373, 401n, 414; Union mass meetings, 402, 415; U.S. Military Academy, 350; U.S. Naval Academy, 406; Wabash College, 415

Wallace, Lew, III, [v], 398

Wallace, Susan E. (Mrs. Lew), 7n, 24, 277, 309, 310, 315, 316, 317, 318, 349, 350, 359, 371, 388, 397, 398, 412, [417]–446

Wallace, Susan E., biography of, 438

Wallace, Susan E., letters from New Mexico, 439; from New York, 445

Wallace, Susan E., letters to: Cousin, 434n; Editor, *Crawfords-*

ville Journal, 442; family, 440; Mrs. E.A. Grosvenor, 440; Harpers, 317, 318, 439; Editor, *Journal*, 446; Joanna (Mrs. Henry S.) Lane, 440; Elizabeth P.H. Little, 444; Editor, *The Locket*, 445; Rose Blair Marsh, 444; Editor, *Rochester Post-Express*, 446; sister, 425; Henry Lane Wallace, 356, 425–426, 440
Wallace, William, 8
Wallace Souvenir, M.O.L.L.U.S., 389
Walt Whitman and the Critics, 256
Walt Whitman's True Value, 252
Walters, William T., 169
Walton, Izaak, 268
Wanted: A Political Emetic, 167, 171
War against the Classics, The, 279
War Bond Best of Good Things, 164
War of the Carolinas, The, 102
War of the Rebellion, 353, 368, 374, 376, 377, 380, 381, 383, 384, 385, 386, 387, 388, 389, 390, 392
War Papers Read before the Indiana Commandery, Loyal Legion, 141
War-Time Horror, A, 43
Ward, Herbert, 265n, 266n, 269n
Was She a Boy?, 179
Washington, [George]: His Place in History, 264
Washington and Lee University, 170
Washington Chronicle, 415, 446
Washington Effigies, The, 39n
Washington Letter, 59
Washington Post, 415
Washington State Bar Association Report, 296, 299
Washington State Legislature, 295, 296
Watching for an Otter, 251
Watching the World Go By, 77, 91
Water or Wine, 263
Watson, O'Neal, 393
W.A.W. (see Western Association Writers)
W.A.W. Souvenir, 245
Way of the World, The, 68
Wayward Muse, The, 93
W.C.T.U. Convention, 45
Weaklings to the Rear, 274
Weatherly, 261
Webb, John J., 405

Wedding Customs in the East, 430
Week of Funerals, 25
Weekly New Mexican, The, 354, 355, 356, 360, 415
Wells, H.G., 156
Wells, Ida B., 49
Werner's Reading & Recitations, 350
West, 92
West Point, 381, 433, 444n
Western Association Writers, 139, 244–245
Western Frontier Stories, 251
Western Literary Outlook, The, 256
Western Literature and Art, 275n
Westerners Brand Book, The, 355, 397
Westminster Abbey, 433, 434
Weston, E.B., 300, 302
What a Good Bow Has Done, 302
What American Authors Think about International Copyright, 243
"What America's Most Famous Authors Say," 150
"What I Tried to Do," 103
What Is a Drama?, 252
What Is Criticism?, 266
What Is Prose Style?, 269
What Is the Utmost Flight of an Arrow?, 301
What Parepa Sang, 441
What Sort of an Arrow Should Be Used?, 301
What the Babies Say, 79
What the Birds Told, 64
What the Child Jesus Saw and Heard, 436
What the Crickets Say, 57, 64
What the Monument Means to Us, 162, 163
What the Victory or Defeat of Germany Means, 164
What We Gain in the Bicycle, 256
What We Like to Read, 280
What Will the Baby Be?, 64
What Would You Do?, 169
Wheeler, L. May, 139, 244
Wheeler, Otis, 265n
Wheelman, The, 192n, 282
When Friends Are Parted, 76, 132
When Knighthood Was in Flower, 249
When My Dream Comes On, 283

When Papaws Are Ripe, 269
When Spring Comes, 60, 61
When the Boss Gets Back, 162
Where and When Shall the Second Grand National Meeting Be Held?, 301
Where Away, 76
Where Did You Get That Hat?, 153
Where Four Winds Meet, 92
Where Love Was Not, 78
Where the Fault Lies, 266
Where the Mocking-Bird Sings, 219
Whereaway, 76
White, Gilbert, 268
Whitman, Walt, 252, 256, 265n
Whittier, John Greenleaf, 36, 165n, 190n
Whittlesey, Charles, 353
Who Is to Blame?, 264
Who's Who, 391
Who's Who in America, 11, 37, 144, 248, 299, 391, 438
Whose Business Is It?, 156
Whose House Is Burning?, 164
Why Send for the Doctor?, 109
Why We Color Eggs at Easter, 436n
Wicks, Frank S.C., 127
Wide Margins, 92
Widow Selby, The, 16, 58
Wife of General Canby, The, 444
Wild Boy of Wallahee, The, 257
Wild Eden, 162
Wild Honey, 192
Wildcat at Home, A, 257
Wilds of Wisconsin, 43
Wildwood Archery, 282
Wilkes, Charles, 67
Will Imagination Run Dry?, 259
Will Not Go, 40
Will You Hoard for Hitler!, 170
Williams, A. Dallas, 213n
Williams, Ben Ames, 380
Willson, Elizabeth Conwell, 81
Willson, Forceythe, 81
Wilson, Alexander, 279
Wilson, James Grant, 399n
Wilson, Robert Burns, 77
Wilson, S.C., 415
Winchester, L.W., 404
Wind and the Rain, The, 64
Wind at Whitsuntide, The, 92
Wind Patrol, The, 92, 140, 142

Winslow, Amy, 151
Winston, Arthur Randolph, 136n
Winter Forecast, A, 270
Winter Is Over, 64
Winter Reverie, A, 276
Winter Ritual for Writers, A, 253
Winter Song, A, 259, 268
Winter Sports and Pastimes, 256
Winter Swallow, A, 158, 161
Winter Walk, A, 268
Winter Wind in the Rockies, The, 92, 142
Winter Wolves, 258
Wirz, Henry, 369n, 370
Wisconsin Wilds, 43
Wissler, A.J., 357, 382
Witchery of Archery, The, 180–183; Pinehurst Edition, 182, 228–230, 299
With a Wine Cup, 445
Witherbee, Sidney A., 141, 248
Without Benefit of College, 112, 132
Without Prejudice, 168
Woman and Home, 66
Woman's Kingdom, 25, 40, 41, 42, 43, 44, 45, 46, 47, 48, 49, 50, 51, 52, 53, 54, 55, 56
Woman's New Field, 48
Woman's place, 442
Woman's Press League, 44
Woman's Rights This, 57
"Woman's Sphere," 68
Woman's View, A, 39
Woman's Way, A, 278
Woman's Work and the Fair, 47
Women Abroad, 56
Women and Men in Literature, 264
Women in Novels, 252
Women in Politics, 25
Women in the Orient, 437
Women of Hawaii, The, 39
Women Poets, 163n
Wood, H.L., 242
Wood, William Allen, 144
Wood Duck Shooting, 283
Wood Violet, The, 64
Woodberry, George E., 79, 80, 107, 162
Woodcock Shooting, 257
Woodland Archery, 278
Woodland Battle, A, 258
Woodland Mood, A, 259

Woodward, Wilbur W., 57
Wooing of Malkatoon, The, 307, 314, 345–347
Woollen, Evans, 105, 172
Word and the Phrase, The, 263
Word of the King, The, 63
Word to Southern Tourists, 269
Worden, Mrs. Commodore, 445
Wordsworthian Influence, The, 252
Work That Counts, The, 157
World Praise, 57
World's Fair, 46, 47
World's Sharp Edges Shape Man, 132
World's Work, The, 172
Writing the Record, 271
Written on a Fly-Leaf of Theocritus, 192
Wrong Number, 123

Y.M.C.A., 166
Yale Review, The, 172

Ye Sylvan Archer, 237n, 255n
Yea, Wabash!, 167
Year in Journalism, A, 59
Yesterday, 60, 61
Yew Bow and Clothyard Shaft, 302
Yohn, F.C., 105, 220
You Simply Must Come Back, 147
Young Men the Strength of the Nation, 279
Youth, 160
Youth and Winter, 92
Youth's Companion, The, 172, 415, 446

Zelda Dameron, 84–86
Zenobia, 256
Zimmerman, Charles, 366n
Zoro, 263
Zouaves, 308, 367, 371, 405, 407, 408, 413